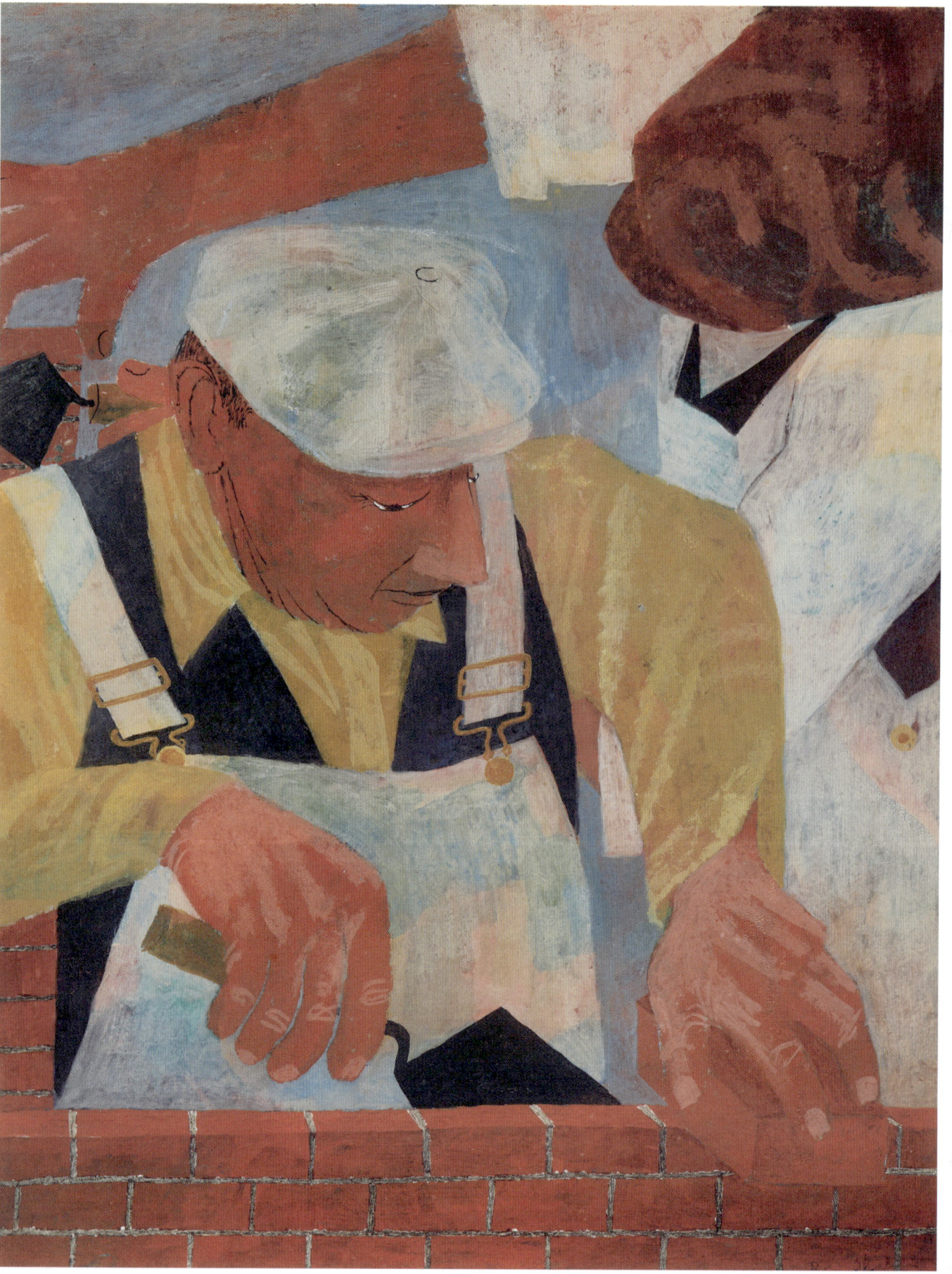

BEN SHAHN
ON NONCONFORMITY

Laura Katzman

With contributions by Beatriz Cordero Martín, Christof Decker, and John Fagg

Jewish Museum, New York
Under the auspices of the Jewish Theological Seminary of America

Museo Nacional Centro de Arte Reina Sofía, Madrid

Princeton University Press, Princeton and Oxford

Published by Princeton University Press in 2025

The first edition of this book was published to coincide with the exhibition *Ben Shahn, On Nonconformity*, curated by Laura Katzman for the Museo Nacional Centro de Arte Reina Sofía, Madrid, from October 4, 2023, to February 26, 2024

This edition has been published to coincide with the exhibition *Ben Shahn, On Nonconformity*

Jewish Museum, New York
May 23 to October 12, 2025

Image credits and copyrights are on page 288

Editors: Donna Wingate with Amelia Kutschbach
Designer: gráfica futura

This book has been printed on Munken Polar White 120 gr (interior), and Woodstock Azzurro, 260 gr (cover)
Set in Tiempos typeface

Printed by Graphicom in Italy

Jewish Museum
1109 Fifth Avenue
New York, New York 10128
thejewishmuseum.org

Museo Nacional Centro de Arte Reina Sofía
Calle Santa Isabel, 52
28012 Madrid, Spain
museoreinasofia.es

Princeton University Press, Princeton and Oxford
41 William Street
Princeton, NJ 08540
USA

99 Banbury Road
Oxford
OX2 6JX
UK
press.princeton.edu

Library of Congress Control Number: 2024949619

ISBN 978-0-691-27311-2
Ebook ISBN 978-0-691-27312-9

British Library Cataloging-in-Publication Data is available

Cover image
Italian Landscape, 1943–44.
Tempera on paper, 27 ½ × 36 in.
Walker Art Center, Minneapolis. Gift of the T. B. Walker Foundation, Gilbert M. Walker Fund, 1944

Page 2
Bricklayers, c. 1951
Tempera on paper
14 × 11 in.
Collection of Debra and Michael Skolnick, Elkins Park, Pennsylvania

10 9 8 7 6 5 4 3 2 1

EDITORIAL NOTE

Regarding Ben Shahn's photographs of a "medicine show" from 1935 (pp. 97, 112, 113), we are aware that the display and reproduction of such problematic images may cause offense in a contemporary context. We also recognize the historical value of Shahn's documentation and his sensitivity to racial discrimination, which is evident in even a cursory analysis of his photograph series of a disturbing phenomenon in the culture of the United States.

In the fall of 1935 Ben Shahn traveled to the Jim Crow South for the Resettlement Administration to photograph struggling rural workers. In Huntingdon, Tennessee, he recorded a traveling medicine show, a carnival-like event led by "quack" medicine men who entertained audiences to lure them into buying dubious miracle cures. Performers were often white men in "blackface" (minstrel show makeup now widely accepted as racist) or dressed as stereotyped Indigenous Americans. Moving inconspicuously around the crowd, Shahn keenly observed racial dynamics from the edges of the scene and poignantly focused on one Black performer in blackface. (For many complex reasons, including limited opportunities, even Black entertainers engaged in the pervasive practice.) Staring enigmatically at the photographer, the Black man exists in triangular tension with a white boy mesmerized by a Black puppet. With such layered visual complexities, Shahn's series compels reflection, reading more as a poignant critique than a blatant exposé of a most demeaning form of racial exploitation.

Contents

Foreword

Ben Shahn, On Nonconformity showcases the extraordinary work of the artist Ben Shahn, a pioneering figure whose commitment to social justice during particularly challenging times in American history could not have greater relevance today. In 1906, while he was still a child, Shahn immigrated to the United States from Russian-controlled Lithuania with his working-class Jewish family. In his new home he grew to achieve prominence among the progressive social realist artists of his time.

In response to the horrors of World War II, Cold War anticommunist crusades, and the rise of art movements such as abstract expressionism, Shahn shifted from documentary approaches to more poetic and lyrical idioms that employed allegory, symbolism, and myth in search of universal expression. At the same time, he never abandoned figuration or social content and became an articulate spokesperson for humanism in art. Even his later spiritual work, which reembraced the Hebrew language and biblical stories, tapped into a long-cherished tradition of activism on behalf of social justice within the worlds of observant and secular Judaism. For Shahn, socially engaged art placed freedom of expression at its core, fueling throughout his work his credo of "nonconformity" as a precondition for all important art and great historical change.

The Jewish Museum, with a long tradition of addressing the history of the global Jewish diaspora over 3,500 years, welcomes this exhibition to its landmark site on Museum Mile in New York. In 1947 when the Museum moved to its current location in the Warburg Mansion on Fifth Avenue, Shahn's eleven watercolors inspired by the Haggadah came into its collection from Edward M. M. Warburg. The Museum has since developed rich holdings of Shahn's oeuvre, organizing and presenting signature exhibitions of his work. In 1976 at the time of the United States Bicentennial and during the heyday of minimalism and conceptual art, the Museum hosted a major Shahn exhibition—the last comprehensive retrospective of his art in the United States. To mark Shahn's centenary in 1998, the Jewish Museum curator Susan Chevlowe organized *Common Man, Mythic Vision: The Paintings of Ben Shahn*, focusing on the role of allegory in the artist's later, lesser-known paintings. Twenty-two years later, the conceptual artist Jonathan Horowitz curated *We Fight to Build a Free World*, which situated Shahn's work at the heart of an exhibition devoted to current artists resisting social injustice. *Ben Shahn, On Nonconformity* extends the legacy of this pathbreaking project, highlighting Shahn's contemporary social relevance and the underappreciated complexity of his aesthetic vision across many media.

The Jewish Museum has organized *Ben Shahn, On Nonconformity* in close collaboration with the Museo Nacional Centro de Arte Reina Sofía in Madrid and Laura Katzman, Professor of Art History at James Madison University in Harrisonburg, Virginia. Dr. Katzman has served as the guest curator of the exhibition in both Madrid and New York and is the lead author of the catalogue, copublished with Princeton University Press. Dr. Stephen Brown, Curator at the Jewish Museum specializing in European and American modernism, has collaborated with Dr. Katzman. We are grateful for their curatorial vision and tireless effort as well as that of the wider exhibition team led by Darsie Alexander, Senior Deputy Director and Susan and Elihu Rose Chief Curator. We warmly thank all of the exhibition's lenders, listed on page 5, whose generosity has helped realize this substantial and timely project.

Our deep appreciation goes to our colleagues at the Museo Reina Sofía: Manuel Segade, Director; Teresa Velázquez, Head of Exhibitions; Beatriz Velázquez, General Coordinator of Exhibitions; and Alicia Pinteño Granado, Head of Editorial Activities, who skillfully assisted us in restaging this long overdue retrospective of Shahn's work for audiences in the United States at this especially meaningful time.

James S. Snyder
Helen Goldsmith Menschel Director
Jewish Museum

Acknowledgments

It has been my privilege to have served as guest curator for *Ben Shahn, On Nonconformity*, at the Jewish Museum in New York and for the original retrospective at the Museo Nacional Centro de Arte Reina Sofía in Madrid. I am grateful to the leadership of the Jewish Museum and its dedicated staff. James S. Snyder, the Helen Goldsmith Menschel Director, and Darsie Alexander, Senior Deputy Director and Susan and Elihu Rose Chief Curator, have powerfully reaffirmed Shahn's social justice vision in our own time. Claudia Nahson, the Morris and Eva Feld Senior Curator, identified the significance of the Museo Reina Sofía's exhibition for the Jewish Museum. For their care and diligence in carrying out the complex logistics of the project, I thank Megan Witko, associate exhibitions manager; Nelly Benedek, deputy director of education and programs; Derya Kovey, associate registrar; Katherine Danalakis, assistant director of collections; Ellen Croisier, collections manager; Amelia Kutschbach, editor of publications; and Jenna Weiss, manager of public programs. Chelsea Garunay, exhibition designer, and Poliana Duarte, graphic designer, created stunning spaces for Shahn's prolific production. Stephen Brown, curator, deserves abundant gratitude for his exceptional curatorial eye, which was critical for the presentation of Shahn in this exhibition.

Sincere thanks are extended to staff members of the Jewish Museum who supported the exhibition at every stage. I gratefully acknowledge Kennedy Anderson, Lyndsey Anderson, Shira Backer, Rebecca Frank, Collin Garrett, Caroline Harvey, Jody Heher, Mason Klein, Julie Maguire, Rebecca Merriman, Christopher Motley, Genesis Mullis, Jannette Reichel, Anne Scher, Samantha Schott, Rebecca Shaykin, Michael Stafford, Gocha Tsinadze, Aviva Weintraub, and Sari Weisenberg. I thank Beatriz Cordero Martín, Christof Decker, and John Fagg for contributing their deep scholarship to this publication and as well as Frances K. Pohl for sharing her immense knowledge of Shahn. For their encouragement of my decades-long work on Ben Shahn, I thank also the Ben Shahn family, Nicholas Acker, Michael Berg, and my colleagues at James Madison University and the Madison Art Collection, who have championed my research and my participation in this exhibition.

At the Museo Reina Sofía, I am indebted to Manuel Borja-Villel, former director, for conceiving a Shahn exhibition on a grand scale and for recognizing its timeliness for global audiences. Manuel Segade, current director, lent his unwavering support, ensuring an enthusiastic public reception for Shahn in Madrid, where the exhibition was led by Teresa Velázquez and coordinated by Beatriz Velázquez and Ana Uruñuela. The Spanish team brought an extraordinary commitment, sensitivity, and expertise to the project. Under the direction of Alicia Pinteño Granado and the coordination of Mercedes Pineda, the publications team, namely Nicholas Acker, César Ávila, Jonathan Fox, and Pamela Sepúlveda, adroitly produced this scholarly catalogue. My deepest gratitude goes to gráfica futura's design expertise as well as Amelia Kutschbach's and Donna Wingate's editorial and professional wisdom in bringing this second English edition to fruition.

The Shahn exhibition at the Jewish Museum was made possible by the generous support of donors and lenders, private and institutional, who contributed to our project. Their participation enabled the cross-cultural reshaping of the originating Madrid installation for the New York exhibition. This transatlantic journey constitutes a kind of homecoming, and is entirely fitting, since New York was indeed the city that shaped Shahn: where he was raised, educated, and politicized. New York is thus entral to the formation of Ben Shahn's identity as an artist and activist, who developed into one of the most fascinating and consequential cultural figures in the history of the United States in the twentieth century.

Laura Katzman
Guest Curator

ESSAYS

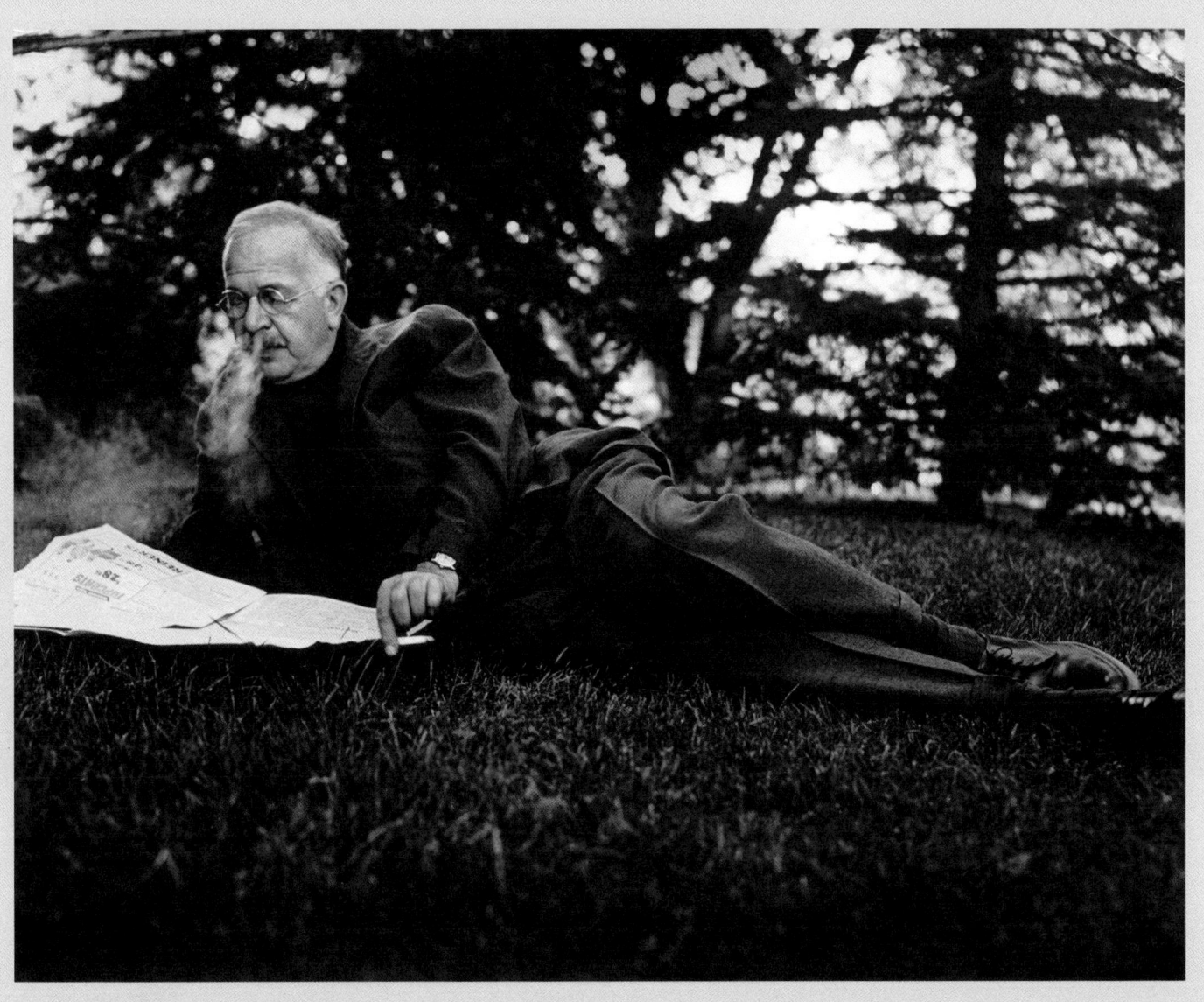

ART AND ACTIVISM: THE CURRENCY OF BEN SHAHN

Laura Katzman

1. Albert Christ-Janer, "What Moves You, Ben Shahn," *Response* 8, no, 2 (1966): 82.

2. Helen Langa, *Radical Art: Printmaking and the Left in 1930s New York* (Berkeley: University of California Press, 2004), 4–5.

3. Susan Chevlowe et al., *Common Man, Mythic Vision: The Paintings of Ben Shahn* (New York: The Jewish Museum and Princeton University Press, 1998); Deborah Martin Kao, Laura Katzman, and Jenna Webster, *Ben Shahn's New York: The Photography of Modern Times* (New Haven: Yale University Press, 2000); and Alejandro Anreus et al., *Ben Shahn: The Passion of Sacco and Vanzetti* (Jersey City: Jersey City Museum and Rutgers University Press, 2001).

4. John Davis, "The End of the American Century: Current Scholarship on the Art of the United States," *The Art Bulletin* 85, no. 3 (September 2003): 568–69, 579, note 109.

5. The Jewish Museum in New York hosted a traveling retrospective (1976–78). The Museum of Modern Art's International Circulating Exhibitions Program hosted a retrospective and a graphics exhibition (1961–63). Japanese museums have mounted large solo exhibitions in 1970, 1991, 1996, 2011–12, and 2015–16, among other years.

6. Megan Cole Paustian, "A Postcolonial Theory of Universal Humanity: Bessie Head's Ethics of the Margins," *Humanity* 9, no. 3 (January 15, 2019): abstract, 343–62.

This essay is dedicated to the memory of Bernarda Bryson Shahn, Jonathan Shahn, Ezra Shahn, and to all Shahn family members and friends in Roosevelt, New Jersey, who for over thirty years have encouraged and aided my research. Special thanks to Jasper Shahn and Zachary Shahn for giving permissions from the Ben Shahn Estate and to Nicholas Acker, Mary Jane Appel, Michael Berg, Beatriz Cordero Martín, Jessica Davidson, Christof Decker, John Fagg, Olmo Masa, Ani Rosskam, Jeb (Jean) Shahn, and Abby Shahn for offering invaluable insights. Frances K. Pohl generously contributed her immense expertise on Shahn.

[William] Blake, in "Marriage of Heaven and Hell," said that righteous indignation over injustice was the truest worship of God. And I guess I am filled with righteous indignation most of the time…. [M]y fear of absolutism, whether in religion, science, politics, or in art…. is the strongest fear I have. And then I feel I must make a statement. I feel that every direction has its right…. but the danger immediately becomes apparent when a particular direction is recognized as the only direction. Then I will raise my voice, as Blake said, at the injustice of this kind of absolutism.—Ben Shahn, 1966 [1]

INTRODUCTION

Ben Shahn, On Nonconformity / Ben Shahn. De la no conformidad, hosted by the Museo Nacional Centro de Arte Reina Sofía, proposes a fresh and wide-ranging look at Ben Shahn (1898–1969) on the 125th anniversary of the artist's birth. The exhibition examines the multifaceted art of this Jewish immigrant from Russian-controlled Lithuania and his endurance as one of the most prominent, prolific, and progressive of the "social viewpoint" artists in the United States from the 1930s through the 1960s.[2] Shahn was celebrated in his lifetime and has been the subject of many exhibitions, television programs, and publications. His centenary generated multiple thematic exhibitions, including those at New York's Jewish Museum, the Harvard Art Museums, and the Jersey City Museum.[3] This "renewed art historical scrutiny" constituted a constellation of influential scholarship—a "collaborative enterprise" deemed the Shahn "project."[4] Yet Shahn's art has not been explored in a career-spanning retrospective in an art museum in the Western world since 1978, nor has his work been seen on a large scale in Europe since 1963.[5] No Shahn retrospective has previously been mounted in Spain. Such a project is thus long overdue and, as this essay discusses, particularly timely in our current sociopolitical and cultural moment.

Ben Shahn, On Nonconformity highlights the currency of Shahn's art and its continued relevance by focusing on the artist's commitment to social justice, through the lens of contemporary diversity and equity perspectives. In so doing, the exhibition presents Shahn as a champion of the underdog, a promoter of the rights of workers and immigrants, among other marginalized or persecuted people, and a critic of the abuses of the powerful and the privileged. The exhibition opens with Shahn's emergence as a radical artist on the left in the dark days of the Great Depression and charts the evolution of, and challenges faced by, his art and politics from the New Deal through the height of the Vietnam War era. The show demonstrates how Shahn interpreted—with compassion and purpose—the most pressing issues of his day, illuminating critical aspects of twentieth-century history, domestic and foreign: the stock market crash of 1929 and the ensuing economic crisis; the Dust Bowl; Jim Crow racism; the rise of European fascism; World War II atrocities; Cold War repression of individual liberties; threats of nuclear annihilation in the atomic age; and the postwar struggles for labor, civil, and human rights when decolonization movements were sweeping the globe. This, in turn, reveals the values of Shahn and other leftists of his generation, such as universal humanism—an ideal that has "come under intense scrutiny for its Western bias and neglect of cultural and historical difference."[6] What did social justice look like to Shahn? What remains relevant today?

Given the broad scope of this thematic retrospective, audiences will be able to trace Shahn's social justice concerns as incisive threads that weave through the fabric of his art—concerns that are detailed in the catalogue's focused essays by Christof Decker, John Fagg, and Beatriz Cordero Martín, who examine Shahn's World War II poster art, labor-related work, and engagement in postwar aesthetic debates, respectively. Drawing on media studies, cultural studies, and art-historical approaches, each text brings new insights to Shahn's progressive vision and to his fight against injustice and inequality, which formed the core of his practice. This remained true even as he shifted from documentary, representational styles to more poetic, lyrical, and elegiac idioms that employed allegory, symbolism, and myth—secular and religious—in search of universal expression. Such changes came in part from Shahn's own disillusionment with Marxist theories and the limitations of "art for the masses" and from his response to the Cold War climate. Social realist styles and overt engagement in radical politics fell out of favor in avant-garde art circles after the war, as certain critics, curators, and gallerists began to promote abstraction and as reactionary politicians persecuted artists for leftist activities and affiliations.

The exhibition shows how Shahn attempted to stay true to his own vision but also remain relevant. Even as his harshest critics denigrated his art as mere propaganda, as "illustration" or "journalism" (and hence, not "high art"), his postwar work was in demand with private collectors and major museums and appreciated by noted critics as well as by particular sectors of the public in the U.S. and Europe. (Abstract expressionism was not "codified" until the later 1950s.) Shahn won accolades, such as the Charles Eliot Norton Professorship at Harvard University in 1956 and honorary degrees in the 1960s. He continued to make meaningful art in the midst of attacks from right-wing politicians and publications like *Counterattack*, as well as interrogation by the Federal Bureau of Investigation (FBI) and the House Un-American Activities Committee. What remains fascinating, as Frances Pohl has so cogently detailed, is how Shahn was able to appeal artistically to the pro-labor left and the business-oriented or moderate right.[7] Equally intriguing is how Shahn engaged with artists far from his own aesthetic ideology, such as conceptual composer John Cage, abstract expressionists Robert Motherwell and Barnett Newman, and the younger abstractionist Cy Twombly, the latter of whom Shahn mentored. This happened despite his protestations against abstract and non-objective art as noncommittal and divorced from human values and his mocking comments on pop art, happenings, and minimalism.[8] Conversely, Dada-inspired pop artists like Andy Warhol, in his early commercial work, emulated Shahn's trademark "blotted line." Pop art has even been linked to the populist folk and graphic design of Shahn's generation.[9] (Shahn admired the whimsically irreverent abstraction of Paul Klee and Alexander Calder as much as the trenchant realism of Francisco de Goya and Honoré Daumier.)

Ben Shahn, On Nonconformity also looks at how Shahn shaped his social justice content. Shahn adapted the stylistic formalism of modern European art to U.S. subject matter in his social realist work (i.e., School of Paris modernism, French and Italian surrealism, and German expressionism), affirming, as Jody Patterson has argued, that realism and modernism were not as polarized in the 1930s as canonical narratives have suggested. Shahn's postwar palimpsest techniques and allegorical subject matter align with the gestural styles and mythic, existential themes of abstract expressionism.[10] Yet his layered visual language and adoption of modernist conceptual strategies—often linked to his use of photography—remain underappreciated by a wide swath of the public. Current scholars have laid the foundation for such exploration, by considering Shahn's use of montage techniques, framing devices (art within art), multiple temporalities, and storefront reflections and commercial signage (as in his photographs), among other reflexive elements that offer metacommentary on the process of the work's creation or the nature of representation itself.[11] While Shahn's narrative approach may seem anti-modernist, his innovative use of lettering and integration of word and image tie his art to the experimental, modernist poets with whom he connected or collaborated, such as E. E. Cummings, William Carlos Williams, Charles Olson, and Mirella Bentivoglio.[12]

7. Frances K. Pohl, *Ben Shahn: New Deal Artist in a Cold War Climate, 1947–1954* (Austin: University of Texas Press, 1989).

8. For debates on abstract art and humanism, see "Contemporary Documents: Modern Art—1950," *College Art Journal* 9, no. 3 (Spring 1950): 339–40. On Shahn's views of avant-garde art, see Ben Shahn, *The Shape of Content* (Cambridge, Mass.: Harvard University Press, 1957), 55–67; Interview with Ben Shahn by Forrest Selvig, September 27, 1968, transcript, 13–19, Smithsonian Archives of American Art.

9. Blake Stimson, "Ben Shahn," in *Citizen Warhol* (London: Routledge, 2014), 124–45; Thomas Crow, *The Long March of Pop: Art, Music, and Design, 1930–1995* (New Haven: Yale University Press, 2015).

10. Jody Patterson, *Painters, Politics, and Public Murals in 1930s New York* (New Haven: Yale University Press, 2020); Stephen Polcari, "Ben Shahn and Postwar American Art: Shared Visions," in Chevlowe et al., *Common Man, Mythic Vision*, 67–109.

11. Examples are Katzman, "Deconstructing Documentary: Ben Shahn's *Contemporary American Photography*," in Joseph C. Schöpp and Martin Klepper, eds., *Transatlantic Modernism* (Heidelberg: Universitatsverlag C. Winter, 2001), 173–90; Diana L. Linden, "Ben Shahn's *Contemporary American Sculpture*," gallery brochure (New York: Jonathan Boos, 2017); and Christof Decker, "Fighting for a Free World: Ben Shahn and the Art of the War Poster," *American Art* 33, no. 2 (2019): 84–105. Sara Blair has read Shahn's New York photographs of the Jewish Lower East Side as meditations on modernity, immigrant assimilation, and on the ontology of photography itself. See "Spirituality, Identity, and the Hebrew Bible" in this catalogue.

12. Frances K. Pohl, *Love and Joy About Letters: The Work of Ben Shahn and Mirella Bentivoglio* (Claremont: Pomona College Museum of Art, 2003).

13. See note 11 and essays by Katzman: "The Politics of Media: Ben Shahn and Photography," in Kao, Katzman, and Webster, *Ben Shahn's New York*, 97–117, 142–46; "Mechanical Vision: Photography and Mass Media Appropriation in Ben Shahn's *Sacco and Vanzetti* Series," in Alejandro Anreus et al., *Ben Shahn and the Passion of Sacco and Vanzetti*, 51–80, 126–35; and "Source Matters: Ben Shahn and the Archive," *Archives of American Art Journal* 54, no. 2 (Fall 2015): 4–33. See also Tetsua Sakai et al., *Ben Shahn: Cross Media Artist/Photographs, Paintings and Graphic Arts* (Tokyo: Bijutsu Shuppan-Sha Co., Ltd., 2012); chapter 3 in Christof Decker, *Imaging the Scenes of War: Aesthetic Crossovers in American Visual Culture* (Bielefeld: transcript Verlag, 2022), 61–89; and John Fagg, "Ben Shahn and Jacob Lawrence: Beyond Genre Painting," in *Re-envisioning the Everyday: American Genre Scenes, 1905–1945* (University Park: Pennsylvania State University Press, 2023), 159–77.

14. Frederick Kaufman, "Ben Shahn's New York," *Aperture* 162 (Winter 2001): 74.

15. Davis, "The End of the American Century," 569. While Shahn believed all images were equal, whether made with the brush, pencil, or camera, painting was the medium in which he felt he could most fully express himself. Shahn, "In the Mail: Art versus Camera," *New York Times*, February 13, 1955, sec. 2, 15.

16. Part of the tempera revival (1930s–1950s), Shahn preferred tempera's fast-drying, matte qualities to the glossiness of oil paint. He used a complex paint mixture applied in layers (often onto paper) to achieve the tightness, clarity, and range of textural contrasts he desired. While tempera is a long-lasting medium, many of Shahn's paintings have suffered from cracking in the paint film and significant paint loss.

17. Shahn produced fresco murals during the New Deal and later mosaic murals, along with stained glass, sculpture, and scenography. In the 1930s, he even briefly engaged in film, which he called the "master medium."

18. Editor Russell Lynes quoted in Howard Greenfeld, *Ben Shahn: A Life* (New York: Random House, 1998), 322. As noted below, Greenfeld also discussed the less-flattering sides of Shahn, who could be egotistical and overbearing.

Shahn's complex use of photography—his own New York City street photographs and Resettlement Administration-Farm Security Administration (RA-FSA) photographs, as well as those of others—to create art in other media is a rich topic that has generated scholarly inquiry. But given the pervasiveness of the practice within his oeuvre and the new discoveries continually emerging from his photo source archive and clipping files, much remains for researchers to mine.

Although Shahn distanced himself from his own photography in the late 1940s, privileging his painting, he continued to refer to or draw on camera images for the entirety of his career. As this author has argued elsewhere, and as Decker and Fagg have shown in their essays for this catalogue, the ways that Shahn used his source photographs reveal his research, thinking process, sociopolitical concerns, and depth of understanding about the topics he explored.[13] Further, the way Shahn recycled and repurposed documentary and mass media photographs—along with the resulting afterlives of the appropriated images—affirms what one influential critic asserted: "Shahn looms as a post-Modern avatar, relevant in our present-day debates over originality and what constitutes artistic 'work.'"[14]

Shahn's layered visual language, with its "competing systems of pictorial logic," emerges across the media he breathtakingly mastered, gravitating to those that could reach mass audiences. He generally rejected a hierarchy of media.[15] The retrospective thus includes easel paintings and mural studies (gouache, watercolor, and his unique type of tempera that emulated the look of fourteenth- and fifteenth-century Florentine frescoes)[16]; drawings in ink or pencil (the backbone of his art); 35 mm photographs (a medium that he first took up for sketching but in which he quickly became an innovator); and prints (lithographs and screen prints made for mass-produced posters or for fine art editions). To amplify and contextualize this work, the exhibition features Shahn's source material, archival ephemera, and commercial design production, such as hand-scripted, illustrated books; magazine commissions; television advertisements; and press and newspaper photographs that he collected, catalogued, used, and reused in a myriad of ways.[17]

The artist's embrace of accessible and reproducible media coincided with his wide patronage—federal, state, and city governments; labor unions; corporations; political campaigns; religious organizations; universities and other nonprofits; and private art collectors. With each agency or project, Shahn surged to the forefront as a leader with far-reaching vision. A force of inexhaustible energy and drive, the warm, gregarious artist cut a charming figure as a raconteur in his prime and was remembered at the end of his life as "a generous, affectionate, wise and humorous giant of a man."[18] Even as he faced ideological clashes, dismissals, censorship, and blacklisting, Shahn never lost his conviction that art should be integral to society as a moral tempering force for science. Believing that the poet was as essential as the physicist, he praised attempts to revive the humanities in the early atomic age. Such beliefs resonate today, given the divestment in the arts and humanities by governments and educational institutions and the intense focus on science, technology, engineering, and math to prepare younger generations for the high-tech global economies of our time.

CONTEMPORARY RELEVANCE AND RESONANCE

While each generation since Shahn's death could find his work timely, his art has taken on new urgency in the current polarized political climate in the U.S. and beyond, with the seismic disruption of conventional politics. Shahn's relevance surfaced vividly in the powerful exhibition *We Fight to Build a Free World* hosted by the Jewish Museum in New York (2021–22). Curated by conceptual artist Jonathan Horowitz, the exhibition addressed the resurgence of antisemitism in the U.S., tying it to the broader institutional racism and the rise of xenophobia and authoritarianism erupting around the world, including in long-standing democracies. Horowitz was invited to organize this show in the wake of the violent "Unite the Right" rally in 2017 that mobilized far-right extremist groups in protest of the proposed removal of the statue of Confederate General Robert E. Lee in Charlottesville, Virginia and in support of white supremacy.[19] The curator situated Shahn's work *We Fight for a Free World!* (c. 1942) (p. 152) at the heart of his installation. This painting was created to promote a never-realized series of anti-fascist posters Shahn envisioned for the Office of War Information (OWI) during World War II. It presents the proposed posters by artists of Japanese, Jewish, and German descent, featuring not the enemy but the "methods of the enemy"—a propaganda strategy intended to announce the dangers of Nazism to the U.S. population and strengthen domestic support for the war effort.

"Inspired by Shahn's attempt to incorporate multiple voices across years and cultural identities," Horowitz commissioned thirty-six contemporary artists to create their own posters—making reference to Shahn if desired—to respond to the struggles of our own day, such as gun violence, climate change, and Islamophobia.[20] The curator's own meta-installation of the resulting posters was complemented by his expert selection of other socially and politically engaged art, much of it contemporary, from a critical perspective. Recognizing the prescience of Shahn's warnings about threats to democracy, Horowitz underscored the relevance of Shahn's art to the twenty-first-century art of resistance. He keenly grasped the provocation of Shahn's textual language, implicating viewers' moral conscience (who is the "We"?), and of his framing of "art within art," which uses propaganda to comment on the very nature of propaganda.[21]

While the Jewish Museum exhibition was underway in 2018, the Los Angeles County Museum of Art opened *Shahn, Mooney, and the Apotheosis of American Labor*. A small, focused exhibition curated by Ilene Susan Fort, celebrating the museum's purchase of *Apotheosis* (1932–33), it reunited several paintings and source material from Shahn's series on Tom Mooney. Mooney was a San Francisco labor leader wrongly convicted of a bombing during the Preparedness Day parade in 1916 (in anticipation of the U.S. entrance into World War I). His persecution became a *cause célèbre* that generated mass protest on the left and mass media sensationalizing of corrupt witnesses, self-serving politicians, and, according to critic Shana Nys Dambrot, "high-profile defenders having a proxy culture war." The exhibition opened at a time when the U.S. saw an upsurge in major strike activity and an increase in public support for labor unions—a notable fact since organized labor has been on the decline in the U.S. since the 1970s.

Stressing Shahn's contemporary relevance, Nys Dambrot wrote, "what truly makes the [Mooney] project come alive is its readily apparent resonance with our current political situation. After all, mass demonstrations, government corruption, an epidemic of incarceration ... and the domination of old white men in policymaking are commonplace now," noting Shahn's painting of the conservative California Supreme Court as "particularly heartbreaking" (p. 72). Nys Dambrot asserted that "at our own crucial moment of political strife," art like Shahn's is "one of the most powerful tools in the fight to reach people and change minds." His artistic voice, she concluded, is "one that a new generation of activists would do well to study, as the fearless man of principle and honored art-historical trailblazer he remains."[22]

In the year following the tumultuous 2016 U.S. presidential election, this author curated for the Duke Hall Gallery of Fine Art at James Madison University (JMU) in Harrisonburg, Virginia, *Drawing on the Left: Ben Shahn and the Art of Human Rights*. The show interpreted Shahn's graphics as "a blueprint for speaking out against hatred, bigotry, inequality, and injustice" and "a clarion call for all citizens to stand in solidarity with

19. Marchers brandished torches reminiscent of those in Ku Klux Klan rallies, chanting: "Jews will not replace us."

20. Laura Feinstein, "We Fight to Build a Free World: A History of Artists Resisting Intolerance," *The Guardian*, October 8, 2020, theguardian.com/artanddesign/2020/oct/07/we-fight-to-build-a-free-world-jewish-museum-new-york.

21. Interview with Jonathan Horowitz by the author, October 27, 2022. Horowitz's exhibition *The Future Will Follow the Past* (2022–23), Weitzman National Museum of American Jewish History, Philadelphia, also put *We Fight for a Free World!* at its core.

22. Shana Nys Dambrot, "A Powerful Look at One Artist's Quest for Social Justice," *L.A. Weekly*, October 18, 2018, laweekly.com/a-powerful-look-at-one-artists-quest-for-social-justice-more-than-80-years-later/.

23. Katzman, *Drawing on the Left: Ben Shahn and the Art of Human Rights* (Harrisonburg: Duke Hall Gallery of Fine Art, James Madison University, 2017, 2018), 16.

24. See also *For All These Rights We've Just Begun to Fight: Ben Shahn and the Art of Resistance*, Snite Art Museum, University of Notre Dame, 2017, and *The World Through My Eyes: Celebrating the Legacy of Ben Shahn*, University Galleries, William Paterson University, 2019.

25. Betsy Gomberg, "Iconic Works by Artist and Activist Ben Shahn Go on View at Spertus," *JUF News*, April 5, 2017, juf.org/news/arts.aspx?id=442176. Diana L. Linden's *Ben Shahn's New Deal Murals: Jewish Identity in the American Scene* (Detroit: Wayne State University Press, 2015) is relevant to current immigration issues. It also sparked Kathy Lynn Grossman, "How Ben Shahn's Art Anticipates Bernie Sanders," *Religious News Service*, May 19, 2016, religionnews.com/2016/05/19/how-ben-shahns-art-anticipates-bernie-sanders/.

26. Notably, 2015 saw 1.3 million Syrian refugees risking their lives to cross the Mediterranean, seeking asylum from civil war, who along with refugees from Africa and South and Central Asia triggered a humanitarian crisis of epic proportions within the European Union.

27. Tirdad Derakhshani, "Nakashima's Arts Building Turns 50 with a Gala Ben Shahn Retrospective," *The Philadelphia Inquirer*, May 2, 2017, inquirer.com/philly/entertainment/George-Nakashimas-Arts-Building-to-mark-its-50th-anniversary.html.

28. Aruna D'Souza, "Who Speaks Freely?: Art, Race and Protest," *The Paris Review* (May 22, 2018), theparisreview.org/blog/2018/05/22/who-speaks-freely-art-race-and-protest/.

29. Roberta Smith, "Should Art That Angers Remain on View?," *New York Times*, March 28, 2017, C1.

vulnerable communities to ensure the future of democracy, pluralism, and even civilization itself."[23] Three years later, in the months leading up to the November 2020 presidential election, the Madison Art Collection at JMU launched the digital exhibition *Ben Shahn: Art as Civic Engagement*. Featuring Shahn's work related to voting as the cornerstone of a democracy, the display coincided with actual and proposed U.S. legislation in the name of "election integrity," which, in fact, restricted access to voting by economically disadvantaged communities—legislation facilitated by the 2013 Supreme Court decision that struck down major portions of the Voting Rights Act of 1965.[24]

Another noteworthy Shahn exhibition, from 2017, *Ben Shahn: If Not Now, When?*, appeared at the Spertus Institute for Jewish Learning and Leadership in Chicago. Curator Ionit Behar offered this raison d'être for the modest show: "Ben Shahn's images of immigrants, refugees, labor organizers, and civil rights workers are as powerful today as they were during his lifetime. It is critical to exhibit Shahn's works in these times, in this country, in Chicago, and at a Jewish institution. His commitment to debate and social change is inspiring, a much-needed feeling here and now."[25] The "here and now" may be a veiled reference to the controversial 2017 "Muslim ban," a U.S. presidential executive order that blocked refugees from several Muslim-majority nations from entering the U.S., in their attempt to escape poverty, dictatorships, and in the case of Syria, a bloody civil war.[26] In this climate, a larger graphics exhibition opened in 2017 in New Hope, Pennsylvania, celebrating the fiftieth anniversary of the Nakashima Arts Building, which today houses the Nakashima Foundation for Peace chaired by Mira Nakashima. The daughter of Shahn's friend, the architect and woodworker George Nakashima, who endured a World War II Japanese internment camp, Mira Nakashima told the press that "she was deeply disturbed by recent calls from conservative pundits for Arab Americans to be detained" and by "a rising [global] tide of racial prejudice and xenophobia."[27]

Finally, some influential New York art critics have in recent years asserted that Shahn's art can speak to our moment. Roberta Smith of the *New York Times* invoked Shahn's *The Passion of Sacco and Vanzetti* (1931–32) (p. 70 left) in her March 2017 article "Should Art That Angers Remain on View?" It addresses the scandal at the Whitney Biennial surrounding Dana Schutz's abstract painting of the casket showing Emmet Till, the fourteen-year-old who was lynched by the Ku Klux Klan on August 28, 1955—a heinous crime that galvanized civil rights activism. Smith weighed the range of positions (including calls for censorship and the destruction of the painting) regarding whether a white artist today, at a moment when, in the words of Aruna D'Souza, "Black people are still subject to extrajudicial violence," has the moral authority to depict the mutilated body of this Black boy.[28] Smith stated that the controversy brought to mind artists like Shahn (white and Jewish) "who crossed ethnic lines in their depiction of social trauma." (Shahn, in fact, shared with Sacco and Vanzetti an identity as an immigrant.) One example of Shahn's cross-ethnic visual commentary is found in what Smith described as the artist's "stinging commentary on the trial of the [Italian, Catholic, and anarchist] immigrants Nicola Sacco and Bartolomeo Vanzetti." They were executed in 1927 for a murder in Massachusetts for which they were denied a fair trial—and which many believe they did not commit. Smith's words suggest that Shahn's approach manages to avoid exploitation and voyeurism, and even does justice to the horror and pain experienced by others.[29]

Relatedly, in his November 2020 blog commentary "MoMA Hangs a Ben Shahn," Blake Gopnik, a regular contributor to the *New York Times* and biographer of Warhol, also used a canonical work by Shahn—*Willis Avenue Bridge* (1940) (figs. 1–2)—to underscore Shahn's currency. His excitement over viewing a Shahn painting in MoMA's new installation of its permanent collection left him "wanting a whole show of them."

Like Smith, Gopnik highlighted a classic Shahn work that shows his success at depicting people with identities different from his own. *Willis Avenue Bridge* exemplifies Shahn's "Sunday Paintings" series, which reflects his shift from an "art for the masses" to one that features the daily rituals of ordinary individuals—often waiting—as well as the artist's keen observations about their human and material conditions. This image of two Black women sitting on a bench that seems to float before a bridge connecting Manhattan to the Bronx over the Harlem River was created from Shahn's own New York photographs. While the transparent tempera layers evoke pathos and highlight the bony ankles of the elderly woman's thin body, the alarming red girders of the bridge and sturdy crutches of the disabled woman anchor the picture. The older woman's proud bearing, stylish cape, and elegant pearl necklace exude dignity.

Shahn's compassion for struggling individuals, shown with respectful honesty and without idealization, was noticed by Gopnik, who was writing several months after the racial justice protests by Black Lives Matter and allied groups following the horrific Minneapolis police murder of George Floyd. Readers can thus link Shahn's racially sensitive work to a new era of racial reckoning in the U.S. and globally, focused on an epidemic of police brutality that has disproportionately harmed people of color. Indeed, as Gopnik wrote: "In our current moment of social consciousness, Shahn is one artist who deserves another look.... In the 1940s and '50s, he was considered one of the giants of American art—Warhol and his classmates in art school were mad for him—and I for one would like to see him get a proper (MoMA? Whitney?) retrospective."[30]

BEN SHAHN IN SPAIN

The Museo Reina Sofía is a propitious place for such a retrospective. It is the home of Pablo Picasso's *Guernica* (1937), which is at the core of the museum's collection, and which remains the most famous and arguably the most riveting visual condemnation of the atrocities that crushed the fragile, young Spanish Republic during the Spanish Civil War (1936–39). Incorporating collage allusions, abstraction, and surrealism to capture the devastation of the Basque town (a bastion of Republican Loyalist resistance) bombed by Nazi German and Fascist Italian air forces on behalf of General Francisco Franco and the Nationalist government, *Guernica* is also at the heart of the Reina Sofía's mission. The museum has dedicated much space to rethinking the meanings, contexts, and global manifestations of this influential artistic statement.[31] Shahn was one of many left-wing New York artists who fervently tracked the events of the Spanish Civil War and supported the Republican cause. Along with Japan's invasion of Manchuria and Italy's invasion of Ethiopia, the Spanish Civil War politicized progressive U.S. artists in the 1930s, spawning a radical internationalism against fascism. Many saw the Francoist actions in Spain as a prelude to world war. Shahn, according to Diana Linden, "followed these events with consternation and alarm."[32]

While Shahn was not among the estimated 2,800 Americans who fought (with Republican militias) on Spanish soil in units such as the Abraham Lincoln Brigade, as an artist of Jewish heritage he understood what was at stake in Spain.[33] Shahn likely shared the socialist, anti-Stalinist perspective of George Orwell in the British author's personal account of the Spanish Civil War, *Homage to Catalonia* (1938). Undoubtedly, he read André Malraux's *L'Espoir* (*Man's Hope*) (1937)—a despairing political novel about the war's tragedy as a symbol of the human condition; he owned many of Malraux's books and pictured the fearless, pro-Republic artist on the cover of *Time* magazine in 1955. Shahn worked closely during World War II with poet-activists Muriel Rukeyser and Archibald MacLeish. Rukeyser's poem *Mediterranean* (1937) and MacLeish's co-written scenario for the film *The Spanish Earth* (1937) circulated in Shahn's orbit. He was part of the committee in summer

30. Blake Gopnik, "MoMA Hangs a Ben Shahn, and Leaves Us Wanting a Whole Show of Them," *Blake Gopnik on Art Blog*, November 18, 2020, blakegopnik.com/post/635164096125403137.

31. See *Rethinking Guernica*, launched by the Museo Reina Sofía in 2017: https://guernica.museoreinasofia.es/en.

32. Linden, *Ben Shahn's New Deal Murals*, 33. See Helen Langa, "New York Visual Artists and the Spanish Civil War," in Peter N. Carroll and James D. Fernández, eds., *Facing Fascism: New York and the Spanish Civil War* (New York: New York University Press, 2007), 102–19.

33. "The Spanish Civil War had a special meaning for Jews.... Spain, the country of the Inquisition, had permanently expelled Europe's largest Jewish population, a thousand-year-old community, in 1492. Jews were vastly overrepresented in the International Brigades, comprising about one-quarter of their ranks." Stephen H. Norwood, *Antisemitism and the American Far Left* (New York: Cambridge University Press, 2013), 152. Franco wanted to save Spain "from a deadly conspiracy of Bolsheviks, Freemasons, and Jews." Adam Hochschild, *Spain in Our Hearts: Americans in the Spanish Civil War, 1936–1939* (Boston: Mariner Books, 2017), 28. See also Paul Preston, *Architects of Terror: Paranoia, Conspiracy and Anti-Semitism in Franco's Spain* (London: William Collins, 2023).

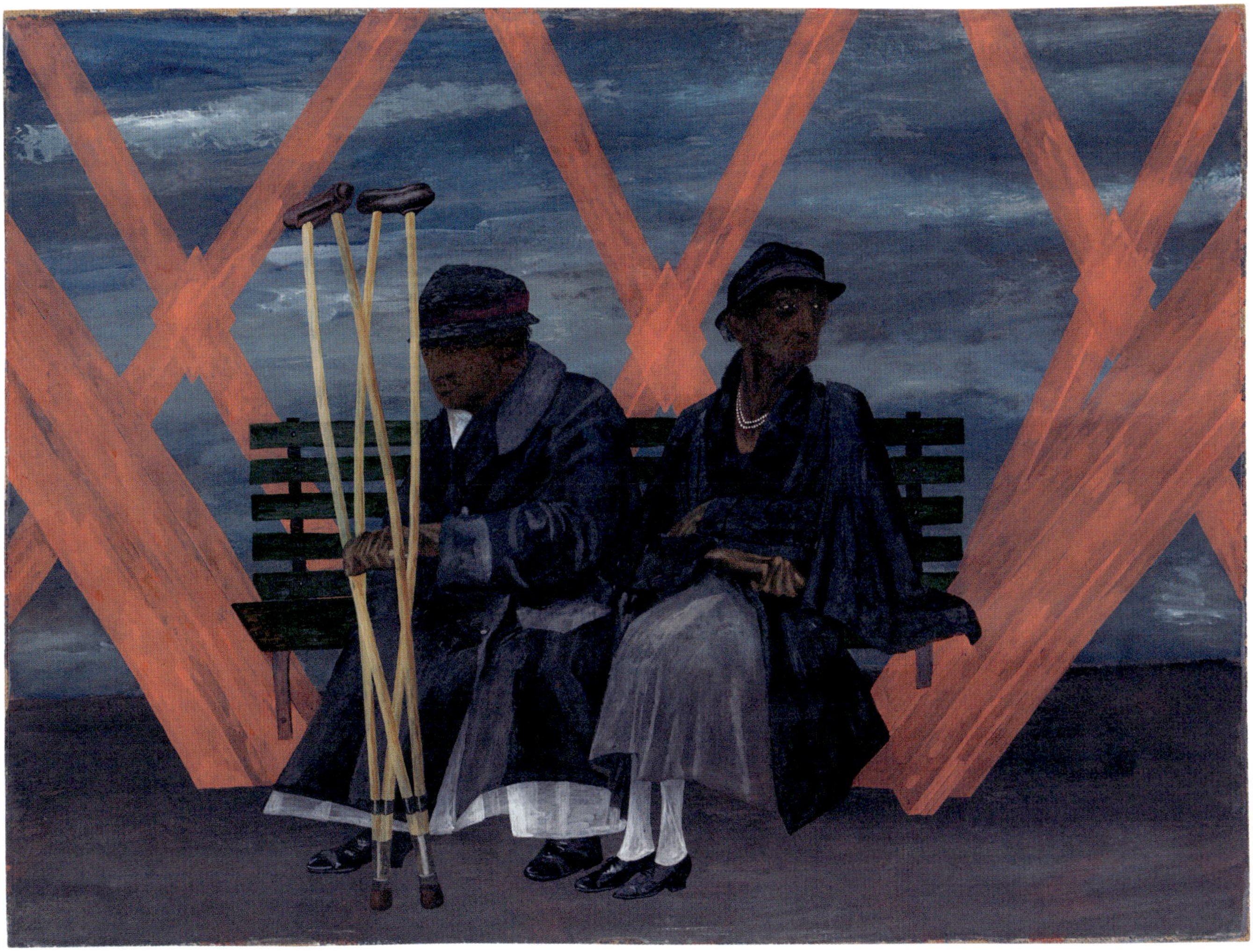

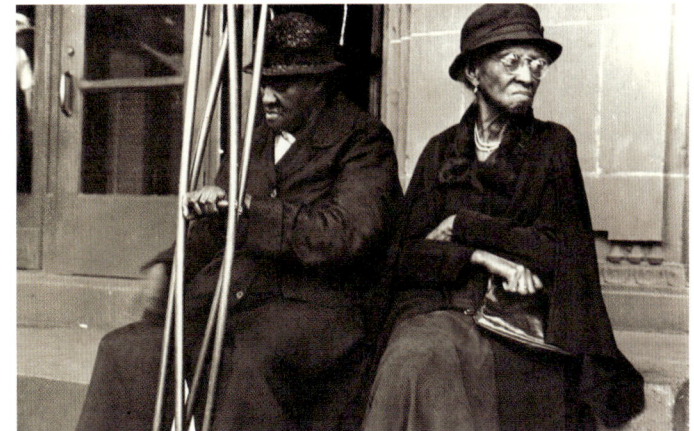

1
Willis Avenue Bridge, 1940

2
Untitled [Welfare Hospital, Welfare Island, New York City],
1934–35

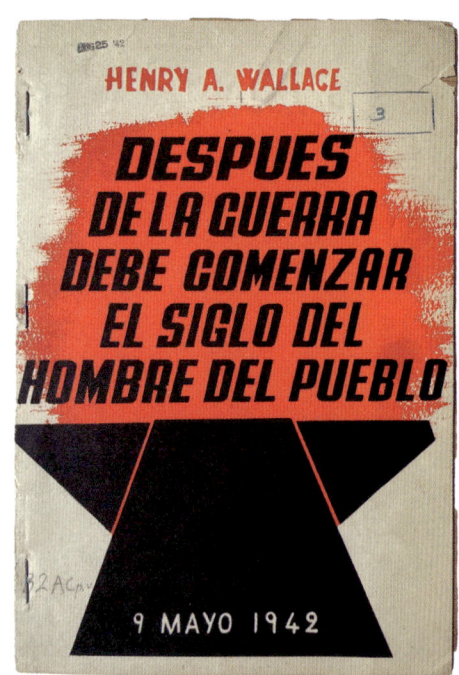

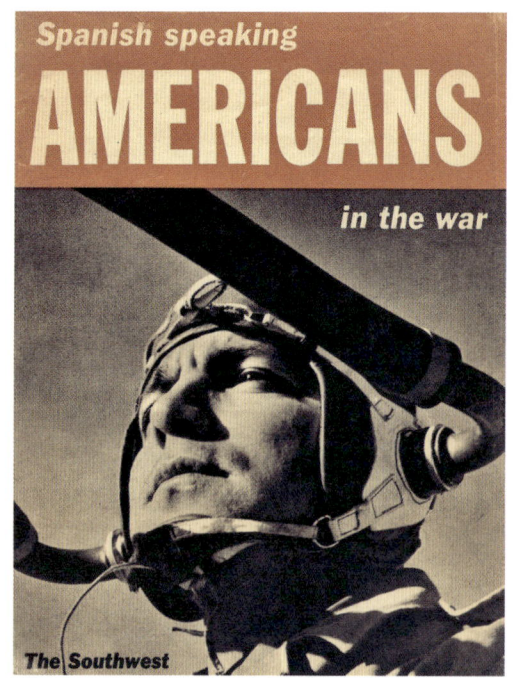

3
Henry A. Wallace, with cover design by Ben Shahn
*Después de la guerra debe comenzar el siglo del hombre
del pueblo.* Mexico City: Publicaciones de la Universidad
Obrera, 1942

4
Charles Olson and Ben Shahn
Spanish Speaking Americans in the War: The Southwest.
Washington, D.C.: Office of the Coordinator of Inter-American
Affairs, 1943

34. Matthew Baigell and Julia Williams, eds., *Artists Against War and Fascism: Papers of the First American Artists' Congress* (New Brunswick: Rutgers University Press, 1986), 9, 47–52. The Congress helped bring *Guernica* from Paris to New York in 1939.

35. Elliott Paul, "Quintanilla and Satire," *Art Front* 1, no. 3 (February 1935): 4–5, Ben Shahn papers, Smithsonian Archives of American Art (BSP-AAA). On the October 1934 Revolution, see Brian D. Bunk, *Ghosts of Passion: Martyrdom, Gender, and the Origins of the Spanish Civil War* (Durham: Duke University Press, 2007).

36. Interview with Ben Shahn by Saul Benison and Sandra Otter, Oral History Research Project, Columbia University, 1957, transcript, 78–79 (Columbia interview). Dan Belgrad, *The Culture of Spontaneity: Improvisation and the Arts in Postwar America* (Chicago: University of Chicago Press, 1998), 24.

37. For Shahn's recollections of this book, which the author discovered in her research for this exhibition, see Columbia interview, 1957, 78–79. The Falange was an extreme nationalist political group founded in 1933 by José Antonio Primo de Rivera, which became the sole official political party under Franco in 1937, when it was forcibly merged with traditional right-wing elements.

38. Columbia interview, 1957, 79–80; Belgrad, *The Culture of Spontaneity*, 25.

39. Shahn, *The Shape of Content*, 82–83.

40. James Thrall Soby, *Ben Shahn: Paintings* (New York: Braziller, 1963), 27; Conversation with Ben Shahn and Elkan Allan, February 10, 1956, transcript, 3, BSP-AAA.

1935 that rewrote the "Call" for the first American Artists' Congress against War and Fascism, which he signed.[34] He served as an early editor and designer of *Art Front*, the organ of the Artists' Union, which published articles on Spanish artist Luis Quintanilla, whose imprisonment due to his role in the violent October 1934 Revolution (quelled by Franco) mobilized aid from the global intellectual community.[35] Shahn photographed Artists' Union members marching at the Spanish Consulate in New York City in spring 1935, carrying signs declaring, "Free Quintanilla and Other Victims of Spanish Fascism." The pictures show U.S. leftist solidarity with the radical activity of Quintanilla and his colleagues, who opposed the entry of right-wing forces into the Spanish Republican government (pp. 94–95).

Shahn kept a file he titled *Refugees* within his photo source archive, which contains mostly newspaper clippings of Spanish Civil War refugees fleeing violence—images he later used to create moving paintings on the devastation of war-torn Italy such as *Italian Landscape* (1943–44). In addition to his better-known anti-Nazi posters for the OWI, he produced wartime propaganda for Nelson Rockefeller's Office of the Coordinator of Inter-American Affairs (OCIAA), which focused on Latin America and on Americans of Latin American heritage. For example, Shahn's work targeted the U.S. Southwest with, in his own words, "our concepts of democracy" in order to counteract "fascist influence" and "the Spanish Falangist propaganda that had reached up there very solidly." This Spanish propaganda, along with that of the Axis nations, "encourage[d] minorities to question their stake in an American victory."[36] Toward these ends, Shahn enthusiastically agreed to design a book with a Spanish translation of then-Vice President Henry Wallace's "Price of Freedom" or "Common Man" speech (*Después de la guerra debe comenzar el siglo del hombre del pueblo*) (fig. 3). Wallace had delivered the speech in 1942 to boost U.S. morale in fighting the Axis powers. In 1943, as part of a goodwill tour, he gave the speech in Spanish in Latin American countries, including those where European fascist and Spanish Falangist ideas had circulated. Little known to Shahn scholars, and much to Shahn's frustration, this Spanish book faced resistance from certain people in the OCIAA who believed that the "concept of Wallace's speech should not be made popular." Even though the text promoted U.S. democracy, Wallace's perspective was apparently seen as too socialistic.[37] (Shahn would go on to support Wallace in his 1948 bid for president on the Progressive Party ticket.) Shahn also collaborated in the OCIAA with poet Charles Olson on *Spanish Speaking Americans in the War* (1943), a bilingual pamphlet illustrated with press and government photographs. Shahn called it "a sympathetic piece" for Latino soldiers in U.S. states like New Mexico, which bore the brunt of the U.S. casualties in the notorious Bataan Death March in the Japanese-controlled Philippines (where Filipinos disproportionately lost their lives). Such pamphlets promoting ethnic or racial equality also "fomented congressional opposition" from conservative forces (fig. 4).[38]

Shahn was invited by Alfred H. Barr, Jr. to participate in a conference on *Guernica* at the Museum of Modern Art (MoMA) on November 25, 1947, when his own retrospective was on view there. Shahn admired Picasso and was moved by *Guernica* as a "passionate testament [of the artist's] sympathies," an art of "intransigent sentiments," and a symbol of artistic nonconformity.[39] Yet as Cordero Martín has discussed in her essay for this catalogue, Shahn also publicly critiqued the painting as ineffective in speaking to the layperson. While Shahn did not directly address atrocities of the Spanish Civil War, as did Picasso and Shahn's fellow left-wing artists, he created what appears to be a portrait of Franco, barely disguised within the painting *Defaced Portrait* (1955) (fig. 5). The work, "ferocious in its antimilitary acrimony," was inspired, Shahn said, by his fear over the 1955 rearmament of the West German army.[40] The image strikingly resembles not a German general but rather the Spanish General, as seen in a famous photograph from 1954. Exaggerating the shoulders of the pompous official, who dons a dense display of regalia on his ornate coat—which dwarfs the general's tiny hands and small head—Shahn used his palimpsest technique to efface the medals with black thrashing X's, allowing traces of the shiny medals to remain. This scathing portrait, and a related drawing, were made when official U.S.-Spanish relations had shifted from mutual disdain in the immediate postwar years to rapprochement as the Cold War proceeded. (The U.S. had ostracized Spain as an Axis ally, at least in official policy and rhetoric, and Spain attacked the harshness of U.S. capitalism.) The Pentagon saw Spain as strategically useful in the anti-communist crusade and as a military bulwark against Soviet influence in Europe.[41] The resulting Madrid Pact of 1953 was *realpolitik* to which progressives like Shahn ardently objected, as they continued to condemn Franco's dictatorship in their activities and in journals like *The Nation*.

In fact, in 1963, according to an FBI report, "Shahn joined other artists in an exhibit to help the Abraham Lincoln Brigade's campaign to aid imprisoned opponents of Franco Spain."[42] In early 1969, in what would be his last interview, Shahn reinforced his anti-Franco stance. After stating, "I'm not a pacifist," he suggested that the U.S. and Western allied powers should have militarily aided Republican forces to defeat the Nationalists in the Spanish Civil War.[43] Most poignantly, close to his death on March 19, 1969, Shahn created what were likely his last drawings: life-sketches of world-renowned Spanish, Catalan, and Puerto Rican cellist Pau (Pablo) Casals (fig. 6). They met in Puerto Rico, where the legendary Spanish Civil War refugee settled circa 1956 after a long self-imposed exile in Prades, France. With his stuttered line, Shahn captured the restrained intensity of the musician's thick fingers moving his bow with surprising delicacy. Drawn to the focused expression of a fellow artist in the act of creating art, Shahn admired *el maestro* for his humanitarianism, bringing great music to ordinary people and crusading for world peace. Indeed, Casals' fame came not only from his restoration of Bach's cello music to the classical repertory and his innovative bowing and fingering techniques, but also from his impassioned support for the Spanish Republic and fellow exiles, his long-term refusal to perform in countries that recognized Franco, and his pledge to never return to Spain until democracy was restored.[44] Like Casals, Shahn avoided travel to Francoist Spain.

However, Shahn had ventured to pre-Second Republic Spain, in 1925 and again for about one month in 1929, as a struggling artist on his second European pilgrimage (when he lived in Paris and in North Africa, mostly on the Tunisian island of Djerba). In April 1929, he was in Málaga, planning to visit Granada, Córdoba, Seville, Madrid, and Toledo—which he called "the tourists' itinerary," as his main goal was to see the great museums. The Prado is where Shahn first saw the paintings of Goya.[45] Decades later, he paid tribute to this paragon of *l'artiste engagé* in *Goyescas* (1956) (p. 210), which shows a four-handed, empty-eyed Napoleonic general of Goya's era. He clasps one set of hands in anguished concern, and with the other callously plays a game of cat's cradle while trampling on "the strewn corpses of his victims." Exposing the duplicity of many political and military leaders—possibly referring to the USSR's repression of the Hungarian Uprising—*Goyescas* invokes Goya's *Los caprichos* (1796–98) and *Los desastres de la guerra* (1810–20). Indeed, in his artistic treatise *The Shape of Content* (1957), Shahn called Goya's unflinching protest "the most unforgettable indictment of the horrors of religious and patriotic fanaticism that has ever been created in any medium at all."[46]

Coincident with this homage to Goya, and as an ironic result of the thawing Cold War relations between Spain and the U.S., some Shahn works were shown in Spain, for example, at Barcelona's Palacio de la Virreina (III Bienal de Arte Hispanoamericano), which hosted a traveling exhibition of American paintings, sculptures, and prints organized by MoMA's International Council, *50 ans d'art aux États-Unis* (1955). His solo and group exhibitions in

41. "Franco's regime appreciated the prospect of U.S. economic aid and tourism, and international acceptance." Claudia Hopkins, "Bienvenido! Welcoming American Art in Francoist Spain, 1950s–1963," in Hopkins and Iain Boyd Whyte, eds., *Hot Art, Cold War—Southern and Eastern European Writing on American Art, 1945–1990* (New York: Routledge, 2021), 59. On the U.S. engaging Spain covertly to normalize relations as early as 1947, see Miguel González, "America's Shameful Rapprochement to the Franco Dictatorship," *El País*, October 23, 2018, english. elpais.com/elpais/2018/10/22/ inenglish/1540219578_899934.html.

42. Herbert Mitgang, *Dangerous Dossiers: Exposing the Secret War Against America's Greatest Authors* (New York: Ballantine Books, 1989), 215.

43. Richard Kostelanetz, "Ben Shahn: Master 'Journalist' of American Art (1969)," in *On Innovative Art(ist)s: Recollections of an Expanding Field* (Jefferson, N.C.: McFarland & Company, 1992), 169.

44. Bernarda Bryson Shahn, *Ben Shahn Drawings*, unpublished book, circa early 1970s, 218–19. Bernarda Bryson Shahn papers, Smithsonian Archives of American Art (BBSP-AAA). Casals was criticized by fellow Spanish exiles and other leftists for playing for the John F. Kennedy White House in 1961 and living in a U.S. territory. Ironically, he was simultaneously under FBI surveillance for his international peace work and alleged sympathies with the USSR. His support for his native Catalonia and Spanish democracy never waned. See Pedro Reina-Pérez, "A Cellist in Exile: Pablo Casals and the Cold War," *Revista* 15, no. 2 (Winter 2016), revista.drclas.harvard.edu/a-cellist-in-exile/.

45. Shahn to Philip Shan, April 19, 1929, BSP-AAA; Bryson Shahn, *Ben Shahn Drawings*, n.p.

46. Soby, *Ben Shahn: His Graphic Art* (New York: Braziller, 1957), 20; Shahn, *The Shape of Content*, 8, 83.

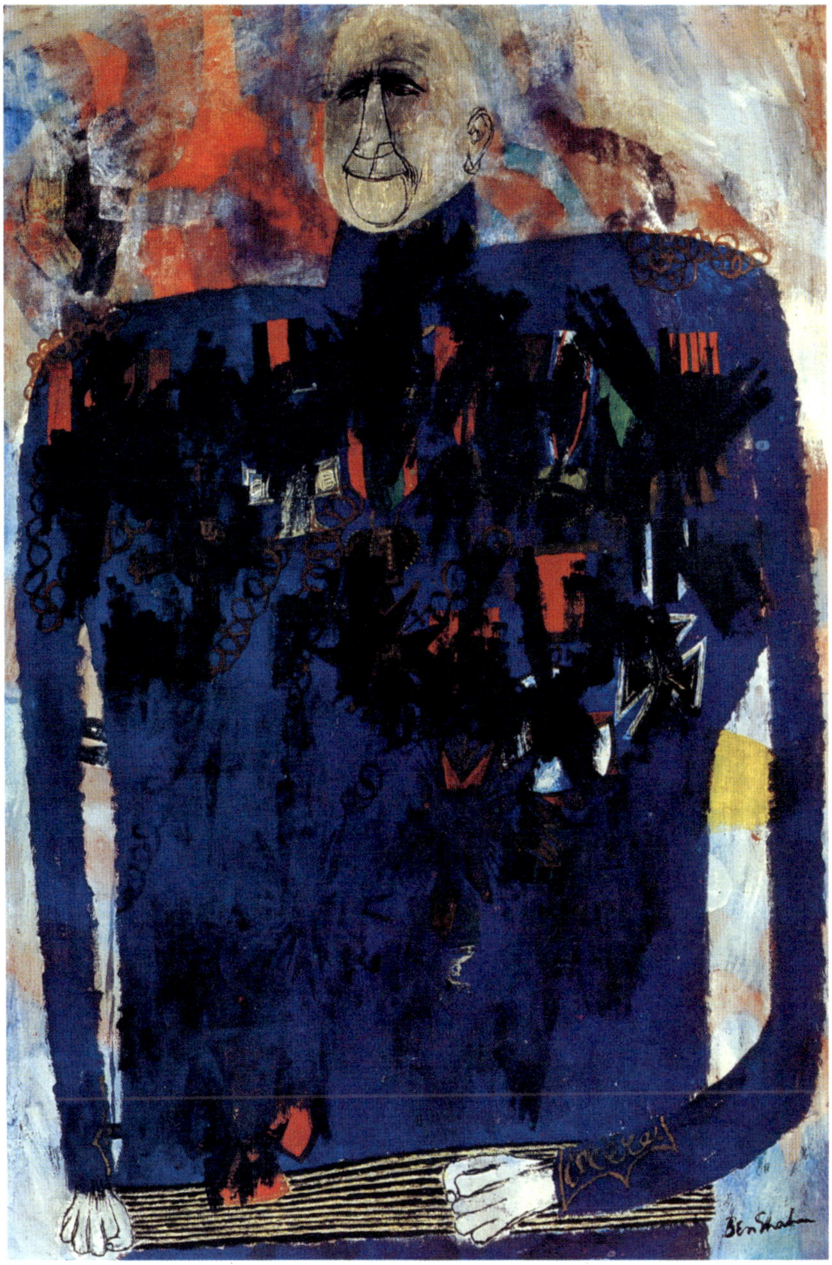

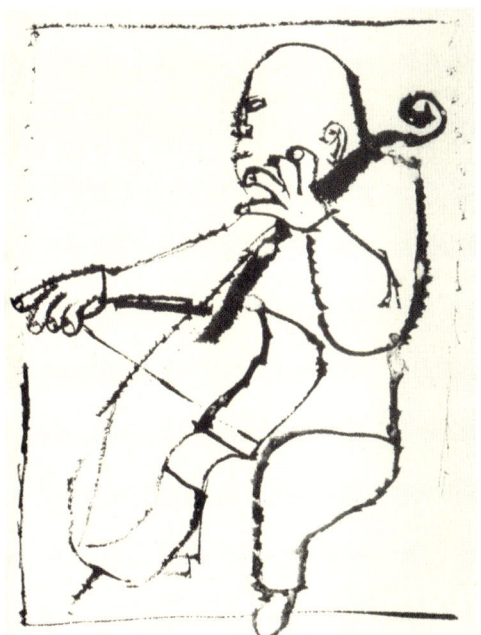

5
Defaced Portrait, 1955

6
Casals with Cello, 1969

Europe and the U.S. were noted circa 1954–64 in the Spanish art journal *Goya*, which was founded in 1954 and regularly featured American art. And while Shahn's social realism was praised by Vicente Aguilera Cerni, "an important voice for American art in Spain," in his book *Arte norteamericano del siglo XX* (1957), it was generally U.S. abstract art (i.e., abstract expressionism) that found a more "welcoming context" in Spain. As Claudia Hopkins has stated: "Paradoxically, as is now well known, the conservative Francoist regime, craving international acceptance, promoted Spanish abstraction in international exhibition contexts in order to project a positive image of Spain" as a place of creative freedom.[47]

Shahn was better known in the 1950s and 1960s in other European countries—in the United Kingdom and especially in Italy. Despite his involvement in controversies regarding a cancelled 1947 U.S. State Department exhibition and subsequent attacks by right-wing congressmen on "communistic" modern art, Shahn was selected by MoMA in 1954, along with abstract expressionist Willem de Kooning, to represent U.S. painting at the Venice Biennale. (Shahn was favored by critics for his sincerity, his sympathy for oppressed people, and his individualistic style.) In 1956, MoMA and the U.S. Information Agency funded Shahn's trip to the Institute of Contemporary Arts in London. As argued by Pohl, Julia Tatiana Bailey, and others, Shahn's figurative realism and social content served as a symbol of U.S. freedom in the early Cold War—as much as abstract art did.[48] Between 1961 and 1963, a Shahn retrospective and a graphics show, sponsored by MoMA's International Council, traveled to Israel and Japan and throughout Europe, but conspicuously not to Spain.[49] *Ben Shahn, On Nonconformity* will thus introduce Shahn's art on a large scale to Spanish audiences and reintroduce his work to new generations of European audiences.

There is some precedent for the Museo Reina Sofía exhibition. In 1984, in the early years of Spain's transition to democracy—when the social democratic government was dealing with an economic crisis and integration into the European community—the country saw its first solo exhibition on one aspect of Shahn's work. *Ben Shahn: Dibujos y fotografías de los años treinta y cuarenta*, organized by the Dirección General de Bellas Artes y Archivos (BAA), was shown at the Salas Pablo Ruiz Picasso in Madrid and was scheduled to travel to Valencia, Oviedo, and Barcelona. The director general of the BAA noted that Franklin Delano Roosevelt's New Deal (the economic context of Shahn's social realism) was "an era of experimentation ... [that] holds particular relevance for today's Spain."[50] Since 1992, four Shahn paintings have been part of the Museo Nacional Thyssen-Bornemisza in Madrid. More recently, the Museo Reina Sofía included a few Shahns in exhibitions such as *Black Mountain College: Experiment in Art* (2002–03) and *Encounters with the 1930s* (2012–13), which honored *Guernica*'s seventy-fifth anniversary. In 2020, the museum acquired its first Shahn work, *We French Workers Warn You* (1942) (p. 148 bottom), a multilayered propaganda poster circulated by the OWI, that holds great relevance for Europeans. Related to one of the Thyssen-Bornemisza paintings, the image shows workers protesting the labor decree on a "poster within a poster," issued by the Nazi-collaborationist Vichy regime, whose security forces held close watch over Spanish Civil War refugees in France during World War II.

Displaying this striking graphic within the present retrospective of Shahn's socially and politically engaged art comes at a critical moment in the history of Western European art museums, many of which are grappling with the legacies of imperialism and autocracy. The Museo Reina Sofía, rethinking its role and "responsibilities as a 21st-century cultural institution," inaugurated in 2021 a "rereading" of its permanent collection, evocatively titled "Communicating Vessels." Indeed, the museum has been committed for some time to diversifying its holdings and expanding its exhibitions to be more inclusive of female artists, Latin American artists, and forgotten Spanish exile-artists of the Franco era. Innovative—and often conceptual— curatorial investigations have addressed global

47. Hopkins, "Bienvenido!," 60–63. Thanks to Beatriz Cordero Martín for her research on the journal *Goya*.

48. Pohl, *New Deal Artist*, 147–72; Julia Tatiana Bailey, "'Realism Reconsidered': Ben Shahn in London, 1956," in *Modern American Art at Tate 1945–1980* (2019), tate.org.uk/research/publications/modern-american-art-at-tate/essays/realism-reconsidered. See also essays by Chiara Di Stefano.

49. The retrospective (1961–62) traveled to Holland, Belgium, Italy, and Austria; the graphics exhibition (1962–63) to Germany, Yugoslavia, Slovenia, Sweden, Israel, and Japan. The largely positive press reviews are housed in the Museum of Modern Art Archives.

50. Manuel Fernández Miranda, Foreword, in Eugenia Cucalón et al., *Ben Shahn: Dibujos y fotografías de los años treinta y cuarenta* (Madrid: Salas Pablo Ruiz Picasso, 1984), 5.

51. Sam Jones, "How a Small Photo of a Bomb Site Took Its Place Alongside Picasso's *Guernica*," *The Guardian*, December 10, 2021, theguardian.com/world/2021/dec/10/reina-sofia-museum-reorganisation-robert-capa-photo. These efforts might further be examined in the context of Spain's Historical Memory Law of 2007 and the Democratic Memory Law of 2022, both aimed at addressing the legacy of the Franco era.

52. Pohl, *New Deal Artist*, 111.

53. Shahn to Baskerville, Septembèr 26, 1946, BSP-AAA; Belgrad, *The Culture of Spontaneity*, 10; Michelle Kelley, "Fun and Facts about America: Postwar Corporate Liberalism and the Animated Economic Educational Film," *Journal of Cinema and Media Studies* 61, no. 1 (Fall 2021): 154.

54. Maurice Berger, *Revolution of the Eye: Modern Art and the Birth of American Television* (New Haven: Yale University Press, 2014); Pohl, *New Deal Artist*, 138–39.

55. Shahn, "The Artist and the Politicians," *Art News* 52, no. 5 (September 1953): 6; Shahn, "Remarks to *The New Republic*," in John D. Morse, ed., *Ben Shahn* (London: Secker & Warburg, 1972), 212–13.

environmental crises as well as those related to migration, exile, colonialism, and cultural imperialism.[51] The exhibiting of Shahn's far-reaching art, contextualized in thematic episodes with archival documentation—and featuring the scholarly perspectives of catalogue essayists from the U.S., Spain, Germany, and the United Kingdom—offers yet another powerful way to further such timely explorations.

COMMITMENTS AND CONTRADICTIONS

While Shahn was ahead of his time (which partly explains his continued relevance), he was also of his time. He was a man of paradoxes who remains as fascinating for his contradictions as for his commitments. Shahn's biographers, as Pohl has stated, have long noted Shahn's paradoxical nature: "that he was popular with both labor organizations and big business, that he defended the primacy of content at the same time as he engaged in formal experimentation, that he was both political and spiritual."[52] Shahn was as comfortable speaking Yiddish with his working-class neighbors in the New Deal cooperative town of Jersey Homesteads (later Roosevelt), New Jersey, his home from 1939 to 1969, as he was conversing with Nobel prize-winning intellectuals at nearby Princeton University and "well-bred" curators at MoMA. In our current moment, other paradoxes or dualities emerge as we ask different questions of his art. For example, how did Shahn square his sharp critique of capitalism (and class privilege) in the 1930s with his embrace of commercial work in the postwar period? How do we make sense of his biting caricatures of General Motors president Alfred P. Sloan or the scandalous media mogul William Randolph Hearst alongside his commissions from *Time*, *Fortune*, *Harper's*, CBS Broadcasting, Container Corporation, Upjohn Company, and Volkswagen, among other corporations?

These questions must be asked because when Shahn worked for the OWI, he and other New Deal liberals and progressives vehemently opposed the takeover of the agency by corporate advertising executives. And in 1946 Shahn rejected a commission from the Chrysler Corporation, stating that industry should not stipulate content and that the artist can only make work "if he feels a powerful urgency in a situation." But given the massive scope of Shahn's commercial production, how did he navigate what Dan Belgrad has called "the triumph of a corporate-liberal advertising culture" in the postwar years? How did his work interface with, affirm, and/or subvert the growing power of large, monopolistic corporations and the ways big business sought "to sell Americans on the merits of U.S. capitalism?"[53] We know, for instance, that Shahn raised the level of commercial design to a high art, exerted a towering influence on the field, and invented a widely appropriated folk alphabet. He worked for television but also noted its menacing influence on culture. He even criticized how U.S. consumer products were promoted overseas in the postwar years, as this reinforced the nation's reputation as philistine and materialistic in European eyes.[54]

Shahn not only called out the rising economic imperialism of the U.S. abroad but also the increase in U.S. military interventions overseas. Although he saw U.S. democracy as "the most appealing idea that the world has yet known" and was a critic of the Soviet Union, he railed against U.S. military involvement in Southeast Asia. In a 1964 talk for *The New Republic*, he wittily highlighted "the folly of our tactics" in Vietnam and predicted that the U.S. military would do the same in Indonesia, regretting that "artists will not be consulted in time to prevent bloodshed."[55] In 1967, he further expressed his protest of the Vietnam War in the *New York Times* with a peace message that paired his image of Gandhi with an antiwar quotation by Mark Twain. But it is unlikely that Shahn would have used the current language of colonialism or subscribed to the concept of "internal colonialism," as voiced by activists in his own time to refer to Black, native, and Latino peoples living in urban blight or on reservations as "colonized" citizens within the U.S. Seeing its greatest popularity in the late 1960s and early 1970s with the radicalization of the civil rights movement led by Black nationalist groups, this theory represented for Shahn a militancy that, despite his progressive views on race and his potent images of the movement's pioneers, he did not seem to share.[56]

Shahn's anti-colonial work focused on the older European empires of Belgium, France, and Great Britain, the latter of which was the largest the world has known. He thereby supported the sweeping postwar decolonization movements in Asian and African countries. As early as 1925 in Tunisia, Shahn "join[ed] briefly the native 'underground' movement against the French."[57] In *India* (1943), he pictured the victims of the 1943 Bengal famine in British India (today's Bangladesh), which is based on a *New York Times* photograph of a family "ravaged by starvation"—in a tragedy that recent research has shown was exacerbated by British wartime colonial policies (figs. 7–8).[58] Over twenty years later, Shahn memorialized Gandhi, whose nonviolent disobedience strategies against British rule inspired Martin Luther King, Jr. and U.S. civil rights struggles (pp. 246–247). Shahn illustrated advertisements for "Reports from Africa" (1954–56), Edward R. Murrow's *See It Now* CBS television series featuring "the rising resistance to colonialism." One of Shahn's drawings includes stylized if not exoticized images of faceless African porters carrying baskets on their heads—abstracted figures revealing little cultural insight into the peoples depicted. Others include a more pensive, individualized portrait of an unidentified African man who faces the viewer, and a somber rendering of a South African family shown with overt signs of Apartheid-era discrimination (pp. 248–249). For the CBS film *Satchmo the Great* (1957), Shahn made spirited drawings from press photographs of renowned trumpeter Louis Armstrong and his All-Stars' European and African tours, including the life-changing visit of this "jazz ambassador" to Accra in the Gold Coast (today's Ghana) in May 1956. Shahn recognized Armstrong's support of the African nation's civil disobedience campaign for freedom from Britain, which it achieved in March 1957 (p. 249 left).

Further, Shahn supported the United Nations (UN) from its inception in 1945, with its founding charter based on "respect for the principle of equal rights and self-determination of peoples." His haunting commissioned painting of the late UN Secretary-General, *Dag Hammarskjold* (1962) (fig. 9), must be seen in the context of the decolonization of the Belgium Congo. The isolated Hammarskjold is flanked by a flaming beast symbolizing nuclear destruction and an excerpt of a speech—his response to Nikita Khrushchev's demand for his resignation over his handling of the Belgian-Congolese violence, which erupted in the wake of Congo's declaration of independence in 1960. Shahn's work is a defense of his friend—more philosopher than politician—after his death on September 18, 1961, in a mysterious plane crash in then-Northern Rhodesia (today's Zambia). Strong evidence suggests that this was an assassination by Congolese separatists and European mercenaries funded by Belgian mining interests (with possible assistance from U.S. intelligence agencies) who opposed Hammarskjold's peace mission in the new independent Republic of Congo.[59]

Shahn's critique of European empire coexists—or stands in tension with—his love of European culture, which he held as a high ideal. His art training at New York's National Academy of Design and at Parisian art academies was Eurocentric. His wartime paintings lament the destruction of classical landscapes in Italy, based on the premise that European culture was the heir to ancient Rome. Shahn revered Italian Renaissance art, designed stage sets for a Jerome Robbins ballet at the 1958 Festival of Two Worlds in Spoleto, Umbria, and at the time of the 1954 Venice Biennale called Italy "the home place." Indeed, Italy, along with France, was a favorite travel destination of Shahn's in the postwar years, when he advised art students to "go to Paris and Madrid and Rome and Ravenna and Padua"

56. Charles Pinderhughes, "Internal Colonialism," in B. S. Turner, ed., *The Wiley-Blackwell Encyclopedia of Social Theory* (2017), onlinelibrary.wiley.com/doi/10.1002/9781118430873.est0187.

57. Selden Rodman, *Portrait of the Artist as an American, Ben Shahn: A Biography with Pictures* (New York: Harper & Brothers, 1951), 141.

58. Michael Safi, "Churchill's policies contributed to 1943 Bengal famine-study," *The Guardian*, March 29, 2019, theguardian.com/world/2019/mar/29/winston-churchill-policies-contributed-to-1943-bengal-famine-study.

59. United Nations Charter, Chapter 1: Purposes and Principles: Article 1 (2) (signed on June 26, 1945); Colum Lynch, "What Really Happened to Dag Hammarskjold's Plane," *Foreign Policy* (February 15, 2022), foreignpolicy.com/2022/02/15/hammarskjold-plane-crash-united-nations/.

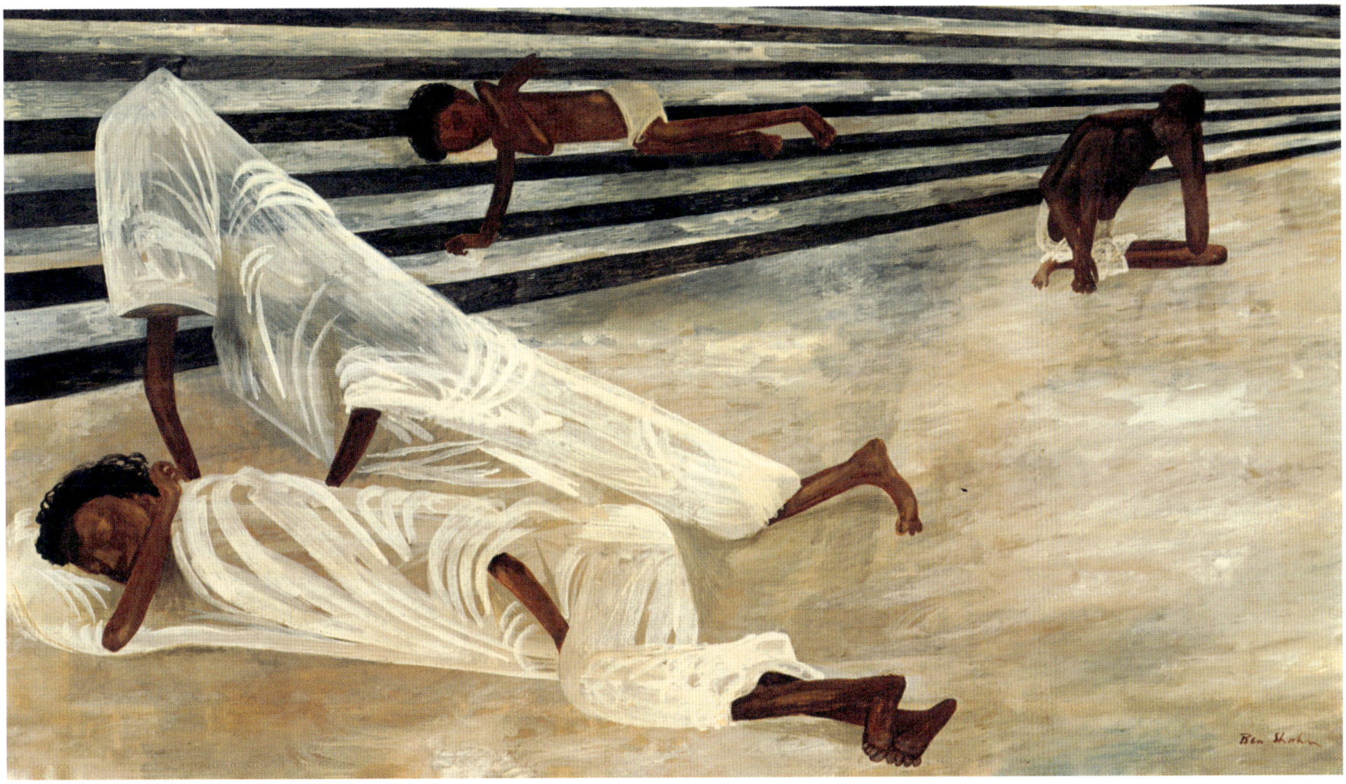

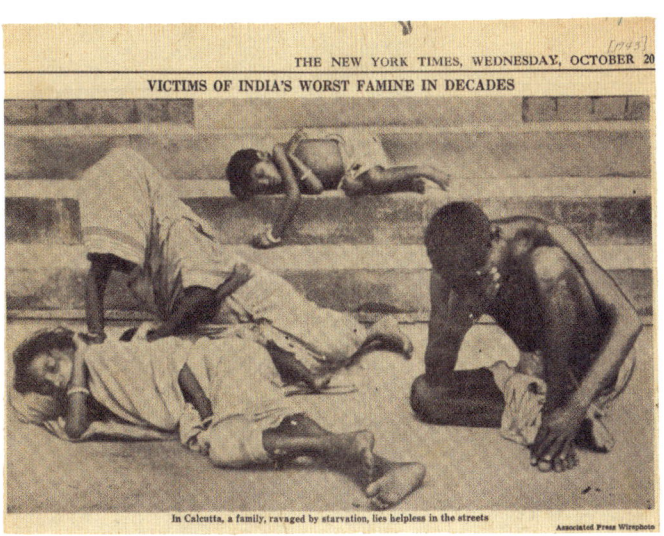

7
India, 1943

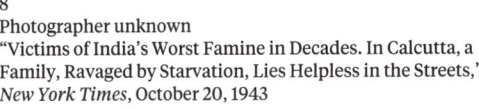
8
Photographer unknown
"Victims of India's Worst Famine in Decades. In Calcutta, a
Family, Ravaged by Starvation, Lies Helpless in the Streets,"
New York Times, October 20, 1943

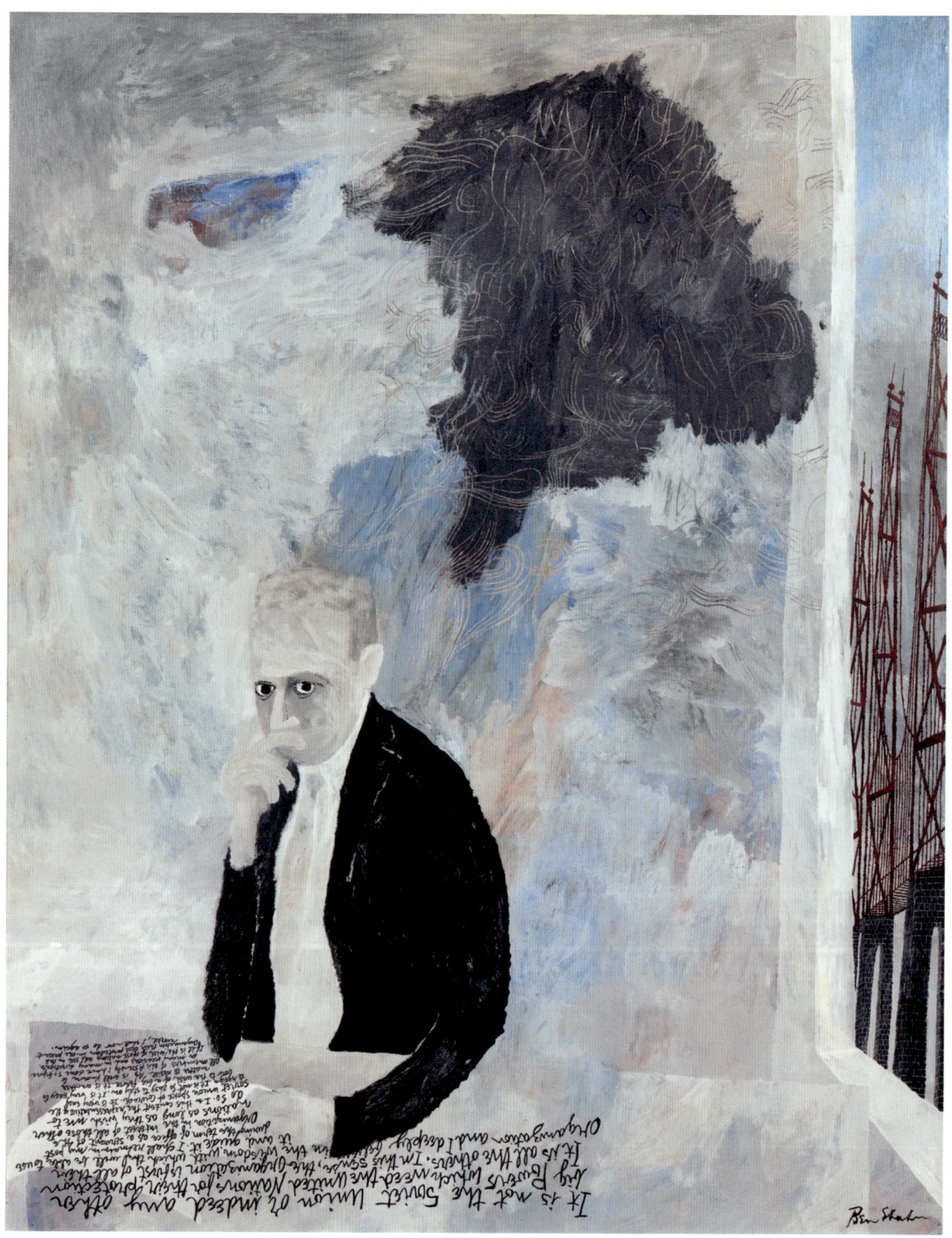

9
Dag Hammarskjöld, Doctor of Philosophy, Public
Government Official, United Nations Secretary-General,
1962

60. Pohl, *New Deal Artist*, 158; Shahn, *The Shape of Content*, 113–14; Greenfeld, *Ben Shahn*, 292–98; Shahn, "The Artist and the Politicians," 34–35, 67.

61. Shahn to Philip Shan, April 19, 1929, BSP-AAA; Shahn, *Love and Joy About Letters* (New York: Grossman, 1963), 46, 27; Katzman, "The Politics of Media," 105–6, 144, note 22.

62. Columbia interview, 1960, 127–29; Sakai et al., *Ben Shahn: Cross Media Artist*, 213–17.

and to "read Sophocles and Euripides and Dante and Proust." Fluent in French, Shahn insisted that aspiring artists should "know French" and he spent much (frustrated) energy in the late 1950s trying to enhance his reputation across Europe through Arnold Fawcus of Trianon Press, which produced deluxe editions of his illustrated books *Haggadah* (1966) and *Ecclesiastes* (1967). Finally, Shahn cared about European intellectuals' perceptions of the U.S., quoting existentialist writers like Jean-Paul Sartre who feared U.S. influence on French culture at a time when the reactionary "sinister attack against art" and "official acts of suppression" rendered U.S. democracy hypocritical in the eyes of European allies.[60] European high culture thus remained an enduring reference point for the artist for much of his creative and political life.

It is critical to note, however, that Shahn did embrace the art of many non-Western cultures. His extended stay in Djerba may be attributed to his fascination with its ancient, Arab-speaking Jewish community, memories of which informed his 1931 watercolors for a *Haggadah*. But with scant information about Shahn's North African travels, along with his romanticist words about following in Eugène Delacroix's footsteps in Algiers and his quoting of Gustave Flaubert's *Salammbô* (set in ancient Carthage), he did not seem to push beyond Eurocentric, orientalist stereotypes of Arab and/or North African peoples as "exotic," sensual "others." Shahn collected non-Western art, including Hindu gouaches and pre-Columbian sculpture, and was fascinated by Mayan glyphs. As a child learning Hebrew and a young teenager training to be a lithographic engraver, he gained a deep and abiding love of lettering, which grew to include the Sanskrit and Arabic alphabets and Khmer script. He was especially drawn to Chinese and Japanese calligraphy, seeing the latter as "the honorable heirs to action painting" and to Western abstractionism. Shahn even planned a book on the legendary origins of certain Chinese ideograms—passions fueled by his travels in 1960 to New Zealand, Tahiti, Indonesia, Cambodia, Singapore, Hong Kong, and Japan. This excursion inspired Shahn to pick up the camera again, photographing street scenes, storefronts, and signage, with a special focus on the exquisite carvings and stone sculptures of monuments, temples, and other religious sites. Although he joked about being a tourist photographer, his 35 mm snapshots are far from conventional postcard views. They reveal his cultural awareness that Eastern "esthetic and religious principles are so highly fused."[61]

Shahn drew similarities between the ancient Japanese city of Kyoto and interwar Paris. His special affinity for Japanese culture began as early as the mid-1940s, when he collected source material related to Japan and World War II. An International News photograph of August 9, 1945, from Hiroshima, "Atom's Destruction"—showing a modern building with "steel girders twisted into grotesque shapes"—became a symbolic motif in certain Shahn works that convey the destructive potential of science. He made drawings and paintings to commemorate the 1954 *Lucky Dragon* nuclear disaster at Bikini Atoll (1957–62) (pp. 230–233). In Japan he had a chop created of the Hebrew alphabet, which he stamped on new and even older works. Shahn collaborated with Nakashima, who in the 1960s designed additions and furniture for Shahn's International Style modernist home, synthesizing modern principles and traditional Japanese craft methods. Such admiration was reciprocal, as Shahn's art has long been revered in Japan—influential to Japanese graphic art during its postwar economic growth. (One aim of his 1960 trip was to review Japanese printmaking.) Indeed, Japan has organized numerous solo exhibitions on Shahn; notable collections of his work are held by the Marunuma Art Park and the Fukushima Prefectural Museum of Art; and Japanese writers have made pilgrimages to Shahn's homes in the U.S. and Europe.[62]

Shahn's worldliness was informed by a universal humanist philosophy of the Western liberal tradition—a "new humanism" associated with the Franz Boas school of cultural anthropology that recognized and appreciated the cultural differences of peoples across the globe but affirmed their common human identity. These concepts were critical to the Cold War political integration of diverse countries under the umbrella of a "free world" alignment against authoritarian regimes. According to Cécile Whiting, Shahn's adherence to such a "pluralistic humanism" and shift (in his antinuclear and post-Holocaust work) to a more symbolic style that "minimized signs of racial and ethnic identity" enabled him to "extend compassion across national, ethnic, and racial divides" and "affirm a shared humanity." Yet as also articulated by Whiting, who referenced postcolonial theories, universal humanism has its pitfalls and limitations. This is evident in its "tendency to eradicate cultural specificity in the quest for an ideal of sameness ... defined by the dominant culture" and to ignore the historical particularities of the suffering of distinct individuals or groups and of targeted genocides.[63]

How universal was Shahn's humanism? Like many leftist male artists of his generation, Shahn was more attuned to race, ethnicity, and class than to gender. Male figures dominate his paintings, posters, and murals about immigration, rural and industrial life, and the labor movement, as well as works dealing with the McCarthy era, civil rights struggles, and nuclear disaster.[64] When shown, women are often depicted as protective mothers, worried wives, grieving widows, or other vulnerable figures. In certain prints, women appear as ancient Roman goddesses with mysterious, supernatural powers. Notable exceptions are found in Shahn's photographs of Black female workers in Arkansas cotton fields or more privileged white female artist-activists in New York City. Women protesting to keep alcohol illegal are prominent in his *Prohibition* mural (pp. 130–131). The image of a sole woman toiling in a textile mill in the Bronx Central Post Office mural (by Shahn and Bernarda Bryson), according to Linden, both "corresponds to the marginalization of women in the [industrial] workforce" and stands out as "an exception in New Deal art."[65] Yet Shahn's art of the 1930s and 1940s, for example, does not reflect the increasing numbers of women taking jobs during the Depression in domestic service, teaching, and clerical fields (as "women's work" was less affected by the economic crisis). Nor does his art address the millions of women hired into the U.S. industrial labor force to support the World War II effort, when millions of men were drafted or enlisted into the military.

What is remarkable about this relative absence in Shahn's art of women engaged in wage work beyond the domestic sphere is that the artist was surrounded by strong, independent career women whom he respected, who inspired him, and who helped launch and maintain his career, years before the second wave of feminism began circa 1963. His first wife Tillie Goldstein, who shared with him a Jewish immigrant upbringing in Brooklyn, was a smart and politically engaged woman who worked as a bookkeeper to help pay for Shahn's travels abroad. His second spouse, Bernarda Bryson (later Bryson Shahn), who hailed from a more privileged Scottish, Christian family in Ohio, was a printmaker, illustrator, and writer, who as president, then secretary, of the Artists' Union and a one-time communist, influenced Shahn's political radicalization. Theirs was passionate love between equals, rooted in leftist affinities, ranging from their fascination with Russian newsreels to the socialist speeches of Norman Thomas to the labor histories of Samuel Yellen. Working to build a world closer to their own beliefs, they collaborated for the Resettlement Administration, the U.S. Treasury's Section of Fine Arts, and the Congress of Industrial Organizations-Political Action Committee.[66]

Shahn deeply admired RA-FSA photographer Dorothea Lange; New York Public Library superintendent Romana Javitz; MoMA curator Mildred Constantine; critic Betty Chamberlain; poet Muriel Rukeyser; and until their relationship deteriorated in the 1960s, his longtime dealer Edith Halpert of the Downtown Gallery. In a 1957 interview Shahn spoke of Halpert as "the dean of American art," a pioneer responsible for the careers of many

63. Cécile Whiting, "Ben Shahn: Aggrieved Men and Nuclear Fallout during the Cold War," *American Art* 30, no. 3 (Fall 2016): 5, 12–13, 18. On how Shahn in his 1950s work avoided the "naïve humanism" that is often associated with MoMA's *Family of Man* exhibition (1955), see Christof Decker, "A Unique Universalism: Ben Shahn and the Rhetoric of Visual Anecdotes," in James Dorson et al., *Anecdotal Modernity: Making and Unmaking History* (Berlin: De Gruyter, 2020), 263–78.

64. Whiting argued that Shahn countered the antinuclear movement's stereotypical use of images of women and children as victims of nuclear disaster, creating works that reflect a "compassionate masculinity." See note 63.

65. Linden, *Ben Shahn's New Deal Murals*, 85–86; Langa, *Radical Art*, 122–27, 213–19. Shahn's *The Clinic* (1944) (p. 183) and *Convention* (1949), which address the need for decent obstetrics/neonatal care and the existence of sexual harassment, respectively, speak to his concern for improving certain oppressive conditions for women.

66. See Shahn-Bryson correspondence, undated (c. 1936–early 1940s), BBSP-AAA.

67. Columbia interview, 1957, 108–9, 112.

68. See Rodman and Greenfeld biographies, and Edwin Rosskam, *Roosevelt, New Jersey: Big Dreams in a Small Town and What Time Did to Them* (New York: Grossman, 1972). Shahn's closest friend in later years, Rosskam noted his arrogance, but also his kindness and brilliance. Bryson Shahn's perspectives are gleaned from Interviews with Bernarda Bryson Shahn by the author, Roosevelt, New Jersey, 1989–2002, untranscribed.

69. Shahn, "Aspects of Realism," Black Mountain College, 1951, lecture transcript, BSP-AAA; Shahn, *The Shape of Content*, 38.

70. Shahn, "The Problem of Artistic Creation in America Today" (1953), in Morse, ed., *Ben Shahn*, 210.

prominent artists who did "a brilliant job" in bringing "primitive art" to the fore; he was grateful for their long artist-dealer relationship. He praised art director Cipe Pineles as one of "the most courageous, the most inventive minds" in the commercial art world. [67] Yet Shahn biographers have also acknowledged his strong patriarchal side, noting his bitterness, anger, arrogance, and self-centeredness. Shahn caused much suffering to his first wife, daughter, and son, whom he essentially abandoned in New York City in the middle of the Depression (he saw the children sporadically in their early years) to start a relationship with Bryson Shahn, with whom he would raise three children and spend the rest of his life. Despite their enduring intellectual companionship, their mutual stubbornness led to volatile conflict, and she too suffered as a result of Shahn's dominant personality. She had to fit her career in and around the care of her family and Shahn's career, which she nurtured and protected, while hosting a constant stream of Shahn admirers. Like many progressive women of her generation, Bryson Shahn relied on her wit and cleverness to "negotiate" with her partner more space and time in their house to pursue her own creative and political work.[68]

CONCLUDING REMARKS

Addressing the contradictions and dualities of Ben Shahn's art and life allows one to understand the artist holistically. Shahn neither glorified nor romanticized the ordinary people who populate his pictorial worlds. His subjects—waiting or working, suffering yet persevering, melancholic and hopeful—are pictured with feeling and restrained dignity. It seems fitting that Shahn and his art should be approached with the critical eye and compassionate heart with which he saw the world. As artist-activist-philosopher, Shahn left an extraordinary body of work that incisively chronicles the forgotten (as well as the famous) figures and events of much twentieth-century U.S. and global history. In so doing, he engaged in and expanded on what he called "aspects of realism." He experimented with old and new styles, drawing and redrawing on a rich trove of photographic and literary sources to make moving social statements and penetrating political commentary. Ultimately, Shahn used real-world particularities (or what he called "individual peculiarities") to create universal symbols for his time.[69]

Perhaps Shahn's greatest gifts are not the answers that his art offers to society's problems, though such answers are evident, for example, in his labor posters that announce the basic needs required for a decent existence. Rather, his most impactful legacy may lie in the questions that he asks of art: What are the roles that artists can play in society? What modes of art best communicate human experiences? And how can art aid in the perpetual struggle for a more just future? It is Shahn's musing on these profound questions in his compelling images and words that has endured. He extolled the power of art to stir the moral conscience of viewers, to elicit empathy for others, and to create meaning. As he eloquently said in 1953— notably at the height of the McCarthyite assault on civil liberties—it is the artist's "values, his judgments, made with love, or anger, or compassion that live in the work of art and make it significant to the public."[70] For Shahn, artists were not only creators who construct meaning, but also "truth-tellers"—catalysts in the quest for social justice. His faith in this latter role is "a much-needed feeling" at this crucial moment, as reactionary forces have severely tested the democratic experiment in the United States, as well as in other established and aspiring democracies in Europe and around the world.

WORKING AND WAITING: BEN SHAHN'S PICTURES OF AND AFTER LABOR

John Fagg

1. Walter Abell, "Art and Labor," *Magazine of Art* 39, no. 6 (October 1946): 262.

2. Ben Shahn, "Artist's Statement," in Dorothy C. Miller and Alfred H. Barr, Jr., eds., *American Realists and Magic Realists* (New York: The Museum of Modern Art, 1943), 52. Elsewhere Shahn said he started the trade at age fourteen.

3. Shahn, *Love and Joy About Letters* (New York: Grossman, 1963), 15.

4. Diego Rivera, "The Revolutionary Spirit in Modern Art," *The Modern Quarterly* 6, no. 3 (Fall 1932): 51–57, here 56. See Alejandro Anreus et al., *Ben Shahn and the Passion of Sacco and Vanzetti* (Jersey City: Jersey City Museum and Rutgers University Press, 2001).

Commercial and industrial projects can't hold out the spiritual comfort that work with labor gives. —Ben Shahn, 1946[1]

Before mark-making was art for Ben Shahn, it was work. Born into a family of woodcarvers and potters in Lithuania and following his family's migration to the United States in 1906, he was apprenticed at age fifteen to Hessenberg's lithography workshop in Lower Manhattan.[2] There Shahn began working toward the active, artisanal line that would come to characterize his drawing, printmaking, and painting. He later explained that this early experience of "cutting" lines onto lithographic stones meant that in his mature art, "I found that this chiseled sort of line had become a necessity, a sort of temperamental fixture, so that even when I drew with a brush the line retained that style."[3] Shahn put that line to work, delineating laborers' shirt sleeves hitched at the elbows; faces worn with toil and strain; and most strikingly hands, whether grasping hammers, raised as fists, or contorted in expressions of worry and grief. His career spanned from before the Red Decade of the 1930s, when trade unionism and socialism came close to mainstream politics, to after the second Red Scare of the 1950s, when suppression and persecution of the left ran rampant. He witnessed the shift from the producer economy (grounded in coal and steel) of the prewar years to the emerging consumer culture of the 1960s, which changed the nature and meaning of work in the U.S. Even as the political landscape shifted and Shahn's thematic and stylistic concerns evolved, the cause of labor always remained embedded in his thinking and in his artistic gestures.

Shahn's first deep investment in the form and theme of labor manifests in his paintings on the Sacco and Vanzetti and the Mooney scandals. In the early years of the Great Depression he turned from what he saw as the disengaged avant-garde art he encountered on two European trips in the 1920s to a directness and simplicity that he developed circa 1930–31 in depicting the infamous Dreyfus Affair and then applied to other *causes célèbres*. The case of Nicola Sacco and Bartolomeo Vanzetti, Italian immigrants and anarchists executed in 1927 for a murder many believe they did not commit, spoke to Shahn's sense of justice and inspired the series of twenty-three paintings that he exhibited at the Downtown Gallery in 1932. Shahn presented Sacco, a shoemaker, and Vanzetti, a fish peddler, as ordinary, dignified laborers in the context of their working-class, immigrant Boston community. In *Bartolomeo Vanzetti and Nicola Sacco* (1931–32) (p. 71), the men sit side by side, the composition centered on Vanzetti's left wrist cuffed to Sacco's right—strong working hands denied by force the right to work. Using a montage of elements, Shahn created the horizontal panel *The Passion of Sacco and Vanzetti* (1931–32), which he submitted to a mural competition at the Museum of Modern Art (MoMA) in New York. At left, Sacco and Vanzetti stand alongside Parisian demonstrators: linked arms, raised placards, and one man's red scarf wrap the victims in the embrace of international solidarity. These aspects led Mexican muralist Diego Rivera to observe that Shahn's paintings "possess the necessary qualities, accessibility, and power to make them important to the proletariat."[4] The ideal Rivera pursued in his murals and saw in Shahn's work was an art at once *of* and *for* working people.

While the Sacco and Vanzetti series may have been motivated by Shahn's abhorrence of injustice, which he attributed to an intense childhood reaction to an Old Testament test of faith,[5] he directly engaged the labor politics of the interwar years with the Tom Mooney case. Mooney, a San Francisco union organizer, had been convicted for a 1916 bombing, despite perjured testimony and a strong alibi. In his Mooney series, as in *Tom Mooney Handcuffed* (1932–33) (p. 73), Shahn again showed a worker denied work, picturing Mooney—an iron molder by trade—imprisoned and inert. In *Apotheosis* (1932–33), Mooney is framed by a carceral architecture of bleak brick walls that cut him off from his mother (whose sash proclaims, "My son is innocent"), the bland bureaucrats who adjudicate his fate, and the passionate crowd gathered to demand his release. At the height of the Depression, and with labor in the fore of public and political consciousness, this was a widespread demand, as evident in a 1934 folk song that cast Mooney's story as the "Ballad of the American Dreyfus Case" and in a 1938 *Life* magazine piece that named him "America's Most Famous Prisoner." Shahn's series claims Mooney's cause as the cause of labor and the left, whose raised fists in *Apotheosis* embody their protest. Shahn repeated this image of protest in another painting from the series, *Demonstration* (1933), and based both on an Associated Press photograph of a communist demonstration from the *New York Telegram*, found in Shahn's source archive. The act of repurposing photographic images to insinuate the politics of the original context into new settings would become a defining feature of Shahn's multilayered art.

This artistic practice found full expression when Shahn began painting from his own photographs. Equipped with a Leica camera and hurried instructions from his studio mate Walker Evans, and following a foundational stint as a New York street photographer,[6] Shahn set off in late 1935, with his future second wife Bernarda Bryson at the wheel, on a documentary road trip for the New Deal government's Resettlement Administration (RA). Traveling south through the coal mining workscapes of Pennsylvania and West Virginia, Shahn stopped at Scotts Run, West Virginia—a cluster of Appalachian towns that had become a notorious symbol of the Depression's devastating economic impact on mining communities.[7] Shahn's RA photographs from this trip, including *Striking Miners, Scotts Run, West Virginia* (1935) (p. 122 top) and *Payoff at Pursglove Mine, Scotts Run, West Virginia* (1935), were repurposed in the temperas *Scotts Run, West Virginia* (1937) (p. 123) and *Unemployed* (1938) (p. 119).

The paintings' titles strip away the specific details of mining and striking that the source photographs and their captions record. *Scotts Run, West Virginia* shows three men seemingly loitering without purpose in a railroad yard (p. 123). The men's inactivity; the desolate, scrubby yard; and the coal dust-stained company houses create an image of the malaise and degradation of working people's lives, which elides the picketing workers' proactive protest of their condition. Shahn's painting thus appears to be a passive document of everyday life in the Depression that avoids the kind of politics that might have made the Whitney Museum of American Art, which purchased it in 1938, uncomfortable. But traces of the confrontational atmosphere of the *Striking Miners* photograph linger in *Scotts Run, West Virginia*, in the piercing squint of the tallest man and in the central figure's left hand (p. 122 top). Here Shahn's lithographic line cuts through the tempera paint, taking on the graphic physicality of left-wing cartoons where proletarian muscles bulge and flex, hinting that the thumb pressed to forefinger might curl into a fist. The election posters interpolated from other Shahn photographs also suggest a political subtext to the scene. Shahn's painting, like much of his social realist work, wrestled with the question: How could artists on the left meaningfully express their politics in paint?

Shahn's RA road trip was part of a much larger New Deal program of federal patronage for the arts, for which he worked not only as a photographer but also as a muralist, graphic artist, exhibit designer, and advisor. Regarding this program, in a 1933 letter to President Franklin Delano Roosevelt (FDR), artist George Biddle cited Rivera's claim that the Mexican mural movement "was only possible because [President Álvaro] Obregón allowed Mexican artists to work at plumbers' wages in order to express on the walls of the Government Buildings the social ideals of the Mexican revolution." His suggestion that a similar scheme would enable young American artists to express their awareness of the "social revolution

5. John D. Morse, "Ben Shahn: An Interview," *Magazine of Art* 37, no. 4 (April 1944): 136.

6. See Deborah Martin Kao, Laura Katzman, and Jenna Webster, *Ben Shahn's New York: The Photography of Modern Times* (New Haven: Yale University Press, 2000).

7. On mining workscapes, see Thomas G. Andrews, *Killing for Coal: America's Deadliest Labor War* (Cambridge, Mass.: Harvard University Press, 2008), 125.

8. Quotes from George Biddle, "An Art Renascence Under Federal Patronage," *Scribner's Magazine* 93, no. 5 (May 9, 1933): 428, 430.

9. See Diana L. Linden, *Ben Shahn's New Deal Murals: Jewish Identity in the American Scene* (Detroit: Wayne State University Press, 2015).

10. Howard Greenfeld, *Ben Shahn: An Artist's Life* (New York: Random House, 1998), 188, 193.

11. Warren Carter, *Figuring the New Deal: Publics and Ideology in Treasury Section Painting and Sculpture in Washington, D.C., 1934–1943* (PhD diss., University College London, 2013), 242.

that our country and civilization are going through" instigated the 1934 Public Works of Art Project and subsequent programs that employed artists to make easel paintings, graphics, and public murals for schools, hospitals, and federal buildings. In a magazine article, Biddle further explained: "For the first time in our history the government has recognized the social necessity of art in life. Not only does it recognize the same responsibility to indigent artists as to indigent plumbers or bricklayers, it accepts a further responsibility to foster art and keep it alive during the depression."[8] U.S. government policy, at least for a brief moment, acknowledged the kinship between fine art and craft labor to which Shahn was committed: art could be purposeful, decently paid work.

Shahn's immersion in the practice and politics of mural painting came during his work as one of Rivera's assistants on the ill-fated 1933 mural commission at Rockefeller Center. There he learned—through masterful example—wall-scale composition and fresco technique, but also witnessed the breakdown of the professional working relationship between artists and patrons of opposing political ideologies. Rivera's mural was censored (and later destroyed) when it was found to contain a portrait of communist leader Vladimir Lenin. Shahn then conducted his own, largely successful fresco mural for an RA commission for Jersey Homesteads, the New Deal cooperative town built for Jewish garment workers that became the location of the Shahn family home from 1939 to the end of his life. There he depicted Eastern European Jewish immigration to the U.S. intertwined with labor union history, both critical to the formation of the town. Building on these experiences, Shahn would also place labor at the heart of the two coveted mural commissions he won from the U.S. federal government's Section of Fine Arts.[9]

In the mural *Resources of America* (1938–39), painted by both Shahn and Bryson, the towering figures of textile workers, gleaners, cotton pickers, and engineers dominate large panels in the main hall of the Bronx Central Post Office. In *The Meaning of Social Security* (1940–42), scenes of unemployment and destitution give way to the labor of New Deal infrastructure and social improvement projects along the main corridors of (what was briefly) the Social Security Building in Washington, D.C. (pp. 140–141, 143). Making art in public spaces and on the federal payroll came with demands, expectations, and controversies: the Walt Whitman quote Shahn chose for his Bronx mural was censored and some boosterish aspects of New Deal ideology are found in his Social Security mural. For many artists on the left, these conditions created an insurmountable tension with their commitment to an art of class struggle. For other painters of the period, the bureaucratic and collective culture of federal patronage was at odds with their individualistic artistic expression. By contrast, Shahn was relatively comfortable and successful in this environment, able to work within its structures and strictures to realize major mural projects. On completing his Social Security mural in 1942, Shahn brought the same collaborative spirit to work within government restrictions as Senior Liaison Officer in the Graphics Division of the Office of War Information (OWI), although there he was eventually thwarted by the "labyrinth of cross purposes" and petty bureaucracy that so often characterize white-collar work.[10]

The *Resources of America* and *The Meaning of Social Security* did not involve fundamental compromise for Shahn. While he contributed to the radical *Art Front* journal and other Popular Front activities linked to the Communist Party USA, his politics aligned with the "interventionist" and "progressive" public works projects of the early New Deal and he held deep respect for FDR.[11] Moreover, Shahn's commitment to labor was based on an ingrained, intergenerational feeling—a personal, visceral connection to work and workers that lay outside formal politics. Much of what he wanted to say about work could be expressed within the terms of a government commission, as seen in the Bronx mural study *Riveter* (1938). The tonal harmony of the Black worker's body and functional overalls mesh man and work. His strong forearm creates a line of force that runs through the power tool he wields with great precision—the product of a steady concentration that binds hand and eye. This is meaningful mental and manual labor, the proud expression of the whole person who performs it. The worker is to be valued, elevated to the larger-than-life scale of the Bronx Central Post Office's high ceilings, though not above the stoop labor of the cotton picker or the managerial work of the engineer featured in other panels. The mass of the composition is balanced by Shahn's delicate yet deliberate line, imbued with the same commitment to craft that the riveter displays.[12] Shahn's New Deal representations of work fit the strain of populist thought that Michael Kazin has termed "producerism"—an emotive investment in industrial and agricultural labor that was common currency across the U.S. political spectrum for much of the twentieth century.[13]

Making art *of* and *for* working people was not, however, an unproblematic endeavor. Where Biddle could write directly to FDR given their bond as classmates at the prestigious Croton School and make detached, theoretical claims about art, labor, and social revolution, Shahn—with his working-class Brooklyn upbringing and ongoing dialogue with working people—had a grounded, at times cynical, perspective. The construction workers who seemed enthralled by Rivera's Rockefeller Center mural told him they were willing to destroy it as they "would do anything for time and a half." Revisiting *Resources of America*, Shahn asked the post office service crew foreman if he liked the mural. "Not particularly, but I'm sure glad you put all these guys in overalls up on the walls," came the reply. "It helped me organize the building crew. Made 'em think they were important."[14] This was not quite what Rivera meant by an art "important to the proletariat," and such responses, which punctuate Shahn's recollections of the period, must have caused him to question the accessibility of his murals and whether they were truly *for* the working people they were *of*.

Those became pressing questions when Shahn began to work under the more means-ends logic of public communications and political campaigning, first for the OWI and then for the Congress of Industrial Organizations-Political Action Committee (CIO-PAC). Where the hierarchies and internal politics of the OWI tested Shahn's capacity to make art in an institutional setting, the CIO-PAC work was a labor of love that, especially during the 1944 campaign to reelect Roosevelt, aligned his political allegiance to the president with visual representation of work and workers. His best-known CIO-PAC poster, *For Full Employment After the War, Register, Vote* (1944), utilizes elements of his earlier imagery and working practice. Shahn took Alfred T. Palmer's OWI photograph of ship welders, which he obtained for his source files, and repurposed it for the political campaign (pp. 187 top, 186). As Laura Katzman has discovered, Shahn replaced one of the white welders from the photograph with a Black worker (from another photograph), thus picturing a diverse and unified work force—a yet-to-be-realized goal of the labor movement and the Democratic party.[15] (The interracial image was rejected for an earlier OWI poster.) The controversy generated by claims of the white welder's likeness to FDR emphasized the need for clarity in political communication. Indeed, Shahn would distill, even simplify, his motifs of labor in other CIO-PAC posters, such as *For All These Rights We've Just Begun to Fight* (1946) (p. 194), in which a worker's fist is raised amidst a density of slogans and banners.[16]

Shahn's energetic images of active New Deal and wartime workers were at odds with his own lived experience of work. As a documentarian whose instinct was to engage directly with the people he photographed, Shahn saw that periods of purposeful labor, moments of solidarity, or opportunities to take pride in a job well done were rare and fleeting. Alongside his mural projects he developed a type of easel painting that he described as "personal realism" and exhibited as "Sunday Paintings." This name evokes the artworks' contrast with

12. See John Fagg, "Unit and Gross: Picturing Individual Workers and Collective Labor," in David C. Ward and Dorothy Moss, *The Sweat of Their Face: Portraying American Workers* (Washington, D.C.: Smithsonian Books, 2017), 45–46.

13. Michael Kazin, *The Populist Persuasion: An American History* (Ithaca: Cornell University Press, 1994).

14. Shahn, "Artist's Statement," in Miller and Barr, eds., *American Realists and Magic Realists*, 53; Morse, "Ben Shahn: An Interview," 140.

15. Katzman, "Source Matters: Ben Shahn and the Archive," *Archives of American Art Journal* 54, no. 2 (Fall 2015): 21–25. See John Ott, "Graphic Consciousness: The Visual Cultures of Integrated Industrial Unions at Midcentury," *American Quarterly* 66, no. 4 (December 2014): 883–917.

16. On Shahn's CIO-PAC work, see Frances K. Pohl, *Ben Shahn: New Deal Artist in a Cold War Climate, 1947–1954* (Austin: University of Texas Press, 1989), 9–33.

17. Katzman identified and discussed Shahn's unofficial RA photographs from his source files in the Archives of American Art. Negatives are in the Harvard Art Museums. See Katzman, "Source Matters," 19–20, 33.

18. Quoted in Selden Rodman, *Portrait of the Artist as an American, Ben Shahn: A Biography with Pictures* (New York: Harper & Brothers, 1951), 77.

19. On Shahn's "Sunday Paintings," see Fagg, *Re-envisioning the Everyday: American Genre Scenes, 1905–1945* (University Park: Pennsylvania State University Press, 2023), 159–97.

20. John Bartlow Martin, "The Blast in Centralia No. 5: A Mine Disaster No One Stopped," *Harper's Magazine* 196, no. 1174 (March 1948): 193–220.

21. Martin, "The Blast in Centralia No. 5," 219.

22. "Interview (1957): Ben Shahn and Nadya Aisenberg," in John D. Morse, ed., *Ben Shahn*, (London: Secker & Warburg, 1972), 55.

his government commissions and their stylistic borrowings from amateur or "folk" art. In works such as *Puddlers' Sunday* (1937 or 1938) and *Sunday Morning* (1938–43), male workers stand or sit around at leisure, their stasis accentuated by their moribund surroundings. Both repurpose elements from Shahn's RA photographs; *Puddlers' Sunday* derives from one shot in a series of striking workers (figs. 1–3). Here the original context of the photograph, the violent confrontations between strikers and strikebreakers of the July 1937 Little Steel Strike in Ohio, is largely suppressed, buried beneath the banality of what appears to be a workers' excursion to the countryside.[17] On viewing these "Sunday Paintings" exhibited at the Julien Levy Gallery in spring 1940, one critic observed: "Everybody sits around dejected, grim as though waiting for something to happen to them—and something not very inspiring at that."[18] This was a Depression-era reality for relief clients and laid-off workers as well as for longshoremen and cotton pickers hoping to make the day's crew, not to mention desk-bound government employees waiting to meet the next boss. Even taking strike action often meant simply doing nothing.[19]

Waiting bound to working also underpins the series of paintings Shahn developed from his illustrations for John Bartlow Martin's 1948 *Harper's Magazine* article on a mine disaster in Centralia, Illinois.[20] In the postwar period, Shahn began to take assignments from mass-market magazines, as well as from advertisers such as the Container Corporation of America and the Columbia Broadcasting Company (CBS), finding new ways to be a working artist after federal patronage ended and his involvement with the CIO-PAC waned. Shahn took great care over the terms of these projects and preferred those that fit his personal and political convictions, hence his interest in Martin's work.

Detailing the bureaucratic inertia and indifference regarding the failings in mine safety that led to the buildup of coal dust and culminated in a mine explosion that claimed 111 lives, Martin immersed readers in the micropolitics of industrial relations. The long article ranges across the bland language of corporate, union, and local government buck-passing, the miners' passionate plea to "save our lives" in a whistleblowing letter, and the fatalistic folk speech of grieving families. Shahn's response, a burst of creativity that produced over one hundred line drawings, of which *Harper's* used twenty-four, instigated a period of friendship and collaboration with Martin. Here was an understanding of labor and the state that matched Shahn's own broad purview and that moved beyond partisan union politics. A story that demanded a hundred drawings and that occupied the most space *Harper's* had ever allocated to a single article contrasts sharply with the short slogans and truncated imagery of the CIO-PAC posters. Moreover, Martin did not hold back on indicting the United Mine Workers of America as part of the "vast, unapproachable, insensate organism" that meant no one individual or entity took responsibility or intervened to close the mine.[21]

Shahn's line drawings present straight portraits of key figures in the story, in the manner of his earlier Dreyfus series (p. 181 bottom). They punctuate the thicket of acronyms and agencies into which Martin's investigation descends with the figure of a fallen miner. They visualize the mining community's folk fatalism with a simple shrine to a lost husband and son. "My wife comes from mine country and I have been down mines," Shahn told an interviewer, and his varied experiences of the mining workscape informed his response.[22] But the drawings also repurpose photographs, including those from Shahn, other New Deal documentarians, and *Life* magazine (pp. 179–180). The drawings and their textual and photographic sources were, in turn, employed across a series of mine paintings. *Miners' Wives* (c. 1948) (fig. 4)—showing women waiting for news from below with their loved ones' clothes hoisted above their heads—takes imagery from his mine drawing, itself derived from a *Life* photograph. The central woman's wrung hands are appropriated from the figure of fretful waiting Shahn devised in his line drawings. Her straight-lipped stoicism

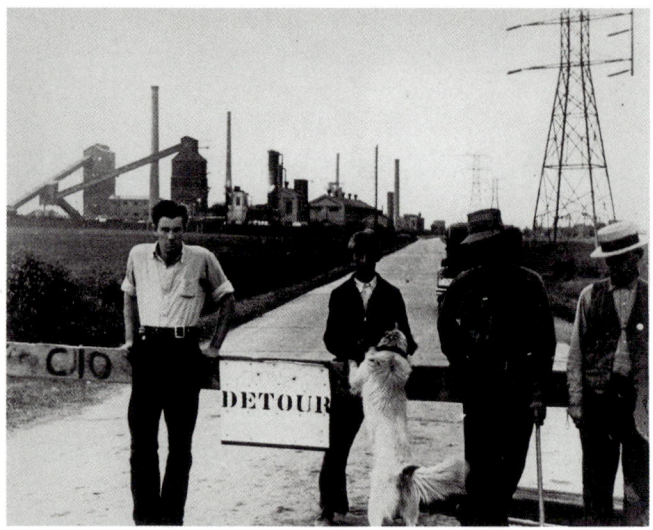

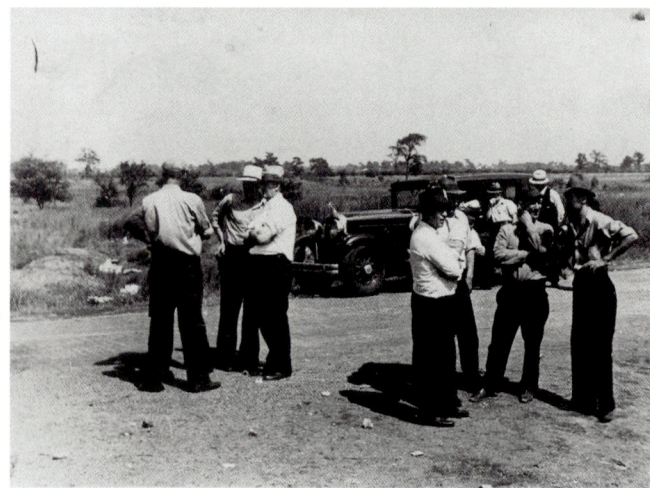

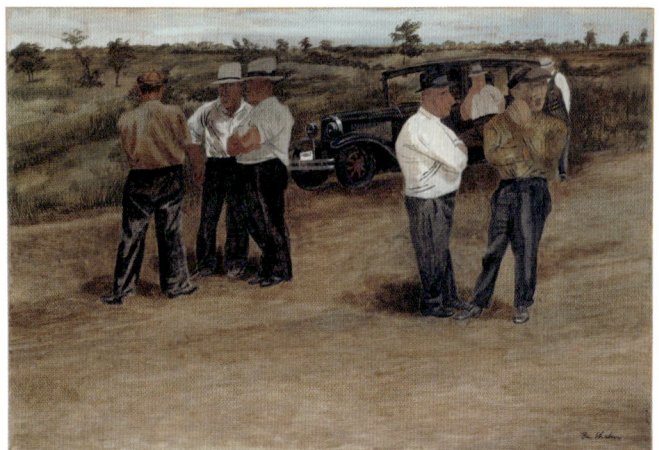

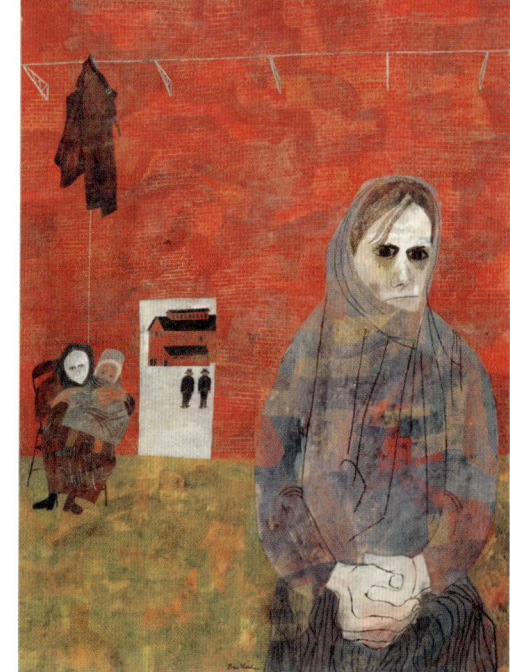

1 and 2
Untitled [Steel Strike, Warren, Ohio], Summer 1937

3
Puddlers' Sunday, 1937 or 1938

4
Miners' Wives, c. 1948

23. Martin, "The Blast in Centralia No. 5," 220, 219.

24. Carol DeCamp, "DeCamp Discusses Cage, Shahn; Their Approach to Art," *The Vassar Chronicle*, March 6, 1948, 3, 6.

25. "Interview (1957)," 47.

26. See Edwin Rosskam, *Roosevelt, New Jersey: Big Dreams in a Small Town and What Time Did to Them* (New York: Grossman, 1972).

27. Shahn, *The Shape of Content* (Cambridge, Mass.: Harvard University Press, 1957), 113.

corresponds to Martin's article, where one of the miners' wives told him, "them accidents happen, seems like it just has to be," while the "vast, unapproachable, insensate organism" of bureaucracy registers in the turned backs of the suited men and, metaphorically, in the vast brick wall.[23] While research is required to trace these specific sources, if *Miners' Wives* succeeds, it is because Shahn's layered understanding, informed by many kinds of knowledge about the working world, remains a tangible presence in the painting itself.

In February 1948, shortly after completing the *Harper's* illustrations, Shahn told the National Inter-Collegiate Arts Conference at Vassar College that "he works at a variety of jobs. His source of income is potato-raising and not the result of undivided attention to the brush and easel." This may have been a reference to the workers' cooperatives at Jersey Homesteads or a joke likening the menial aspects of his CIO-PAC and commercial illustration work to agrarian labor. Either way, Shahn clearly intended to project a workingman's identity to an audience that included students from Yale, Princeton, and Harvard universities. When pressed on what "the real question today for the artist is," he reportedly responded, "How am I going to feed myself and my family?"[24]

The conference at Vassar was among the first of Shahn's many engagements at elite northeastern universities, exemplified by his appointment as the Charles Eliot Norton Professor at Harvard in 1956. During this period, Shahn befriended academics, including the Smith College art historians Oliver Larkin and Edgar Wind; taught at the experimental Black Mountain College; and in other ways participated in the movement—or retreat—of left-wing intellectuals into the academy. "There always has been, and I am afraid there will always have to be some kind of patronage," Shahn explained in a 1957 interview. "Willy-nilly, the universities are becoming the patron—if not of concept, of economic aid."[25] If moving in these circles pulled Shahn further from his working-class roots, that was tempered by his long residence in Jersey Homesteads (renamed Roosevelt in 1945). But this locale was changing too, as many resettled Jewish garment workers returned to New York and were replaced by young families and artists attracted to the bucolic setting and affordable housing, as well as Shahn's presence.[26] Against this turning tide, Shahn told Harvard students who aspired to become artists: "Get a job in a potato field; or work as a grease monkey in an auto repair shop. But if you do work in a field do not fail to observe the look and feel of earth and of all things that you handle—yes, even potatoes! Or, in the auto shop, the smell of oil and grease and burning rubber."[27] Seemingly inventing the "gap year," Shahn urged on his audience the experiential and olfactory sensations of manual work as if to instill in Ivy League graduates the identification with labor that had been the wellspring of his own art.

The communal experience of migration and striving that shaped Shahn's artistic approach, the solidarity among workers forged on the production line and fostered by the trade unionism of the interwar years, and even the very nature of the skilled agricultural and industrial jobs pictured in Shahn's New Deal murals were becoming the stuff of old folks' memories and history books in the postwar period. If a detachment from Shahn's working world was emerging for mid-twentieth-century audiences of his art, it is a gulf of understanding today. Rather than allowing his art to fall into the kind of nostalgia that makes 1930s denims and overalls a contemporary menswear trend, we might focus on the way that Shahn adapted to different mediums, political climates, and creative contexts without losing his core commitment to the values of work and workers. Those values might then be productively adapted to the ever-shifting, varied, and global nature of work in our current moment.

DIGNITY, GRIMNESS, URGENCY: BEN SHAHN AND THE POSTER ART OF WORLD WAR II

Christof Decker

1. Ben Shahn, "The Future of the Creative Arts," *University of Buffalo Studies* 19, no. 4 (February 1952): 125.

2. The poster shows Broadway lyricist Mack Gordon—adapted from a photograph in Hans Diebow's antisemitic brochure *Die Juden in USA* (Berlin: Franz Eher Verlag, 1941). An example of modernist art hangs next to a grotesquely convoluted statue of Mary and Jesus—caricatured examples of Nazi-deemed "degenerate art." "Low-brow" literature is shown as well as a racist depiction of an African American musician. "Kultur" in quotation marks indicates a cliché, predating the Nazi period, that U.S. culture was debased and vulgar.

3. Heartfield deconstructed Nazi terminology, in this case "Übermensch." An x-ray reveals Hitler to be a fake and a liar, controlled by outwardly invisible yet powerful forces. See David King and Ernst Volland, *John Heartfield: Laughter Is a Devastating Weapon* (London: Tate Publishing, 2015), 86–87.

4. On the history of war posters, see G. H. Gregory, ed., *Posters of World War II* (New York: Gramercy Books, 1993); Peter Darman, *Posters of World War II: Allied and Axis Propaganda, 1939–1945* (Barnsley: Pen & Sword Military, 2011); and Steven Luckert and Susan D. Bachrach, *State of Deception: The Power of Nazi Propaganda* (Washington, D.C.: United States Holocaust Memorial Museum, 2011).

5. See "Posters for Defense," *The Bulletin of the Museum of Modern Art* 8, no. 6 (September 1941): 3–8.

During the last war, the work of American artists was effectively harnessed to the war aims. Indeed we felt our cause strongly, so much so that in some cases the art of war posters and illustrations rose above immediate use to achieve the universality and deep feeling of truly great art.—Ben Shahn, 1952[1]

INTRODUCTION

During World War II visual communication was shaped by films, illustrated magazines, and newspapers, among other types of mass media. As part of this ensemble, posters played a special role. They employed dynamic forms and colors, were produced quickly and in multiples, were printed in huge sizes, and were presented in public spaces. Instantly visible and often ubiquitously displayed, posters could dominate the public sphere and impact the minds of large audiences. These features, combined with how they compress complex ideas into recognizable combinations of image and text, made wartime posters the precursors of today's meme culture. During the 1940s, however, posters were part of a slower-paced world of visual communication and their artistic potential—as exemplified in the work of graphic artists like Ben Shahn—was a topic of lively discussion in the art world.

In the United States, poster art had historically evolved in the fields of advertising and politics. But when World War II began, with Germany's invasion of Poland on September 1, 1939, the U.S. was lagging behind other countries in the creation of posters containing visual information or propaganda. In Great Britain, Germany, Italy, the Soviet Union, and Spain, the political radicalization and extremism of the 1930s, and the start of the war, produced a constant outpouring of posters. Authoritarian regimes, in particular, developed new designs aimed to appeal to a public relying not only on newspapers for information but also on posters, photographs, films, and mass gatherings in public places for affective attachments. In Germany, Adolf Hitler's persona was crafted through campaigns presenting him as a savior, warrior, or leader of the German nation. Similarly, the targeting of the Jewish population was promoted by German poster campaigns. These works played on established antisemitic tropes like the "Eternal Jew" (as in a 1937 exhibition advertised by a prominent poster) and updated other stereotypes. In a 1942 series of posters reacting to the U.S. entry into the war on December 7, 1941, anti-American sentiments merged with antisemitism to perpetuate the myth that U.S. society was dominated by Jews. Mixing photography and caricature, posters such as *Kultur* claimed that finance, media, and culture were *verjudet* ("jewified")—a typical example of Nazi hate speech.[2] The authoritarian elite in Germany, the fascist regime in Italy, and the communist leadership in the Soviet Union spawned the development of poster traditions based on the respective political ideologies of each nation, as did the warring Loyalist and Nationalist factions in Spain during its civil war. State-sponsored and politically extremist poster production also provoked innovative visual counterattacks in anti-fascist works such as John Heartfield's *Adolf, der Übermensch: Schluckt Gold und redet Blech* (1932) (fig. 1).[3]

At the outbreak of World War II, European governments reacted quickly with poster art production, while American institutions realized the need to develop their artistic endeavors as rapidly as possible.[4] A case in point is the 1941 *Posters for Defense* exhibition at the Museum of Modern Art (MoMA) in New York. It showcased Great Britain's use of posters in the Allied war effort and inspired one of many competitions to jump-start U.S. poster work. It was inadequate for the U.S. to continue to rely on advertising models, older designs from World War I, and European examples. Public tastes had changed, and as MoMA's *Bulletin* explained, poster art had to meet higher aesthetic standards.[5] Several government agencies and private manufacturing companies prioritized utilitarian purposes for posters to promote wartime needs: saving resources, boosting military production, or cautioning the public against endangering U.S. security, as in Henry Koerner's *Someone Talked!* (1942) (fig. 2).[6] But it soon became clear that poster production required centralization at the Office of War Information (OWI) and a focus on more complex issues to help the public identify allies and enemies and to craft a compelling image of the American nation on the home front around which citizens could rally.

BEN SHAHN AT THE OFFICE OF WAR INFORMATION

Shahn joined the Graphics Division of the OWI in fall 1942—a critical time in the war that saw major battles in Europe and Asia as well as the systematic persecution of the Jewish population across Nazi-occupied Europe. Shahn worked on various poster campaigns and brochures for the OWI and other war-related agencies. Yet it appears that when he left the OWI in summer 1943, only two of his posters had been used for public circulation while other projects were aborted.[7] Shahn's political convictions—his progressive and humanist concerns—were not always compatible with the official line of the OWI. Further, his approach to artistic creation relied on the autonomy and subjective vision of the artist, which soon conflicted with institutional routines that were ultimately modeled on the commercial advertising of corporate publicity departments.[8] Still, Shahn's time at the OWI was a crucial transition in his artistic trajectory and it introduced him to important media-world figures, among them Francis E. Brennan (art director at *Fortune* magazine) and William Golden (art director at CBS), both of whom he continued to collaborate with after the war.

In an early discussion with Golden at the OWI, as recalled by Shahn after Golden's untimely death, they tried to define the nature of a war poster: "It must be neither tricky nor smart. Agreed. The objective is too serious for smartness. It has to have dignity, grimness, urgency. Agreed. It has to be unblinkingly serious; agreed."[9] These ideas were part of a broader effort at the OWI to define visual communication from an American perspective.[10] They seemed to rule out two powerful European traditions that had emerged in the climate of political extremism: the hate propaganda of the Nazi regime and the biting satire of the anti-Nazi Heartfield school. And yet, if dignity, grimness, urgency, and seriousness constituted a form of visual rhetoric that addressed the audience as human beings, what this *democratic* idea of propaganda should look like as an effective tool of communication was less clear. The projects that Shahn managed to complete or had to abort, therefore, allow us to explore how this search for a complex, challenging, and urgently appropriate form of poster art developed during a key phase of World War II.

ATROCITIES IN LIDICE

This is Nazi Brutality (1942) (p. 144) is the first Shahn poster used during the war, reflecting the artist's response to the destruction of the town of Lidice, Czechoslovakia (today's Czech Republic) on June 10, 1942. After the assassination of Reinhard Heydrich, Deputy Reich Protector of Bohemia and Moravia, in Prague, German units perpetrated revenge killings in Lidice. Importantly, the German military did not attempt to hide the atrocities at the time but made them known in a public statement, featured prominently in Shahn's poster. The work shows an anonymous hooded man in a black suit standing in front of a red brick wall, his clenched and shackled fists signifying desperation and defiance. The view from below guides the viewer's attention to the ticker tape message from "Radio Berlin" that puts the "Nazi brutality" on display. The brutality applies both to the act of murdering hundreds of innocent civilians and to making the crime publicly known. While the brick wall opens up to a patch of blue sky, it also delimits the space where the man will be shot. A typical element in Shahn's work, the exquisitely painted wall, creates a sense of entrapment.

6. Koerner's poster cleverly combines the smallness of the proverbial "man in the street" with a massive, guilt-inducing finger. The newspaper headline allowed Koerner, who fled Austria for the U.S., to make his point in a highly compressed manner. The poster won first prize in a 1942 poster competition sponsored by Artists for Victory, the Council for Democracy, and the Museum of Modern Art.

7. For an in-depth discussion of Shahn's OWI work, see Christof Decker, "Fighting for a Free World: Ben Shahn and the Art of the War Poster," *American Art* 33, no. 2 (Summer 2019): 84–105. Shahn also worked for the Office of the Coordinator of Inter-American Affairs, officially and in a freelance capacity, circa 1942–45.

8. On Shahn's often contentious tenure at the OWI, see Howard Greenfeld, *Ben Shahn: An Artist's Life* (New York: Random House, 1998), 187–96. On Shahn's move from the OWI to CIO-PAC, see Frances K. Pohl, *Ben Shahn* (San Francisco: Pomegranate, 1993), 21–22, 68.

9. Shahn, "Bill," in Cipe Pineles Golden et al., eds., *The Visual Craft of William Golden* (New York: Braziller, 1962), 126.

10. See Decker, "Fighting for a Free World," 94–95.

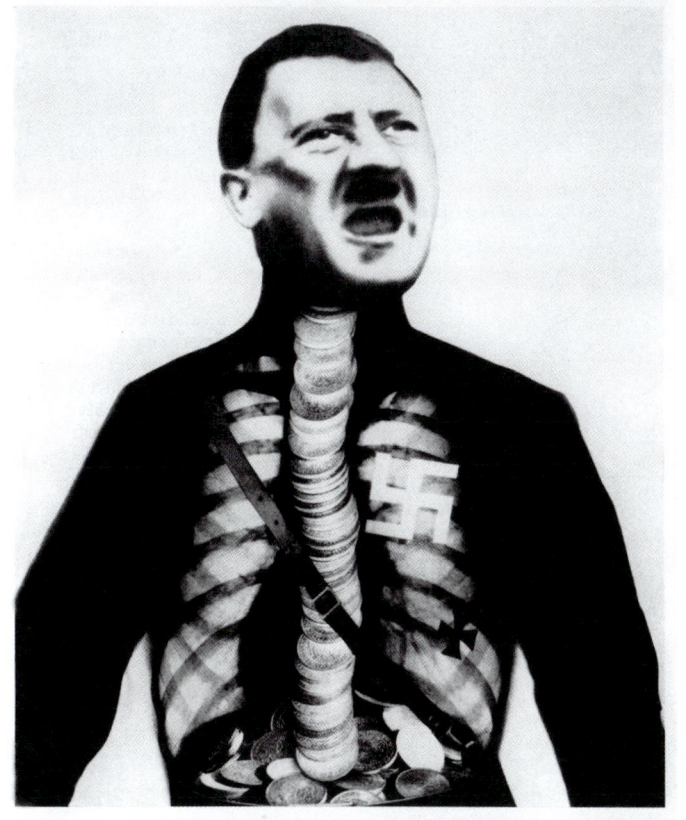

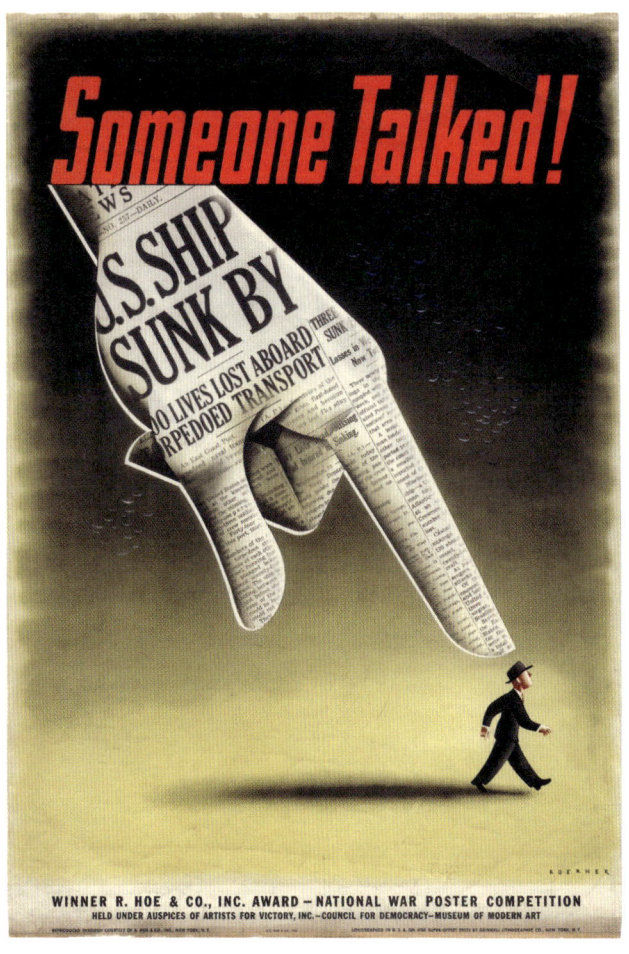

1
John Heartfield
Adolf, der Übermensch: Schluckt Gold und redet Blech
(Adolf, the Superman: He Swallows Gold and Spouts Junk), 1932

2
Henry Koerner
Someone Talked!, 1942

An impenetrable piece of cloth forms the massive, suffocating hood drawn over the man's head, compelling viewers to imagine the horror of his facial expression, as he appears to be staring down at the onlookers.

The combination of textual, figurative, and aesthetic elements made *This is Nazi Brutality* a fitting example of the war poster conception that Shahn and Golden had envisioned. Its sense of urgency comes from the contemporaneousness of Nazi revenge killings, while the horrific grimness lay in the fate of a victim of such war crimes who faces his cruel and senseless death blindfolded. The poster highlights the dignity of the man despite his vulnerability amidst the unfathomable terror. Well-dressed and upright, he expresses his final gesture of resistance in his stance and through his hands—defiant opposition to the most evil acts of humanity.

THE MENACE OF FORCED LABOR

We French Workers Warn You (1942) (p. 148 bottom) is the second Shahn poster known to have been used by the OWI. Here Shahn also reacted to current events, in this case those reported by the *New York Times* on September 14, 1942, regarding the Vichy government, which—in collaboration with the Nazi regime—had issued a decree for compulsory labor.[11] Shahn depicted four workers with hands raised standing before a wall displaying the Vichy labor decree. This public announcement in black letters on a red background appears as a *mise en abyme* element, a "text within a text" or a play of signifiers within a text. The men's hands and the poster's slogan partially block the text of the decree, which was probably taken from the English translation published in the *New York Times*. (The preparatory painting of the same scene [p. 148 top] exists without the slogan.) The decree ruled: "All persons of masculine sex between the ages of 18 and 50 and unmarried persons of female sex between the ages of 21 and 35 can be obliged to execute any work the government may judge necessary in the superior interests of the nation."[12] Shahn's slogan reads: "We French workers warn you... defeat means slavery, starvation, death." He thus likely interpreted the labor decree along the lines of the newspaper as an attempt by the German government to requisition forced labor in France.

The poster's messages, however, are more ambiguous. Nearly all the workers, who display similar features, turn their backs to the viewer and to the decree. The most visible worker in white overalls and a gray and white cap stares inscrutably into the distance. The whole group appears to be frozen in time and place, their collective gestures suggesting defiance (or possibly defeat) in response to the official announcement. Characteristically, Shahn emphasized the strong, finely textured yet massive hands of the workers, and again included a small patch of blue sky in the background. While the hooded male figure in *This is Nazi Brutality* could be a stand-in for the victims of the Lidice massacre, the men in *We French Workers* appear as an empowered unit claiming agency, as if waiting to enter the annals of history. Framing the scene as a warning asserts the message that to avert surrender, one must prevent defeat by all means. Here too, Nazi rule created the cramped, walled-in space of terror, but in this instance, the overlapping figures of the workers—the collective body and voice of "we"—uphold a vision of resistance.

Even though Shahn discussed the idea for this poster with Golden, his final version differs substantially from what they had conceived. As Shahn remembered, Golden did not like the result: "Bill's reaction to what I had created was apoplectic. It wasn't what we had talked about or what we had agreed upon. If (I said to myself) he expected me to labor and belabor an idea that was neither visual nor valid, he was working with the wrong artist."[13] Shahn used the then-topical event of the Vichy labor decree to connect it with themes and motifs common to his work, and he was adamant about following his own

11. Lansing Warren, "Forced Labor Law at Vichy Opens Way to Supply Nazis," *New York Times*, September 14, 1942, 1, 4.

12. "The Text of Vichy's Labor Decree," *New York Times*, September 14, 1942, 4.

13. Shahn, "Bill," 126.

14. Pohl, *Ben Shahn: New Deal Artist in a Cold War Climate, 1947–1954* (Austin: University of Texas Press, 1989), 22.

15. In a related, seemingly unfinished work, *French Workers* (1942) (p. 147), a long line of prisoners waits behind the barbed wire fence of a labor or concentration camp. They are flanked by German guards; a French restaurant is in the background. It remains unclear if Shahn intended to use this work in OWI campaigns.

16. Muriel Rukeyser mentioned the conflicts to Francis E. Brennan. See "Memo. Poster tie-up with bureau of intelligence reports," typescript, February 19, 1943, Muriel Rukeyser papers, The Henry W. and Albert A. Berg Collection of English and American Literature, New York Public Library.

17. As Laura Katzman has discussed, in creating the poster Shahn replaced one of the white welders from one source photograph with a Black worker from another photograph to serve his message of promoting an interracial workforce. See Katzman, "Source Matters: Ben Shahn and the Archive," *Archives of American Art Journal* 54, no. 2 (Fall 2015): 21–25.

18. It is unknown if Shahn intended the painting itself to be a poster on its own.

artistic vision. *We French Workers* shares the layered textuality with *This is Nazi Brutality*, yet the event depicted was likely less known to the American public. Viewers at the time needed to understand that the Vichy labor decree posed a direct threat to French laborers, who could be forced to work for the Nazi government. A further complication is that the U.S. maintained diplomatic relations with the Vichy regime.[14] But Shahn was apparently convinced that the poster was a most suitable design to highlight urgency regarding the decree, the grimness of forced labor, and the dignity of the collective gesture of the raised hands of the workers—unified in their response to their threatened freedom.[15]

IMAGING THE AMERICAN WORKFORCE

As these two published posters show, Shahn designed work in reaction to war-related events overseas. But he also joined campaigns aimed at increasing U.S. war production and motivating the workforce at home. His OWI poster *Our Manpower* (c. 1943) (p. 187 bottom), a collaboration with poet Muriel Rukeyser in the Graphics Division, resulted from these efforts and responded to reports that some U.S. factories had seen racial conflicts among their workforces.[16] Shahn's composition depicts two welders seen from below, and relates to a painting entitled *Welders* (1943). Both figures were adapted from OWI photographs taken by Alfred T. Palmer on various shipyards that Shahn collected for his photo source archive.[17] Protected by helmets and goggles, the white welder, with his hand clearly visible, appears as the larger of the two figures in the right foreground, looking at a steel structure reflected in his glasses. Behind and next to him, a Black welder stands without goggles, his facial expression of intense concentration thus more fully visible. Against the light blue sky, the workers stand in close proximity as a team cooperating in war production activity.

This close collaboration between Black and white workers in the U.S. war effort was clearly one of the main ideas behind Shahn's design—its message reinforced by the slogan, which spoke to the racial disputes that had marred this effort: "Our Manpower: 1/5 of our strength must not be lost through discrimination." An explanation at the bottom of the poster states that the nation's strength included "12,900,000 Negroes, 4,800,000 Jews, 11,400,000 Foreign born." Yet neither this poster nor a related design with the caption "A Need For All In The War, A place for all in the peace," were used by the U.S. government. Shahn's and Rukeyser's attempt to create a propaganda of inclusion on the home front—promoting a vision of interracial solidarity—was ultimately not accepted within the OWI. Eventually, the image of the same two workers was used for one of the "Register, Vote" campaigns of the Congress of Industrial Organizations-Political Action Committee (CIO-PAC), for which Shahn worked after his departure from the OWI. The slogan under the welders in the labor union poster, which doubles as its title, is *For Full Employment After the War, Register, Vote* (1944) (p. 186 top). The promotion of the dignity of workers, particularly in interracial cooperation, therefore needed a different political context to be presentable to the American public.

THE NATURE OF THE ENEMY AND THE FIGHT FOR FREEDOM

During his time at the OWI, Shahn worked on a series of posters on the topic of the nature of the enemy; this endeavor too was never realized. As the division's internal correspondence indicates, Shahn began work on this project in late 1942, aiming to produce a number of posters covering violent enemy actions. His proposed posters combined images from several artists with various slogans, many of which were tested out on preliminary designs. In his painting *We Fight for a Free World!* (c. 1942) (p. 152), Shahn brought together five central motifs—suppression, starvation, slavery, torture, and murder—as he himself had planned to present them, even if they were intended as a series of individual posters.[18]

In the painting, the "enemy method" contrasts with the graffiti-like slogan "We Fight for a Free World!"—juxtaposing the desire for freedom with its powerful enemy. The five motifs appear in posters by artists of different heritages, adding diversity and aesthetic complexity to the layout. Suppression is represented by Edward Millman; starvation by Käthe Kollwitz; torture by Yasuo Kuniyoshi; and murder by Bernard Perlin. To signify slavery, Shahn included in the middle his own poster of a man standing behind a barbed wire fence confronting the viewer with a deeply worried expression.

These motifs create a dynamic arrangement envisioning the authoritarian threats to freedom. The multiple artistic styles in the posters glued to the red brick wall not only establish pictorial variety, but also highlight the representational process itself. In a reflexive gesture, Shahn used meta-referencing, often found in modernist art and literature, to at once underscore the enemy's crimes and foreground the numerous ways of imaging the unimaginable. His own poster at the center of the painting is the only design whose figure confronts the viewer's gaze. As he often did, Shahn modeled this man on the image of Sam Nichols, a tenant farmer from Boone County, Arkansas, whom he photographed while working for the Resettlement Administration (RA) in 1935 (p. 150). He based the toiling prisoners in the background on his RA photographs of levee workers from Plaquemines Parish, Louisiana.[19] In the poster, the farmer, with his troubled face and furrowed brow—his eyes looking into an uncertain future and his massive hand covering his mouth—becomes a working man forced into captivity. For a U.S. audience, the reference to slavery has overt connections to the enslavement of Africans in American history, but in the context of World War II, it would have suggested forced labor in European concentration camps. Indeed, when Leo C. Rosten organized an exhibition at New York's Rockefeller Center called *The Nature of the Enemy* in 1943, he used Shahn's poster as one inspiration for his three-dimensional tableau entitled "Concentration Camps."[20]

Even though different slogans were tried out in individual posters envisioned by Shahn, the OWI did not use the series and it was abandoned. Yet *We Fight for a Free World!* remains a painting in line with Shahn's other wartime work. The grimness of the enemy method is obvious in the poster designs represented, while the urgency demanded of viewers is implied in the graffitied declaration on the brick wall. And although this series of anti-fascist posters sought to address the most inhumane aspects of the war, dignity is still present. Shahn focused on the victims, not the perpetrators of violence, as he believed that successful poster art needed to compassionately depict the people who were being oppressed. While other OWI posters of the era include menacing Nazi symbols, Shahn took an alternative approach. His work demonstrates that effective war posters must feature the human beings whose very humanity and individuality are under threat.

Shahn transformed his slavery poster within *We Fight for a Free World!* into a separate painting, *1943 AD* (c. 1943) (p. 151), which shows the same scene but without some sections of the barbed wire fence. This omission renders a kind of crown of thorns around the man's head, which, along with the title, alludes to a Christ-like martyr.[21] In his CIO-PAC poster *Warning! Inflation Means Depression* (1946) (p. 193), Shahn again used the motif, eliminating the working men in the background and changing the central figure's shirt from dark gray and brown to light blue. Keeping the man's concerned, anxious look, Shahn appropriated the figure to suggest crisis within the postwar labor movement. Thus, the image of an impoverished U.S. farmer in the Depression, used to represent a prisoner forced into labor in a European concentration camp during World War II, returns to being a symbol of U.S. poverty and economic desperation after the war. Indeed, in the labor poster, the man evokes American workers' fears about enduring another cataclysmic Depression.

19. See Decker, "Fighting for a Free World," 96–101. On Shahn's use of photography, see Katzman, "The Politics of Media: Painting and Photography in the Art of Ben Shahn," in Deborah Martin Kao, Laura Katzman, and Jenna Webster, *Ben Shahn's New York: The Photography of Modern Times* (New Haven: Yale University Press), 97–117, 142–46; Katzman, "Source Matters," 4–33; and Decker, "In Search of a Common Vision: Ben Shahn, Photography, and *The Family of Man* Exhibition in 1955," in *Imaging the Scenes of War: Aesthetic Crossovers in American Visual Culture* (Bielefeld: transcript Verlag, 2022), 61–89.

20. See Decker, "Imaging Axis Terror: War Propaganda and the 1943 *The Nature of the Enemy* Exhibition at Rockefeller Center," in *Imaging the Scenes of War*, 35–59.

21. Pohl, *New Deal Artist*, 23.

Through such repurposing of potent images, Shahn showed in a nutshell how the aesthetic crossovers and complex resignifications of his art worked during the 1940s.

CONCLUSION

Ben Shahn's poster art from World War II represents a critical phase in his work, as Shahn would never again return full-time to the U.S. federal payroll. This work also constitutes an important contribution to U.S. graphic art in the twentieth century. As this essay has argued, to understand Shahn's contribution, the small number of his posters used during his OWI tenure must be examined within the larger context of all the projects he worked on during the war years. Shahn maintained his autonomy from the OWI and found it difficult to adjust to its working methods. He attempted, with frustration, to accommodate his political convictions to the requirements of wartime propaganda. Remarkably, he showed how questions of racial discrimination, antisemitism, and labor unrest were not only relevant to Nazi Germany and Nazi-occupied Europe, but also to the U.S. as it entered the global conflict.

The most significant aspect of Shahn's wartime posters, however, lies in their aesthetic legacy. Whether he was creating art on the nature of the enemy or about workers in Europe or the U.S., Shahn followed neither the path of hate propaganda nor of "smartness" and cynicism. Instead, he aimed to define the contours of a propaganda of inclusion, based on the need for a shared feeling of belonging and identity among viewers. In condemning Nazi war crimes against civilians, Shahn emphasized the experience of innocent victims. Making the causes and consequences of their suffering palpable to U.S. citizens was one of the main approaches he took in creating motifs of grimness and urgency. Shahn's designs did not therefore focus on ridiculing or vilifying the perpetrators. His concern for human vulnerability was at the center of an aesthetic that claimed equality and inclusion as a precondition for the common goal of freedom imagined by the posters. Shahn also created complex visual designs—employing source photographs and reflexive strategies that require viewers to pay close attention to grasp the layered meanings. Through using multiple media and by testing the limits of showing physical abuse for a 1940s audience, Shahn sought to challenge viewers intellectually while at the same time appealing to their humanity. In so doing, he affirmed the dignity of his subjects as ordinary people who deserve respect, regardless of race, religion, ethnicity, or nationality.

BEN SHAHN AT MOMA IN 1947: REFLECTIONS ON AESTHETIC DEBATES IN THE EARLY COLD WAR ERA

Beatriz Cordero Martín with Laura Katzman

1. Ben Shahn, "The Future of the Creative Arts," *University of Buffalo Studies* 19 (February 1952): 128.

2. Shahn, "Realism Reconsidered," *Perspecta* 4 (1957): 31.

3. Shahn quoted in Henry Brandon, "Nightmare: Goya Gets a Guggenheim: A Conversation with Ben Shahn," in *As We Are* (New York: Doubleday & Company, 1961), 83.

4. Shahn has been central to studies of New Deal social realism and studies of twentieth-century Jewish art.

5. Frances K. Pohl, *Ben Shahn: New Deal Artist in a Cold War Climate, 1947–1954* (Austin: University of Texas Press, 1989); Julia Tatiana Bailey, "'Realism Reconsidered': Ben Shahn in London, 1956," in *Modern American Art at Tate 1945–1980* (2019), tate.org.uk/research/publications/modern-american-art-at-tate/essays/realism-reconsidered.

6. Howard Greenfeld, *Ben Shahn: An Artist's Life* (New York: Random House, 1998), 215.

7. John D. Morse, "Ben Shahn: An Interview," *Magazine of Art* 37, no. 4 (April 1944): 138.

It is the mission of art to remind man from time to time that he is human, and the time is ripe, just now, today, for such a reminder. —Ben Shahn, 1952[1]

If Social Realism seeks to impress upon art a rigid aesthetic of subject matter and point of view, there also exists another opposite camp which seeks with equal rigidity to exile from art all meaning—to keep it free from any content whatsoever. That is the camp of Pedantism. —Shahn, 1957[2]

I use abstraction as a tool, as I use realism as a tool. —Shahn, 1960[3]

Ben Shahn, who was central to the social realist movement of the New Deal era in the United States, was also among the most compelling and multifaceted artists of the post-World War II period. Even though canonical studies of postwar avant-garde American art have tended to exclude extensive analysis of his work, he and fellow social realists should be better integrated into that vanguard history.[4] The postwar art world, as scholars have shown, was more pluralistic than many earlier examinations have acknowledged. Abstract expressionism, for example, did not take over the U.S. art world in the mid-1940s; its dominating presence was not felt in full force until the later 1950s. Realist, figurative, and representational styles were still practiced and appreciated. Artists like Shahn, as demonstrated by Frances Pohl and others, continued to exhibit and sell art and make the lists of the top U.S. artists in magazines like *Art News* and *Look*.[5] Intense aesthetic debates transpired in the increasingly oppressive climate of the early Cold War era in the U.S.—defined in foreign policy by the anti-communist struggle and nuclear arms race with the Soviet Union and informed at home by the Red Scare tactics of Senator Joseph McCarthy and of the House Un-American Activities Committee, the latter of which blacklisted many liberal and progressive cultural figures for their allegedly subversive activities and affiliations.

This essay offers reflections on Shahn's contributions to these postwar aesthetic debates in the context of early Cold War ideology. It focuses on key Shahn-related events at New York's Museum of Modern Art (MoMA) in the pivotal year of 1947—deemed by historians the first year of the Cold War. The Truman Doctrine, announced by President Harry S. Truman on March 12, 1947, aimed to prevent the spread of communism and Soviet influence in Europe and Asia. It ushered in an era decidedly more conservative than the New Deal era of Truman's predecessor, Franklin Delano Roosevelt. The year 1947 was also when the young yet already venerated MoMA hosted a midcareer retrospective on Shahn, bestowing national attention on a political realist—"the youngest American painter to be accorded such a distinction in the history of the museum."[6] That same year, during Shahn's exhibition in fact, MoMA organized a watershed conference on Pablo Picasso's *Guernica* (1937), securing its meanings for the museum and its singular place at the forefront of modern art.

Shahn is an ideal figure through whom to examine the U.S. artistic and political tensions at midcentury. Although he was antagonistic toward new abstract art movements and rarely abandoned figuration, he admired much abstract art (especially sculpture) and was attentive to formalist concerns in his own work, which transcends any literal social realist content. In a 1944 interview, Shahn spoke about how he worked abstractly when making paintings, even holding his pictures upside down to work out all the textures, patterns, colors, spatial relations, and compositional structures.[7] His hard-to-define style embodies formal complexity; his pictures are, in the words of John Davis, "topical and grounded in place but temporally and spatially ambiguous; media-inspired and collagelike but artisanal in facture."[8] After the war, and following Shahn's critical stint in 1951 at Black Mountain College, where he collaborated with cutting-edge dancers, poets, and musicians, he increasingly experimented with abstract expressionist techniques in layered palimpsest temperas that embody improvisation and spontaneity.[9]

Relatedly, Shahn participated in spirited debates about humanism in modern art, which preoccupied artists across the stylistic spectrum, along with art critics, museum directors, and curators. Myriad dilemmas unfolded about the fate of human civilization—dilemmas unleashed by the global horrors of World War II—from the shocking realities of death camps to the destruction wrought by atomic bombs. To cope with this new world order, many artists became introspective, using allegory, symbolism, and myth to ponder urgent questions.[10] What stylistic forms and symbols best captured the experience of postwar modernity? How could artists balance the particular and the universal, the subjective and the objective, to speak in intelligible terms? Should modern artists connect with the individual or aim to reach all audiences? What was the meaning of reality, if art focused on individuality and there are as many realities as artists? Not only did Shahn ruminate on these questions in his studio, but he also lectured on them widely at universities, museums, and art centers across the U.S. and abroad, and published his views in his book *The Shape of Content* (1957) and in liberal and leftist publications. Reflecting on the role, purpose, and destiny of the artist, Shahn believed art could carry forth humanism and individualism, especially at moments when free expression was under threat. He wrote: "Perhaps Humanism and Individualism are the logical heirs to our earlier, more mystical beliefs.... If we are to have values, a culture, these things must find their imagery and their interpretation through the arts."[11]

Shahn's example further illuminates these postwar debates because of his strong yet at times contentious relationship with MoMA. As a champion of modern art in the U.S. and abroad, and as a formidable force in establishing a historical canon of modern art, MoMA was a focal point for the realism-abstraction debates and was attacked from both sides of that continuum. MoMA also entered the conversation on humanism, as it pushed back on the reactionary backlash against modern art. In 1950, for example, curators from MoMA, the Whitney Museum of American Art, and the Institute of Contemporary Art in Boston signed "A Statement on Modern Art," defending the "freedom of expression inherent in a democratic society," and emphasizing the "humanistic value of modern art even though it may not adhere to academic humanism with its insistence on the human figure as the central element of art." They identified "the humanistic value of abstract art, as an expression of thought and emotion and the basic human aspirations toward freedom and order"—a declaration that contributed greatly to the acceptance of abstract expressionism as having humanistic content.[12] This connection, however, would be contested by Shahn, who thought that abstract and non-objective art were disengaged, "absorbed in [their] own plastic [and technical] problems, and not involved with the human prospect."[13]

Such ideas are exemplified by Shahn's "first public disagreement" with abstract expressionist painter and theorist Robert Motherwell at a MoMA-sponsored symposium of March 19, 1949, "Art Education 1949-Focus on World Unity," which was followed by a "verbal altercation." (fig. 1).[14] In the session "The Artist's Point of View," according to Pohl, Shahn "reiterated his appeal to all artists to work together in order to bring new dimensions to the spirit and imagination of men and women." But he was critical of the "non-objectivist," whose "disassociated form" and delineation of "shapes and colors and lines" as "the object of painting," was "not the stuff of man's ultimate values."[15] Motherwell, annoyed at his critics for disparagingly labeling him an intellectual and possibly anticipating a confrontation with Shahn, spoke with passionate intensity about

8. John Davis, "The End of the American Century: Current Scholarship on the Art of the United States," *The Art Bulletin* 85, no. 3 (September 2003): 569.

9. Katherine Markoski, "Aspects of Realism: Ben Shahn's Palimpsest Paintings," unpublished lecture, Savannah College of Art and Design Fifth Biennial Art History Symposium, 2014.

10. Stephen Polcari, "Ben Shahn and Postwar American Art: Shared Visions," in Susan Chevlowe et al., *Common Man, Mythic Vision: The Paintings of Ben Shahn* (New York: The Jewish Museum and Princeton University Press, 1998), 67–109.

11. Shahn, *Paragraphs on Art* (New York: The Spiral Press, 1952), unpaginated.

12. "Contemporary Documents: Modern Art—1950," *College Art Journal* 9, no. 3 (Spring 1950): 338–40.

13. Shahn, "The Future of the Creative Arts," 127.

14. The conference addressed "the respect for the integrity of the individual as a creative being [as] essential for the establishment of world order." moma.org/momaorg/shared/pdfs/docs/press_archives/1304/releases/MOMA_1949_0018_1949-03-11_490311-17.pdf. See Stephanie Terenzio, ed., *The Collected Writings of Robert Motherwell* (New York: Oxford University Press, 1992), 57.

15. Pohl, *New Deal Artist*, 81; Shahn and Balcomb Greene, "The Artist's Point of View," *Magazine of Art* 42, no. 7 (November 1949): 266, 269.

16. Terenzio, ed., *The Collected Writings of Robert Motherwell*, 62, 58, 61, 58.

17. Dore Ashton and Joan Banach, eds., *The Writings of Robert Motherwell* (Berkeley: University of California Press, 2007), 96. Shahn and Motherwell met again at a Fogg Art Museum symposium on April 12, 1951, at Black Mountain College in summer 1951, and at the Fourth Annual Woodstock Art Conference, August 3–22, 1952.

18. Shahn, *The Shape of Content* (Cambridge, Mass.: Harvard University Press), 58; Brandon, "Nightmare: Goya Gets a Guggenheim," 66–67.

19. Russell Lynes, *Good Old Modern: An Intimate History of the Museum of Modern Art* (New York: Atheneum, 1973).

20. Between 1930 and 1979, Shahn was exhibited at MoMA approximately seventy-six times; from 1980 to 2023, this number drops to twenty-eight. This does not include all of MoMA's international exhibitions. See moma.org/calendar/exhibitions/history/.

21. See moma.org/momaorg/shared/pdfs/docs/press_archives/1119/releases/MOMA_1946-1947_0102_1947-09-30_47930-40.pdf.

art as the "expression of [the artist's] inner life" and as inspiration that rises "unpredictably as the flight of a bird." For him, abstract art "asserts man's courage [and] intellectual daring." He dismissed "discussions of the artist's social responsibility" and said: "I loathe every form of ideology…. I am interested in persons who are independent moral agents."[16] Elsewhere Motherwell defended abstraction for its ability to transmit spiritual values, gaining inspiration from myth and poetry. He expressed the need of artists to alienate themselves from society. He insisted on the incompatibility of any artistic and literary creation with political commitment—an idea he famously defended in the first issue of *Possibilities* in 1947.

In a lecture for the College Art Association on October 27, 1950, Motherwell referred to the 1949 MoMA conference and his "public duel" with Shahn, whom he described as the "leading Communist artist in America." He noted that Shahn had denigrated his art as supposedly having "no content … decorative and good to taste, like a wedding cake." In turn, Motherwell railed against "dogmatic intellectualism" and Shahn's type of politically charged art, calling it "cold, empty, mechanical, and [ironically] alienated from the world," containing "none of the feeling for real humanity, for its capacity for self-realization" that is needed "to liberate humanity."[17] To Shahn, Motherwell stood for all he came to resent: the rigid "paint-alone" aesthetic, with its absolute adherence to pure form, the faddish trends, and the competitiveness of the postwar art world, which he blamed more on critics, theorists, gallerists, and curators than on artists. Seventeen years older than Motherwell, Shahn had benefited from the New Deal federal arts projects and, despite his own work for a wage in commercial art, he believed deeply in such national sponsorship of public art, through which artists "were all leveled" economically.[18]

BEN SHAHN AND THE "GOOD OLD MODERN"[19]
Shahn's retrospective at MoMA (September 30, 1947–January 4, 1948) marked the artist's then-seventeen-year involvement with the museum. From the year after MoMA's opening in 1929 until the artist's death in 1969, Shahn was included in scores of exhibitions held at the museum, was featured prominently in the early years of its International Program, and became a ubiquitous presence in the museum's programming.[20] His work entered the permanent collection as early as 1935. He was respected by MoMA's most influential leaders, from head of collections Alfred H. Barr, Jr. (the museum's first director) to director of photography Edward Steichen. Shahn's 1947 retrospective signaled a definitive turning point in his career. Along with organizing the exhibition, which traveled to the Boston Institute of Modern Art, MoMA curator James Thrall Soby published the first monograph on the artist with the British publishing house Penguin, which became a top seller in its Modern Painters series. Combined with a small traveling exhibition arranged by the Arts Council of Great Britain for London's Mayor Gallery in April 1947 (likely Shahn's first solo show overseas), the MoMA exhibition helped shape the postwar international projection of Shahn's work (fig. 2).[21]

Yet this was not the first time MoMA propelled Shahn into the spotlight. *Murals by American Painters and Photographers*, an exhibition curated in 1932 by impresario and *ex officio* MoMA curator Lincoln Kirstein, brought Shahn into conflict with the museum's wealthy trustees. A number of them were outraged by Shahn's 1931–32 panel *The Passion of Sacco and Vanzetti* (p. 70 left) and its satirical treatment of the trustees' powerful friends, the "pompous" men of the Lowell Committee, who are shown standing over the immigrants' coffins. These easily recognizable men were "either generous donors or potentially generous donors of the new museum." MoMA board members also condemned works in the show by Hugo Gellert and William Gropper for their anti-capitalist and alleged

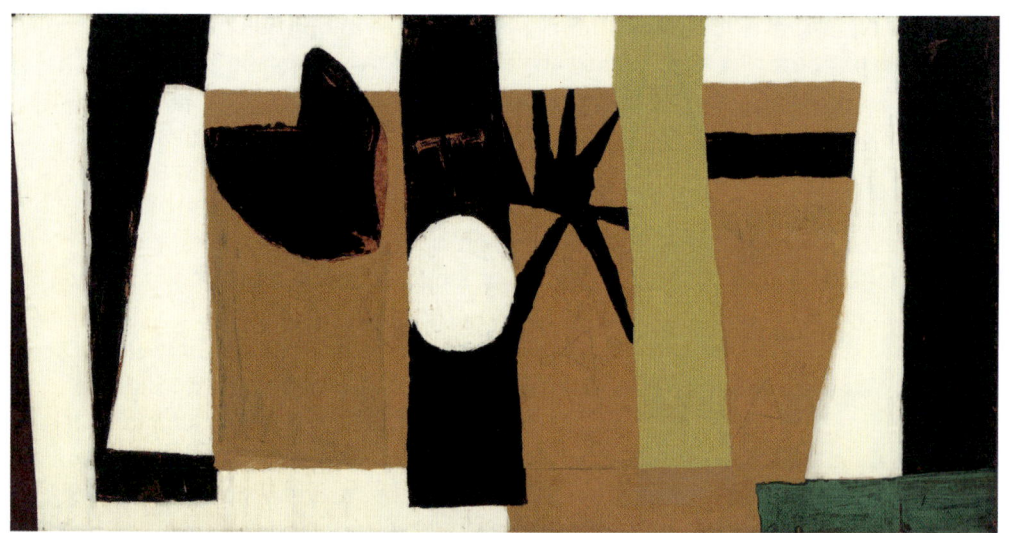

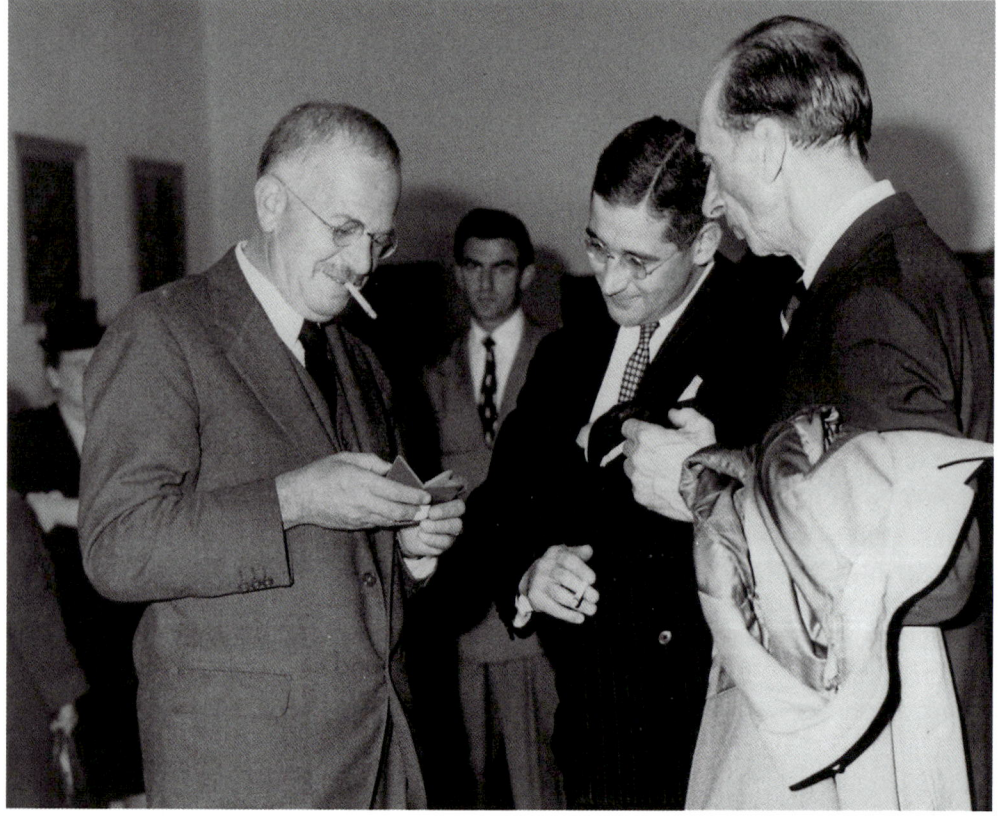

1
Robert Motherwell
The Voyage, 1949

2
Photographer unknown
Ben Shahn, James Thrall Soby, and Amédée Ozenfant
[Opening of the Exhibition "Ben Shahn," The Museum
of Modern Art, New York], 1947

22. Greenfeld, *Ben Shahn*, 82–83. The Lowell Committee reviewed Sacco and Vanzetti's guilty verdicts at the request of the Massachusetts governor, concluding the convictions were warranted and thus clearing the way for the executions.

23. Pohl, *New Deal Artist*, 2–3, 47–48; James Thrall Soby, *Ben Shahn* (West Drayton, Middlesex: Penguin Books, 1947), 3–4, 15–16.

24. Alfred M. Frankfurter, "The Year's Best: 1947," *Art News* 46 (January 1948): 36–37; Pohl, *New Deal Artist*, 48–52; Ralph Pearson, "A Modern Viewpoint: Ben Shahn at the Modern," *The Art Digest* 22 (December 1, 1947): 36.

25. Clement Greenberg, "Art." *The Nation* (November 1, 1947): 481.

26. Scott Bishop et al., *Art Interrupted: Advancing American Art and the Politics of Cultural Diplomacy* (Athens: Georgia Museum of Art, 2012), 33.

27. George A. Dondero, "Modern Art Shackled to Communism," *Congressional Record*, 81st Congress, 1st Session, August 16, 1949, 11586.

communist content; some even called for the cancellation of the exhibition. The controversial pictures were ultimately exhibited, with the support of trustees J. P. Morgan, Jr., Nelson Rockefeller, and Abby Aldrich Rockefeller.[22] (The last, a MoMA founder, had championed Shahn's work during the Depression; she patronized his dealer Edith Halpert of the Downtown Gallery and stood by Shahn's painting until her passing in 1948.)

The criticized Sacco and Vanzetti work was given pride of place in Shahn's 1947 retrospective. Pohl has analyzed how Soby (and MoMA) positioned Shahn in the context of the artistic and political debates of 1947. The curator asserted that Shahn was "the opposite of the 'pure' painter," a propagandist and a humanist, politically and spiritually oriented, with honest, individualist conviction—an artist who, paradoxically, worked for labor unions and corporations, and was appreciated "by collectors of every political hue." Soby called him "an unmistakably American painter"—no doubt to counter Cold War accusations to the contrary.[23] The exhibition received mixed critical response, but it was cited as one of the ten best one-person exhibitions of 1947 in *Art News*. Favorable reviews ranged from those that commented on Shahn's surrealistic techniques or the combination of the particular and universal in his work to those that stressed "the narrative, political element" and his successful embrace of "esthetics and commentary."[24] The most damning negative review, published in *The Nation*, came from the Marxist-turned-anti-communist-liberal Clement Greenberg—a powerful critic who considered Shahn's pictorial work "rarely effective beyond a surface felicity ... lacking ... in density and resonance." He deemed it "not important [and] beside the point as far as present-day painting is concerned." For an influential formalist proponent like Greenberg, such current art meant Jackson Pollock, who in 1947 had begun to create what would become his iconic drip paintings.[25]

Attacks on Shahn circa 1947, beyond the MoMA exhibition, also came from the opposite direction, as right-wing politicians were condemning Shahn and fellow artists who were included in the short-lived U.S. State Department traveling exhibition *Advancing American Art*—initiated in 1946 and cancelled by Secretary of State George C. Marshall in 1947. The artists were called unpatriotic and subversive, accused of presenting a false picture of the U.S. Planned to tour Europe and Latin America, this cultural diplomacy project aimed to portray a positive image of U.S. artistic freedom and democracy—"a demonstration of the heterogenous, global nature of American art and as a weapon against the suppression of intellectual freedoms under communism." The congressional attacks (and those in the Hearst press) referred to the artists' alleged communist affiliations and their pictures as ugly, distorted, and "foreign." Paintings by artists as stylistically diverse as Romare Bearden, Stuart Davis, Georgia O'Keeffe, and Shahn were among the works recalled and sold as surplus property by the War Assets Administration (p. 191). But the pictures had a "second life" when dispersed to many small museums across the country.[26]

Two years later, Republican Congressman George Dondero heightened the attacks to the level of hysteria. Even though he maligned Shahn as "that proponent of social protest in art" and "one of the pets of the Museum of Modern Art," while accusing the institution of propagating communism, Shahn himself did not feel favored by MoMA.[27] In fact, in March 1950, he joined a group of artists, including Raphael Soyer, Yasuo Kuniyoshi, Isabel Bishop, Jacob Lawrence, and Edward Hopper, to discuss current troubling trends among art critics and museums and what they saw as MoMA's disproportionate emphasis on abstract and non-objective art. In a 1951 letter from twenty-two artists that Shahn wrote (but from which he withheld his name as author) to MoMA's director René d'Harnoncourt, the group urged the museum to uphold its official policy of supporting artistic diversity in a democratic society and noted a revival of humanism "in all creative fields." Museum leadership denied the validity of their claims.[28] In spring 1953, the artists published this letter in the first of three issues of *Reality: A Journal of Artists' Opinions*. This issue also featured excerpts from Shahn's 1952 pamphlet *Paragraphs on Art*, which called for "a resurgence of the humanities, a rebirth of the spirit." Shahn ultimately disassociated from the group; he possibly considered it too restrictive aesthetically or too hostile toward MoMA—an institution that had staunchly supported him, especially with the 1947 retrospective.[29]

GUERNICA AT MOMA

At the same time that Shahn's MoMA retrospective was on view, the artist was invited to participate in a November 25, 1947 conference dedicated to Picasso's *Guernica*. The famed mural-scale interpretation of the destruction of the Basque town by the Nazi German and Fascist Italian military in support of the Francoist forces during the Spanish Civil War had been "in exile" at MoMA since 1939. On Picasso's wishes the work would not be moved to Spain until democracy was restored. The conference was organized by Barr and Monroe Wheeler, MoMA's head of the department of exhibitions and publications. Other participants included Josep Lluís Sert, Catalan co-designer of the 1937 Spanish Pavilion in the International Exposition in Paris where *Guernica* was shown originally; Juan Larrea, Spanish poet central to the painting's commission; Jerome Seckler, U.S. abstract painter who interviewed Picasso after the liberation of Paris; Jacques Lipchitz, French and American cubist sculptor who was part of Picasso's Parisian circles; and Stuart Davis, politically engaged U.S. painter influenced by cubism.

According to Andrea Giunta, who has read *Guernica* as "a crucial item in the Cold War's symbolic clashes" between the Soviet Union and the U.S., Barr convened the conference to resolve *Guernica*'s ambiguities—to "establish the painting's ultimate meaning" and its consecrated place in the history of modern art, where it would be "sheltered from harsh political disputes." After Picasso joined the French Communist Party in 1944, Barr confronted the thorny issue of how (in writings, lectures, and exhibitions) "to separate the public man from his work, especially from *Guernica*," to turn him "into a representative of the Allies," and "to change the artist's problematic political affiliation into something less troubling." This is not unlike Soby, who in Shahn's 1947 retrospective stressed the artist's Americanness, aiming in part to shield him from attacks by reactionary critics and to make his leftist politics palatable to mainstream liberal audiences. But by 1947, Giunta argued, Barr was more concerned with "controlling [*Guernica*'s] meanings"—to protect it from an "uncertain interpretive fate" in the Cold War era. Barr tried strenuously (but ultimately failed) to discredit Juan Larrea's new interpretation, which completely reversed a basic agreement around the work's central iconography, namely, that the bull represented the Francoist forces (or brutality) and the horse the Spanish Republican people. Barr recognized, however, that sealing the specific meaning of each element in *Guernica* would place it in a "perilous realm" of illustration or propaganda, or generate a "moralizing reading" associated with social realism. This led to Barr's attempts, Giunta concluded, to "pacify" the painting, downplaying its "potentially explosive consequences ... diminishing its political visuality."[30] (This meant suppressing a communist-inflected anti-fascist view.)[31] Indeed, *Guernica*'s short object label (c. 1955–80), while briefly noting the key historical facts that propelled Picasso to create the painting, offered only a generalized interpretation of the artwork, with no iconographic analysis. The label stated that Picasso denied *Guernica*'s "political significance" and noted only "his abhorrence of war and brutality."[32]

28. Letter drafts (June 1, 1951), Ben Shahn papers, Smithsonian Archives of American Art (BSP-AAA). The letter was attributed to Raphael Soyer. Bailey noted, "in 1953 Alfred Barr railed against the group as 'party-liners' (hence the emphasis on reality and humanism)." Bailey, "Ben Shahn in London," endnote 25.

29. Pohl, *New Deal Artist*, 105–7, 197, endnotes 27–30.

30. Andrea Giunta, "The Power of Interpretation (or How MoMA explained *Guernica* to its audience)," *Artelogie* 10 (October 2017): 2, 4, 5, 2, 12.

31. The authors learned from Miriam M. Basilio that in 1937, under Barr's directorship, MoMA hosted an exhibition of Spanish government posters that are boldly anti-fascist and pro-Republic; it also included U.S. government posters promoting rural electrification. But with many communists in the Republican struggle, and with the Soviet Union having been the main supplier of military aid to the Republican army, by the Cold War era, when the Soviet Union had turned from U.S. ally to foe, overt support for the Republic could be taken as support for communism and/or the Soviet Union. "If the Communist Block had been able to claim [Picasso] as man, Alfred Barr, would claim his work for the [democratic] Free World." Giunta, "The Power of Interpretation," 13.

32. Giunta, "The Power of Interpretation," 12. Barr noted the political importance of *Guernica* in his 1946 study on Picasso; in his 1967 study on *Guernica*, he "marginalized the whole political significance of the mural." See *Rethinking Guernica*: guernica. museoreinasofia.es/en/document/picasso-fifty-years-his-art.

33. Shahn, *The Shape of Content*, 93–95; Brandon, "Nightmare: Goya Gets a Guggenheim," 67.

34. Interview with Ben Shahn by Forrest Selvig, September 27, 1968, transcript, 14, AAA; Selden Rodman, *Portrait of the Artist as an American, Ben Shahn: A Biography with Pictures* (New York: Harper & Brothers, 1951), 26.

35. Jacques Lipschitz and Stuart Davis said that they did not think *Guernica* was Picasso's best work, formalistically.

36. Minutes from "Symposium on *Guernica*," November 25, 1947, The Museum of Modern Art Archives, 73–74.

37. Minutes from "Symposium on *Guernica*," 74, 16.

Shahn's inclusion in the symposium—barely mentioned in the Shahn literature—may be explained by the timing of his retrospective and by the perspective he offered as a non-abstract painter whose art, like *Guernica*, commented on the contemporary scene. Shahn was one of the many leftist artists who closely followed events of the Spanish Civil War and Picasso's artistic and verbal responses, as seen in the October 1937 issue of *Art Front*. Although Shahn never met Picasso (during his stay in Paris in the 1920s, Shahn cancelled an arranged meeting out of "shyness"), the Spanish artist's work powerfully impacted Shahn's style. In *The Shape of Content*, Shahn expressed his admiration for Picasso, whom he elevated far above Salvador Dalí, stating the former had stimulated "almost the whole major art activity within the contemporary styles.... [He] has revitalized myth in his art, has captured the pagan spirit and the primitive spirit, has explored everywhere and found and *created* value." By the late 1950s, Shahn still defended Picasso as "the greatest influence [of] today" and called him "a monument."[33] Regarding *Guernica*, the icon exemplified for Shahn an artist's passions poured into paint—a work that must be grappled with. He invoked the painting in 1968 when discussing his earlier posters for the Office of War Information, where he had aimed to communicate to the "six million who understand Norman Rockwell" as well as to the "sixty [who] understand Picasso's *Guernica*. The work affirmed Shahn's belief that if Picasso's "prodigious inventiveness" were merged with Diego Rivera's "*feeling*" and communicative abilities, "the result would certainly be the greatest art."[34]

At the conference, although encouraged to speak a couple of times, Shahn contributed only modestly to the discussion, and as a discordant voice, perhaps because he did not fully partake in the veneration of the painting.[35] Shahn expressed that *Guernica* was not an effective painting or antiwar poster because it did not speak to the uninitiated layperson. He agreed with an attendee in the audience who wondered if *Guernica* would be "understood" if it emerged in Alaska sometime far in the future. Shahn wittily added that "without the backlog of critical references," it would not be understood if it were found in Brooklyn that same week, "except by this very select audience here." Without such concrete, accessible references, for Shahn, it was impossible to read *Guernica* in relation to the events of the Spanish Civil War. In this regard, and "as a piece of propaganda, for mass use," as Picasso spoke about the painting, it failed.[36]

The few words Shahn did share about *Guernica* during the symposium are meaningful because they are so enigmatic. They read like a puzzle that needs decoding. "As a painting," he said, "it has everything that everybody here said about it. I feel it very strongly"—likely referring to the varying interpretations of the bull and horse in Spanish and Anglo-Saxon cultures. "I think the distinction between nerves, muscles, heart, brain, is very slight"—Shahn continued—"The heart is a muscle; the brain is the terminus of the nerves, and so on, so there is a very, very slight distinction." While the cryptic tone leaves much to interpretation, the "slight distinction" could signal the visual effect of *Guernica*'s composition, generated by Picasso having brought all the figures to the foreground, and the metaphoric overlapping of animals and humans, science and nature, indoor and outdoor space, done with "slight distinction." For Shahn, Picasso formalistically outlined the emergence of feelings (heart), the association of ideas (brain), and the apparition of sensations (nerves), all converging to invoke suffering—the only unquestionable aspect of *Guernica* for many viewers. Stating "I feel that thing because of my own backlog of experience with painting, with Picasso," Shahn evoked Jerome Seckler's earlier comment that "we actually feel the emotional impact of the struggle presented on the canvas through our nerves and our muscles before we understand it with our minds."[37]

In contrast to Picasso, Shahn privileged particularities: the texture of an item of clothing, the configuration of a hairdo, or the style of a hat that he found so revealing of the class or the character of the person depicted. Such particularities would ensure that his increasingly universal messages would not be lost in abstraction. Shahn's own antiwar posters like *This is Nazi Brutality* (1942) (p. 144) starkly announce the specific heinous tactics of the Nazi enemy, while paintings such as *Italian Landscape II: Europa* (1944) intensify details of rubble and a blasted building that he extracted from press photographs to lament more quietly the loss of revered European sites bombed by Axis and Allied powers (pp. 157, 155 top). Such paintings beg comparison with Picasso's unfinished *The Charnel House* (1944–45), painted after Paris' liberation from the Nazis, also with the aid of news photographs and newsreels. The brutally contorted bodies of the massacred family, splayed out under a domestic table, have been linked to a documentary film about a Republican family murdered during the Spanish Civil War and to gruesome photographs of corpses piled up in Nazi concentration camps.[38] While Shahn offered hints of hope in the still-standing mother and child who walk the tortured landscape, Picasso left only existential finality.

Perhaps it is the absence of Shahn-like particularities in *Guernica* (despite content based on documentary reportage and allusions to newsprint) that enabled the work to become a global icon for peace.[39] But for Shahn this absence revealed the weakness of the painting; its abstraction removes it from the actual realities that drove Picasso to expose the atrocities of the totalitarian forces that dropped the bombs on Guernica on April 26, 1937, killing an estimated 1,600 civilians, one-third of the town's population. Tied to various forms of social realism, Shahn did not shy away from the "perilous realm" of propaganda, when used in the service of a "noble" cause. One wonders how Shahn felt about Barr and MoMA's ultimate "neutralization and universalization of [*Guernica*'s] political content" and avoidance of specific references to Picasso's interpretation of the Nationalist-Loyalist struggle in the Spanish Civil War in the museum's presentation of the work.[40] After all, despite his own personal critique of *Guernica*, Shahn knew firsthand what the work had meant to his U.S. compatriots who had embraced the cause of Spanish democracy—protesting and sacrificing their lives on behalf of the Spanish Republic, which for them embodied a larger global struggle.[41]

CONCLUSION

The simultaneity of MoMA's Shahn retrospective and the *Guernica* conference demonstrates that MoMA promoted a "wide-ranging program of diverse exhibitions" and events and that its oft-accused favoring of abstract expressionism and the latter's use in U.S. Cold War cultural propaganda campaigns, while significant, was exaggerated—as argued by Michael Kimmelman in 1994 and amplified by much subsequent scholarship.[42] This dual promotion of figurative and abstract artistic practices was repeated dramatically when MoMA selected Shahn and abstract expressionist Willem de Kooning to represent American painting in the U.S. Pavilion at the 1954 Venice Biennale. Art historians have shown how Shahn symbolized another kind of democratic freedom as distinct from the stylistic freedom signaled by de Kooning—the freedom to speak out against the wrongs of one's own nation. Shahn's vocal anti-Soviet stance and harsh critique of socialist realism, however, also made him useful in such U.S. cultural diplomacy abroad.[43]

MoMA continued to support Shahn throughout the 1950s and 1960s, but as Bailey has noted, theirs remained "a fluctuating relationship ... that was never resolved." Even though MoMA (and the United States Information Agency) funded Shahn's 1956 lecture at the Institute for Contemporary Art in London, Shahn still took aim at the museum, along

38. Lynda Morris and Christoph Grunenberg, eds., *Picasso: Peace and Freedom* (London: Tate Publishing, 2010), 70.

39. Interestingly, Picasso wrote to Shahn in French on November 4, 1950, inviting him to the Second World Peace Conference in Great Britain, BSP-AAA. Picasso's famous peace doves influenced similar imagery by Shahn, who was equally dedicated to the postwar peace and antinuclear movement.

40. Brandon Truett, "*Guernica*, Inc.: Art, Exile, Recirculation," *M/m* 5, cycle 3 (December 9, 2020), modernismmodernity.org/articles/ truett-guernica-inc. Motherwell, while admiring *Guernica*, believed it failed "because of its systemic formal ambivalence, as neither wholly abstract nor figural," as noted by Truett.

41. Shahn and Bernarda Bryson likely saw *Guernica* in 1939 when it arrived in New York, where they had completed a mural for the Bronx Central Post Office. Shahn's contemporaneous comments on *Guernica* are unknown to the authors.

42. Claudia Hopkins and Iain Boyd Whyte, eds., *Hot Art, Cold War— Western and Northern European Writing on American Art, 1945–1990* (New York: Routledge, 2021), xxiii.

43. On MoMA's role in international cultural diplomacy, see the writings by Pohl and Bailey and the groundbreaking studies by Eva Cockcroft, Max Kozloff. Nancy Jachec, Frances Stonor Saunders, and Greg Barnhisel, among others.

44. Bailey, "Ben Shahn in London." In 1956, Alfred Barr defended Shahn (whom he called a "gullible" liberal) from right-wing attacks, echoing his assessment of the dual dangers of communism and reactionary anti-communism. Barr, "Artistic Freedom," *College Art Journal* 15, no. 3 (Spring 1956): 184–86.

with curators and critics, for their role in dismantling the status of realist forms of art.[44] Soby wrote two more books on Shahn, in 1957 and 1963, and, with Mildred Constantine, organized one-man traveling exhibitions through MoMA's International Council between 1961 and 1963. Shahn's stylistic middle ground—between academic realism and non-objectivism—and his social democratic politics, which eschewed left-right extremes, clearly served MoMA well for decades. Yet MoMA has not mounted a solo exhibition on Shahn since his death in 1969, more than half a century ago, even though it holds one of the strongest collections of his work in the world. Why this is the case is an open and probing question—one that merits a separate, in-depth discussion.

WORKS

Hans Namuth
Ben Shahn [Roosevelt, New Jersey]
1964

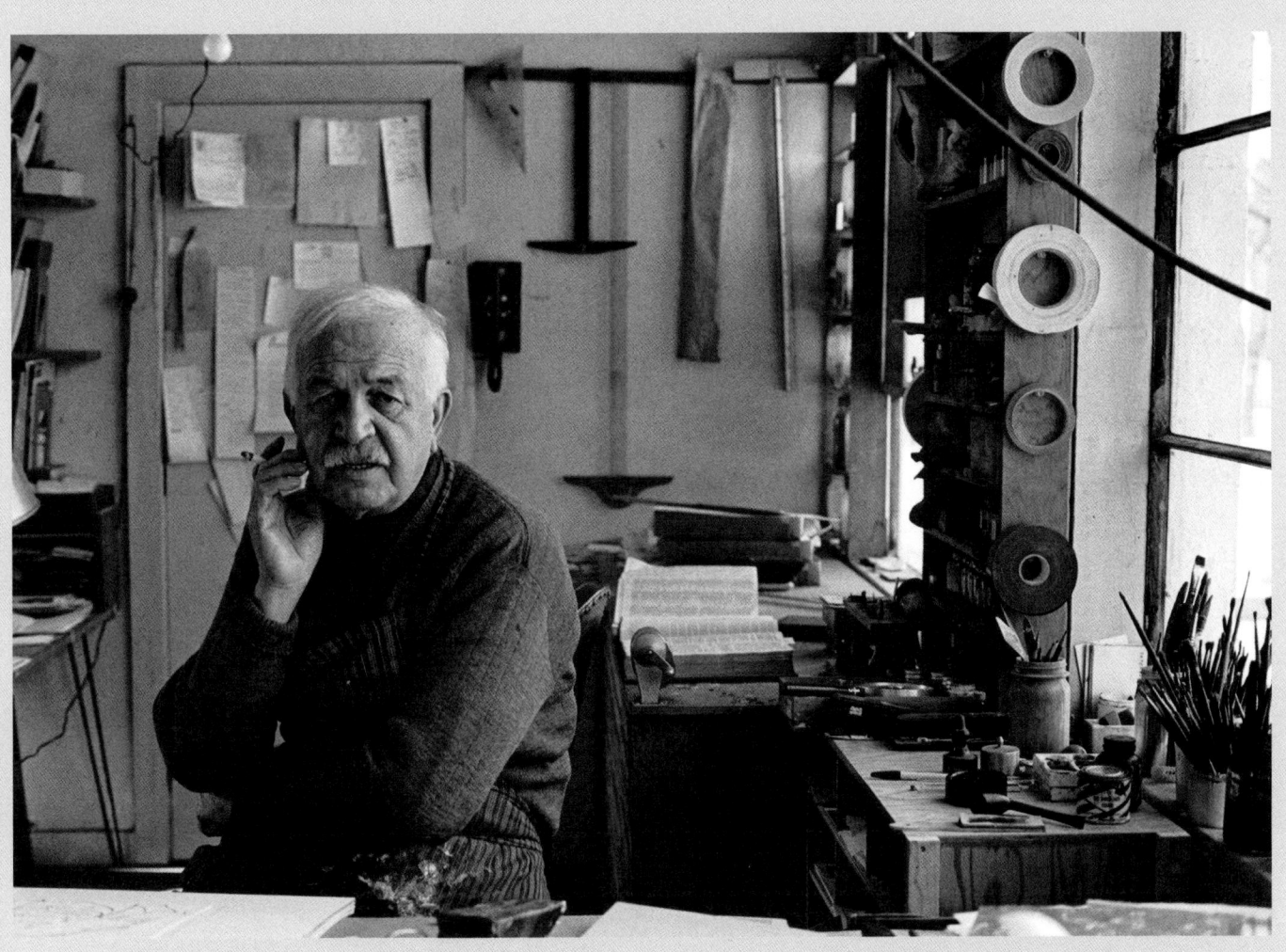

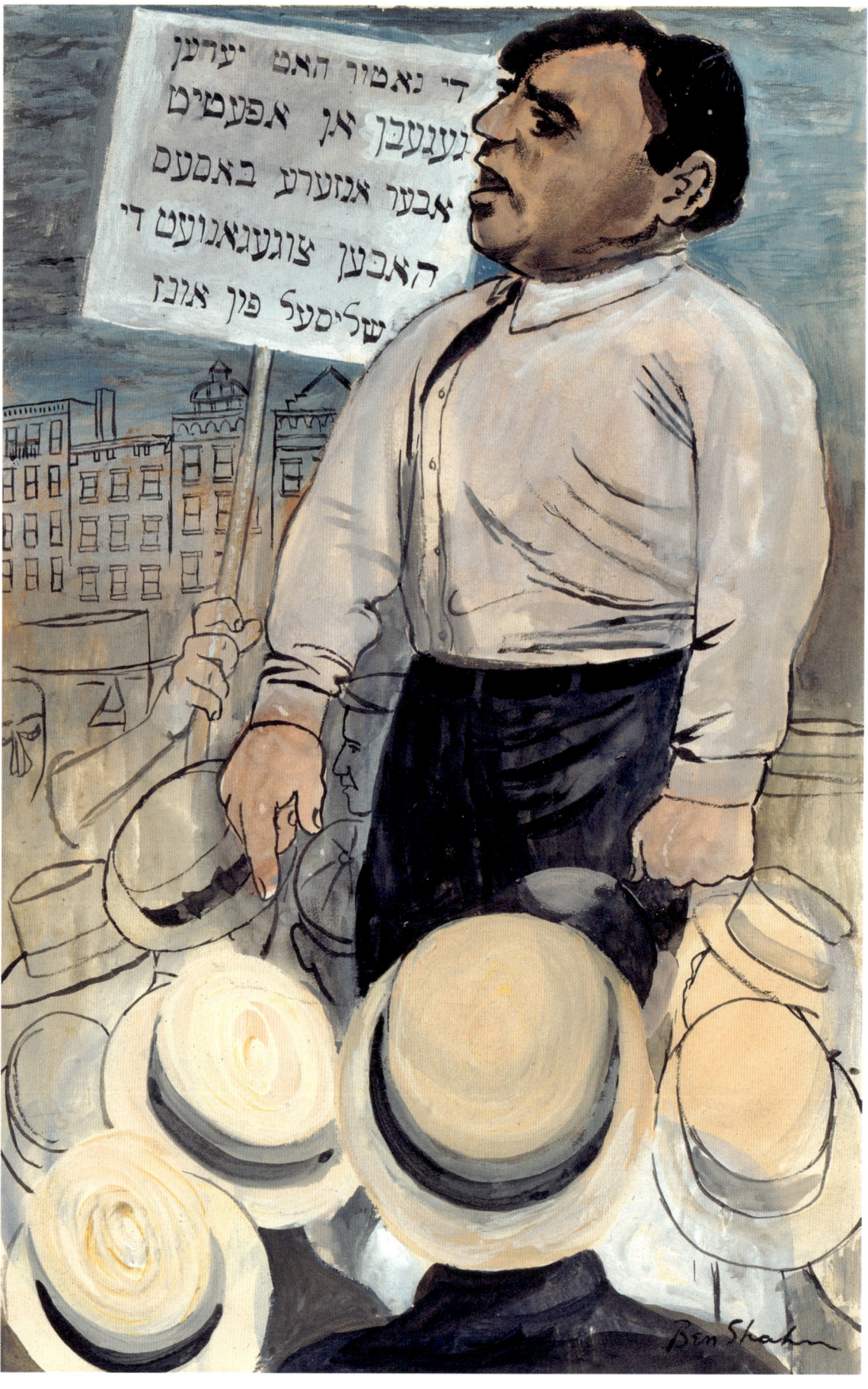

THE ROOTS OF ACTIVISM: BEN SHAHN'S *CAUSES CÉLÈBRES*

The formative education of Benjamin Zwi Shahn (September 12, 1898–March 14, 1969) took place within his working-class, religious Jewish family in Kovno, Lithuania—a major center of Jewish culture and learning—and in the smaller town of Vilkomir. This was part of the "Pale of Settlement," the region in which Jewish people were confined to certain cities and overcrowded shtetls, where harsh conditions and educational and employment restrictions prevailed. Poverty-stricken residents feared pogroms, the organized massacres of particular ethnic groups sanctioned by the ruling Russian Empire.[1] Such persistent social and economic problems fueled the anti-tsarist actions of Shahn's socialist father, Joshua Hessel Shahn, a woodcarver who was exiled to Siberia, made his way to South Africa, and reunited with the family in the U.S. at the time of its emigration in 1906. Shahn grew up in the poor immigrant neighborhoods of Williamsburg, Brooklyn, at a time when Jewish and other Eastern and Southern European immigrants were excluded from the privileges of white Protestants. While drawn to the rich Yiddish culture of Eastern European Jewry, he also fervently wanted to become "American." (Shahn's Americanism, however, would be rooted not in extreme patriotism but rather in critique of a nation falling short of its democratic ideals.)

The artist absorbed his father's intellectual and political ideas and respect for craftsmanship. He was thus enraged when his parents, at the instigation of his strong-willed mother, Gittel Lieberman, who was from a family of peasants, removed him from school as a young teenager so he could earn money for their household of seven. Fortunately, his apprenticeship at Hessenberg's lithography shop on Manhattan's Lower East Side, involving rigorous drawing and engraving, became solid training for an art career. Ambitious and determined, Shahn read voraciously, with the guidance of a public librarian. He studied at the Eastern Evening High School, and took classes at the Art Students League and the Educational Alliance Settlement House.

Shahn also studied briefly at New York University, the Marine Biological Laboratory in Woods Hole, Massachusetts, the City College of New York, and the venerable and conservative National Academy of Design. He made extensive trips to Europe in 1925 and 1928–29, thanks in part to the bookkeeping jobs of his progressive-minded first wife, Tillie Ziporah Goldstein. They ventured to France, Spain, Algeria, Tunisia, Germany, Austria, and Italy, where the proto-Renaissance frescoes of Giotto, with their elegantly clear narratives, moved him deeply. In Paris, he enrolled in either the Académie Julien or the Grande Chaumière and—immersed in the bohemian "lost generation"—he learned the lessons of Cézanne, Picasso, Matisse, and Rouault. He developed an expressive brushstroke and a flat, modernist style, which later gave dynamic shape to his social and political

East Side Soap Box, 1936
Nature has given every [worker] an appetite, but our bosses took away from us the key [to our sustenance].

content. His extended stays on the Tunisian island of Djerba, where a unique Arab-speaking Jewish community had for centuries lived in relative harmony with Muslims, made a lasting impression.[2]

Returning to the U.S. right before the cataclysmic stock market crash of October 1929, which spawned the Great Depression, Shahn sought subjects that resonated with his own experience. He focused on stories of struggle and instances of injustice, responding to the massive unemployment triggered by the global economic collapse and embracing the *causes célèbres* of his time. Inspired by prints in old French military volumes, Shahn created watercolors (or gouaches) circa 1930–31 on the "Affair" of Alfred Dreyfus, the French captain who fell victim to antisemitism between 1894 and 1906. This initiated his method of drawing on news photographs, incorporating text, and working in series that encompassed the major players of the drama. Contemporaneous films and newsreels also informed his practice. Critical recognition came from his series of twenty-three gouaches exhibited at Edith Halpert's Downtown Gallery on another scandal that generated worldwide protests: *The Passion of Sacco and Vanzetti* (1931–32). With a deliberately naive style, simplified forms, and an incisive line, Shahn rendered the working-class Italian immigrants who were executed on August 23, 1927 , for a robbery and murder in a Braintree, Massachusetts shoe factory—having never received due process for a crime many believe they did not commit. Colored by anti-immigrant, anti-Catholic, and anti-anarchist prejudices, the case represented for Shahn and other leftists a travesty of justice—even a Christ-like martyrdom.[3] Shahn next produced a series of fifteen gouaches (and one tempera), with brilliant color and technical acuity, on *Tom Mooney* (1932–33)—the Irish-American labor leader wrongfully imprisoned for a 1916 bombing at a World War I Preparedness Day parade in San Francisco. Both series focus on the humble, ordinary details of the protagonists' lives and relationships.

Such series attracted praise as powerful proletariat art from Mexican muralist Diego Rivera, who hired Shahn in 1933 to assist on his ill-fated Rockefeller Center fresco, *Man at the Crossroads*. The mural's controversial contrast of capitalist greed and communist utopia (led by Soviet leader Vladimir Lenin) contributed to its censorship and ultimate destruction. This censorship, in the context of the global political climate, catapulted Shahn to the forefront of radical leftist activity. The fascism then raging in Adolf Hitler's Germany and Benito Mussolini's Italy, and threatening Spain's Popular Front Republic on the verge of its own civil war, propelled the artist into action. Yet he knew that ultra-nationalist, authoritarian, and antisemitic tendencies were not confined to Europe; he called them out at home, as evident in his biting caricature of *Father Coughlin* (1939). In the manner of Honoré Daumier and Francisco de Goya, and evoking photographs of Hitler giving a speech in Berlin on April 4, 1932, Shahn scathingly satirized the social reformer-turned-reactionary Catholic "radio priest" in the midst of his own hate-mongering rant.

1. "[T]here was [also] a thriving and rich world of public culture in the Jewish Pale of Settlement." See Diana L. Linden, *Ben Shahn's New Deal Murals: Jewish Identity in the American Scene* (Detroit: Wayne State University Press, 2015), 7.

2. On Shahn's early life and influences, see books by James Thrall Soby (1947), Selden Rodman (1951), Mirella Bentivoglio (1963), John D. Morse (1972), Bernarda Bryson Shahn (1972), Kenneth W. Prescott (1973), Frances K. Pohl (1993), and Howard Greenfeld (1998). See also the thoughtful and timely children's book, Cynthia Levinson, *The People's Painter: How Ben Shahn Fought for Justice with Art* (New York: Abrams, 2021).

3. See Alejandro Anreus et al., *Ben Shahn and the Passion of Sacco and Vanzetti* (Jersey City: Jersey City Museum and Rutgers University Press, 2001).

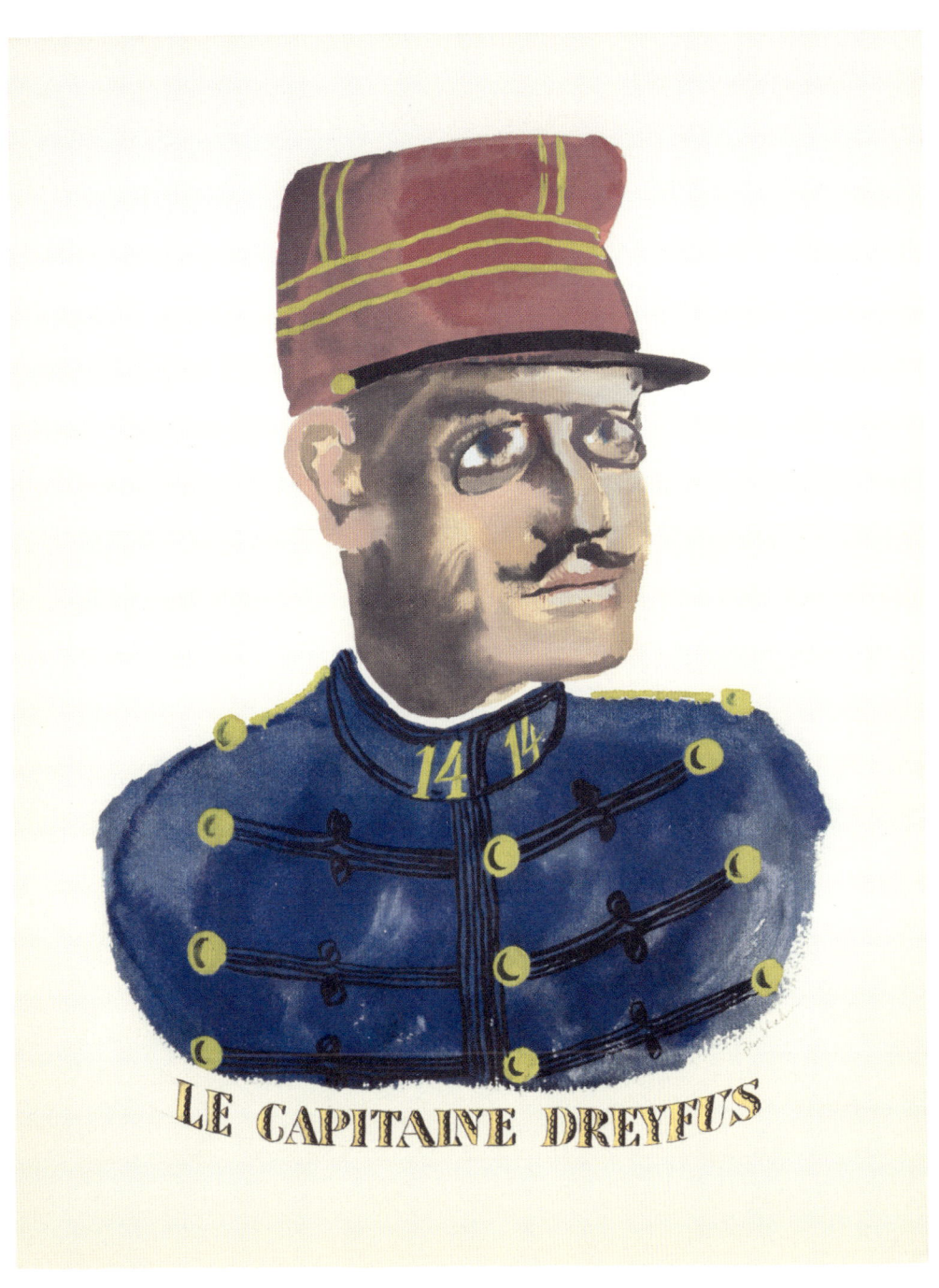

Le Capitaine Dreyfus [from *The Dreyfus Affair* portfolio]
1984 (based on c. 1930–31 watercolor)

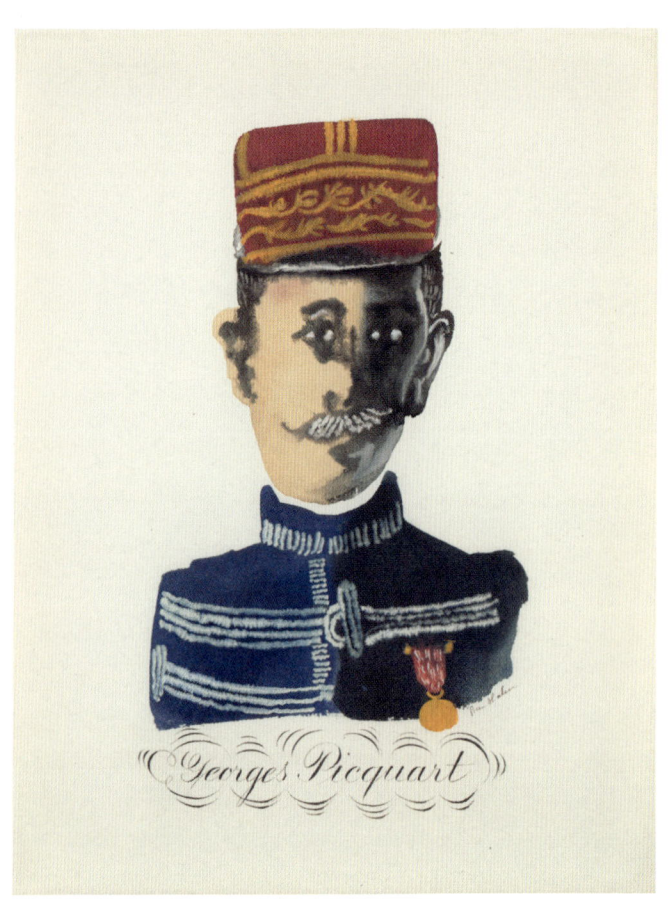

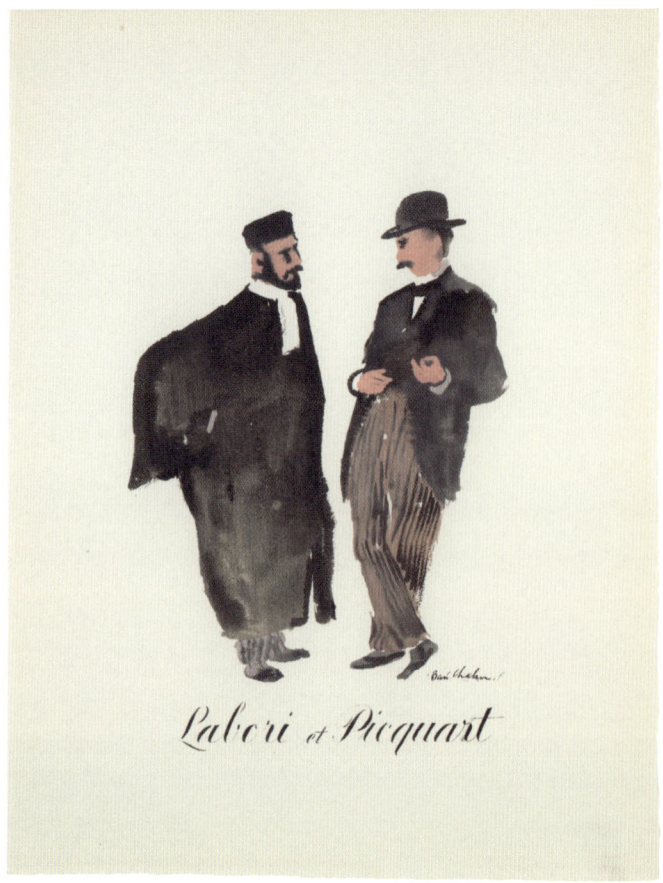

Georges Picquart [from *The Dreyfus Affair* portfolio]
1984 (based on c. 1930–31 watercolor)

Labori et Picquart [from *The Dreyfus Affair* portfolio]
1984 (based on c. 1930–31 watercolor)

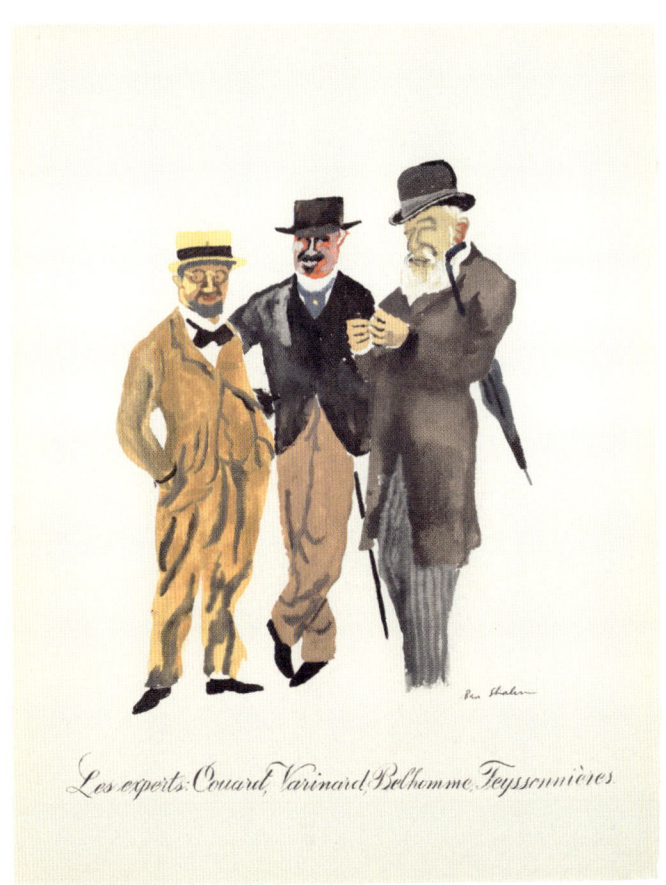

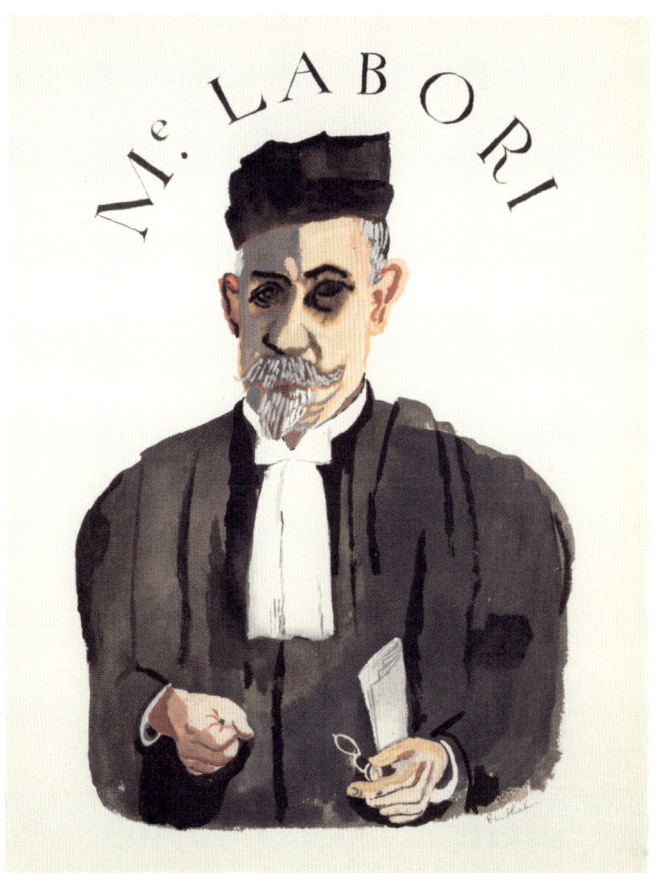

Les Experts: Couard, Varinard, Belhomme, Teyssonnières
[from *The Dreyfus Affair* portfolio]
1984 (based on c. 1930–31 watercolor)

Me. Labori [from *The Dreyfus Affair* portfolio]
1984 (based on c. 1930–31 watercolor)

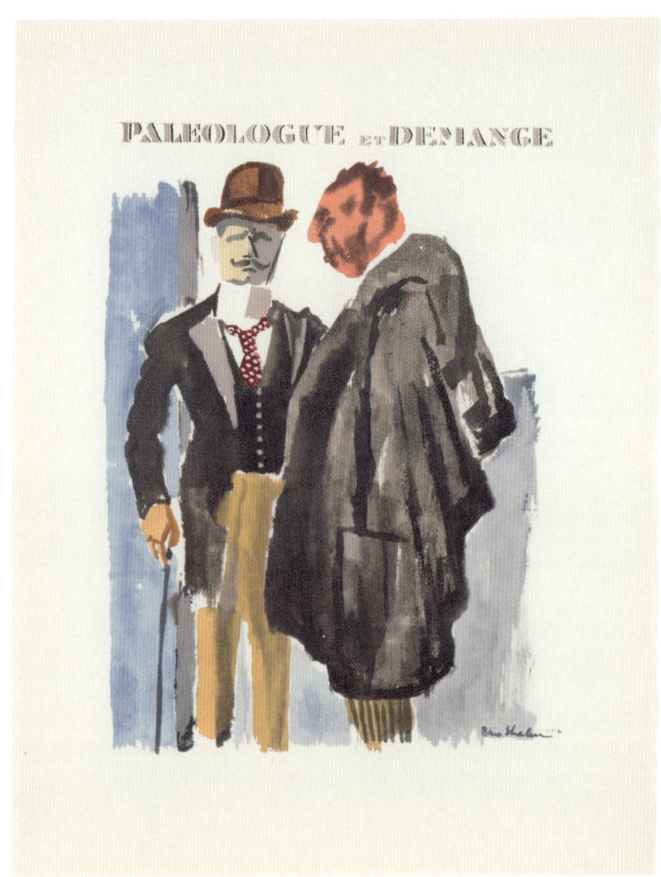

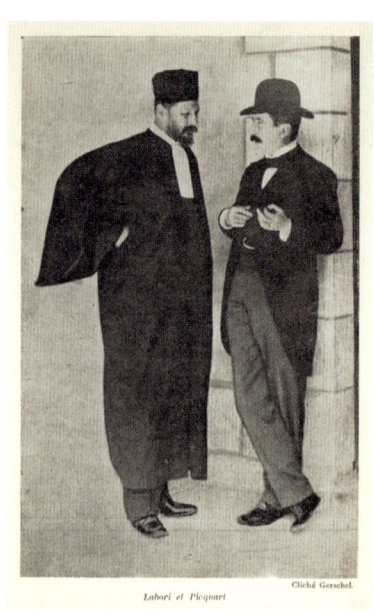

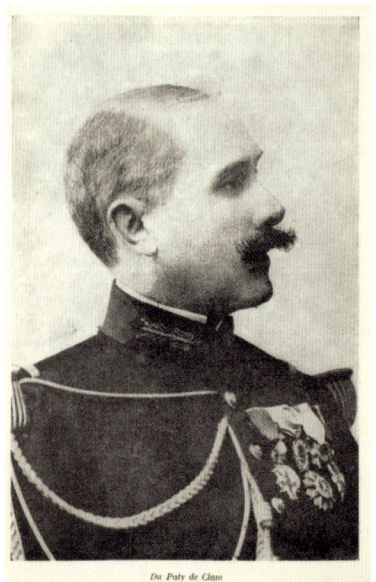

Georges Charensol
L'Affaire Dreyfus et la Troisième République.
Paris: Éditions Kra, "Les Documentaires," 1930

Paleologue et Demange [from *The Dreyfus Affair* portfolio]
1984 (based on c. 1930–31 watercolor)

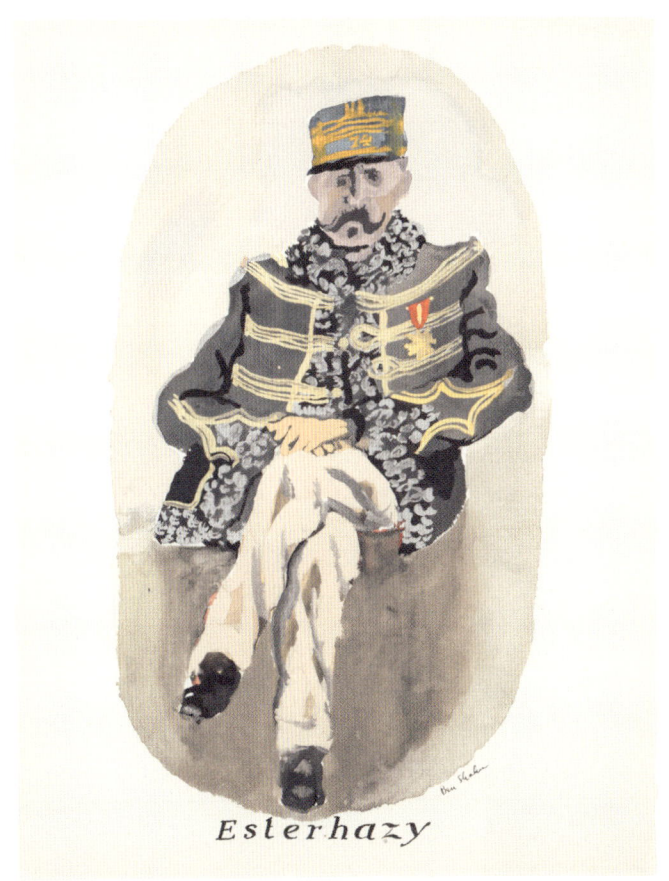

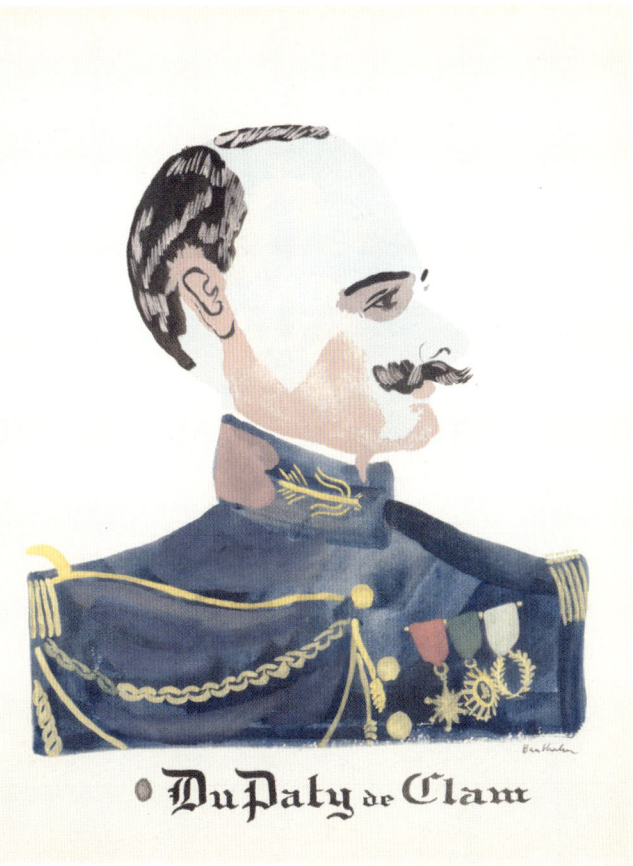

Esterhazy [from *The Dreyfus Affair* portfolio]
1984 (based on c. 1930–31 watercolor)

Du Paty de Clam [from *The Dreyfus Affair* portfolio]
1984 (based on c. 1930–31 watercolor)

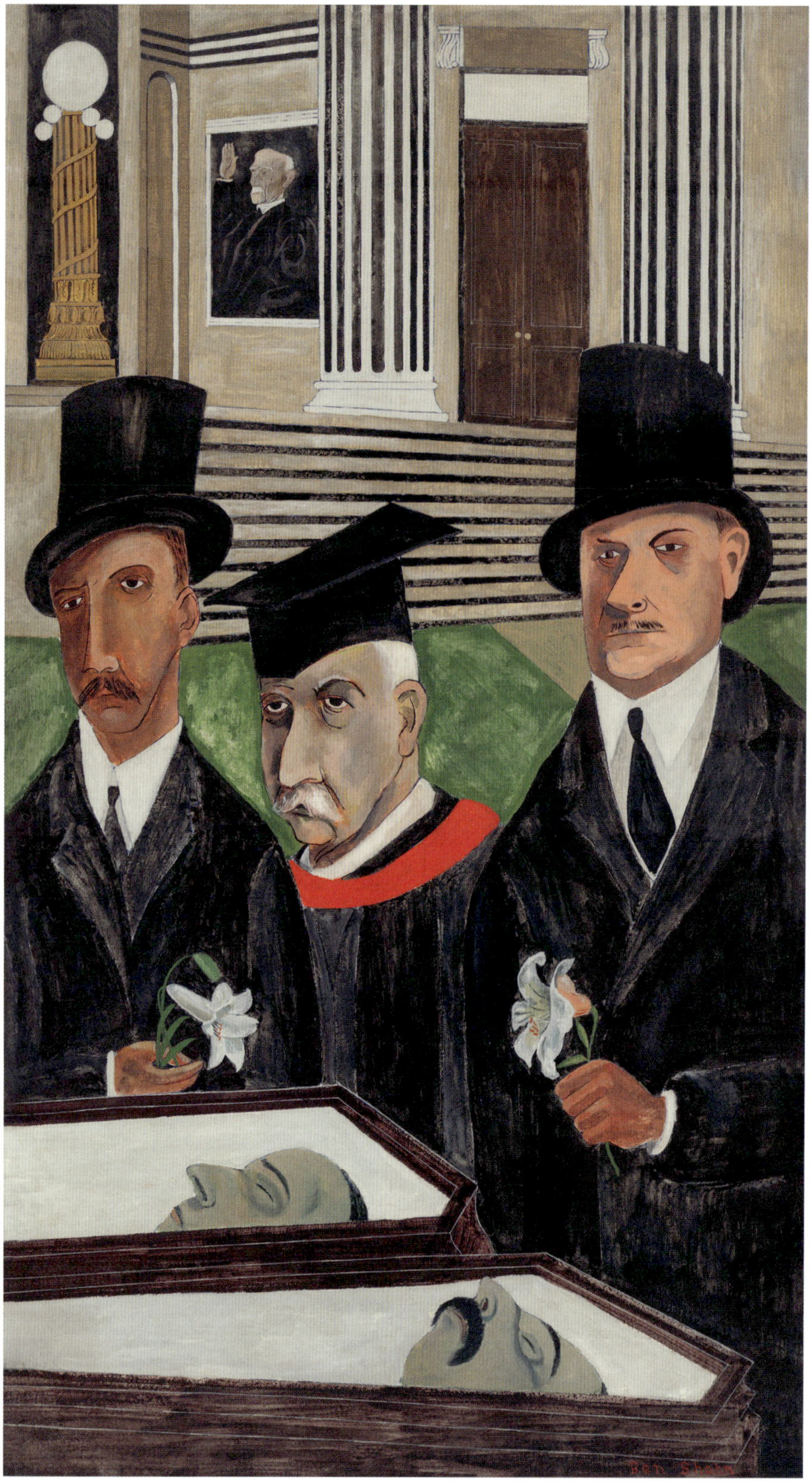

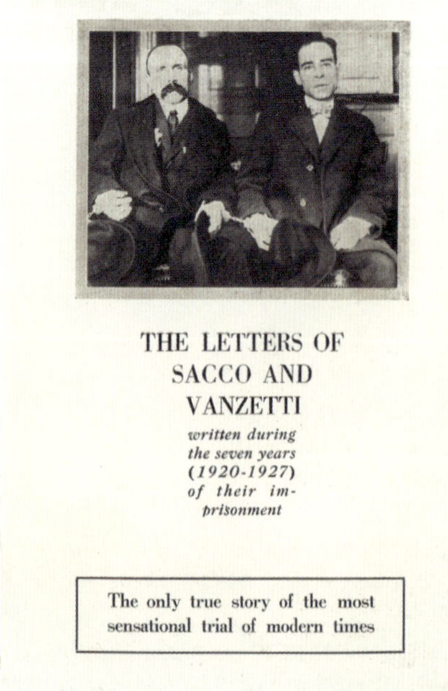

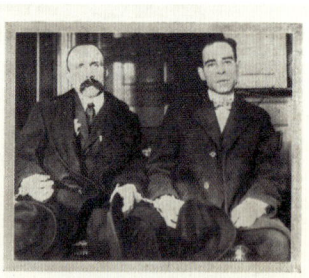

**THE LETTERS OF
SACCO AND
VANZETTI**
*written during
the seven years
(1920-1927)
of their im-
prisonment*

The only true story of the most
sensational trial of modern times

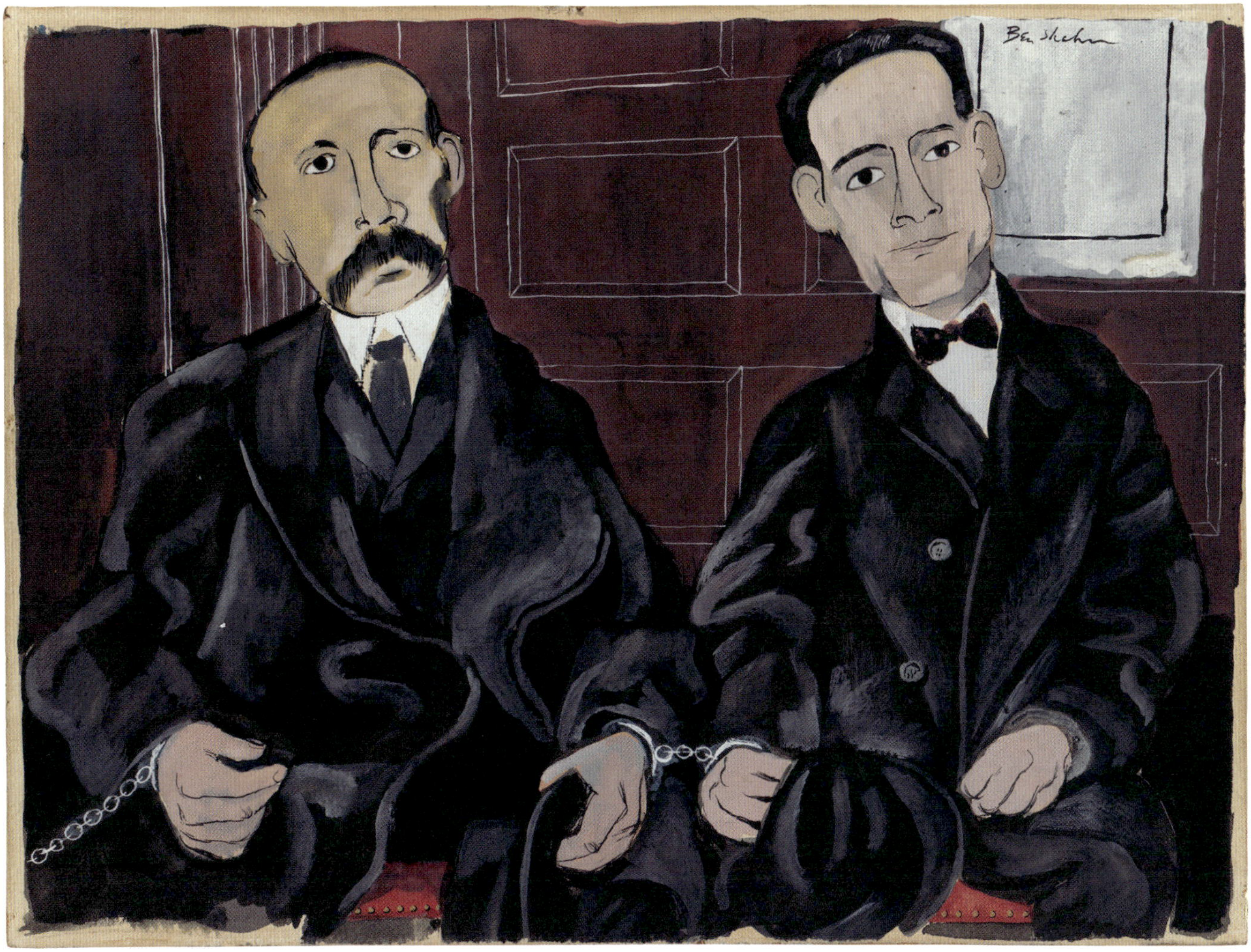

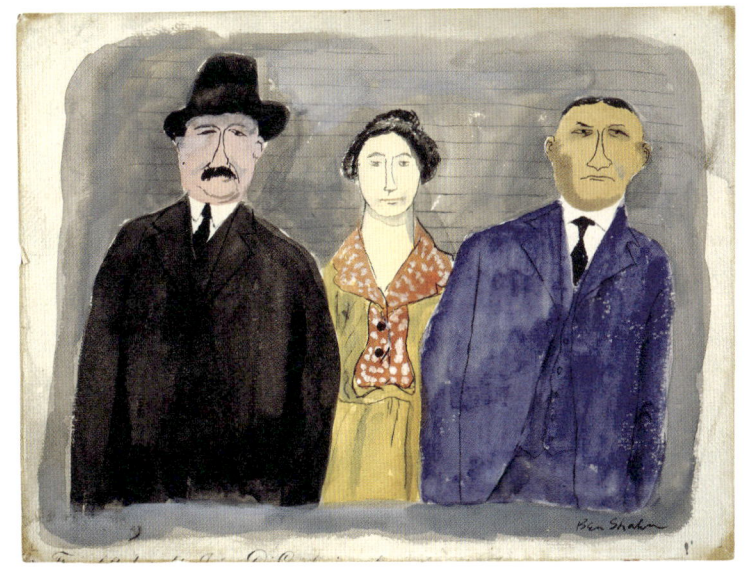

The Passion of Sacco and Vanzetti
1931–32

Marion D. Frankfurter and Gardner Jackson, eds.
*The Letters of Sacco and Vanzetti: Written During
the Seven Years (1920–1927) of Their Imprisonment.*
London: Constable & Company Ltd., 1929

Bartolomeo Vanzetti and Nicola Sacco
1931–32

Three Witnesses
c. 1931–32

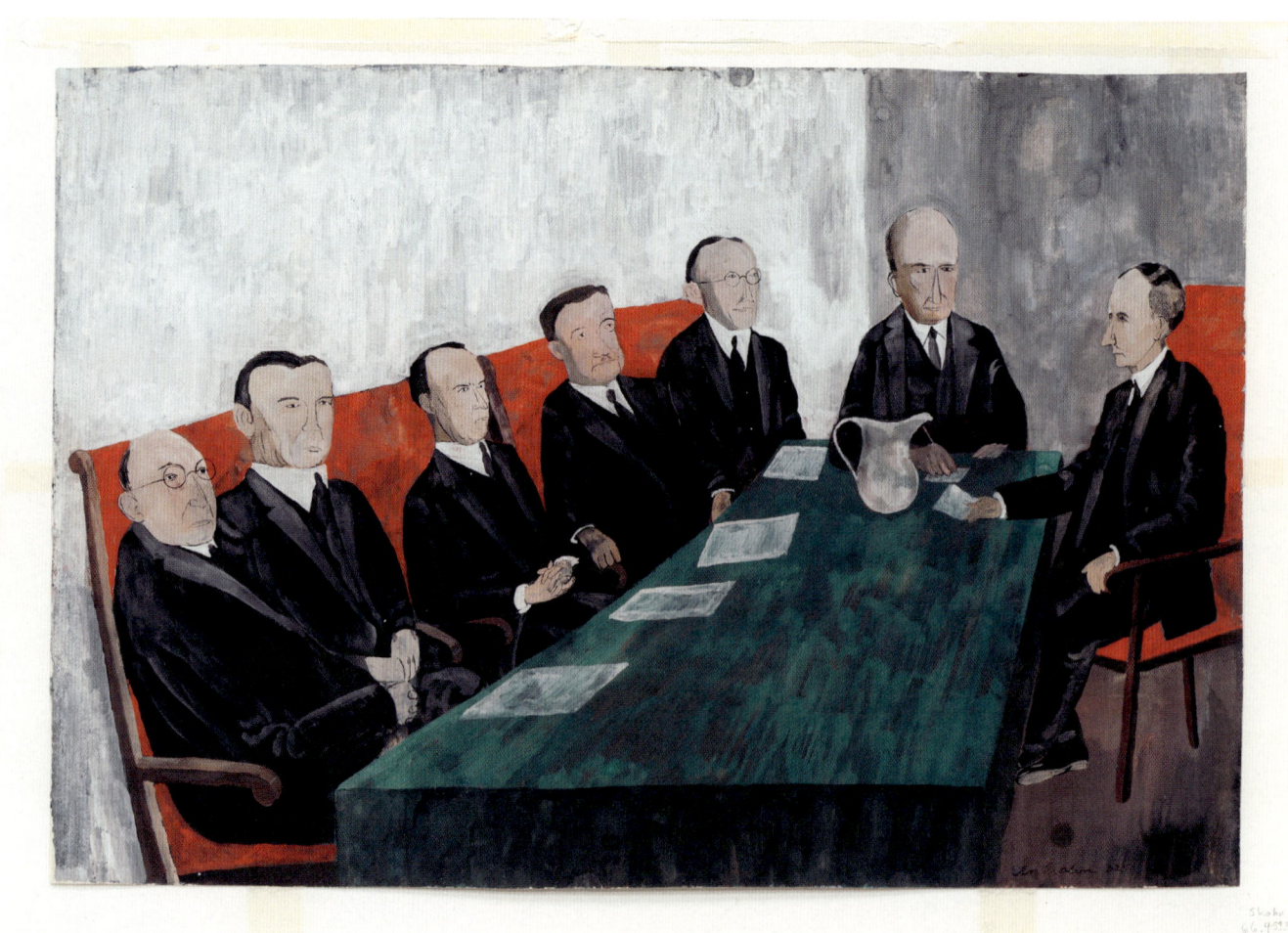

Supreme Court of California: Mooney Series
1932

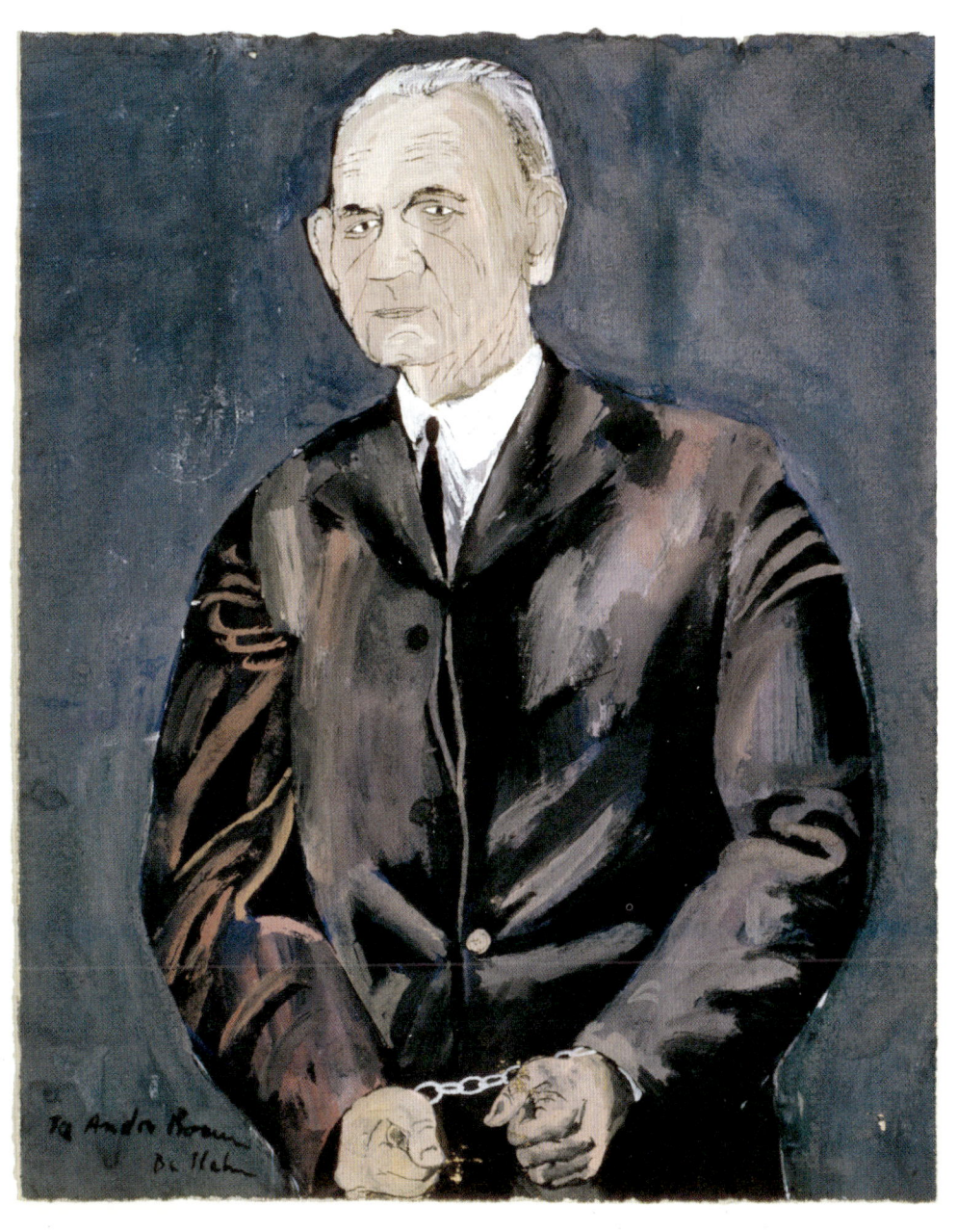

Tom Mooney Handcuffed
1932–33

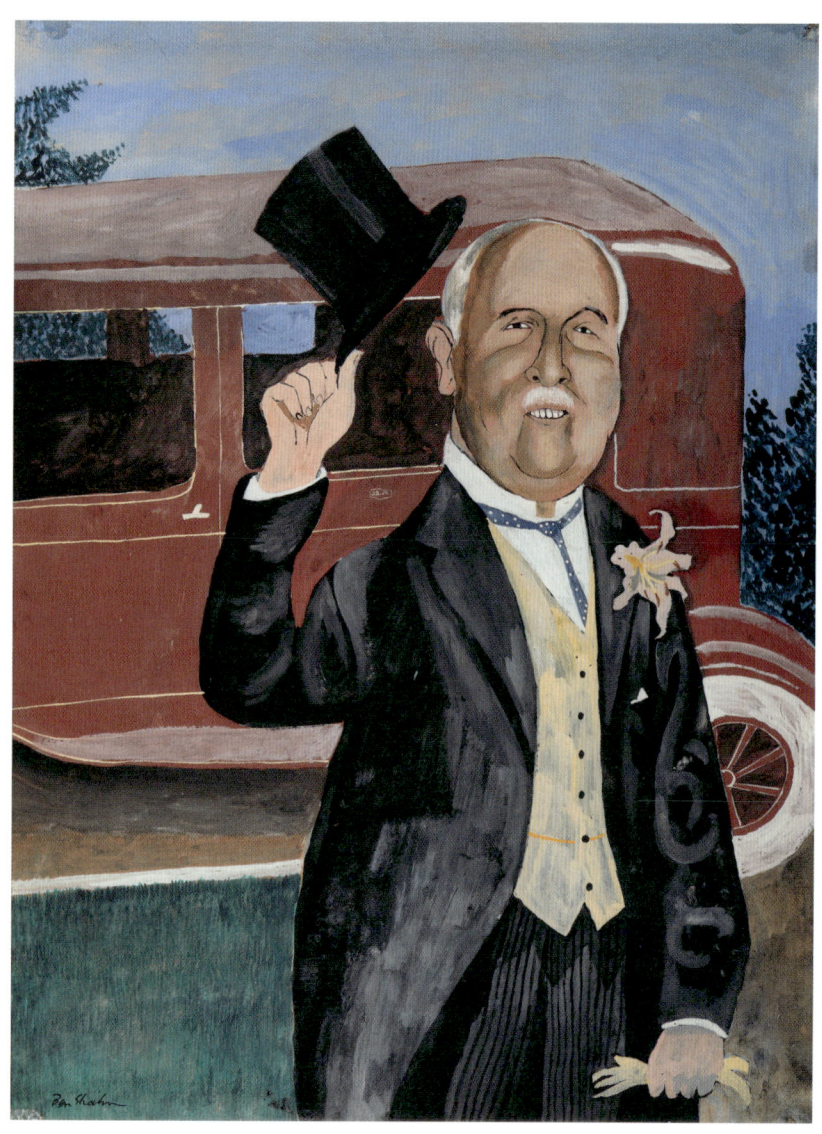

Governor James Rolph, Jr., of California
1932–33

Two Witnesses, Mellie Edeau and Sadie Edeau
1932

Photographer unknown
"Two Blood-Hunting Vultures. Mellie Edeau and Sadie Edeau,
Self-Confessed Perjurers," c. 1919

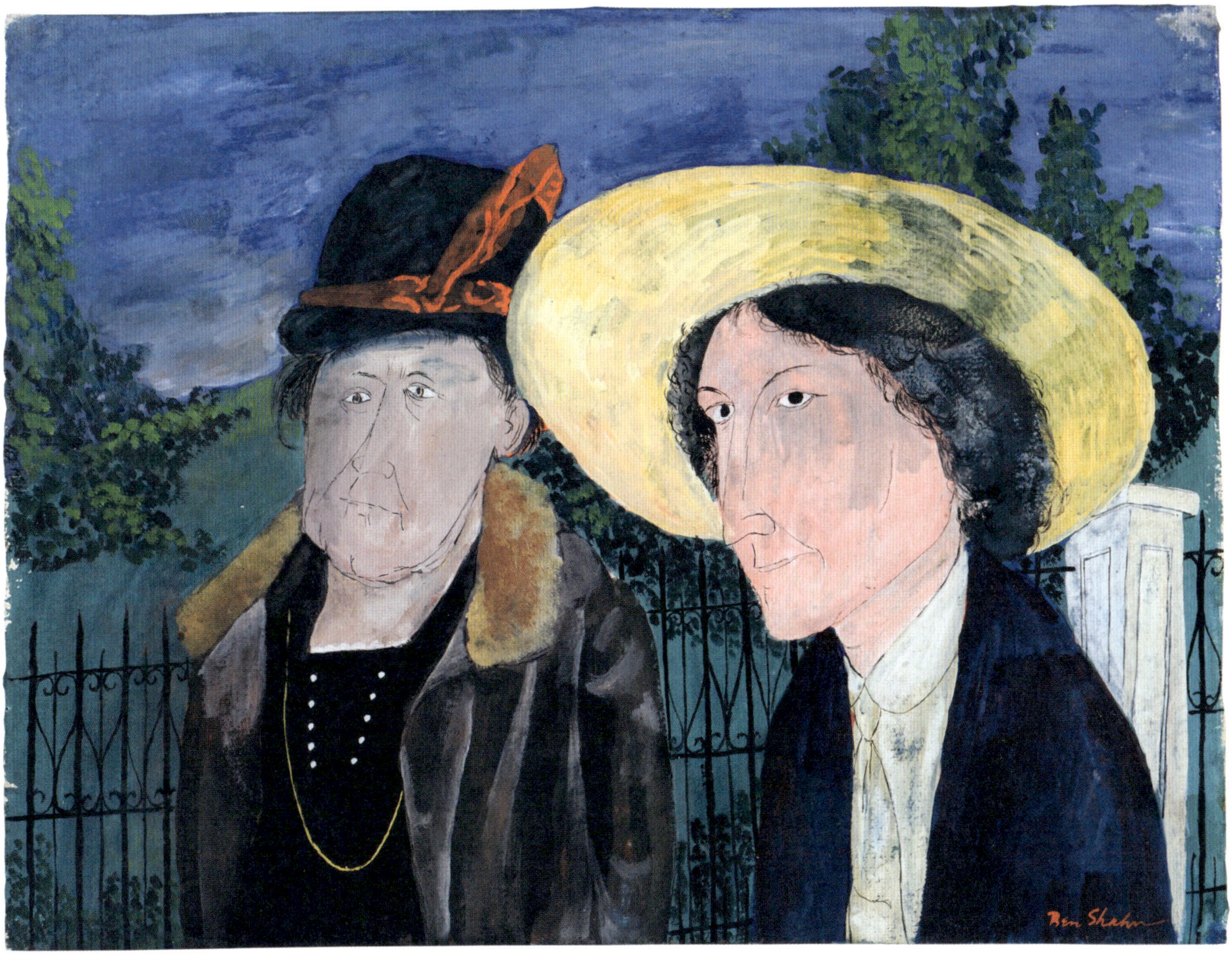

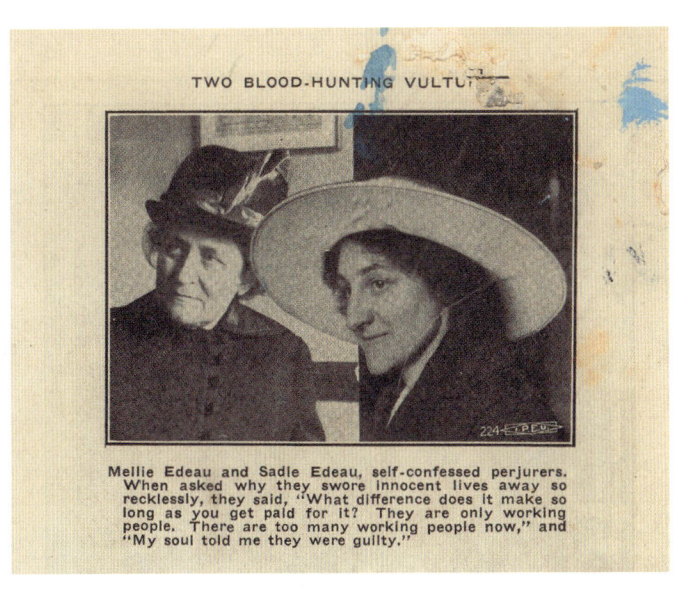

TWO BLOOD-HUNTING VULTU[...]

Mellie Edeau and Sadie Edeau, self-confessed perjurers. When asked why they swore innocent lives away so recklessly, they said, "What difference does it make so long as you get paid for it? They are only working people. There are too many working people now," and "My soul told me they were guilty."

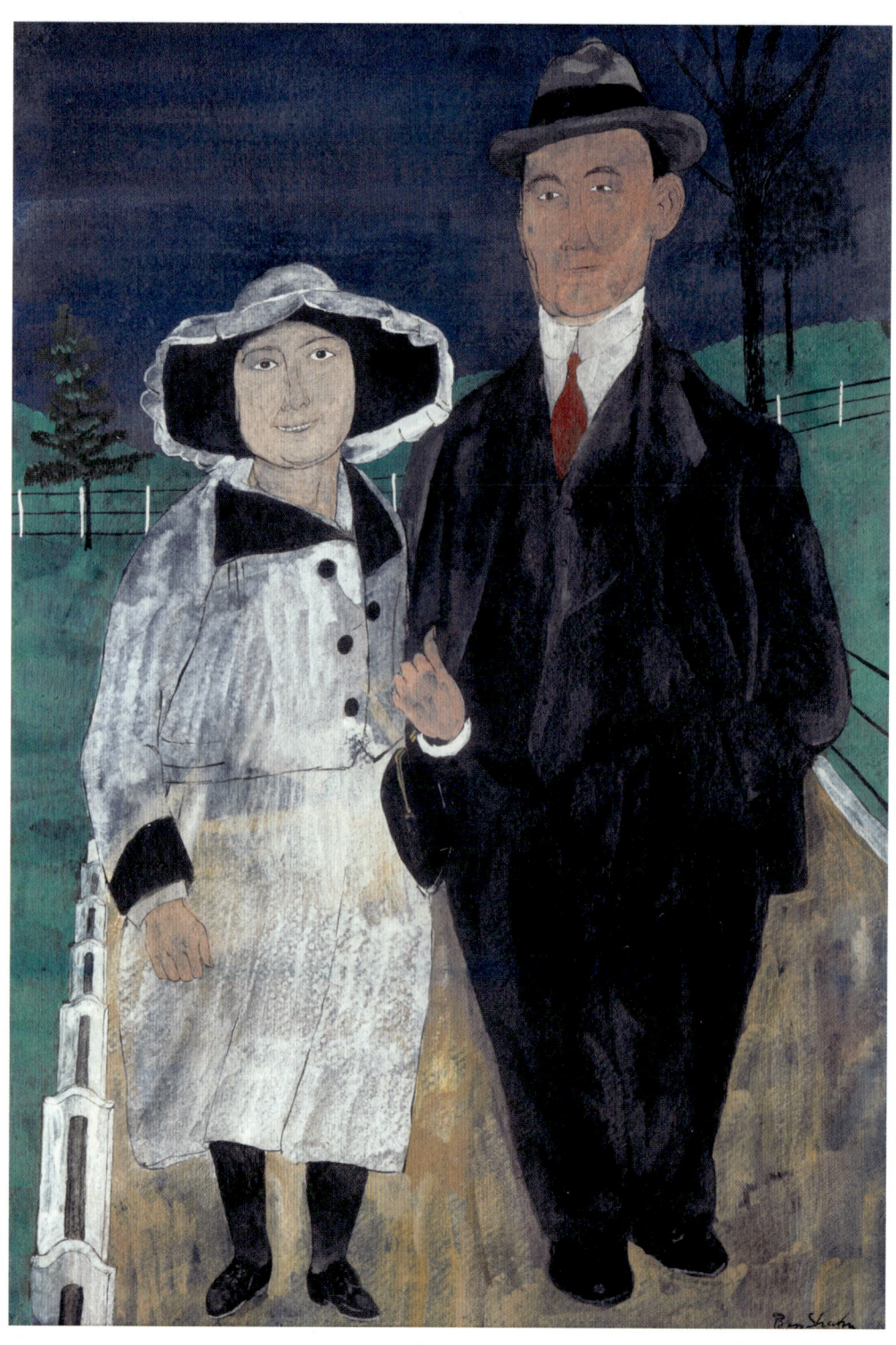

Rena and Tom Mooney
1933

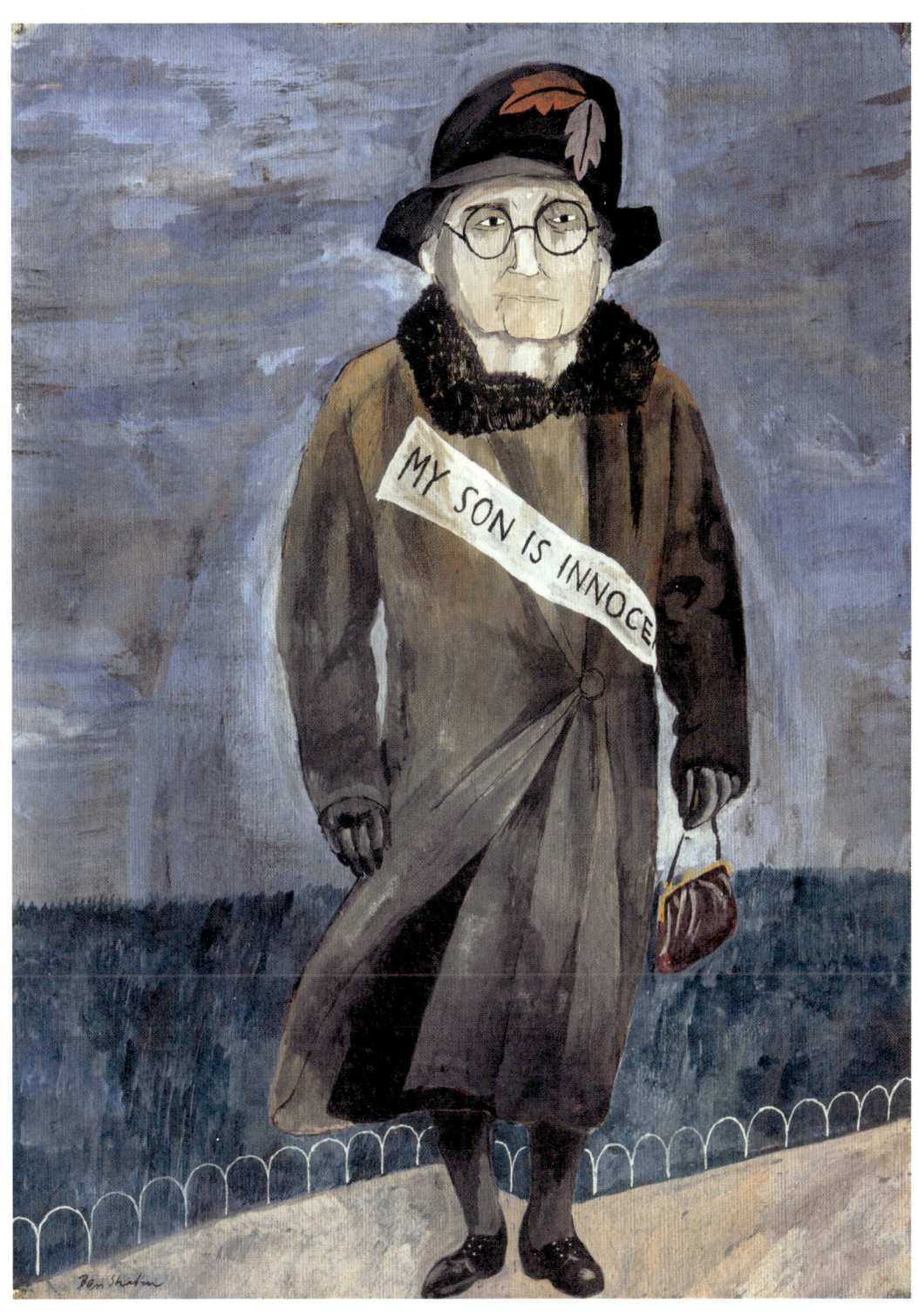

My Son is Innocent
1932

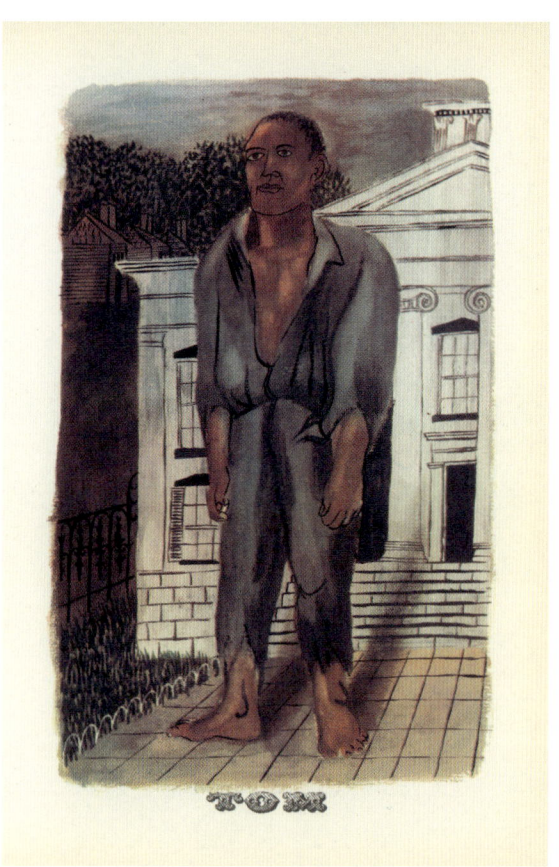

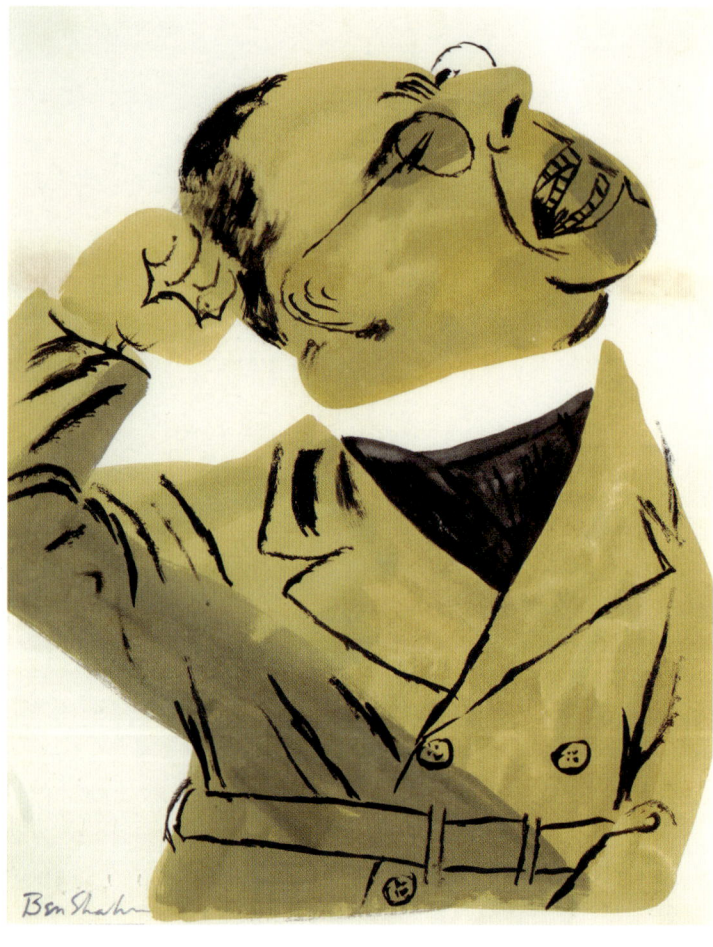

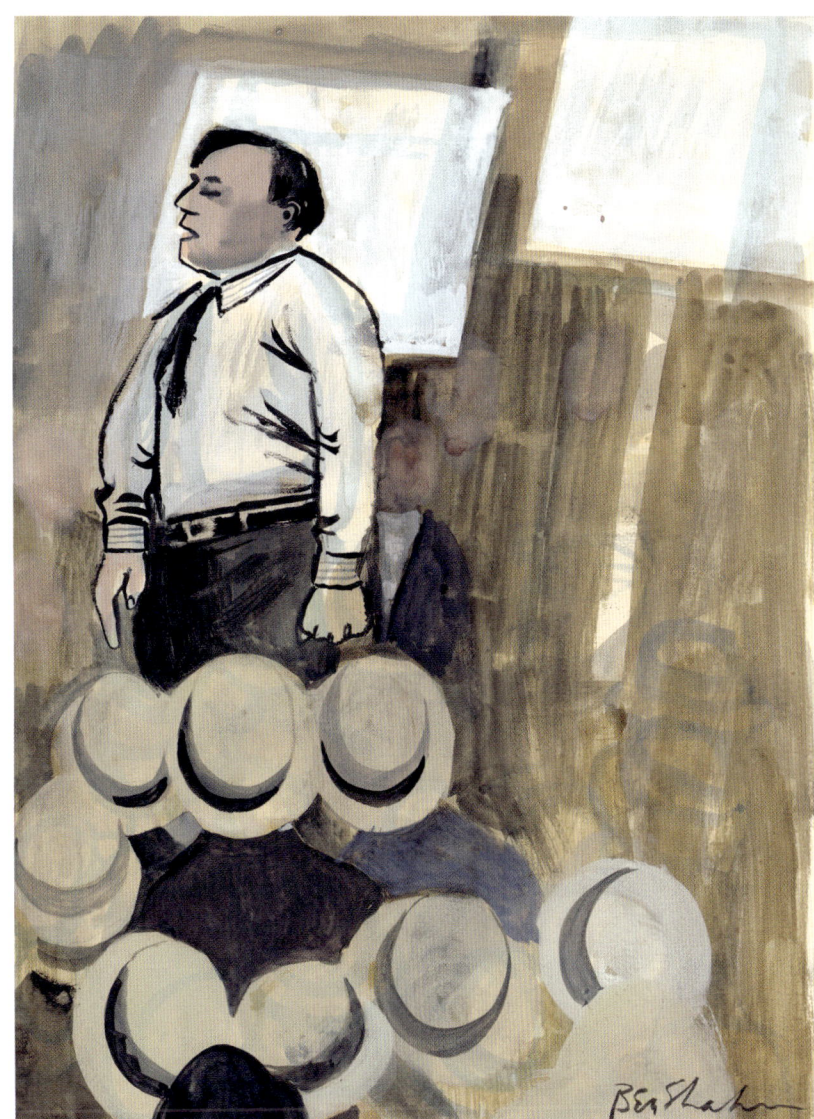

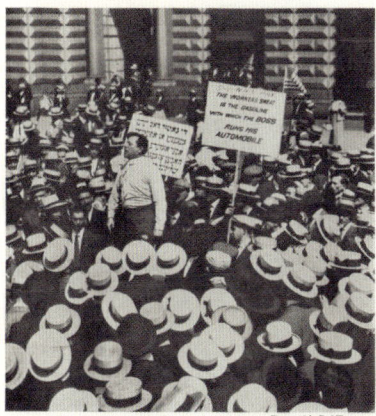

E. E. Cummings, *Tom*. New York: Arrow Editions, 1935

Father Coughlin
1939

Street Corner Speaker
1936

Paul Thompson, "The Soap-Box Orator and His Auditors," *National Geographic Magazine*, July 1918, vol. 34. no. 1, p. 8

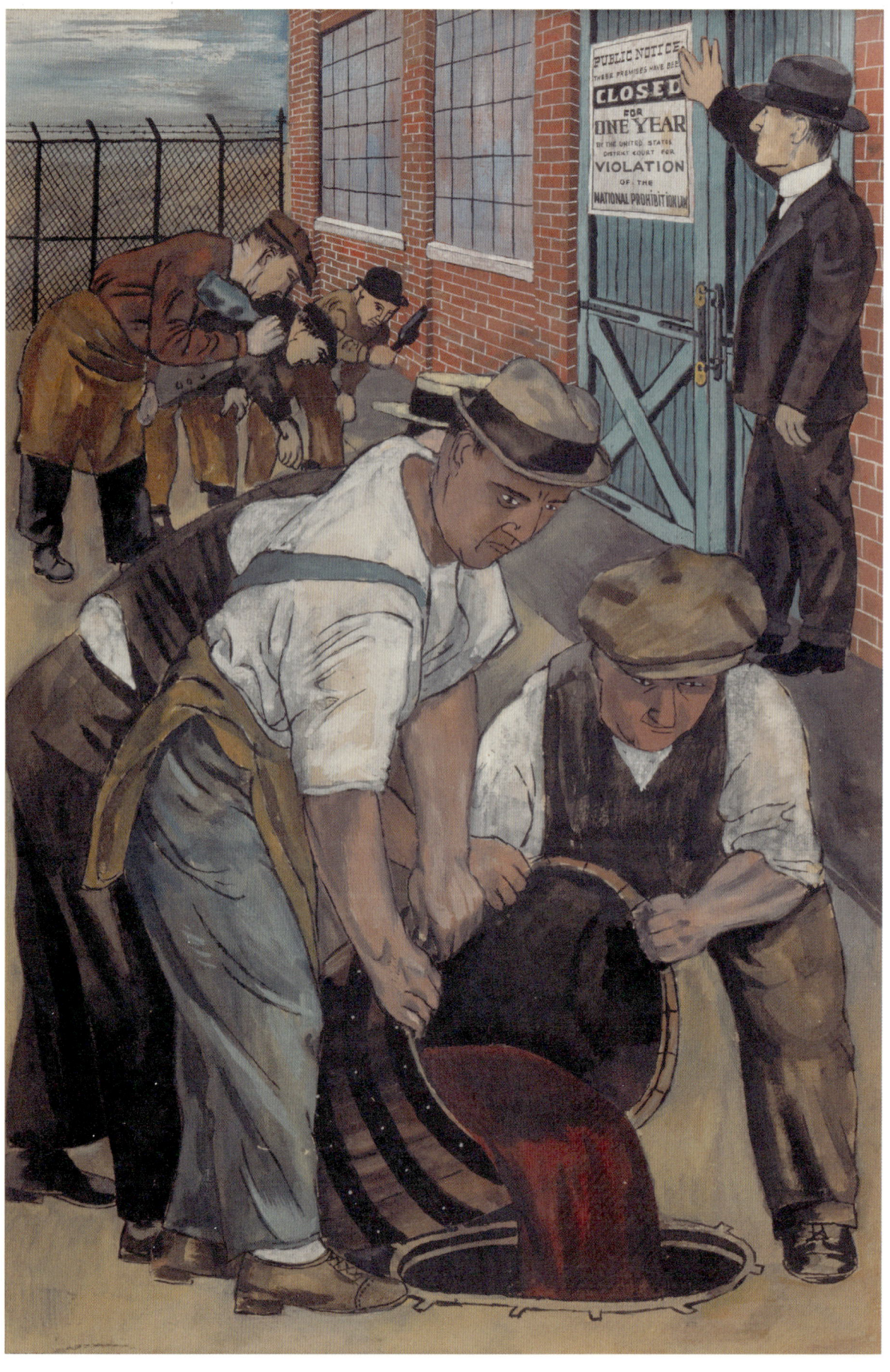

A NEW DEAL FOR ART:
FROM REVOLUTION TO REFORM

With the economic crisis of the Great Depression, many U.S. artists found socialism and communism appealing alternatives to a capitalist system they believed had failed the "common man." Ben Shahn and other leftist artists, such as Lucienne Bloch, Lou Block, Stuart Davis, Stephen Dimitroff, Hugo Gellert, Boris Gorelick, William Gropper, Max Spivak, and Moses Soyer, either joined the U.S. Communist Party (CPUSA) or became "fellow travelers," sympathetic to the party's goals but not formal members. Using his art as a weapon in the class struggle, and with inspiration from his new companion Bernarda Bryson, Shahn joined the Artists' Union circa 1933–34; edited and designed its journal, *Art Front*; and worked briefly for the CPUSA. (He soon rejected the dogmatism and infighting he found within communist circles; the romance with Russia died for many leftists in the wake of Joseph Stalin's show trials.) Shahn took up candid street photography, seeking a reportage aesthetic and "authentic" details for his "social viewpoint" paintings. Armed with his 35 mm Leica and a right-angle viewfinder that captured his subjects unawares, he recorded New Yorkers of various ethnicities and races. He photographed young men incarcerated in New York prisons. He documented artist-activists demonstrating for relief jobs, agitating for a municipal art gallery, and marching in solidarity with fellow workers in May Day parades.[1]

By the middle of the 1930s, Shahn became a staunch New Dealer and moved to Washington, D.C. Like many radicals, he joined with more moderate liberals in Popular Front coalitions to protest fascism abroad. He supported the New Deal of President Franklin Delano Roosevelt, whose unprecedented social programs put millions of Americans back to work. Although right-wing critics decried it as socialism, the New Deal actually preserved the capitalist economy, while adding social safety nets. In September 1935, Shahn and Bryson took jobs with the Special Skills Division of the Resettlement Administration (RA). Later renamed the Farm Security Administration (FSA), the RA aimed to combat the devastation wrought by the Dust Bowl and the nation's dire farm crisis. Both artists designed posters—and Shahn made photographs—to raise public awareness. Their works served as persuasive documentary evidence to prove the need for federal relief programs that relocated and retrained rural workers.

Posters from 1936, such as *Years of Dust* and *A Mule and a Plow*, featuring worried workers in bleak landscapes, were informed by the graphic detail and stark realities embedded in Shahn's iconic RA-FSA photographs: sharecroppers, tenant farmers, and coal miners throughout the South, Midwest, and mid-Atlantic regions. Along with Walker Evans, Dorothea Lange, and Russell Lee, among others, Shahn created a massive and now-legendary photographic file, which was attacked

Federal Agents Pouring Wine Down A Sewer [*Prohibition* mural study for the Central Park Casino, unrealized] c. 1934

by contemporaneous conservative politicians as leftist propaganda and, paradoxically, by later scholars as a sanitized documentation of poverty. Shahn's dynamic and spontaneous photographs are an extraordinary record of a country in crisis, showing hardship and endurance. They are notable for their keen observations and poignant but indirect critique of the racial discrimination and segregationist policies that challenged the nation's democratic ideals.[2] (This must be seen in the context of an oppressive racial order in the 1930s and the New Deal government's prioritizing of economic recovery over racial justice.) Shahn's photographs were also primary source material for his other art, such as his "Sunday Paintings," including *Sunday Painting* (1938) and *Pretty Girl Milking the Cow* (1940), which dignify the ordinariness of everyday people and their mundane activities. Examples of Shahn's "personal realism," these pictures mark a shift in his work from an "art for the masses" to one of individuals, with all their contradictions—a shift he attributed to his revelatory photographic travels around the U.S.[3]

Shahn secured several important New Deal mural commissions, through both his own proposals and public competitions. His unrealized 1934 mural for New York's Central Park Casino (nightclub), sponsored by the Public Works of Art Project, presents the subject of Prohibition. Shahn's dynamic architectural settings provide the stage for witty and satirical commentary on the efforts, often divided by gender, to uphold or repeal the nation's controversial liquor ban.[4] The first mural (*buon fresco*) he completed, circa 1936–38, is a scene of Eastern and Central European Jewish immigration to the U.S., depicting what has been described as a secular, modern-day exodus from Old World persecution to New World promise (via labor unionization and cooperative living). It was funded by the RA for the agro-industrial planned community of Jersey Homesteads (later Roosevelt), New Jersey, established to resettle Jewish garment workers from New York City sweatshops and tenements.[5] Shahn's arguably most successful and prestigious mural (*fresco secco*), *The Meaning of Social Security* (1940–42), was commissioned by the Federal Works Agency's Section of Fine Arts for the then-Social Security Building in Washington, D.C. Shahn included those whom the New Deal's Social Security Act would assist, such as unemployed, elderly, and disabled people. Yet he also subversively pictured those left out of the legislation: farmers and what may be a domestic worker. Although the mural shows industrious construction crews employed in public works projects, it avoids both the glorification of workers found in Soviet socialist realism and the simplistic celebration of the "American way." Despite some censorship Shahn experienced with his murals, and his disdain for the "poverty oath" artists took to secure a Work Projects Administration commission, in a 1964 interview for the Archives of American Art he spoke of being "completely in harmony with the times" and of his "total commitment" to this far-reaching experiment in government-sponsored art.[6]

1. On Ben Shahn's art and politics in the 1930s, see Deborah Martin Kao, Laura Katzman, and Jenna Webster, *Ben Shahn's New York: The Photography of Modern Times* (New Haven: Yale University Press, 2000), and see note 5. Shahn's photographic aesthetic was influenced by his studio mate Walker Evans and by Henri Cartier-Bresson.

2. John Raeburn, *Ben Shahn's American Scene: Photographs, 1938* (Champaign: University of Illinois Press, 2010), 159–76. On Shahn's RA-FSA photographs and race, see the work of Nicholas Natanson and Susan H. Edwards.

3. Katzman, "Source Matters: Ben Shahn and the Archive," *Archives of American Art Journal* 54, no. 2 (Fall 2015): 4–33. On Shahn's "Sunday Paintings" and how they worked within and against the tradition of genre painting, see John Fagg, *Re-envisioning the Everyday: American Genre Scenes, 1905–1945* (University Park: Pennsylvania State University Press, 2023), 159–77.

4. On another ill-fated mural and for an unusual critique of Shahn's progressivism, see Davida Fernández-Barkan, "Of Murals and Men: Carceral Aesthetics and Ben Shahn's Rikers Island Project," *American Art* 31, no. 1 (Spring 2023): 32–57.

5. Diana L. Linden, *Ben Shahn's New Deal Murals: Jewish Identity in the American Scene* (Detroit: Wayne State University Press, 2015), 17, 61–63. On Jersey Homesteads' importance to Shahn, who settled there in 1939, see the doctoral dissertation by Daniel S. Palmer (CUNY, 2021).

6. On Shahn's Social Security mural as symptomatic of the Roosevelt administration's limited commitment to racial justice, see John Ott's forthcoming book, *Mixed Media: The Visual Cultures of Racial Integration, 1931–1954.* The New Deal federal arts projects can be seen as progressive in how they supported struggling artists, but also as conservative in how the artworks promoted traditional values. Many scholars have read the murals as propaganda aimed to boost public morale, instill regional pride, and reinforce national identity during the Great Depression.

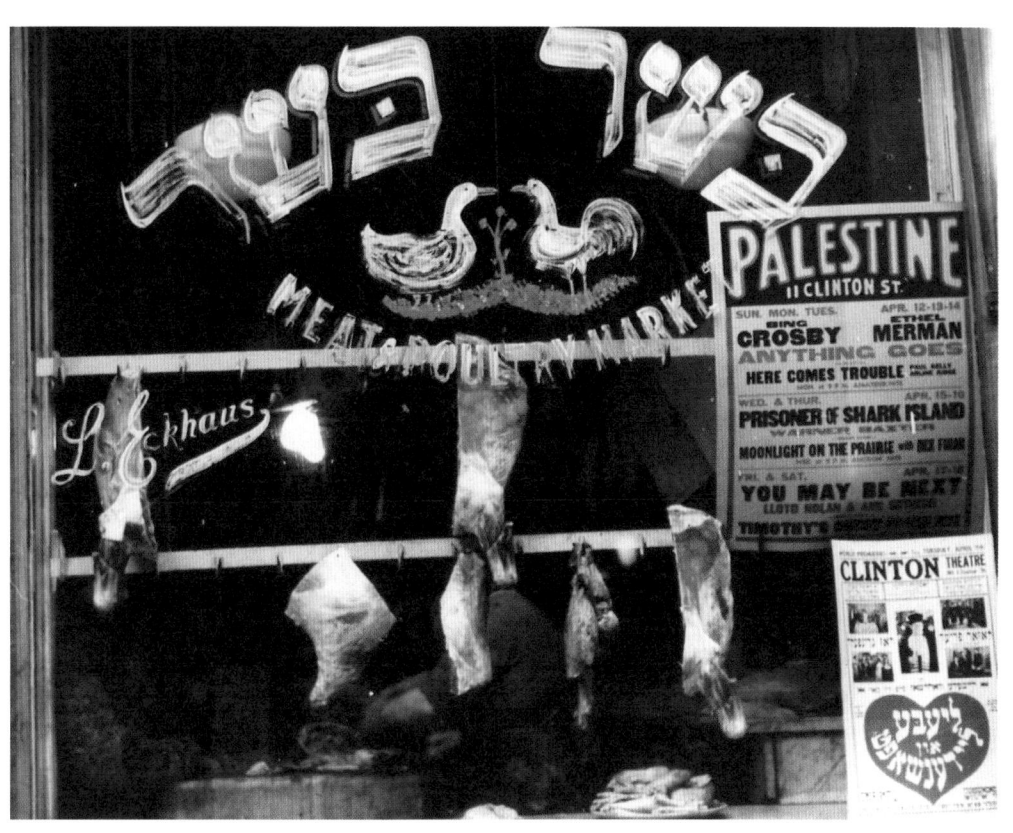

Untitled [Lower East Side, New York City]
April 1936

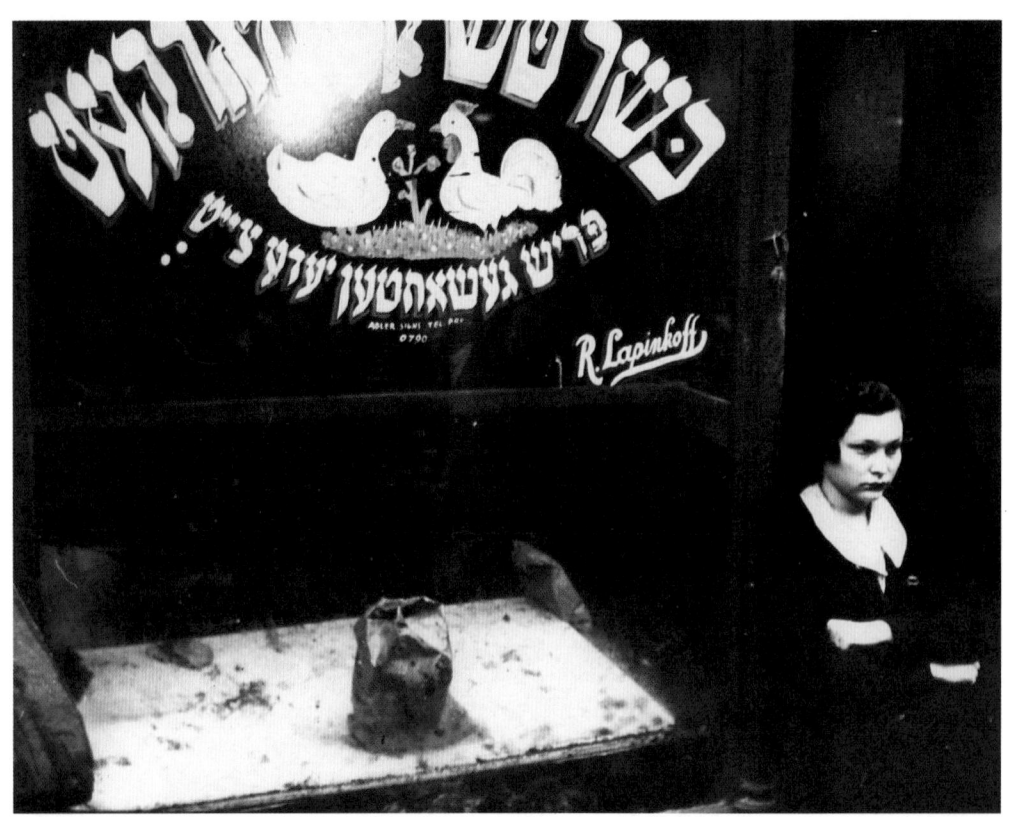

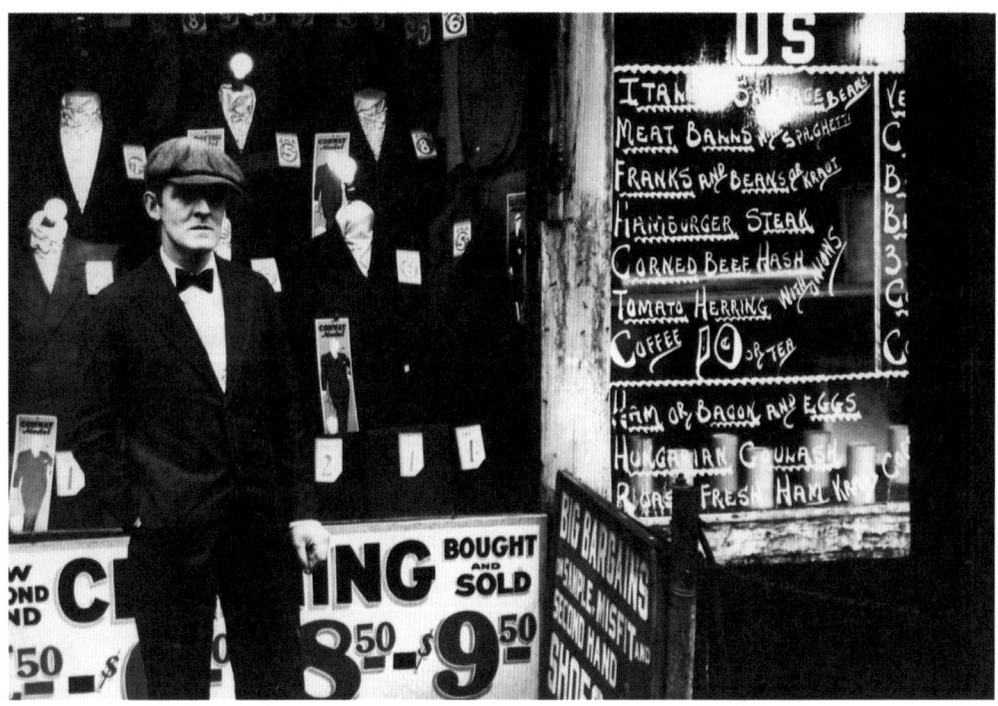

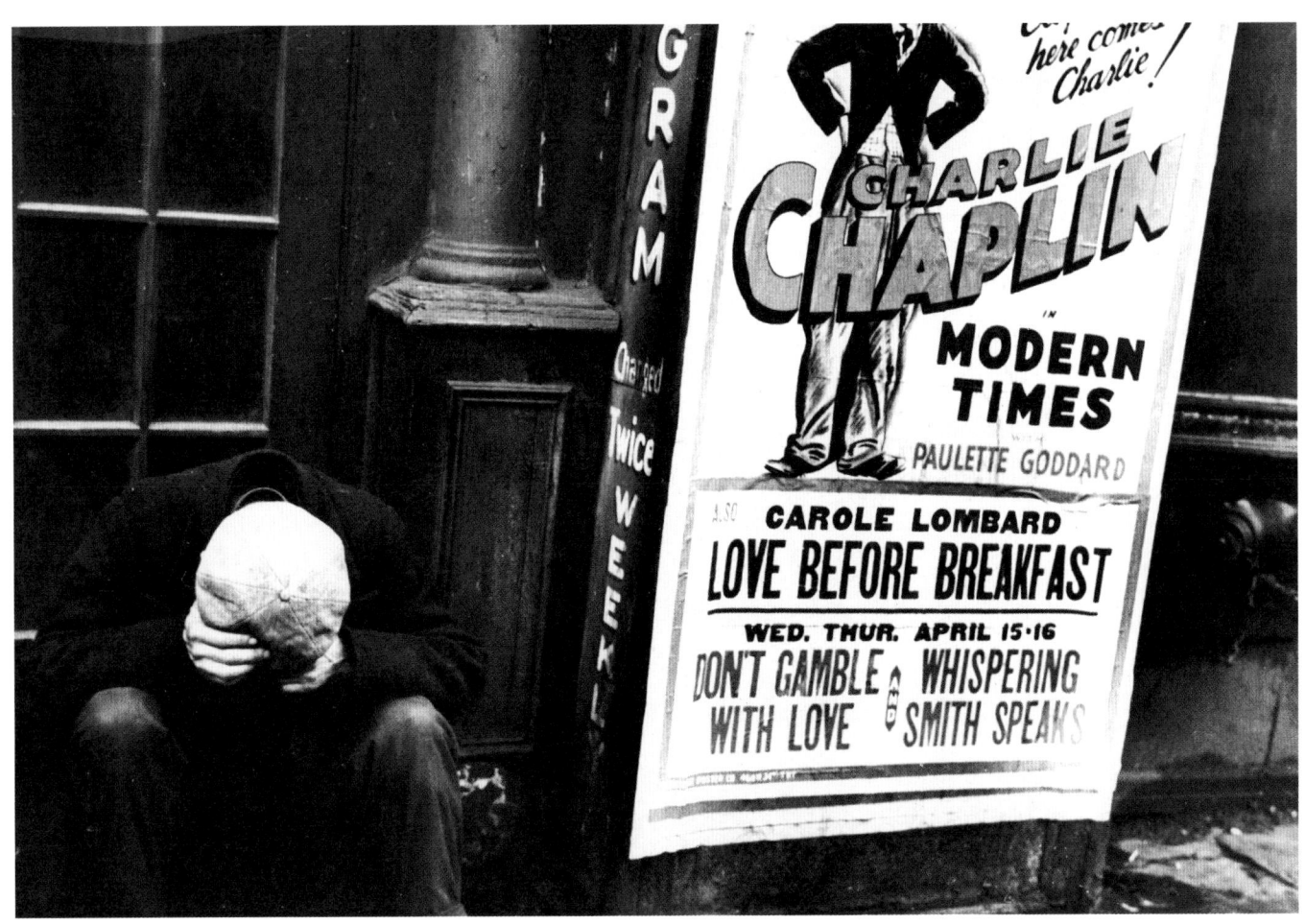

East Side Merchants [Lower East Side, New York City]
April 1936

Bowery [New York City]
April 1936

Untitled [Bowery, New York City]
1995 (from April 1936 negative)

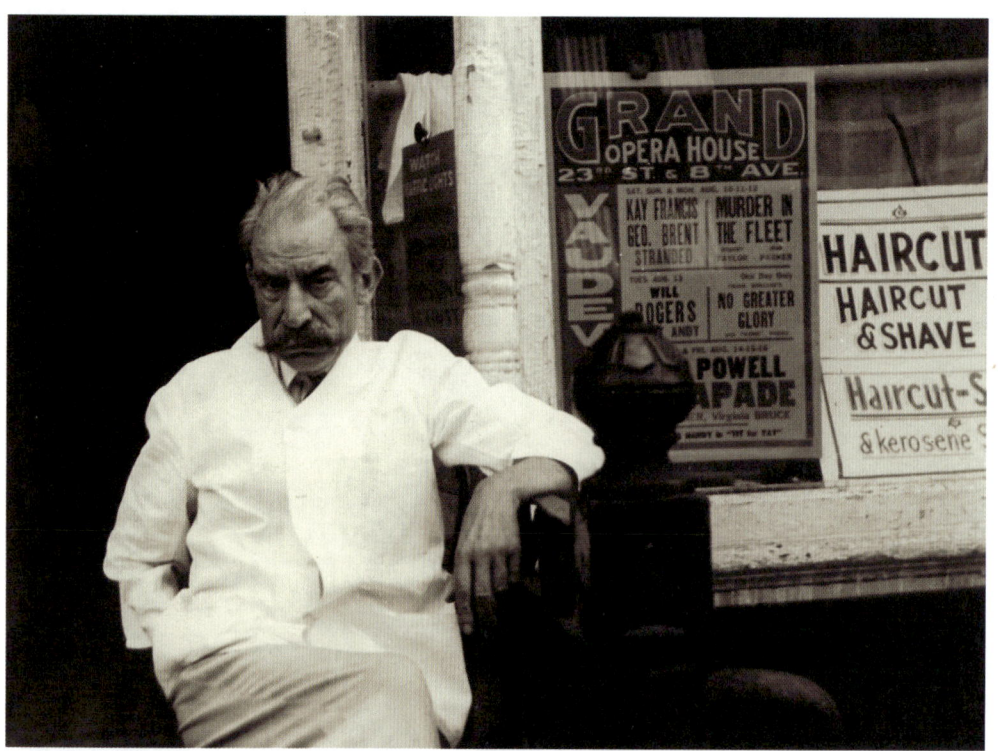

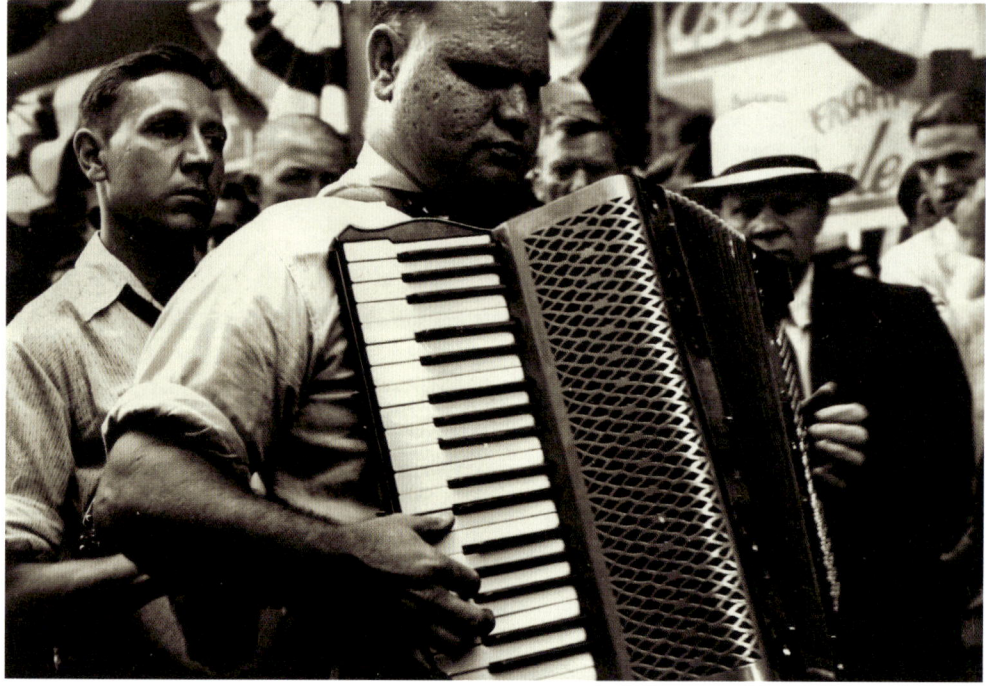

Untitled [New York City]
1935

14th St. [New York City]
1932–34

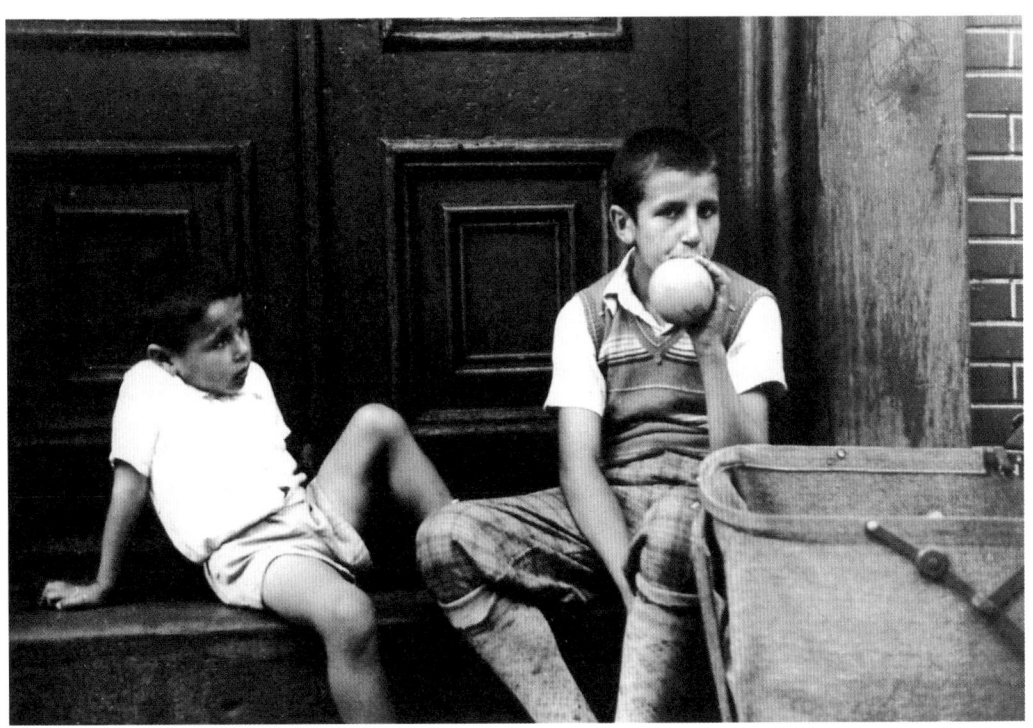

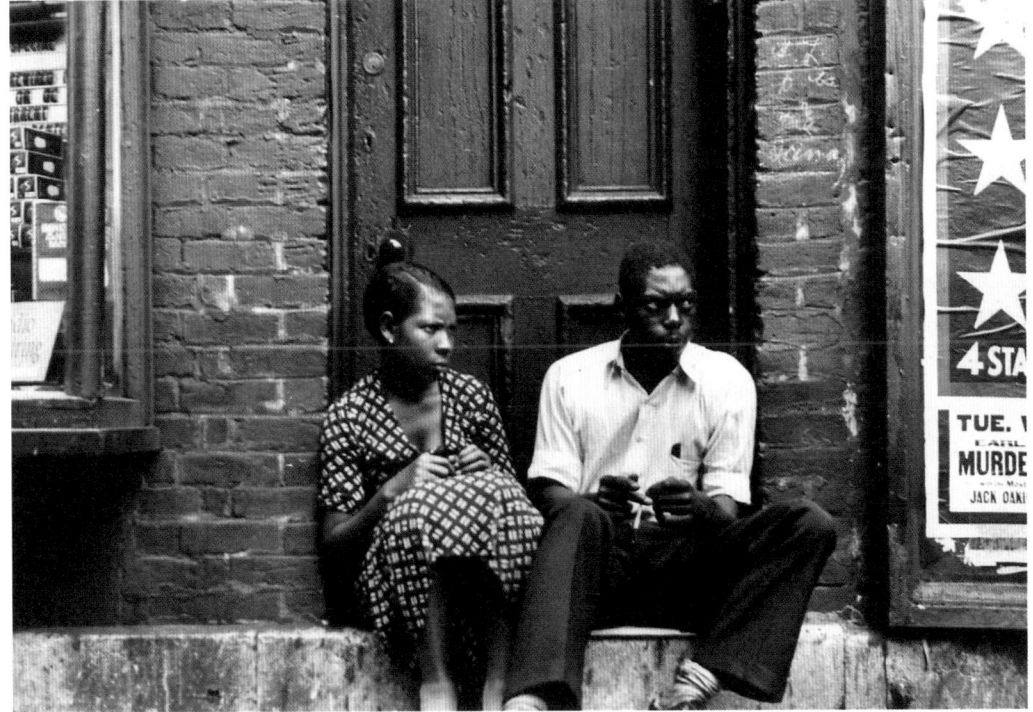

Greenwich Village [New York City]
1932–35

Greenwich Village [New York City]
1932–34

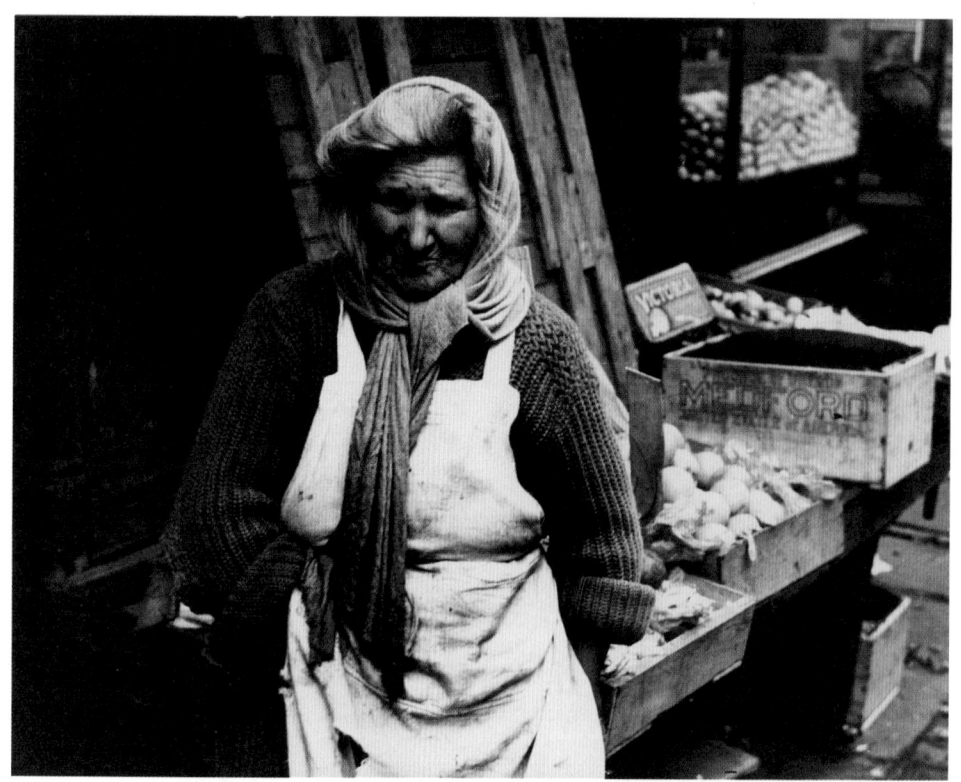

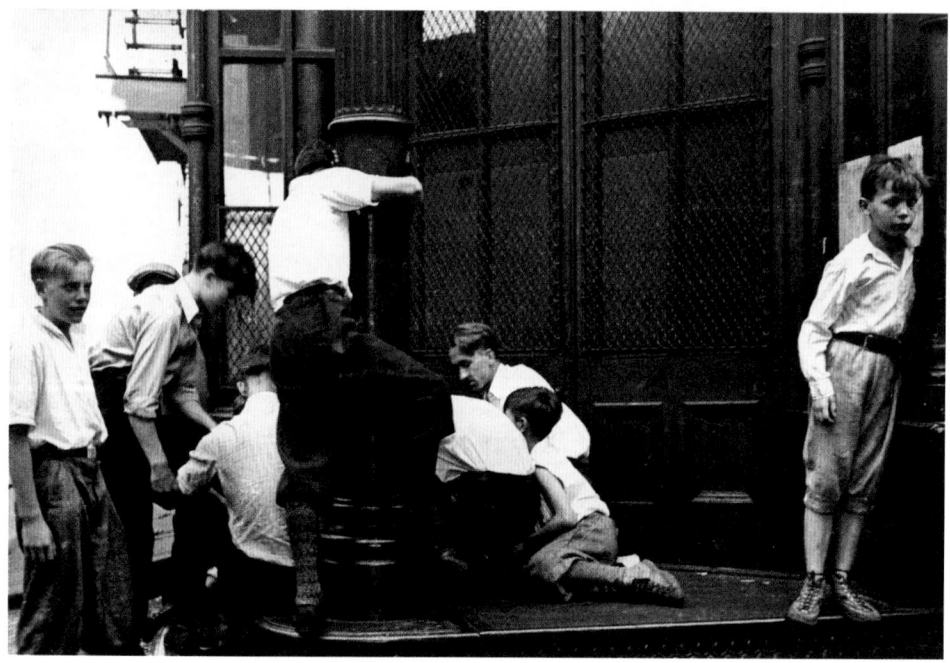

East Side Merchant [New York City]
1932–35

Greenwich Village [Bethune Street, New York City]
1932–35

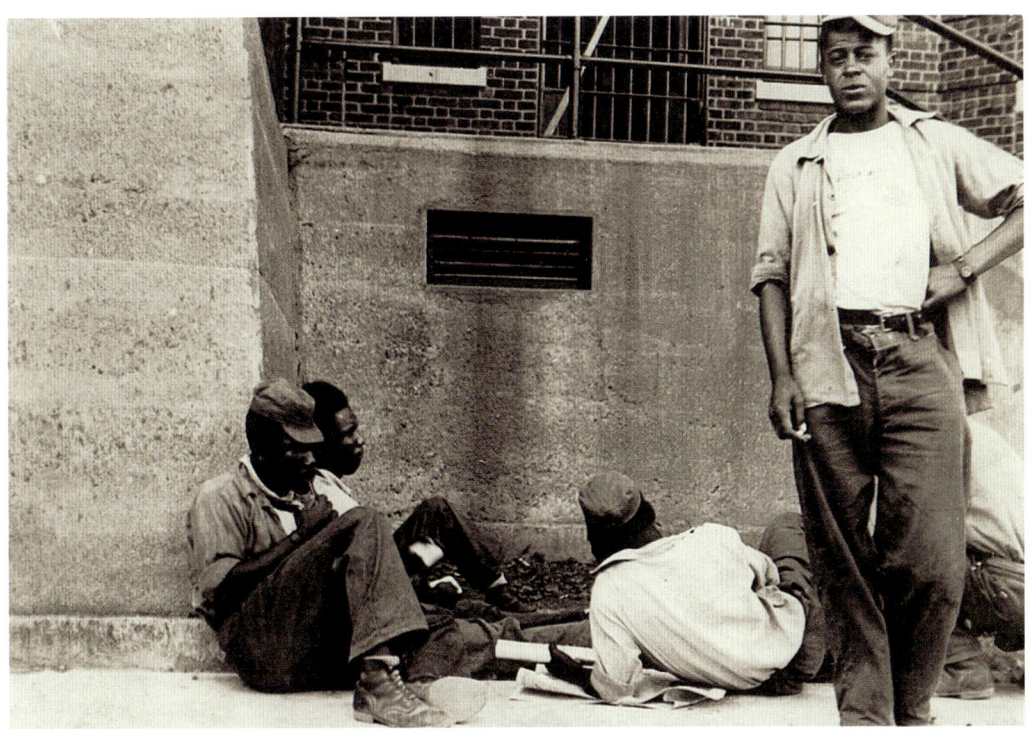

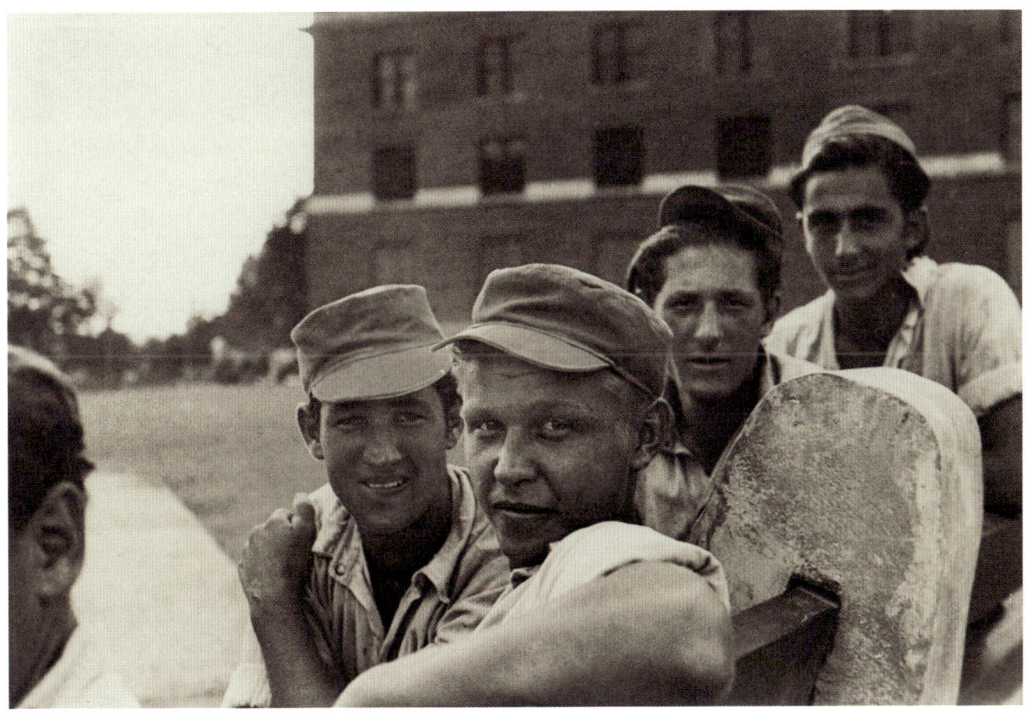

Untitled [New York City Reformatory, New Hampton, New York]
1934

Untitled [New York City Reformatory, New Hampton, New York]
May–June 1934

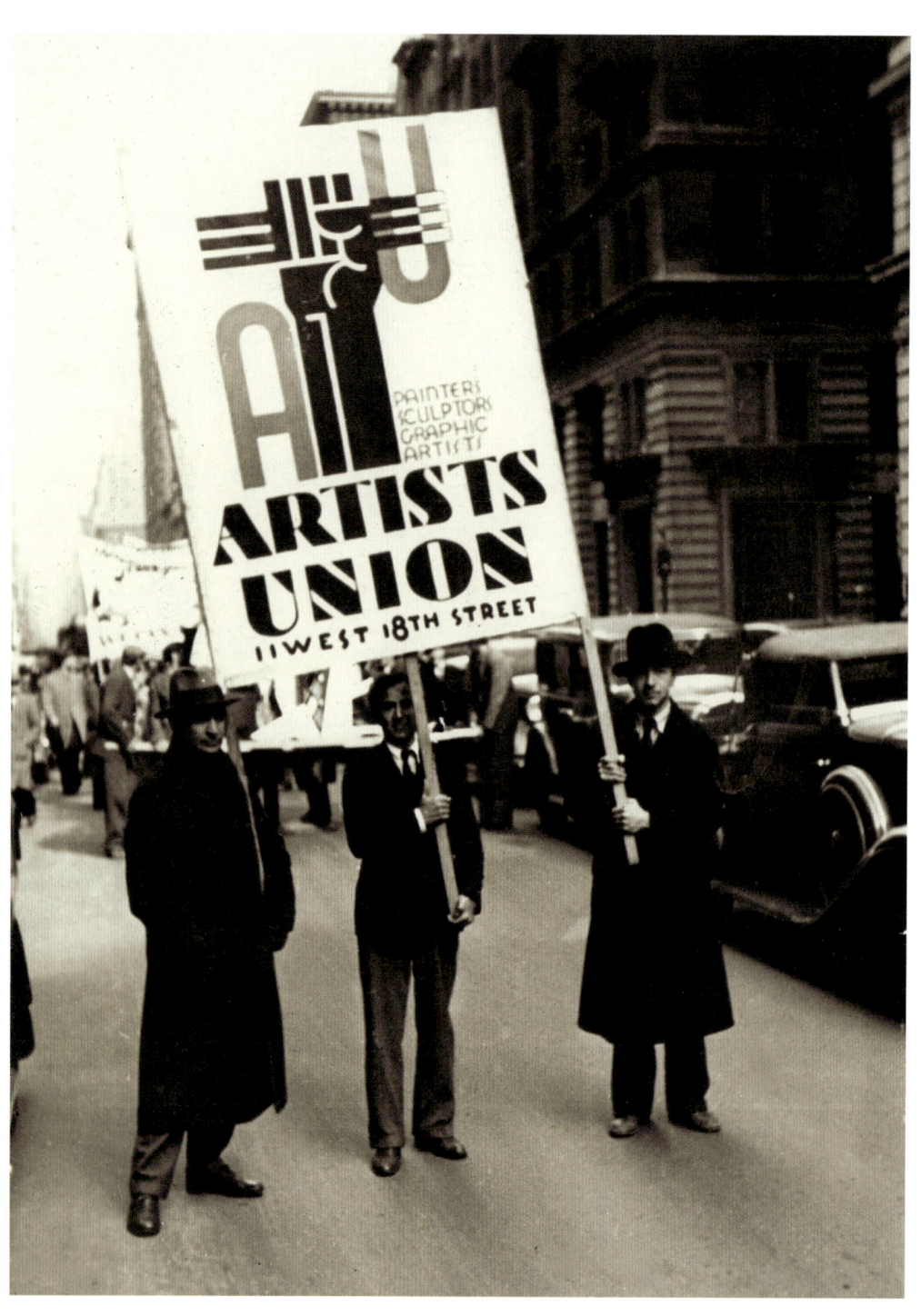

Untitled [Artists' Union and Artists
Committee of Action Demonstrations, NYC]
1934–35

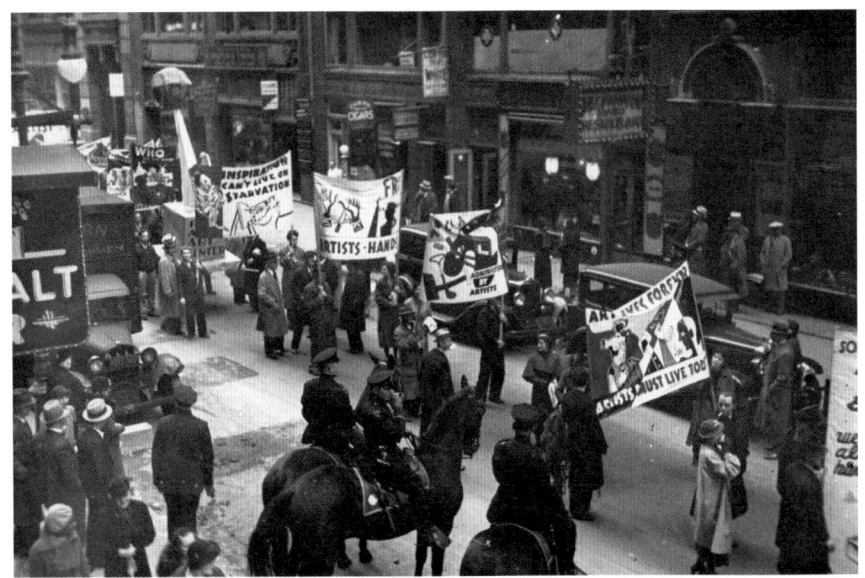

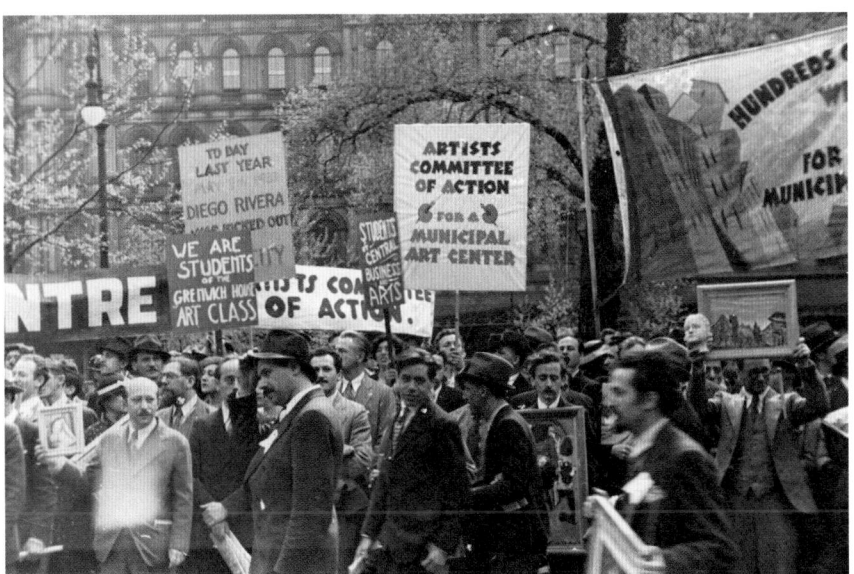

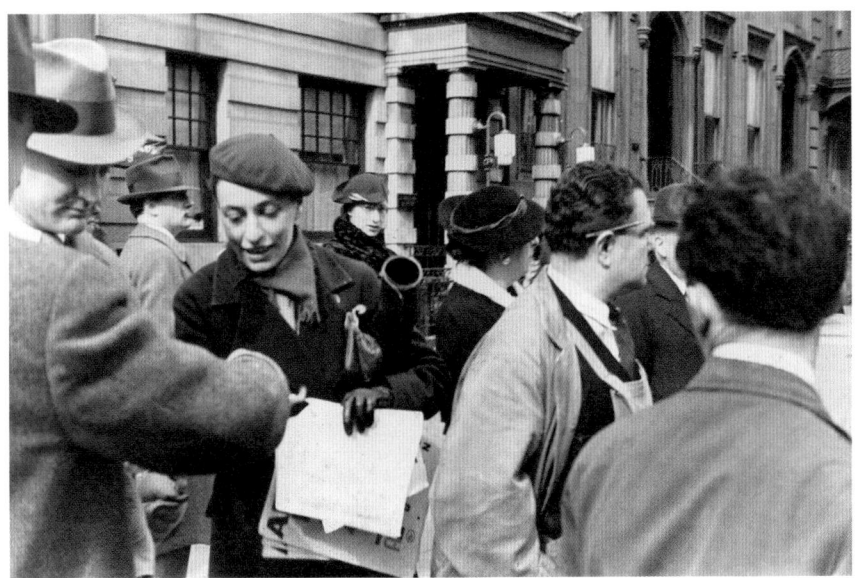

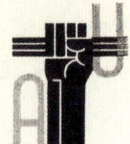

ART FRONT

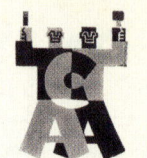

Official Publication of the ARTISTS' UNION, 60 West 15th Street, New York
Editorial Office, ART FRONT, 54 West Eighth Street, New York City

Wages For Artists

WHILE Washington politicians debate about whether it is more dangerous to risk the Administration's displeasure by recognizing prevailing wages in the new $4,880,000,000 Relief Bill, or to flout organized labor by undermining its hard-won wage rates, it becomes apparent that the answer lies with labor itself.

Present developments indicate that the prevailing wage clause will not be written into the Work Relief Bill, but that the Administration will make whatever concessions are necessary in the face of union pressure. That is, wherever relief workers are organized in strong unions they have some chance to retain the union wage scale.

Artists now on art projects receive $24.00 weekly for from 30 to 39 hours' work, that is, about $4.80 per day. It is interesting to compare this wage with that of other skilled workers. Union plumbers, for instance, receive $12.00 per day, house painters receive $11.20, plasterers, $12.00, stone carvers, $14.00. The Artists' Union, after careful consideration of comparative wages, has determined on $2.00 per hour as a fair wage for artists, for a maximum 30-hour, and a minimum 12-hour week. Artists who now receive $24.00 for a 30-hour week will, under the new rate, receive the same sum for 12 hours of work.

It is vital at the present time that artists organize for the creation of new art projects, for the maintenance of desirable working conditions, and for the recognition of the Union wage scale.

Hearn Plan

INVITATIONS were recently sent out by the "Lower New York Art Council" to artists for an exhibition which opened March 4 at Hearn's Department Store. On the eve of the opening, the artists were surprised to learn that this exhibit was being sponsored by Mayor LaGuardia's Municipal Committee of One Hundred, which body had refused to admit duly elected delegates of New York artists to its first and only conference at City Hall.

Artists protested against the first municipally sponsored exhibition last year because it was held in Rockefeller Center where a work of art was destroyed by the owners of the building. After withdrawing their works, the artists sent a delegation to Mayor LaGuardia and presented him with plans for a permanent Municipal Art Gallery and Center.

We protest against this exhibition at Hearn's. It is one precisely of the character that the creation of a Municipal Art Center would prevent. In no way does it serve the interests of artists but is merely instrumental in providing free publicity for a department store.

This time our protest has been effective. On the opening day of the exhibition, six paintings were removed by indignant artists.

During the first week of the exhibition so many more have been removed that the sponsors of the show, in order to cover the bare spaces, have had to resort to hanging the work originally thrown out by the jury as unfit.

Why Mr. Benton!

Editors of Art Front.   February 14th, 1935.
Dear Sirs:

The copy of Art Front which, according to your letter of February 12th, was mailed to me, has not yet arrived.

I am always interested when people criticize me, so I hope you will mail me your sheet.

I am not, however, interested in answering criticisms or in defending myself.

I am in the first place in too strong a position to make that necessary, and in the second place am too sceptical of the nature of critical motives, in general, to take the critical findings of my contemporaries with much seriousness.

The criticisms of artists are unconsciously controlled, for the most part, by impulses that are defensive rather than inquiring.

In the case of an "imitator of imitations" like Stuart Davis, the motives for a criticism of my work or of that of Curry, Marsh or Wood are plain.

No verbiage can disguise the squawks of the defeated and impotent.

Yours sincerely,
THOMAS H. BENTON.

But the next day Mr. Benton read the article. He telephoned—would we ask him ten questions and give him three thousand words? We did. Several days later we received his answers, he telephoned again. Were we answering him in the next issue? If so, he must have five hundred more words of rebuttal.. *Art Front* is limited for space and we could not tell him definitely. Mr. Benton became panicky. He "scooped" us and delivered our questions and his answers to them to *Art Digest*.* THE EDITORS.

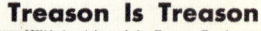

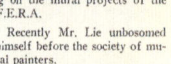

Ben Shahn

Treason Is Treason

WHEN the sluices of the Panama Canal opened in 1912, there rode to fame on the famous waters, Jonas Lie, a little known painter who had set himself the task of immortalizing the great engineering feat.

Never distinguished for the quality or the profoundness of his work, he has nevertheless risen steadily in the world of art. He painted pretty sailboats and became an Associate N. A. He painted more p.s.b. and became a full N.A. He painted still more p.s.b. and became president of the N.A.

He then gave up his struggles with the brush to become painter member of the New York Municipal Art Commission. In normal times the duties of this office would be to choose the proper design for subway kiosks, lamp posts, park benches and garbage cans. But these are not normal times. Under the desperate enterprises of hard-pressed politicians, Mr. Lie finds himself in a key position. That is to pass or reject the murals designed by some hundred and fifty artists working on the mural projects of the F.E.R.A.

Recently Mr. Lie unbosomed himself before the society of mural painters.

He confessed that of the many murals that he had passed during his year in office, he had "passed them with a smile, but there is an awful lot behind that smile." He did not like the murals, but he remembered that the walls could always be whitewashed. Beside, the work was going into "old decrepit buildings that are coming down anyway."

Mr. Lie dislikes modern trends in painting. "If academic painting is on the skids," he cries, "God help American art!" But if he dislikes modern painting, he abominates work dealing with social subject matter. He does not think, for instance, that the achievements of medical science have a place on the walls of hospitals. That prison walls should speak of the injustices of prison life, or depict ideal prison conditions, that the walls of schools should tell children of a better life, or a different form of society is to Mr. Lie propaganda and not art. "Treason is treason," he shouts, "whether in literature or paint!"

To an administration that has been a paragon of economy, that has balanced its budget by the sales tax, by flying squadrons that descend upon the poor and jerk them off relief rolls, that has twice given the excuse of economy to cut the artists' wages, Mr. Lie seems an unusual luxury. We feel that the city cannot afford such a luxury.

There is a move among the artists of New York to demand Lie's resignation, a move which we heartily support.

[As we go to press, a rumor reaches us that Jonas Lie is to be made curator of paintings at the Metropolitan Museum. If this is true, then we can indeed say, "God help all painting!"]

* Our compliments to *Art Digest*, who has twice copiously quoted *Art Front*, once after publication, and once before.

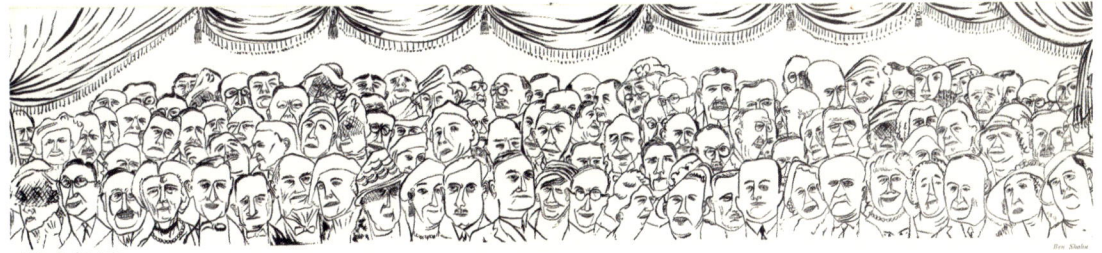

The Committee of 100 count 'em. Ben Shahn

Potted Palms and Public Art

THE cop stationed outside the City Hall was in sore need of a friend. The situation was unprecedented, not to say desperate. Should he send in a riot call?

It was hard to say what the cop feared, perhaps a bourgeois-democratic revolution led by embattled Social-Registrites. City Hall Park was crammed with limousines, and gossiping chauffeurs in nifty uniforms took the places of the usual unemployed.

Inside, amid the potted palms, the Corinthian columns, the crystal chandeliers and draped draperies of the rococo Governor's Room, Culture Defender Fiorello H. La Guardia was giving a select group the low-down on the future course of history.

"I have conceived," he modestly declared, "a plan so startling that I dare not reveal it fully at this time!"

...

Alfred Sinks

Quintanilla and Satire

AS the artist in America turns to the workers to join them in their demand for work, food and recognition, he learns that he must fight ignorance, stupidity and prejudice with every available weapon. Satire is not the least of these.

...

Elliot Paul.

On Work Relief

THE growing animation of artists on work relief projects is meeting with direct opposition by the administration.

...

Project Committee 295

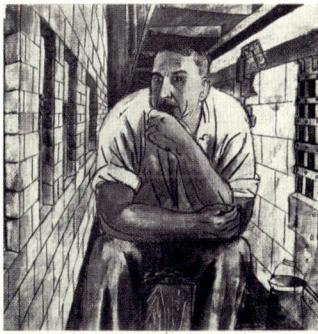

Detail, Prison Mural Ben Shahn

"WE REJECT" — THE ART COMMISSION

THE large mural designed by Ben Shahn and Lou Block for the Riker's Island Penitentiary was rejected by the Municipal Art Commission on the ground of "psychological unfitness."

...

THE SOCIAL STERILITY OF PAINTERS

The following is the conclusions of the article by Jean Lurçat, begun in the last (May) issue of ART FRONT

MERE denials are not sufficient. In the mind of Breton nothing we are decided in 1924. It was not only to insist that he was unable to bend his principles. Suffering from the obscurity of the whole epoch, he prolonged its movements as if in spite of himself.

...

(Continued on page 8)

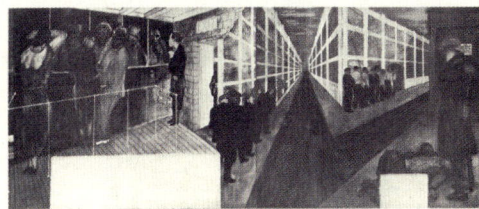

Section, Prison Mural, Left Wall Ben Shahn

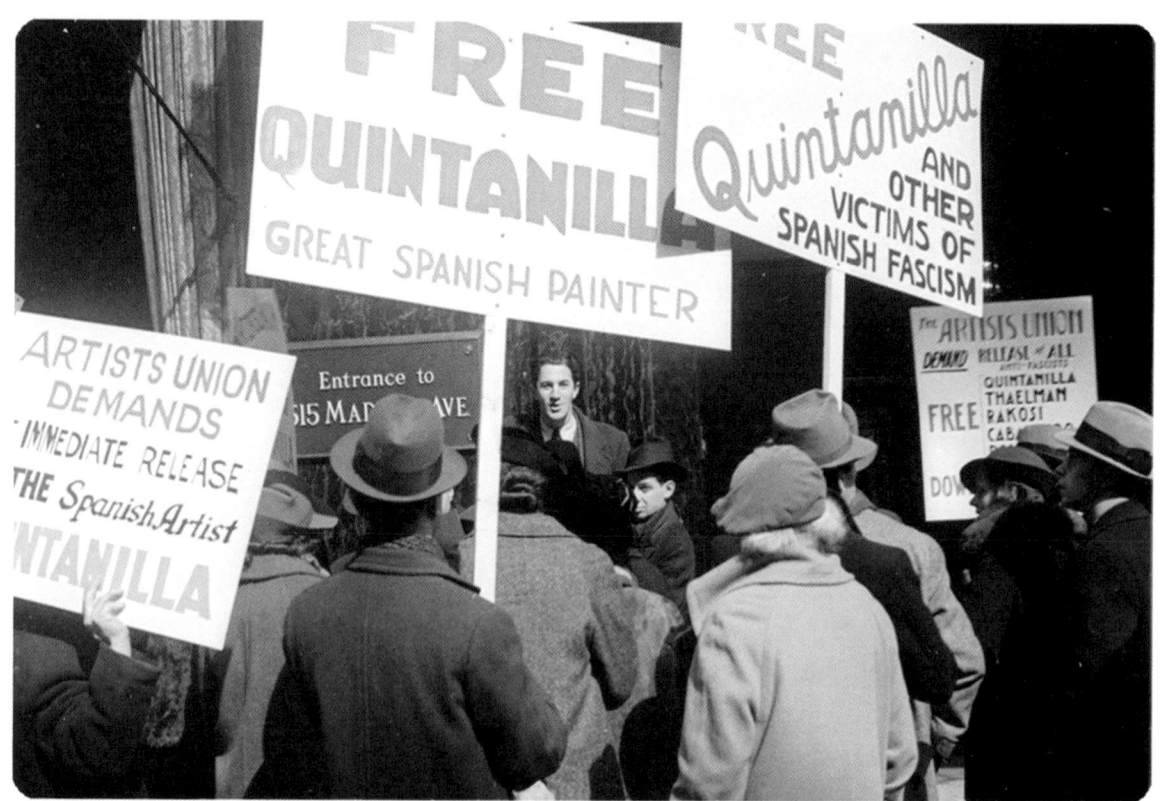

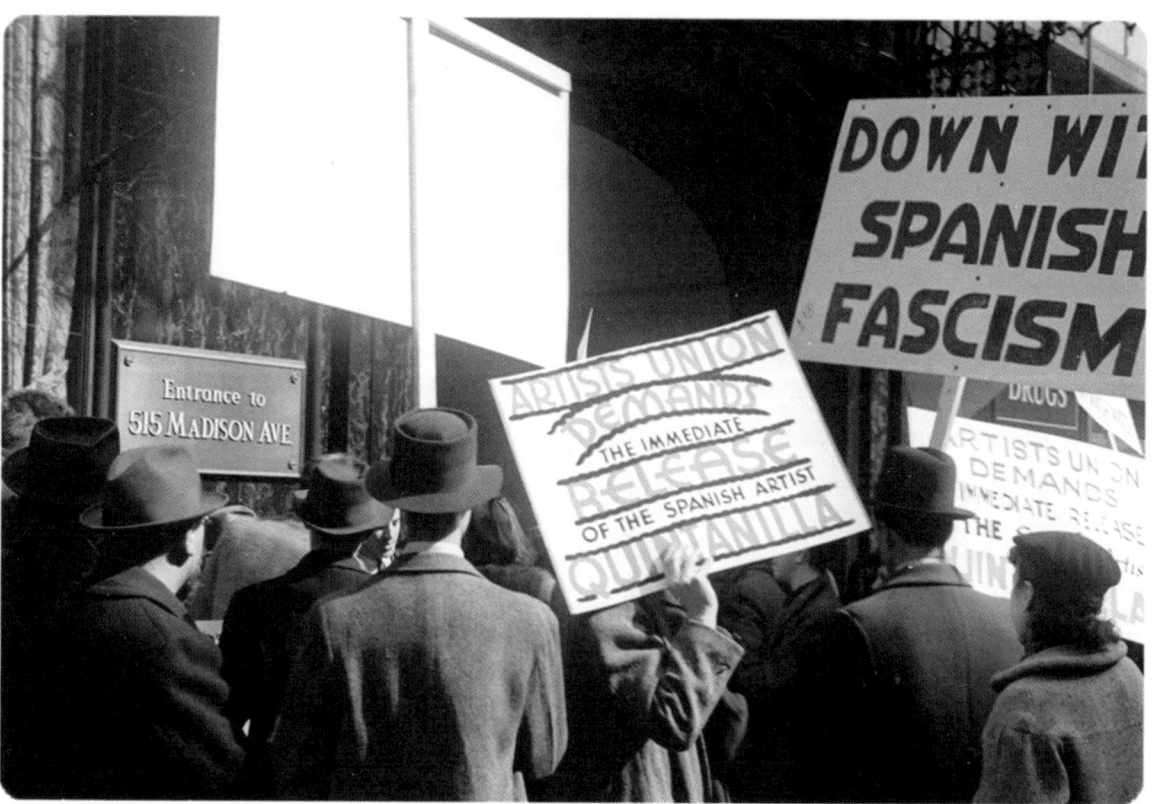

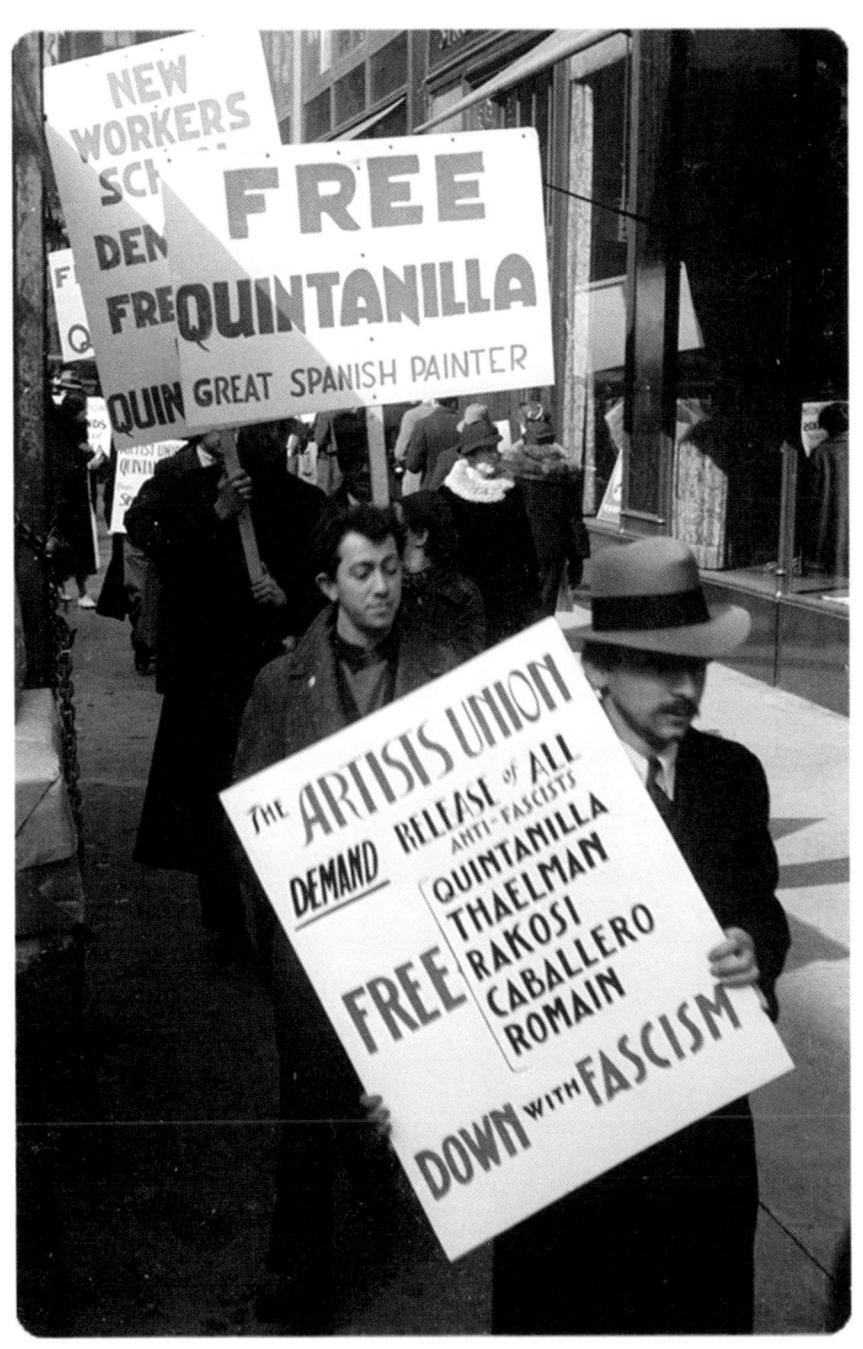

Untitled [Artists' Union Demonstration, Spanish Consulate,
near Madison Avenue and East Fifty-Third Street, New York City]
Spring 1935

Watching Medicine Show, Huntingdon, Tennessee, RA6166-M4
October 1935

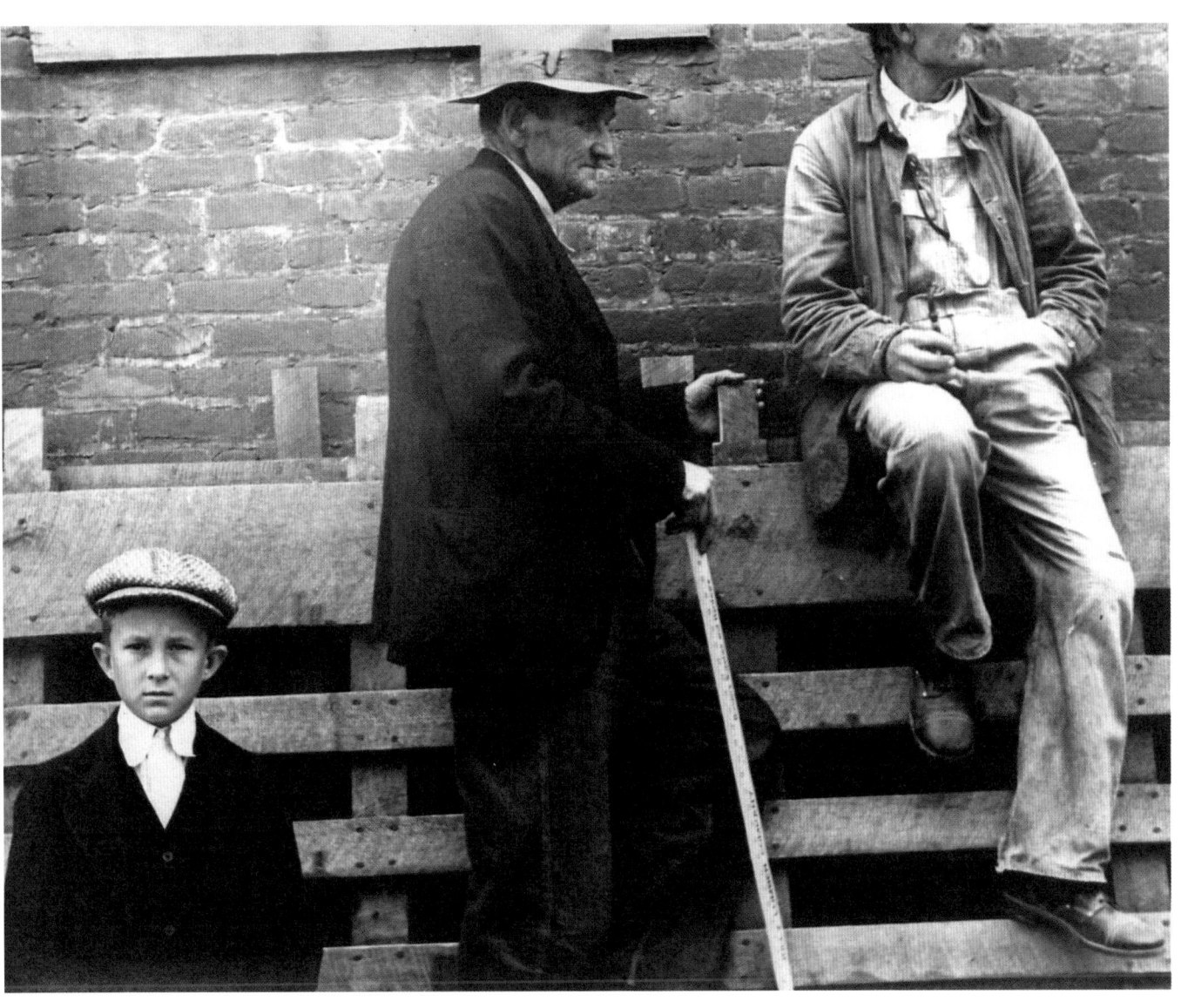

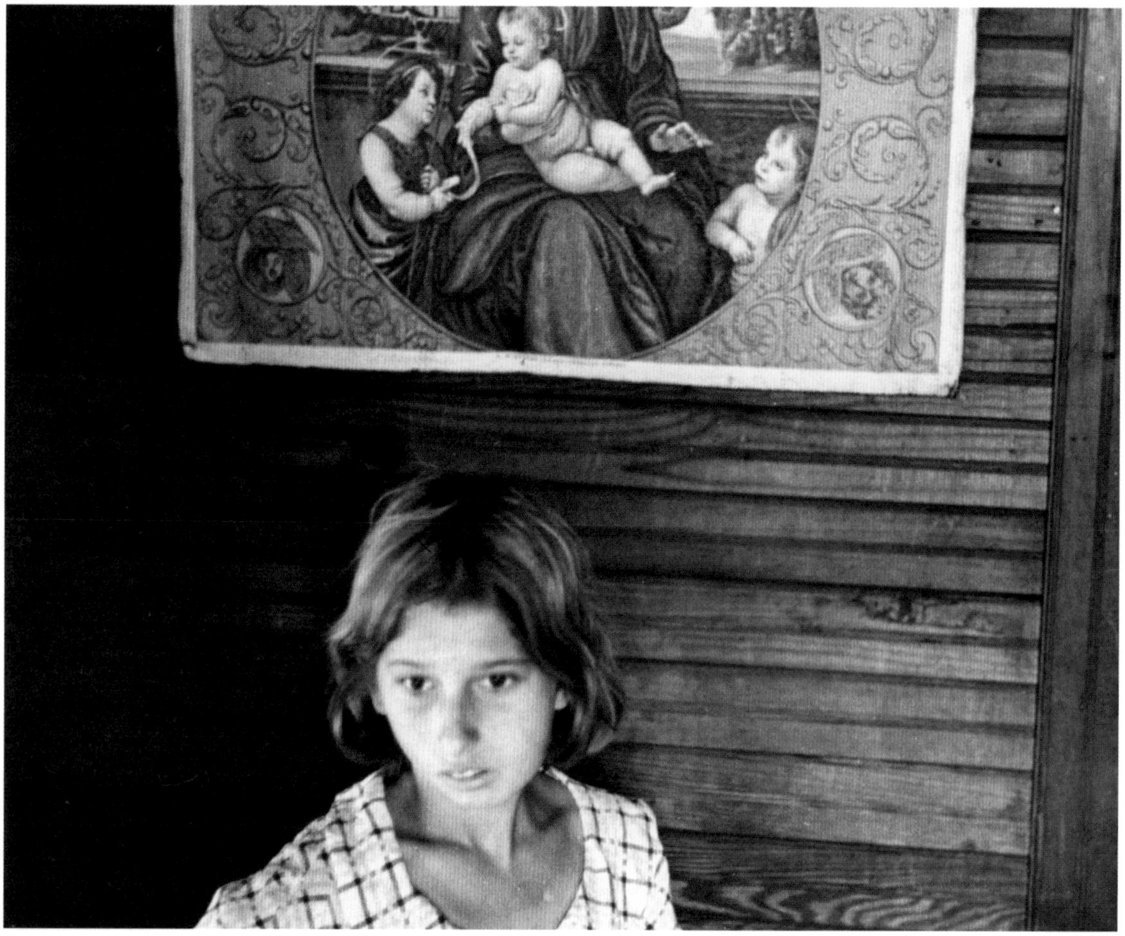

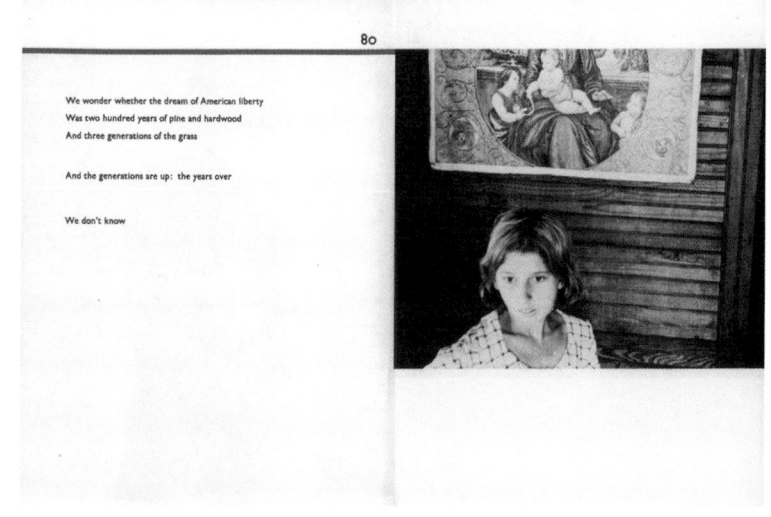

Child of Fortuna Family, Hammond, Louisiana, RA6174-M3
October 1935

Archibald MacLeish
Land of the Free. New York: Harcourt, Brace and Company, 1938, p. 80

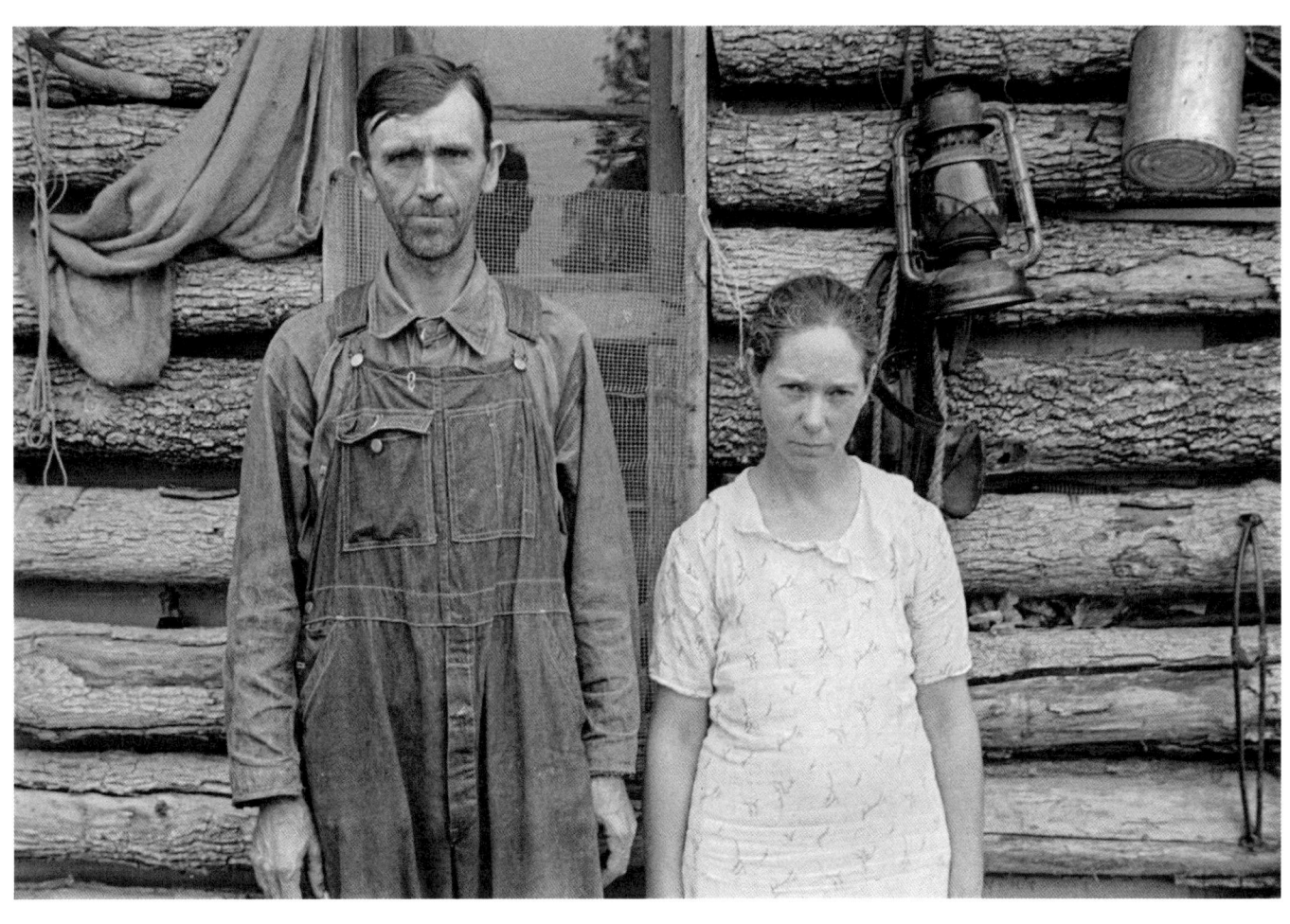

Rehabilitation Clients, Boone County, Arkansas
October 1935

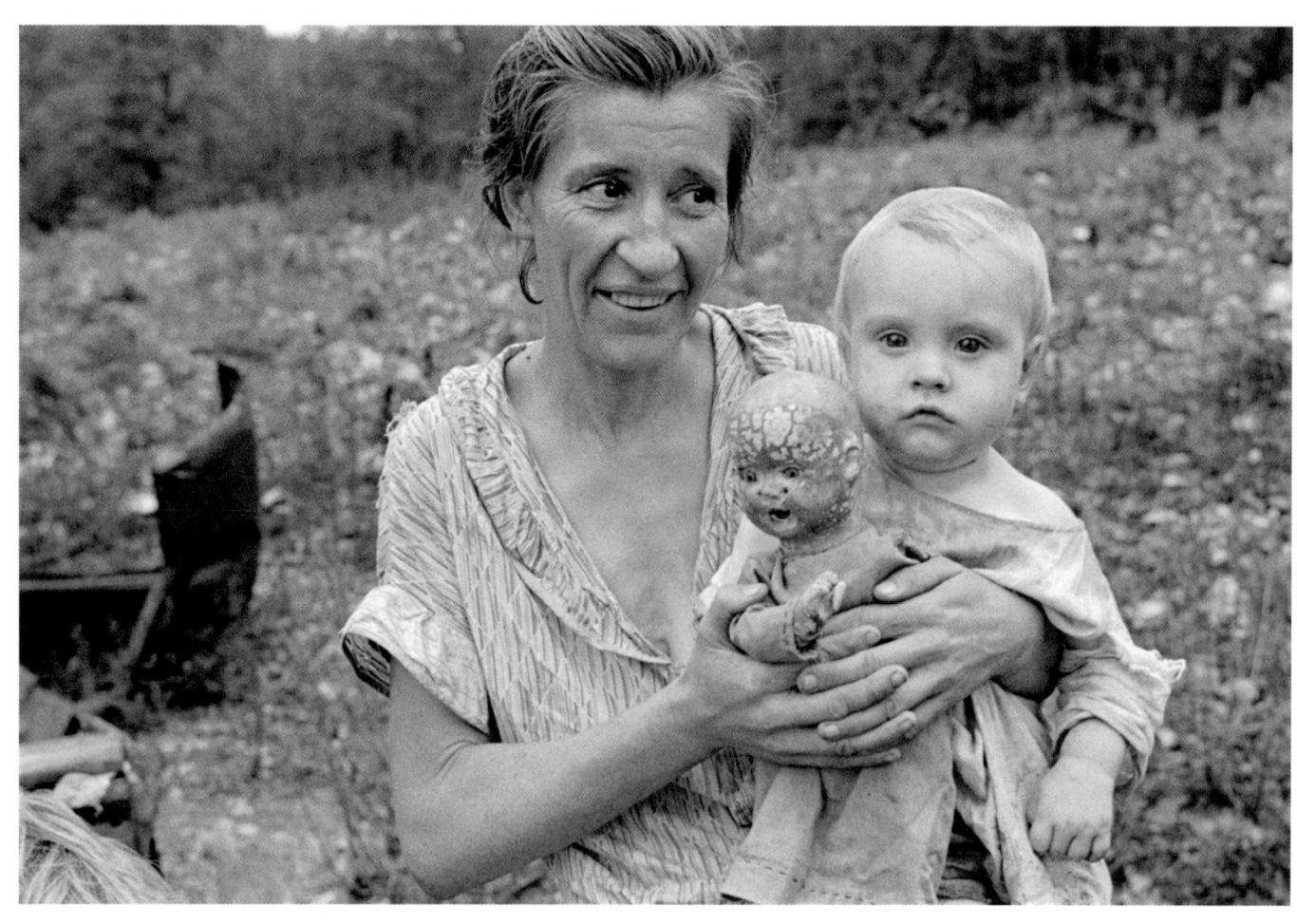

Wife and Child of Sharecropper, Arkansas
October 1935

Children of Destitute Ozark Mountaineer, Arkansas
October 1935

Children of Rehabilitation Client, Maria Plantation, Arkansas
October 1935

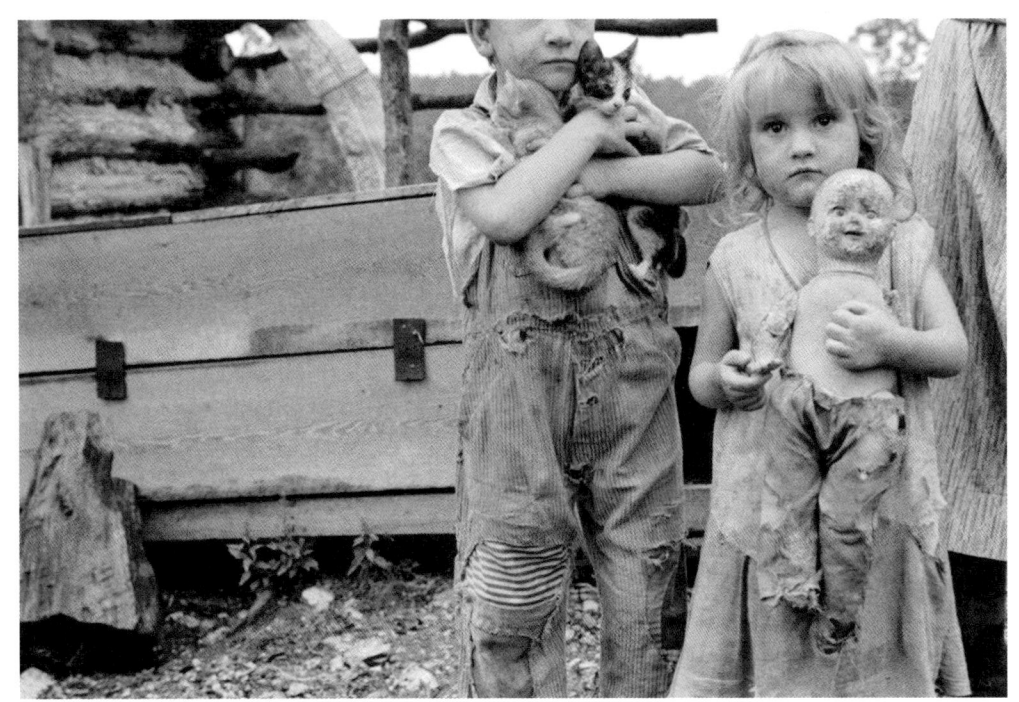

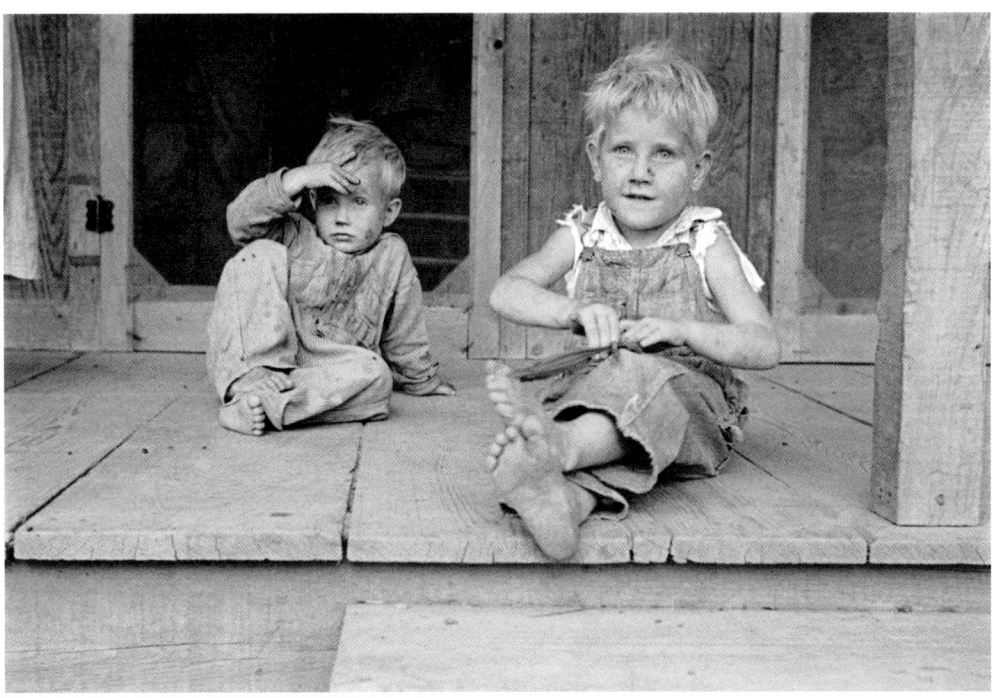

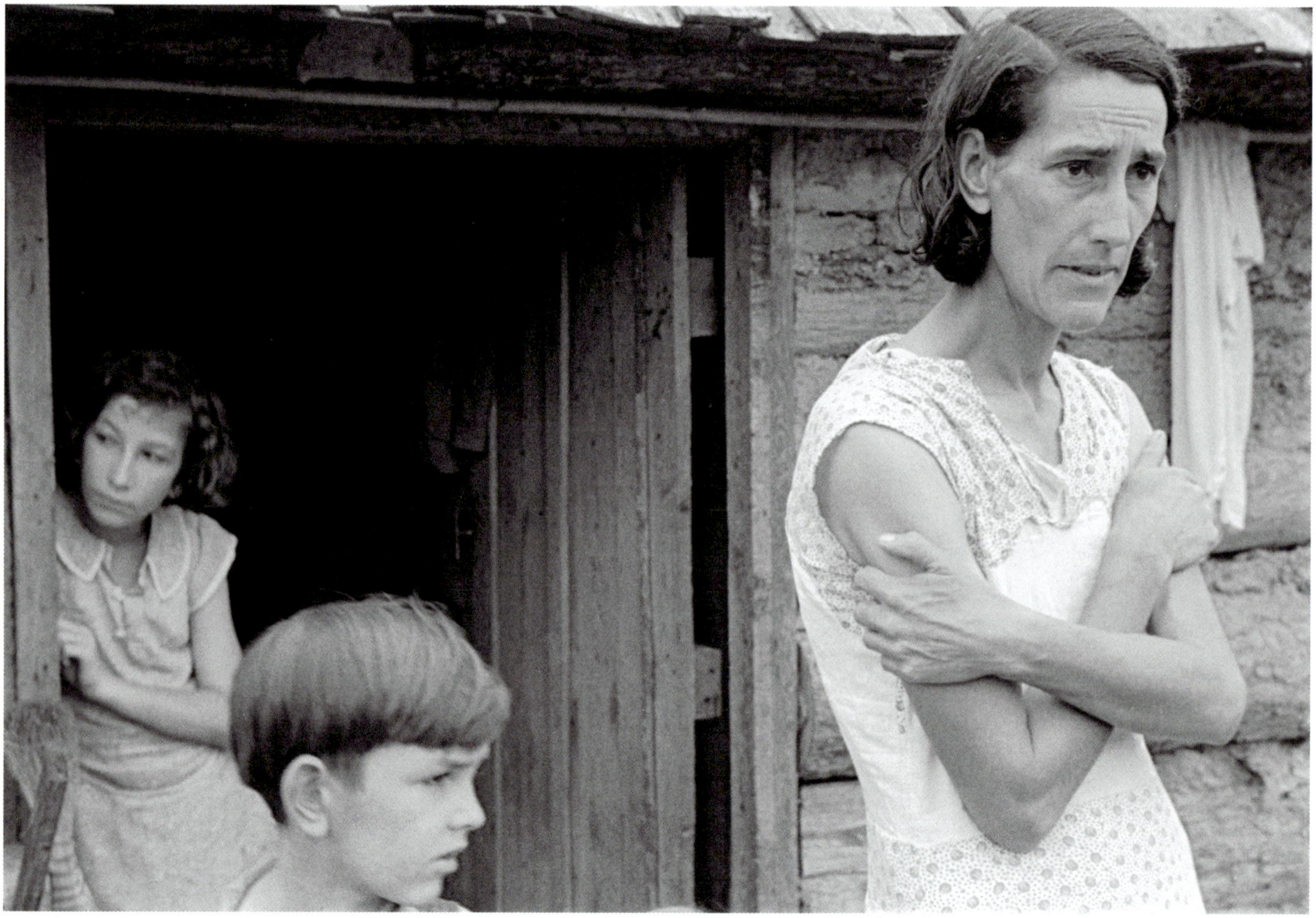

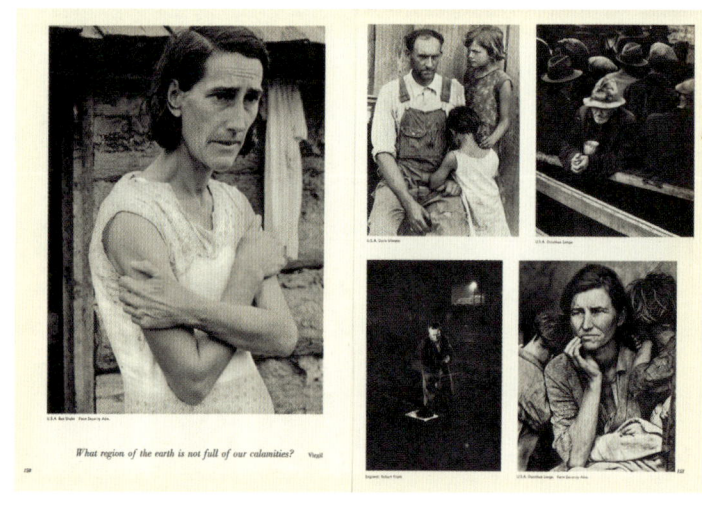

Boone County, Arkansas. The Family of a Resettlement
Administration Client in the Doorway of Their Home
October 1935

Edward Steichen
The Family of Man: The Greatest Photographic Exhibition
of All Time—503 Pictures from 68 Countries—Created
by Edward Steichen for the Museum of Modern Art.
New York: Maco Magazine Corporation for the Museum
of Modern Art, 1955, pp. 150–151

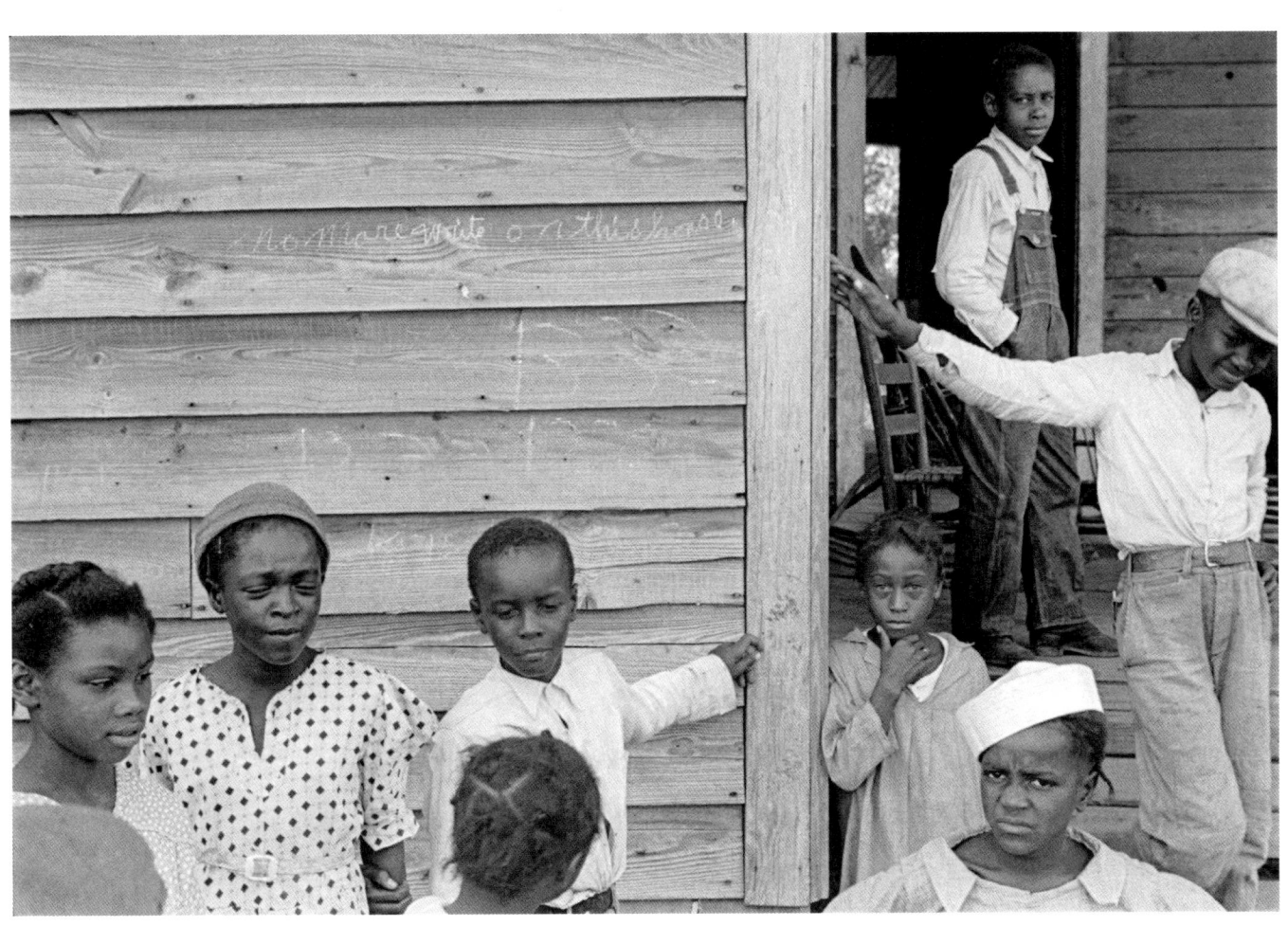

Sharecroppers' Children on Sunday, near Little Rock, Arkansas
October 1935

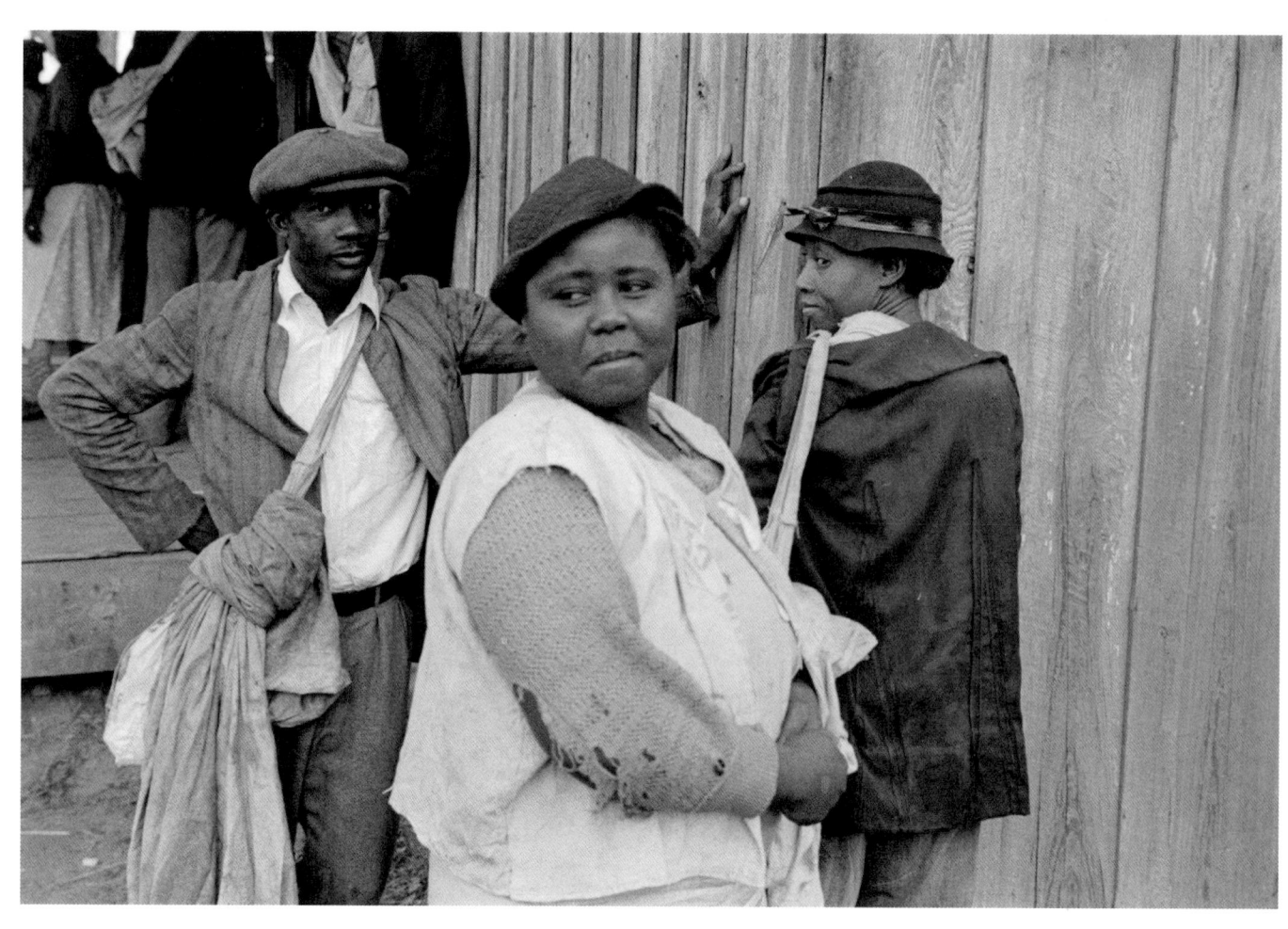

Cotton Pickers, 6:30 a.m., Alexander Plantation, Pulaski County, Arkansas
October 1935

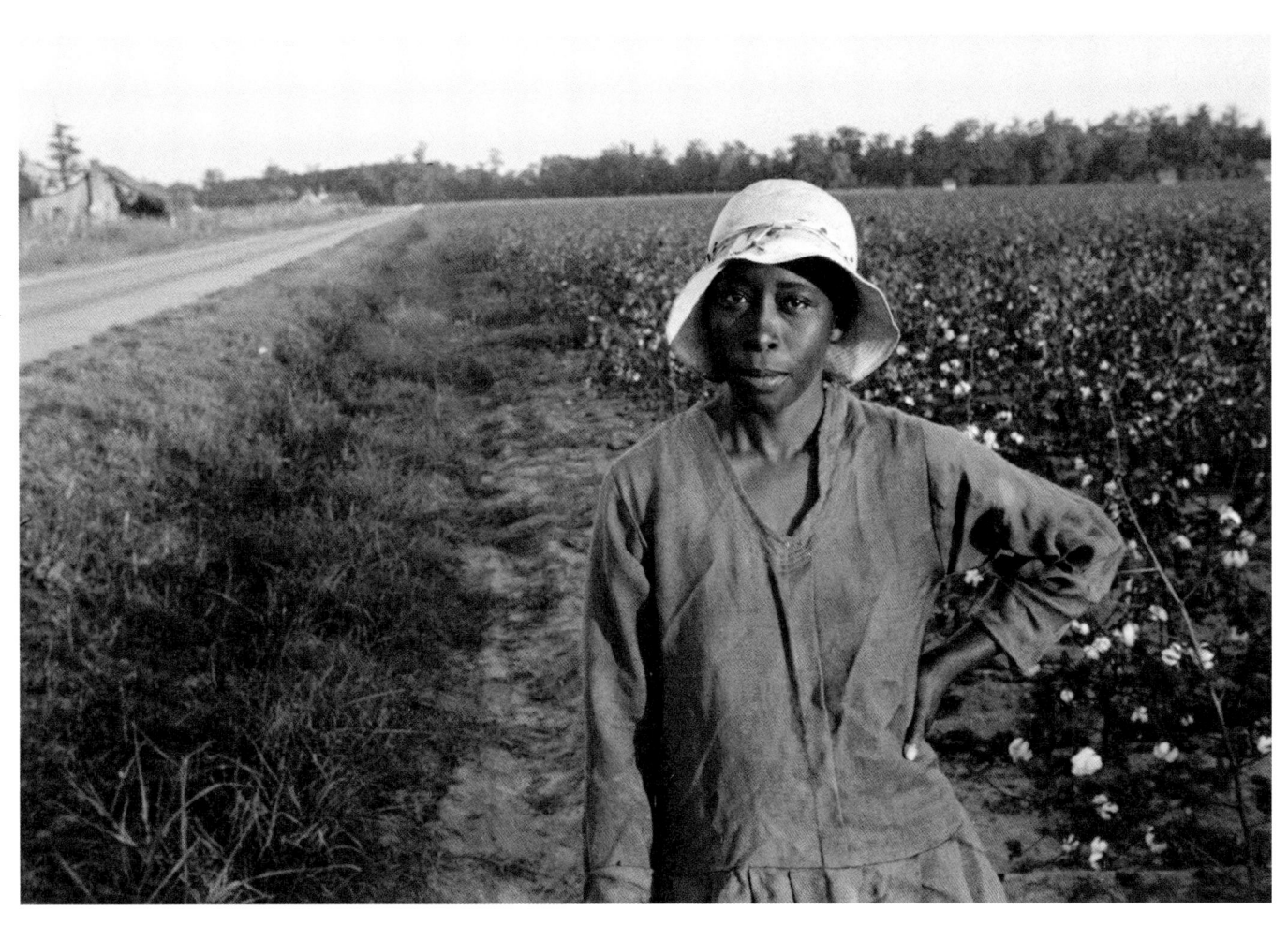

Untitled [possibly related to: *Cotton Pickers, Pulaski County, Arkansas*]
October 1935

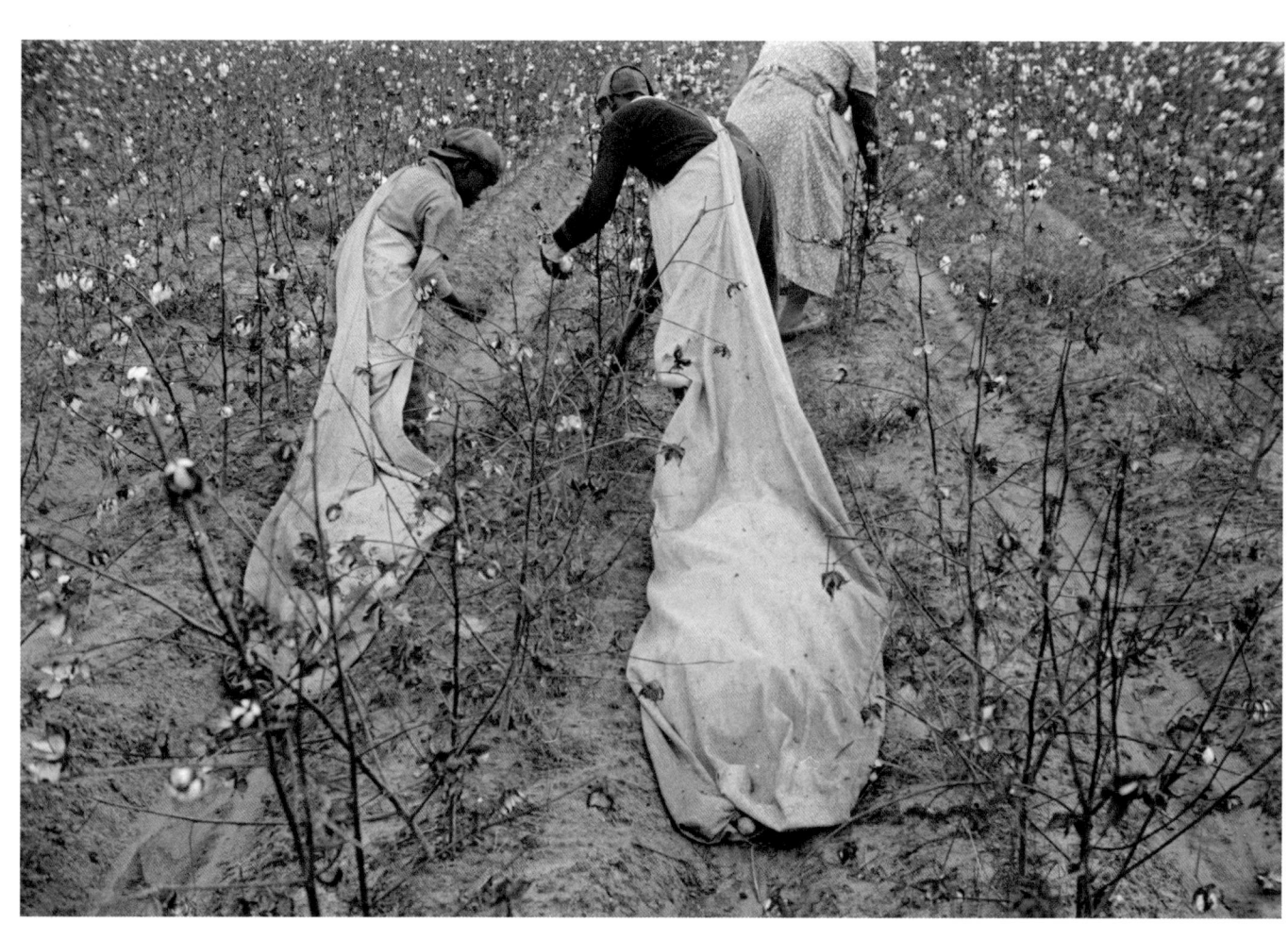

Cotton Pickers, Pulaski County, Arkansas
October 1935

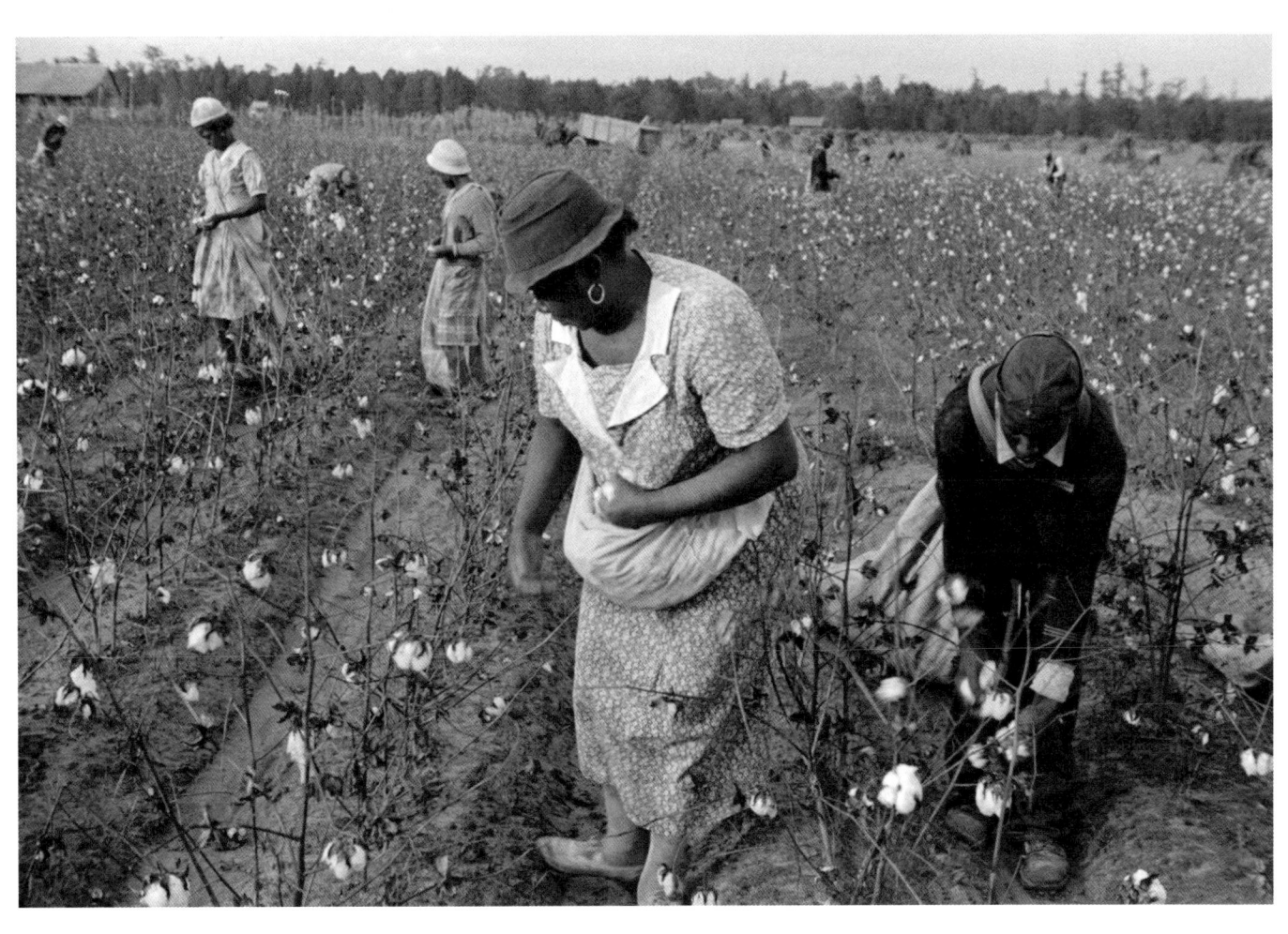

Picking Cotton on Alexander Plantation. Pulaski County, Arkansas
October 1935

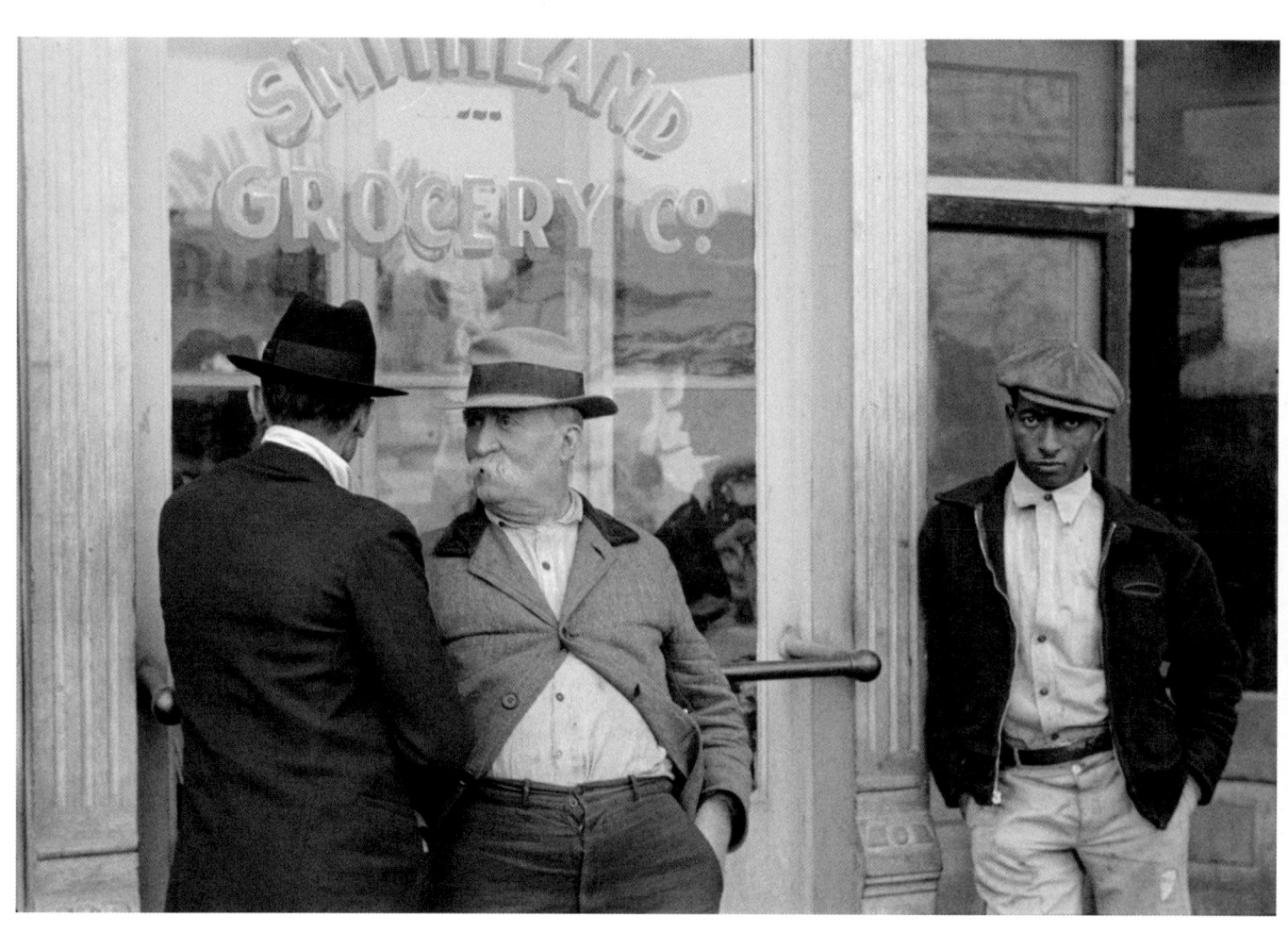

Scene at Smithland, Kentucky
October 1935

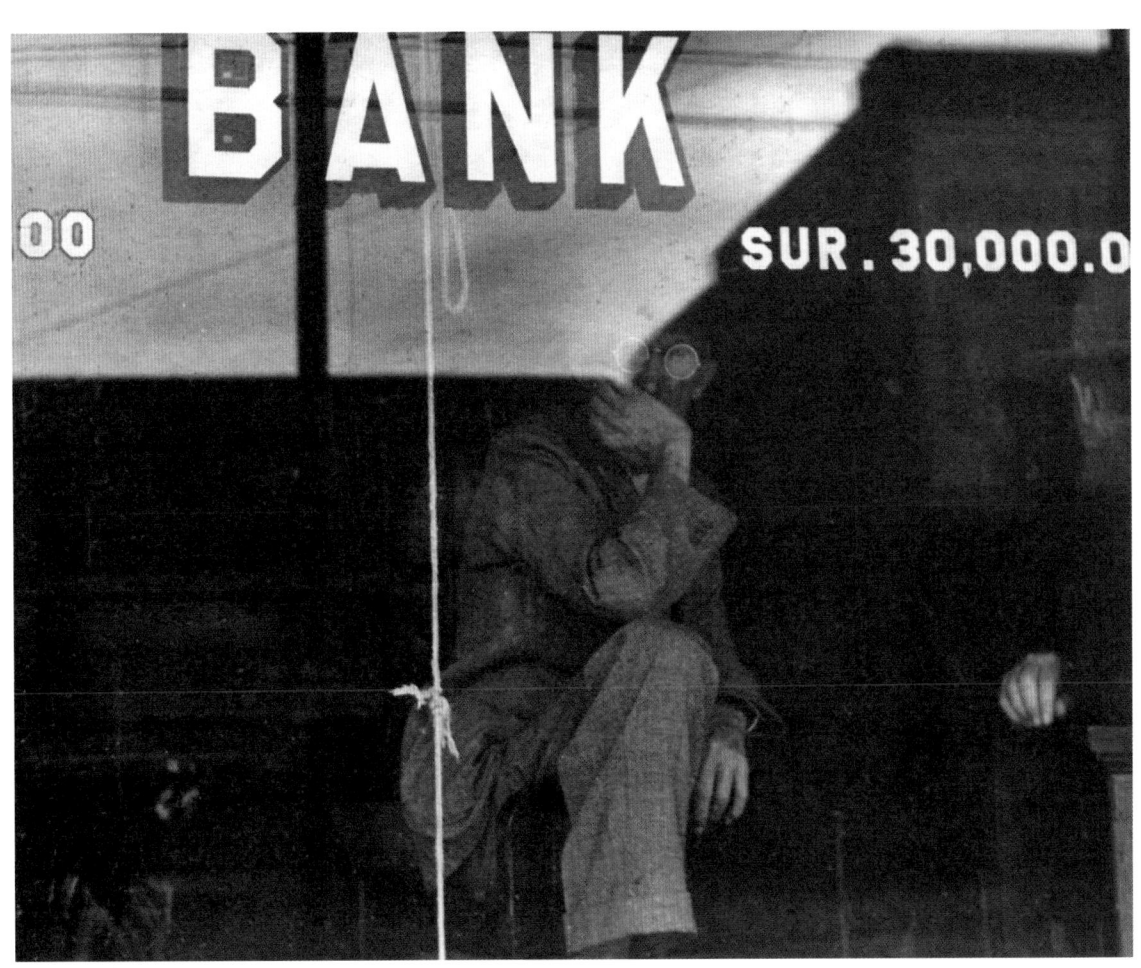

Bank in Smithland, Kentucky, RA6080-M5
October 1935

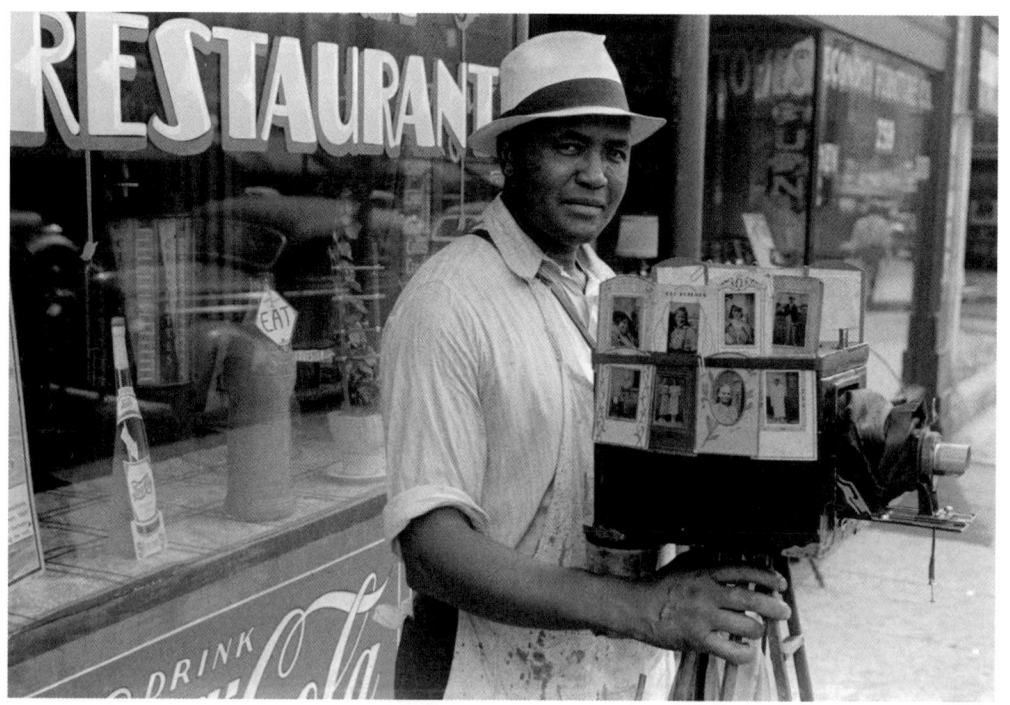

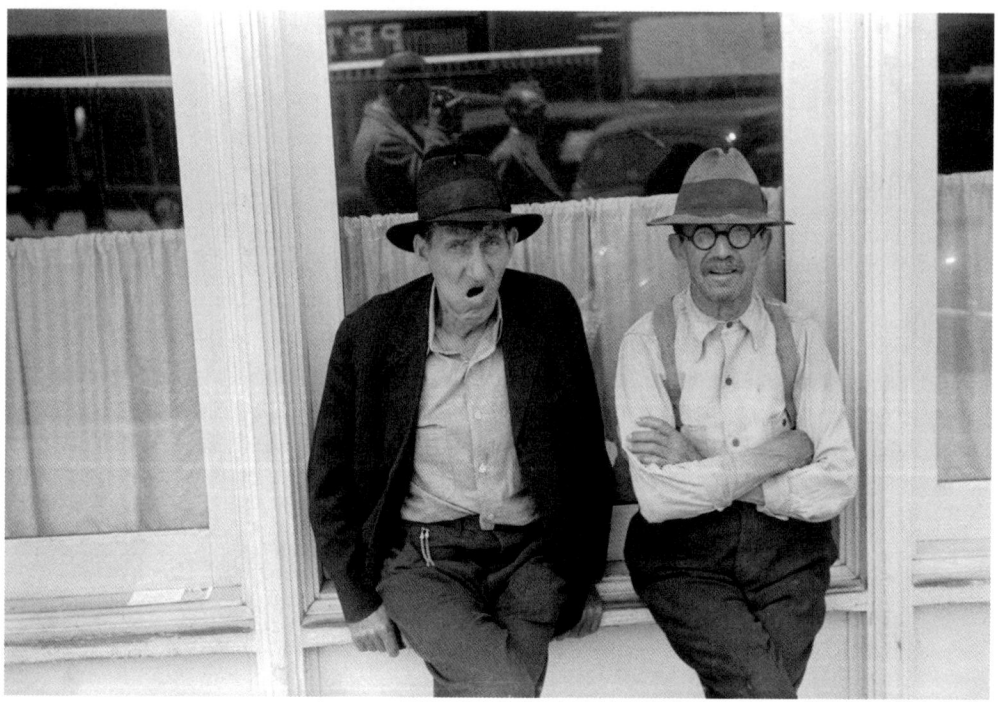

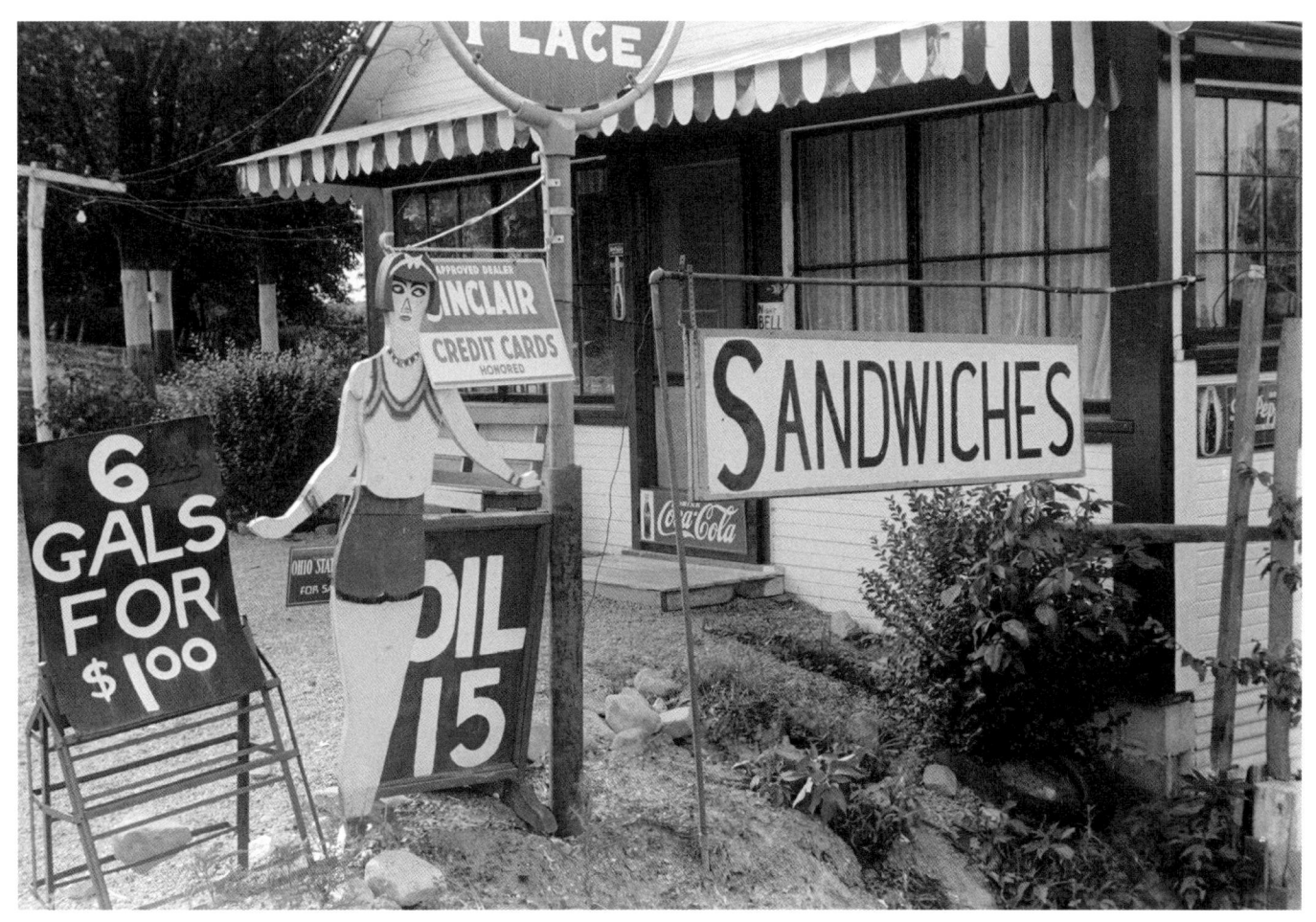

Itinerant Photographer in Columbus, Ohio
August 1938

Street Scene, Circleville, Ohio
Summer 1938

"Roadside Inn," Central Ohio. The Figure of the Body was Originally
Distributed to Advertise the Neward Indian Mounds. Redecorated
Summer 1938

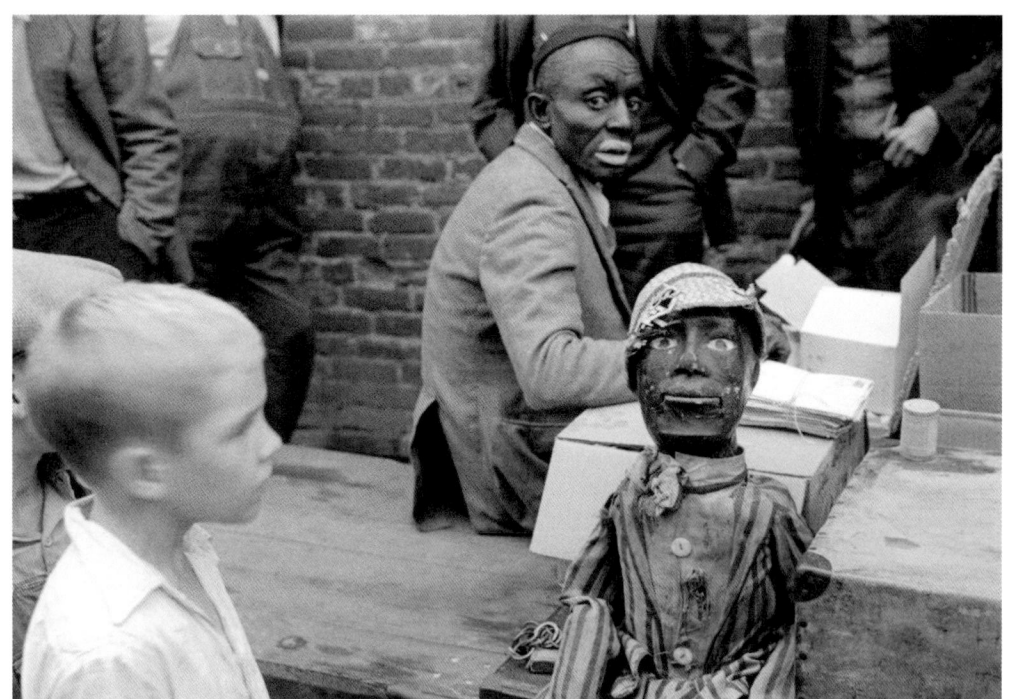

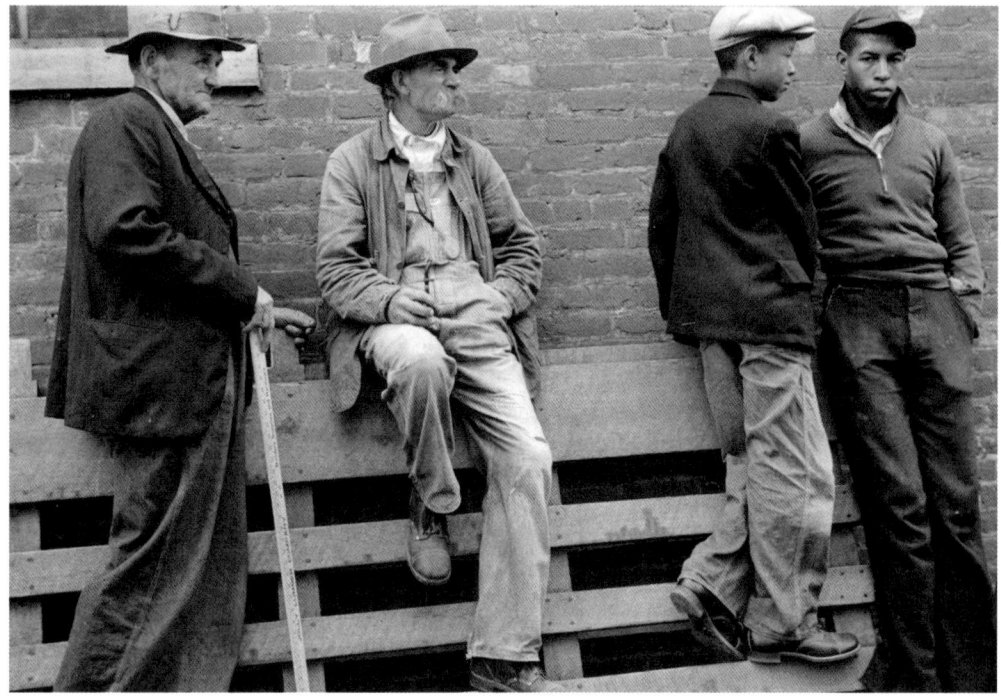

Medicine Show, Huntingdon, Tennessee
October 1935

Huntingdon, Tennessee
October 1935

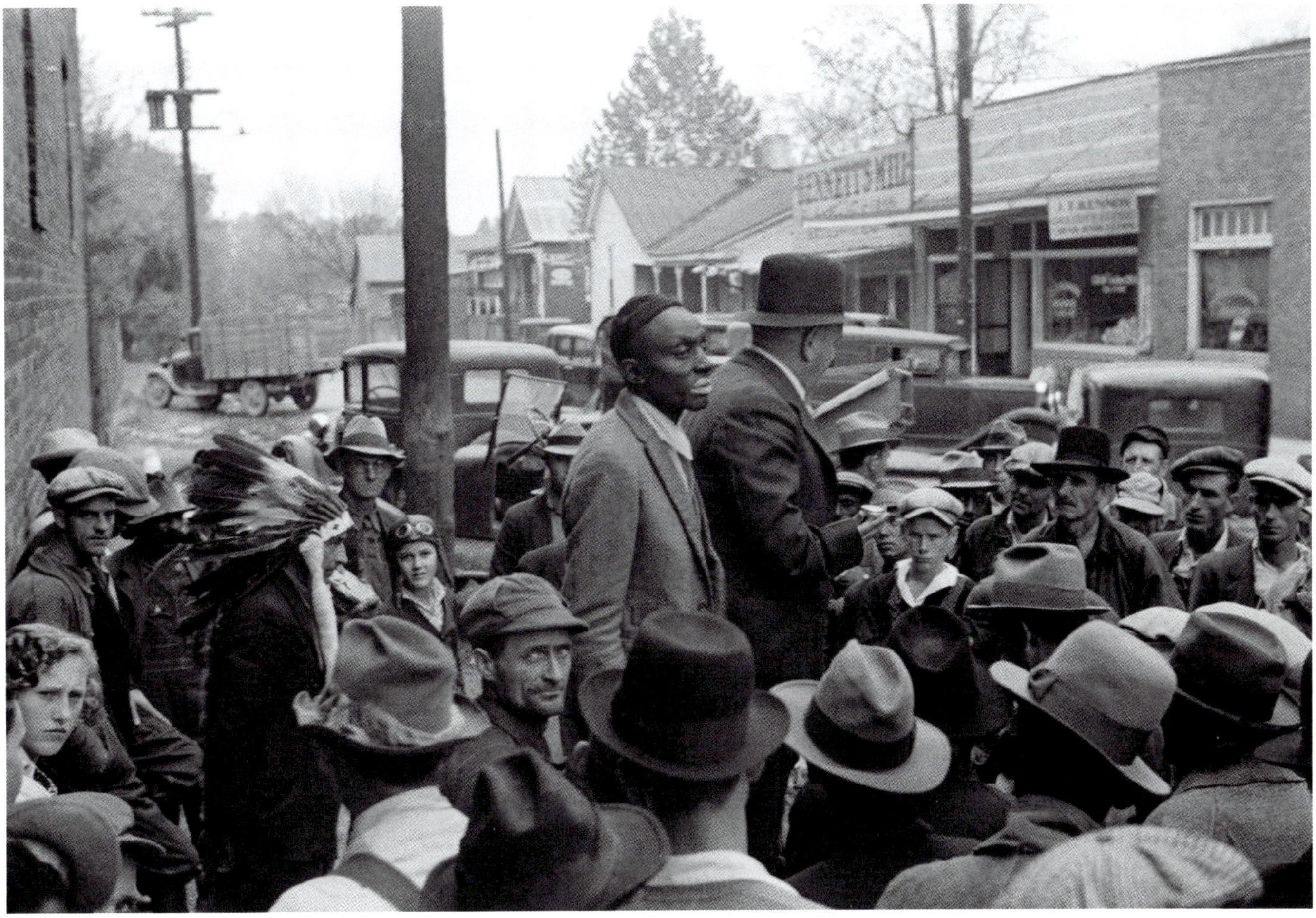

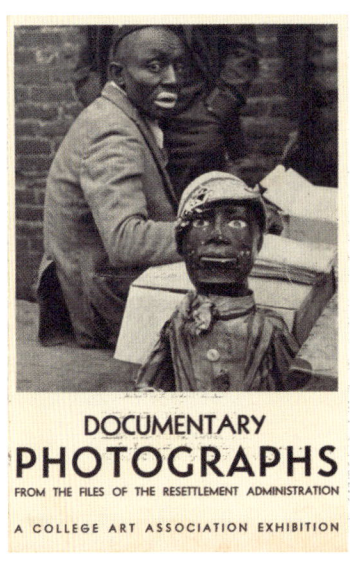

Medicine Show, Huntingdon, Tennessee
October 1935

Documentary Photographs from the Files of the Resettlement
Administration: A College Art Association Exhibition
December 1936

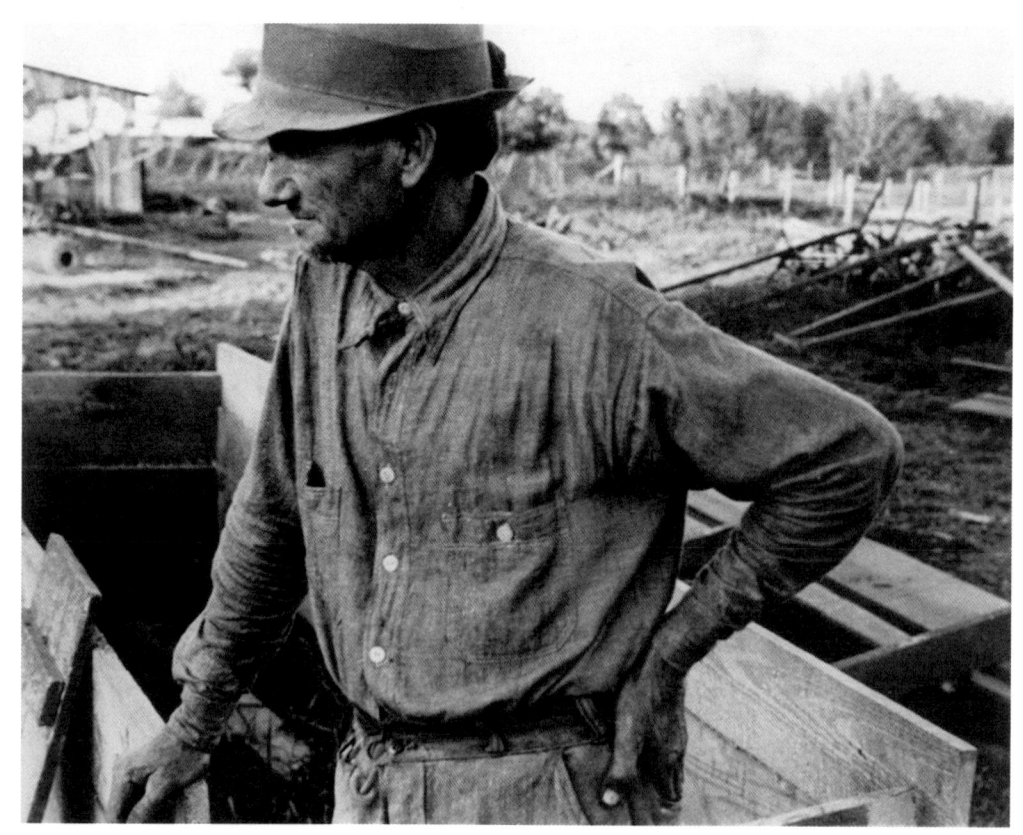

Untitled [Plaquemines Parish, Louisiana]
October 1935

Bernarda Bryson Shahn
A Mule and a Plow
1936

A MULE AND A PLOW

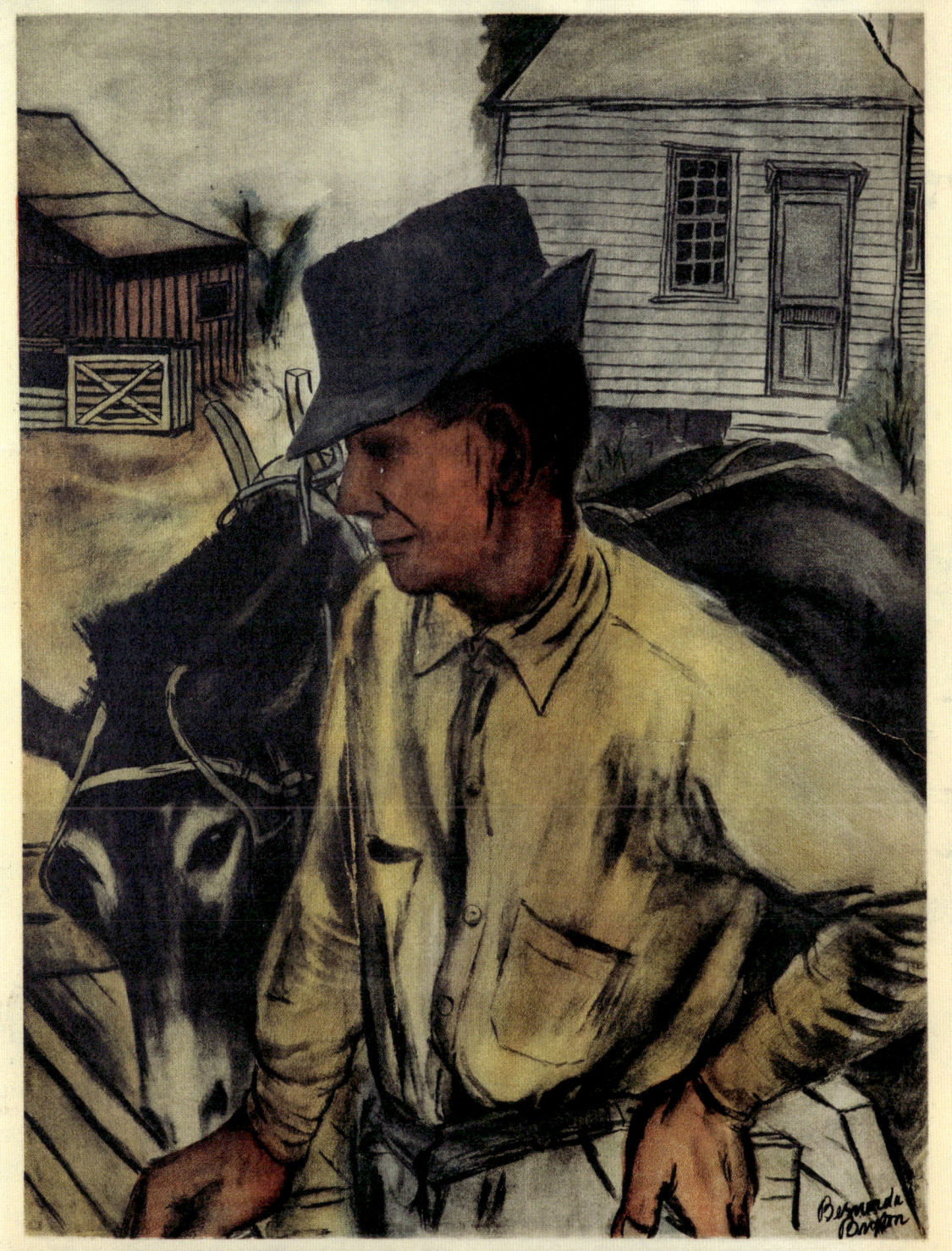

RESETTLEMENT ADMINISTRATION
Small Loans Give Farmers a New Start

YEARS OF DUST

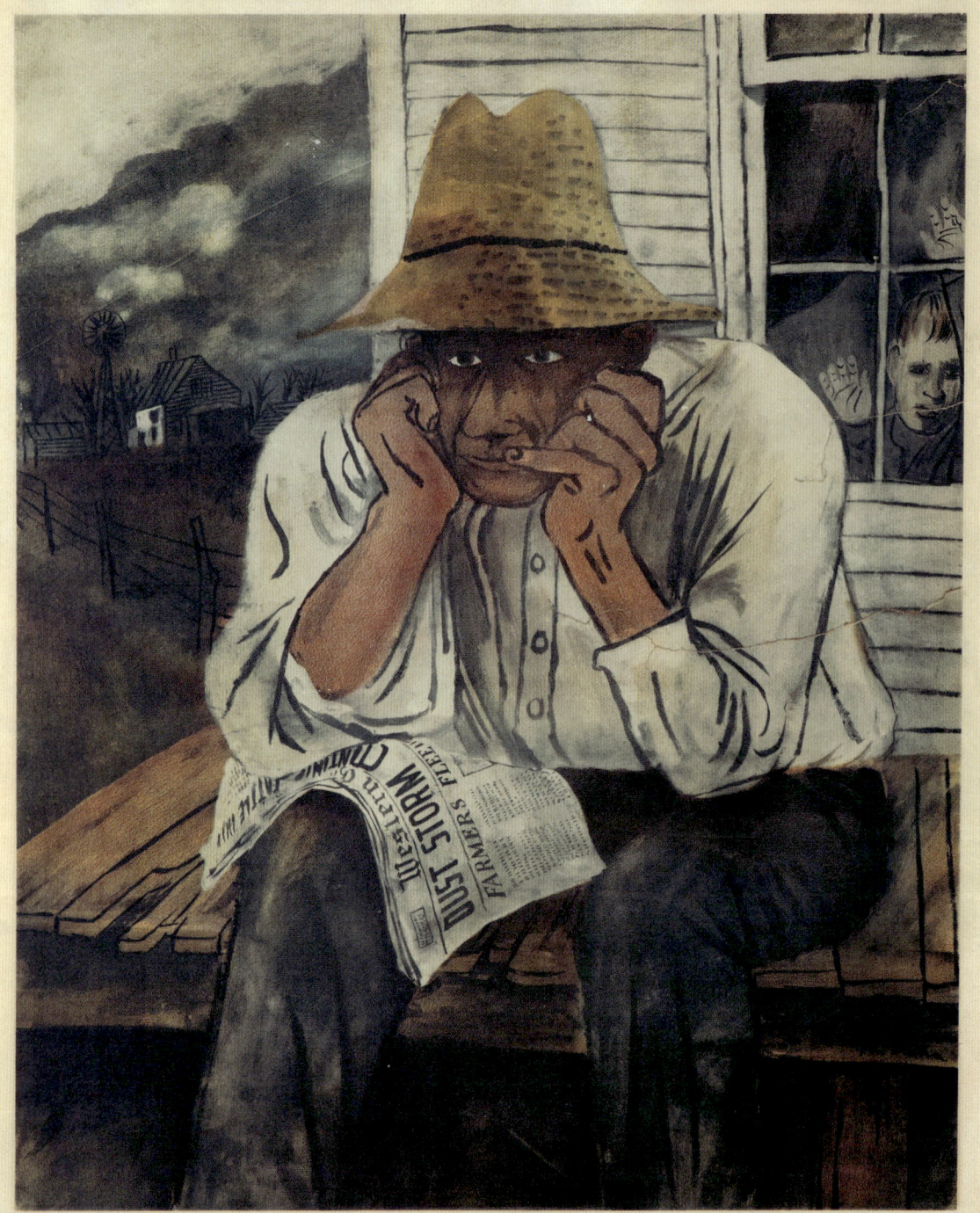

RESETTLEMENT ADMINISTRATION
**Rescues Victims
Restores Land to Proper Use**

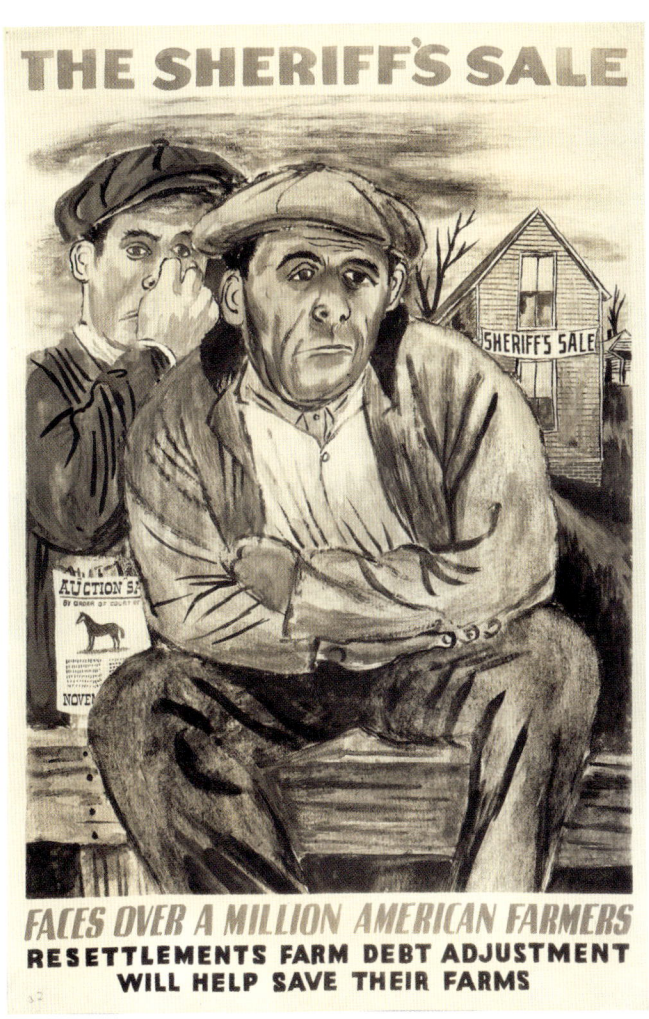

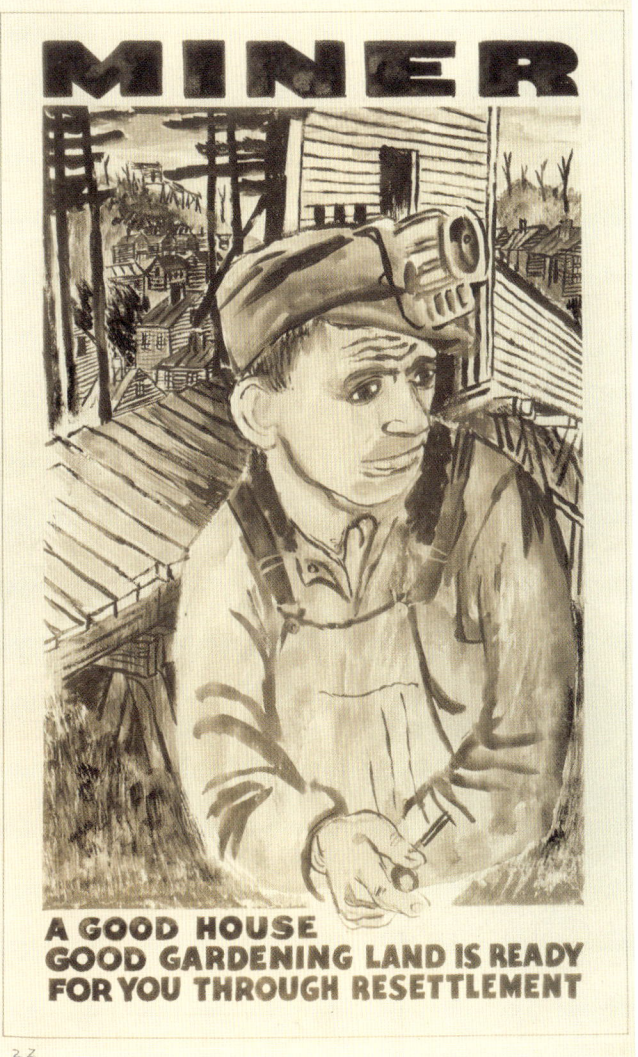

Years of Dust
1936

The Sheriff's Sale / Faces over a Million American Farmers /
Resettlements Farm Debt Adjustment / Will Help Save Their Farms
c. 1936

Miner / A Good House / Good Gardening Land is Ready /
for You through Resettlement
c. 1936

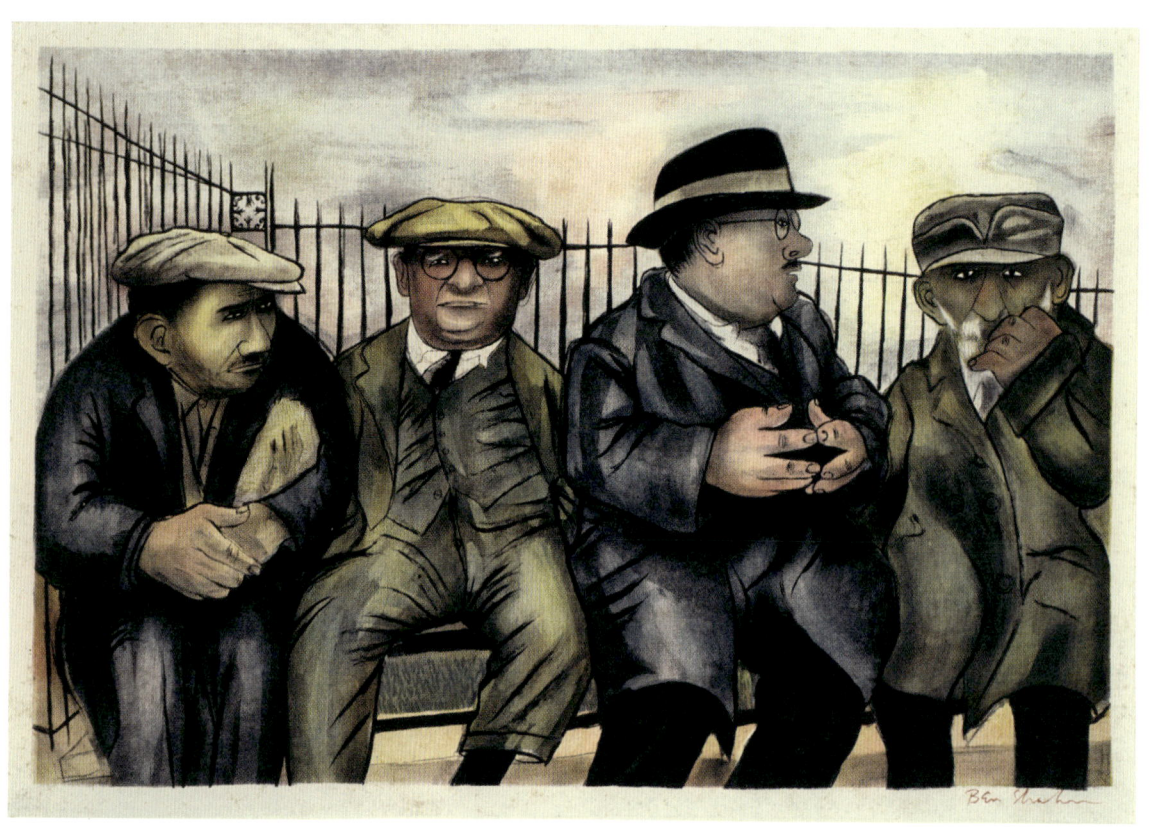

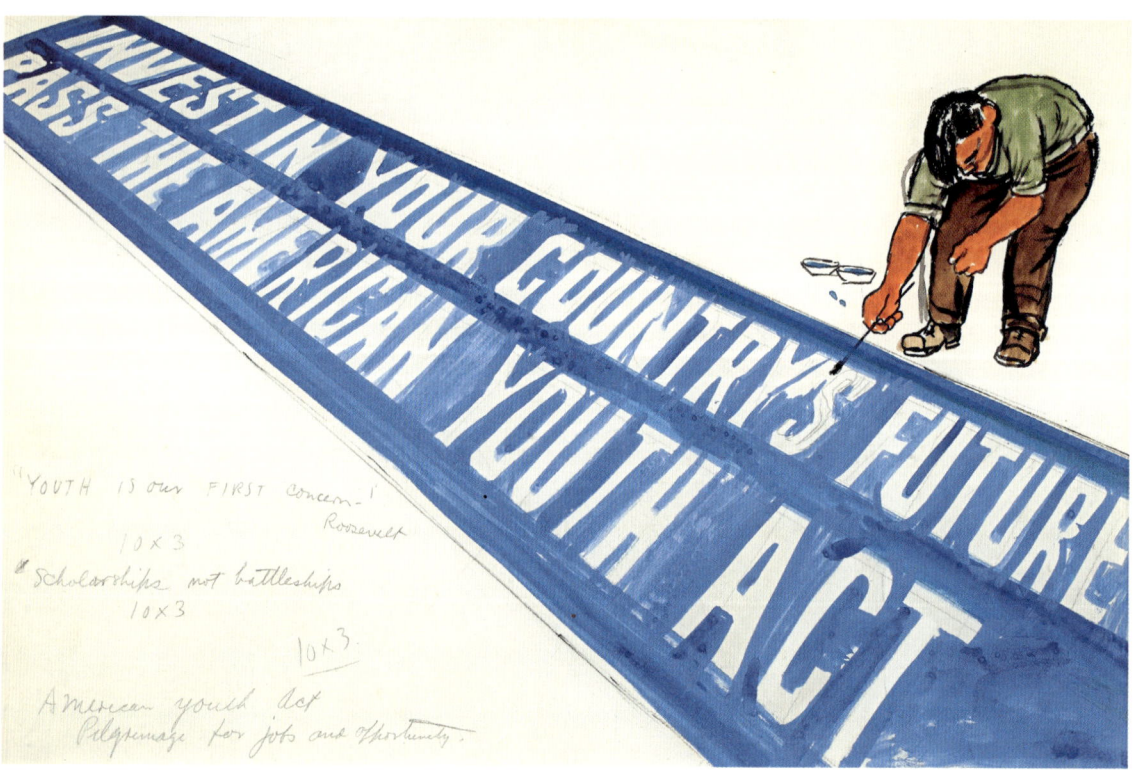

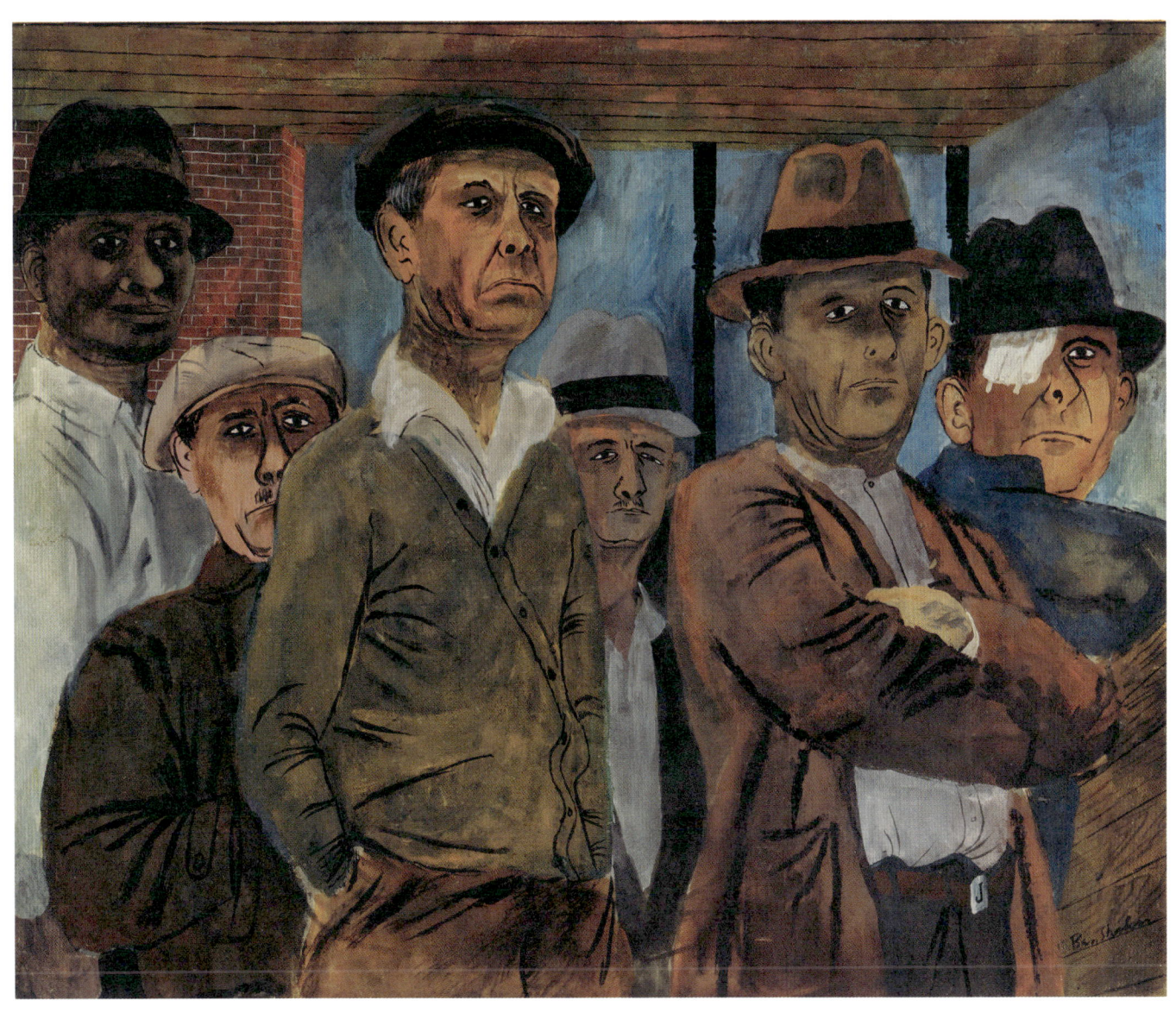

Seward Park
1936

Invest in Your Country's Future, Pass the American Youth Act
c. 1935

Unemployed
c. 1938

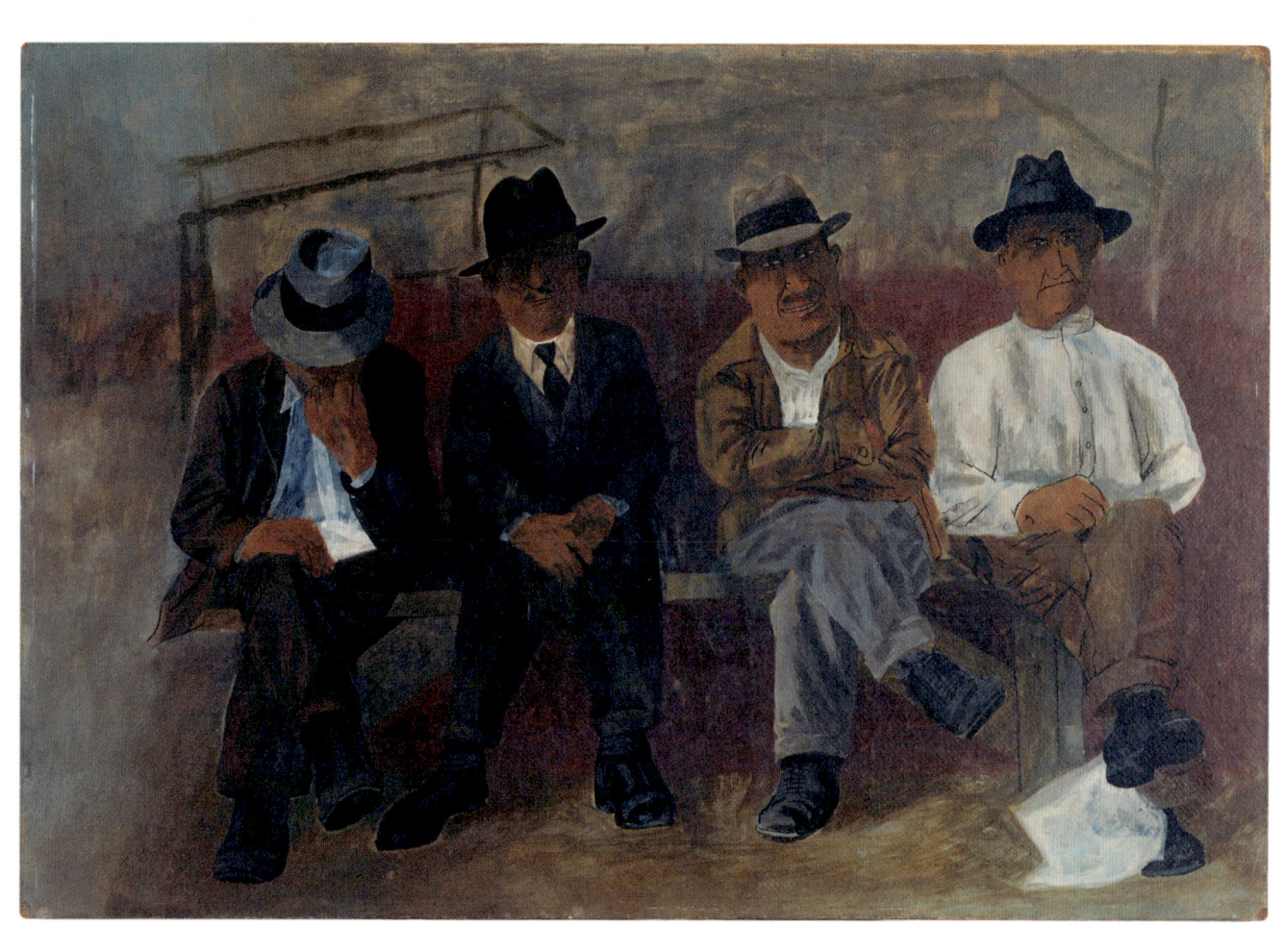

Sunday Morning
c. 1938–43

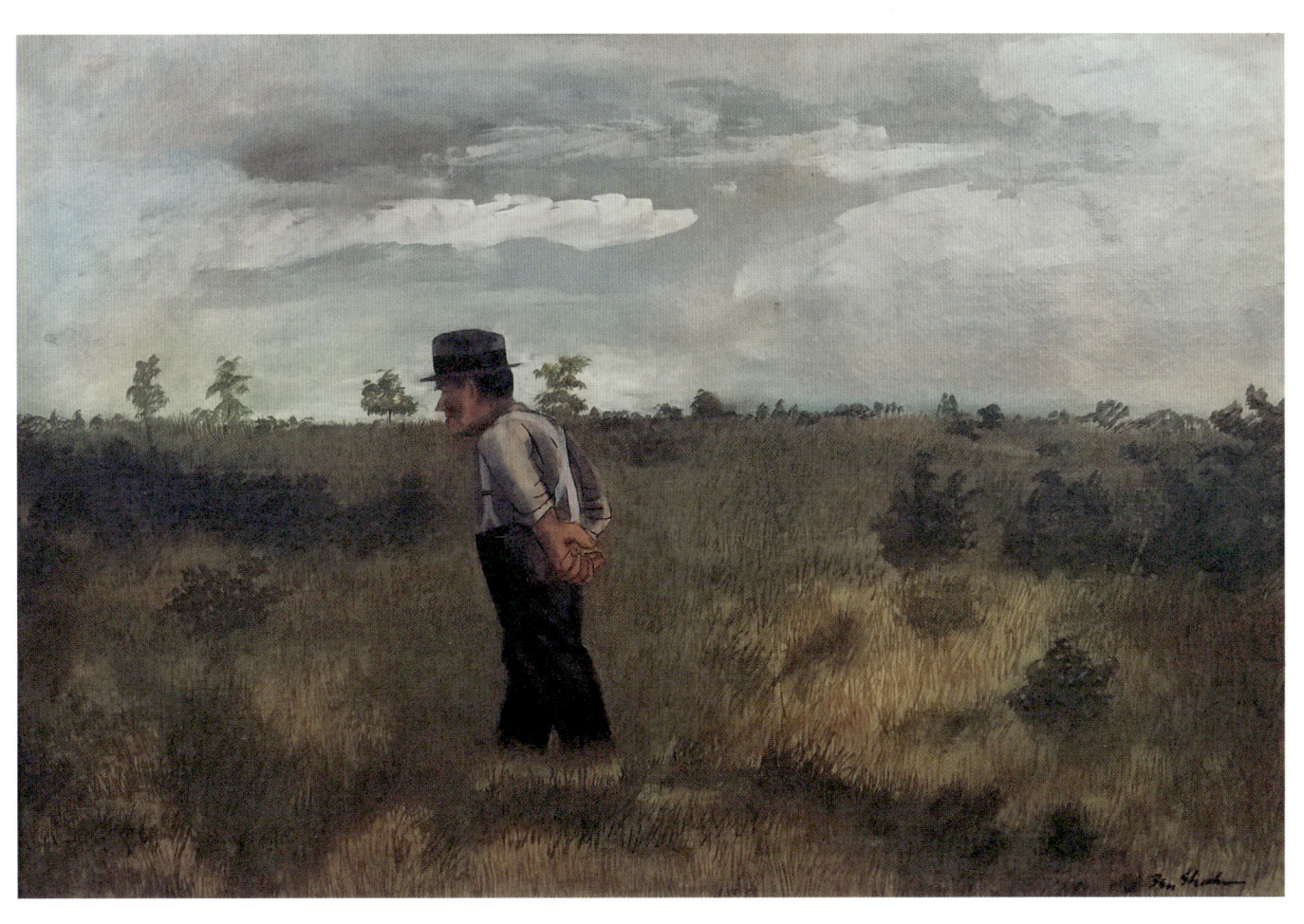

Sunday Painting
1938

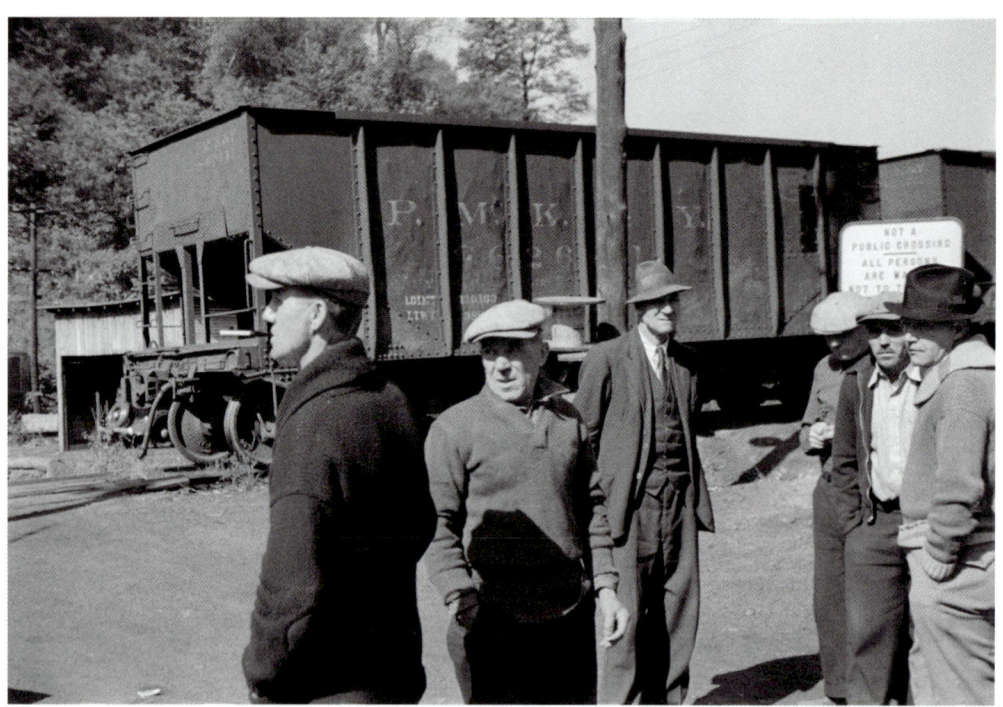

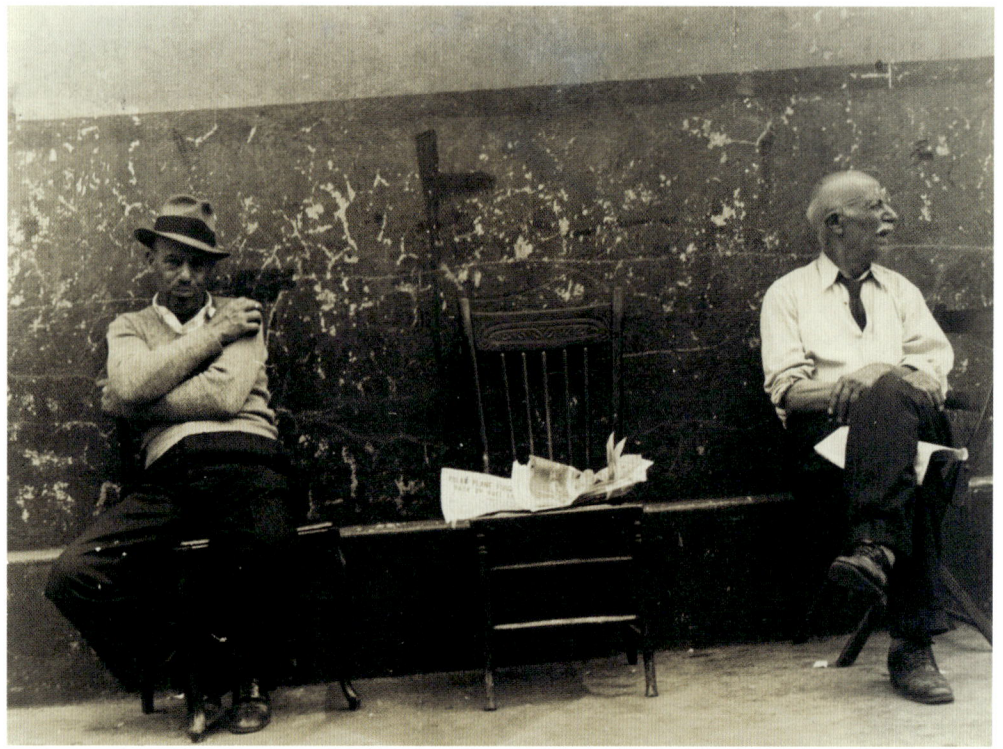

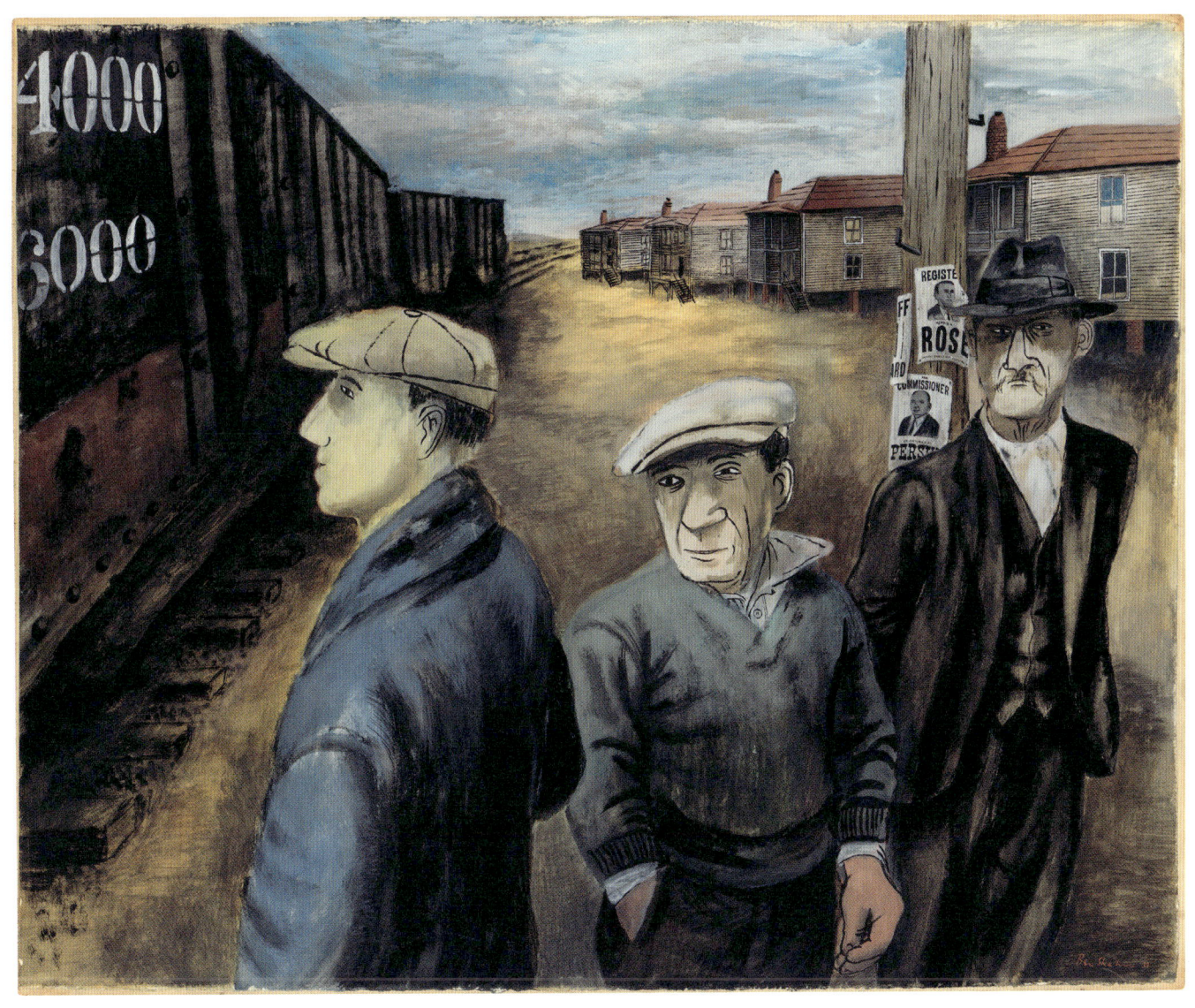

Striking Miners, Scotts Run, West Virginia
October 1935

Untitled [New York City]
1932–35

Scotts Run, West Virginia
1937

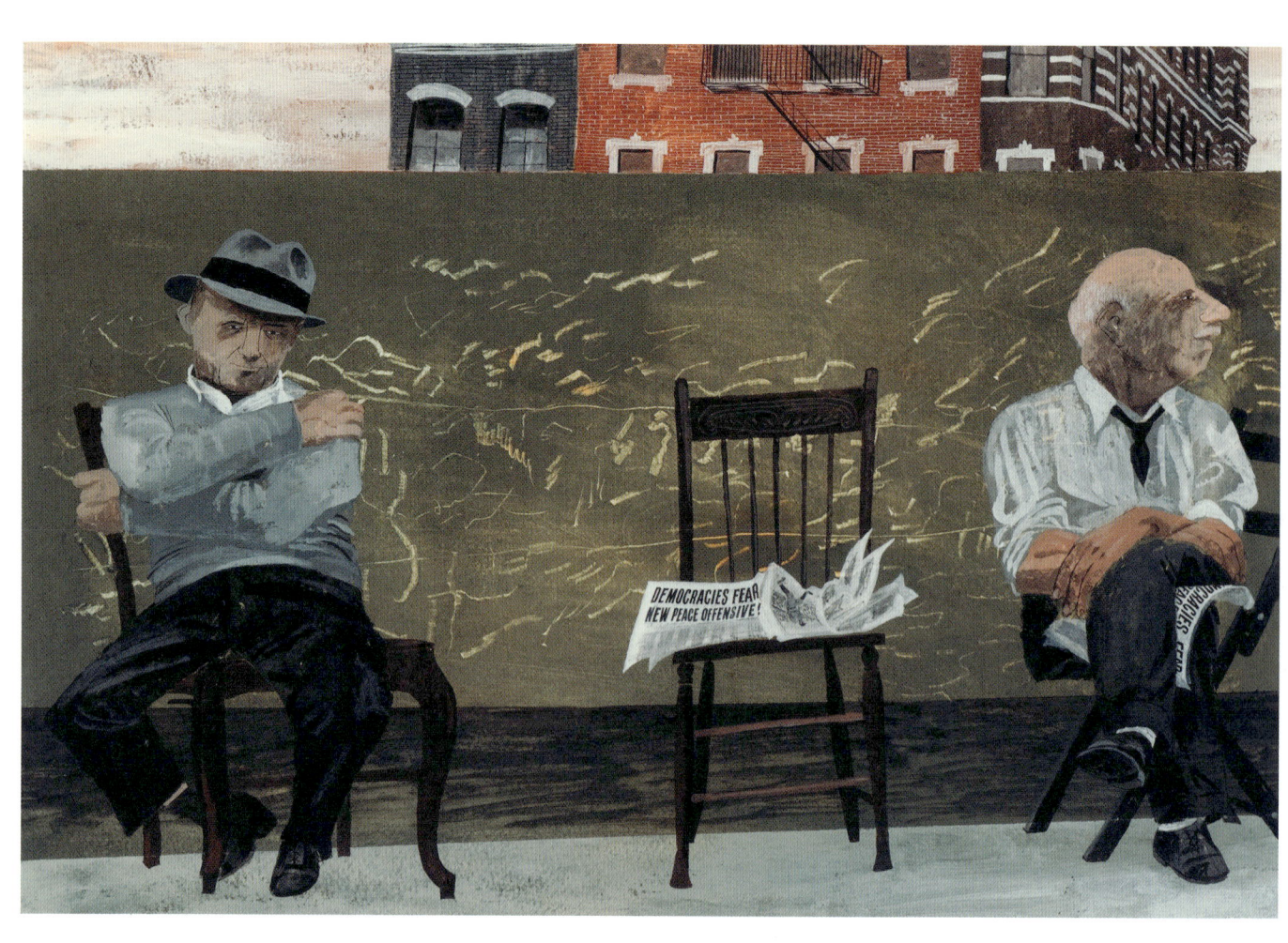

Democracies Fear New Peace Offensive [Spring, 1940]
1940

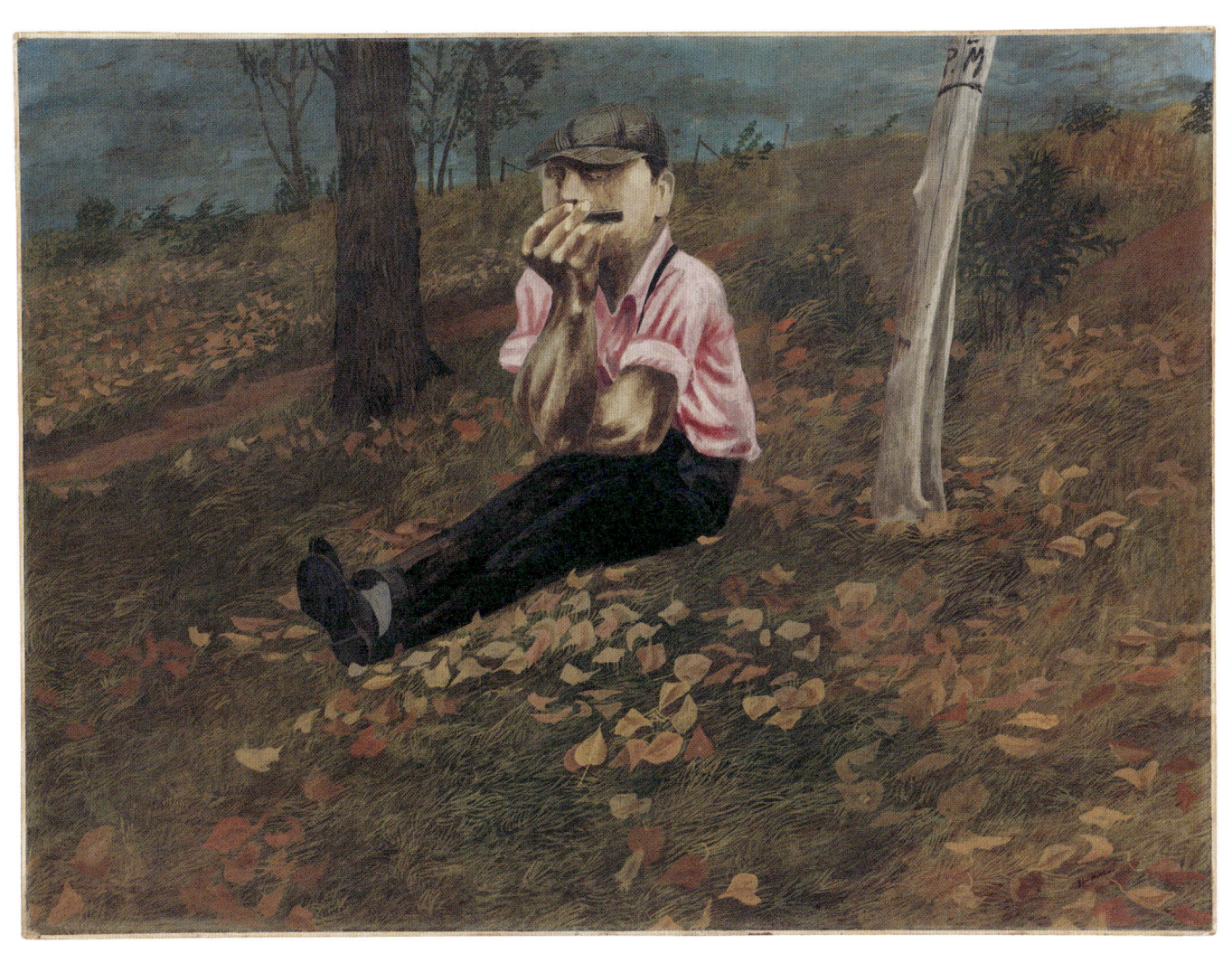

Pretty Girl Milking the Cow
1940

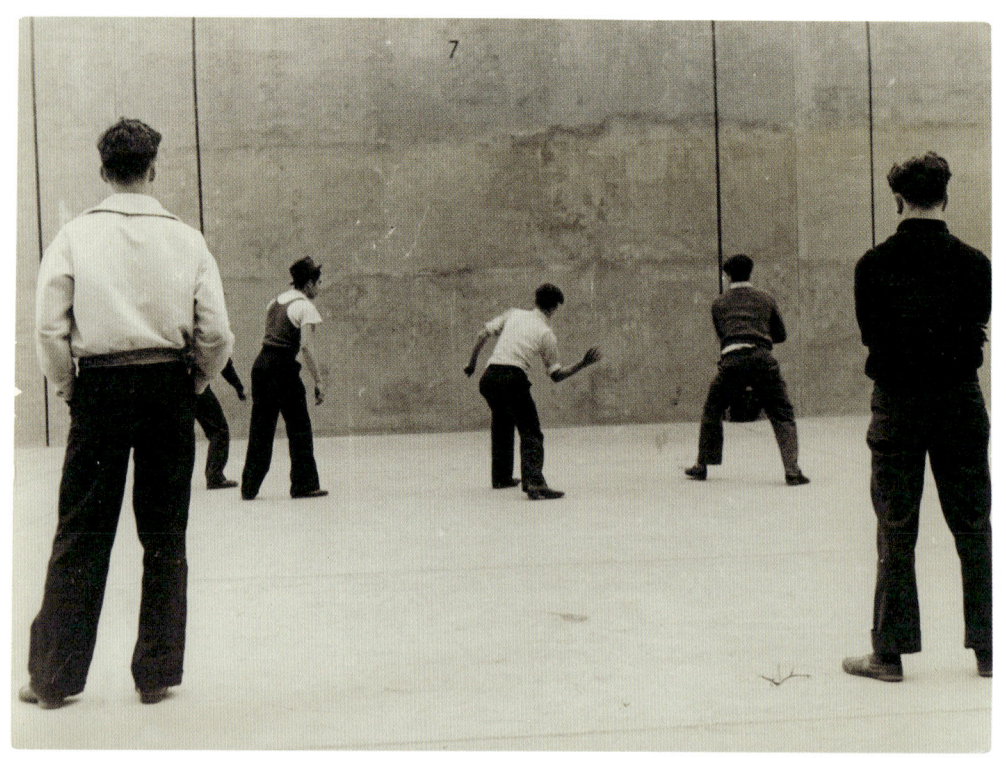

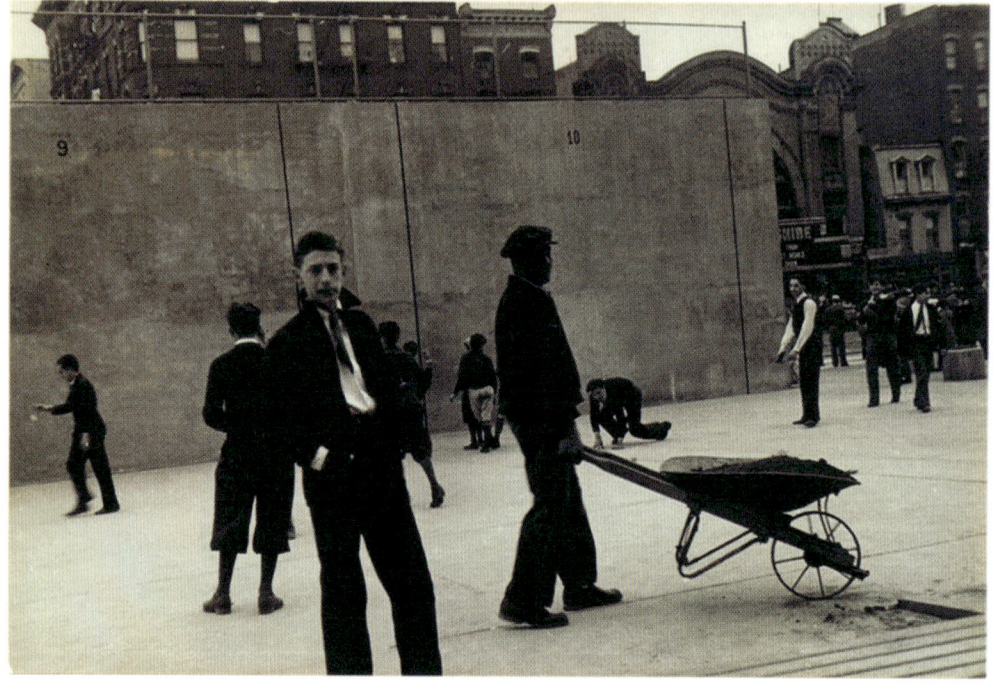

126

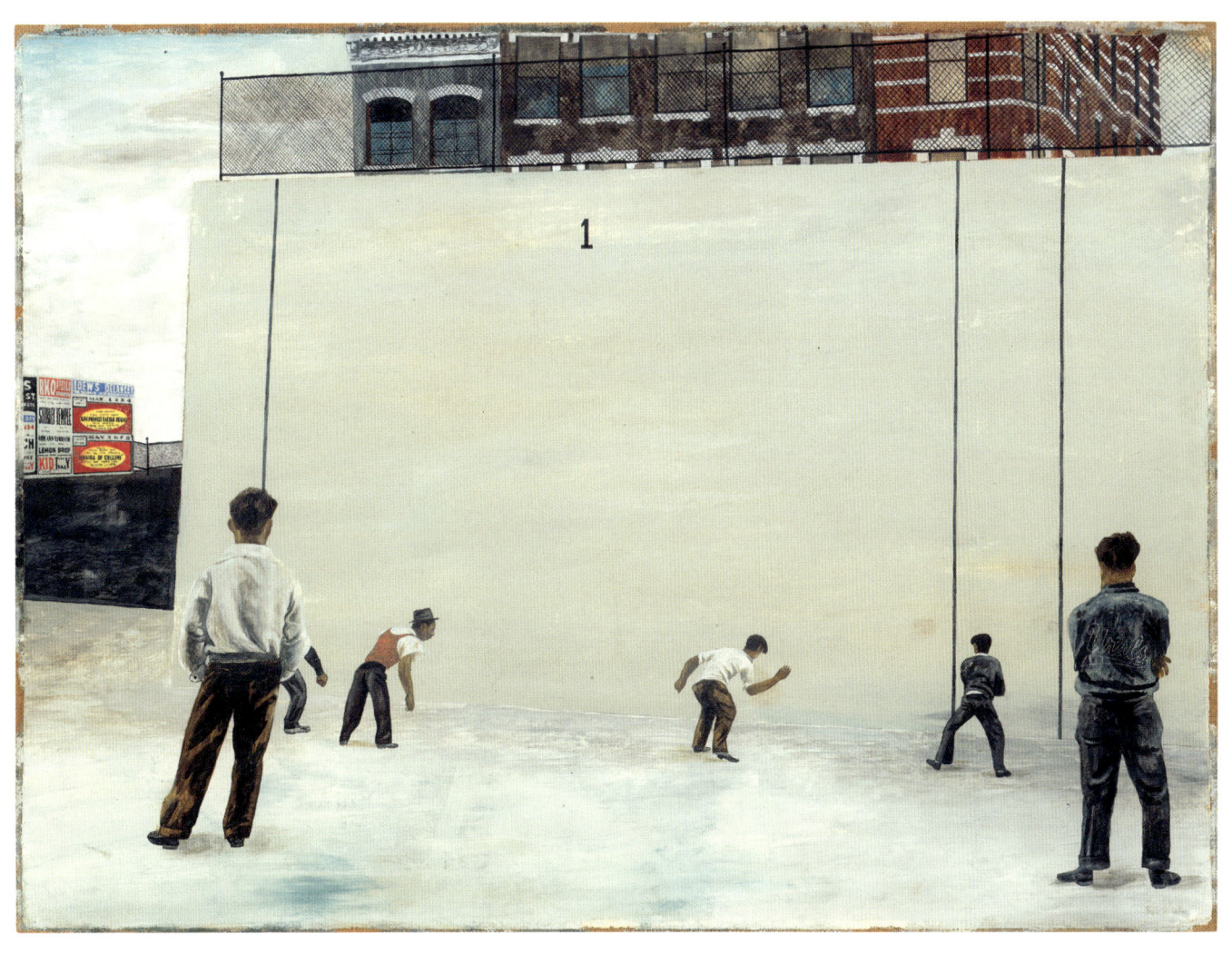

Untitled [Houston Street Playground, East Houston Street, New York City]
1932–35

Houston St. Playground [East Houston Street, New York City]
1932–35

Handball
1939

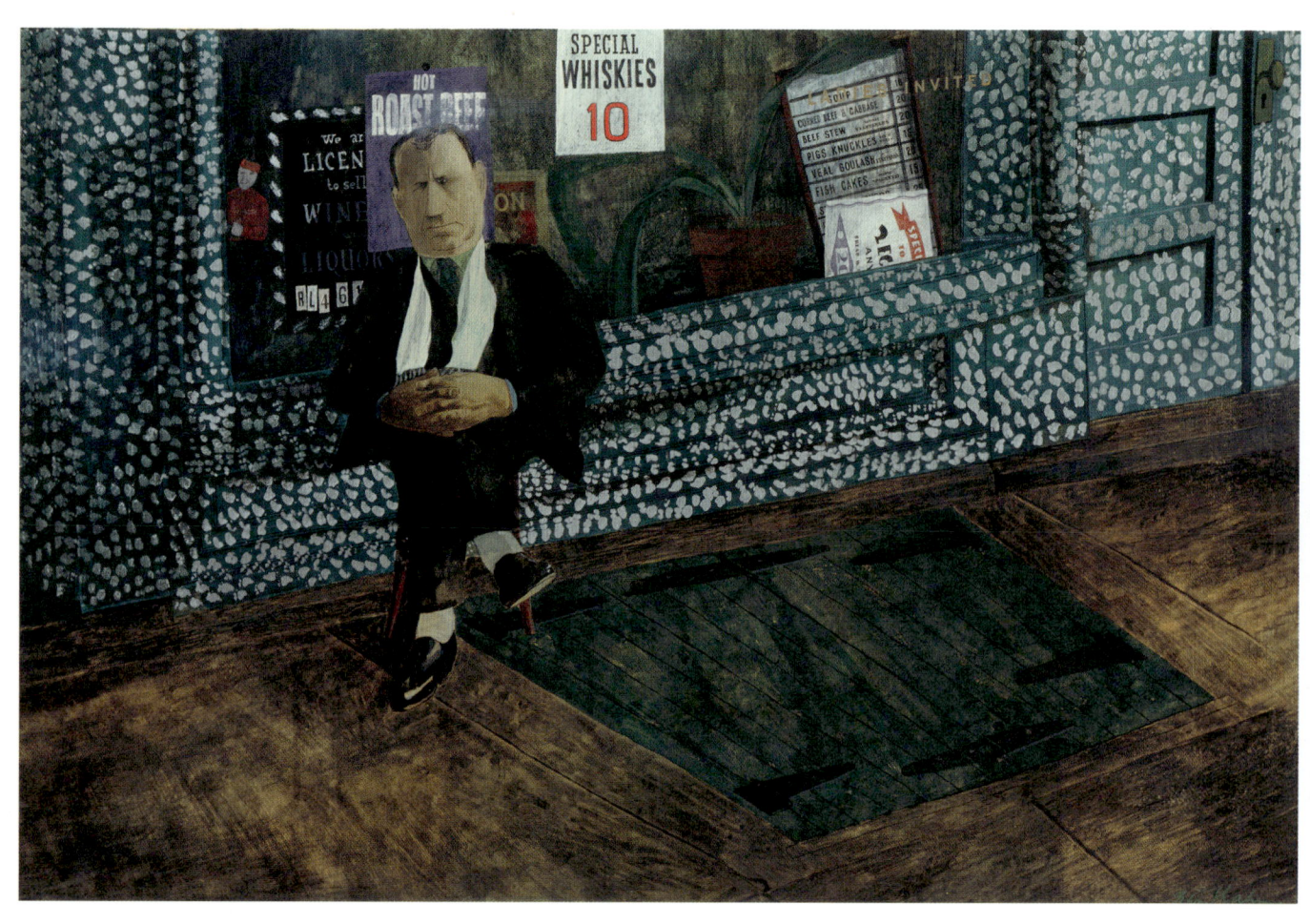

Seurat's Lunch
c. 1939

Untitled [related to *Prohibition* mural, Central Park Casino, unrealized]
c. 1934

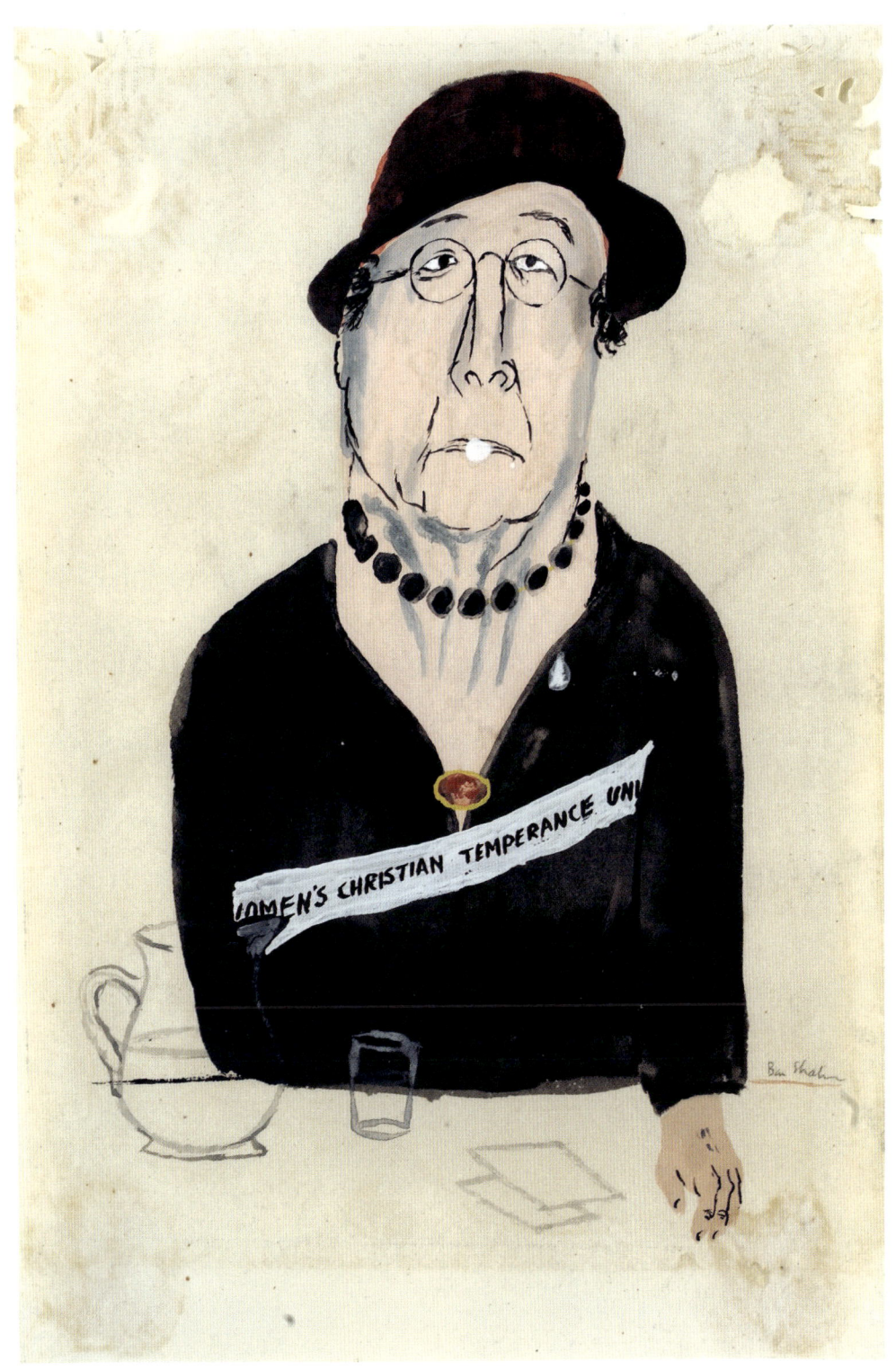

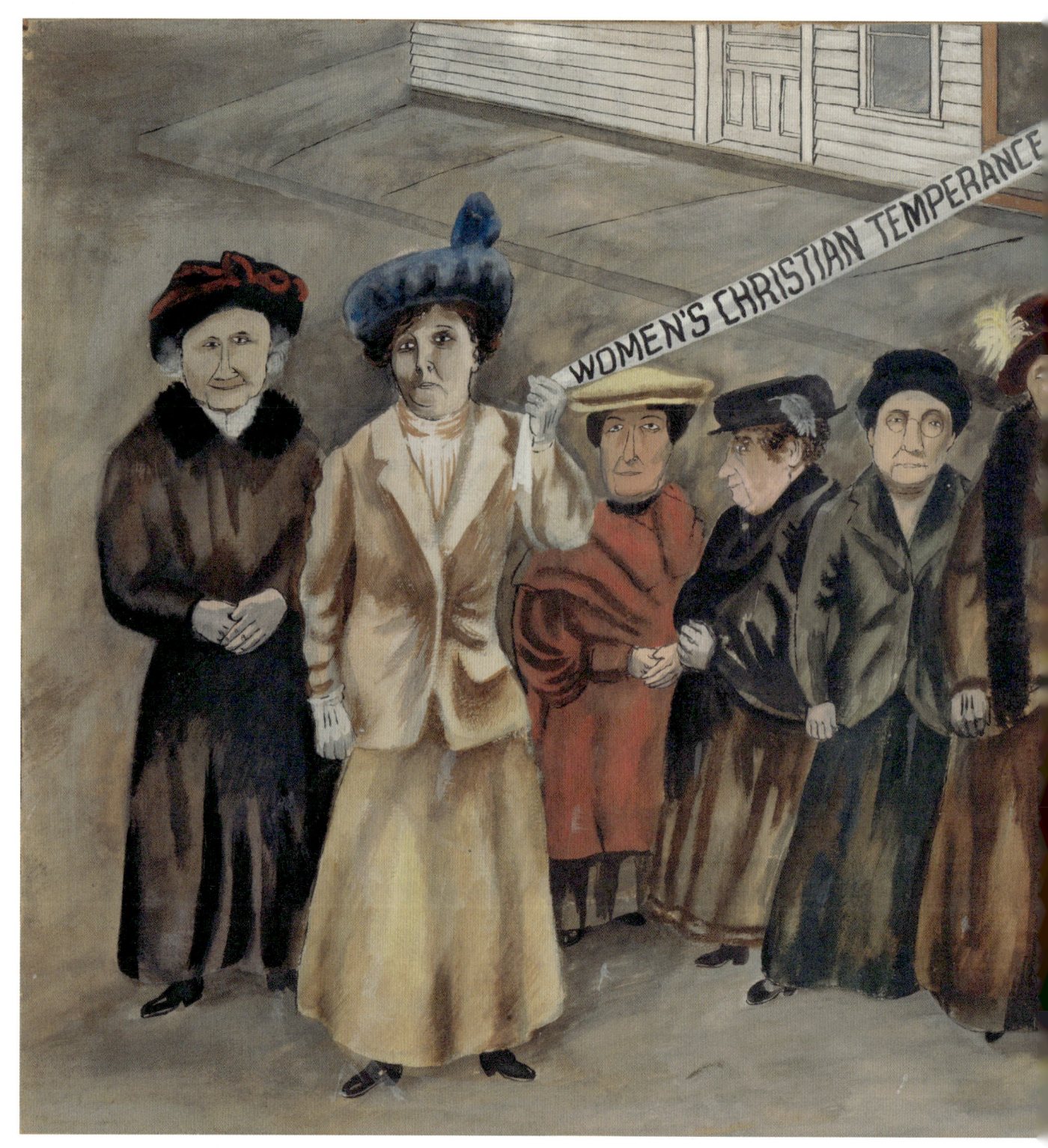

WCTU Parade
[*Prohibition* mural study for the Central Park Casino, unrealized]
c. 1934

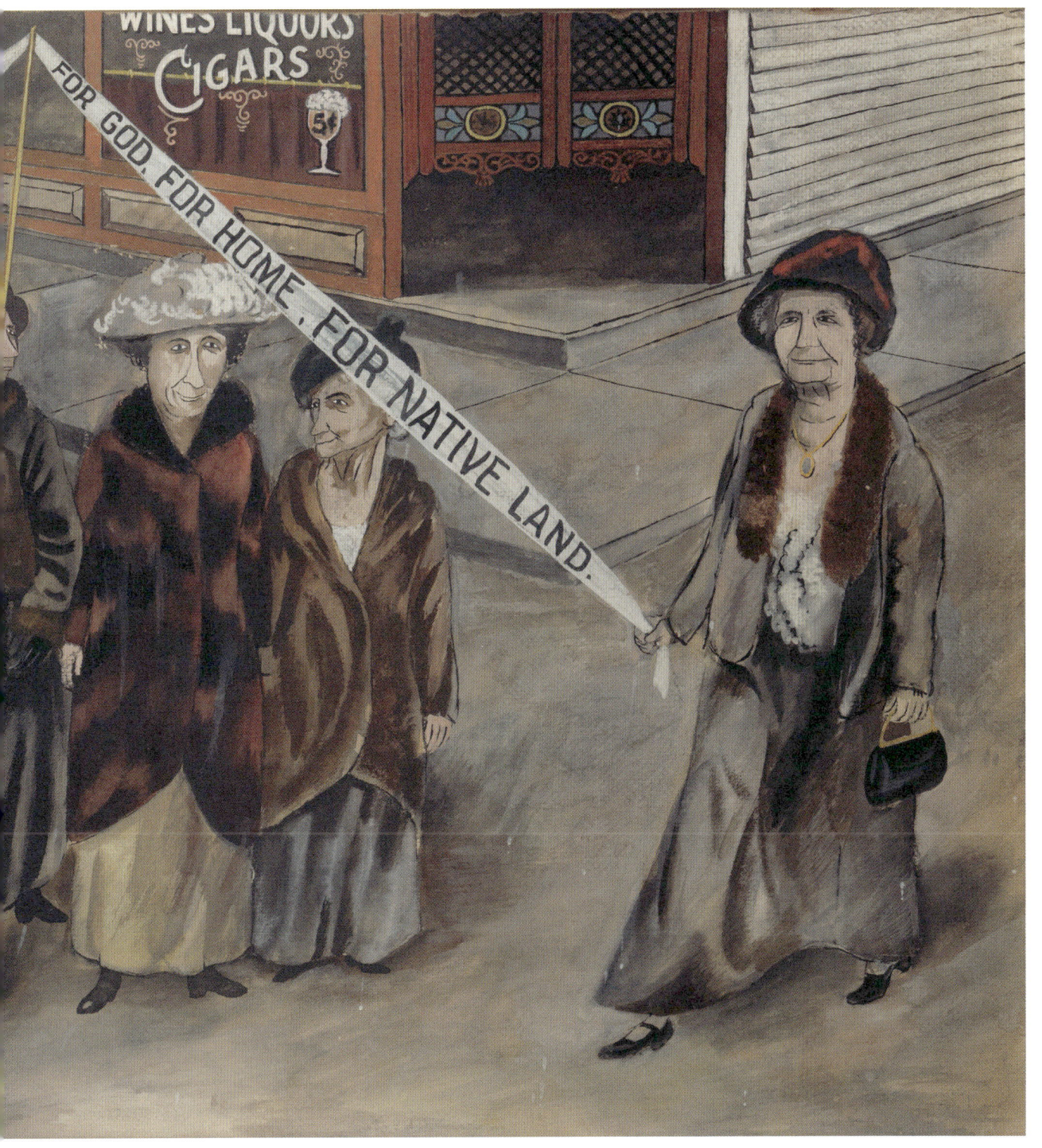

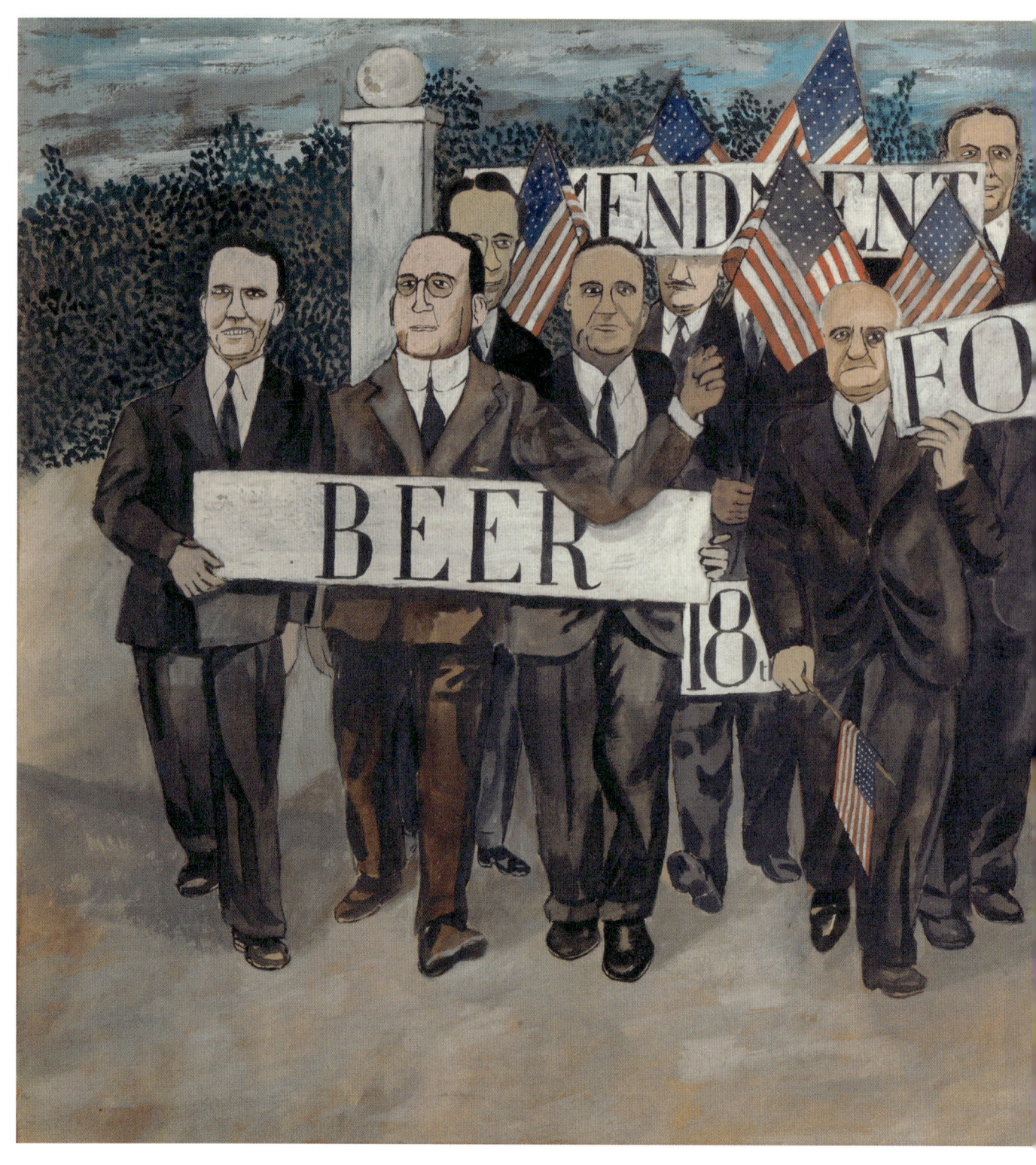

Parade for Repeal
[*Prohibition* mural study for the Central Park Casino, unrealized]
c. 1934

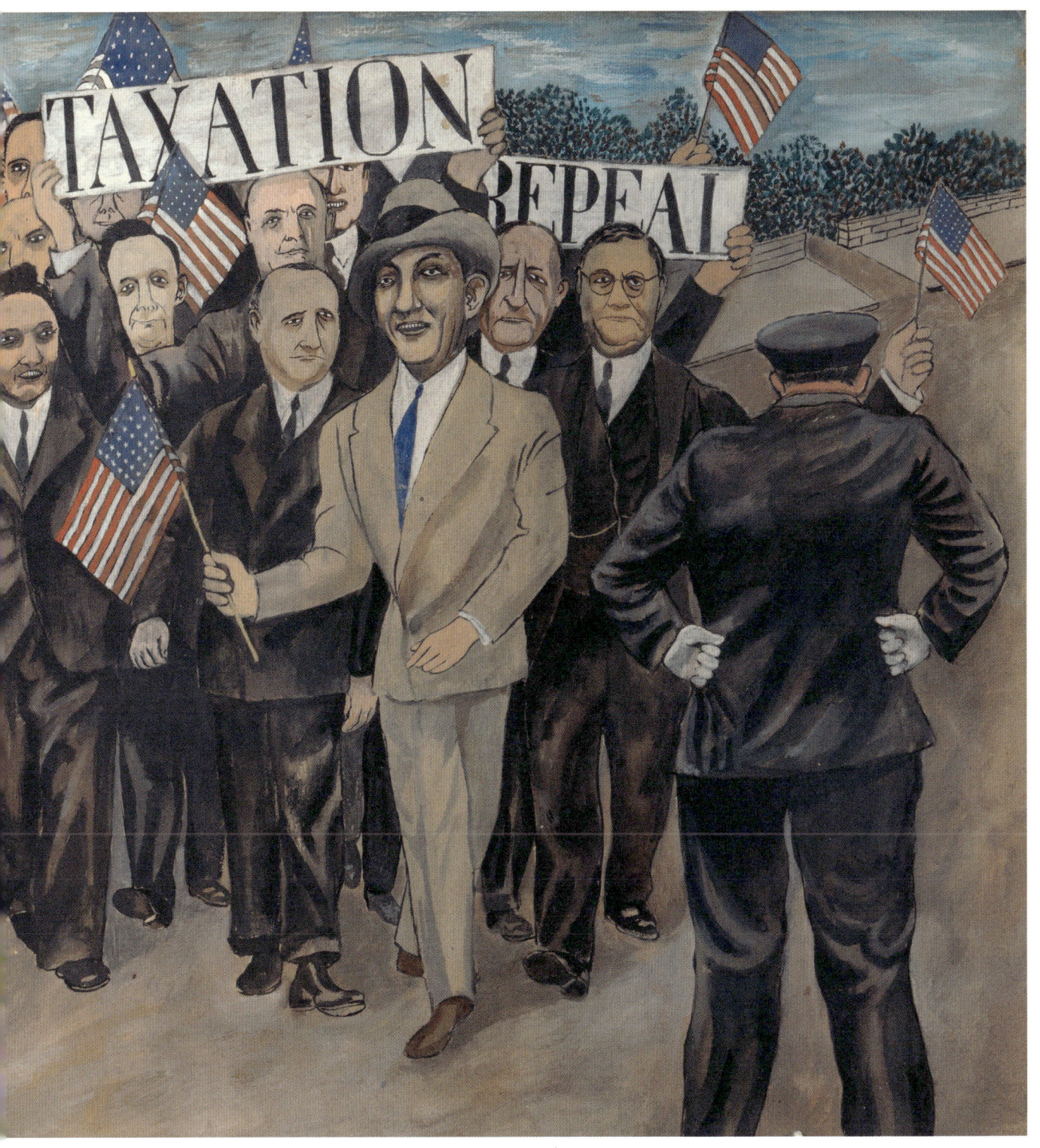

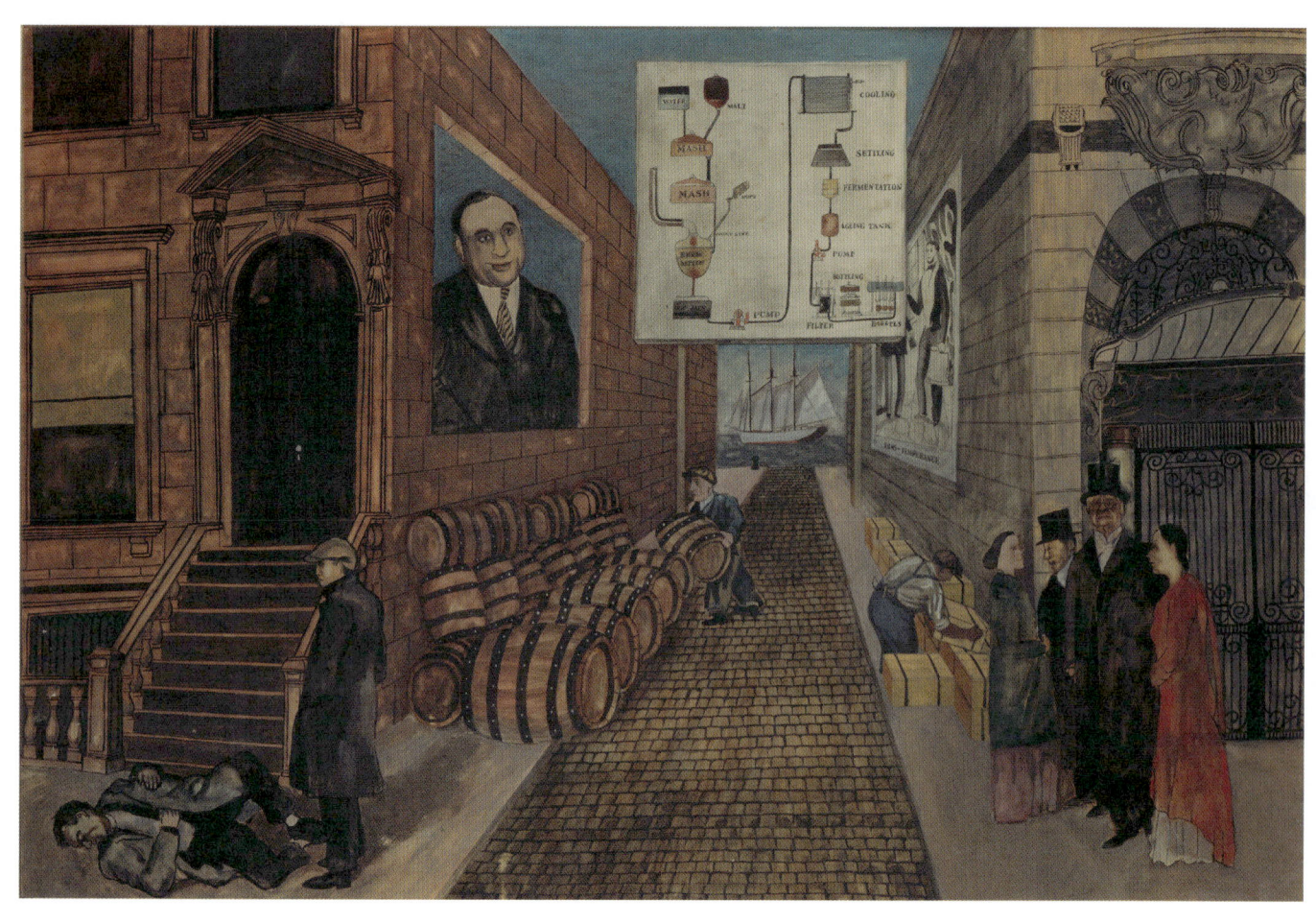

Delivering Barrels
[*Prohibition* mural study for the Central Park Casino, unrealized]
c. 1934

Bootleggers
[*Prohibition* mural study for the Central Park Casino, unrealized]
c. 1934

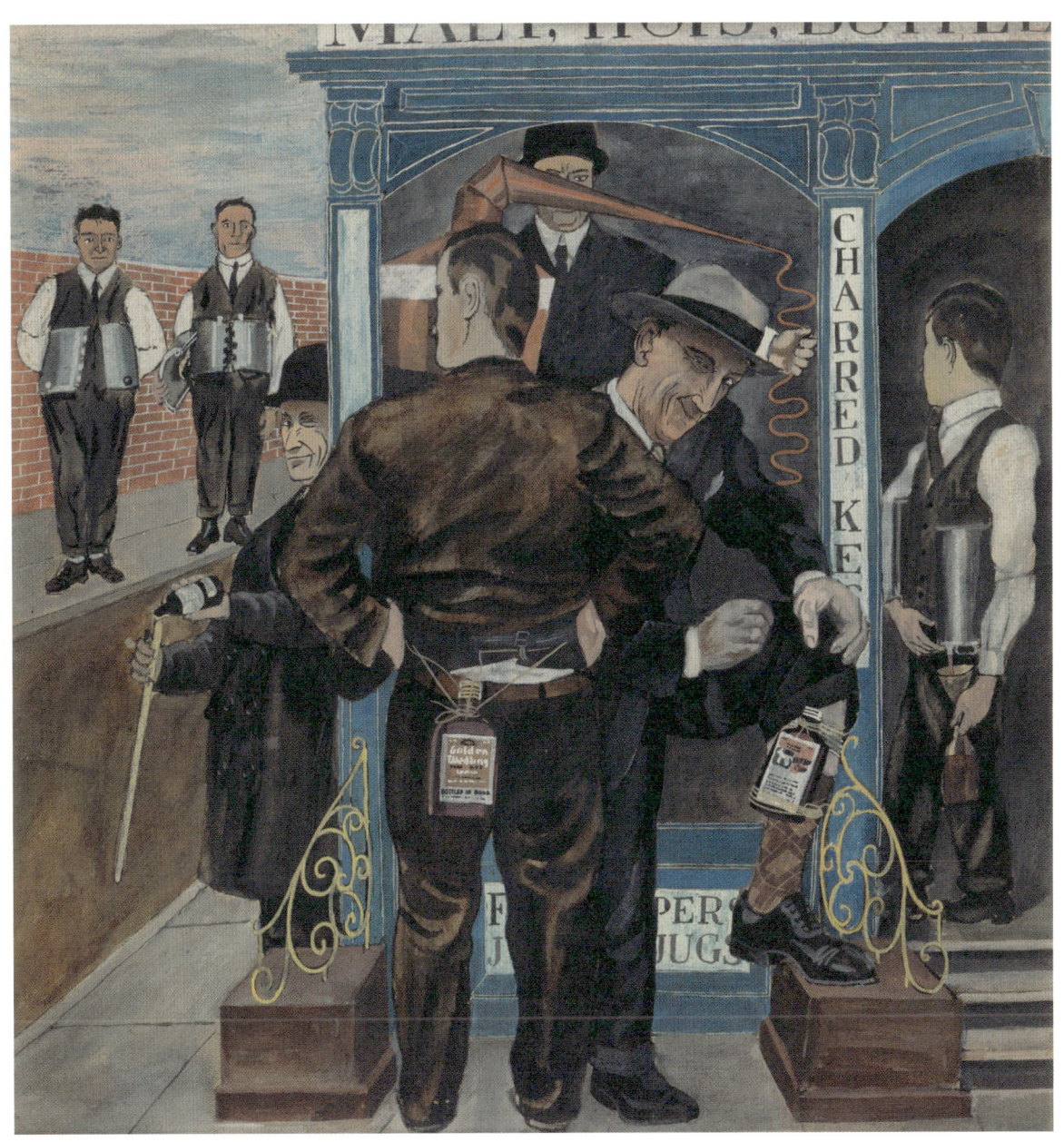

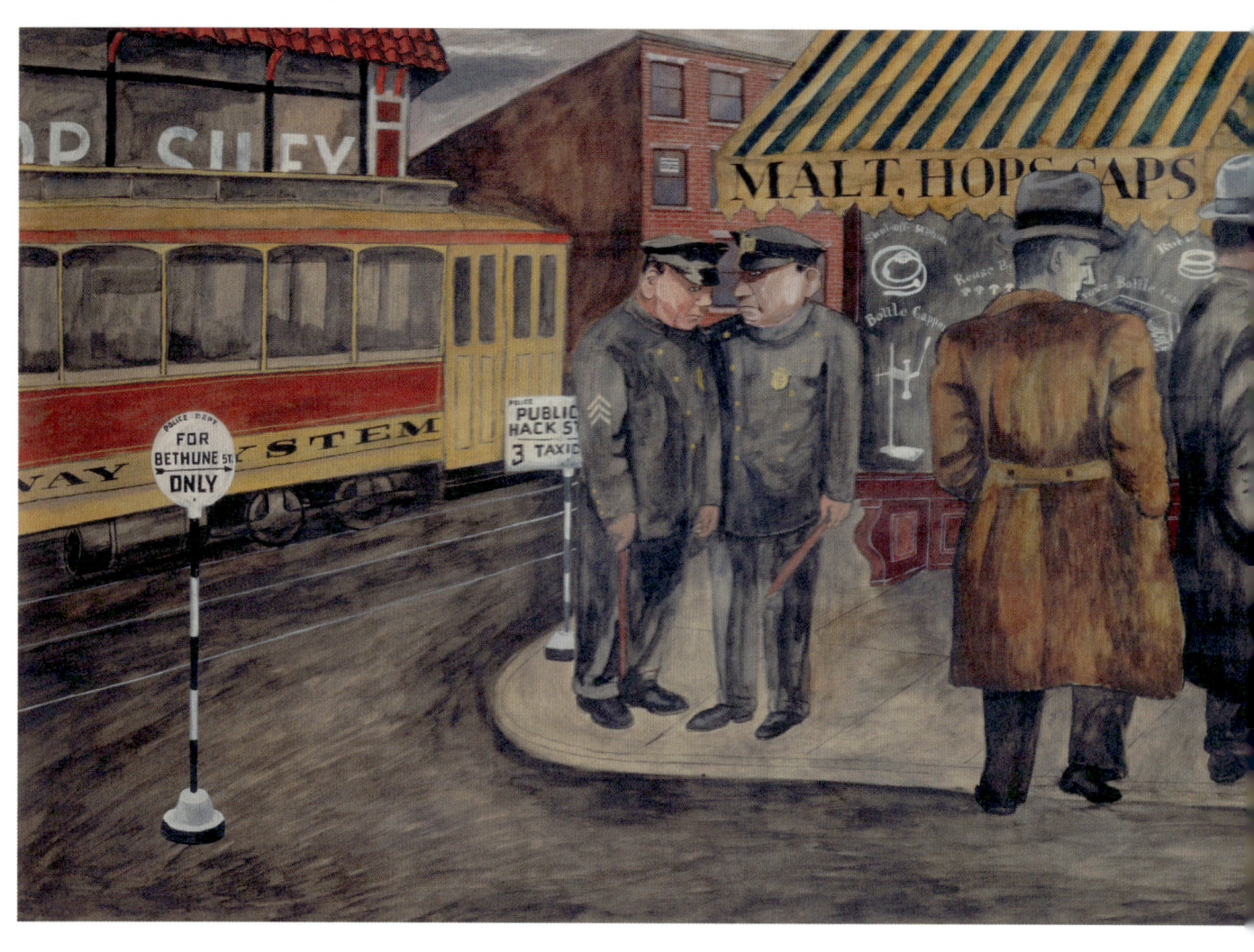

Village Speakeasy Closed for Violation
[*Prohibition* mural study for the Central Park Casino, unrealized]
c. 1934

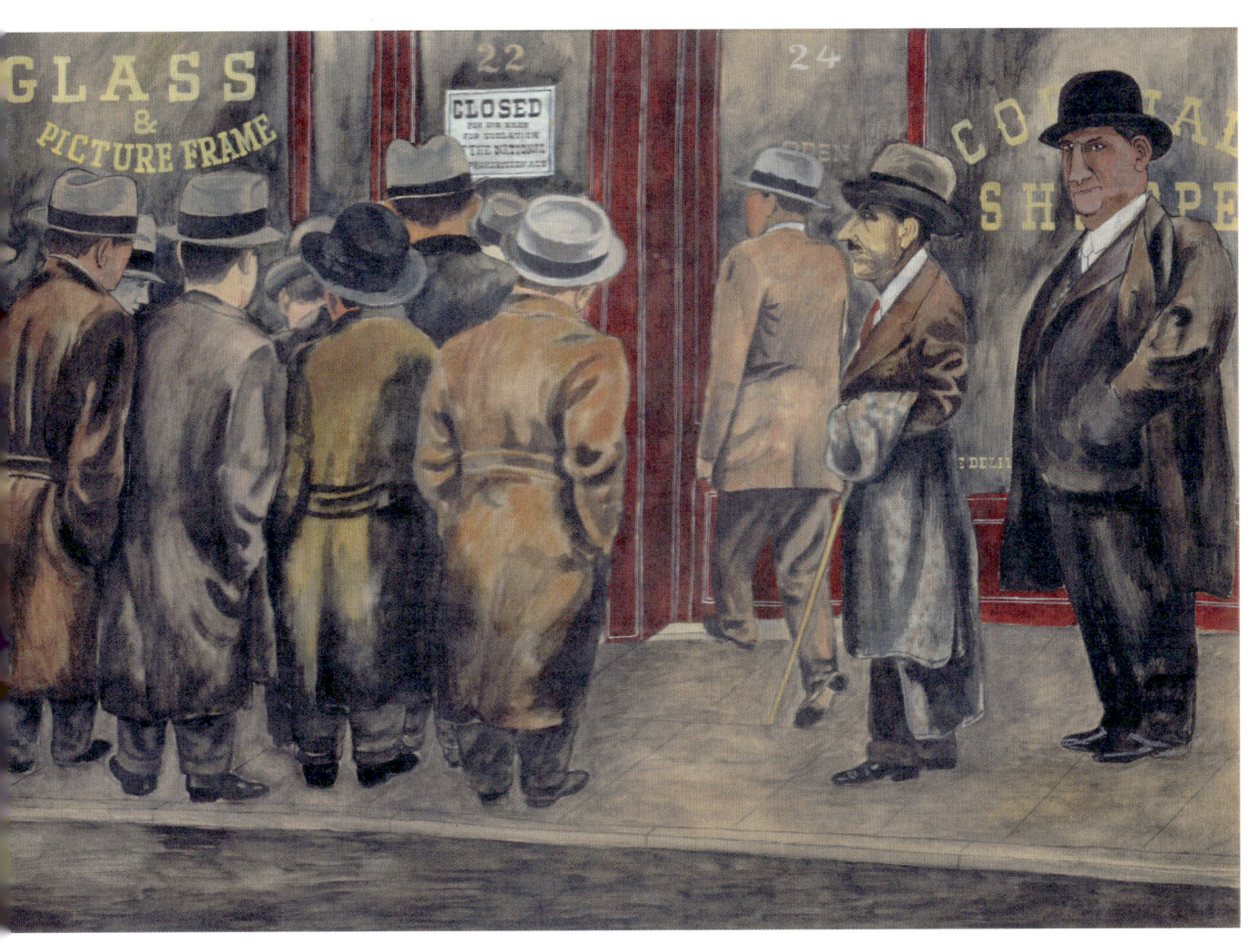

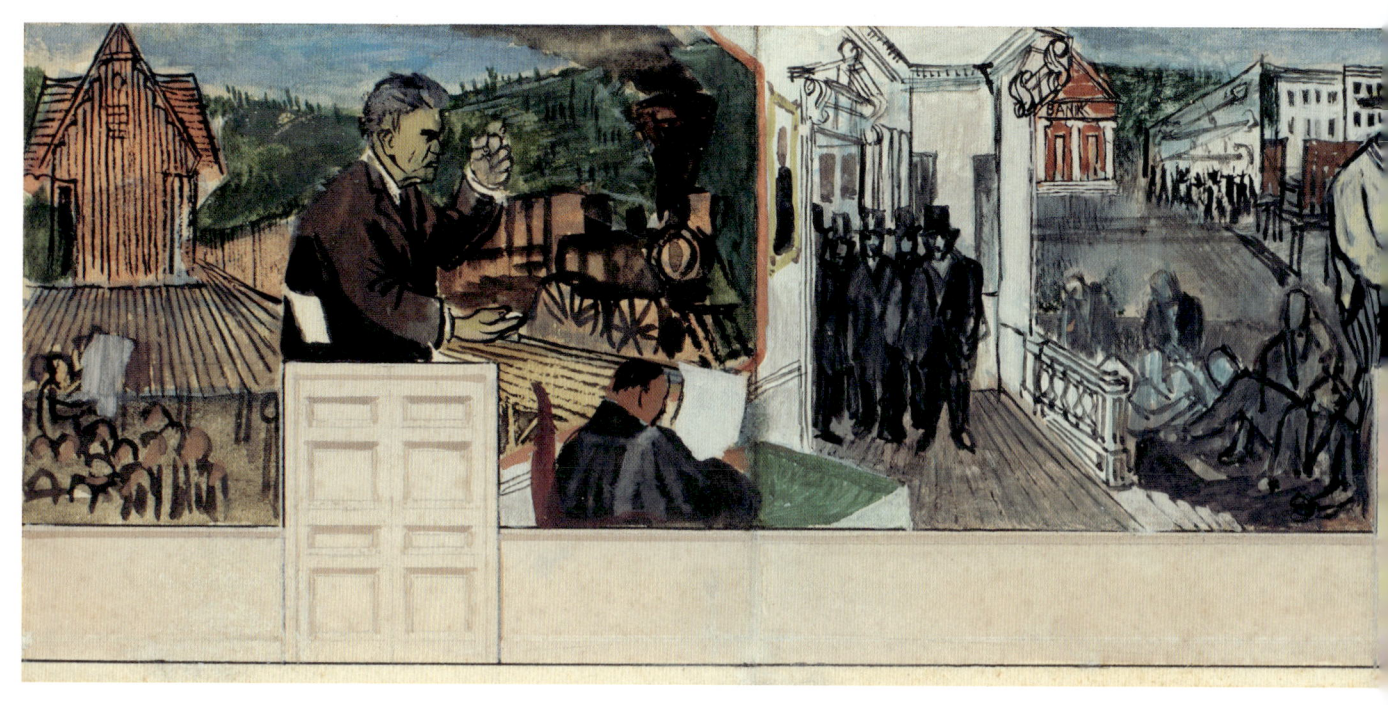

Study for Great State of Wisconsin mural
c. 1937

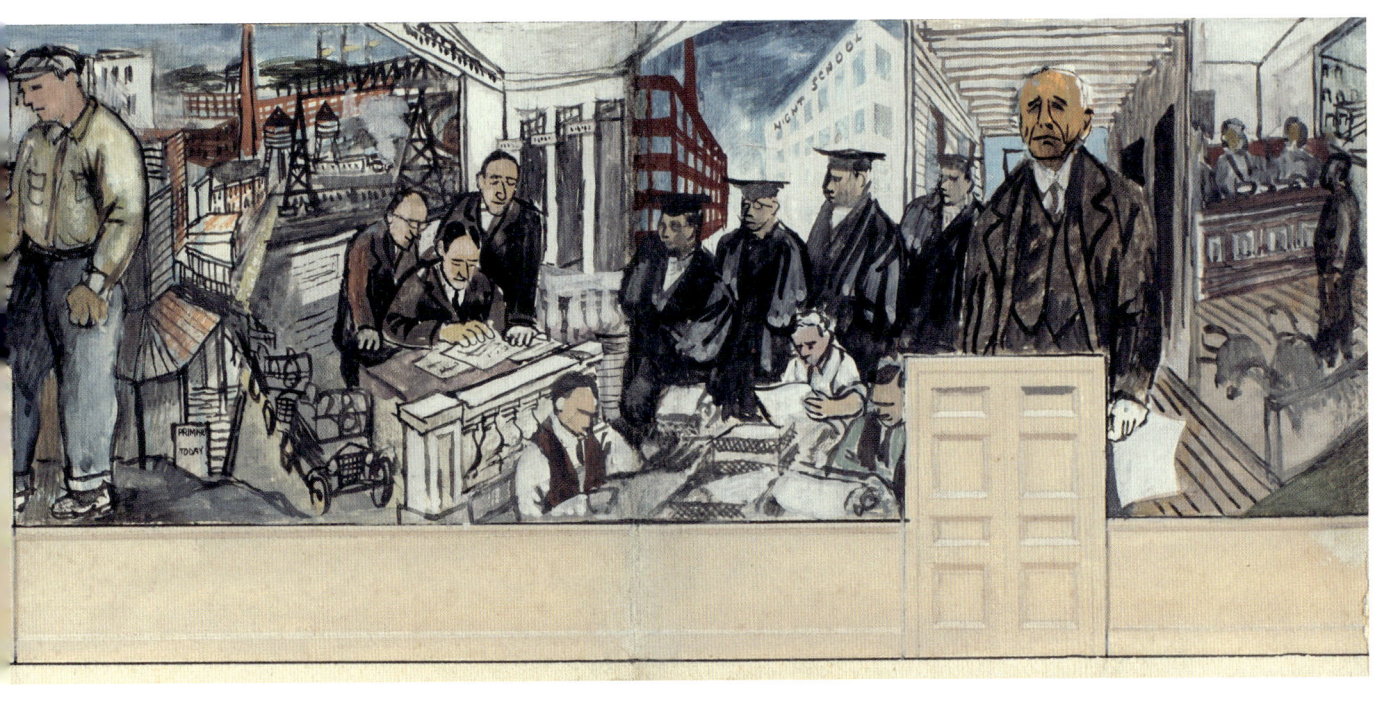

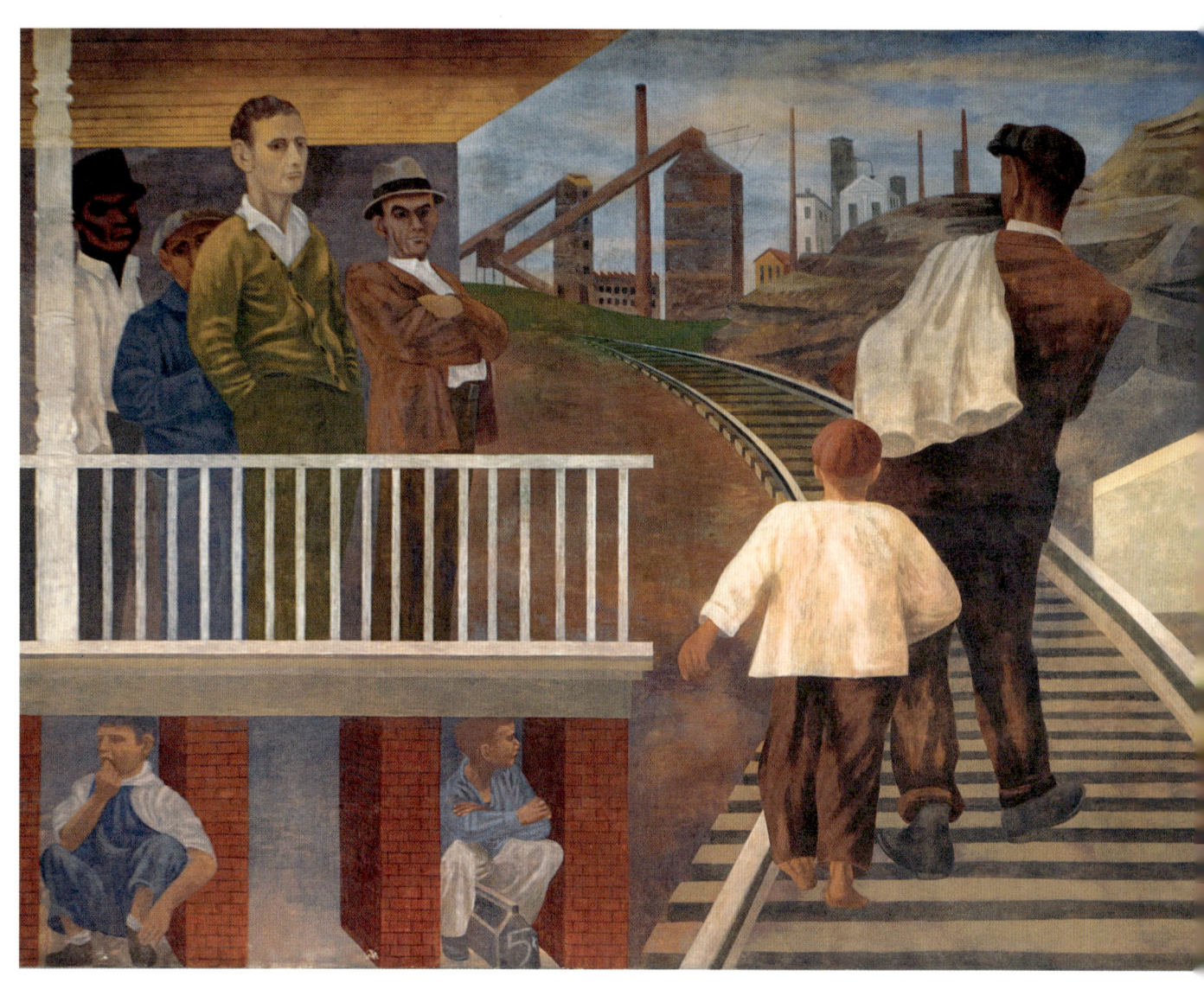

Unemployment [from *The Meaning of Social Security* mural, East Wall]
Wilbur J. Cohen Federal Building, Washington, D.C.
1940–42

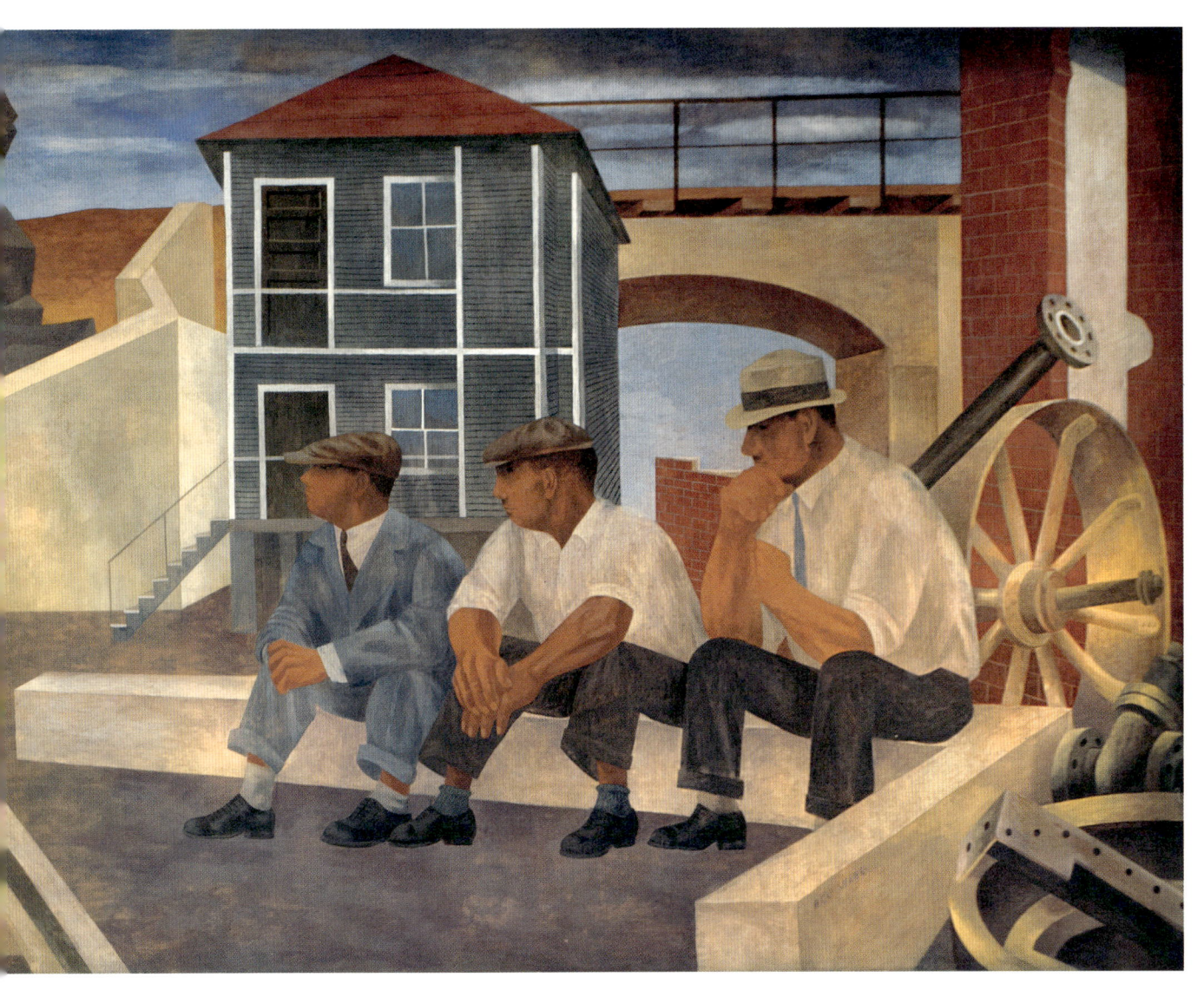

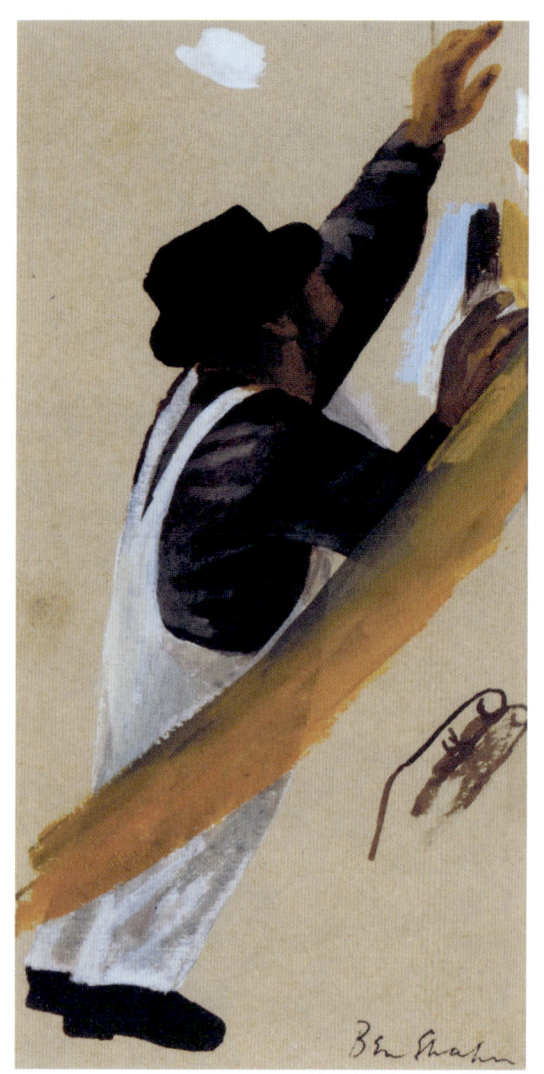

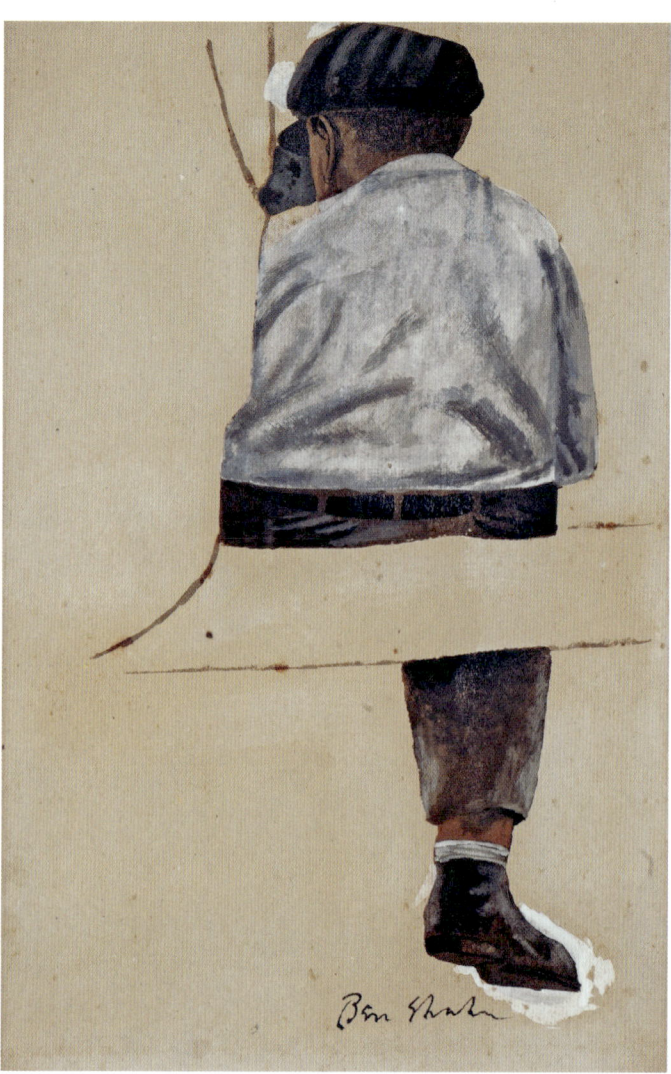

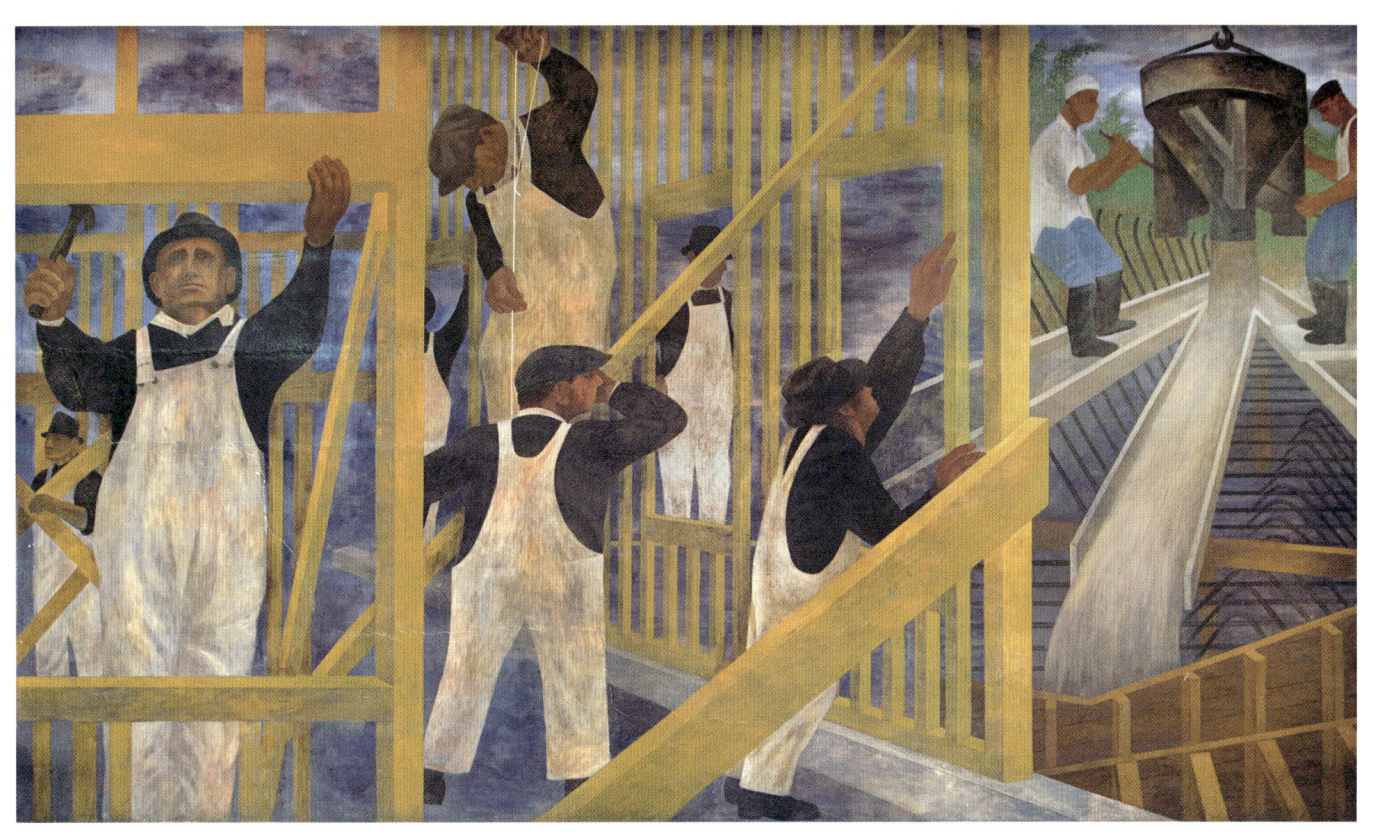

Carpenter's Helper #2
c. 1940–42

Steel Worker
[study for *The Meaning of Social Security* mural, Washington, D.C.]
1940–42

Housing
[from *The Meaning of Social Security* mural, West Wall]
Wilbur J. Cohen Federal Building, Washington, D.C.
1940–42

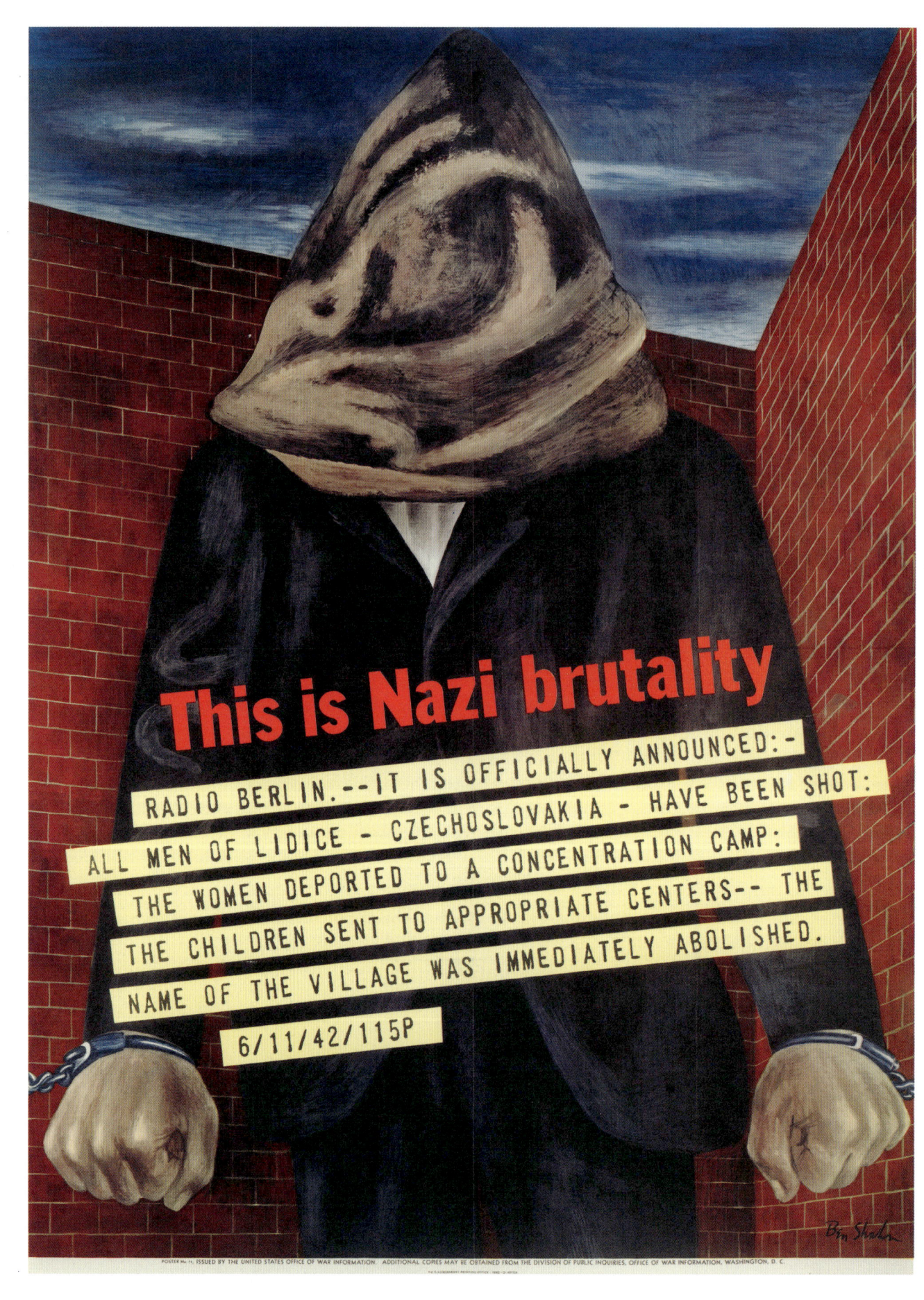

This is Nazi brutality

RADIO BERLIN.--IT IS OFFICIALLY ANNOUNCED:-
ALL MEN OF LIDICE - CZECHOSLOVAKIA - HAVE BEEN SHOT:
THE WOMEN DEPORTED TO A CONCENTRATION CAMP:
THE CHILDREN SENT TO APPROPRIATE CENTERS-- THE
NAME OF THE VILLAGE WAS IMMEDIATELY ABOLISHED.
6/11/42/115P

POSTER No. 1. ISSUED BY THE UNITED STATES OFFICE OF WAR INFORMATION.   ADDITIONAL COPIES MAY BE OBTAINED FROM THE DIVISION OF PUBLIC INQUIRIES, OFFICE OF WAR INFORMATION, WASHINGTON, D. C.

During World War II, Ben Shahn worked for the Bureau of Publications and Graphics of the U.S. Office of War Information (OWI). Established in 1942, after the U.S. entered the global conflict on the side of the Allies in December 1941, the OWI (in its domestic operations) hired artists to design posters, brochures, and other material that functioned as propaganda to encourage U.S. support for the war effort. Shahn also worked for the Office of the Coordinator of Inter-American Affairs to help counter the fascist propaganda of the Axis powers and Francoist Spain that filtered into Latin America. His poster *This is Nazi Brutality* (1942) pictures the horrific tactics used by the Nazis to destroy the entire village of Lidice, Czechoslovakia, and murder or deport most of its inhabitants, in retaliation for the assassination of the high-ranking SS official Reinhard Heydrich by Czech resistance fighters. *We French Workers Warn You* (1942) condemns the forced labor decree issued by the Vichy government in collaboration with Nazi Germany during its occupation of France.

These two posters are the only ones of Shahn's many designs known to have been circulated by the OWI. Most of his posters and pamphlets were criticized as too harsh, violent, or unappealing. Recent scholarship, however, has argued that their "aesthetic intensity and ambiguous messaging" also contributed to their rejection. Shahn's focus on the victims rather than the perpetrators, his avoidance of menacing fascist symbols, and his use of complex textual layering distinguish his posters from those of other OWI artists. Typical wartime posters promoted war production, "victory gardens," and the rationing and recycling of materials—or warned citizens about the dangers of talking to the enemy.[1] Shahn and his OWI colleagues were enraged by the takeover of the Graphics Division by commercial advertising executives who preferred slick publicity over a sincere informational approach to communicating the war's threats to democracy.

Despite Shahn's brief tenure with the OWI (he left in summer 1943), the classified and unclassified photographs he witnessed there left an indelible impression on him. He wrote of "the secret confidential horrible facts of the cartloads of dead; Greece, India, Poland" and of bombed-out European cities—the human devastation wrought by Axis and Allied forces. Such documentation, along with newspaper photographs and newsreels, informed his wartime and postwar paintings dealing with themes of decimation, reconstruction, and the indestructible human spirit. Shahn was particularly grieved by the destruction in his beloved Italy: "the churches destroyed, the villages, the monasteries—Monte Cassino and Ravenna," as seen in *Italian Landscape* (1943–44) and

This is Nazi Brutality
1942

Italian Landscape II: Europa (1944), where widows walk the ruins of war. He searched for a symbolism that could express "the sense of emptiness and waste that the war gave [him], and the sense of littleness of people trying to live on through the enormity of war."[2]

Shahn responded to the immediate postwar moment with pictures such as *Remember the Wrapper* (1945), which depicts the U.S. liberation of an Italian town from Nazi occupation. The energetic scene of soldiers passing out chewing gum to excited children and to a slender, olive-skinned maternal figure poignantly contrasts with the somber background of a lone soldier, blown-up railroad tracks, and barren structures. *Liberation* (1945) shows young girls at the war's end swinging around a pole with wild abandon among a blasted building and piles of rubble. *Carnival* (1946), by contrast, constructed from Shahn's 1938 Ohio photographs of a World War I veterans' homecoming and carnival, a July 4th celebration, and an amusement park, is ironically melancholic, quietly unsettling. It juxtaposes a sleeping stall worker with one couple precariously perched in the seat of a flying swing ride and another couple, whose backs are turned away from the worker, embracing and looking off into the distance—toward an unknown future.

In other postwar works, Shahn referenced the Holocaust—the genocide of the Jewish people perpetrated by Nazi Germany—largely allegorically. Multilayered symbolism abounds in *Allegory* (1948), in which a fiery leonine beast amid flaming red trees looms over a pile of immobile children—an image based on a photograph of victims of Nazi crimes in a Greek government publication Shahn obtained at the OWI. Shahn's memories of devastating fires from his own childhood and his response to a fire that destroyed a Black family in a Chicago tenement in 1947 informed his imagery. Given the painting's date of 1948 and the beast's resemblance to the she-wolf whose suckling of Romulus and Remus in Roman mythology symbolizes the birth of Rome, *Allegory* may also allude to the founding of the State of Israel.[3] The equally enigmatic *New York* (1947) may reflect Shahn's own ethnic identity in America as the full scope of the near extermination of European Jewry was being revealed. A bony boy at the center of the tempera is encircled by an empty tenement and factory, a pike fish, a religious Jewish fish merchant, and a scale—elements extracted from Shahn's photographs of New York's Lower East Side. Floating surrealistically as in a collage, these elements create an evocative dreamscape of Shahn's memories of his immigrant childhood. Such memories—fraught with pain and nostalgia—weighed heavily on his mind in these years. While popular culture was celebrating the triumph of American economic and military power, Shahn and fellow figurative and abstract artists were grappling with the horrors and existential threats of the recent global war and its aftermath.

1. See Christof Decker's essay in this catalogue and "Fighting for a Free World: Ben Shahn and the Art of the War Poster," *American Art* 33, no. 2 (2019): 92, 84–105. See also chapter 2 in Decker, *Imaging the Scenes of War: Aesthetic Crossovers in American Visual Culture* (Bielefeld: transcript Verlag, 2022), 35–59.

2. Ben Shahn, *The Shape of Content* (Cambridge, Mass.: Harvard University Press, 1957), 41–42, 47.

3. On Shahn's *Third Allegory* (1955) as a possible commentary on Israel, see Frances K. Pohl, "Allegory in the Work of Ben Shahn," in Susan Chevlowe et al., *Common Man, Mythic Vision: The Paintings of Ben Shahn* (New York: The Jewish Museum and Princeton University Press, 1998), 132, 134. Shahn's relationship to Israel is complex, analysis of which goes beyond the scope of this text. He did artwork for El Al Airlines (1969) and Zim Israel Navigation Company (1963–64), yet made little public comment on Israel and never traveled there, despite many invitations. In 1969, Shahn said Israel "was probably justified" in its 1967 attack against Arab states in response to threats to destroy the country. See Richard Kostelanetz, "Ben Shahn: Master 'Journalist' of American Art (1969)," in *On Innovative Art(ist)s: Recollections of an Expanding Field* (Jefferson, N.C.: McFarland & Company, 1992), 169.

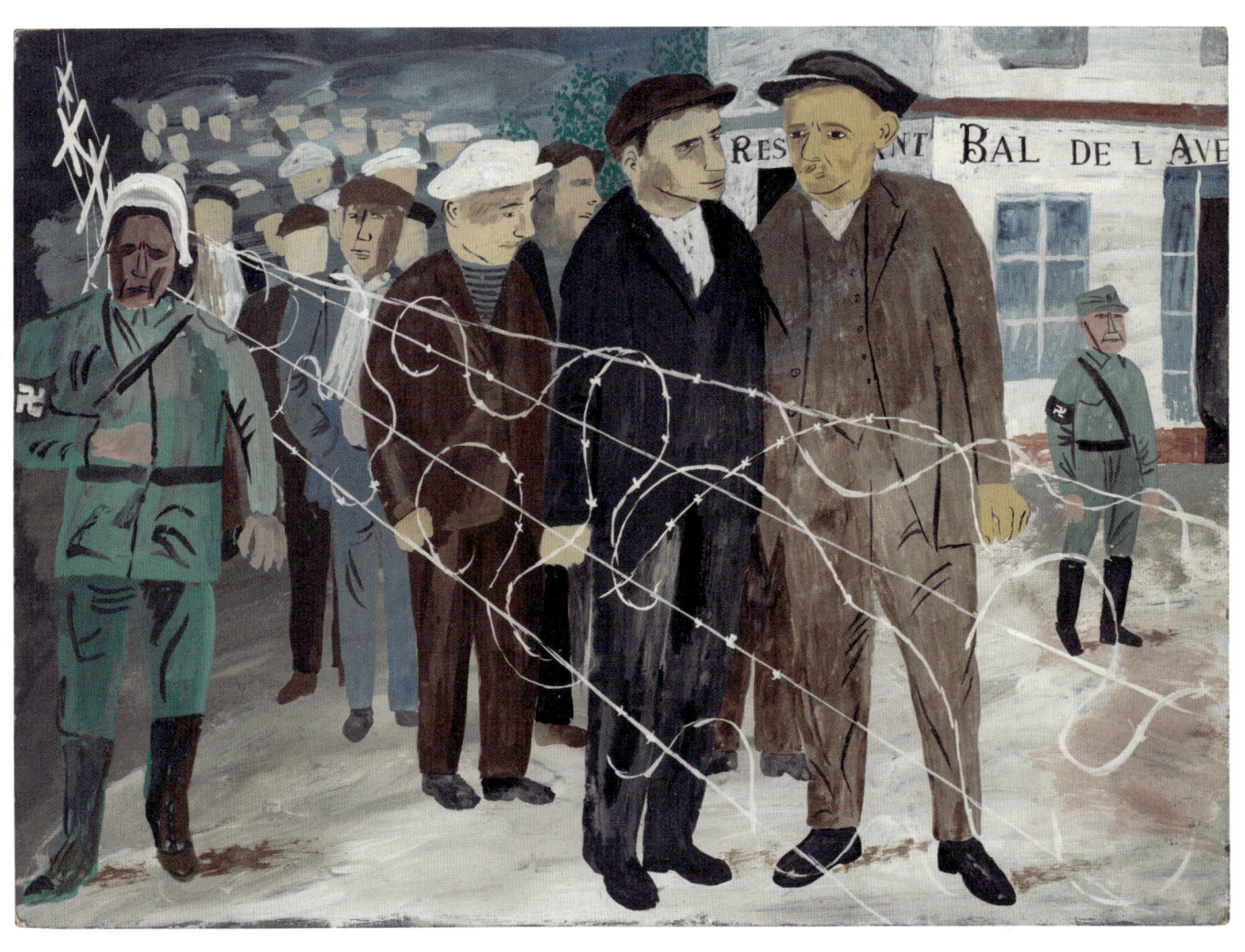

French Workers
1942

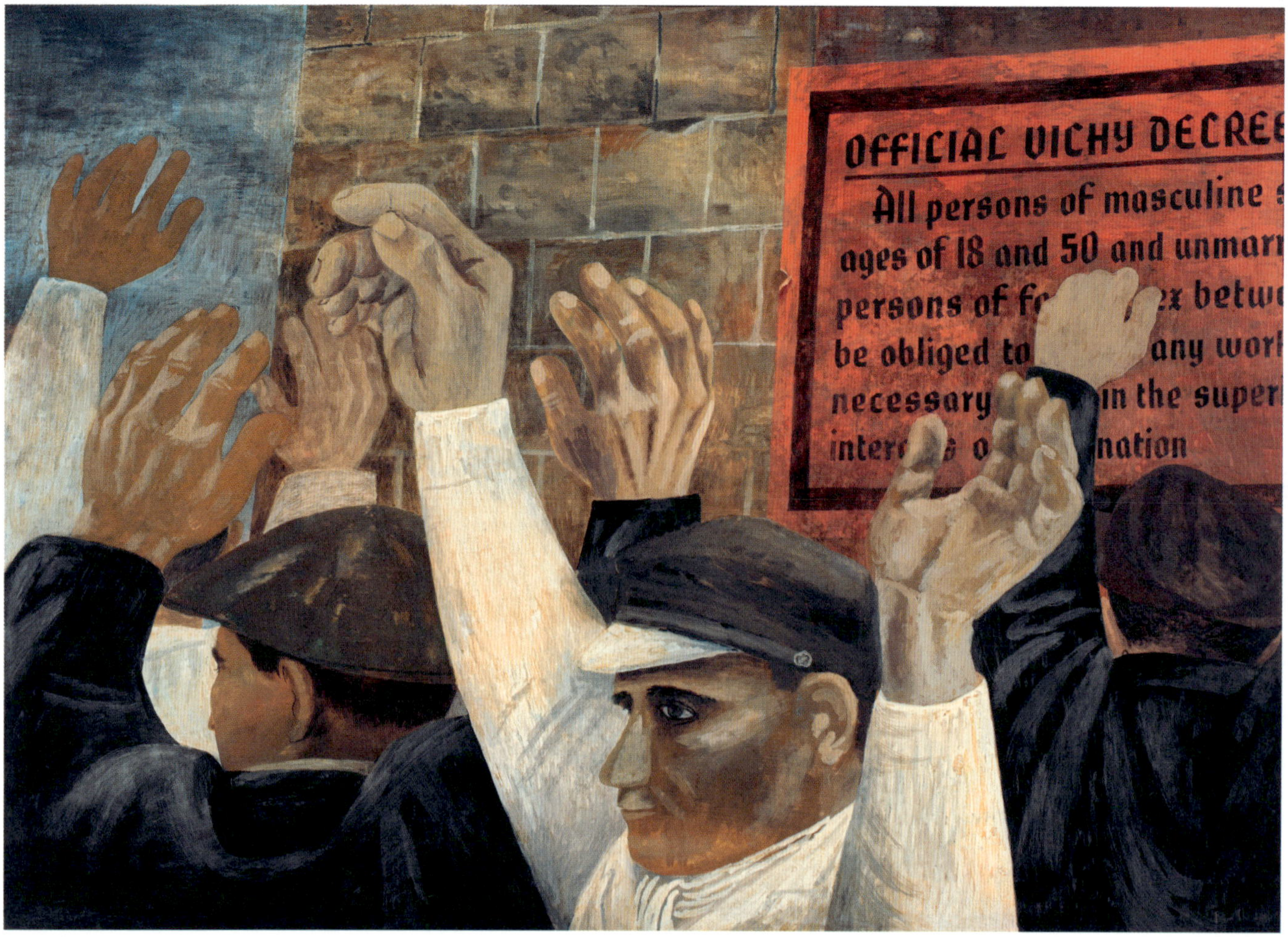

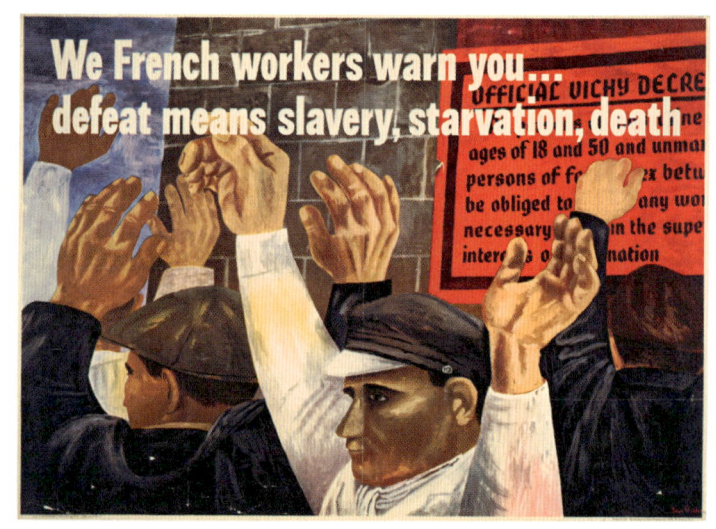

French Workers
1942

*We French Workers Warn You... Defeat Means Slavery,
Starvation, Death*
1942

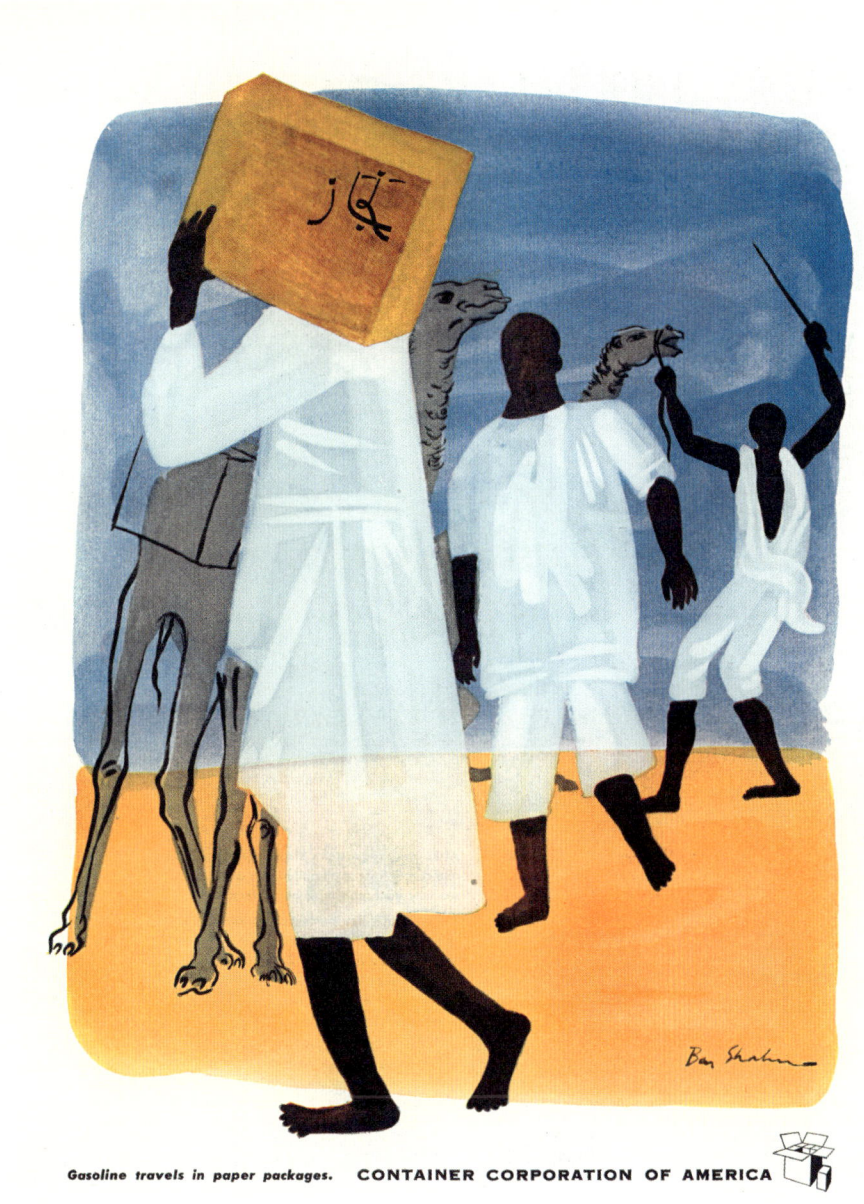

Gasoline travels in paper packages. **CONTAINER CORPORATION OF AMERICA**

"Gasoline Travels in Paper Packages (North Africa),"
Fortune, April 1944, vol. 29, no. 4, p. 219

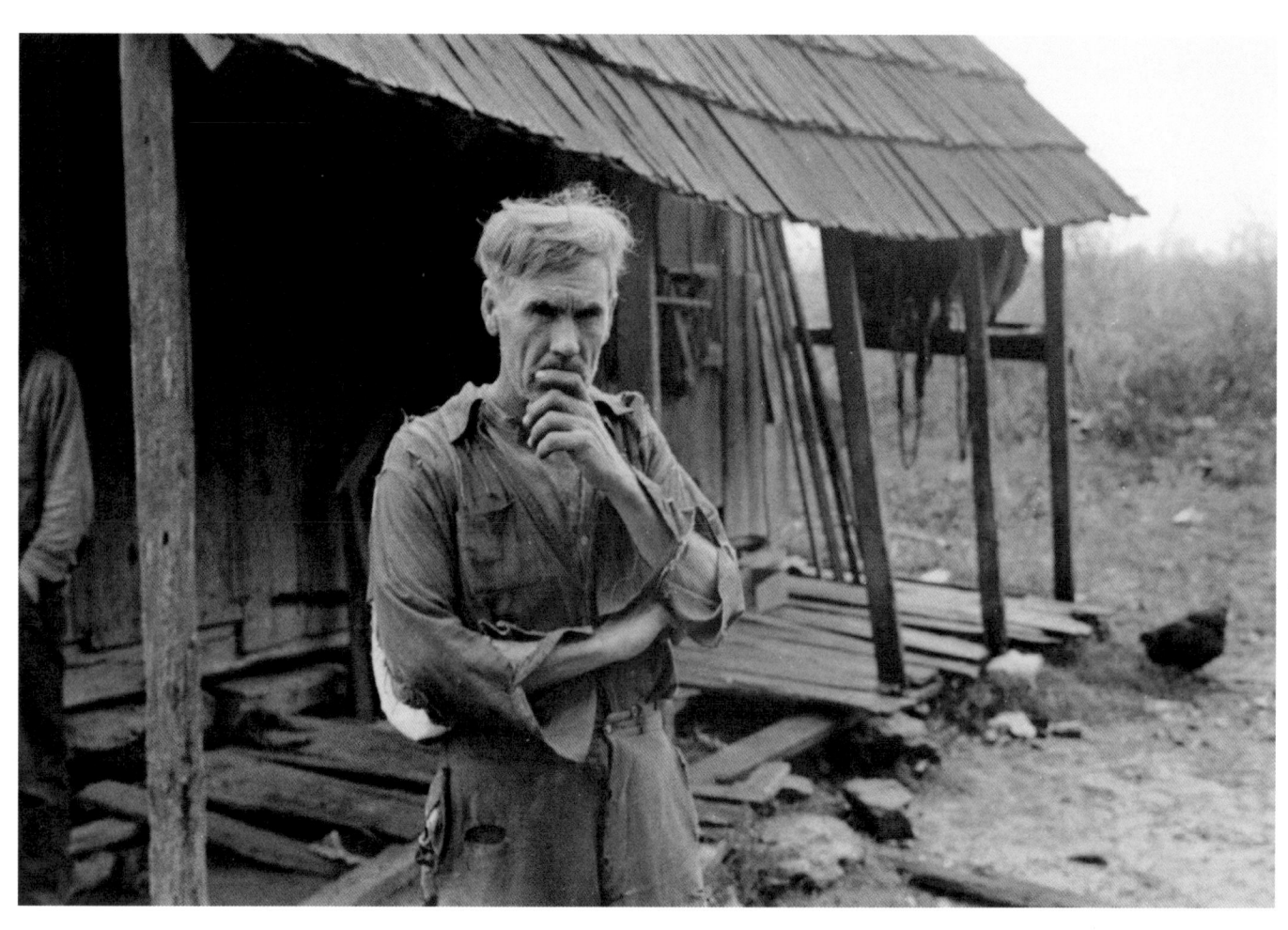

Sam Nichols, Tenant Farmer, Boone County, Arkansas
October 1935

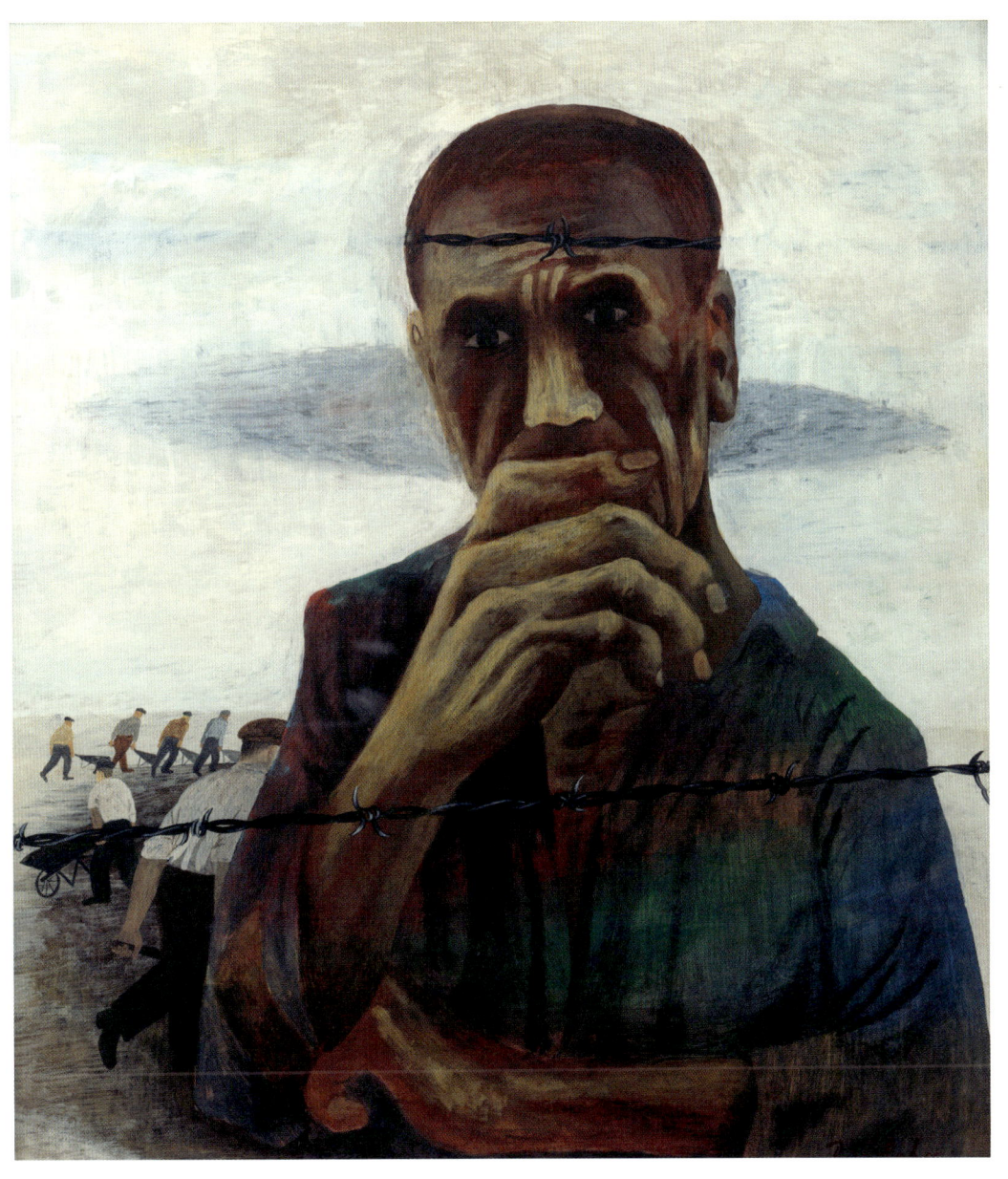

1943 AD
c. 1943

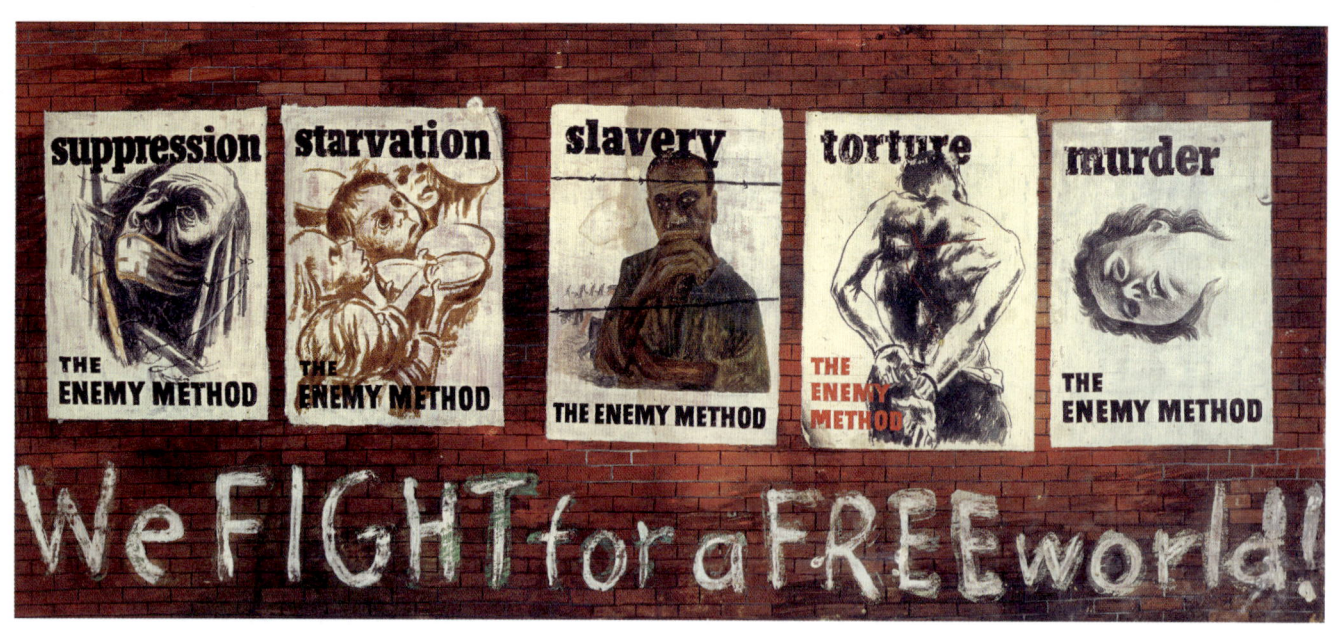

We Fight for a Free World!
c. 1942

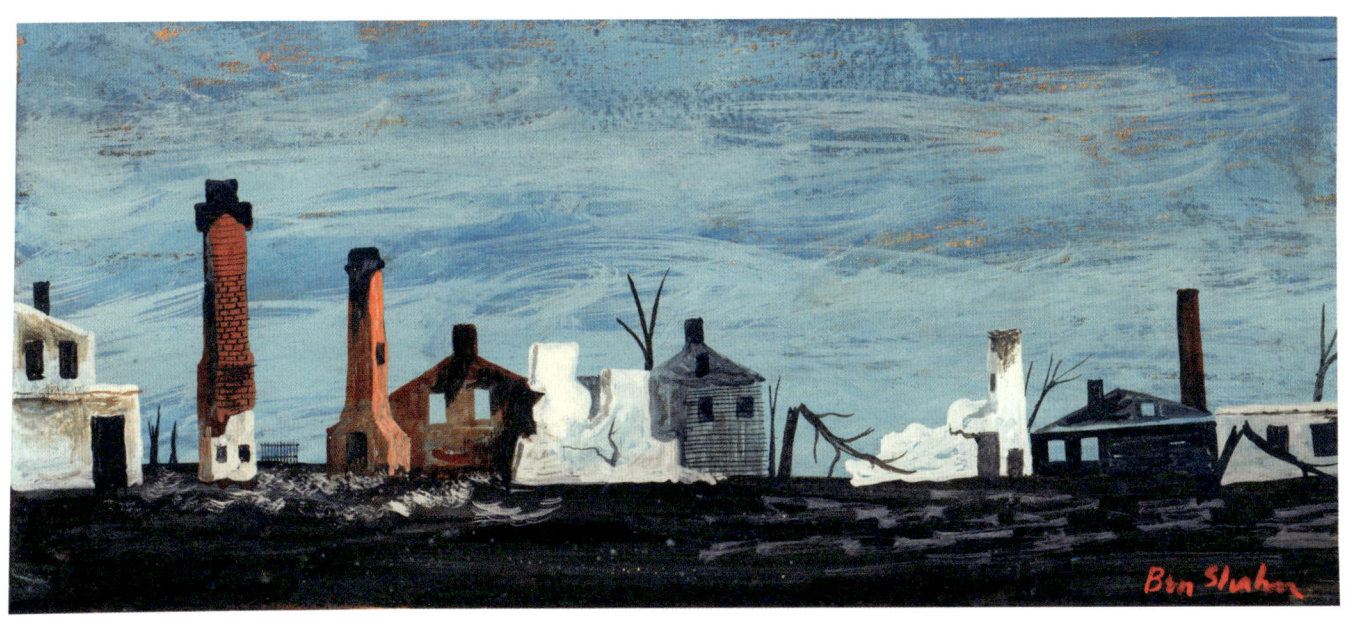

Morning
1943

[Nov. 3, 1936] THE NEW YORK TIMES, TU

INSURGENTS DRIVE NEARER TO MADRID

Continued From Page One

—and that after the death penalty had been resorted to."

In another article the Claridad adds that if the heroic resistance can be maintained for a few more days, the present danger will have disappeared.

Madrid Suburb Is Bombed

By The Associated Press.

MADRID, Nov. 2.—The quiet suburb of Leganes, seven miles southwest of Madrid, felt the brunt of Insurgent bombings and shellings today. The terminal of one of Madrid's street-car lines in Leganes was bombarded, but it escaped serious damage. Government gun crews blazed back at the Insurgents.

With the main line of the Rebel attack on Madrid running from the south to the west, the government also reported heavy fighting on the Guadalajara highroad, about fifteen miles northeast of the capital.

Varela Is 11 Miles From Capital

NAVALCARNERO, Spain, Nov. 2 (P).—General José Varela, after a week-end drive southwest and west of Madrid, commanded a Rebel line about eleven miles from the Spanish capital tonight.

His infantrymen drove tow. d Mostoles, despite heavy government artillery fire, after yesterday's capture of Brunete in a strong offensive in which, the Rebel command said, at least 500 of Madrid's soldiers were killed. Mostoles lies only ten miles southwest of the capital.

An unsuccessful counter-attack by government troops at Parla, eleven miles south of Madrid, cost the lives of 300 militiamen, the Rebels de—

SPANISH REFUGEES ON THEIR WAY TO MADRID

Associated Press Photo.

Mothers and children, forced to leave their homes in the fighting area, on a weary trek toward the capital, whence they hoped to be sent to the coast for safety.

UPHOLDS HIGH TARIFF ON JAPANESE SHOES | **Rebels Bomb Red Cross, Declares Briton in Spain** | **FRENCH ANTI-FASCISTS DENOUNCE MUSSOLINI**

Wireless to THE NEW YORK TIMES

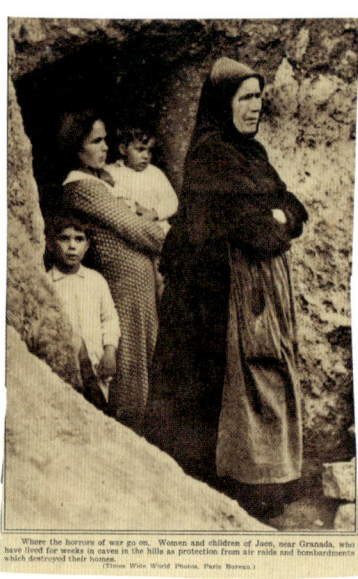

Where the horrors of war go on. Women and children of Jaen, near Granada, who have lived for weeks in caves in the hills as protection from air raids and bombardments which destroyed their homes.
(Times Wide World Photos, Paris Bureau.)

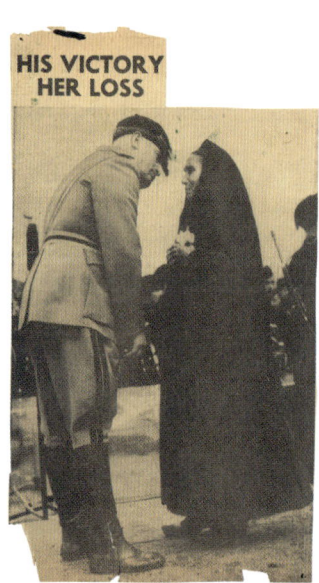

HIS VICTORY HER LOSS

Photographer unknown
"Spanish Refugees on Their Way to Madrid,"
New York Times, November 3, 1936

Photographer unknown, Times Wide World Photos, Paris Bureau
"Where the Horrors of War Go On. Women and Children of Jaen, near Granada ... Air Raids and Bombardments which Destroyed Their Homes,"
c. 1935–36
Unknown source

Photographer unknown
"His Victory, Her Loss," c. 1936
Unknown source

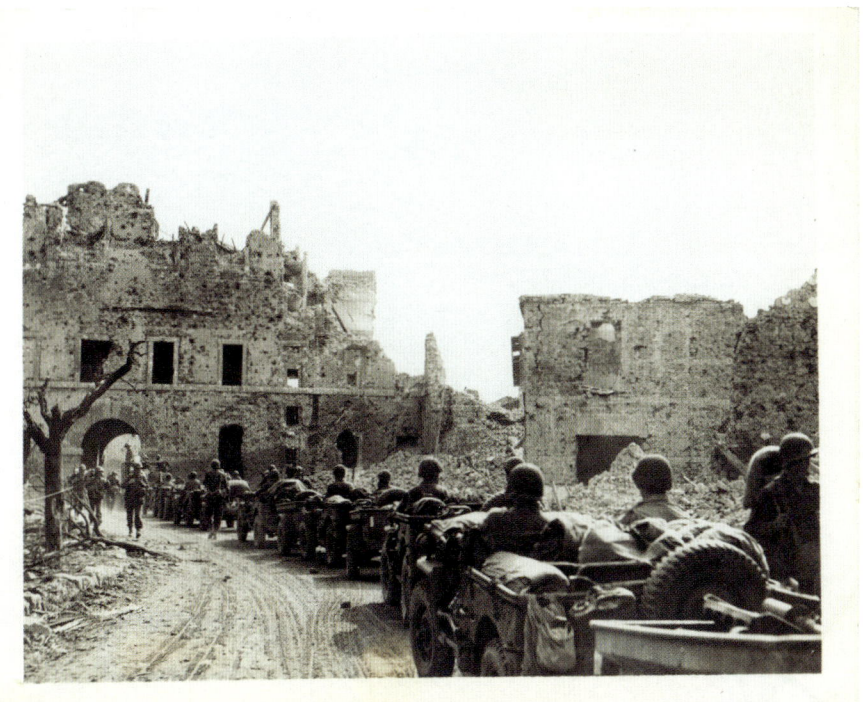

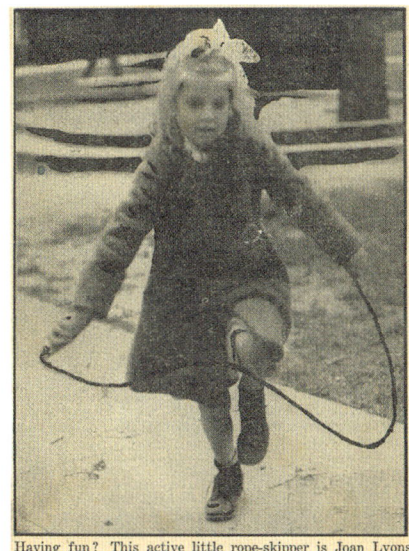

Having fun? This active little rope-skipper is Joan Lyons who lives with her parents, Mr. and Mrs. John H. Lyons, at 1644 21st-st nw.

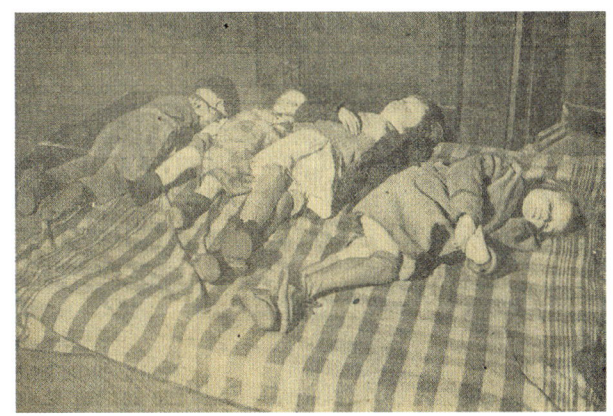

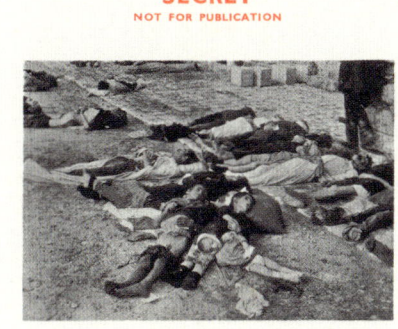

SECRET
NOT FOR PUBLICATION

26

Photographer unknown, ACME
Parade of Jeeps Through Cisterna Castle, Italy, June 9, 1944

Photographer unknown
"Having Fun? This Active Little Rope-Skipper is Joan Lyons...,"
c. 1937
Unknown source

Photographer unknown
"Untitled [Children Sleeping]," c. 1934–44
Unknown source

The Royal Hellenic Government, ed.
Conditions in Greece: Confidential Photographic Record
1942, p. 26

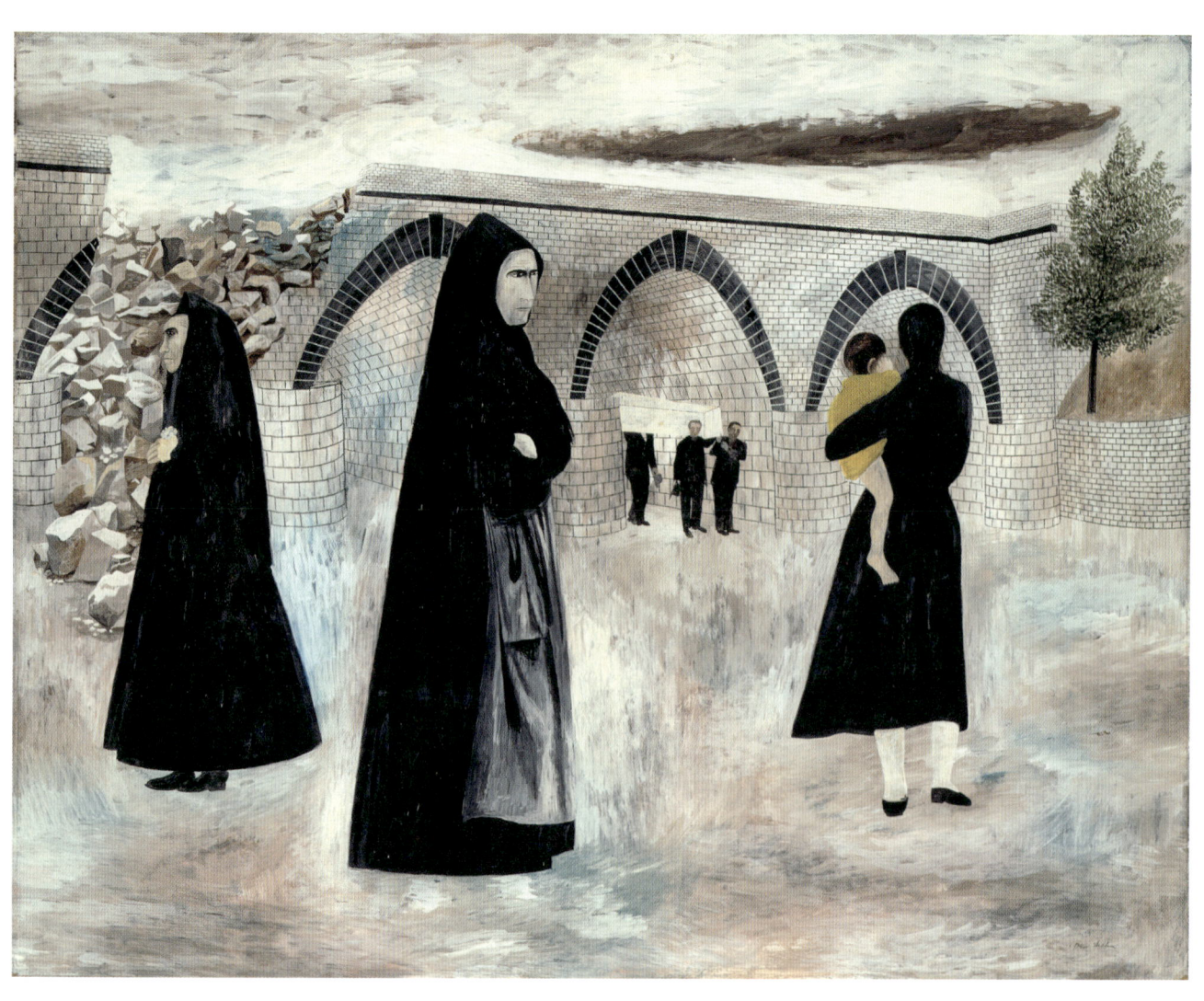

Italian Landscape
1943–44

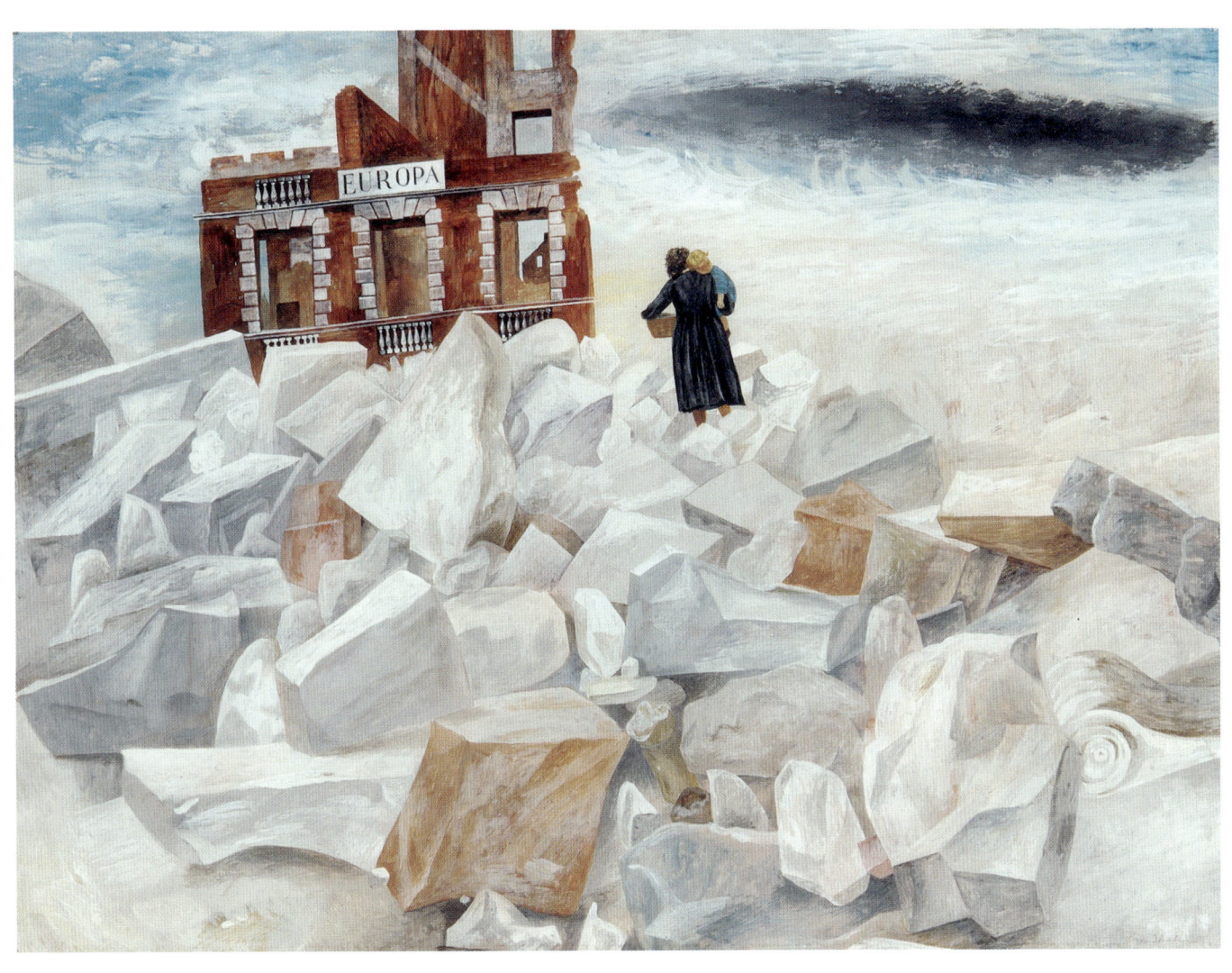

Italian Landscape II: Europa
1944

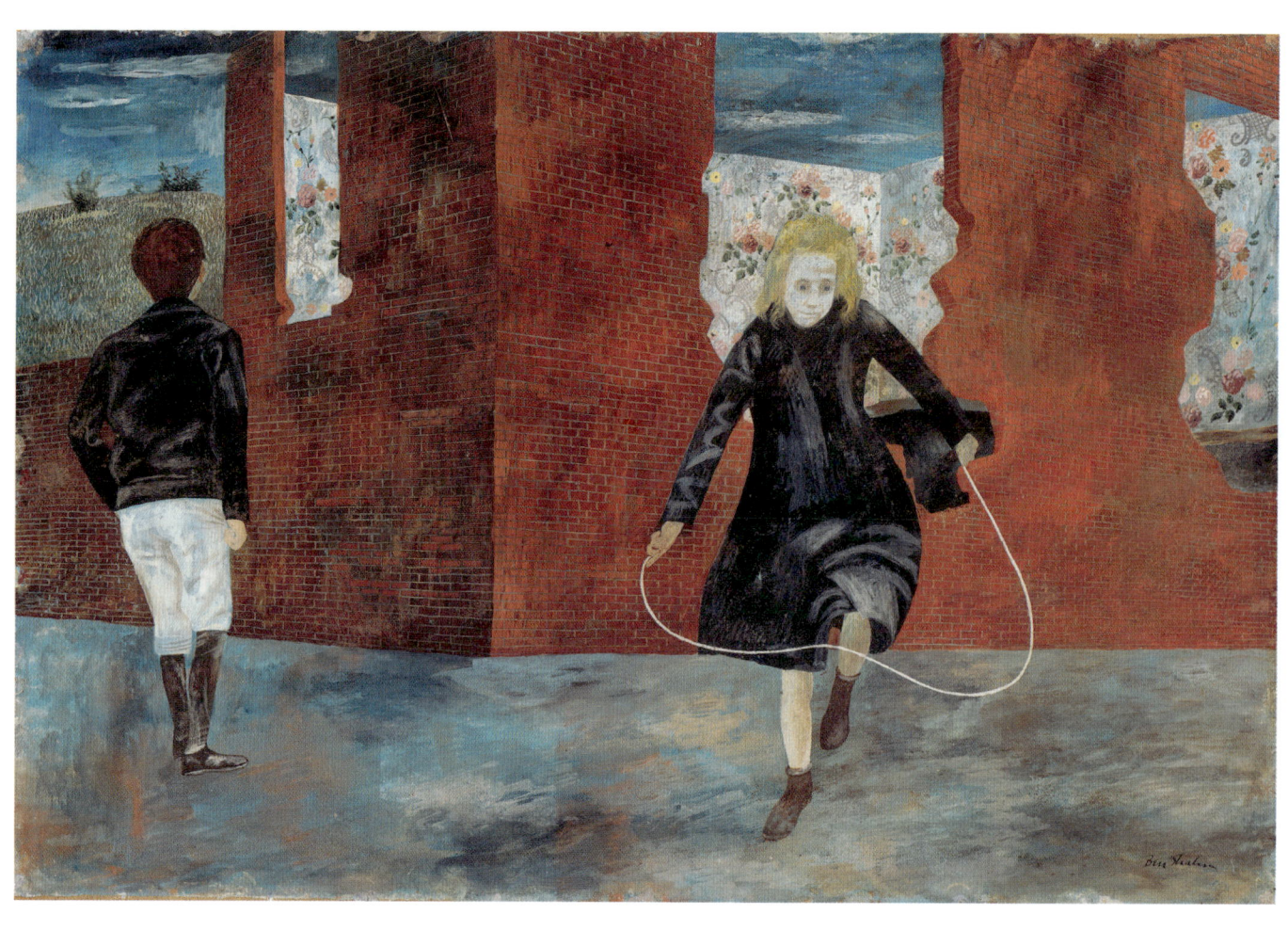

Girl Skipping Rope
1943

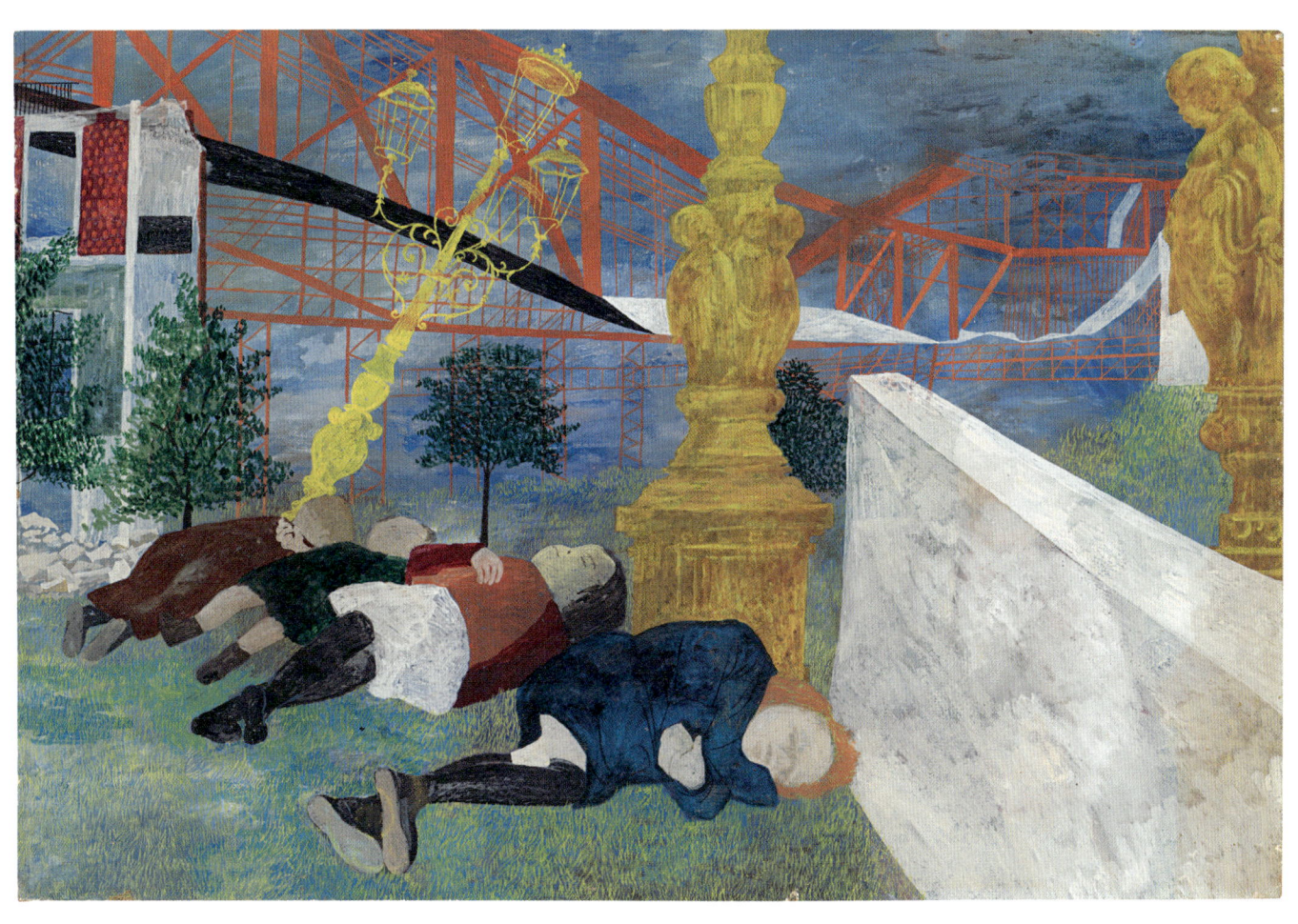

Cherubs and Children
1944

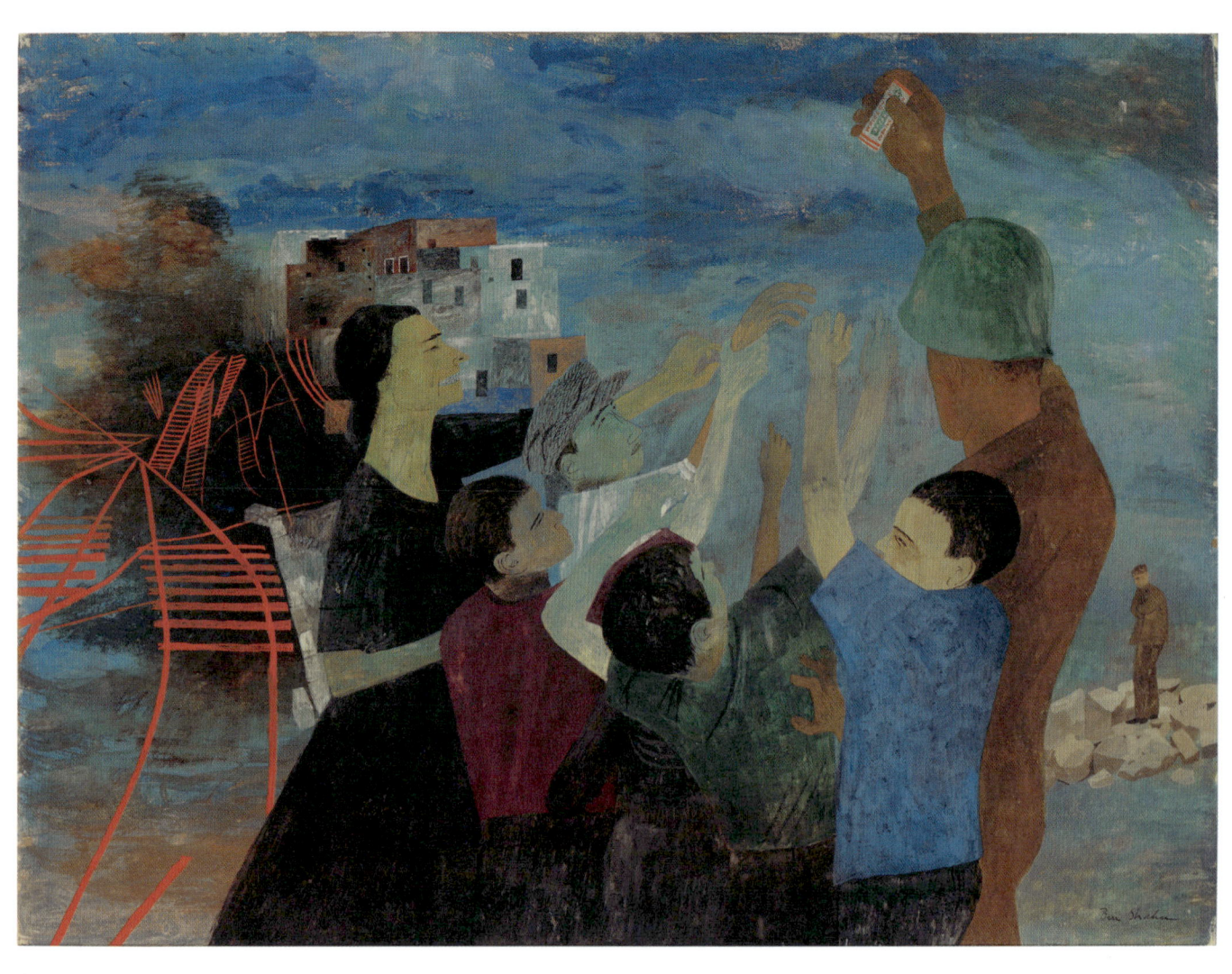

Remember the Wrapper
1945

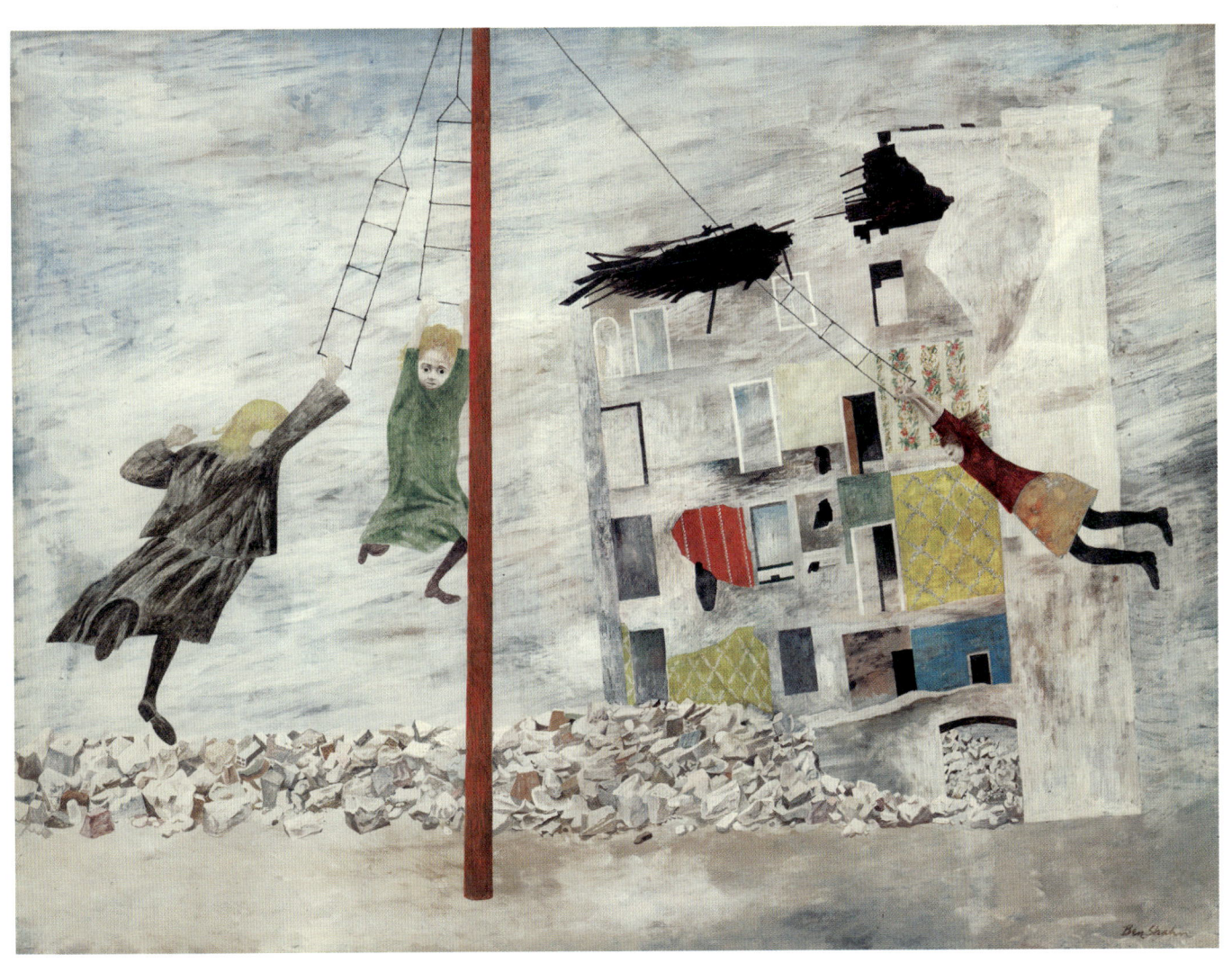

Liberation
1945

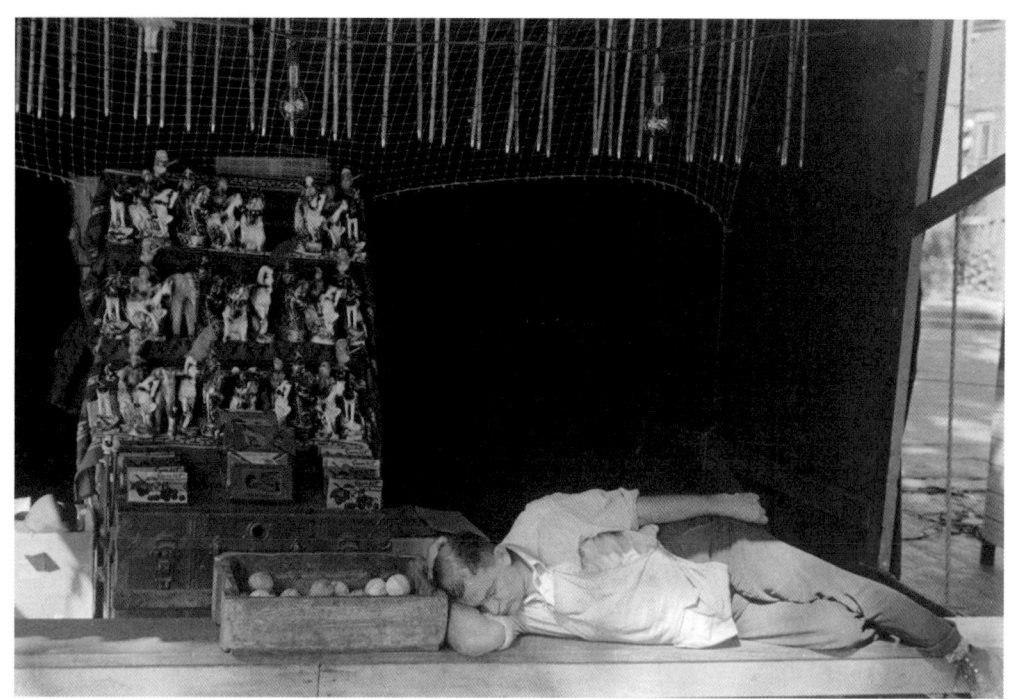

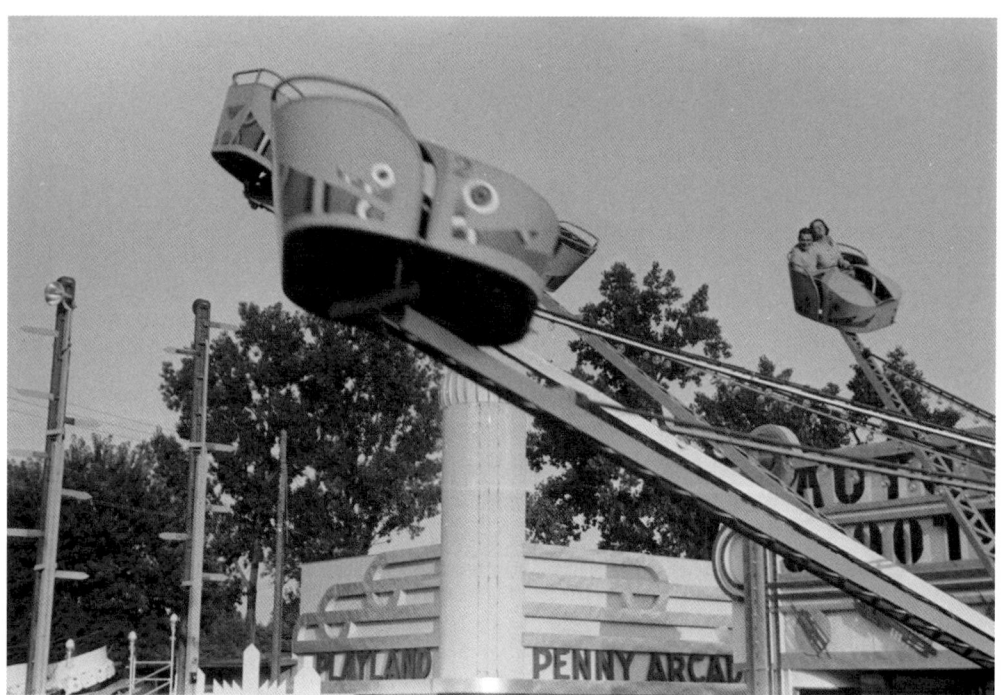

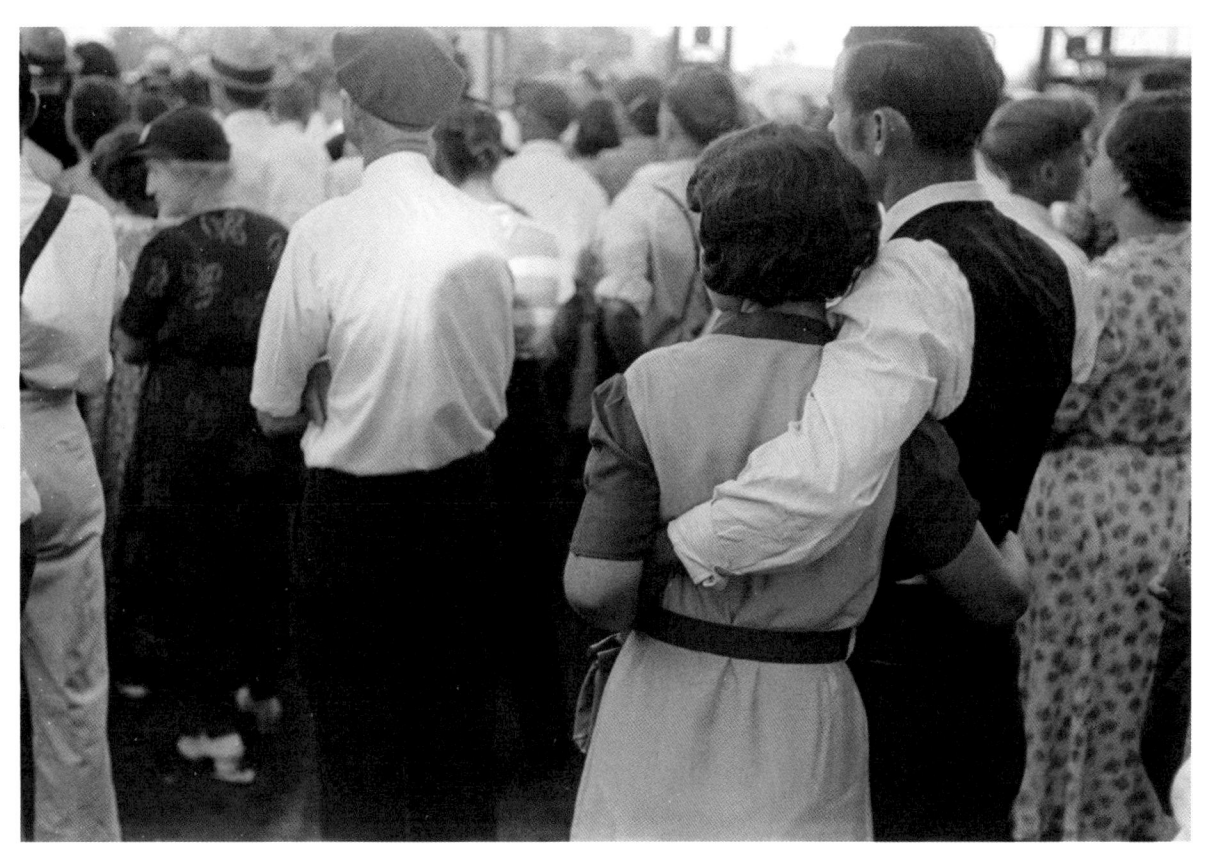

"Business was Bad," World War Veterans' Homecoming and Carnival, London, Ohio
Summer 1938

Scene at Buckeye Lake Amusement Park, near Columbus, Ohio
Summer 1938

At Ashville July 4th Celebration, Ashville, Ohio
July–August 1938

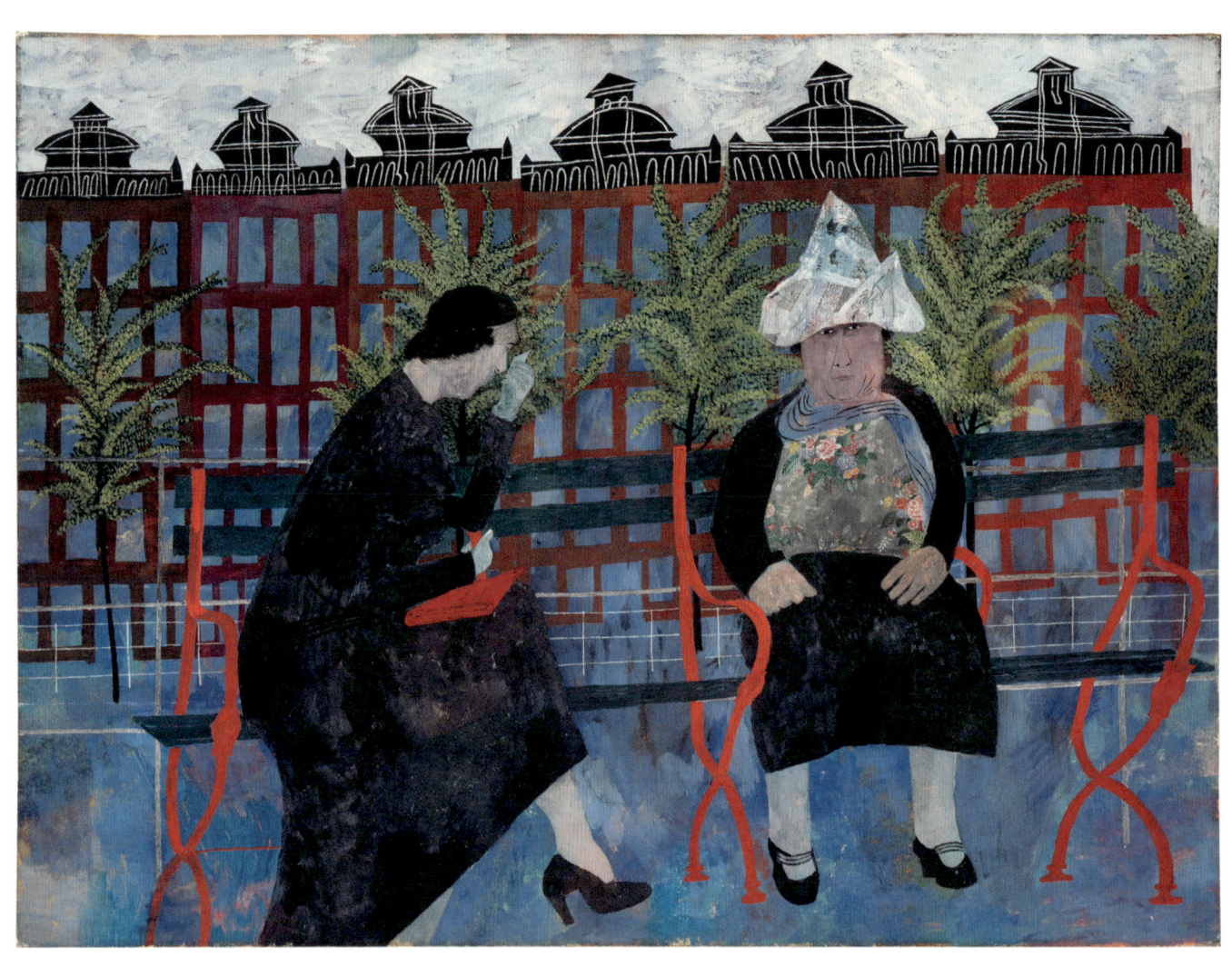

Nearly Everyone Reads the Bulletin
1946

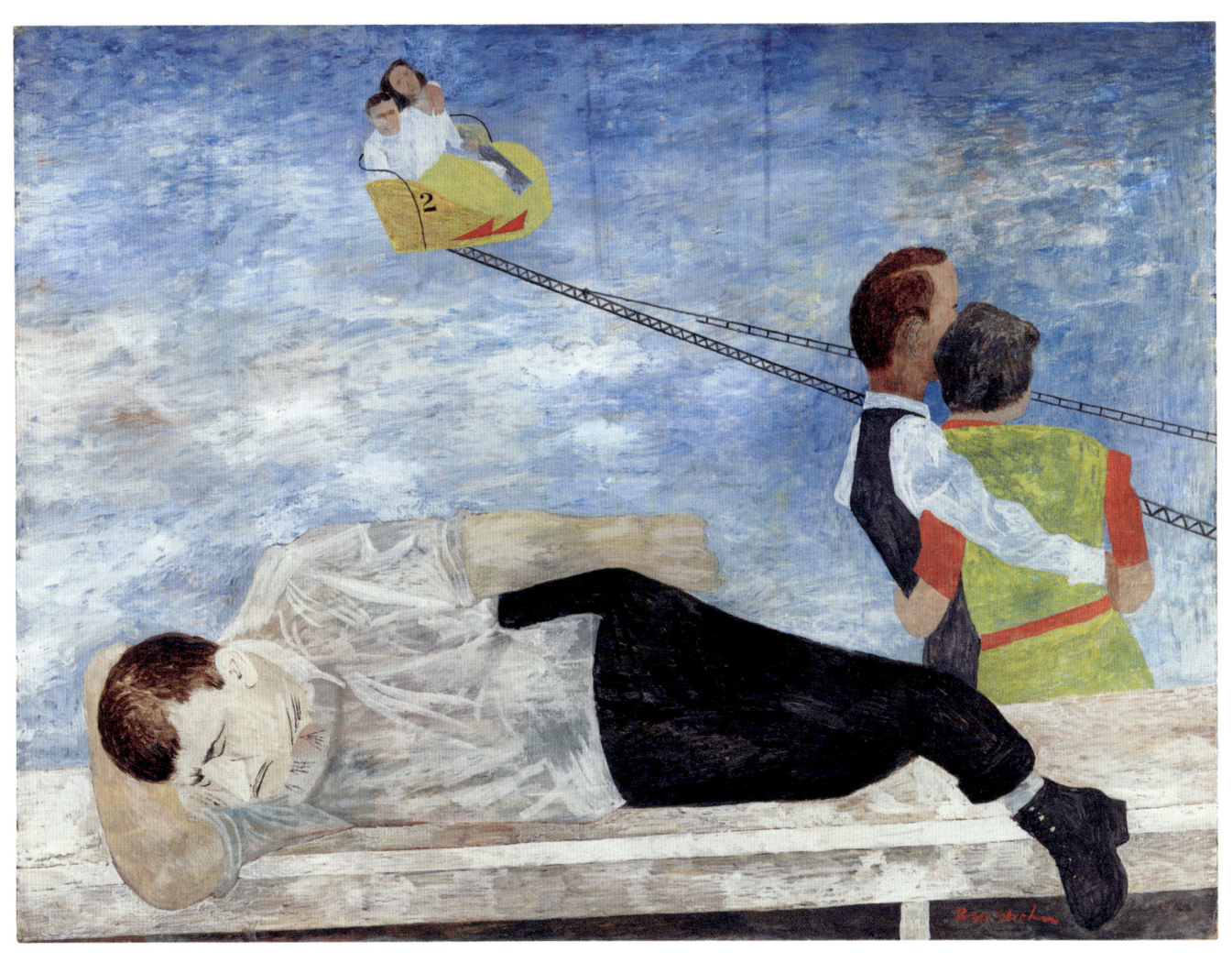

Carnival
1946

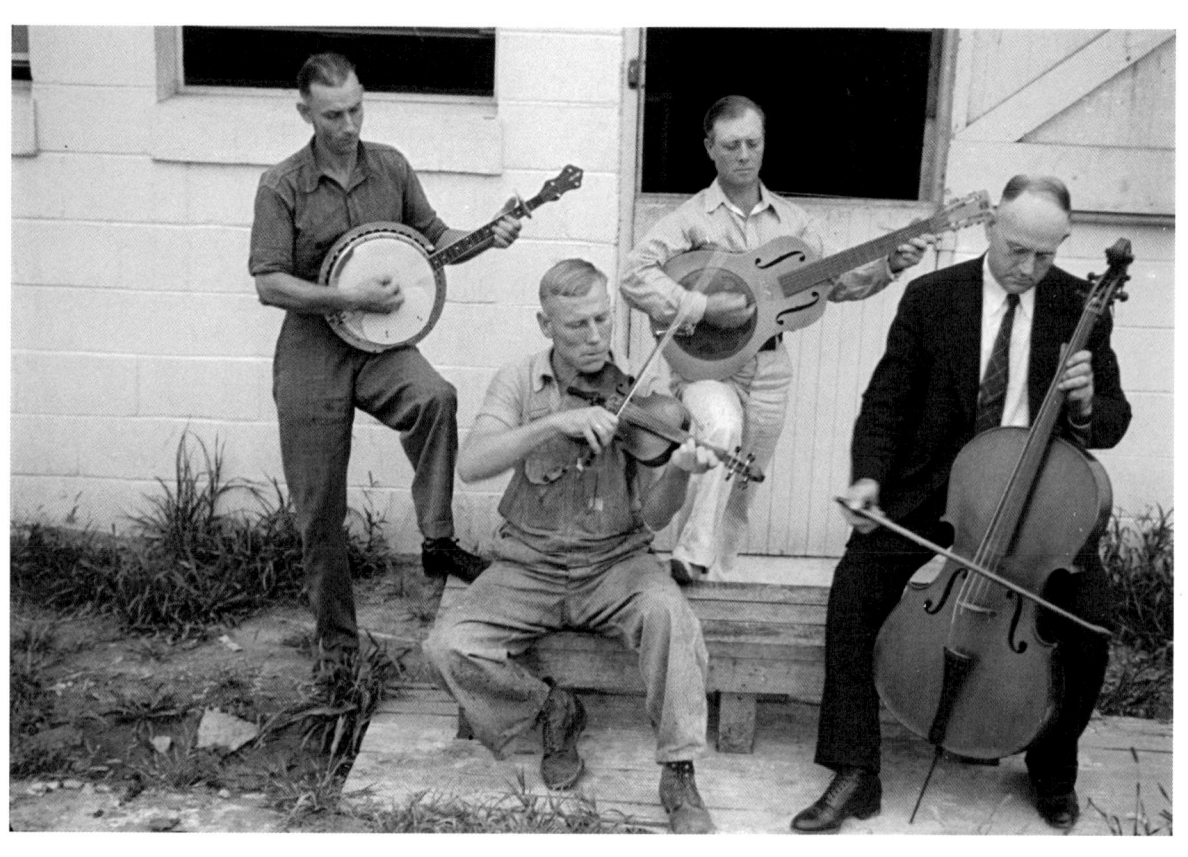

Practicing for the Westmoreland Fair, Pennsylvania
1937

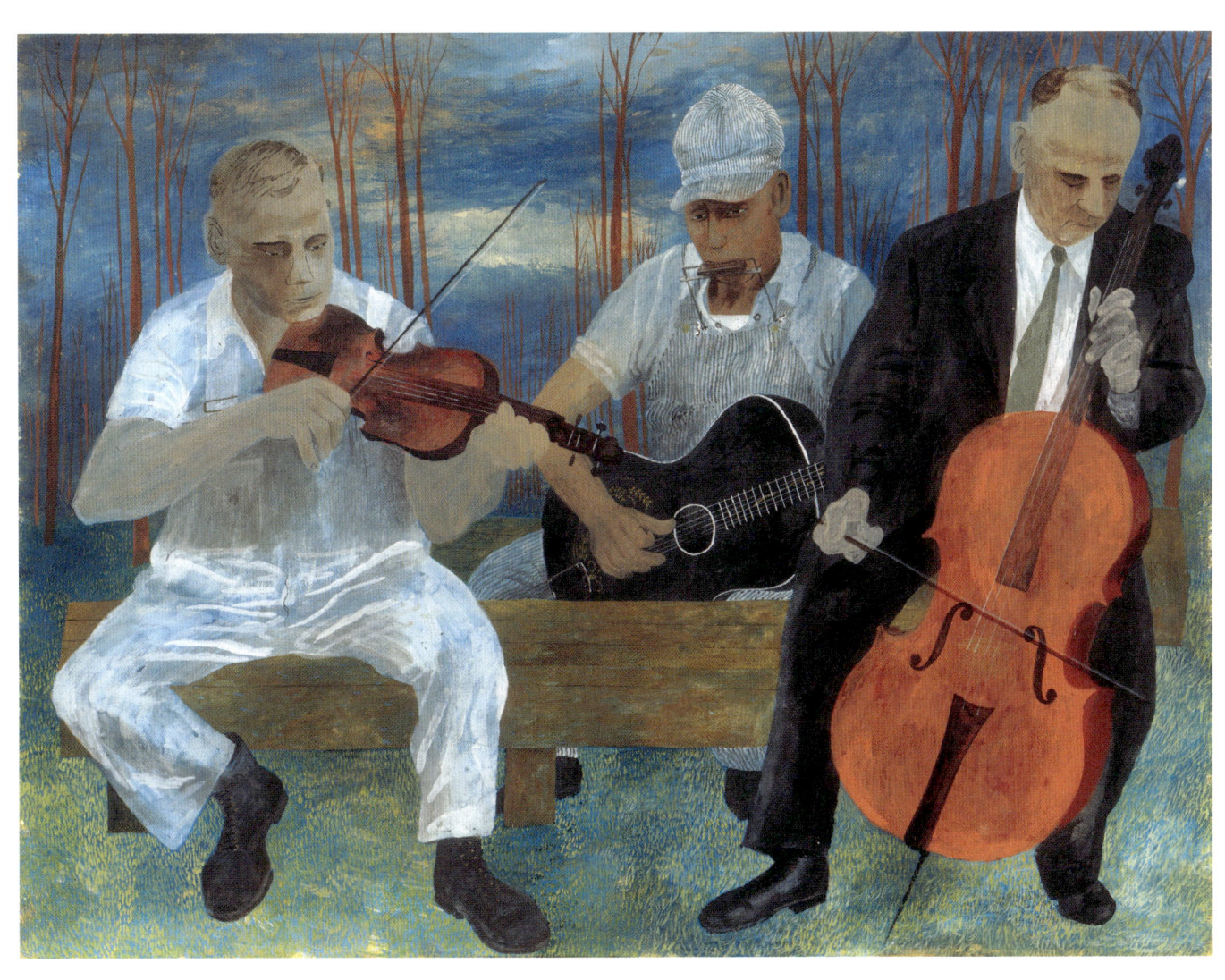

Four Piece Orchestra
1944

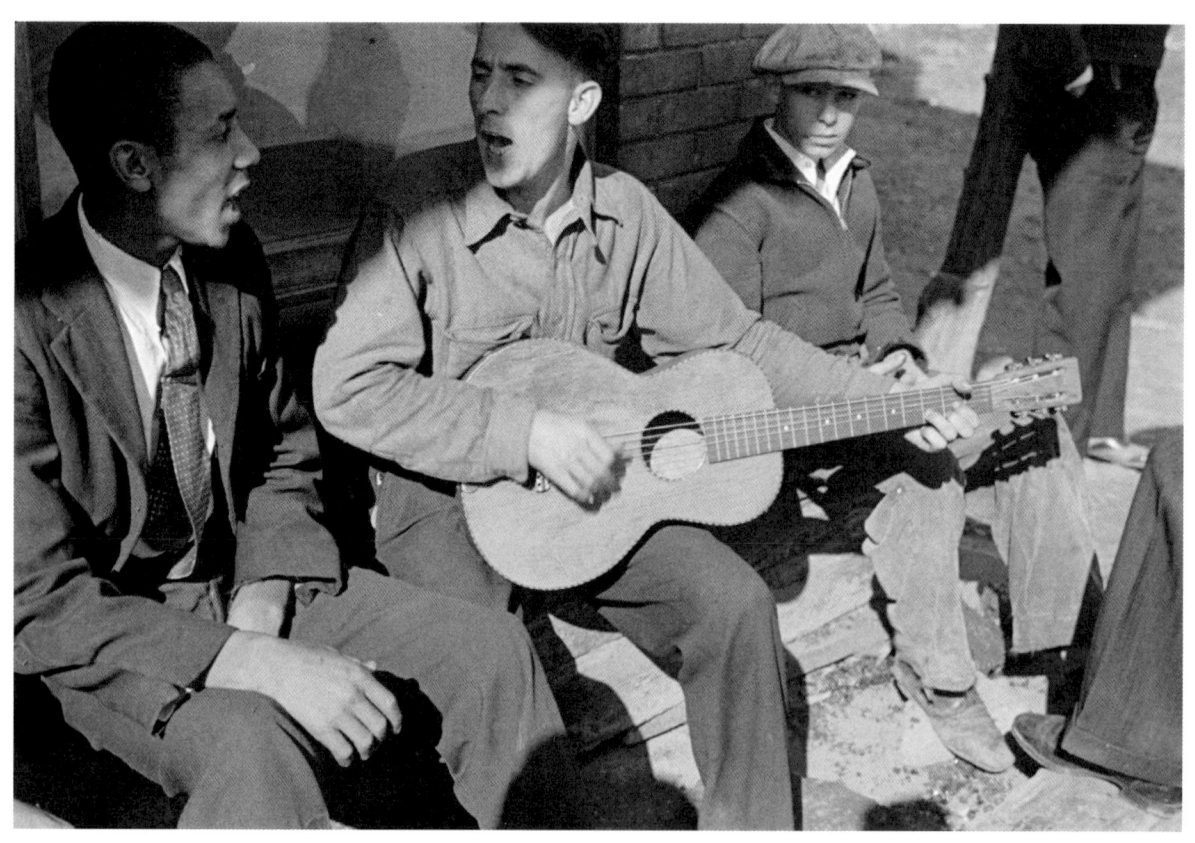

Untitled [possibly related to: *Doped Singer, "Love oh, love,*
oh keerless love," Scotts Run, West Virginia. Relief Investigator
Reported a Number of Dope Cases at Scotts Run]
October 1935

Nocturne
1949

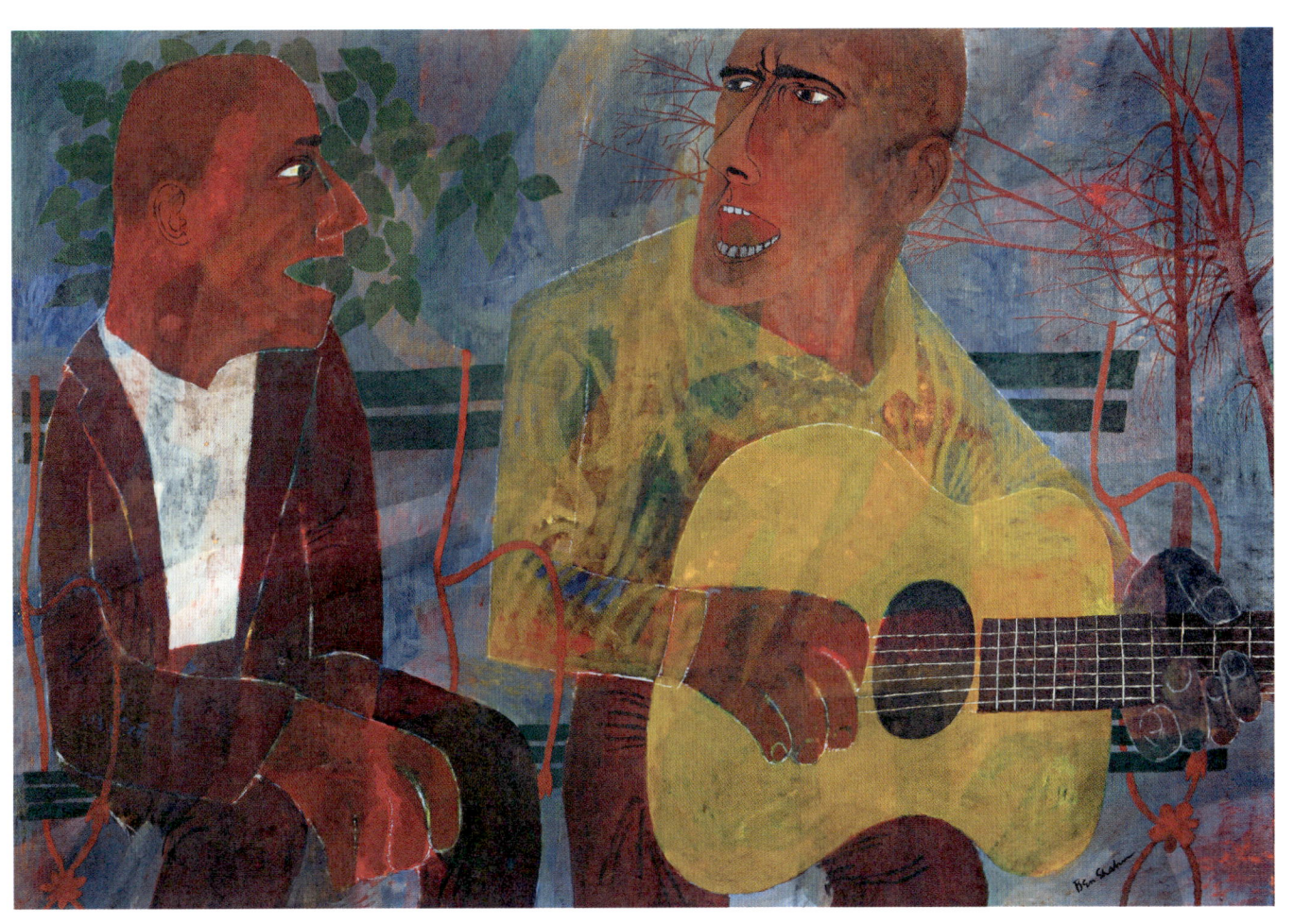

Allegory
1948

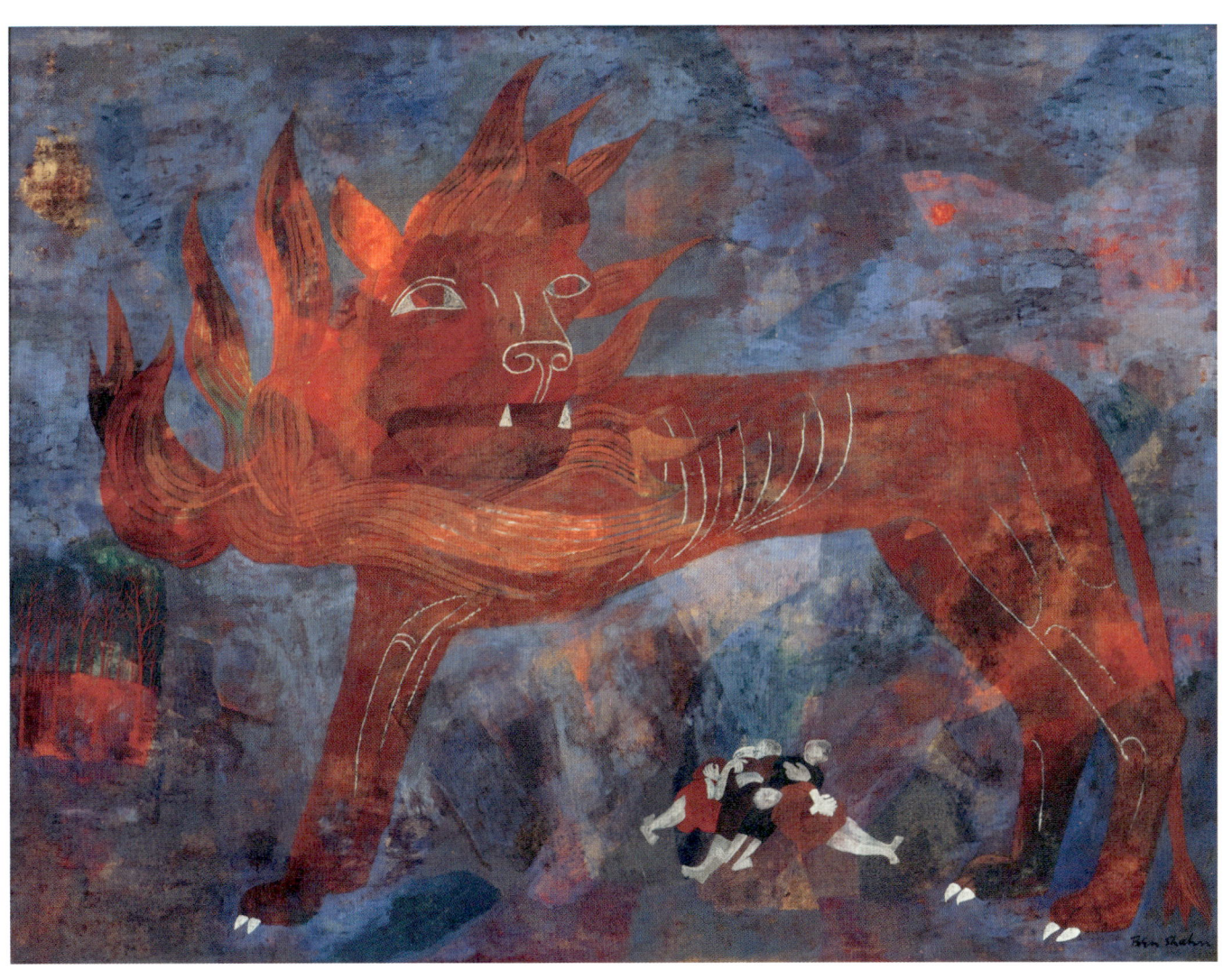

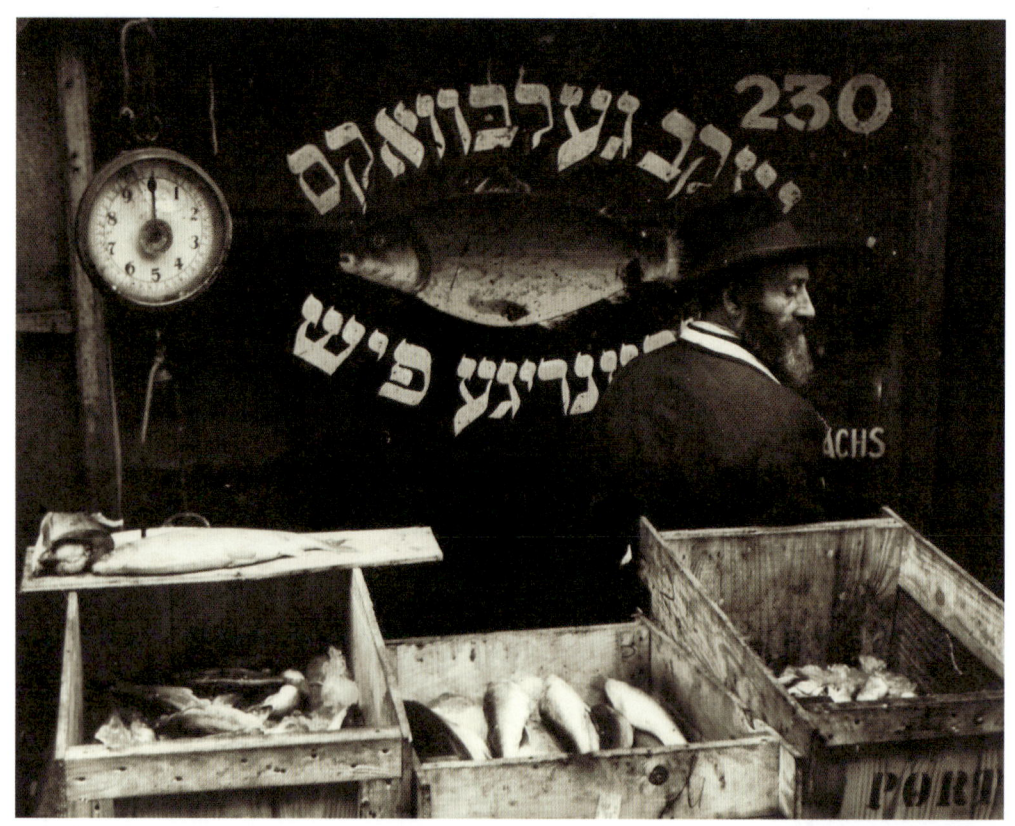

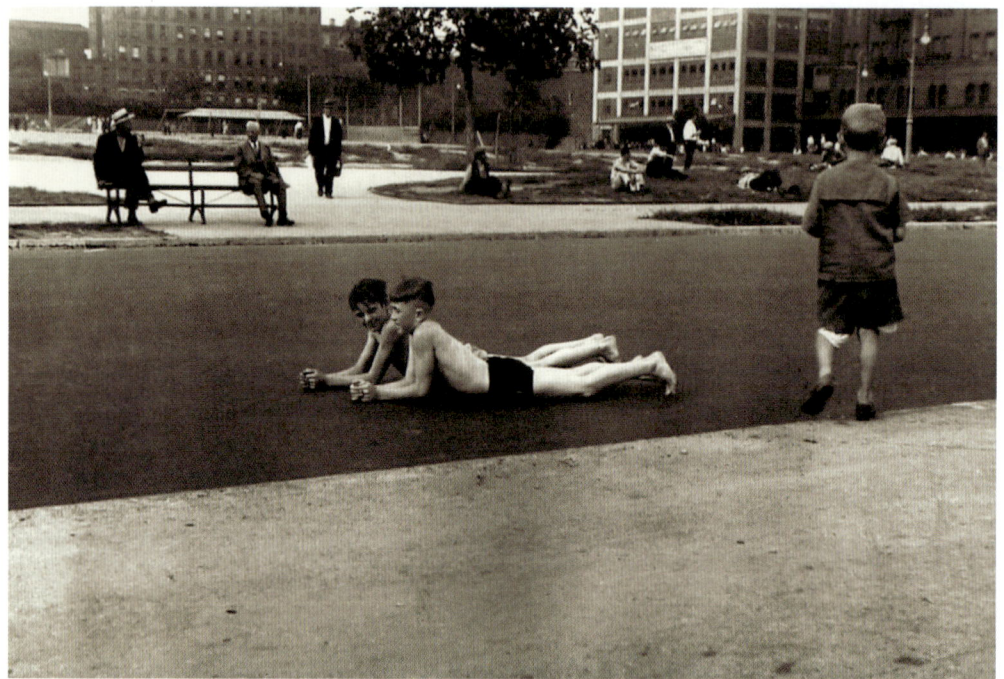

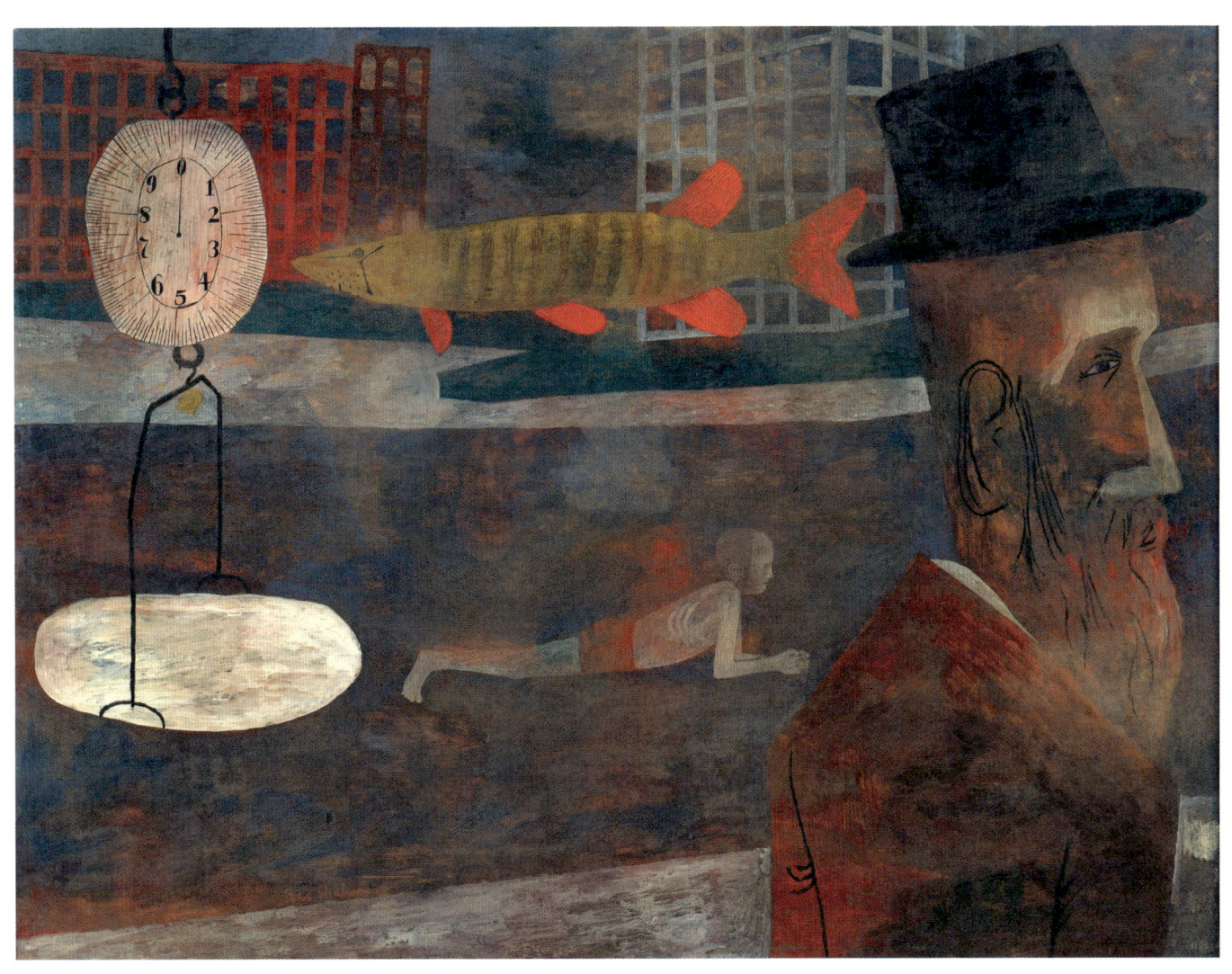

Untitled [Lower East Side, New York City]
April 1936

Untitled [Lower East Side, New York City]
c. 1932–35

New York
1947

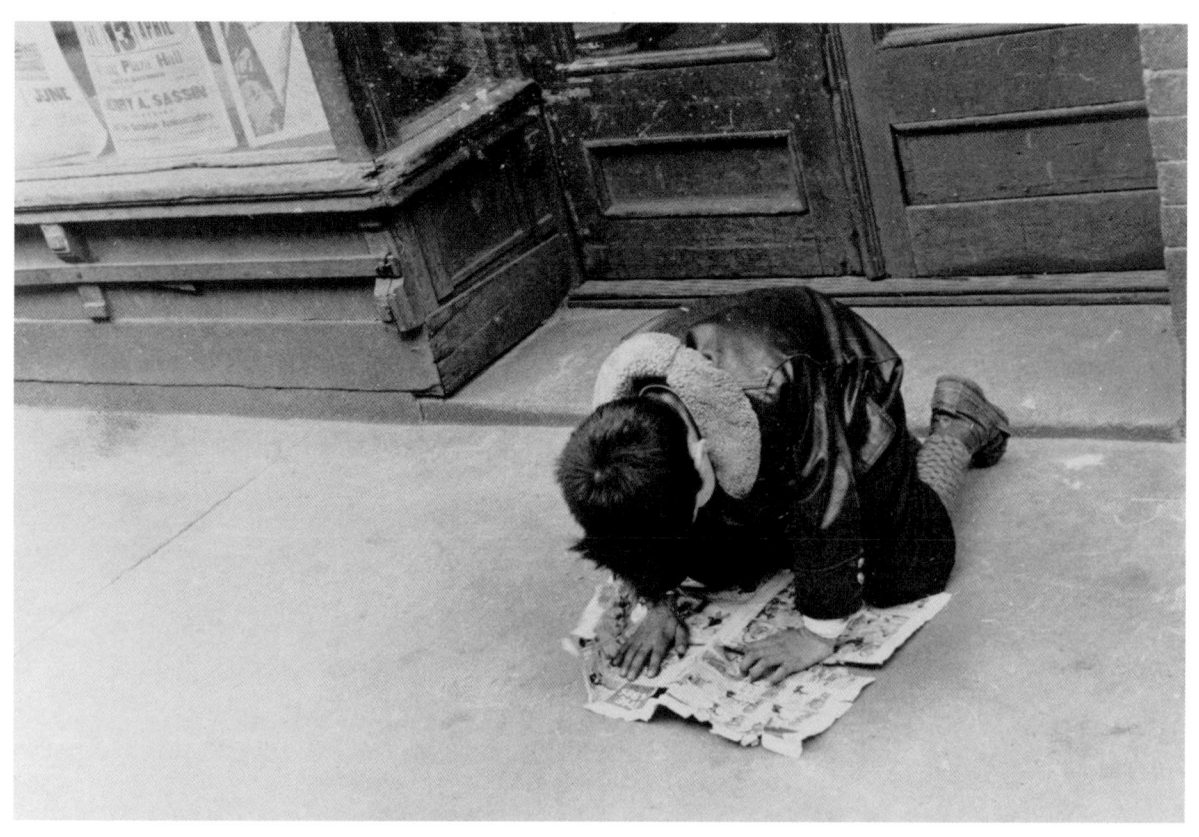

Untitled [Greenwich Village, New York City]
1935

World's Greatest Comics
1946

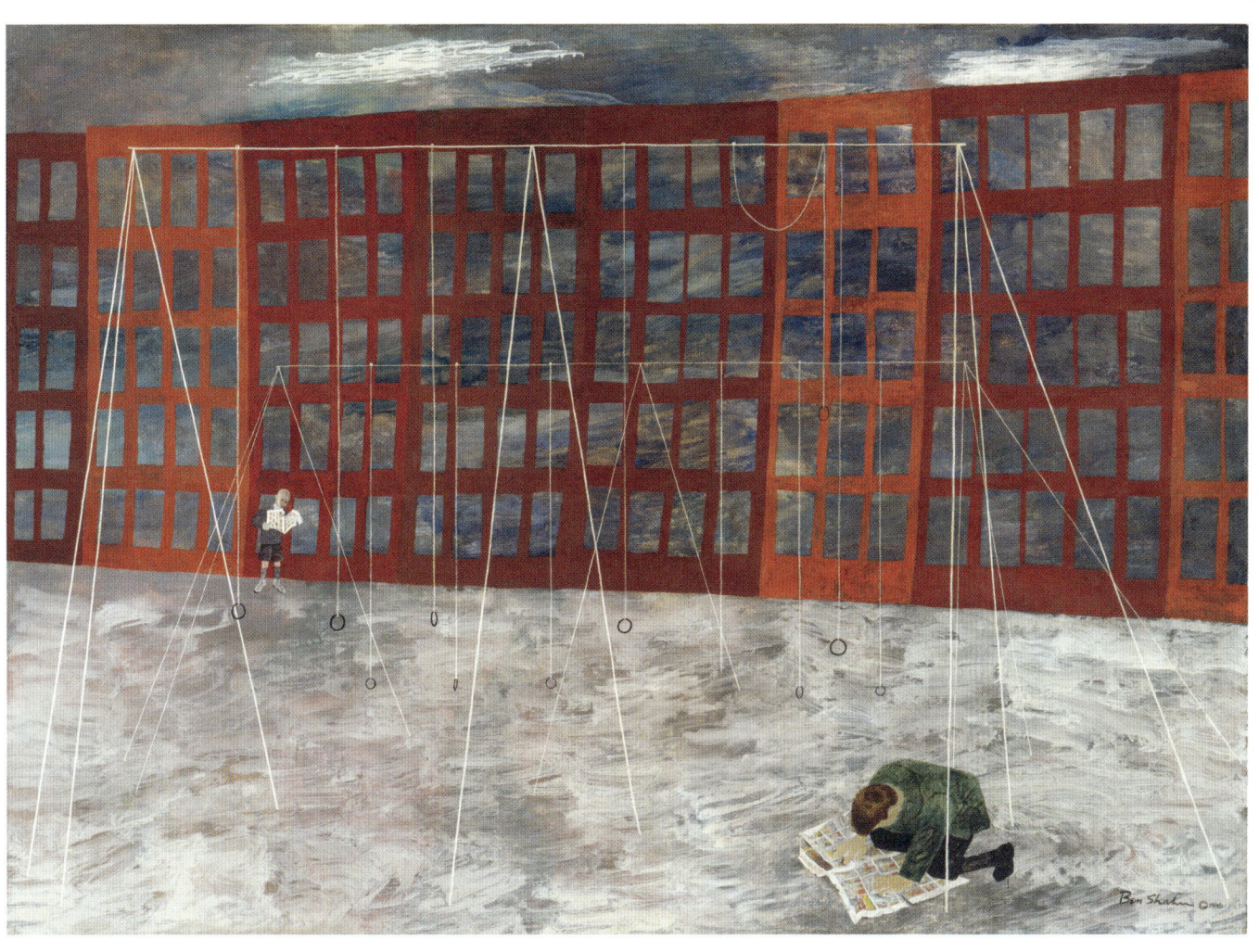

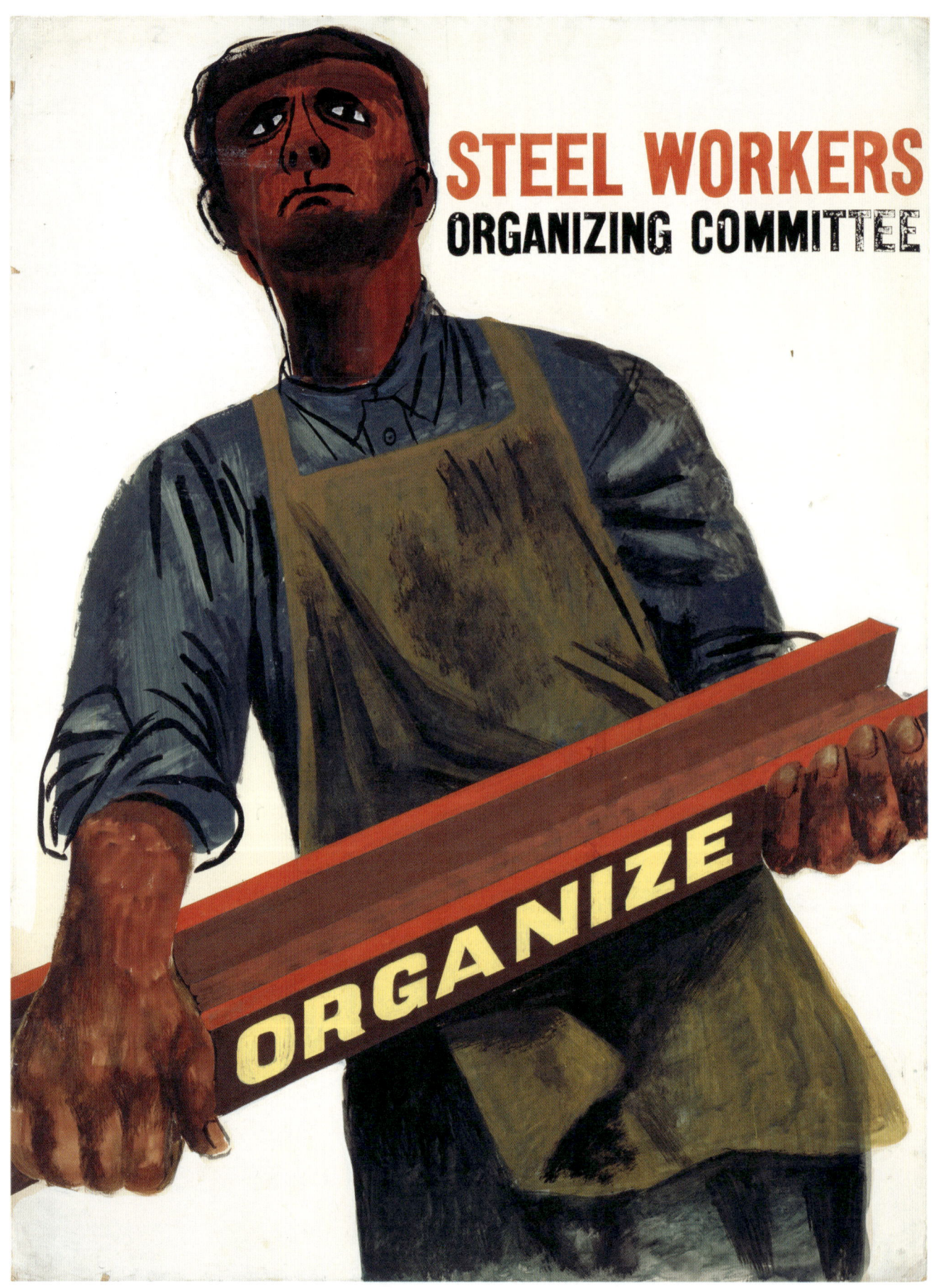

Ben Shahn was committed to the cause of labor in the U.S. as early as the 1930s—inspired by the nationwide upsurge of worker militancy and strike activity that led to the passage of the National Labor Relations Act of 1935. But his labor-related work gained greater attention with the posters he designed between 1944 and 1946, when he served as chief artist and director of the Graphic Arts Division of the Congress of Industrial Organizations-Political Action Committee (CIO-PAC). Established in July 1943, CIO-PAC aimed to circumvent the financial restrictions that unions faced in making contributions to political campaigns. Shahn's posters—with figures featuring large, strong, and hard-worked hands—speak to the dignity of manual labor and to Shahn's values as the son and grandson of woodcarvers, who was himself trained as a craftsman lithographer. These posters, which were often preceded or followed by a closely related painting, also express the centrality of labor issues to the Democratic Party at the time.

The graphics Shahn created in 1944 for CIO-PAC and the National Citizens Political Action Committee were used to champion President Franklin Delano Roosevelt's bid for an unprecedented fourth term, picturing FDR as a friend of labor unions and the working man. Posters like *For Full Employment After the War, Register, Vote* (1944), depicting a Black welder with a downward gaze working alongside a white welder looking upward, sought to promote interracial cooperation in the postwar workforce. Because of the Black man's "anxious expression" and his passive, secondary position within the composition, according to a recent argument, the work "creates a simple racial hierarchy and marginalizes the black worker." It has also been critiqued as "fall[ing] short as political action."[1] Yet Shahn's commitment to an integrated and inclusive workforce is given deeper dimension via examination of his source photographs; for the poster, he replaced one of two white welders from one photograph with the image of a Black welder from another photograph. Also, Shahn earlier used this same interracial imagery in *Our Manpower* (c. 1943), a radical (and rejected) OWI poster design that included various captions touting the racial, ethnic, and religious diversity of the U.S. labor force as its strength. Alas, Shahn's vision was largely aspirational, for although the CIO and affiliated industrial unions pushed for racial integration in the labor movement, discrimination in local unions persisted, especially in the segregated Jim Crow South. The CIO's major campaign of 1946 to organize nonunionized industries in the South ultimately failed, in part because white workers rallied to the rhetoric of white supremacy over the promise of unionization.

By 1946, given that President Harry S. Truman's support of labor unions was ambivalent and that he was hostile to the tactics of its key leaders,

Organize… Steel Workers Organizing Committee
1930s

Shahn's posters, while still backing the Democratic Party, took on a more anxious tone. Instead of showing Truman, they focus on a "greater sense of crisis, of an embattled labor force." They display workers' hands in tension and strife, foreshadowing the weakened position of organized labor in American society. *Break Reaction's Grip* (1946), with its businessman's hand in coat sleeve and shirt cuff gripped by a worker's larger, sleeveless arm, speaks to the struggle between big business and labor.[2] *For All These Rights We've Just Begun to Fight* (1946) refers to FDR's January 1944 Economic Bill of Rights speech. With its defiant figure whose arm is raised amidst colorful protest placards, this militant poster demands every American's right to a job, an adequate wage, a decent home, medical care, economic protection in hardship, and a good education. *We Want Peace* (1946), which repurposes a Shahn wartime painting, poster design, and his Resettlement Administration photographs of coal miners' children in West Virginia, shows a sickly boy reaching out with a pleading hand. Dominating the space, this looming figure signifies the casualties of World War II and suggests the postwar fears of future destruction in the emergent atomic age.

Compounding the problems confronted by labor was the crisis within the labor movement itself. Fueled by the passage of the Taft-Hartley Act of 1947, which restricted the power of labor unions, "conservative forces within the CIO [would] expel communists or suspected communists from the leadership of member unions and from the rank and file." Around 1947 Shahn cut ties with the CIO and turned his attention to the 1948 presidential campaign of the Progressive Party candidate Henry Wallace, whose postwar vision for a "century of the common man" promoted freedom and global peace.[3] He created graphics for this short-lived left-wing party—a safe haven for communists, "fellow travelers," and antiwar liberals in the emerging reactionary political climate. Yet the Progressive Party struggled with infiltration from, and accusations of being controlled by, the Communist Party and Wallace proved to be a complicated, contradictory figure. Despite Shahn's disillusionment, during this time he also fervently embraced another labor-oriented project: drawings for a March 1948 article by John Bartlow Martin in *Harper's Magazine*, which exposed the unsafe working conditions that caused a 1947 coal mining disaster in Centralia, Illinois—a catastrophe immortalized by folksinger Woody Guthrie.[4]

1. John Ott, "Graphic Consciousness: The Visual Cultures of Integrated Industrial Unions at Midcentury," *American Quarterly* 66, no. 4 (December 2014): 903, 901. See also Katherine Mintie, "Art and Politics in the 1940s: Ben Shahn," *Index* (April 22, 2020), harvardartmuseums.org/article/art-and-politics-in-the-1940s-ben-shahn, and Steven Reich's research on race and the U.S. labor movement.

2. Frances K. Pohl, *Ben Shahn* (San Francisco: Pomegranate Books, 1993), 21. See also Pohl, *Ben Shahn: New Deal Artist in a Cold War Climate, 1947–1954* (Austin: University of Texas Press, 1989).

3. Pohl, *Ben Shahn*, 22.

4. On the *Harper's* assignment and on labor and leisure in Shahn's work, see John Fagg's essay in this catalogue. See also Fagg, "Ben Shahn: After the Retrospective and in Response to Disaster," unpublished lecture, "1940s in Focus: American Art during the Decade of Transition," Centre for American Art, The Courtauld Institute, June 3–4, 2021.

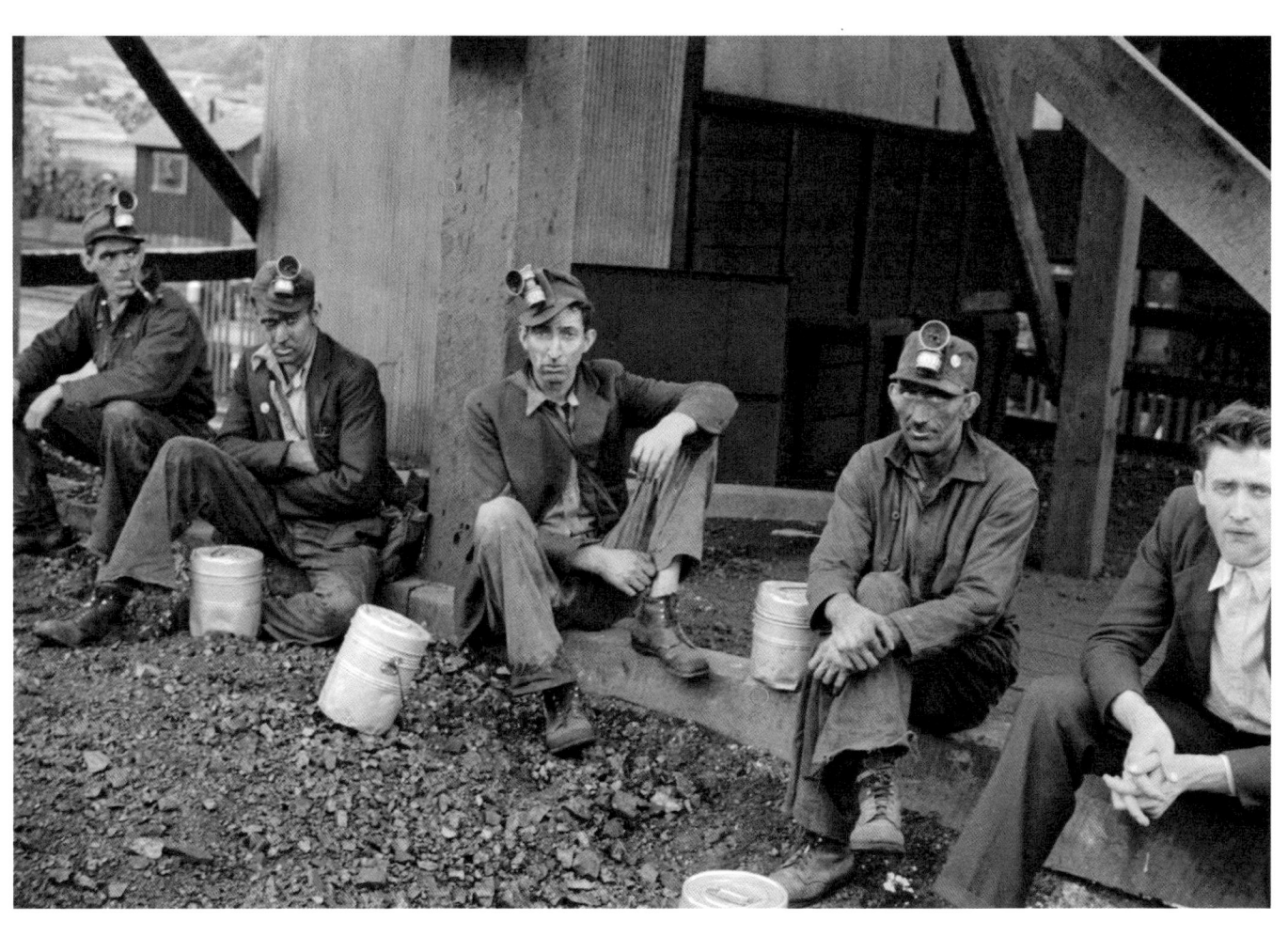

Kentucky Coal Miners, Jenkins, Kentucky
October 1935

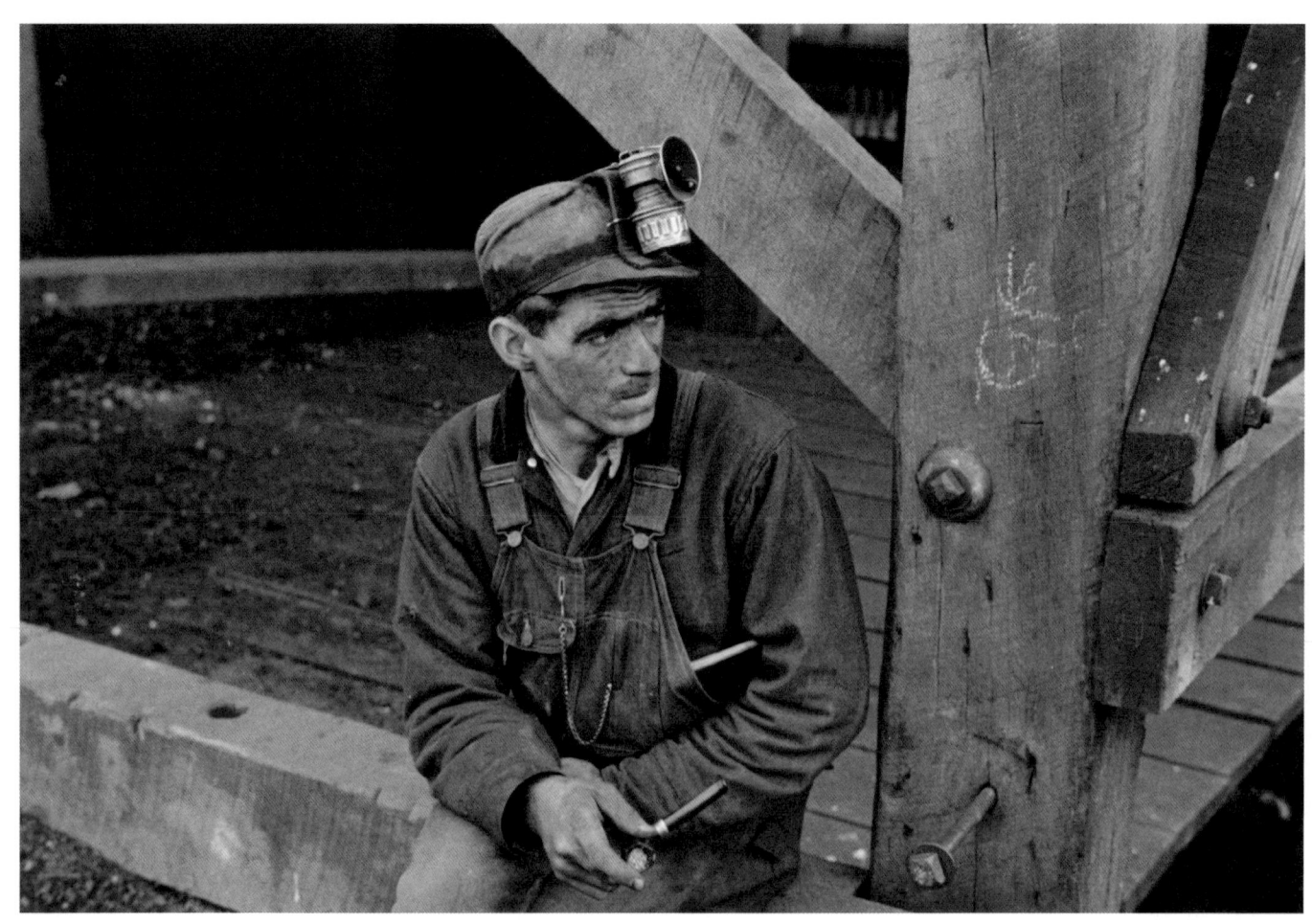

Kentucky Coal Miner, Jenkins, Kentucky
October 1935

Untitled [Grinning Puddler]
c. 1940

The Miner
c. 1948

Harper's Magazine, March 1948, vol. 196, no. 1174, pp. 194–195

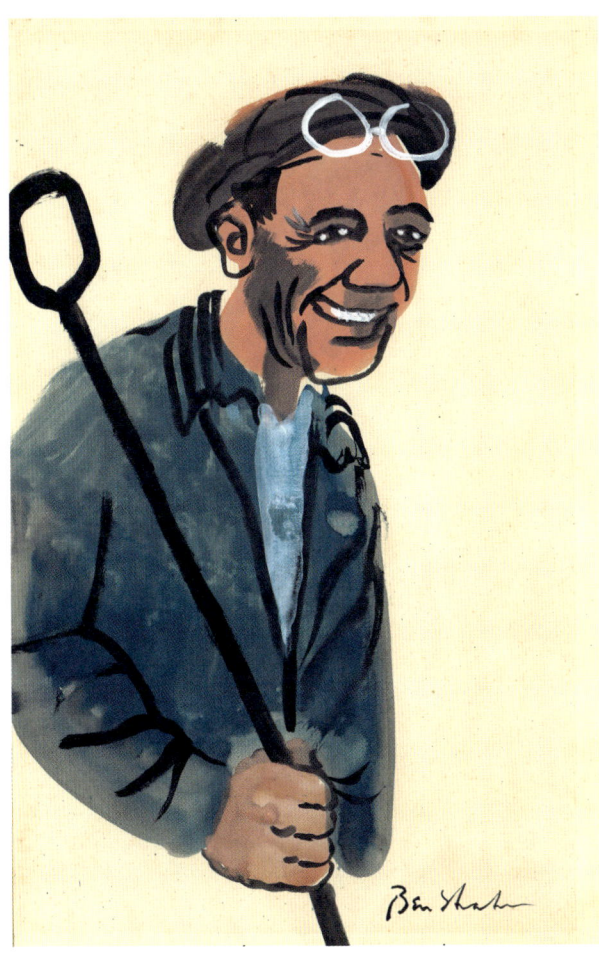

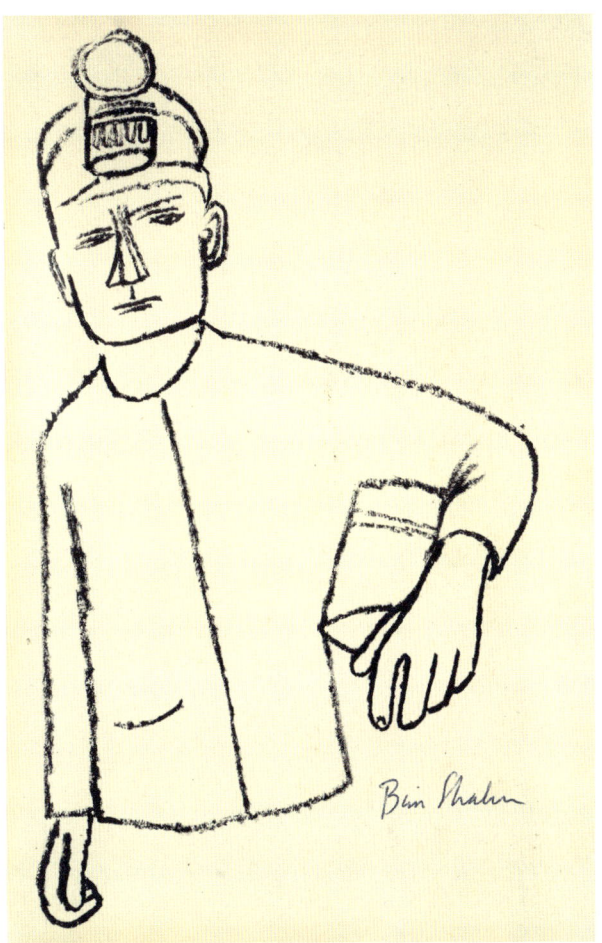

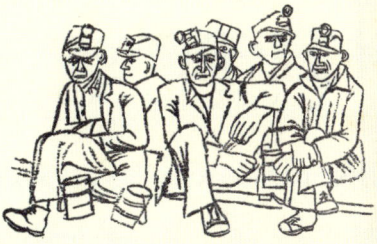

Illinois towns. Nobody knew how bad the explosion was. A sick miner who had just come from underground said he had been walking toward the shaft bottom along the First West Entry when a roaring, smoky wind hit him from behind, and to keep from falling he had begun to run, and he had run all the way to the shaft bottom. Others working near the shaft bottom also had escaped. But more than a hundred men were still below, nearly all of them far back in the mine, and, ominously, nothing had been heard from them.

Superintendent Niermann and several others descended the 540 feet to the bottom. They got aboard a motor, a small electric locomotive used to pull cars of coal, and rode about 1,200 feet south to the intersection of the First West Entry, where the airshaft and fan were located. Here the chunky underground boss, Mine Manager William H. Brown, told them the explosion's great force had knocked out the electric power and reversed the fan; in remedying this Brown had collapsed. Cliff Copple and John Lorenzini, having hauled him to safety, now had gone on down the Main South Entry to look for Cliff Copple's brother. They had not returned. To rescue them Superintendent Niermann sent Rowekamp and two others. Rowekamp, a man of fifty-eight with high cheek bones and thinning hair, headed their motor slowly down Main South through dust and smoke. After a half mile Rowekamp said he saw a light. One of the others said, "Uncle Bill, you are just seeing things," but Rowekamp recalled later, "We got closer and we saw it was a man—Brother Lorenzini." Lorenzini, a wiry agile little man, now was staggering around in the tunnel, flailing his arms, crazed with gas and smoke. Where was his buddy, Cliff Copple? They went a little farther. One of them was getting sick from the fumes. They found water and washed their faces. They reached a place where the roof comes down low. The smoke was billowing through thick. Copple must be beyond. But they would have to crawl; they needed more men and equipment. So they took Lorenzini to the shaft bottom. (Copple died.)

Superintendent Niermann, Mine Manager Brown, and some other men, exploring the First West Entry, had found the pumper, a man of seventy-one. They thought fresh air might revive him but it didn't. They went on. More than a mile back along the First West they found 20 men, 16 dead and four living. The dead were lying on the fireclay floor of the entry as though asleep; gas, not violence, had killed them. The four living were like wild men. One of the rescuers knew that his own father was somewhere back in the mine but they dared go no farther: the corridors were full of gas, the doors and stoppings were scarred by violence—beyond lay the actual area of explosion.

This ended impromptu rescue work. The State Mine Inspector, Driscoll O. Scanlan, took over. It was now 9:00 P.M. on March 25, 1947, five and a half hours after the blast. Thirty-one had come out alive, 17 were known dead. What of the 94 others? This was the question that lay on the minds of those in the crowd all that night and during the succeeding days and nights.

ALREADY the crowd had gathered. Cars clogged the short, black rock road from the highway to the mine, cars bearing curious spectators and relatives and friends of the men entombed. State troopers and deputy sheriffs and the prosecuting attorney came, and officials from the company, the Federal Bureau of Mines, the Illinois Department of Mines and Minerals. Ambulances arrived, and doctors and nurses and Red Cross workers and soldiers with stretchers from Scott Field. Mine rescue teams came, and a federal rescue unit, experts burdened with masks and oxygen tanks and other awkward paraphernalia of disaster.

By now the word had spread all over Centralia, and to other towns and settlements. Centralia is a quiet town on the Illinois prairie, its streets are deserted by nine o'clock, but on this night cars raced late through the streets on terrible errands. Lights burned night-long in the homes of the miners. In a tiny house near a coal mine shaft close by sat a big woman, Mrs. Joe Bryant, surrounded by eight of her children, by relatives and friends, waiting for news of her husband and her first-born son, both trapped; she waited all night, her son's wife with her, both of them pregnant, but there was no news. Some of the miners' women went to the mine. They pressed against the ropes and wires that police had strung to keep them back from the shaft. A bitter, freezing wind was blowing coal dust through the air, and not long after dark it started to rain, a cold winter rain that presently turned to snow, and the hundreds of churning feet and wheels soon whipped the snow and rain and earth into a sticky, gray-tan mud.

When they became too cold the women went to the washhouse, a dim-lit, moist, barnlike building. Here each morning their men donned their working clothes, and now their men's street clothes were hanging from racks by chains and pulleys, so that the washhouse looked like a vast laundry. Each woman—many were widows already, though they refused to believe it—found, without words or prearrangement, her husband's clothes and sat down under them to wait. (This was one place he would surely come if they brought him out alive.) Now and then a rescue worker, exhausted and half-sick with fumes, would come in for coffee or whiskey, and when the door opened the women would look up; but the rescuer would only shake his head, and the women would look back down at the damp concrete floor. Outside, the hoisting machinery would rumble and the cables sway taut and the cage would come up, sometimes with only the rescuers, sometimes with a stretcher; and sometimes nobody could hold back the crowd. Off in the distance the sky glowed red above the Illinois Central shops, and, closer by, the mine buildings loomed black against the sky; but to the east, beyond the lighted taverns, there was nothing but the dark Illinois plains.

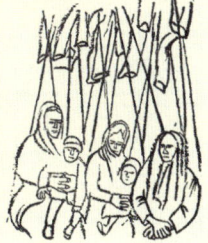

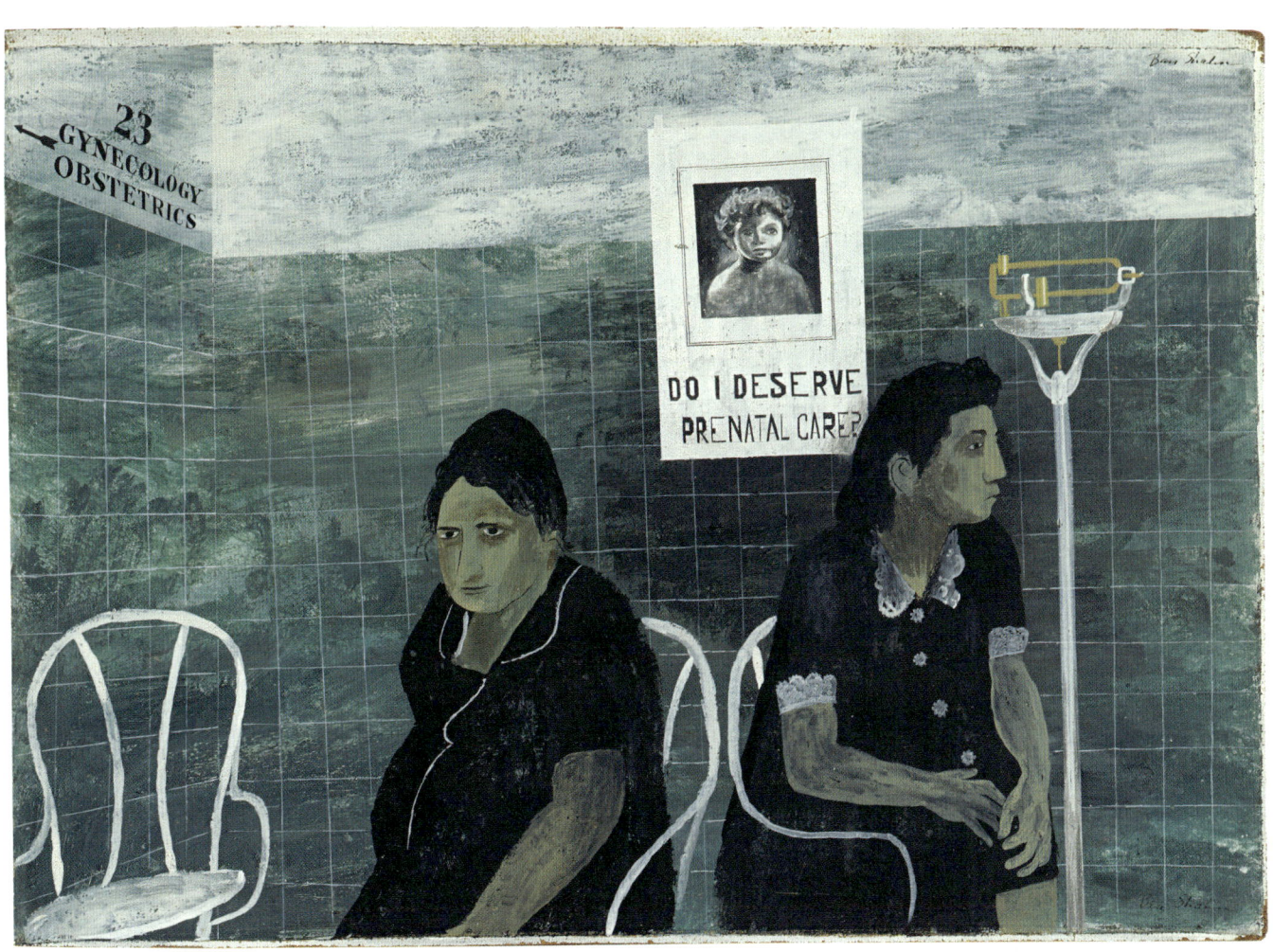

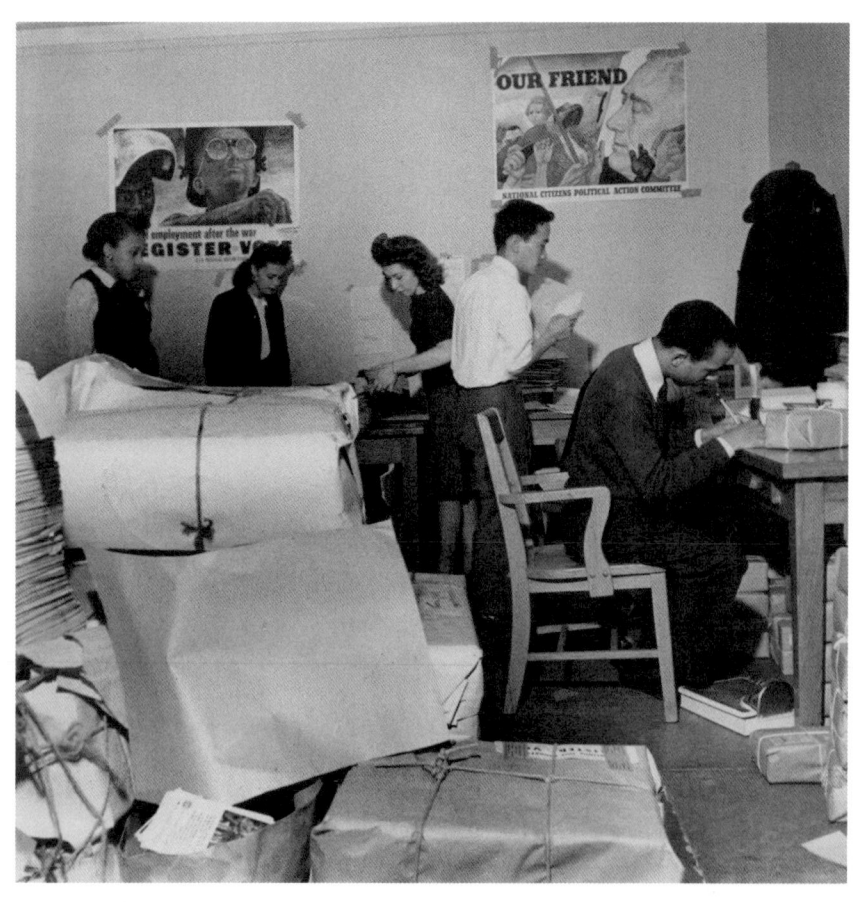

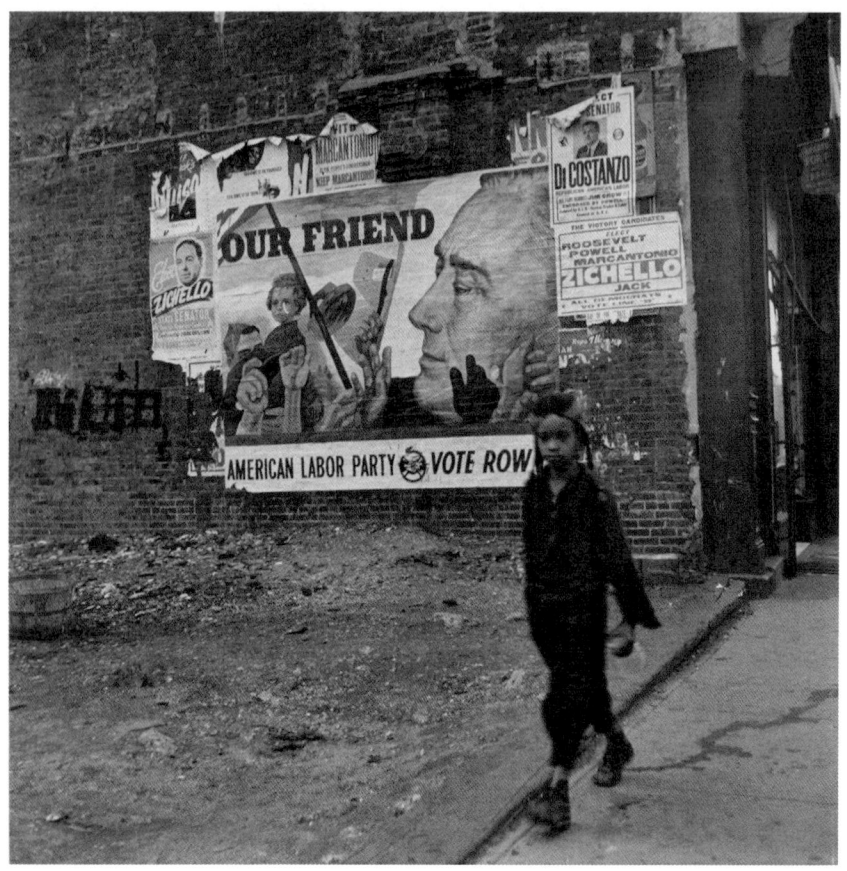

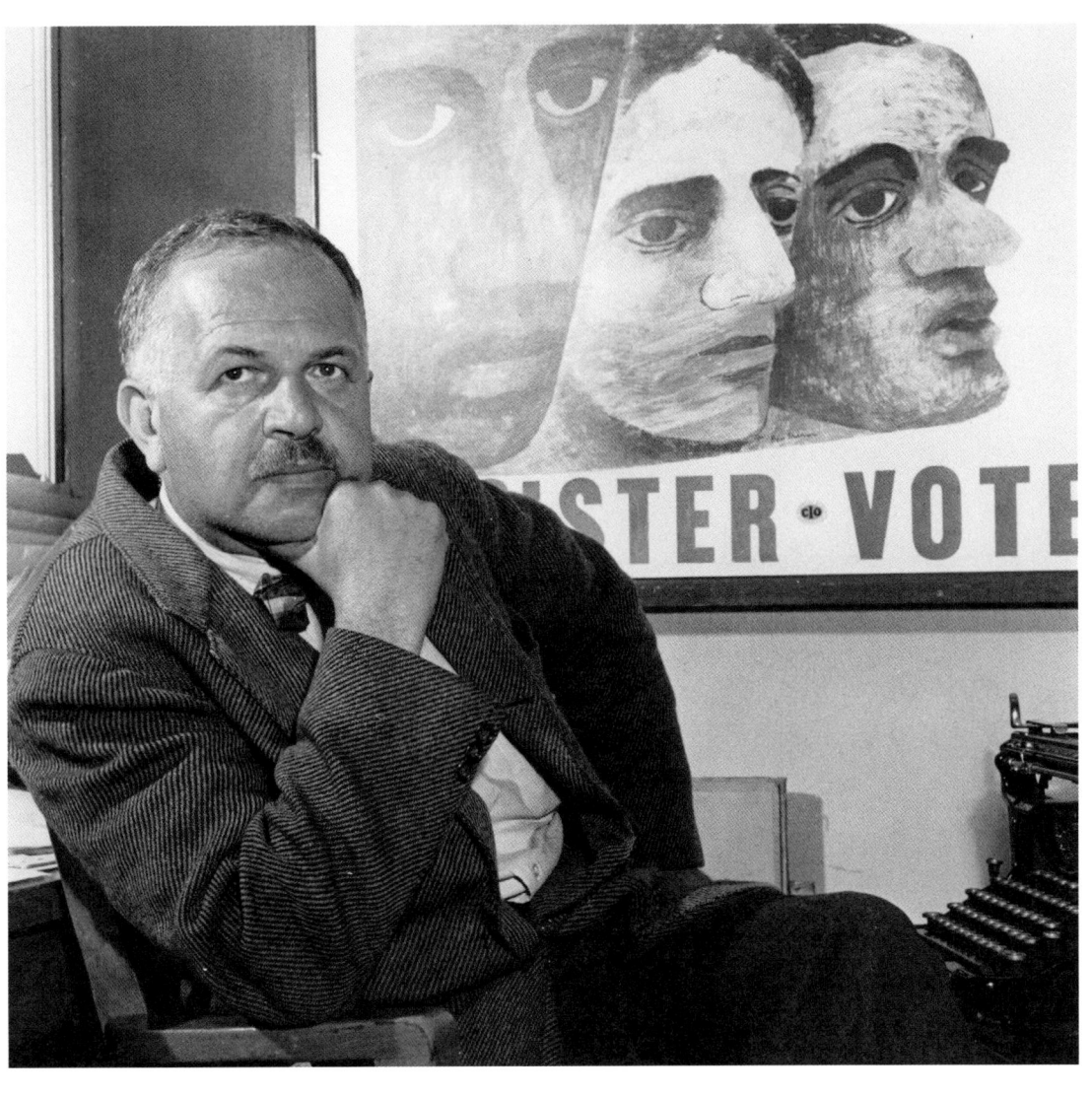

Photographer unknown
Untitled [Workers in CIO-PAC Office, New York City]
c. 1944

Photographer unknown
Untitled [Ben Shahn's CIO Poster on Wall, East Harlem, New York City]
c. 1944

Ronny Jaques
Ben Shahn [CIO-PAC Office, New York City]
c. 1945

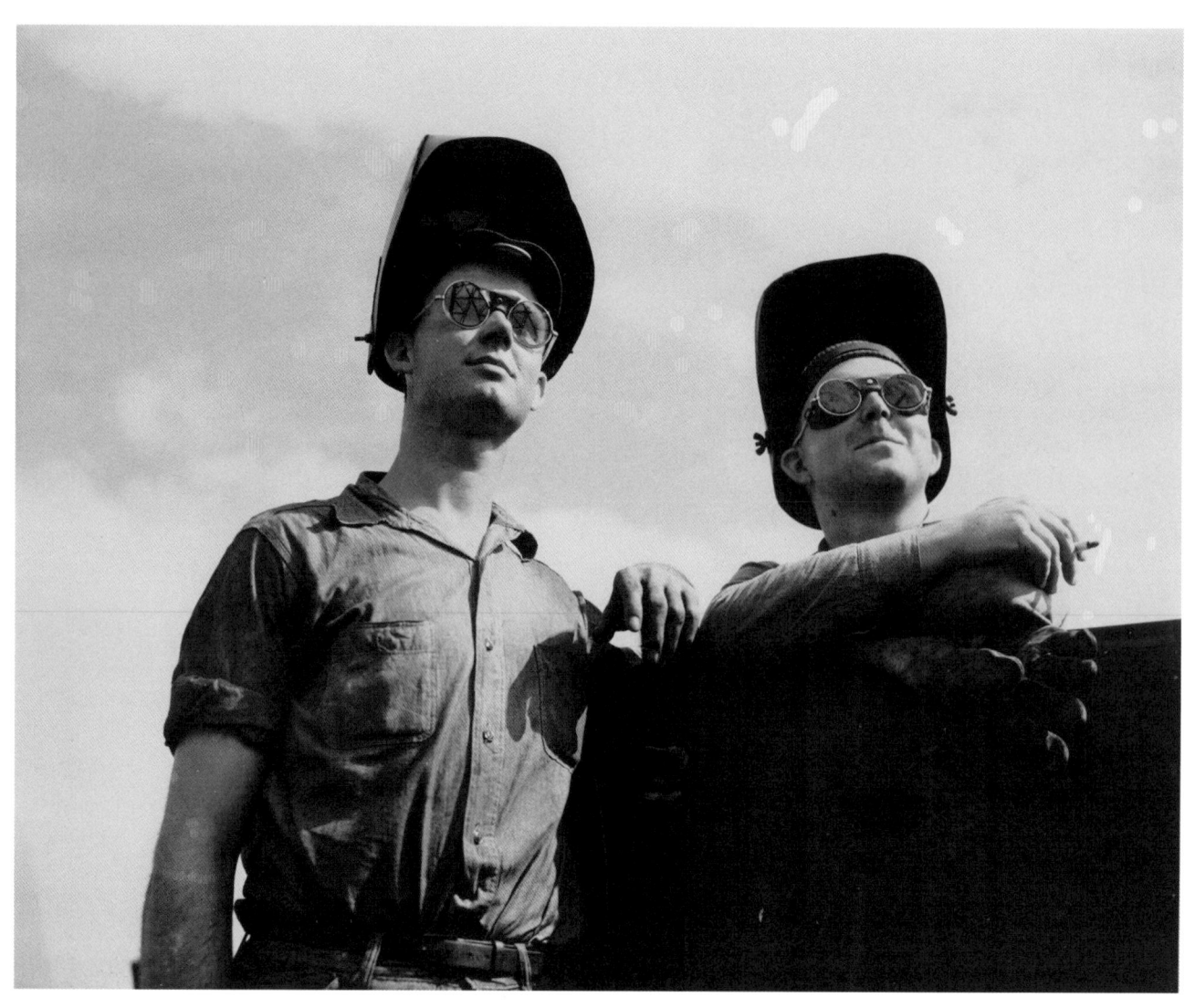

Alfred T. Palmer
*Their Helmets Hoisted Back on Their Heads, These Two Welders Take Time
Out for a Smoke and Breath of Fresh Air. Hundreds of Welders are Employed
in the Building of Uncle Sam's New Navy Craft. Newport News, Va.*
October 1941

For Full Employment After the War, Register, Vote
1944

Ben Shahn and Muriel Rukeyser
Our Manpower
c. 1943

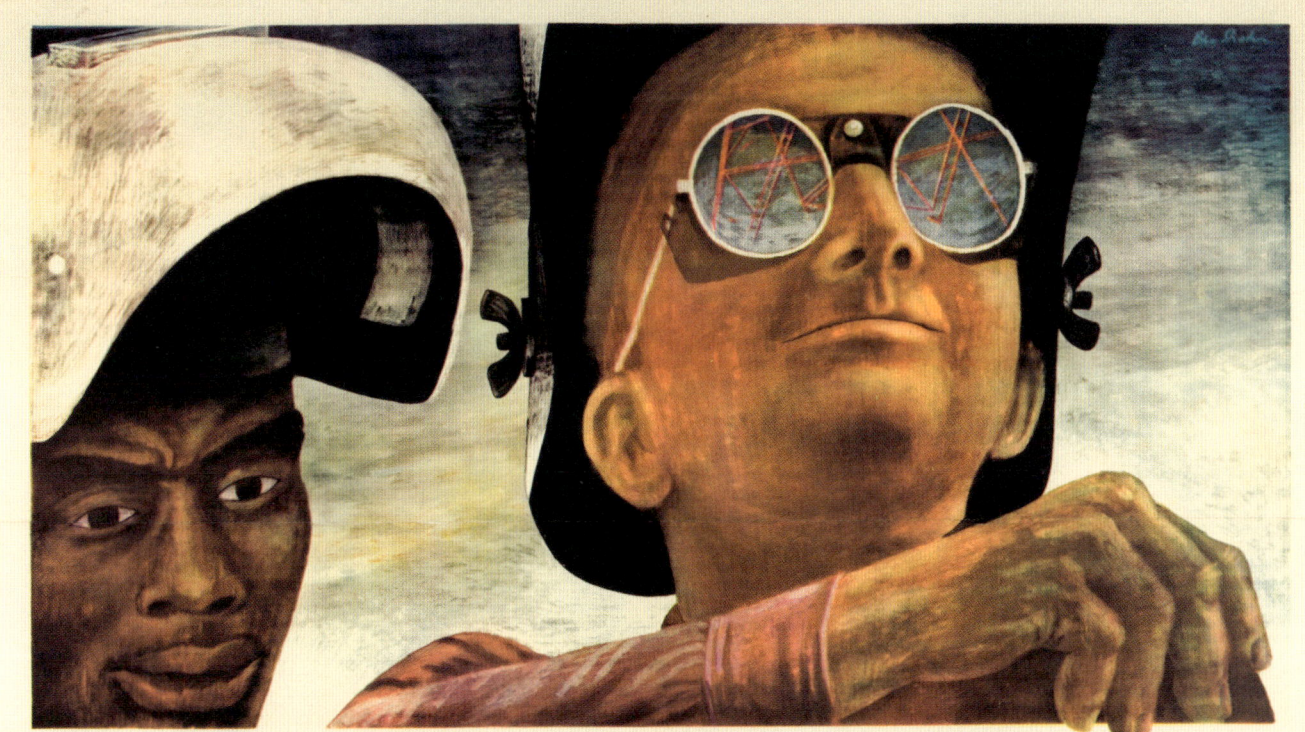

for full employment after the war
REGISTER • VOTE
C I O POLITICAL ACTION COMMITTEE

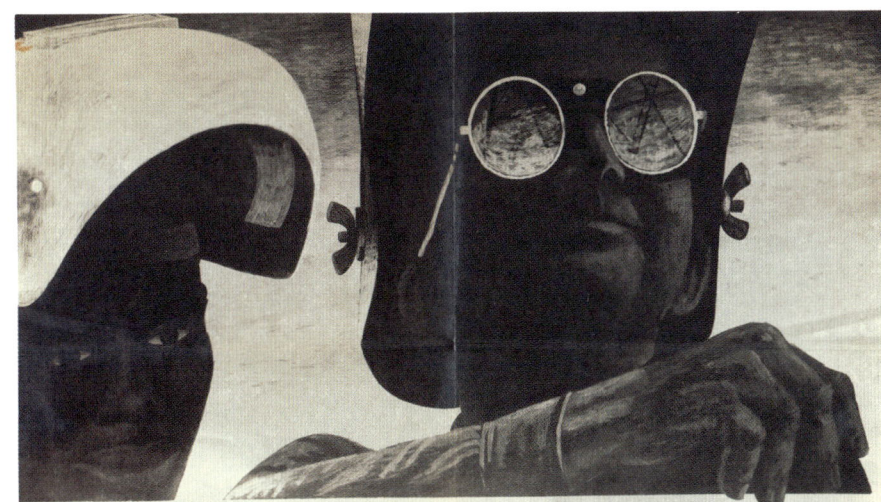

OUR MANPOWER
⅕ of our strength* must not be lost through discrimination
*12,900,000 Negroes, 4,800,000 Jews, 11,400,000 Foreign born

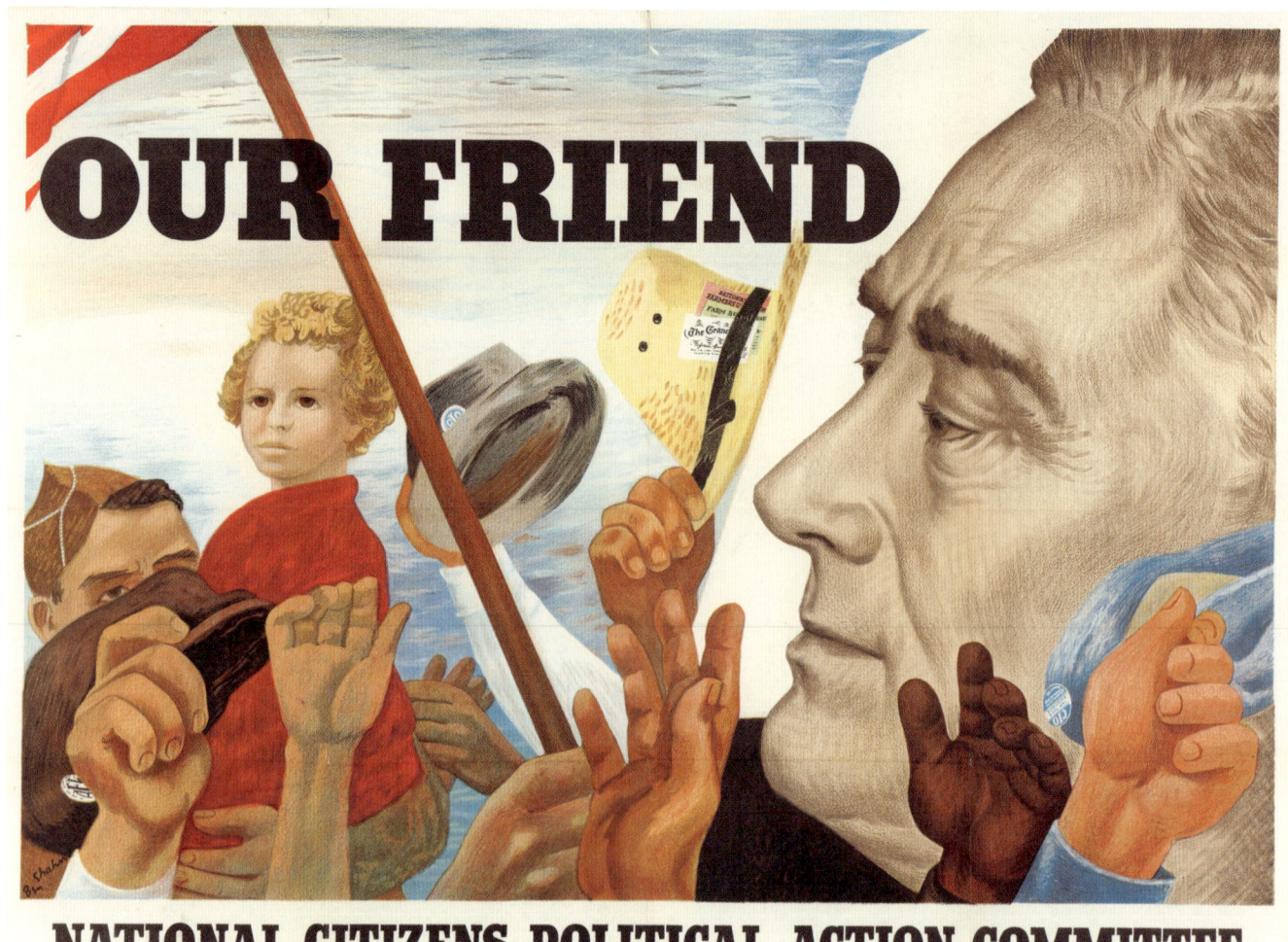

Our Friend
1944

Bountiful Harvest
1944

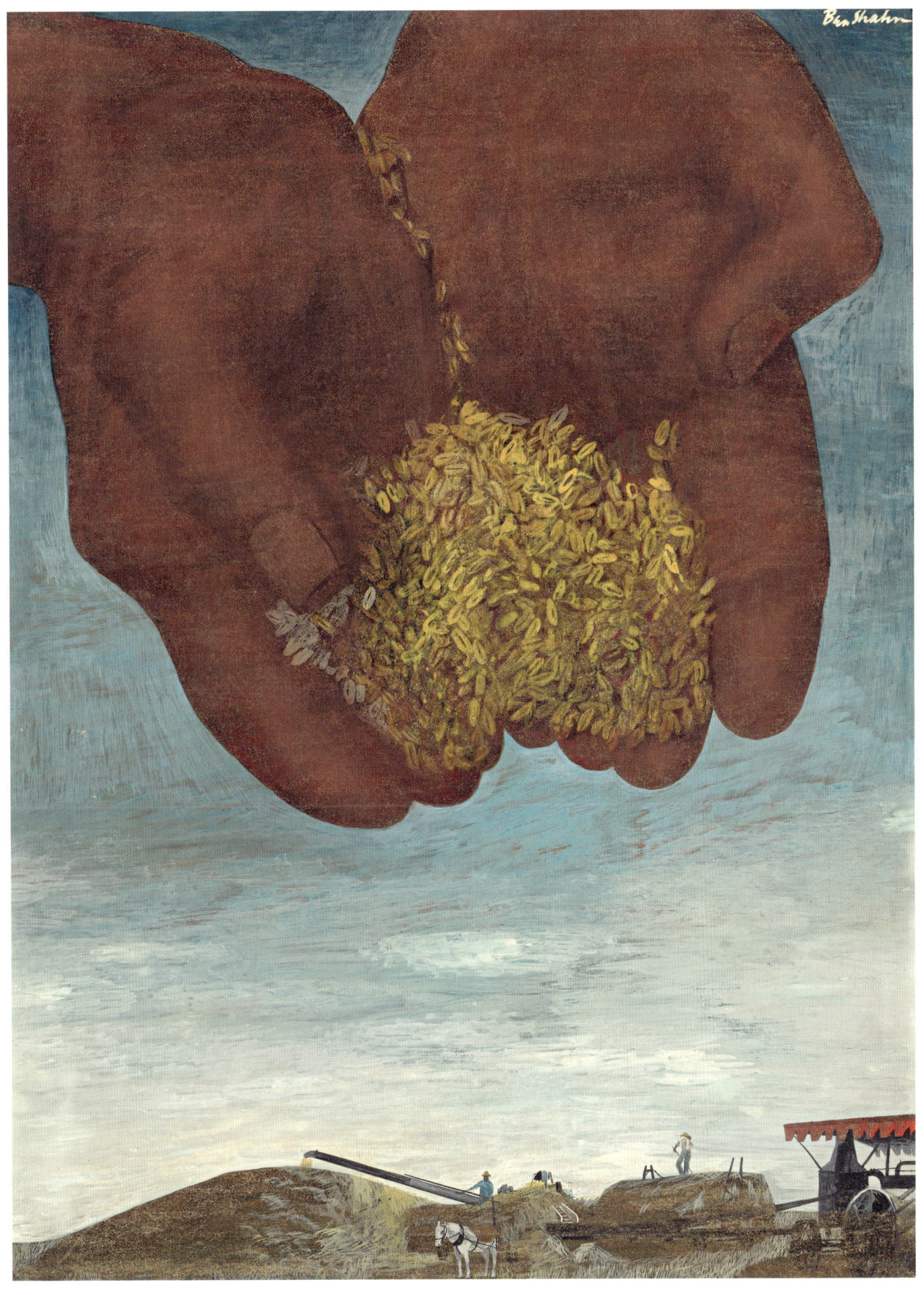

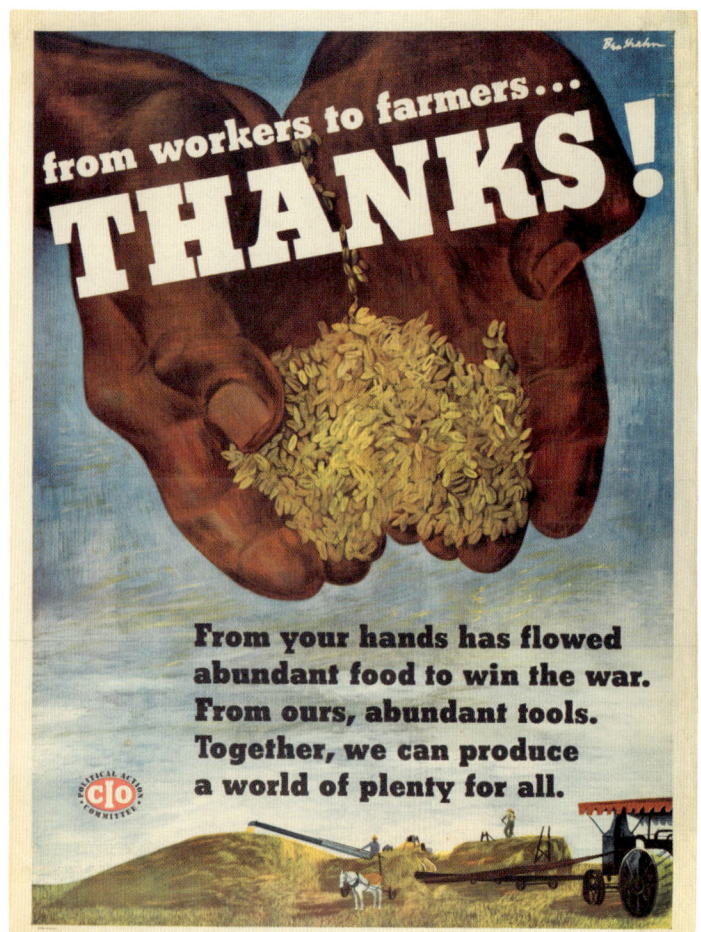

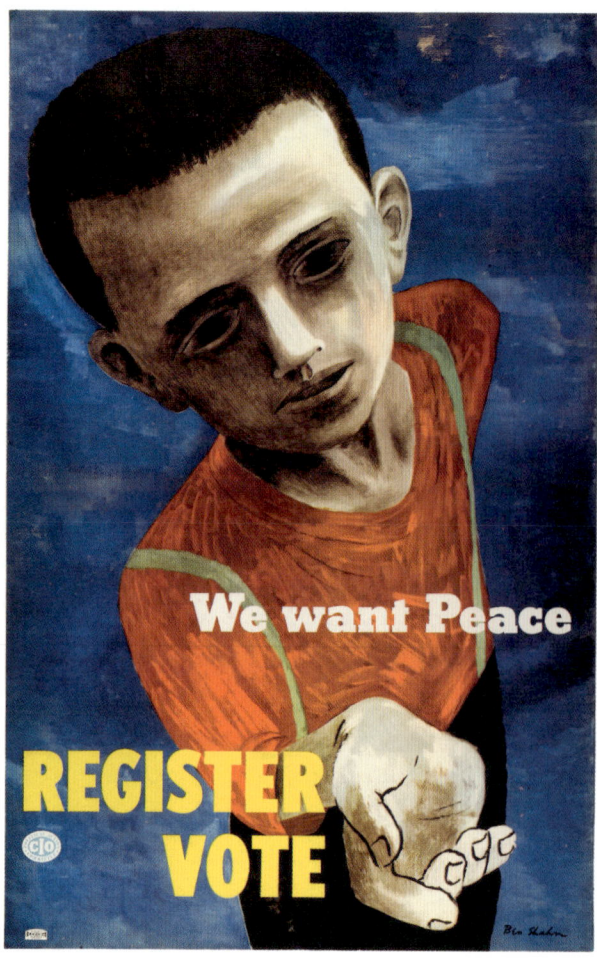

From Workers to Farmers... Thanks!
1944

We Want Peace, Register, Vote
c. 1946

Hunger
1946

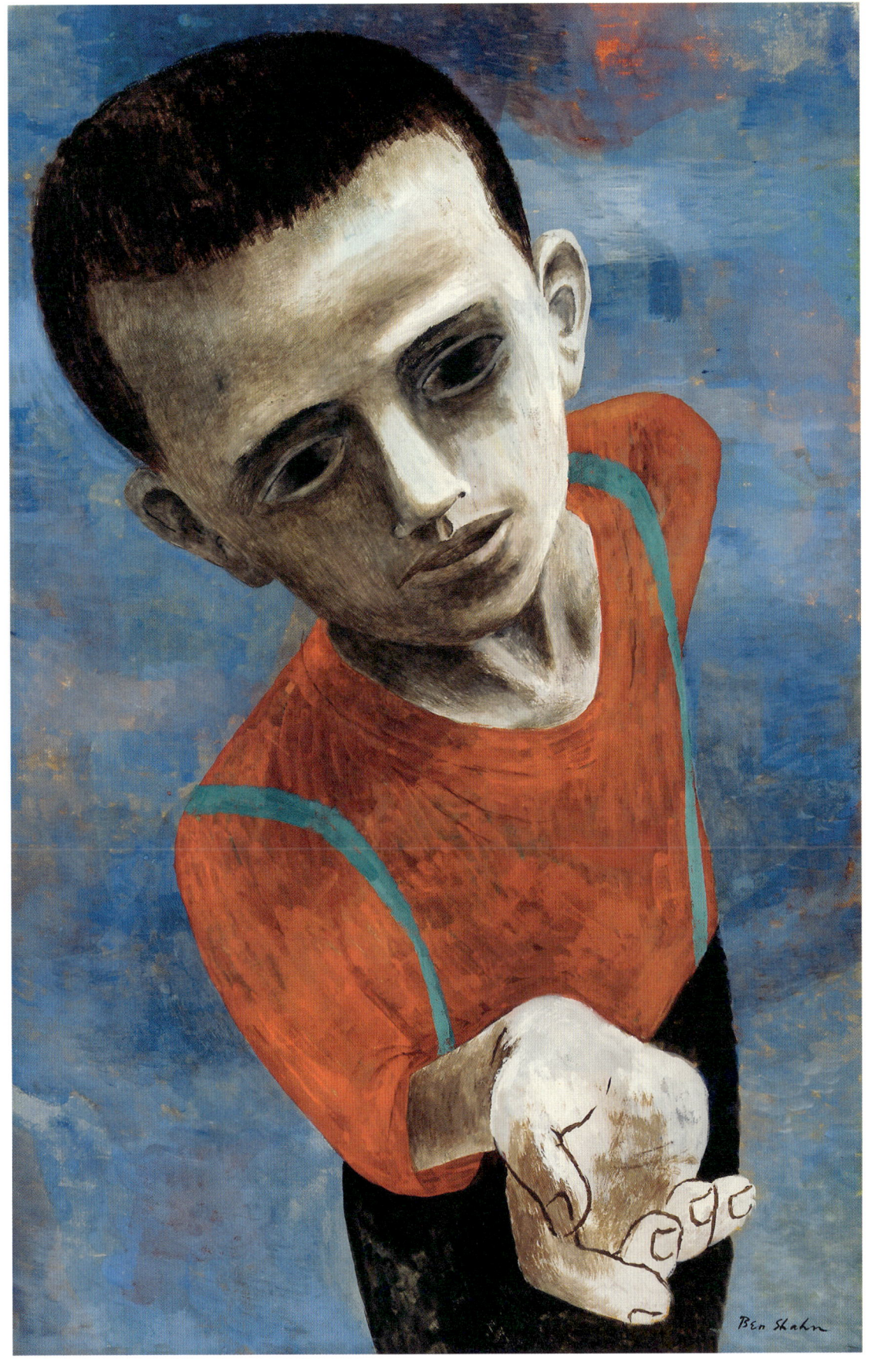

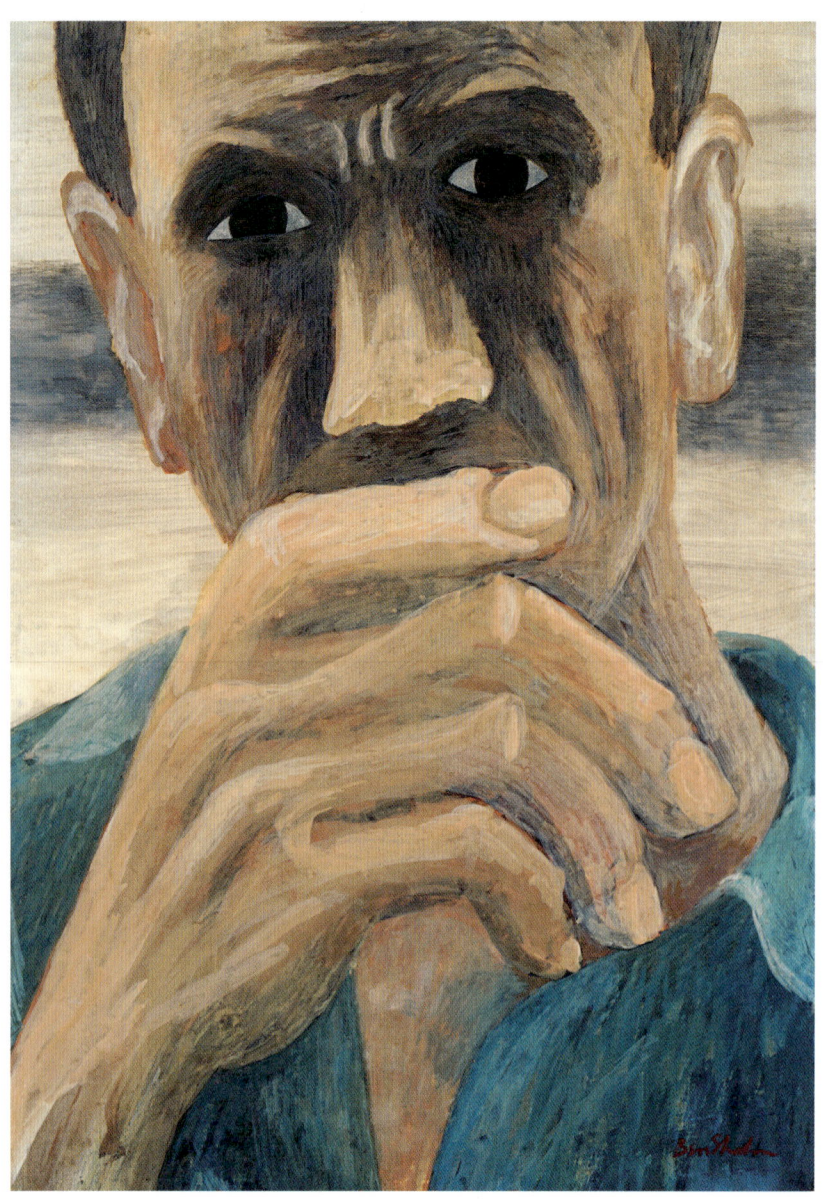

Man
1946

Warning! Inflation Means Depression
1946

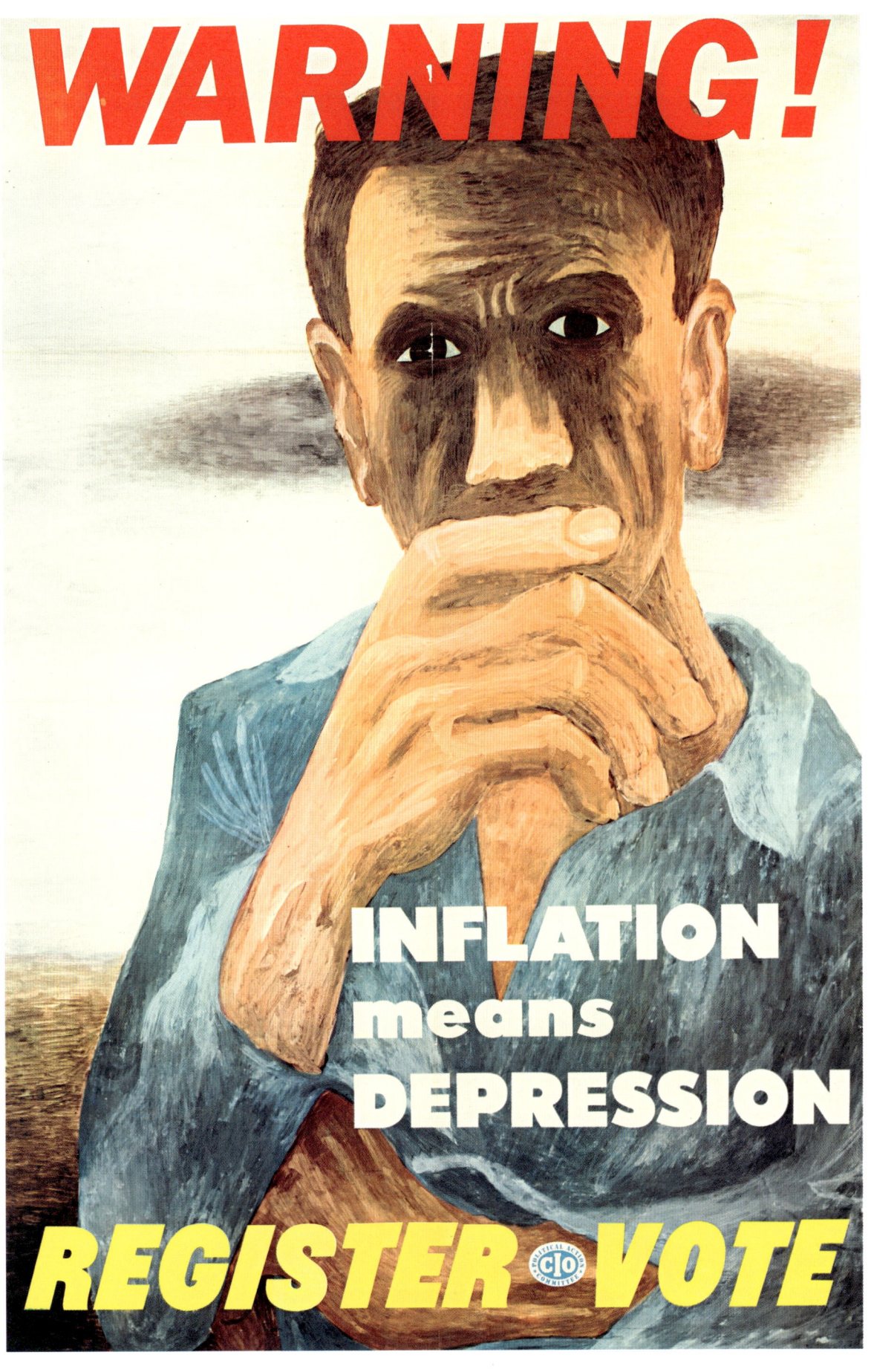

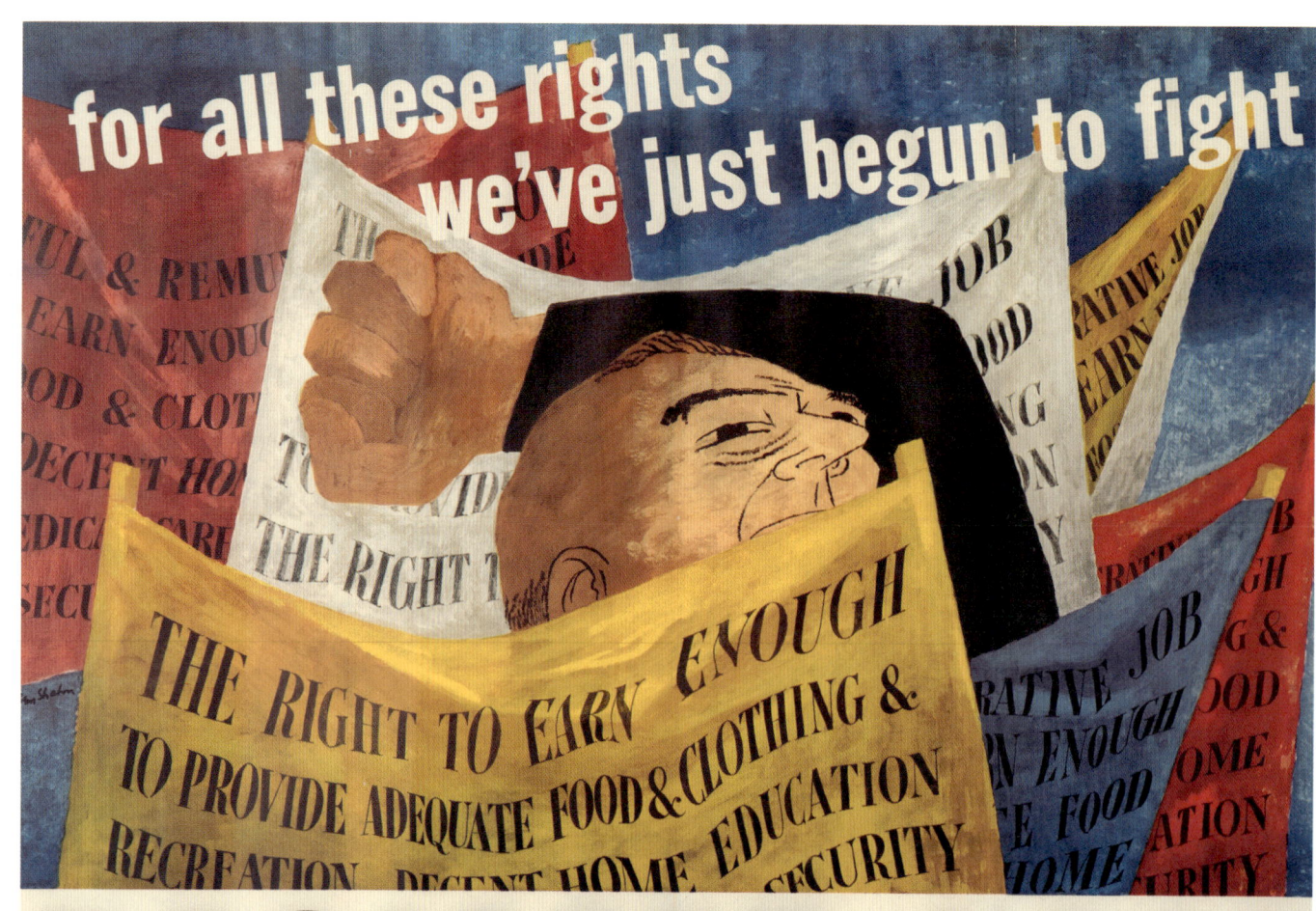

For All These Rights We've Just Begun to Fight
1946

Break Reaction's Grip
1946

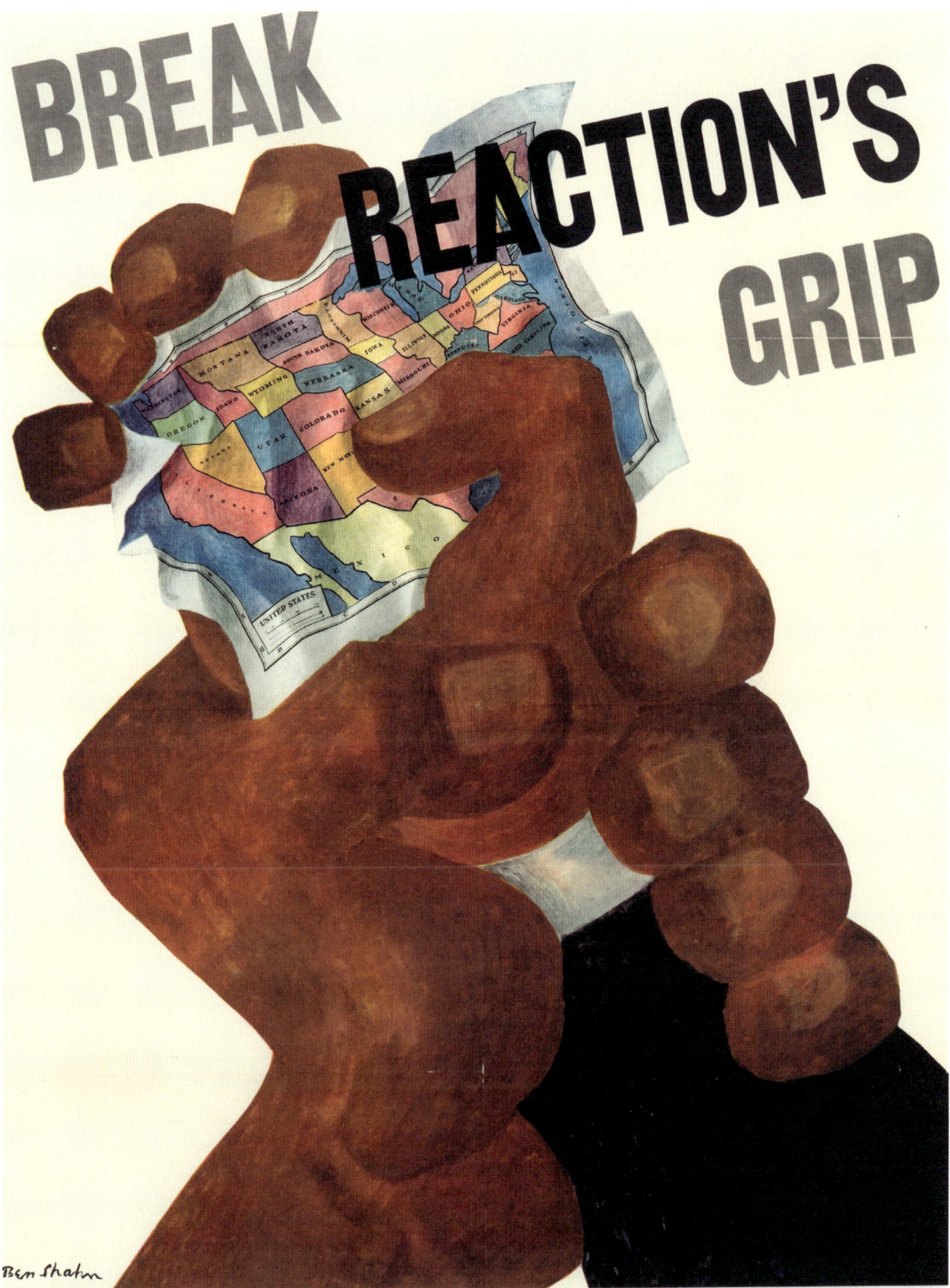

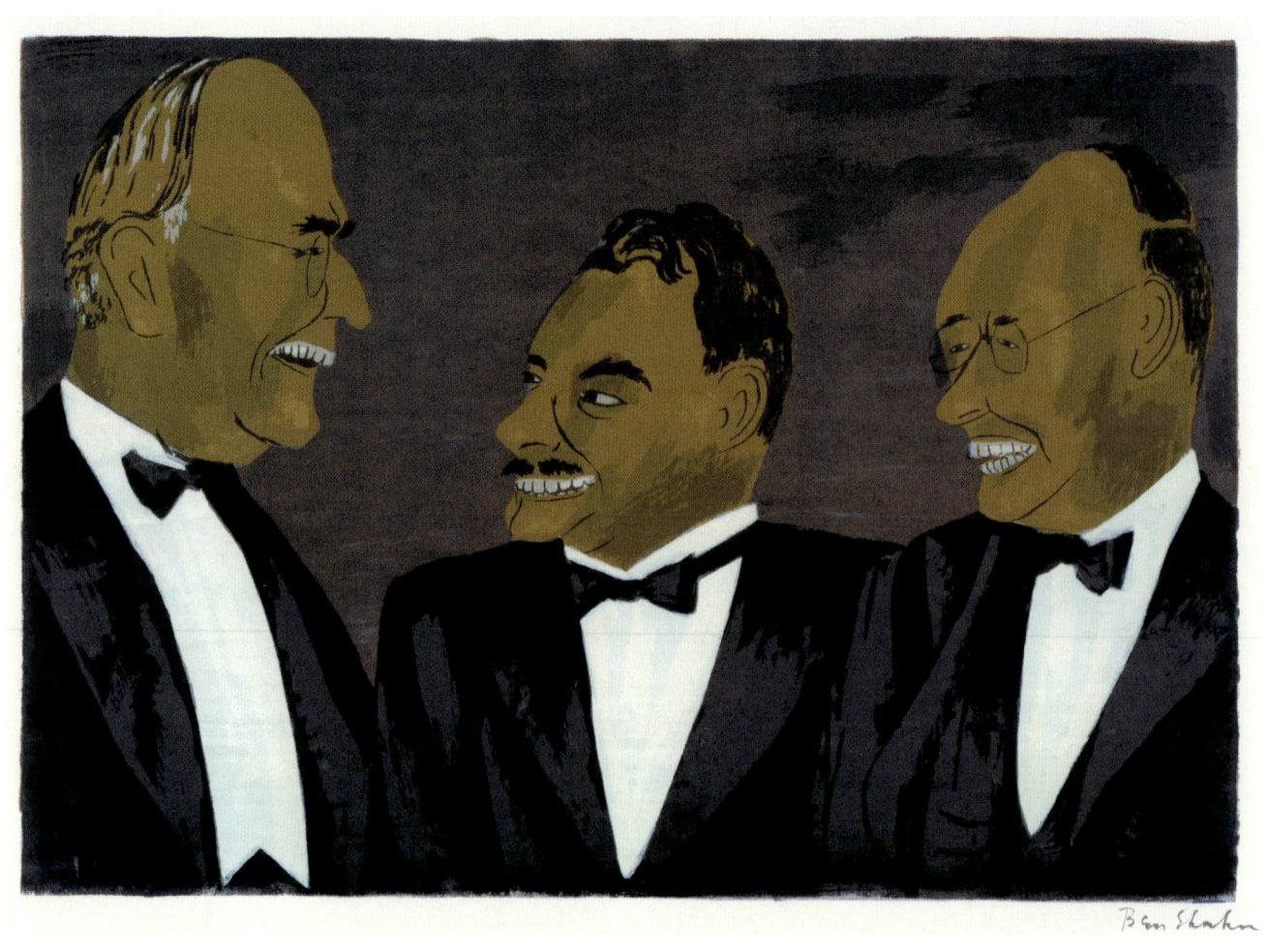

Vandenberg, Dewey, and Taft
1941

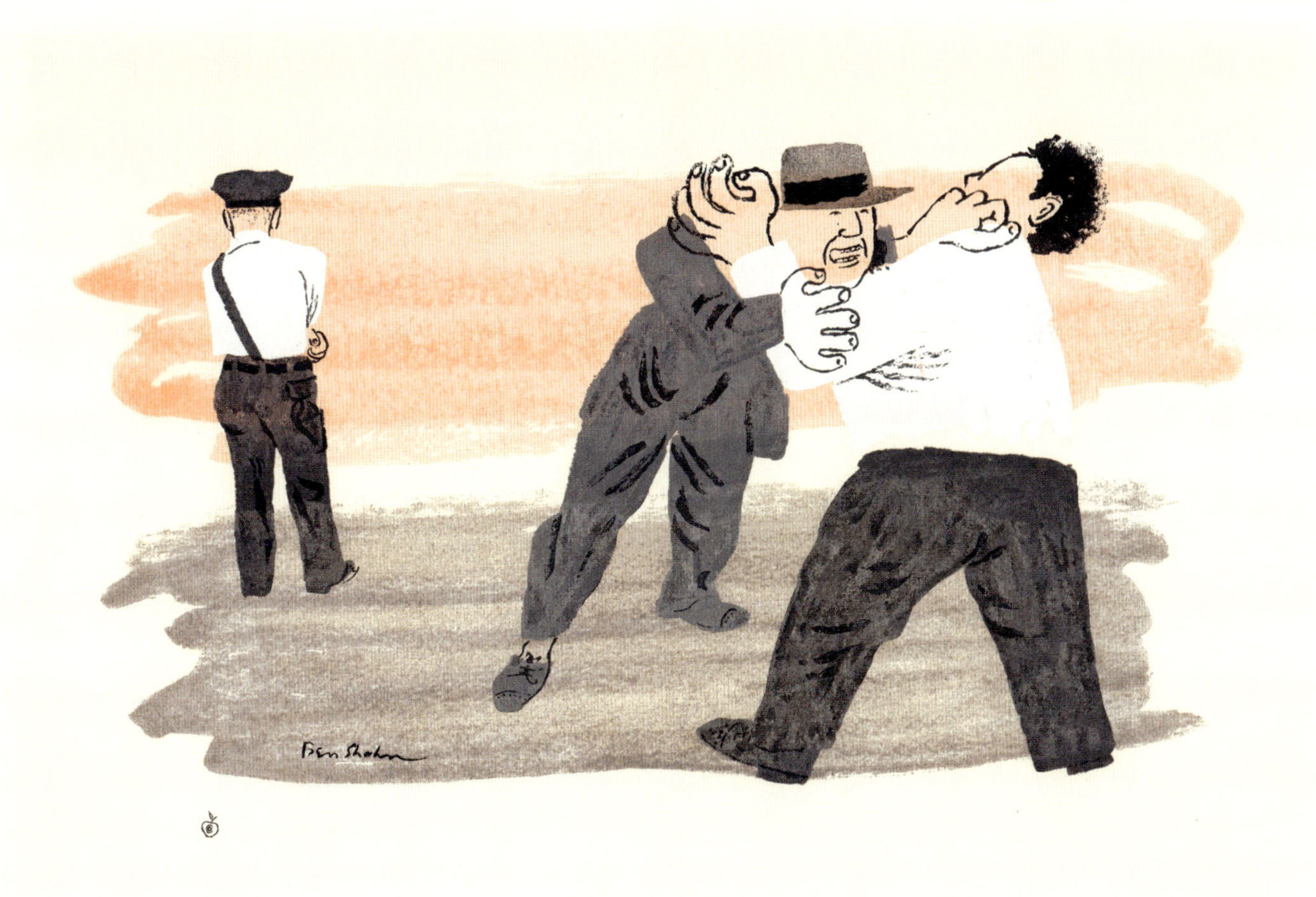

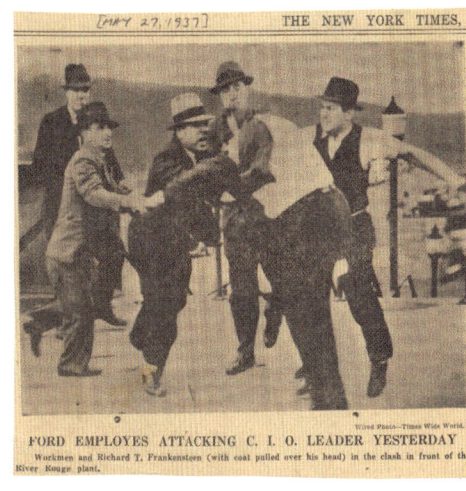

Laissez-faire
c. 1947

Photographer unknown
"Ford Employees Attacking C.I.O. Leader Yesterday,"
New York Times, May 27, 1937

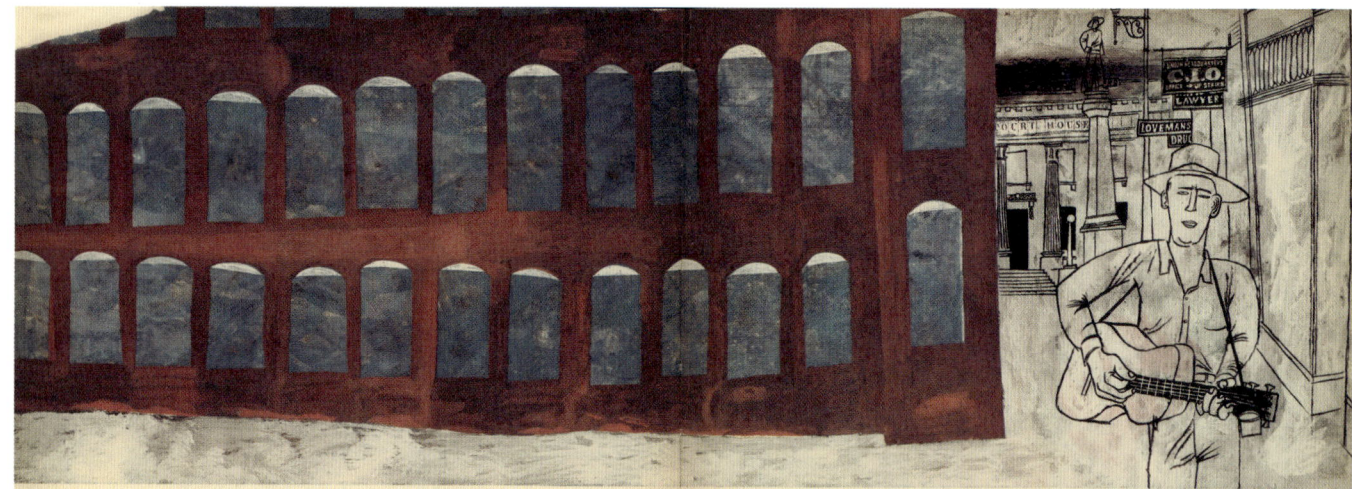

THE CONFEDERATE SOLDIER LOOKS DOWN ON A NEW SIGN OF THE TIMES

Labor Drives South

THE C.I.O., WITH THE A.F. of L. IN FULL PURSUIT, SETS OUT FOR THE LAST U.S. LABOR
FRONTIER · THE QUESTION: CAN THEY MAKE IT BEFORE THE COLLAPSE OF COTTON?

Paintings and drawings: Ben Shahn

In the summer of 1946 the once-lean South was fat and placid. A cool, wet spring had produced the lushest summer in southern memory, and the farms and towns were almost as lush as the countryside. Swarms of new trucks, tractors, and Jeeps buzzed around the freshly painted farm buildings, dazzling under their new aluminum roofs. In the neat little towns and cities, stores put up new fronts, old buildings glistened with new paint, new buildings went up everywhere. For on top of the flood of government money from war wages and Army payments, cotton was selling at 36 cents a pound, and a farmer with a hundred acres of good cotton had a crop worth $15,000 to $20,000. Who cared that cotton's fundamental position had never been so weak?

Across the South money was easy, prices were high, things scarce, wages good, jobs plentiful; and the prosperous combination so bemused and delighted most Southerners that few even took the time to wonder why it came or how long it would last.

In this curiously relaxed atmosphere the two great American labor federations have undertaken the last major organizing job in the U.S. It began when the C.I.O. Executive Board met in February, 1946, and decided to open a southern drive at once. A southern organizing director was chosen in the person of Philip Murray's boyhood chum and trusted lieutenant, Van A. Bittner, veteran of forty years of rough-and-tumble organizing in coal, steel, meat packing, and other industries over the nation.

To conduct a ten-month drive nearly $1,250,000 was raised, primarily among the C.I.O. steel, electrical, auto, clothing, and textile unions. Office space for a southern headquarters was finally secured, after weeks of searching, in an old loft building at 79½ Poplar Street in Atlanta, above Jimmy's Steak House; and by the first part of June there were enough chairs in the office, enough paint on the walls, and enough names on the organization chart for the C.I.O. Organizing Committee to consider its doors officially open for business.

The portents of a C.I.O. southern drive soon called forth a reply from the A.F. of L. (which southern workers almost invariably call the "A.F. & L.," as if it were a branch-line railroad). When some 3,000 A.F. of L. delegates gathered at Asheville, North Carolina, on May 11 and 12, at the Third Biennial Southern Labor Conference, they heard A.F. of L. President William Green open his principal address with the announcement, "Labor is making history here tonight . . . The American Federation of Labor is launching a crusade to organize the unorganized workers of the South." Thereupon Green, supported by George Meany and other A.F. of L. heads, switched the attack to the C.I.O.: "Let me give southern industry this warning

—grow and cooperate with us or fight for your life against Communist forces." Philip Murray snapped testily that Bill Green seemed to be trying to organize southern employers.

The C.I.O. launched its southern drive when it did because it had no alternative. The reasons were three:

1. *Economic:* the competition of unorganized southern plants with C.I.O.-organized northern industries could in time of depression threaten the whole C.I.O. national position.

2. *Bureaucratic:* maintaining their southern locals is an exhausting drain on many C.I.O unions, some of which spend $3 or $4 on the South for every dollar paid back in dues. One national C.I.O. official explained, "The northern part of the C.I.O. is carrying the South."

3. *Political:* despite the official divorce of the C.I.O. drive from politics, a definite long-range factor was the congressional hostility of conservative southern Democrats to labor in general and the C.I.O. in particular.

As for the A.F. of L., it had a southern drive because the C.I.O. was having one (though perhaps the word "drive" is too strong; A.F. of L. chiefs prefer to call it an "intensification of effort"). The C.I.O.'s compelling reasons did not apply to it.

"Labor Drives South," *Fortune*, November 1946, vol. 34, no. 5,
pp. 134–135, 140–141

140

month paid by the county to give them official status; the local doctor, and social-service workers, if any, are on his payroll. In such a village, to lose one's job may mean losing one's home and one's entire place in the community. Hence the interests of the millworker often tend to contract to the limits of the mill village where he lives, and where his father and grandfather may have lived before him.

In August, 1946, a union drive in such a village not far from Macon, Georgia, was making slow progress, for the village mail was distributed in the mill, and any letter with a union return address immediately tagged the union sympathizers. Opposite the mill gates was a little grocery store whose owner, a union sympathizer, made a practice of signing people up in the back of his store. The mill's reaction was symbolic: the store was simply declared out of bounds for all millworkers, and any employee who entered it was "spoken to" the next day.

The younger generation of owners and managers, however, seldom regards unionization as the end of the world. Northern companies owning southern plants look on unionization more matter-of-factly than their southern contemporaries, believing that past a certain point it is not good business to fight the unions. Most susceptible to organization are the converter-owned textile mills, bought in the past few years at fancy prices. As the outlay must be recouped before the end of the seller's market, the owners are in no position to risk a protracted strike. This may account for the scorn in which they are held by old-line millowners, who liken the converters to "black-market fleas who got so rich they went out and bought themselves a dog."

Many southern employers regard unionization as ultimately inevitable, and, influenced by A.F. of L. and other efforts to paint the C.I.O. as Communistic, they tend to prefer the A.F. of L. They are nonetheless interested in staving off organization by anybody as long as possible. Their opposition, however, shows one significant contrast with the free-and-easy thirties: it is generally within the law, despite occasional firings for union activity and some use of supervisory employees for pressure purposes. Moreover, practices that once were common, such as eviction from company houses or the encouragement of company unions, are rare today.

The most widely used employer technique is the "Tube Bending formula,"* involving a series of carefully worded letters to employees just before an NLRB election. Simultaneously, employees may also begin to receive in the mail copies of Sherman Patterson's *Militant Truth* or "Parson Jack" Johnston's *Trumpet*, both little semi-religious newspapers devoted to the propaganda that labor unions are Communistic and hence enemies of religion. The formula seems to be reaching the limit of its usefulness, however, and the little group of southern labor-relations lawyers who operate it expect the day to come when

[Continued on page 230]

*So called because based on a 1942 circuit-court decision in the case of the American Tube Bending Co. of New Haven, Connecticut, defining how far an employer may go in persuading his employees without coercing them.

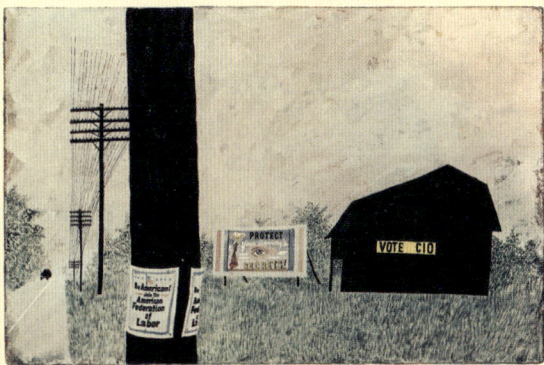

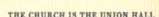

OAK RIDGE ATOM WORKERS after a slam-bang election amid cries of "Red" and "craft union," voted C.I.O. by a narrow margin at the only large plant won by either group. At right, Negro tobacco workers invoke religious sanction for their mass movement into A.F. of L. and C.I.O. THE CHURCH IS THE UNION HALL

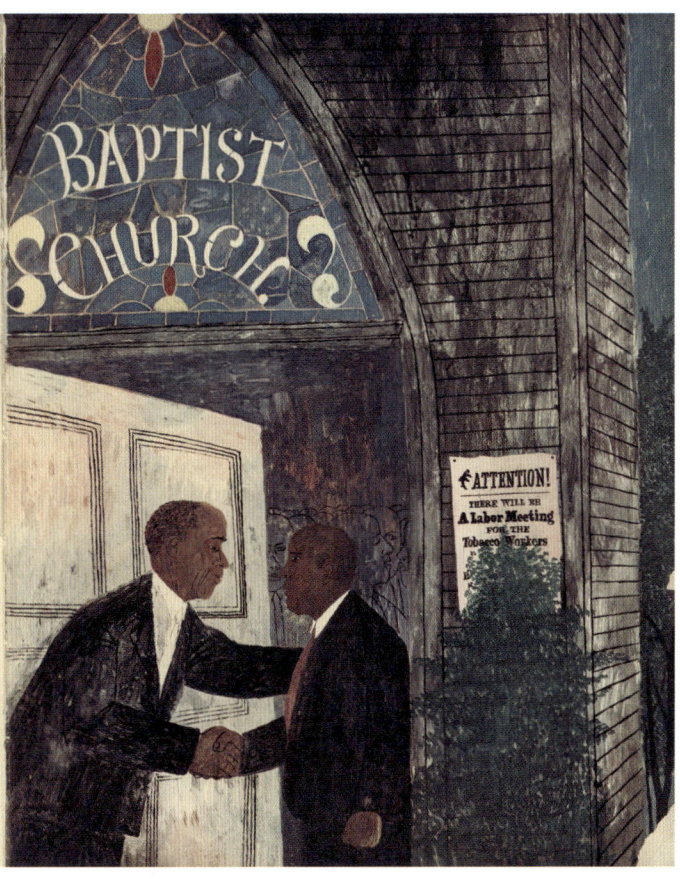

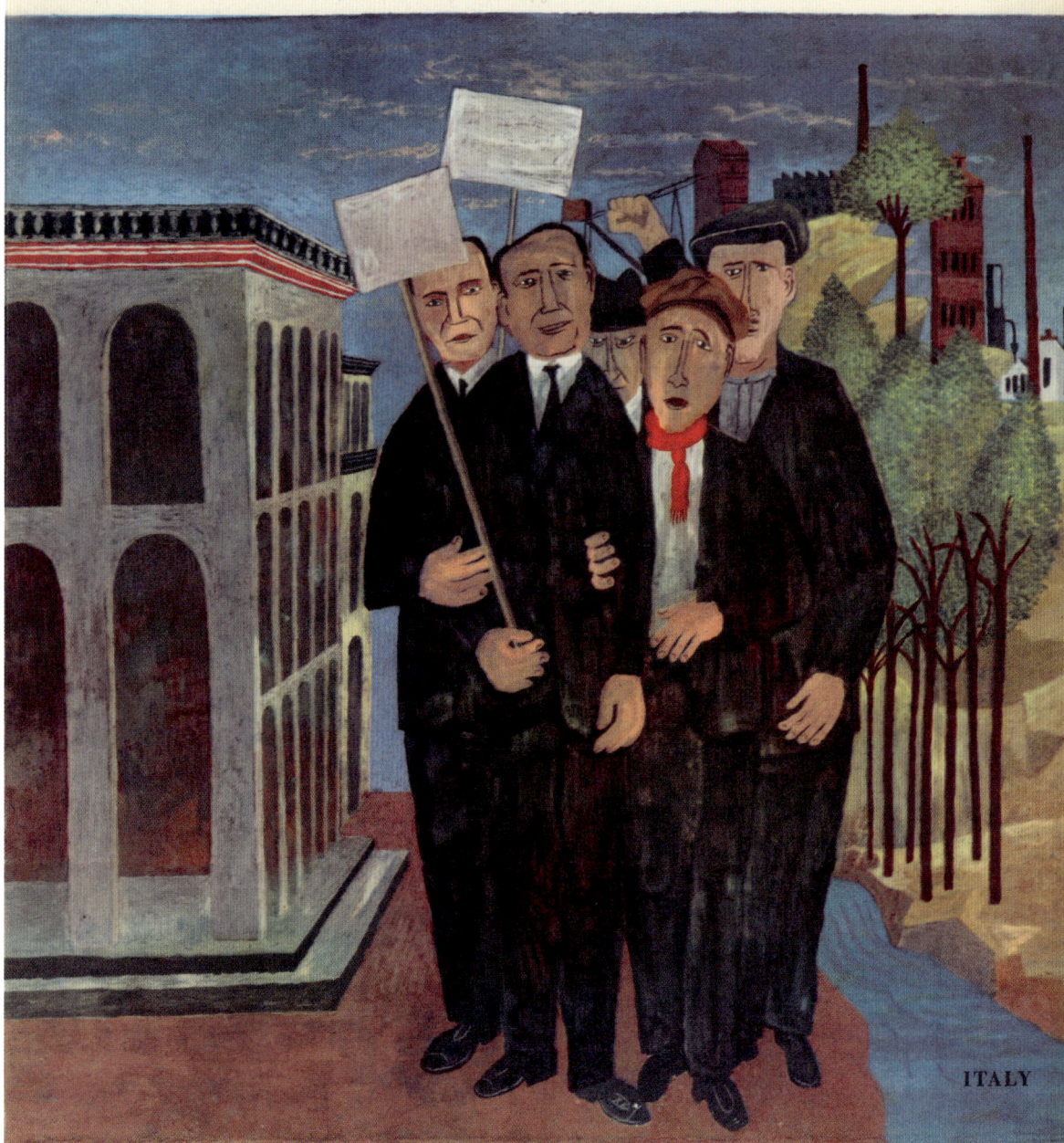

Fortune, August 1947, vol. 36, no. 2

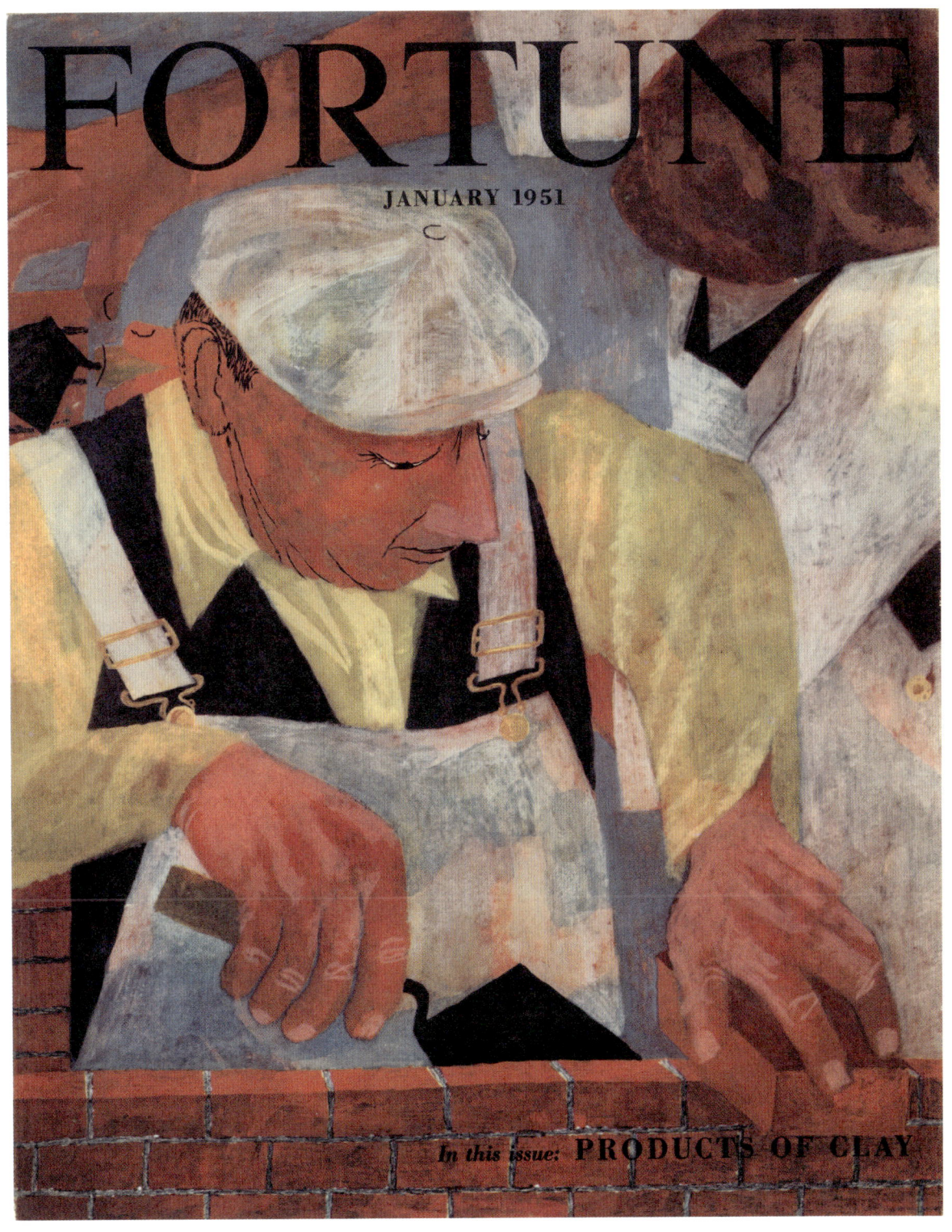

Fortune, January 1951, vol. 43, no. 1

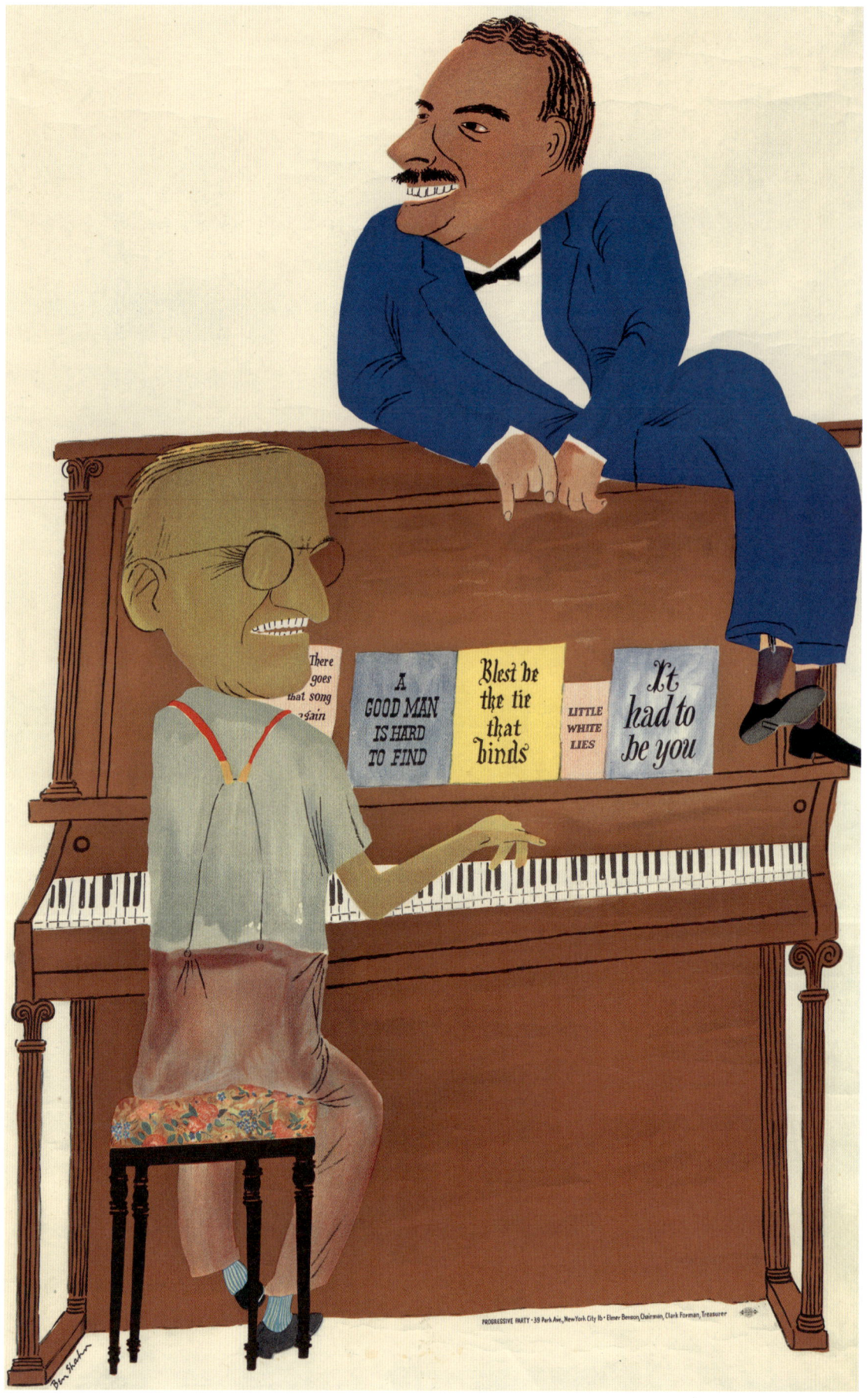

AGE OF ANXIETY:
THE COLD WAR AND CIVIL LIBERTIES

Widespread acclaim came to Ben Shahn in the postwar period: in 1947 New York's Museum of Modern Art honored him with a mid-career retrospective and in 1954 the museum selected him, along with Willem de Kooning, to represent U.S. painting at the Venice Biennale.[1] Yet while Shahn was popular, his type of socially engaged, figurative realism would fall out of favor with certain influential critics, curators, and gallerists, as abstract expressionism and non-objective art took center stage, especially by the late 1950s. Shahn's art and politics were also the subject of reactionary attacks in the oppressive political climate of the early Cold War era.[2] This climate informed *A Good Man is Hard to Find* (1948), Shahn's campaign poster supporting Progressive Party presidential candidate Henry Wallace, which caricatured Democratic nominee Harry S. Truman and Republican nominee Thomas E. Dewey as grinning, ill-proportioned, untrustworthy politicians. After Truman's win, and despite his protection and expansion of Franklin Delano Roosevelt's New Deal policies at home, Truman implemented aggressive, anti-communist policies abroad. This was a time of hostile, declining relations between the U.S. and the Soviet Union—the two superpowers that emerged triumphant from World War II but whose ally-turned-enemy relationship came to be defined by mutual distrust and a nuclear arms race.

American fears of Soviet communism were exacerbated by the "red-baiting" of liberals and progressives by Republican Senator Joseph McCarthy and his allies. The latter took it upon themselves, in the name of national security, to expose suspected communists as well as homosexuals—those in the government of President Dwight D. Eisenhower whom they deemed "subversive" or disloyal to the U.S. Shahn, a social democrat by now, responded with works such as *Artist and Politicians* (1953), which illustrated his eponymous essay that addresses the "two malignant forces" endangering "the great American liberal tradition": communism on the left and the anti-communist crusade on the right.[3] He drew incisive caricatures for *The Nation* of the so-called Army-McCarthy Senate hearings of spring 1954—proceedings that contributed to McCarthy's downfall. Shahn himself was targeted by Republican Congressman George Dondero in 1949 and by the FBI, especially between 1951 and 1953. In 1959, Shahn was interrogated by the House Un-American Activities Committee about his participation in a Moscow art exhibition. From circa 1952 to 1954, he was even blacklisted by CBS Broadcasting, for which he had famously designed advertisements for socially conscious radio and television programs.

A Good Man is Hard to Find
1948

Shahn became a spokesperson for "humanist" content in art and never wavered in his political commitment, even as he increasingly gave such content symbolic and abstract shape. In the 1950s he created paintings that speak to the hysteria of the early Cold War era with its repression of civil liberties, such as *Second Allegory* (1953), in which a vulnerable figure is being attacked by a massive, downwardly pointing finger of accusation. A wreath of flames and crystalline forms rendered in Shahn's layered, palimpsest technique suggest the looming dangers of atomic bombs. In *Discord* (1953), a red-clad figure is overtaken in a physical fight by an enraged figure locking the weaker man's head in his hands— "a commentary on discord in general in 1953 … and a specific commentary on the Red Scare." [4] More cryptic works use wit and satire to present absurd worlds with clowns and labyrinthian architecture. In *Everyman* (1954), an ordinary person and an upside-down harlequin balance themselves on the contorted body of a masked acrobat—a precarious foundation for all. Masks are more prominent in *Conversations* (1958), a watercolor showing two "officials" convening in profile, their multiple masks speaking to an atmosphere of suspicion as well as to duplicity and hypocrisy. Perhaps this is Shahn's veiled critique of democratic leaders meeting with right-wing dictators in the Cold War over shared interests in stopping the spread of communism.

Shahn asserted the power of the individual in his screen print *Credo* (1966). Here he juxtaposed a mystical fire beast image with his vision of Martin Luther holding his 1521 statement to the Diet of Worms, which Shahn hand-scripted. The Protestant leader—deemed a heretic for his attack on corruption and abuses within the Catholic Church—defended his convictions that "No man can command my conscience." Shahn apparently found the Protestant movement "dry and antithetical to art" and surely knew of Luther's virulently antisemitic views, which were widely quoted in the race-based antisemitic Nazi literature. Yet Luther's words nonetheless reflect the artist's own credo—his resistance to the Cold War witch hunts that sought to suppress liberal political speech and his celebration of "nonconformity" as a precondition for innovative artistic creation and great historical transformation. For him, the nonconformist, or the visionary, prevents a society's "fall into decay," as this type of progressive "presses for change, experiment, and venture into new ways." Shahn cogently articulated this credo in his essay "On Nonconformity," from his 1957 treatise *The Shape of Content*.[5]

1. Ben Shahn became a coveted public speaker and appeared on television. He taught at pioneering art schools, among them Black Mountain College and the Skowhegan School of Painting and Sculpture. His honors include the Charles Eliot Norton Professorship at Harvard University (1956–57) and an elected membership in the Academy of Arts and Sciences (1959). In 1970, the year after his death, the New York Philharmonic performed *In Praise of Shahn: Canticle for Orchestra* by William Schuman.

2. See essay by Beatriz Cordero Martín with Laura Katzman in this catalogue. See also Frances K. Pohl, *Ben Shahn: New Deal Artist in a Cold War Climate, 1947–1954* (Austin: University of Texas Press, 1989); Julia Tatiana Bailey, "'Realism Reconsidered': Ben Shahn in London, 1956," in *Modern American Art at Tate 1945–1980* (2019), tate.org.uk/research/publications/modern-american-art-at-tate/essays/realism-reconsidered; and Chiara Di Stefano, "La partecipazione di Ben Shahn alla Biennale di Venezia del 1954," in Francesca Castellani and Eleonora Charans, eds, *Crocevia Biennale* (Milan: Scalpendi, 2017), 181–90.

3. Ben Shahn, "The Artist and the Politicians," *Art News* 52, no. 5 (September 1953): 35.

4. Pohl, *Ben Shahn* (San Francisco: Pomegranate Books, 1993), 119.

5. Bernarda Bryson Shahn, "Introduction," in Ben Shahn, *Hallelujah* (New York: Kennedy Graphics, 1970), unpaginated; Shahn, *The Shape of Content* (Cambridge, Mass.: Harvard University Press, 1957), 76, 84–85, 87. For Shahn's Cold War-era work in the context of art historian Edgar Wind's theories of art and morality, see Ben Thomas, "'The Muses' sterner laws' – W. H. Auden and Ben Shahn," in *Edgar Wind and Modern Art: In Defence of Marginal Anarchy* (London: Bloomsbury Visual Arts, 2020), 117–55.

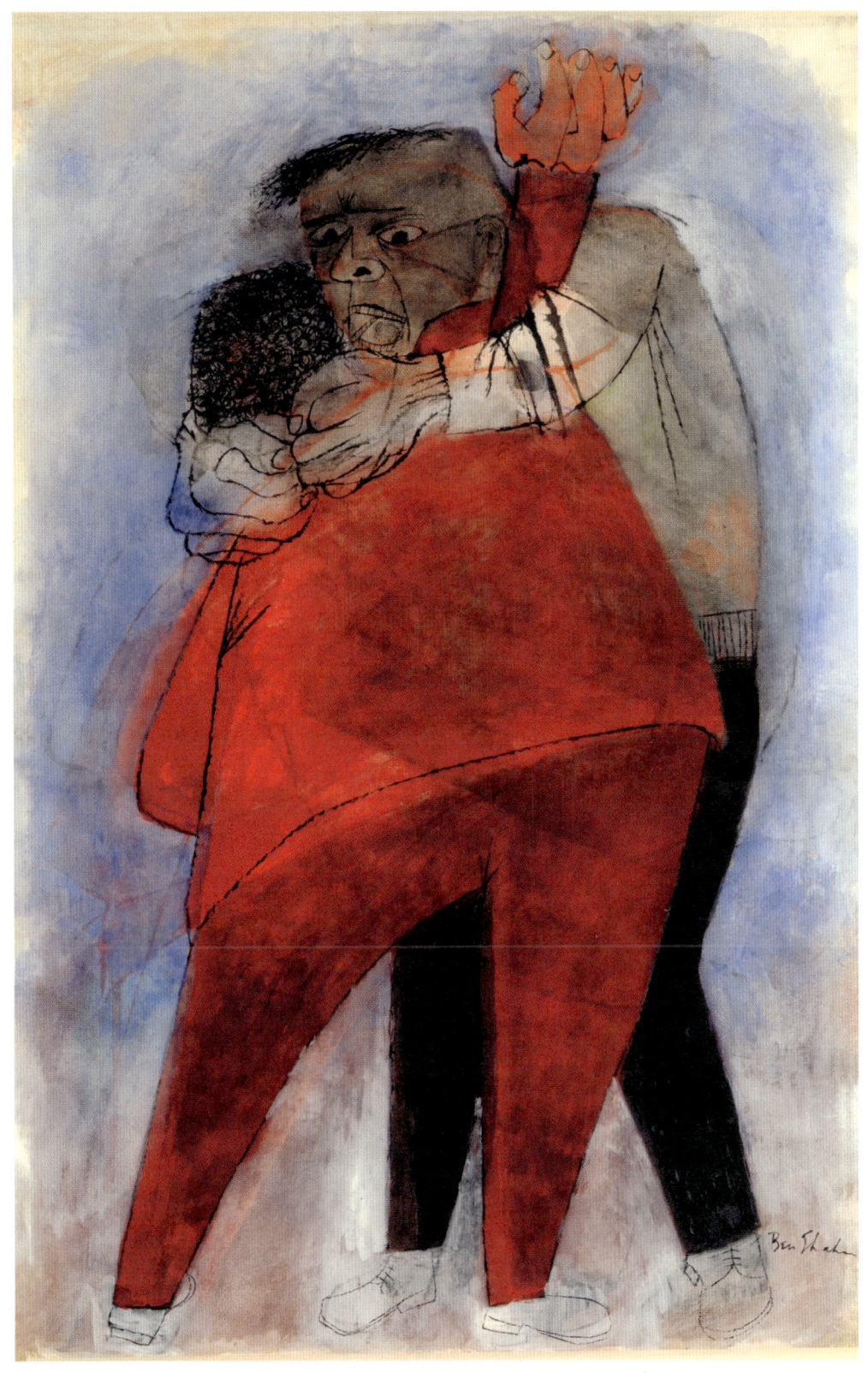

Discord
1953

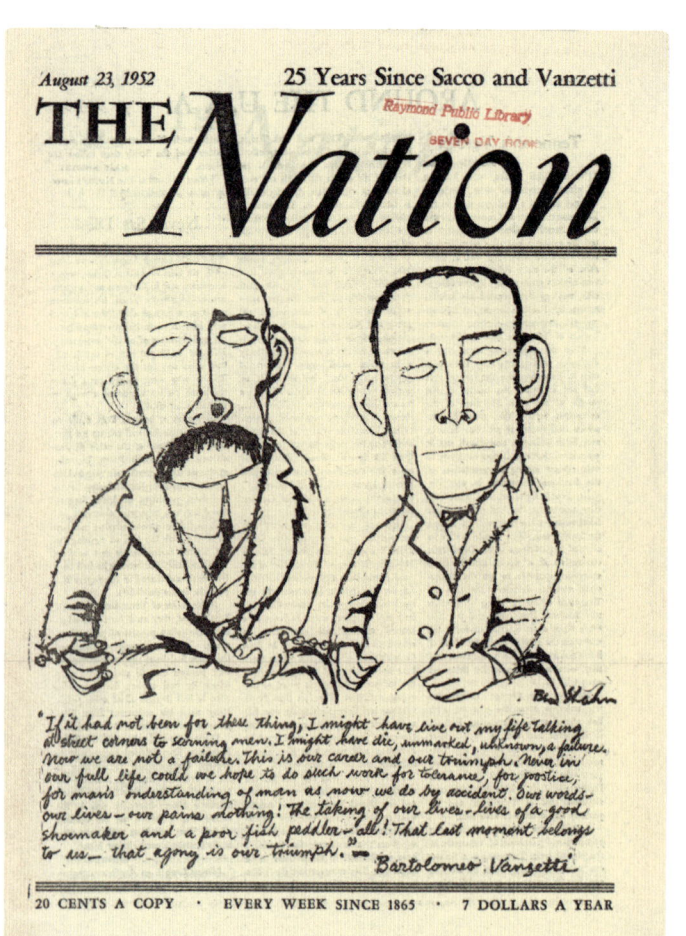

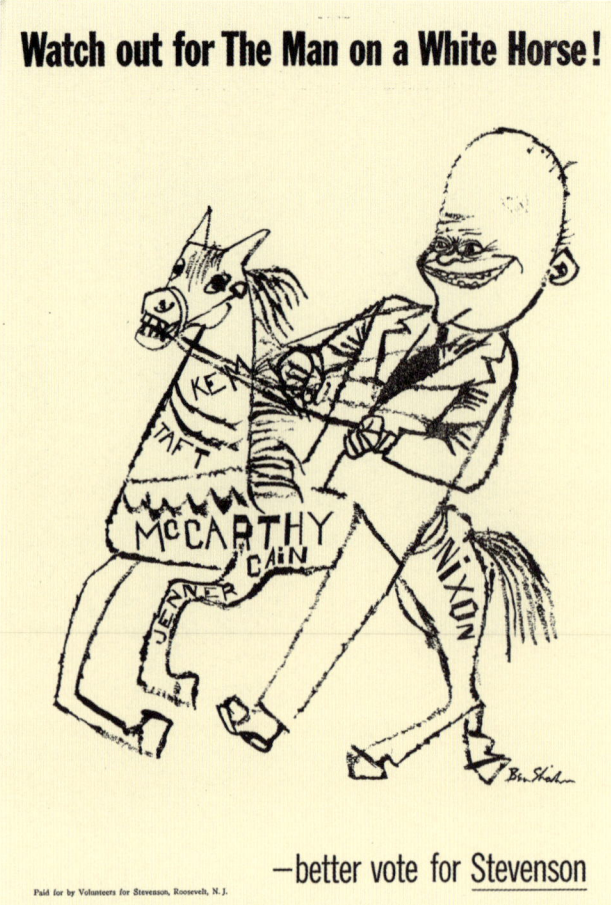

The Nation, August 23, 1952, vol. 175, no. 8

Watch out for The Man on a White Horse!
1952

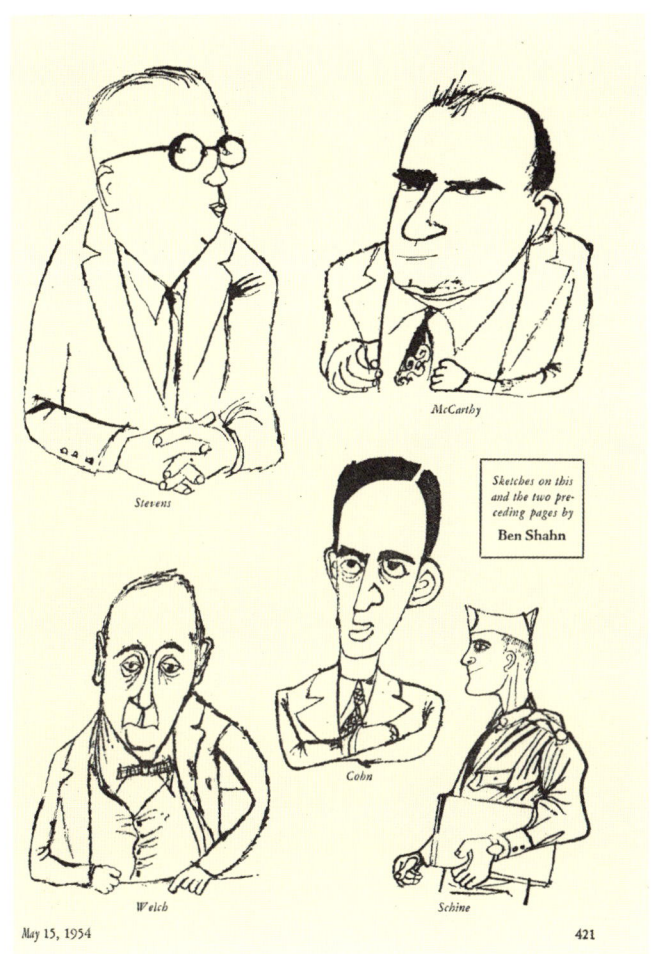

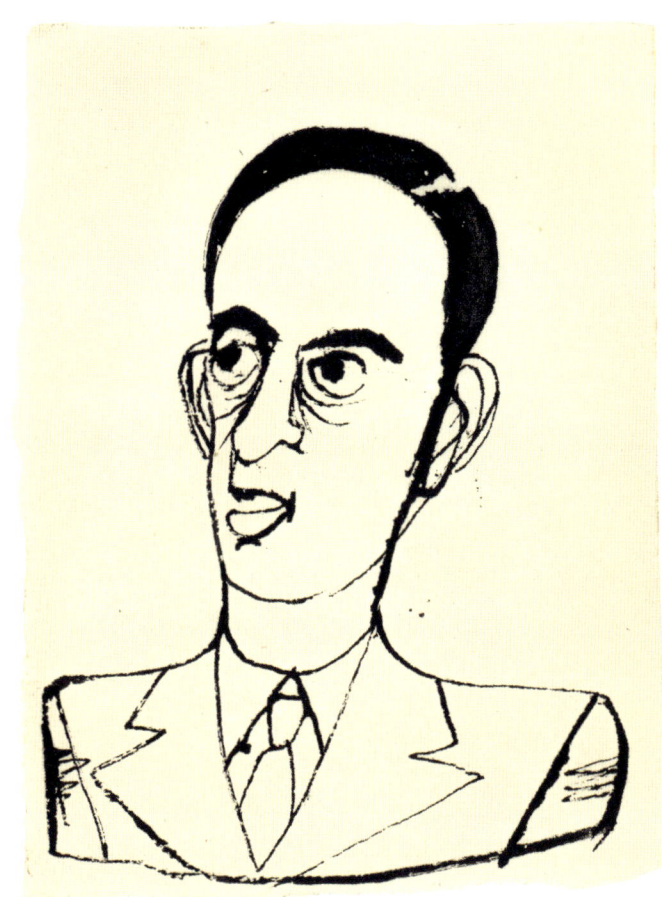

The Nation, May 15, 1954, vol. 178,
no. 20, p. 421

Untitled [Portrait of Roy M. Cohn]
c. 1954

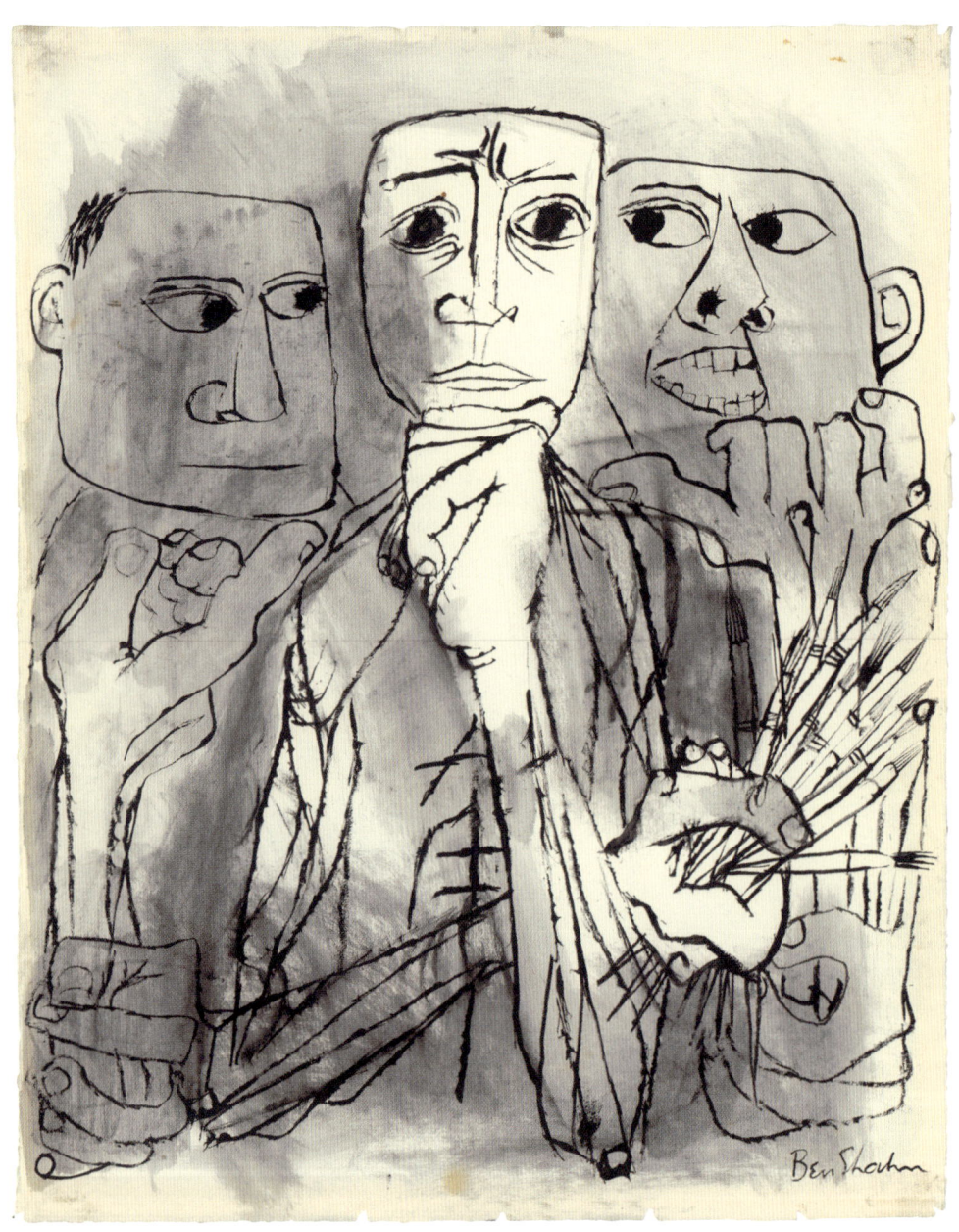

Artist and Politicians
1953

Second Allegory
1953

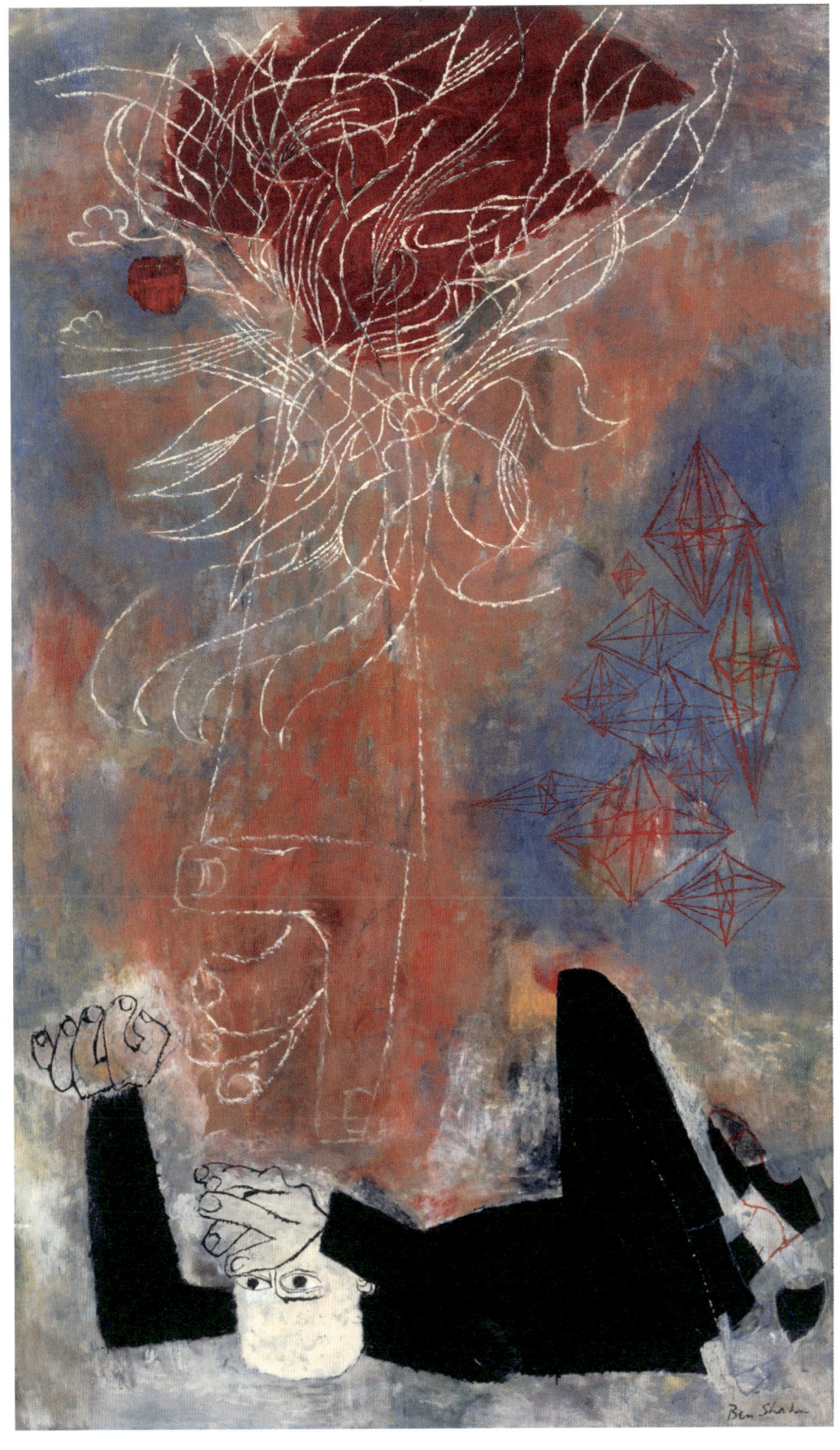

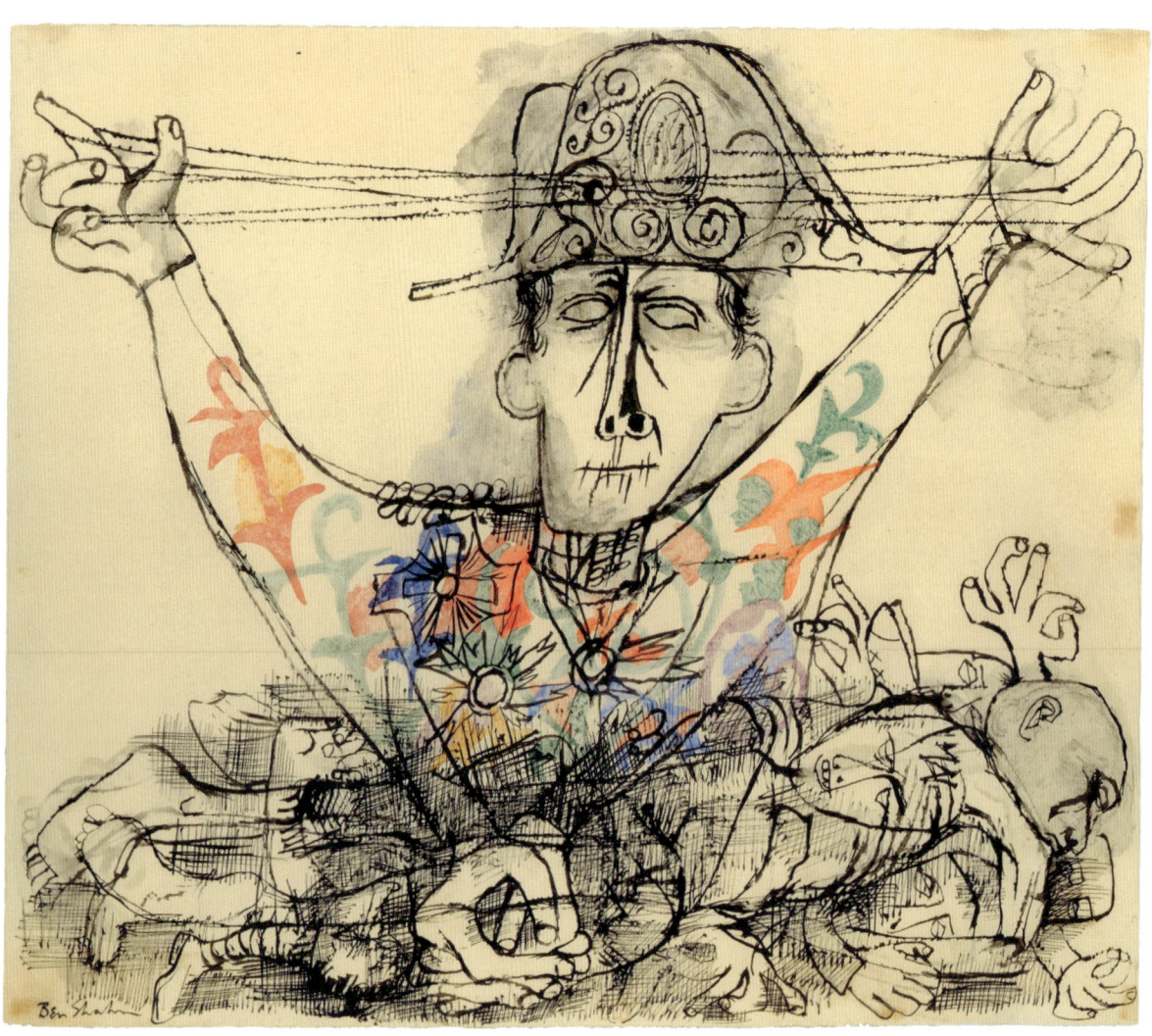

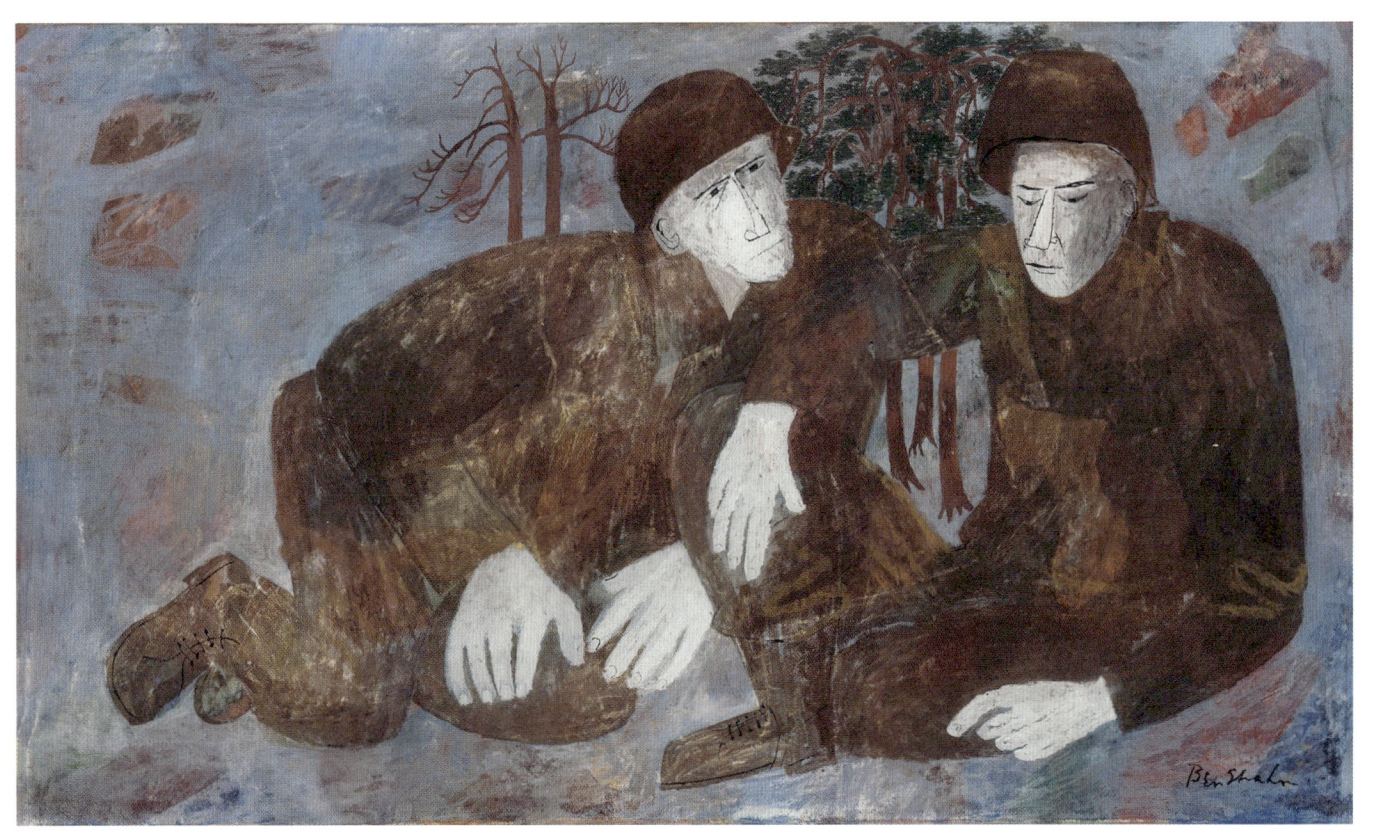

Goyescas
1956

Korea
c. 1958

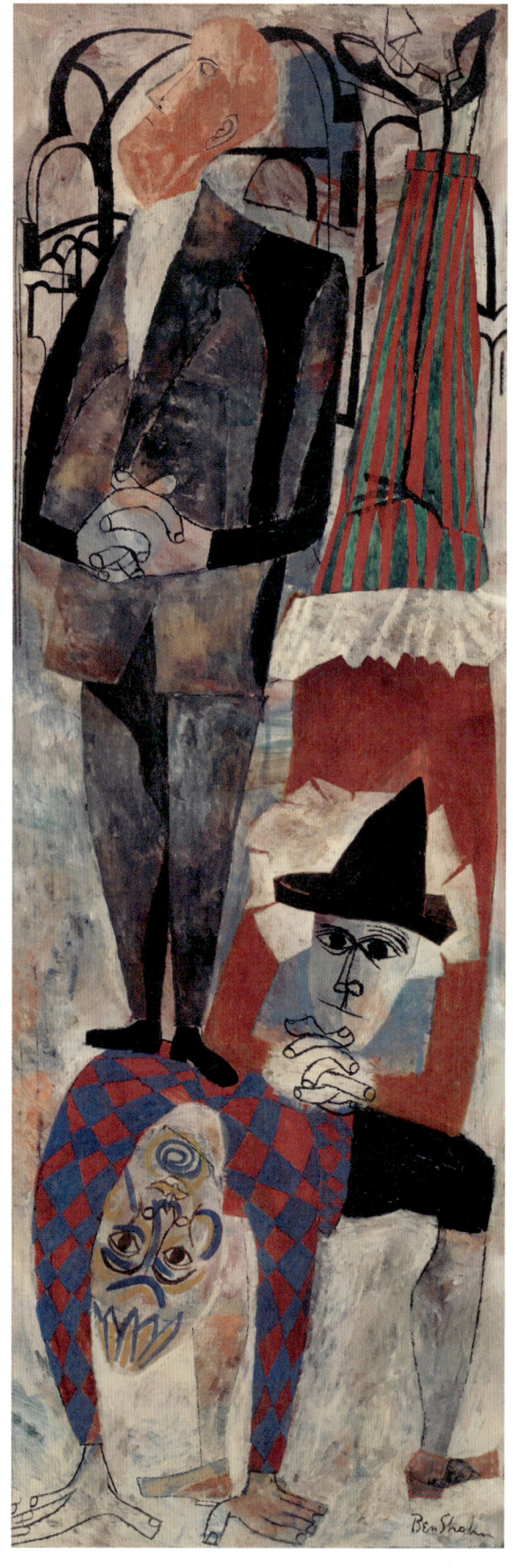

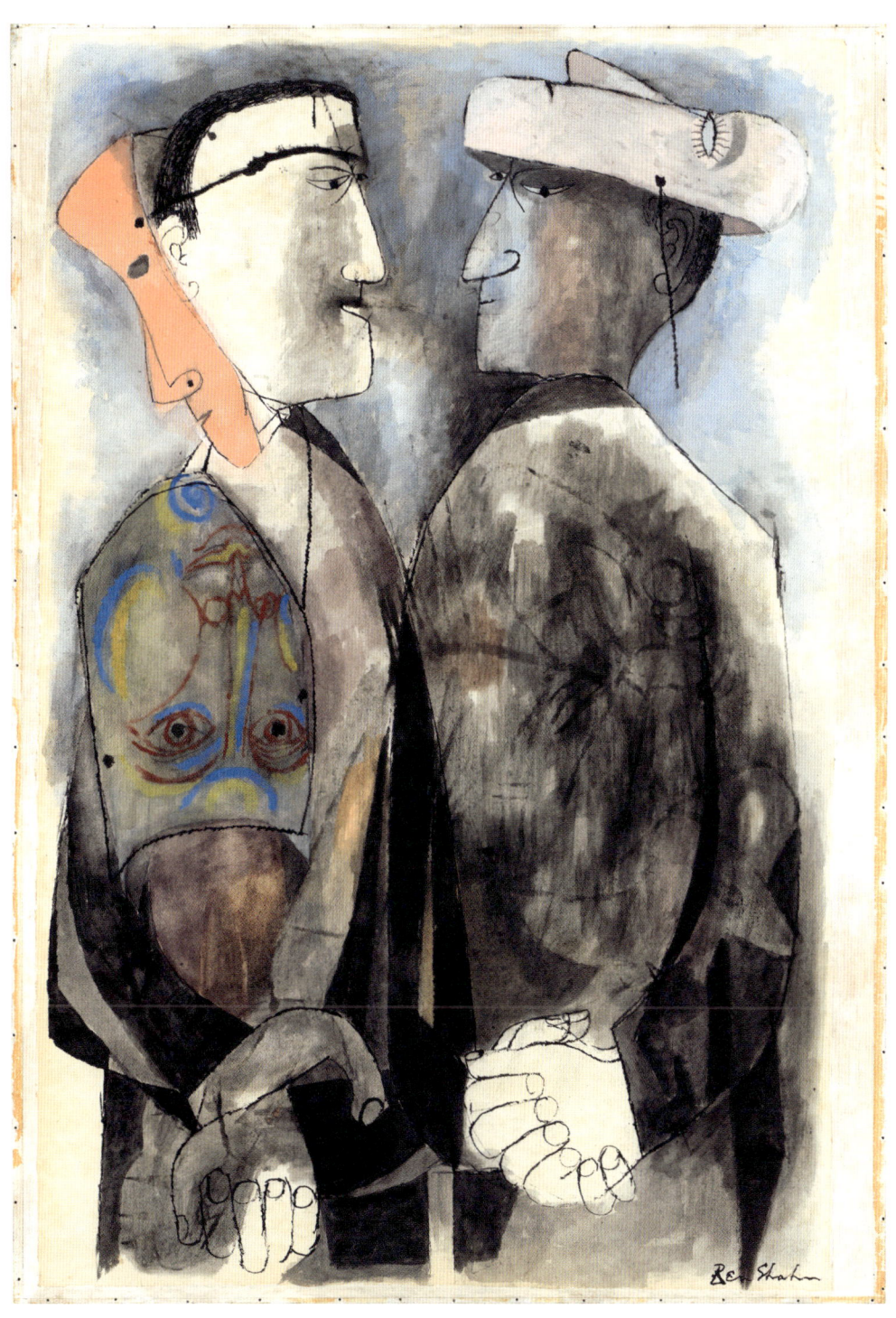

Everyman
1954

Conversations
1958

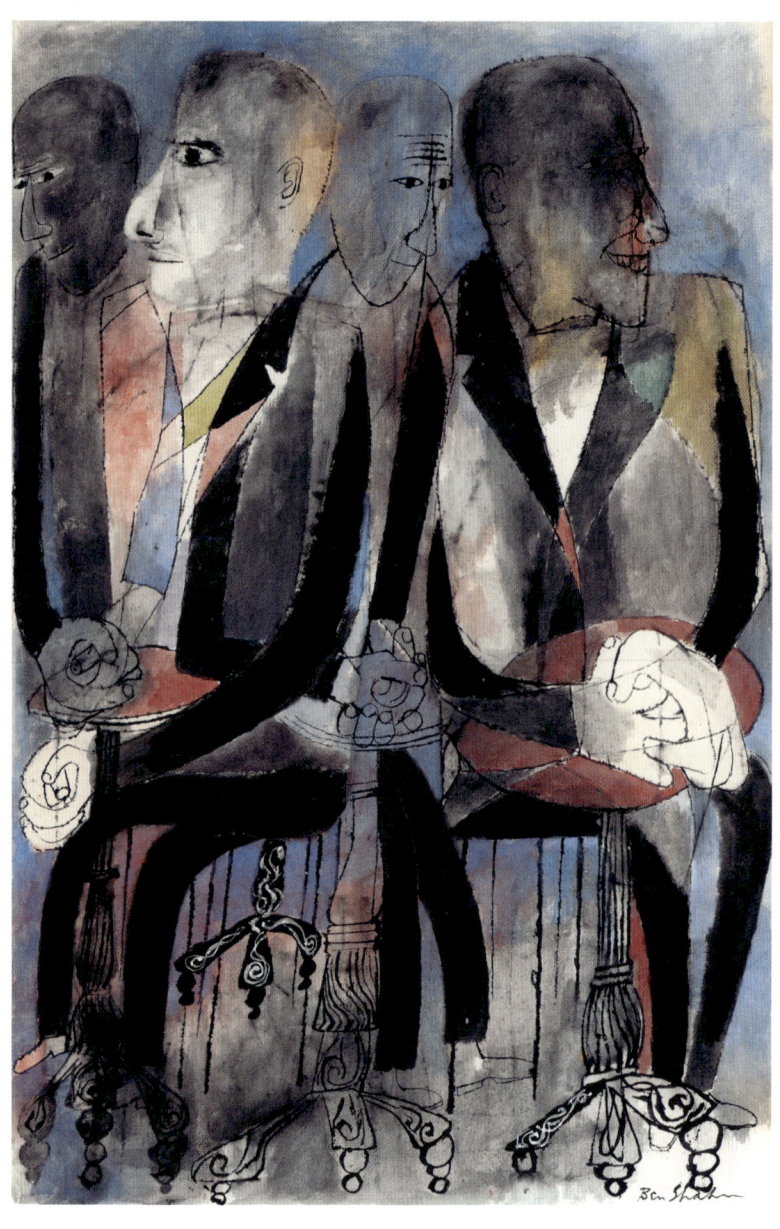

Existentialists
1957

The Atlantic Monthly, September 1957, vol. 200, no. 3

Cat's Cradle in Blue
c. 1959

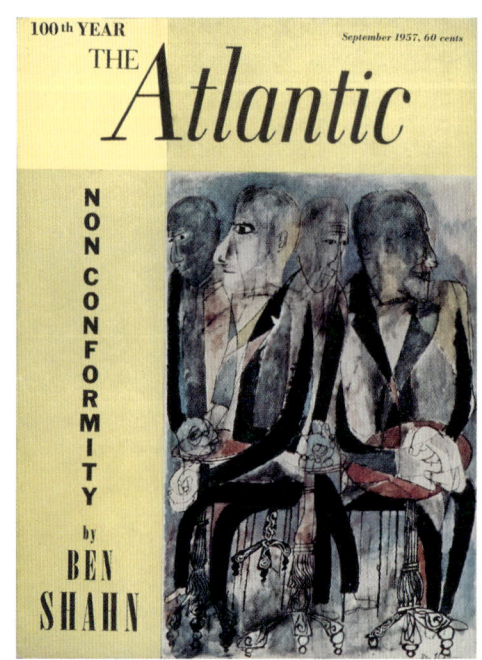

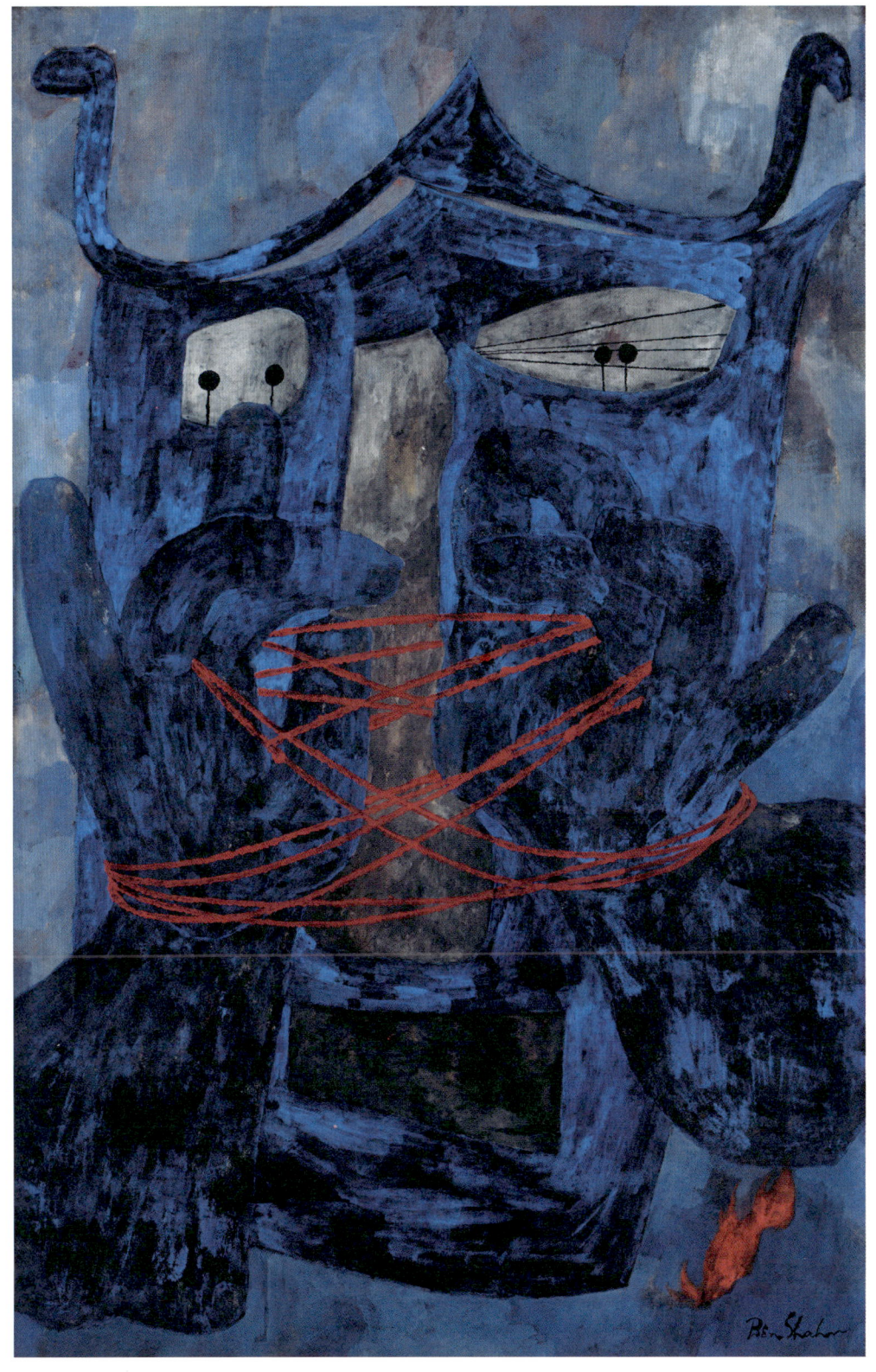

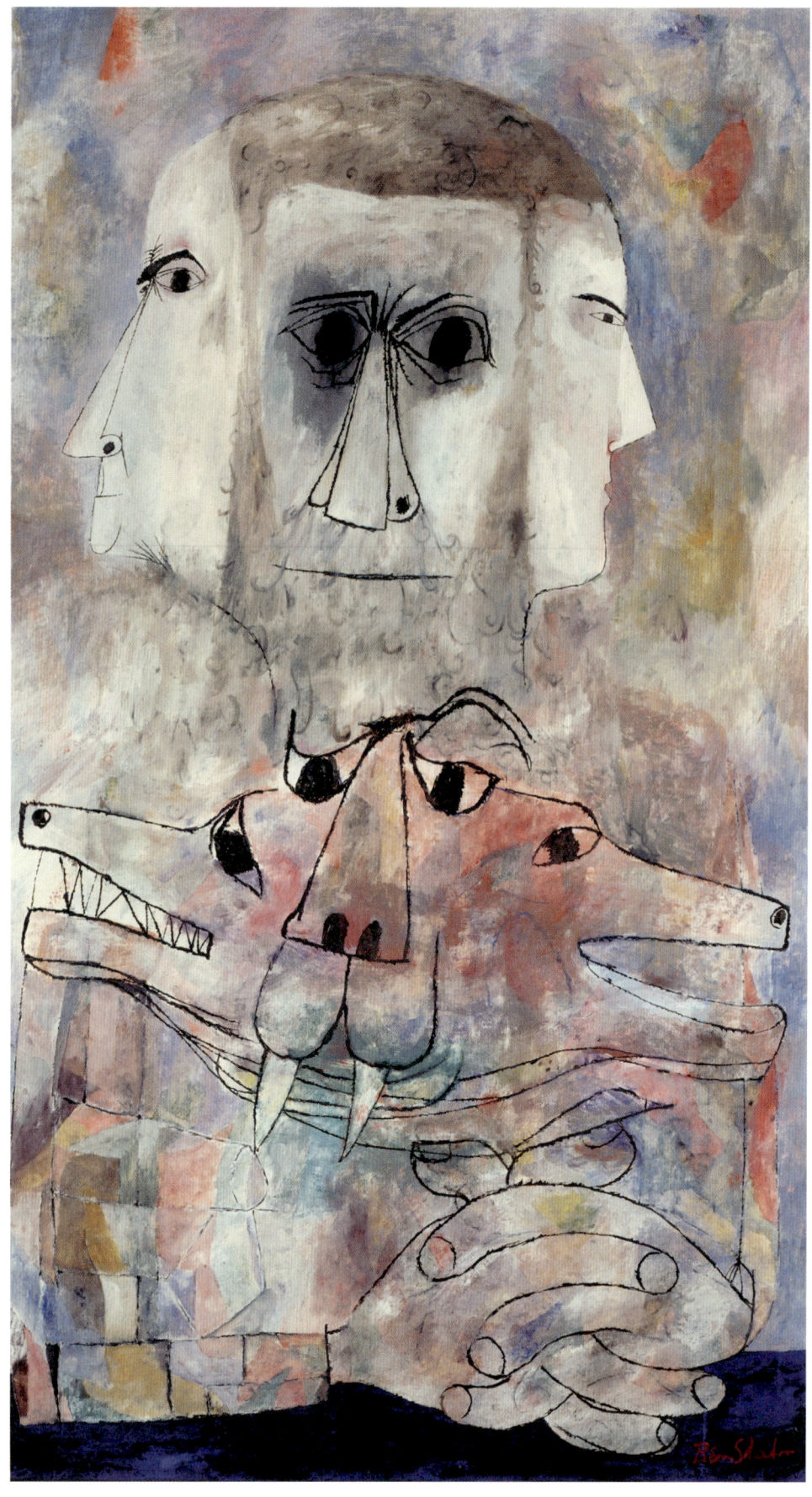

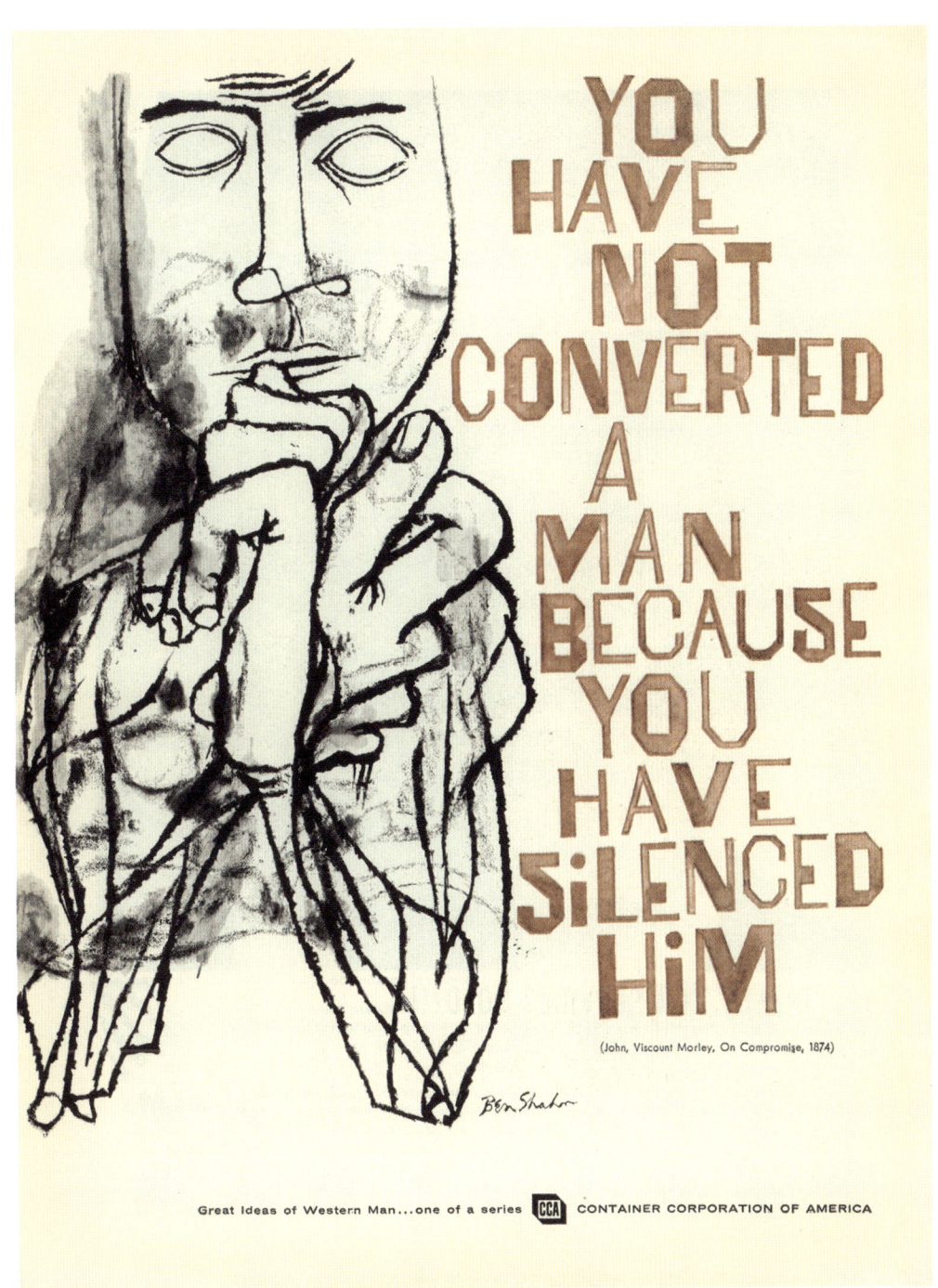

After Titian
1959

Time, April 11, 1960, vol. 75, no. 15, p. 16

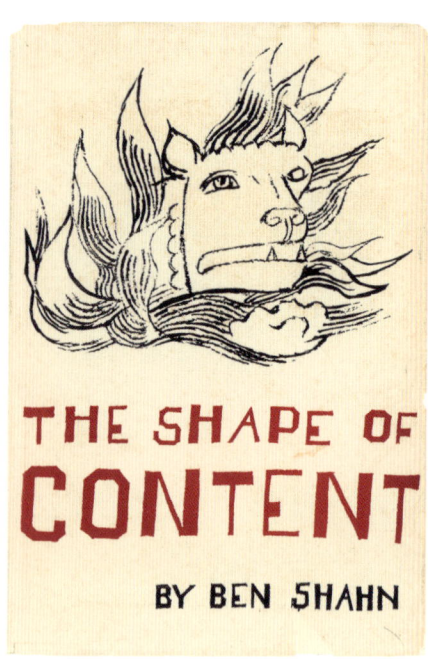

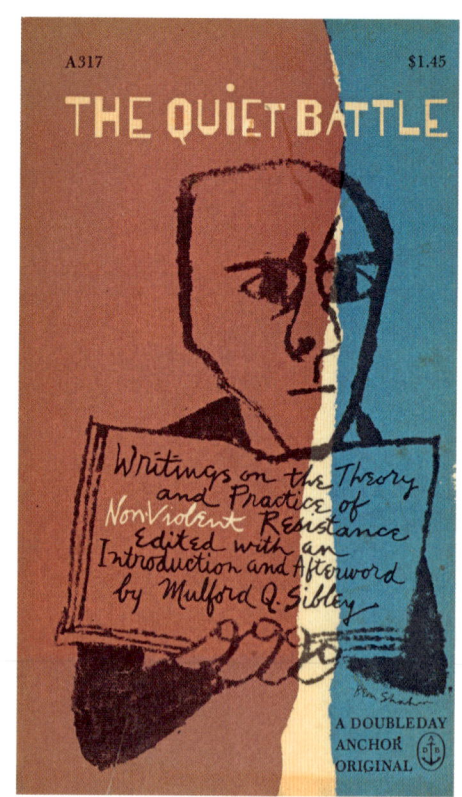

The Shape of Content. Cambridge: Harvard University Press, 1957

Mulford Q. Sibley
The Quiet Battle: Writings on the Theory and Practice of Non-Violent Resistance.
New York: Anchor Books, Doubleday & Company, Inc., 1963

Credo [Martin Luther]
1966

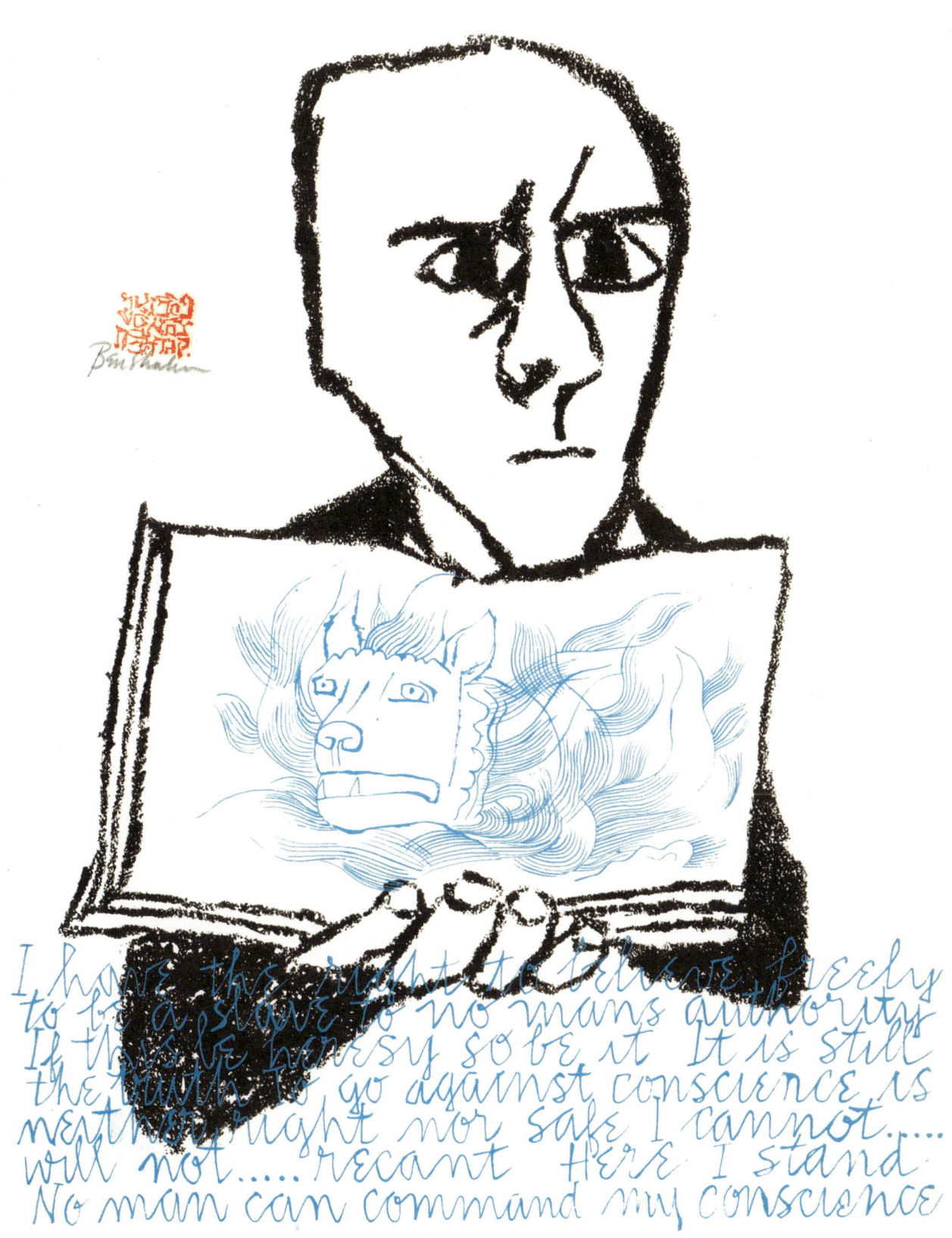

I have the right to believe freely
to be a slave to no mans authority
If this be heresy so be it It is still
the truth To go against conscience is
neither right nor safe I cannot.....
will not.....recant HERE I stand
No man can command my conscience

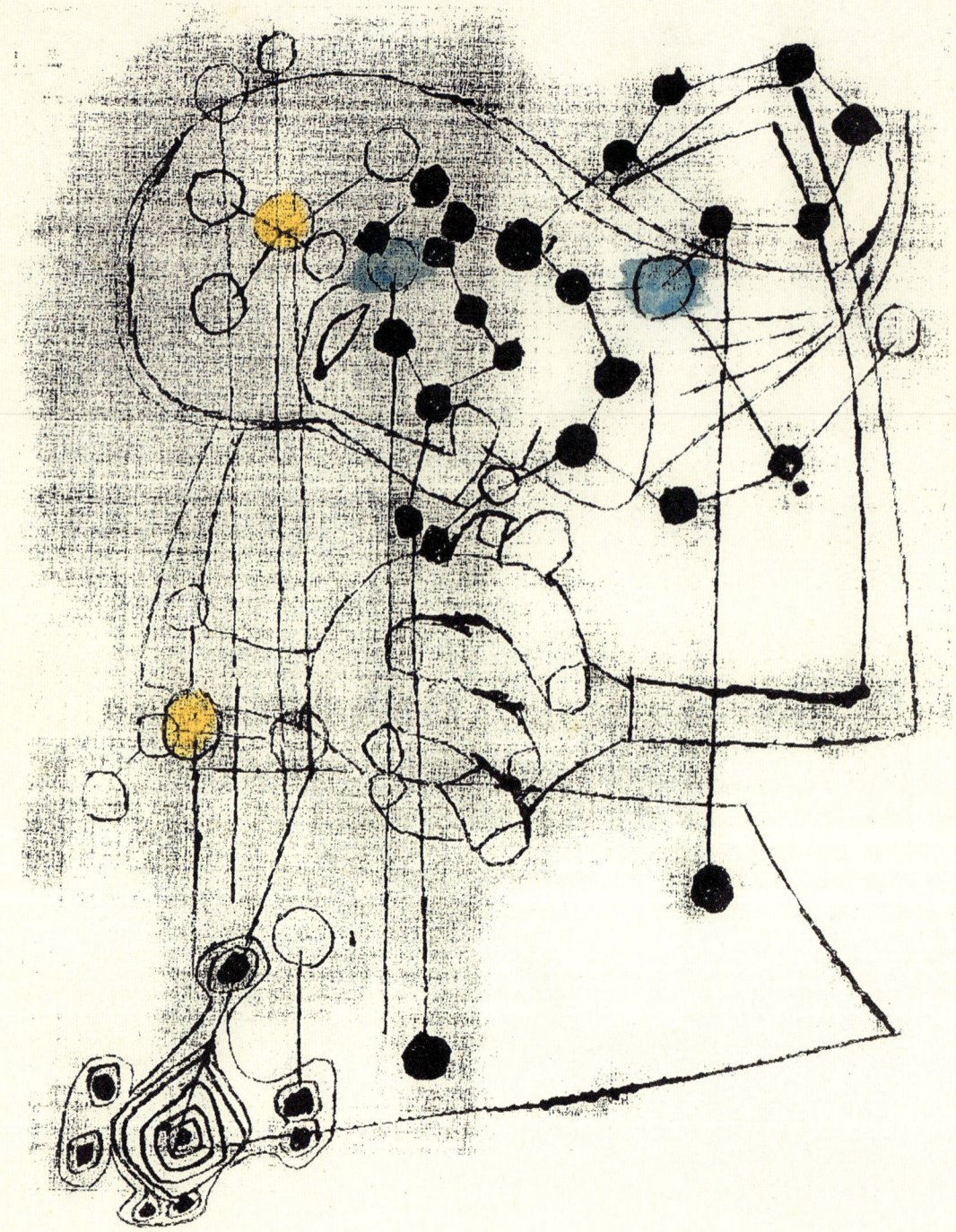

Ben Shahn

Ben Shahn was an active force in the post-World War II peace movement. Fearing that he was "living in a time when civilization has become highly expert in the art of destroying human beings," he spoke out about the dangers of nuclear weapons, supported the Cultural and Scientific Conference for World Peace Alternatives of 1949, and joined the New Jersey Committee for Peaceful Alternatives in 1950. He was skeptical of a "blind, uncritical faith in science and technology" and believed that the arts and the humanities, with their spiritual and philosophical values, must guide materialist, scientific, and technological advances.[1] He doubted whether an atomic or "scientifico-mechanical age" would contribute "to the human spirit" and even connected the "mechanics" of non-objective art with the "absolutism of science and mechanics" of his day. Given that the U.S. peace movement was associated with Soviet "peace offensives" in the Cold War, Shahn's antinuclear work increased FBI suspicions of him as a U.S. security risk.[2]

For a 1958 *New York Times* advertisement for the CBS television program about the effects of radiation, *Fallout*, part 2 of the two-part series *Atomic Timetable*, Shahn made a stark drawing of two hairless men looking upward with worried, anxious expressions—clearly victims of radiation exposure. In 1960, for the National Committee for a Sane Nuclear Policy, he made the monumental poster *Stop H Bomb Tests*, which anthropomorphizes a nuclear weapon itself. Here, the flattened shape of a horned black bull that dominates the space is flanked by an alarming declaration in red that attempts to contain the spreading atomic menace.[3] Equally haunting are Shahn's depictions of "blind botanists"—scientists immersed in their theories, physically threatened by their experiments or molecular structures. *Blind Botanist* (1961), for example, shows one such figure whose face is blocked by a thorny plant with twisted branches. He is accompanied by a quote from *Micrographia* (1665), Robert Hooke's treatise on observations through various lenses.

More intimately, Shahn portrayed famous theoretical physicists such as Albert Einstein and J. Robert Oppenheimer, both of whom he admired for ultimately opposing nuclear weapons on moral grounds and advocating for international control of atomic energy. (Shahn visited both at Princeton University's Institute for Advanced Study, close to Roosevelt, New Jersey, and made drawings of them likely from life.) His drawing of an aging Einstein was used to illustrate the latter's article, "On the Generalized Theory of Gravitation," in the April 1950 issue of *Scientific American*. One of Shahn's Oppenheimer drawings accompanied "An American Tragedy: The Oppenheimer Case" in a September 1954 issue of *The Nation*.

Scientist
1957

He pictured the complicated scientist as a tensely thin figure with hypnotic eyes, furrowed brow, and sunken cheeks—tormented by his lead role in creating the U.S. atomic bombs dropped in August 1945 on Hiroshima and Nagasaki that aimed to end World War II. Causing massive loss of human life, the bombs forecast a terrifying future. Shahn captured the anguish of Oppenheimer at the time of his security hearing conducted in April and May 1954 by the Atomic Energy Commission over his earlier ties to communism and postwar opposition to the development of the hydrogen bomb. This interrogation led to the loss of his security clearance and ended his premier role in advising on government policy.

Shahn's most moving and far-reaching antinuclear statement is *The Saga of the Lucky Dragon*—an eloquent series of ten to fourteen paintings made between 1960 and 1962 and a set of drawings for a three-part article by scientist Ralph E. Lapp in *Harper's Magazine* (1957–58). The work was spawned by the U.S. test of a hydrogen bomb on March 1, 1954, in the Bikini Atoll, which contaminated a crew of Japanese fishermen on their ship, *Lucky Dragon No. 5* (*Daigo Fukuryū Maru*), and several hundred Marshall Islanders. Shahn, who focused on suffering male bodies in his pictures, used schematized figures set against thinly textured backgrounds and subtle tempera washes to create evocative images that speak to the fate of the fishermen and the broader consequences of their tragedy. More typical antinuclear imagery of the time, according to recent research, relied on the stereotype of women and children as innocent victims of nuclear fallout.[4] Apocalyptic in tone, *We Did Not Know What Happened to Us* (c. 1960) features a fanged and clawed dragon dominating a darkened sky, wreaking havoc on the unsuspecting fishermen below. More poignant is *It's No Use to Do Any More* (1961–62), showing two bronze-skinned, spectacled men looking across an amorphous blue space to the *Lucky Dragon*'s radio operator, Aikichi Kuboyama. The men—perhaps doctors, fellow irradiated fishermen, or onlookers—stand as surrogates for viewers who are thus implicated in the scene and in the larger nuclear question. Kuboyama, depicted as a thin black outline floating peacefully on a cloud-like death bed, remains a foreboding symbol of the world's first hydrogen bomb victims.

1. Ben Shahn, "The Artist's Point of View," *Magazine of Art* 42, no. 7 (November 1949): 266; Frances K. Pohl, *Ben Shahn* (San Francisco: Pomegranate Books, 1993), 28, 134.

2. Shahn, *Paragraphs on Art* (New York: The Spiral Press, 1952), unpaginated; Pohl, *Ben Shahn: New Deal Artist in a Cold War Climate, 1947–1954* (Austin: University of Texas Press, 1989), 78–82.

3. Laura Katzman, "Art in the Atomic Age: Ben Shahn's *Stop H-Bomb Tests*," *The Yale Journal of Criticism* 11, no. 1 (1998): 139–58.

4. Cécile Whiting has argued that Shahn created antinuclear imagery that embodies "compassionate masculinity." See Whiting, "Ben Shahn: Aggrieved Men and Nuclear Fallout during the Cold War," *American Art* 30, no. 3 (Fall 2016): 2–25. On the Lucky Dragon series as exemplary of Shahn's complex image-text combinations that sought to convey the universal and global repercussions of nuclear warfare without sacrificing the historical specificity and individual experience of the Japanese victims," see Christof Decker, "A Unique Universalism: Ben Shahn and the Rhetoric of Visual Anecdotes," in James Dorson et al., eds., *Anecdotal Modernity: Making and Unmaking History* (Berlin: De Gruyter, 2020), 263–78.

SEE IT NOW with Edward R. Murrow reports on the question troubling people all over the world—

FALLOUT

In Part II of "Atomic Timetable" a group of world famous scientists present their conclusions on the effects of atomic radiation caused by nuclear explosions today and for future genera- tions. Don't fail to tune to the **CBS** Television Network today from **5 to 6:25** ◎ **CHANNEL 2**

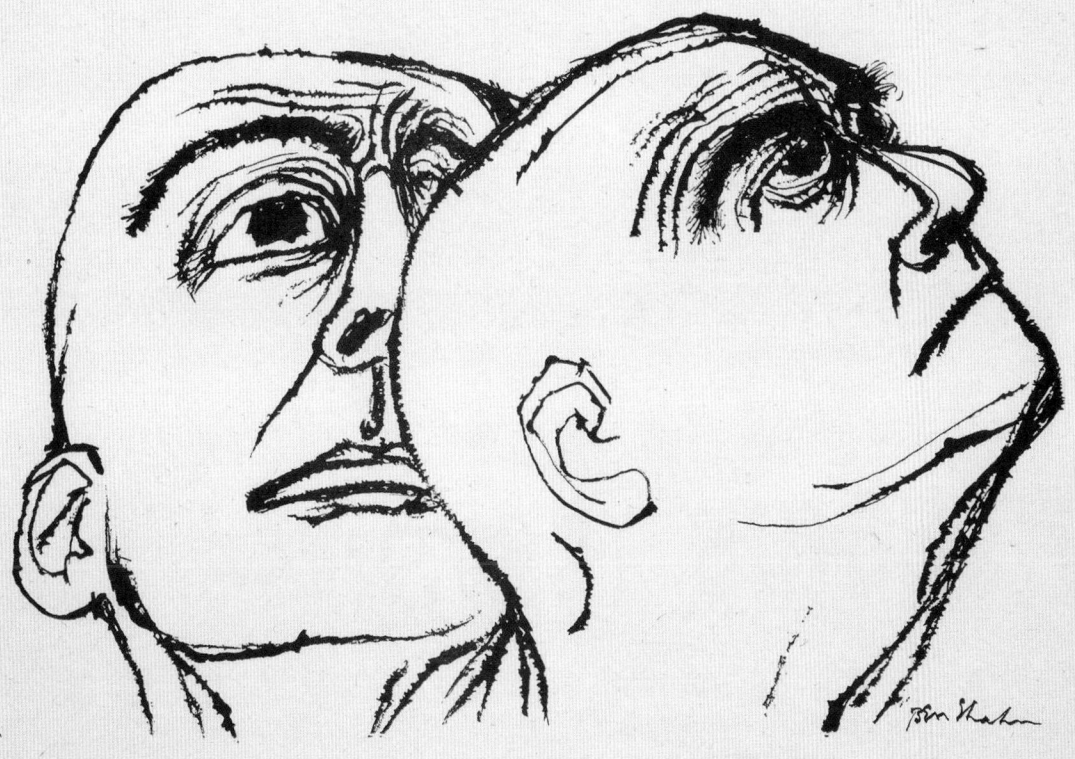

Fallout
[advertisement for CBS]
1958

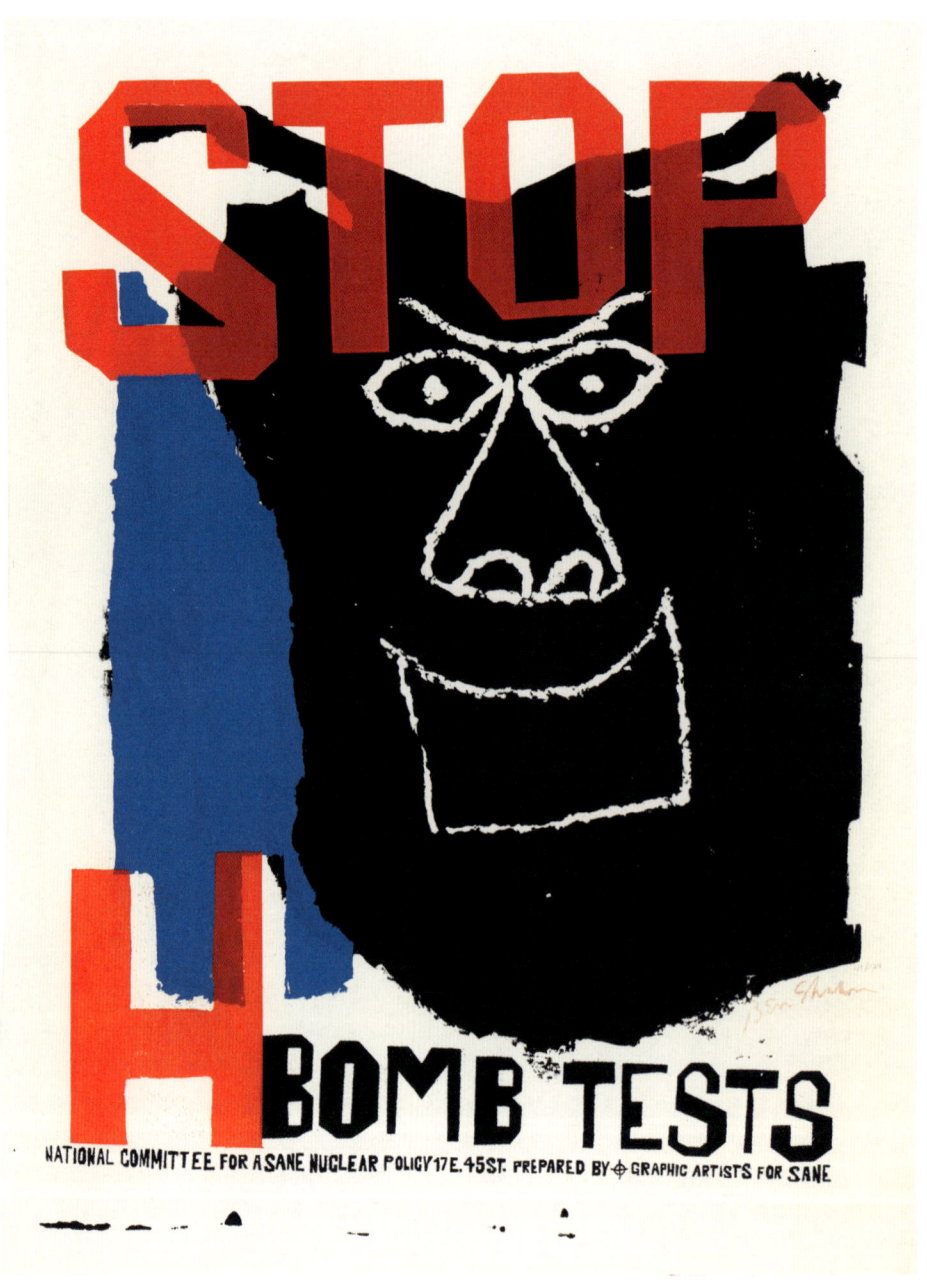

Stop H Bomb Tests
1960

Stewart Meacham
The Social Aspects of Nuclear Anxiety
1964

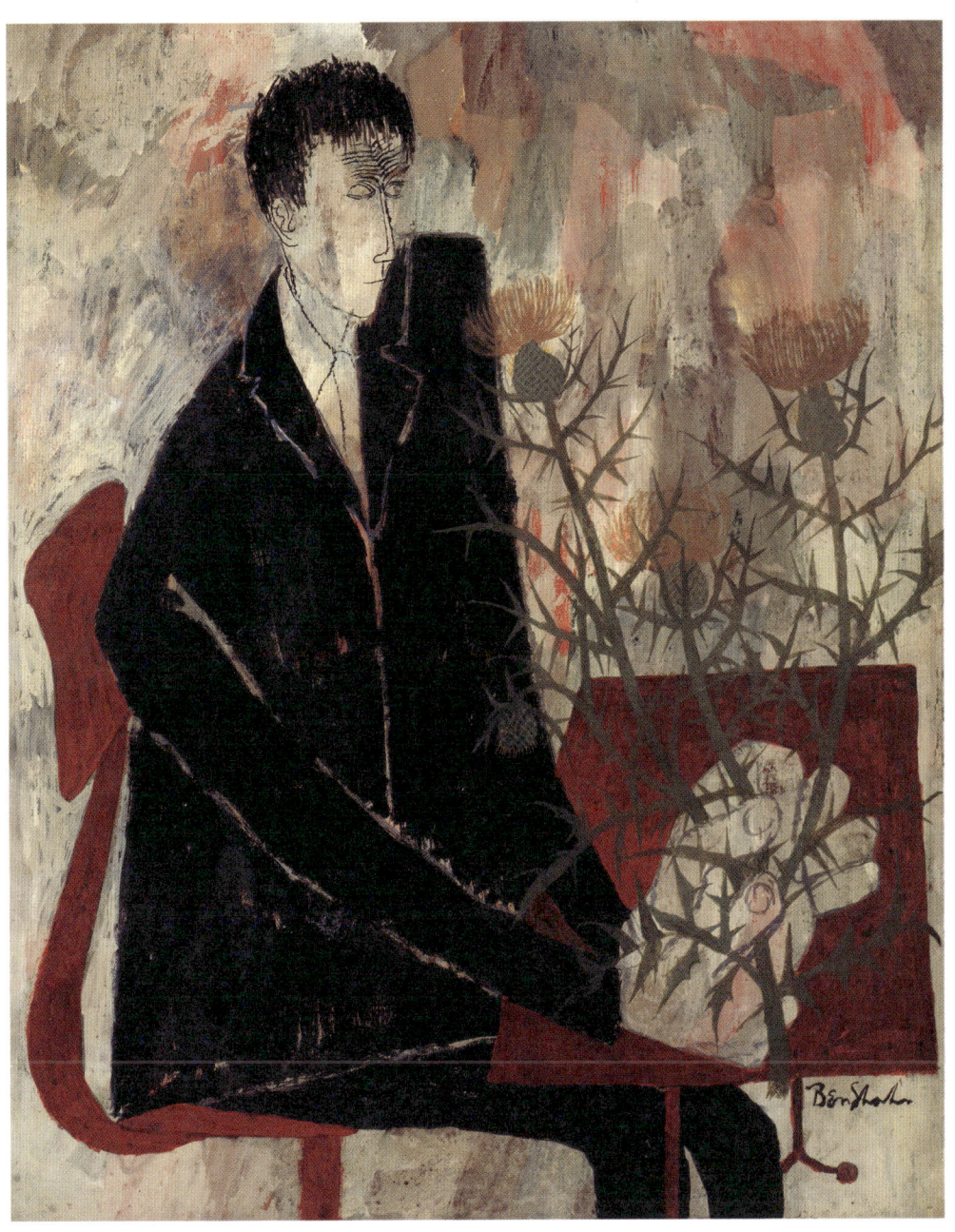

Blind Botanist #2
1954

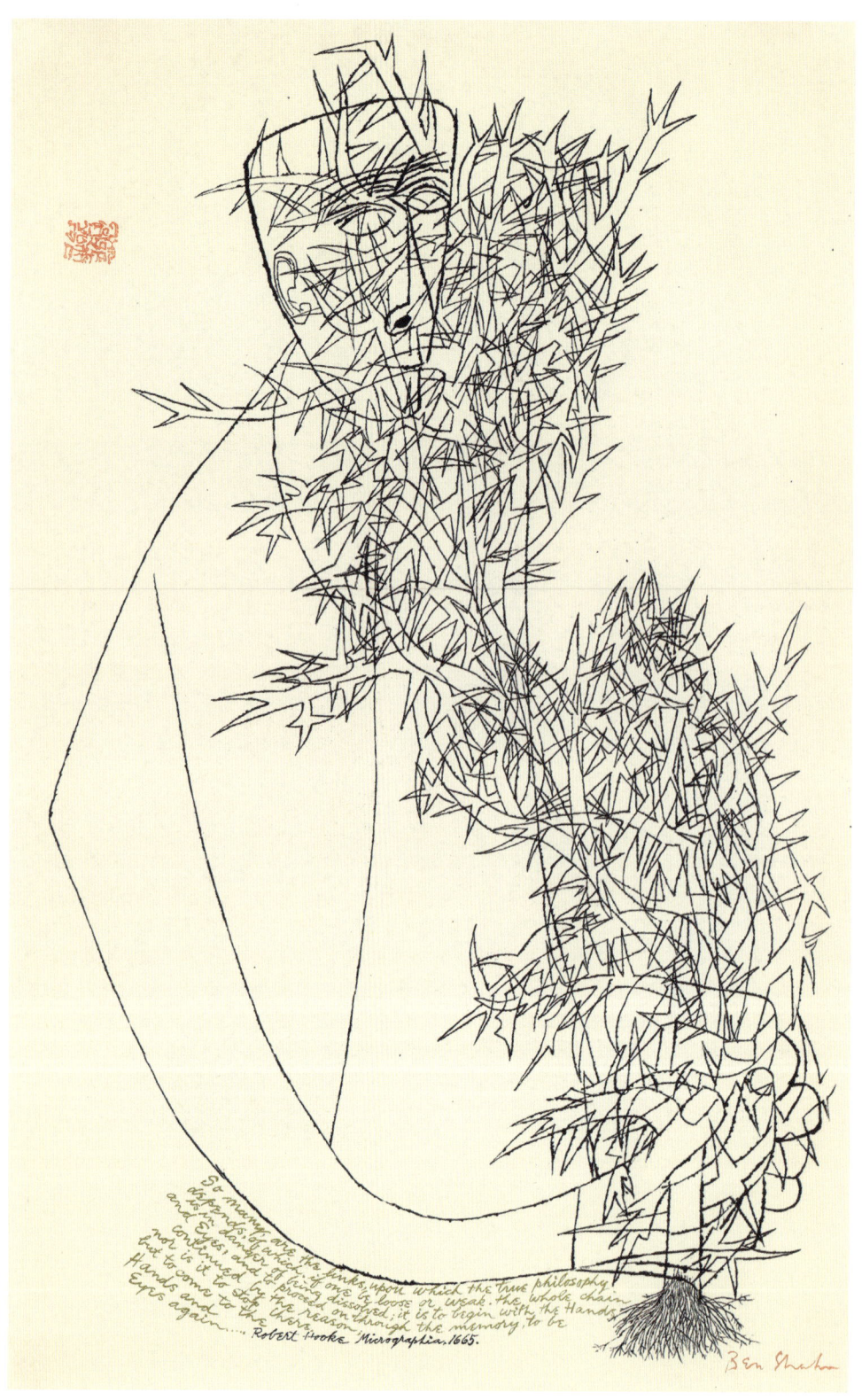

So many are the links, upon which the true philosophy
depends, of which, if any one be loose or weak, the whole chain
is in danger of being dissolved; it is to begin with the Hands
and Eyes, and to proceed on through the memory, to be
continued by the reason; not is it to stop there,
but to come to the Hands and
Eyes again ... Robert Hooke Micrographia. 1665.

Blind Botanist
1961

Blind Botanist
1963

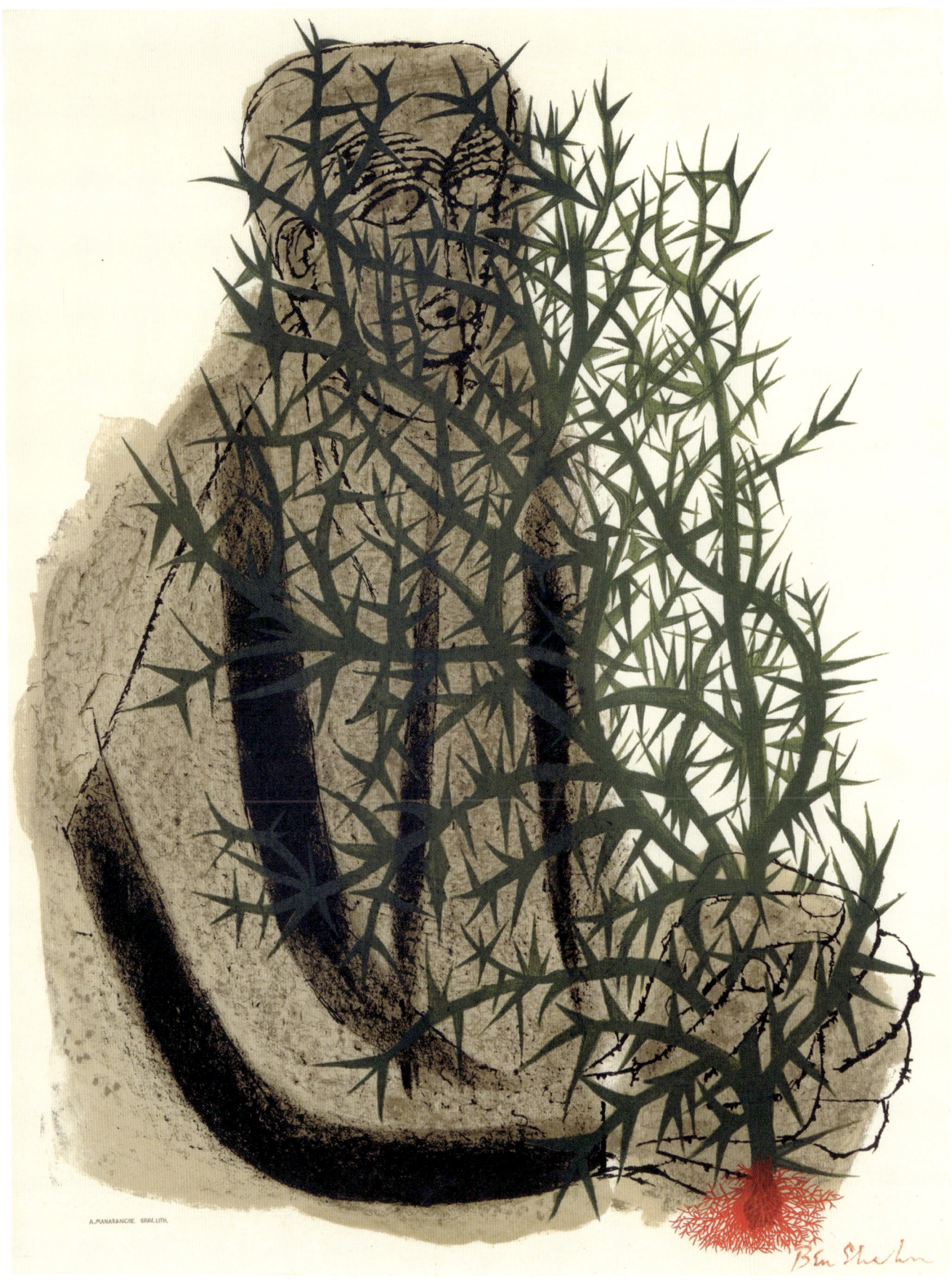

A. MANARANCHE GRAV. LITH.

Ben Shahn

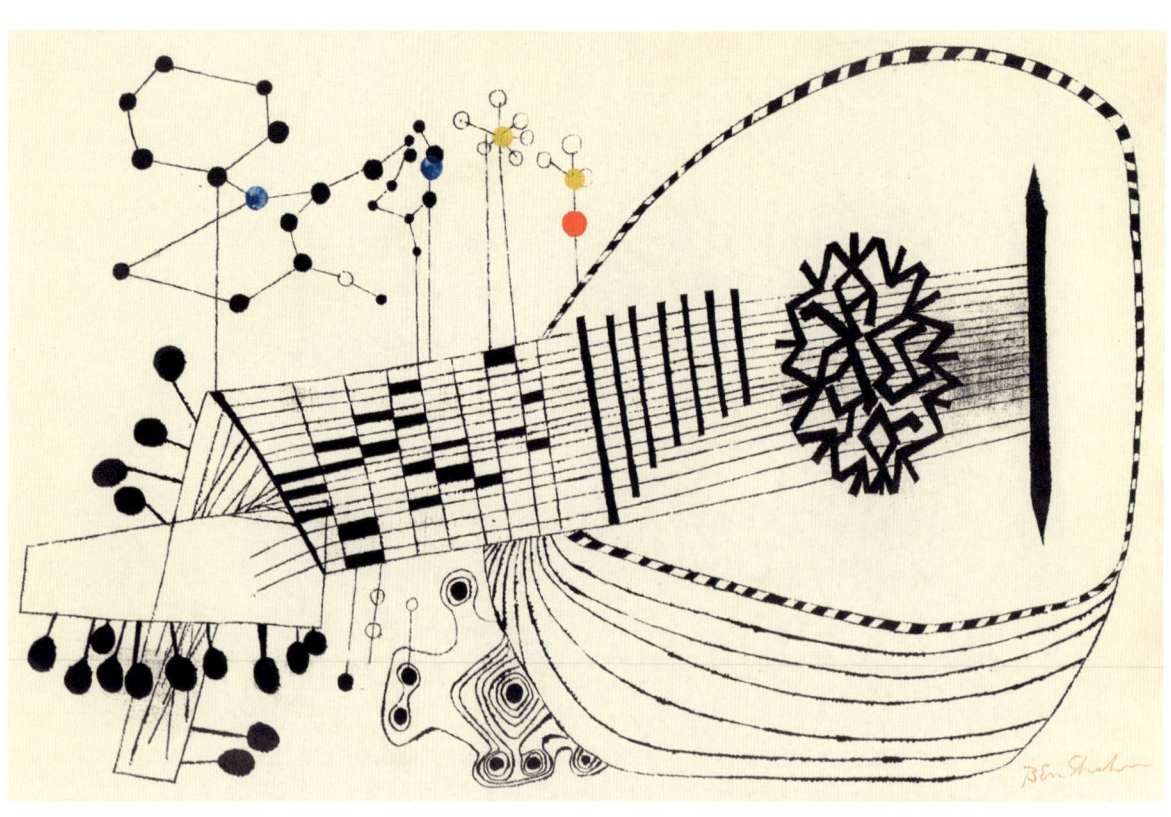

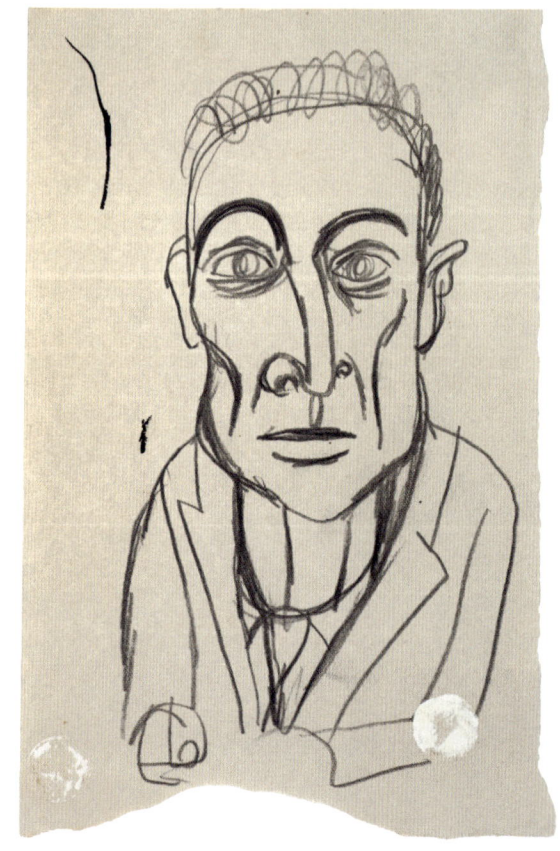

Lute and Molecule #2
1958

Untitled [Portrait of J. Robert Oppenheimer]
c. 1954

J. Robert Oppenheimer
1954

228

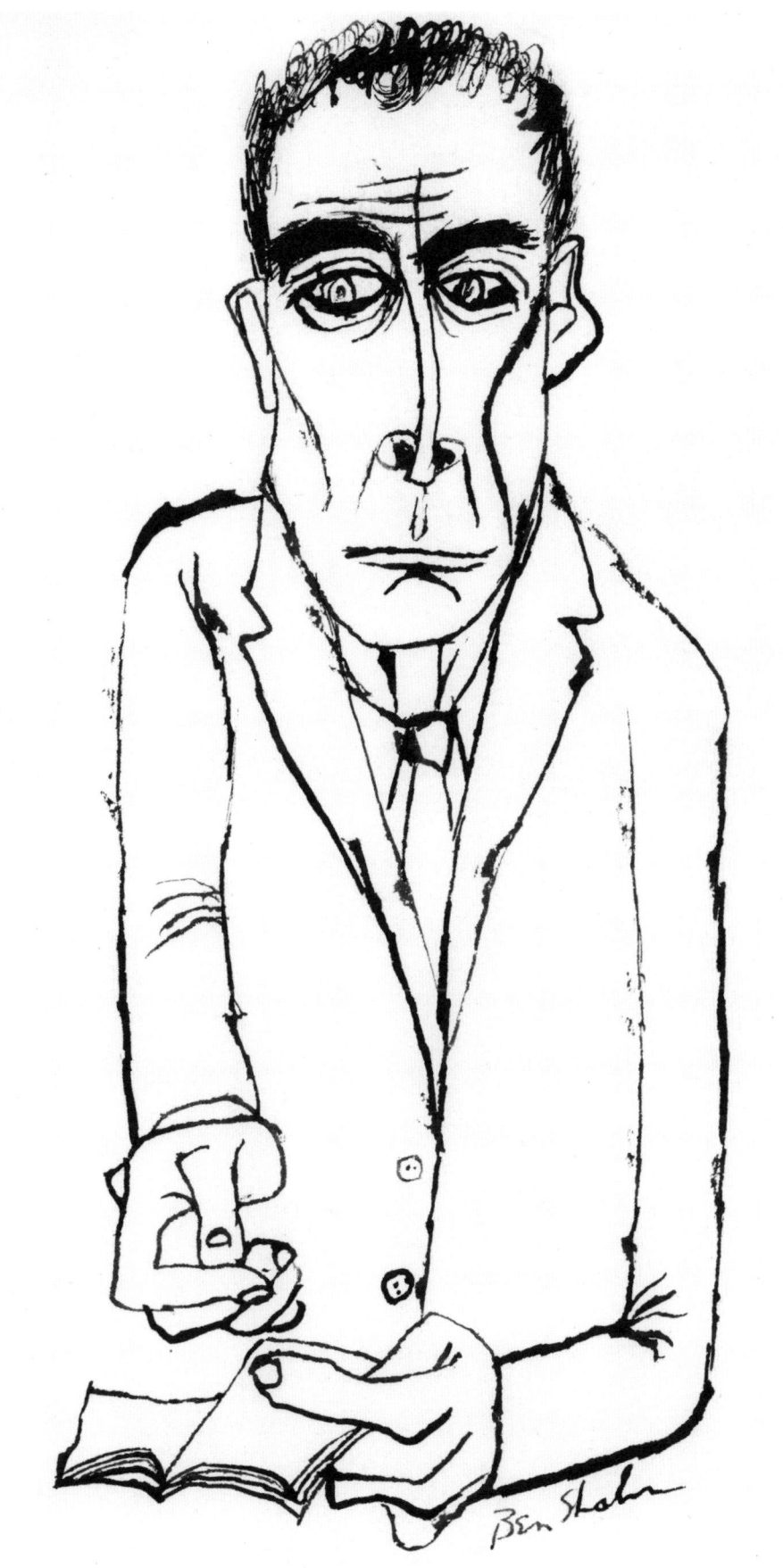

Ben Shahn

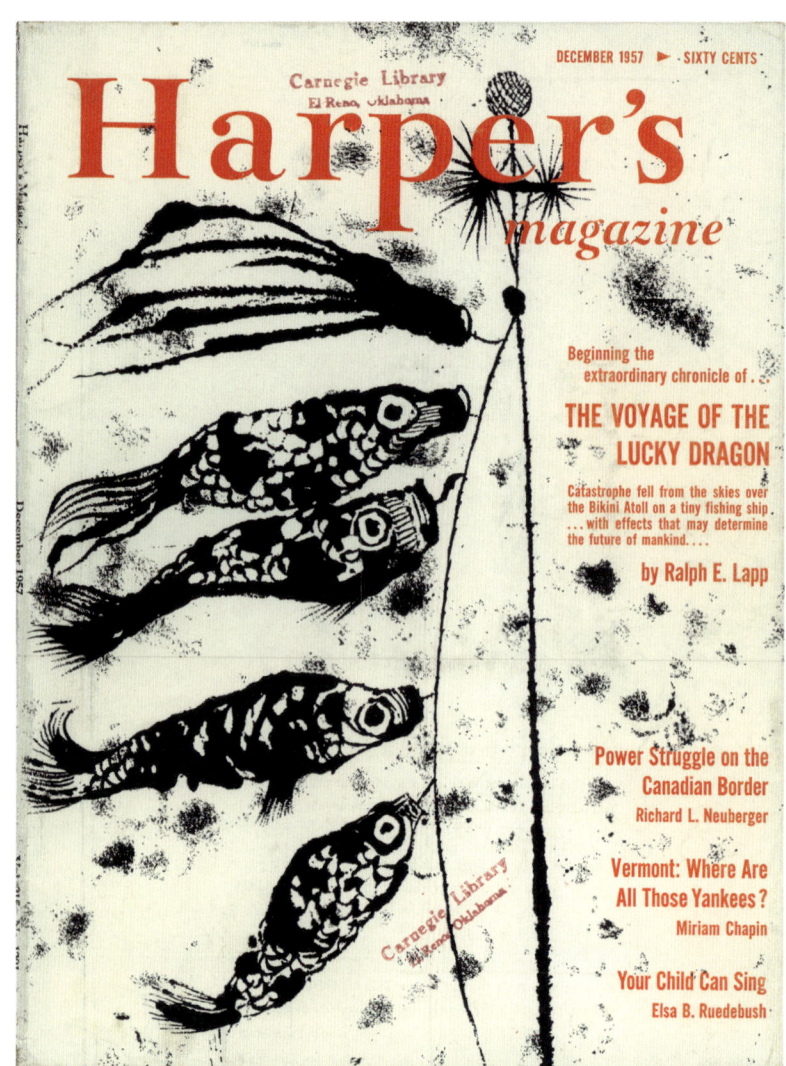

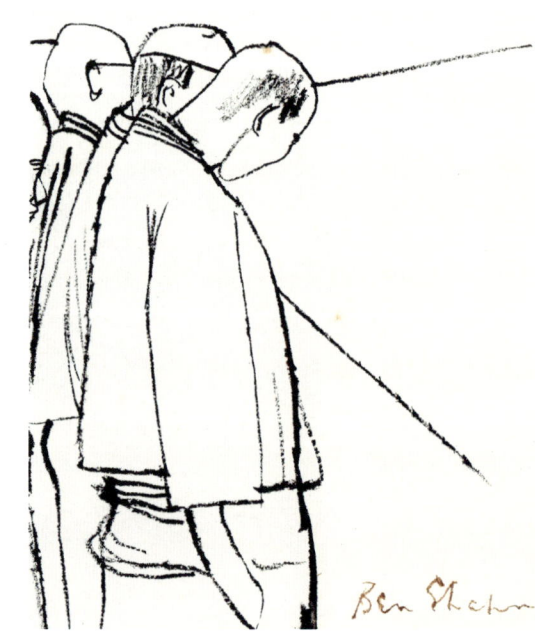

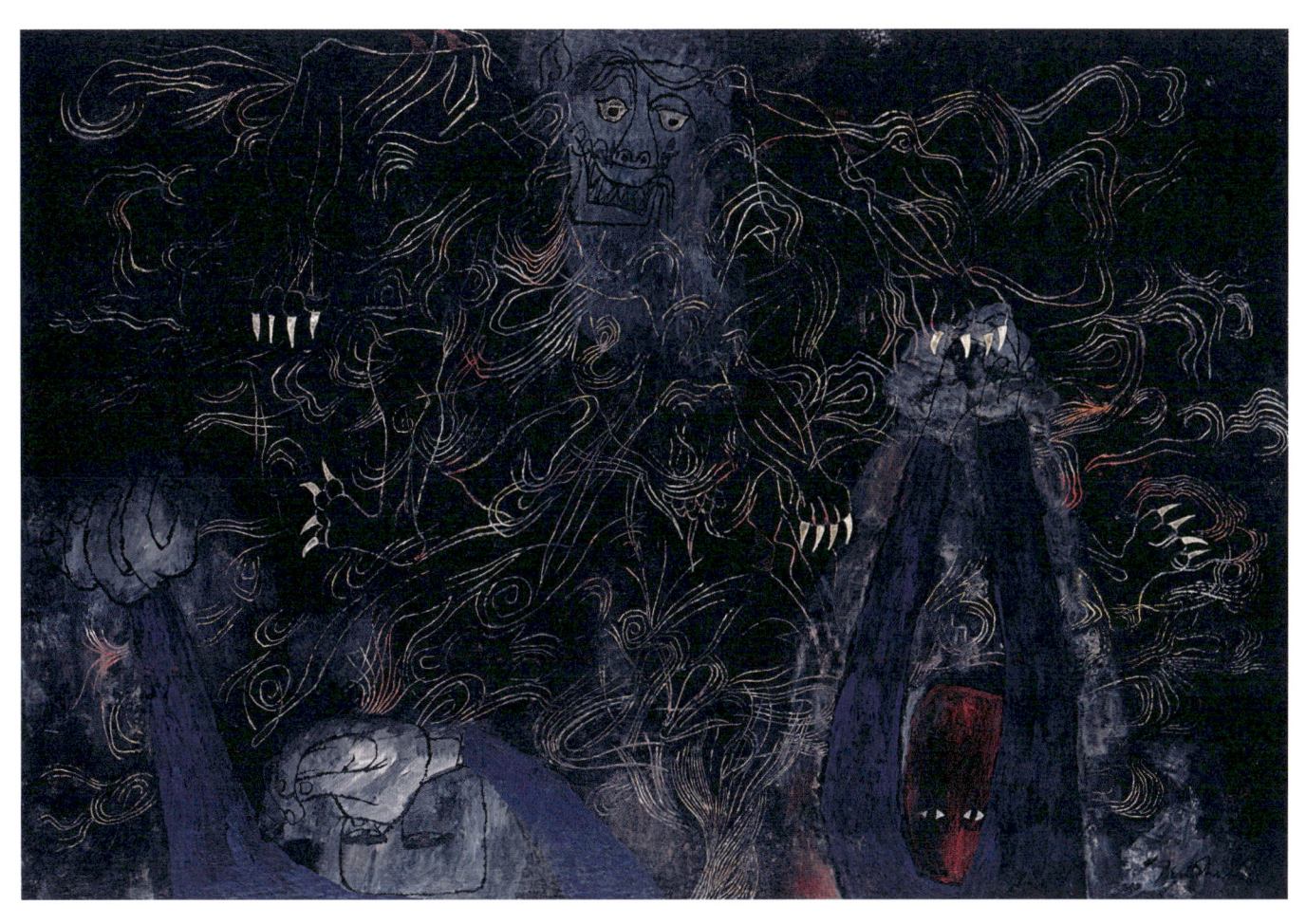

Harper's Magazine, December 1957, vol. 215, no. 1291

The News [from *The Saga of the Lucky Dragon* series]
1957

We Did Not Know What Happened to Us
c. 1960

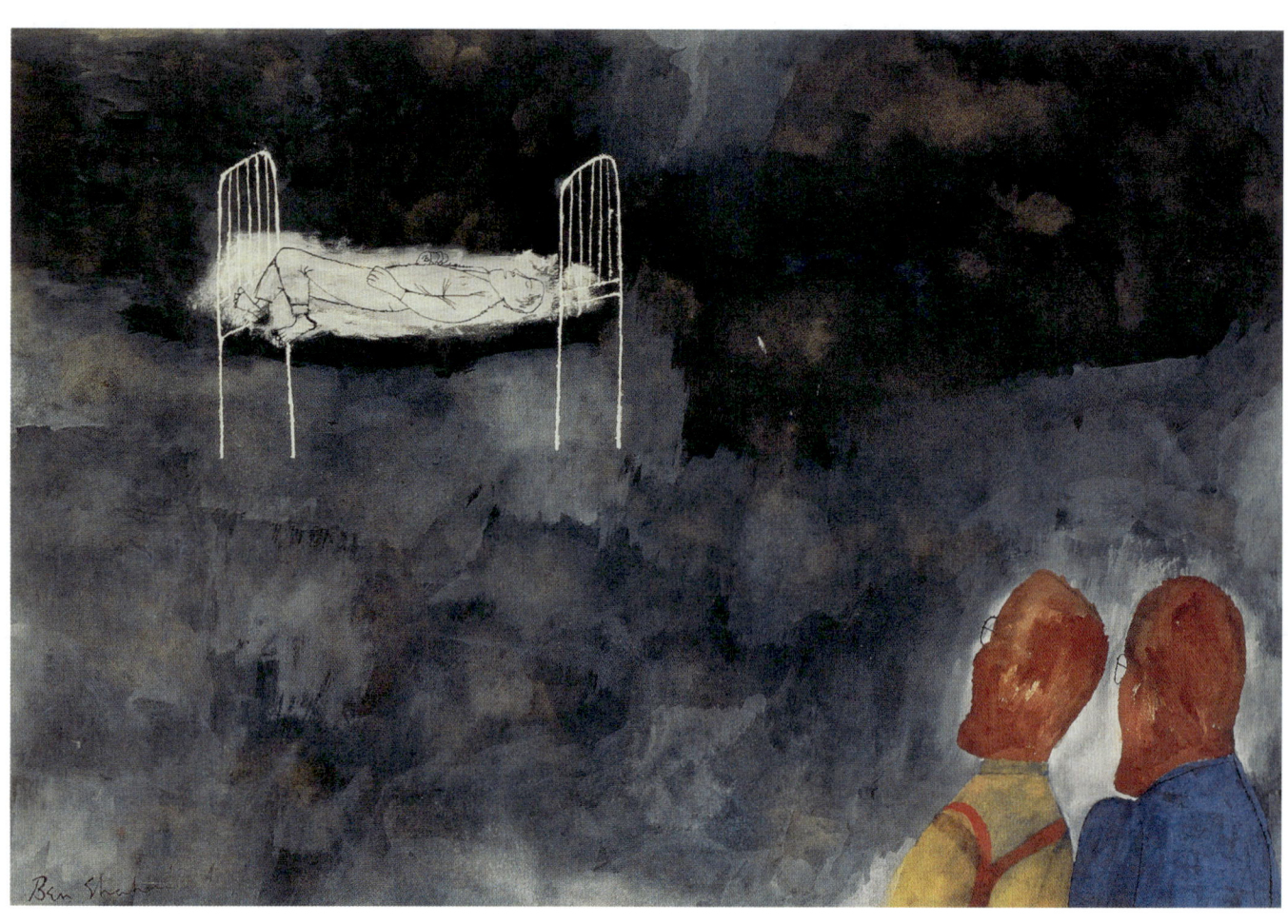

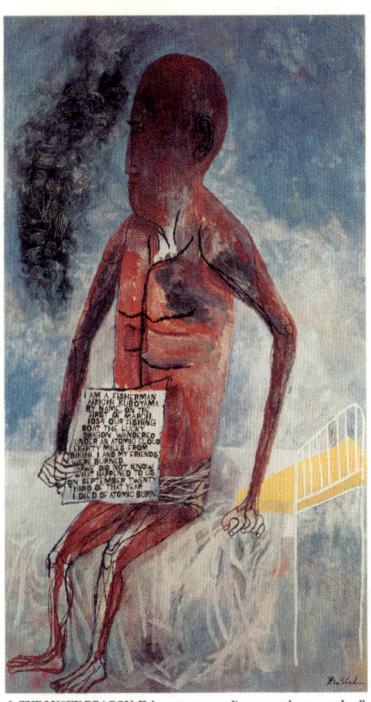

6. THE LUCKY DRAGON. Kuboyama was an ordinary man who measured well against his fellow men.

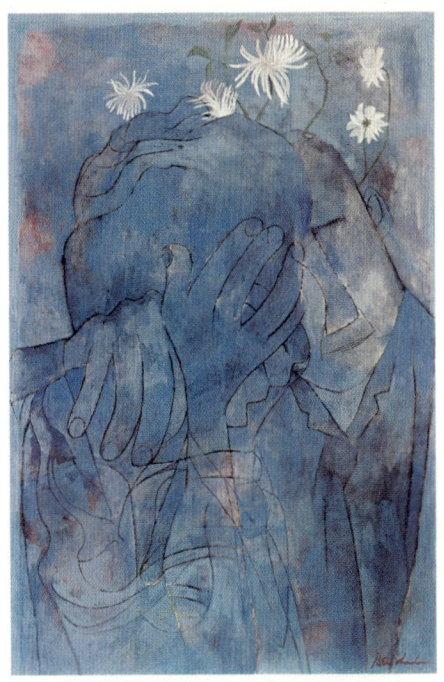

7. I NEVER DARED TO DREAM. His wife told a reporter, "I have worried about his life from the beginning, but alas, the time seems to have come now."

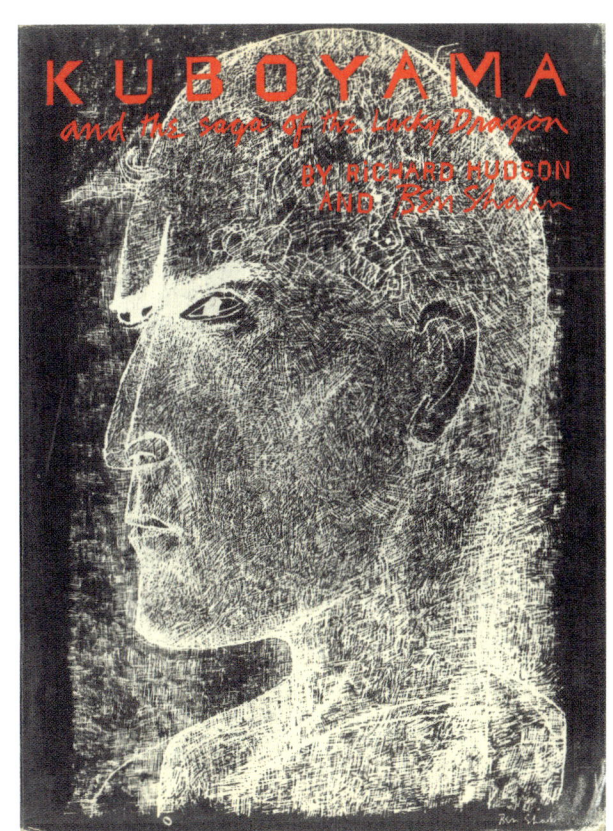

It's No Use to Do Any More
1961–62

Richard Hudson and Ben Shahn
Kuboyama and the Saga of the Lucky Dragon.
New York: Thomas Yoseloff, 1965

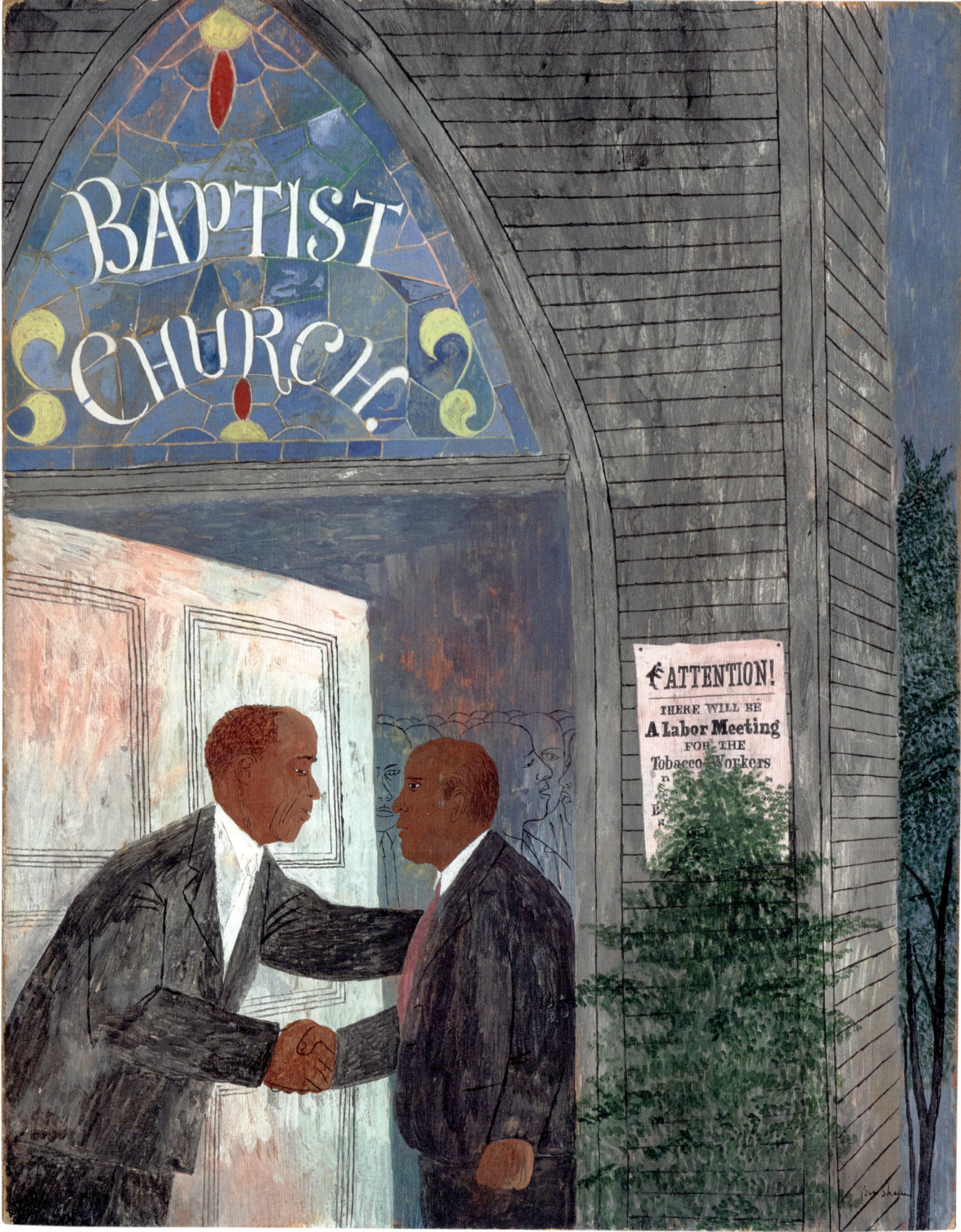

CIVIL RIGHTS AND THE GLOBAL STRUGGLE
FOR FREEDOM

In the 1950s and 1960s, Ben Shahn dedicated himself to the U.S. civil rights movement and to the global struggles of people of color, whose basic liberties had been denied for centuries. But Shahn's involvement in these struggles dates back to the 1930s—a reminder that U.S. civil rights activism predates the landmark 1954 Supreme Court decision (Brown v. Board of Education) that deemed public school segregation unconstitutional. As an American from a Jewish immigrant family who knew antisemitic persecution firsthand, Shahn was committed to combating racism and other forms of discrimination; this was no doubt sparked by the experiences and lessons of his own heritage. The alliance between Jewish and Black people in the "long civil rights movement" has a fertile yet also turbulent history. The era in which Shahn was working has been seen by many historians as a "golden age" of this partnership, which deteriorated in the latter part of the 1960s.[1]

In illustrations for *Harper's Magazine* in August 1948, Shahn exposed the tragic consequences of racial and class segregation and appalling housing conditions faced by Black families in tenements in Chicago, to which southern Blacks had migrated in search of better lives. He addressed Black labor activism in the South in *The Church is the Union Hall* (1946)—composed with figures from his 1938 Ohio photographs that he transformed from white to Black in the painting. He gravitated to Rev. Dr. Martin Luther King, Jr. not only as a civil rights leader of nonviolent action but also as a labor rights strategist; this latter role is often overlooked. He drew King as a spellbinding activist in the course of a stirring oration. (King was under heavy FBI surveillance at this time, considered the most dangerous Black man in America. His alleged ties to communism made him a perceived threat to national security—in contrast with the sanitized, deradicalized image of King today.) Shahn's drawing—commissioned for the cover of the March 19, 1965 issue of *Time* magazine—was seen by readers shortly after "Bloody Sunday," when activists marching from Selma to Montgomery, Alabama, to ensure their constitutional right to vote, were brutally beaten by police and white residents of Selma. King is pictured "not as placid as he was a year ago," as Shahn noted in *Time*. Repurposed for a photolithograph, the portrait appears with Shahn's hand-scripted excerpt from King's April 3, 1968 speech, delivered the day before his assassination. The work was used in a fundraising campaign by the Southern Christian Leadership Conference.

Another fundraising effort—for the Human Relations Council of Greater New Haven, Connecticut—included a 1965 portfolio of Shahn's simple yet haunting line portraits of young civil rights workers accompanied by Edwin Rosskam's text, *Martyrology*. The faces of two white Jewish men,

The Church is the Union Hall
1946

235

Andrew Goodman and Michael Schwerner; and a Black college student, James Chaney, appear under their names, rendered in Shahn's humble folk letters. They were murdered—Chaney the most brutally—by the Ku Klux Klan (KKK) on June 21, 1964, during the "Freedom Summer" campaign aimed at registering Black voters in Mississippi. The men's interracial cooperation and consequent murder helped fuel support for the passage of the landmark Civil Rights Act on July 2, 1964, and the Voting Rights Act on August 6, 1965, both of which reduced but did not end structural racism in the U.S. Shahn's *Integration, Supreme Court* (1963) shows that such legal justice was ironically in the hands of privileged white men on the highest court, who in the painting appear small against the elongated classical columns of their hallowed setting—symbolic of the monumental task before them. This is the Warren Court, considered the most liberal in U.S. history; it decided the 1954 school desegregation case commemorated in this picture.[2]

Notably, Shahn did not depict the powerful, controversial Black nationalist and human rights activist Malcolm X, who was assassinated in 1965. Shahn expressed doubt about whether "the whole Black population" followed Black Power icon Stokely Carmichael's separatist, militant approach toward effecting racial justice and self-determination. And he was apparently "furious" about the use of his King portrait to accompany an article by Black Panther leader Eldridge Cleaver in *Ramparts*, even though the artist staunchly supported that left-wing magazine.[3] Shahn's civil rights world, alas, was largely a male universe. While he honored KKK-slain activist Viola Gregg Liuzzo in his print *I Think Continually of Those Who Were Truly Great* (1965), he did not portray prominent Black women such as Rosa Parks, Ella Baker, or Fannie Lou Hamer, who were instrumental in the fight for civil rights.

Shahn ardently supported the decolonization efforts sweeping the globe in the postwar years, designing advertisements for CBS television programs in the 1950s on resistance movements against European colonial rule in African countries. He memorialized India's struggle for freedom from British rule in his monumental portrait of the "prophet" of nonviolence Mahatma Gandhi, first published in an August 1964 issue of *Look* magazine. Shahn's barbed wire line expresses the moral severity and steady vision of the ascetic leader seated erect in a meditative position. He viewed Gandhi the way King saw him—as a spiritual inspiration and as a profound influence on the civil disobedience strategies of boycotts, sit-ins, and marches. (At the end of his life, Gandhi, like King, faced hatred and opposition by extremists both outside and within his own community.) Just five months after India achieved its independence and in the wake of the horrific trauma and turmoil of the British partition, a Hindu nationalist, condemning Gandhi's tolerance for Muslims, assassinated him on January 30, 1948. Fittingly, Shahn appropriated his own image of Gandhi to protest the Vietnam War in December 1967; he paired it with an antiwar quotation from Mark Twain as a "message for peace" printed in the *New York Times*.

1. Cheryl Lynn Greenberg, *Troubling the Waters: Black-Jewish Relations in the American Century* (Princeton: Princeton University Press, 2006).

2. It should be noted that Ben Shahn's print *Thou Shalt Not Stand Idly By* (1965), showing a white hand lifting up a Black hand, can be read from a contemporary perspective as a "white savior" image.

3. Interview with Ben Shahn by Forrest Selvig, September 27, 1968, transcript, 17, Ben Shahn papers, Smithsonian Archives of American Art (BSP-AAA); Bernarda Bryson Shahn comment on Dugald Stermer's draft, "In Memoriam: Ben Shahn," *Ramparts* (May 1969), BSP-AAA. It is unknown to the author if Shahn recognized the Black Panthers' progressive community work and if he accepted the common misperception that they advocated violence.

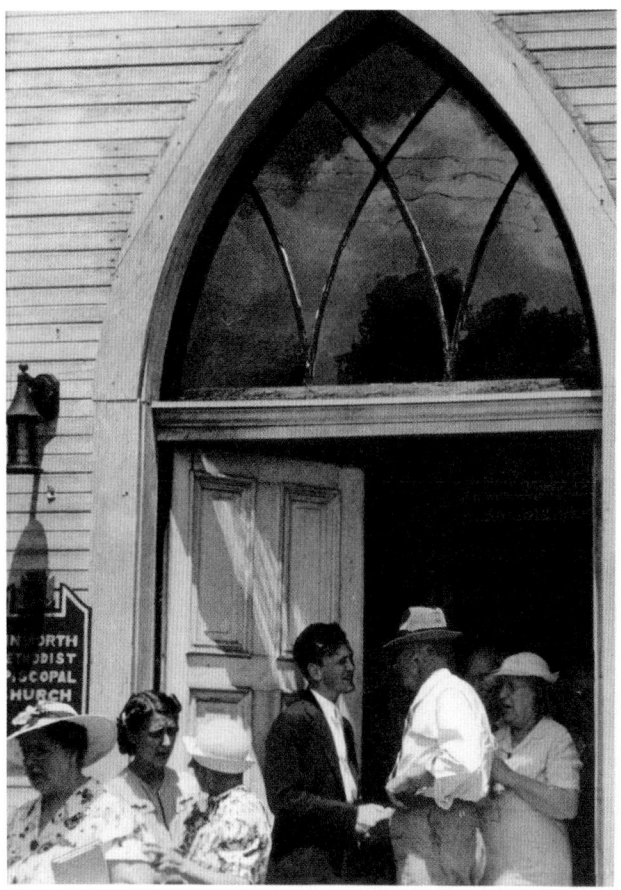

The church you belong to...

122

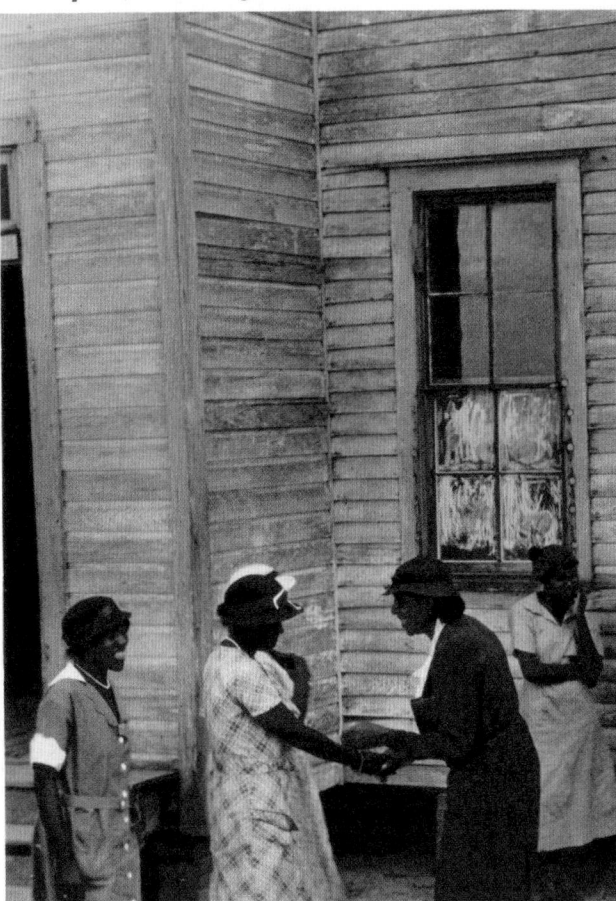

Sherwood Anderson
Hometown. New York: Alliance Book Corporation, 1940, pp. 122–123

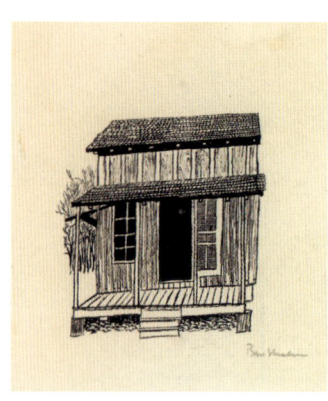 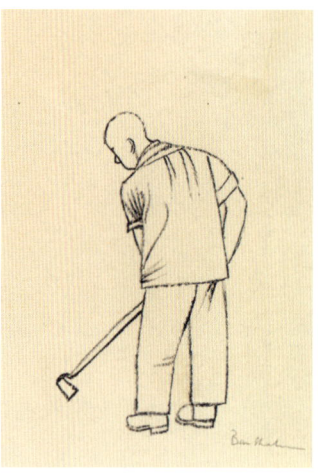 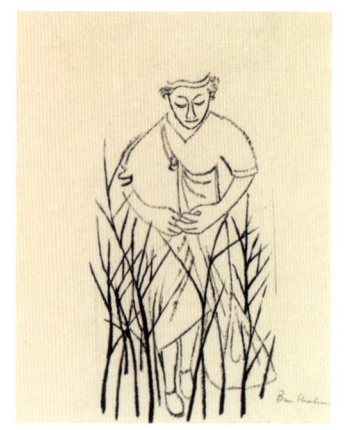 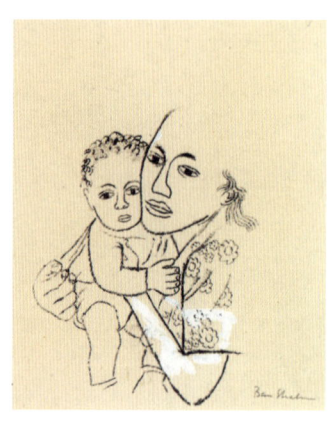

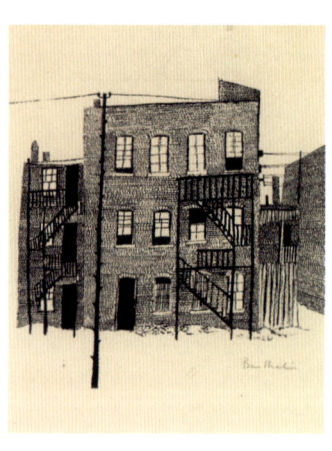 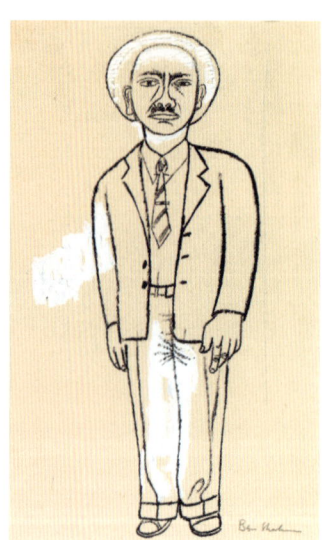 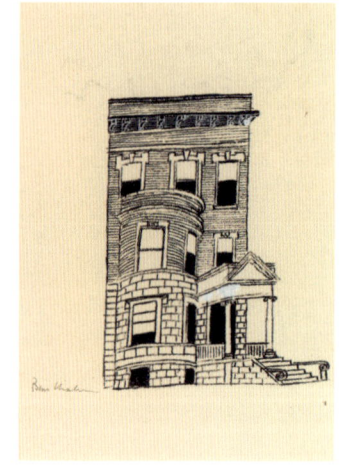 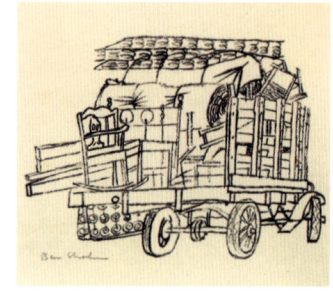

The Hickman Story, 1948

They moved to the Delta, land of milk and honey.

We were anxious to get up North where they had the opportunity to go to school and all these privileges . . .

The plough and hoe and such'll keep knowledge out of a person's head.

How can a black man disappear?

They rarely attended school more than four or five months a year.

. . . drawing rooms and butler's pantries now rented out as "apartments."

She was born in June and she was beautiful.

. . . He got his furniture out of storage, and that night he and his wife hired a taxi and took their six young children there.

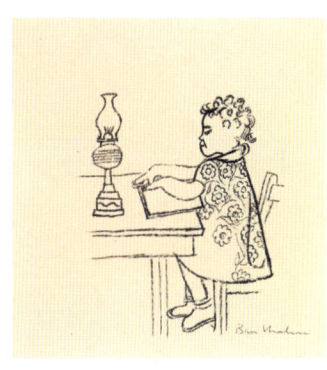 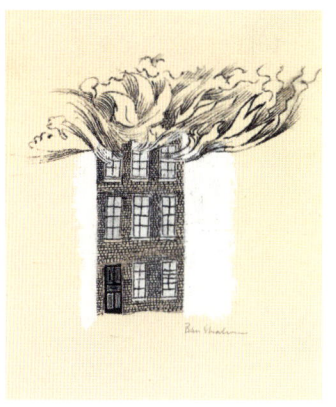 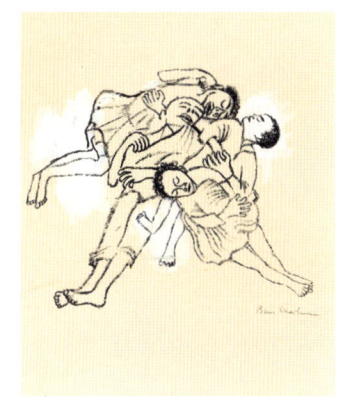 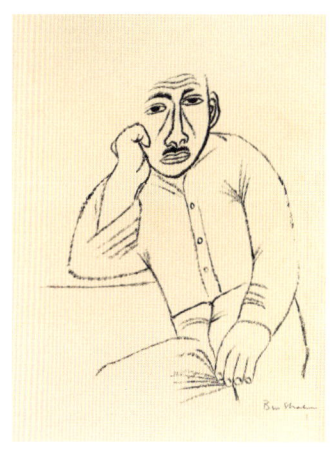

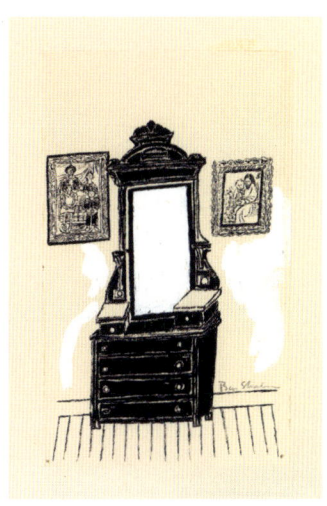 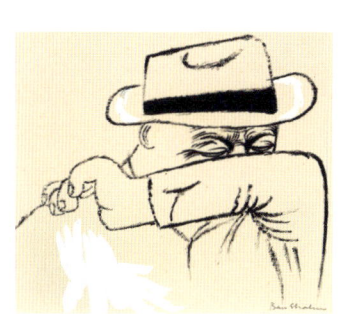 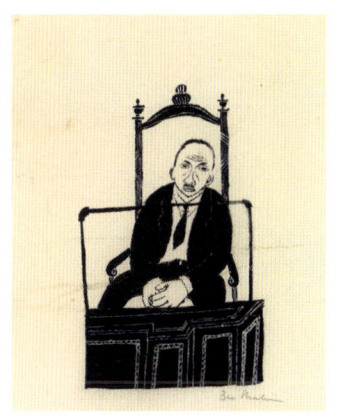 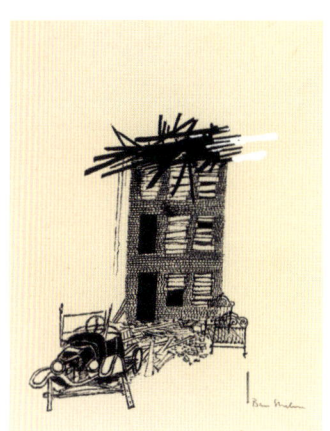

. . . and Velvena was playing at studying though she was only four.

. . . looked at the pictures of the dead children.

I cannot understand how she escaped. . . . It was a miracle. The lord was with her.

. . . and I weakened down to the ground.

Paper was made to burn, coal and rags, not people. People wasn't made to burn.

This was God fixed this. I had raised those children up and God knowed that vow I made to him. . . that these children was a generation to be raised up. God wasn't pleased what happened to them.

When I got to summing up my life I saw my life was unhappy. I was in grief and sorrow.

If they fixed it up, they'll soon be lined up here . . . People got no place to go.

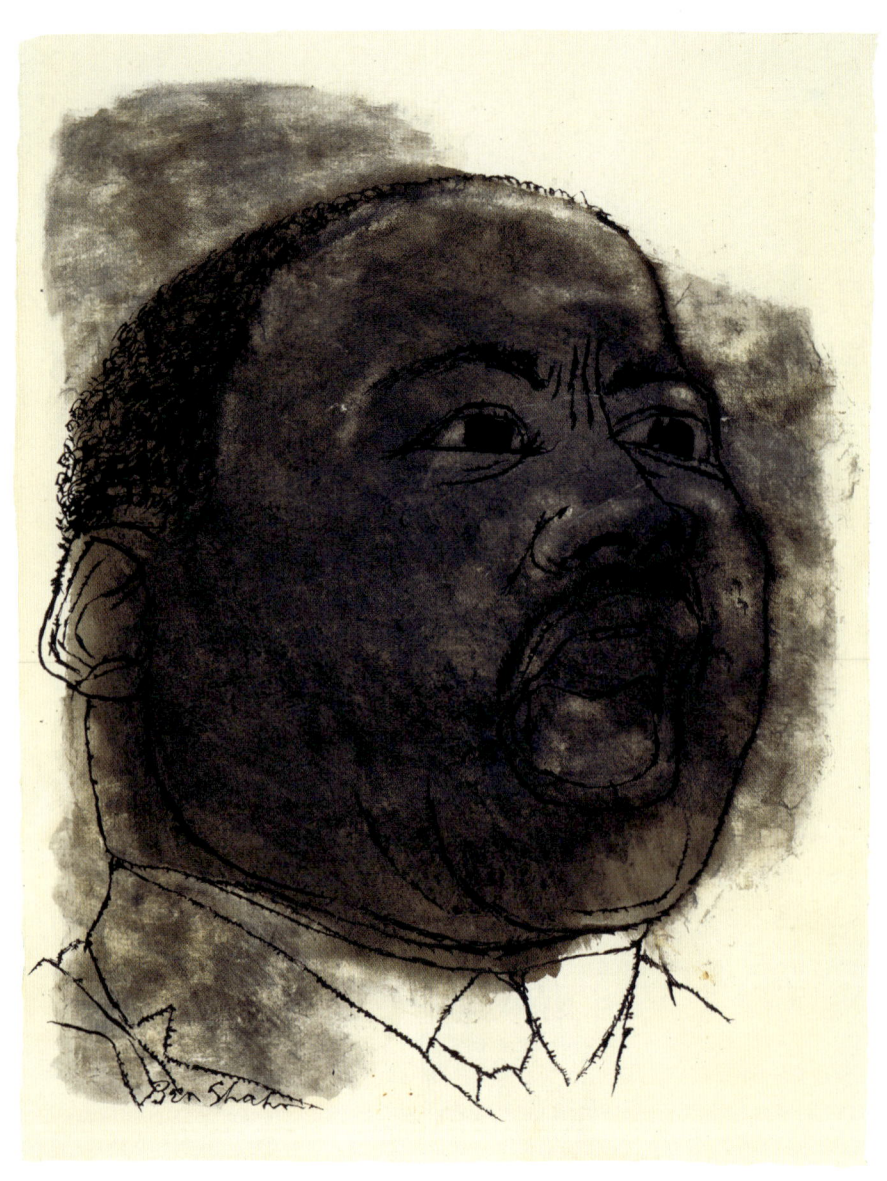

Martin Luther King
1965

Ben Shahn and Stefan Martin
Martin Luther King
1968

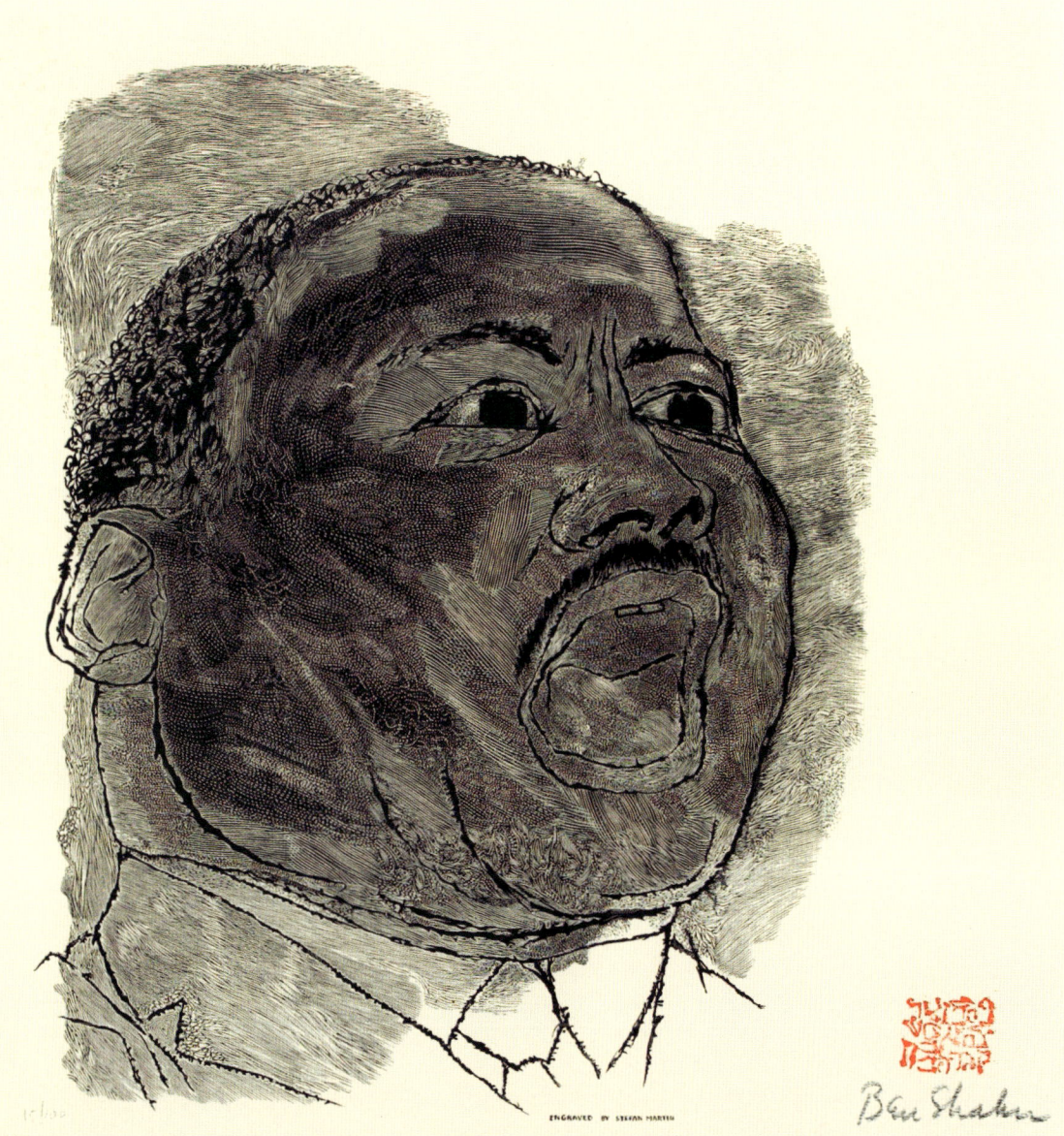

ENGRAVED BY STEFAN MARTIN

Ben Shahn

"I DON'T KNOW WHAT WILL HAPPEN NOW. WE HAVE GOT DIF-
FICULT DAYS AHEAD, BUT IT DOESN'T MATTER WITH ME BE-
CAUSE I'VE BEEN TO THE MOUNTAIN TOP. LIKE ANYBODY ELSE
I WOULD LIKE TO LIVE A LONG LIFE. BUT IM NOT CONCERNED
WITH THAT. I JUST WANT TO DO GOD'S WILL AND HE HAS AL-
LOWED ME TO GO UP THE MOUNTAIN. I SEE THE PROM-
ISED LAND. I MAY NOT GET THERE WITH YOU, BUT I WANT YOU
TO KNOW TONIGHT THAT WE AS A PEOPLE WILL GET TO THE
PROMISED LAND. I AM HAPPY TONIGHT THAT I AM NOT WOR-
RIED ABOUT ANYTHING. I'M NOT FEARING ANY MAN. MINE
EYES HAVE SEEN THE GLORY OF THE COMING OF THE LORD."

Martin Luther King Jr.

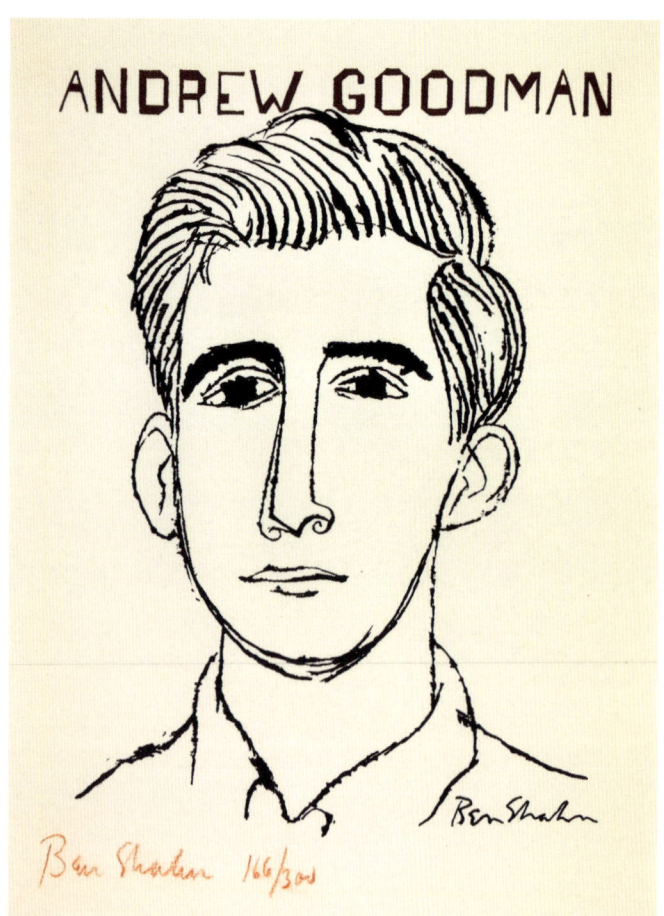

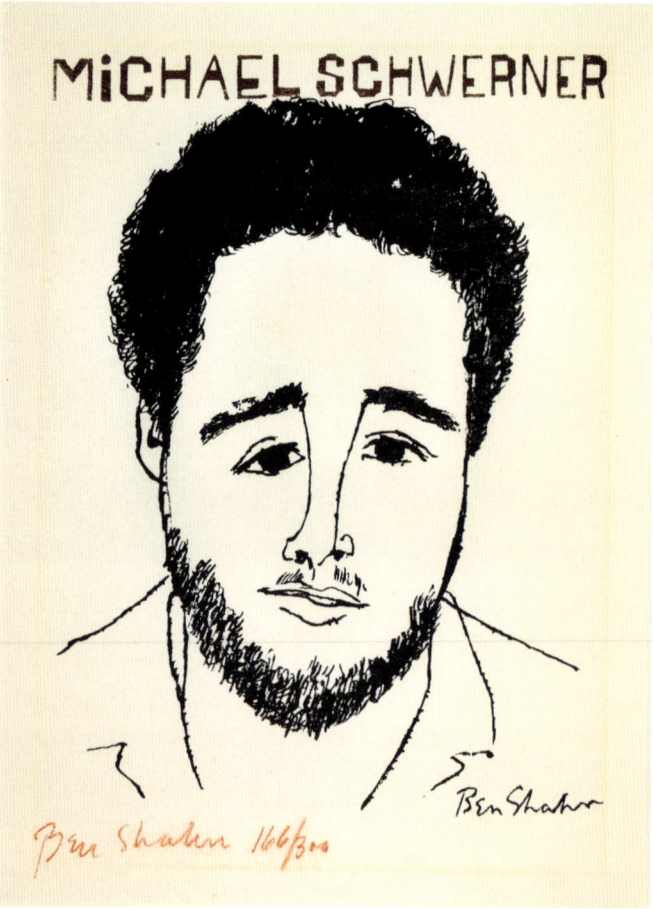

Andrew Goodman [from the *Human Relations Portfolio*]
1965

Michael Schwerner [from the *Human Relations Portfolio*]
1965

242

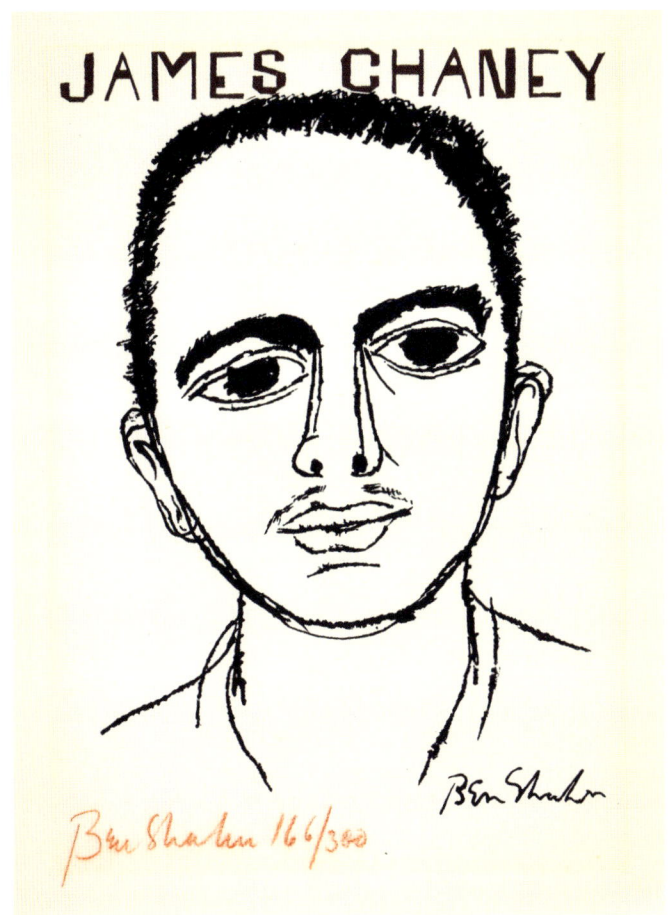

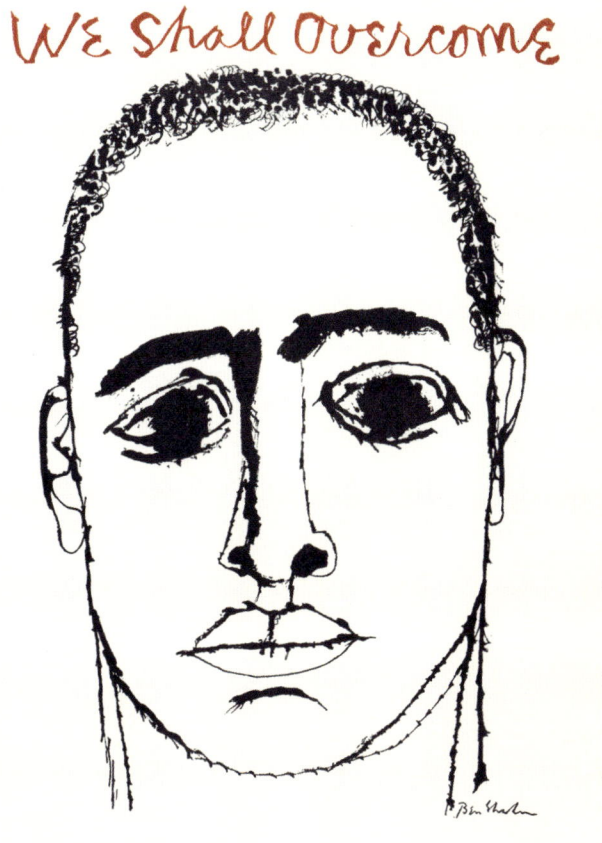

James Chaney [from the *Human Relations Portfolio*]
1965

We Shall Overcome [from the *Nine Drawings Portfolio*]
1965

Integration, Supreme Court
1963

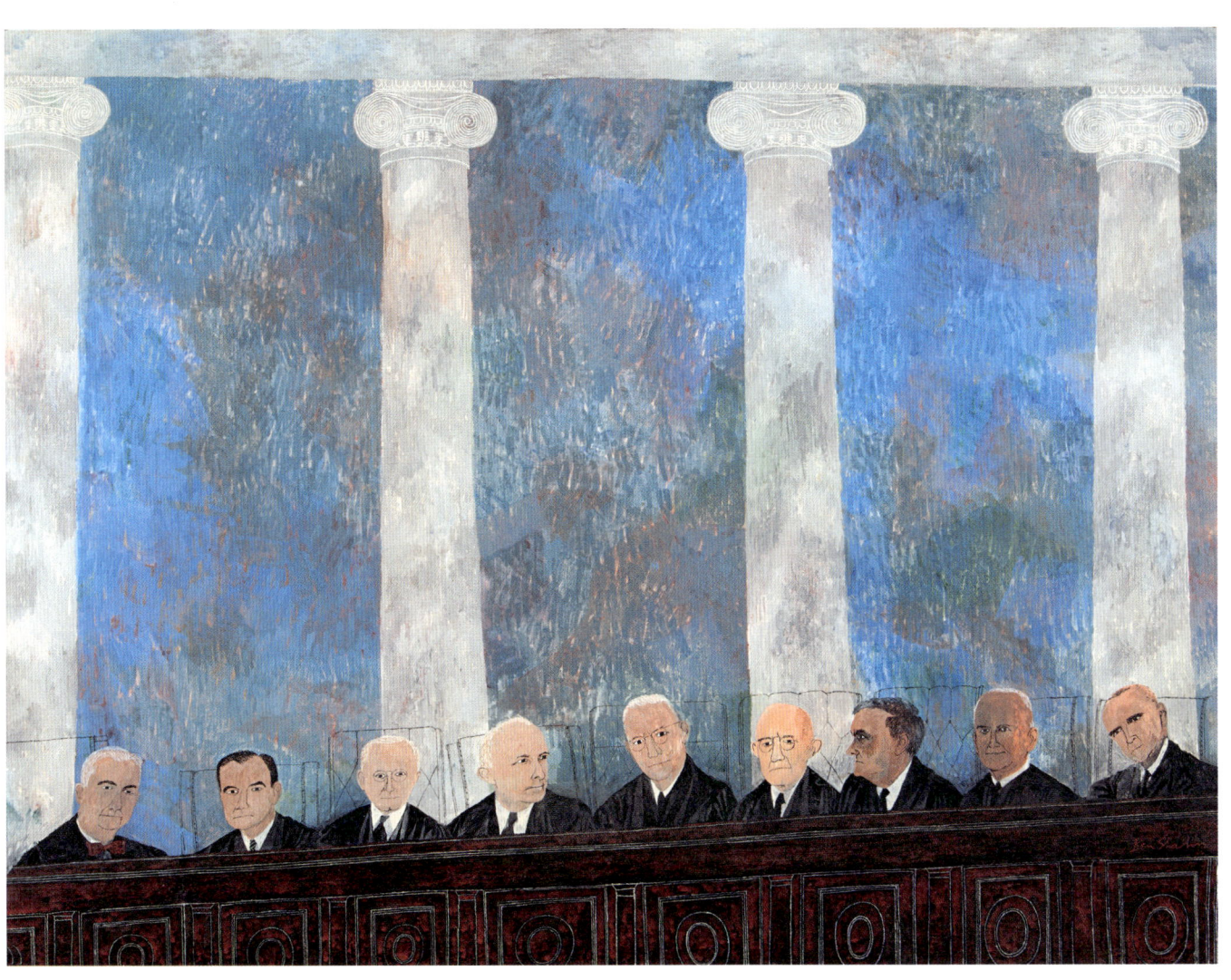

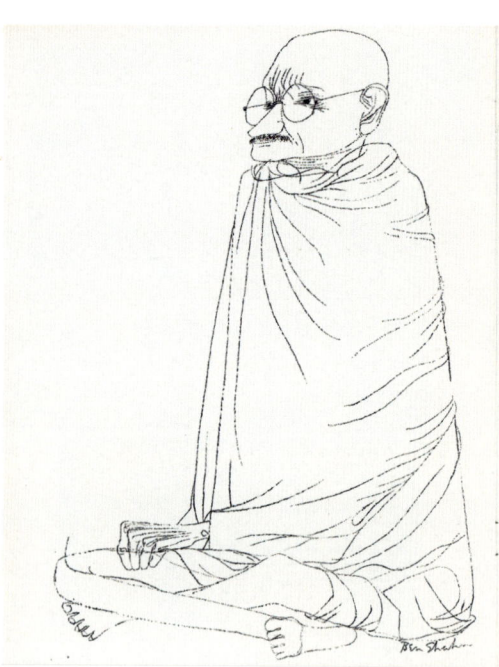

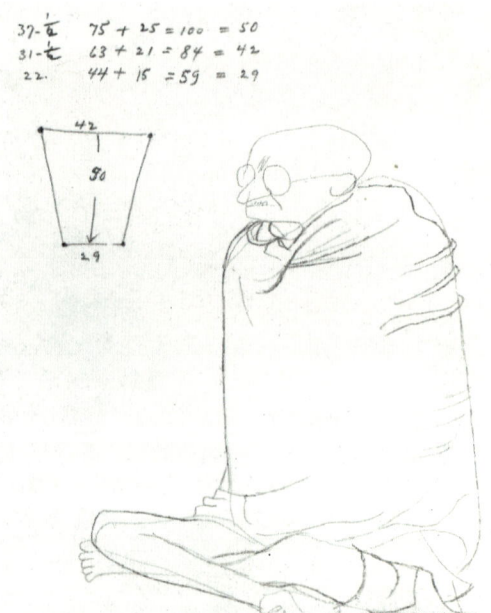

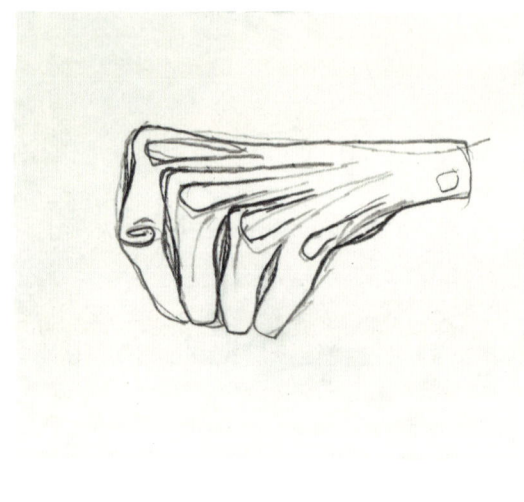

Look, August 25, 1964, vol. 28, no. 17, pp. 60–61

Untitled [Study for Gandhi]
c. 1964

Untitled [Study for Gandhi's Hand]
c. 1964

Gandhi
1965

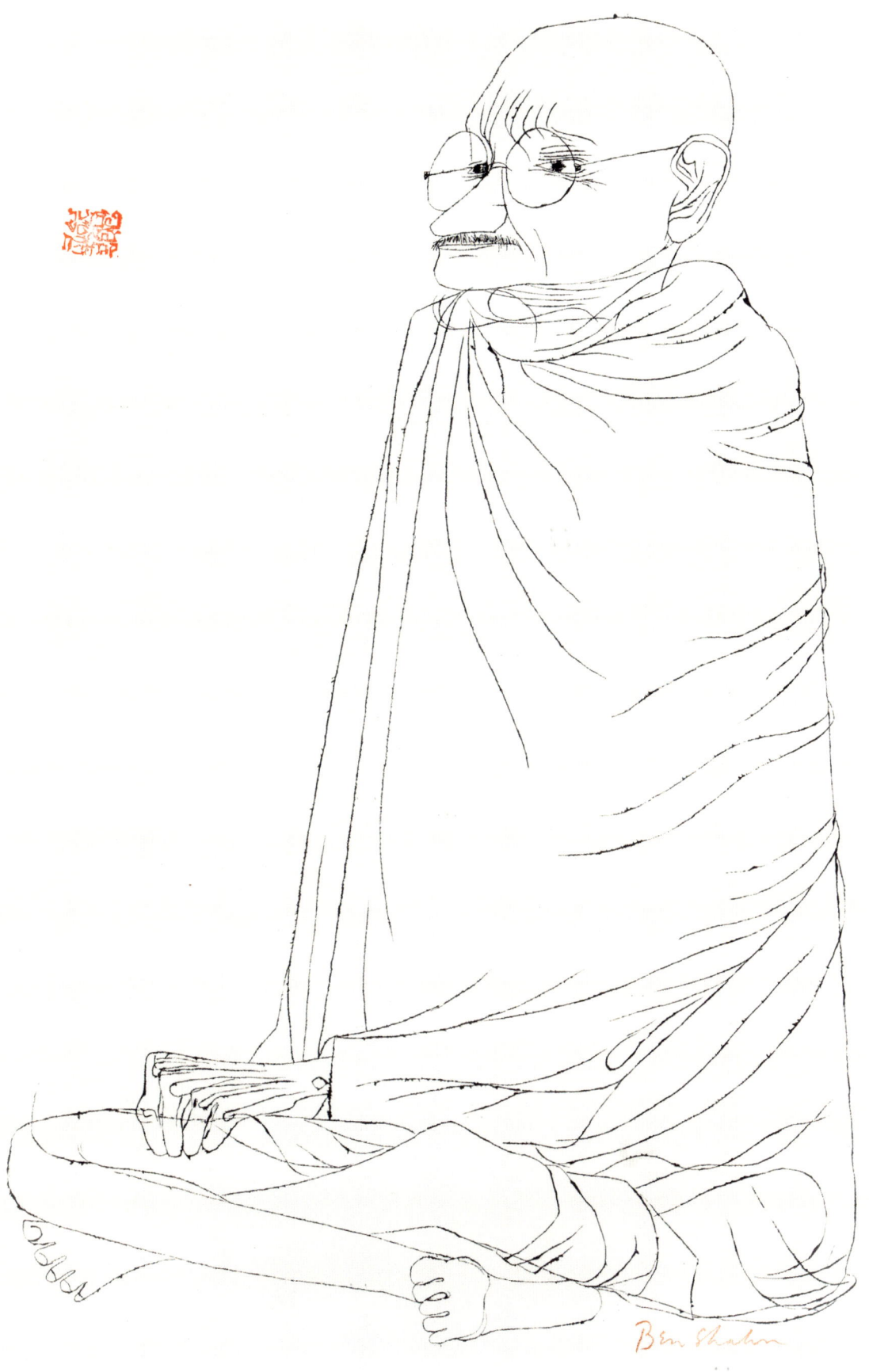

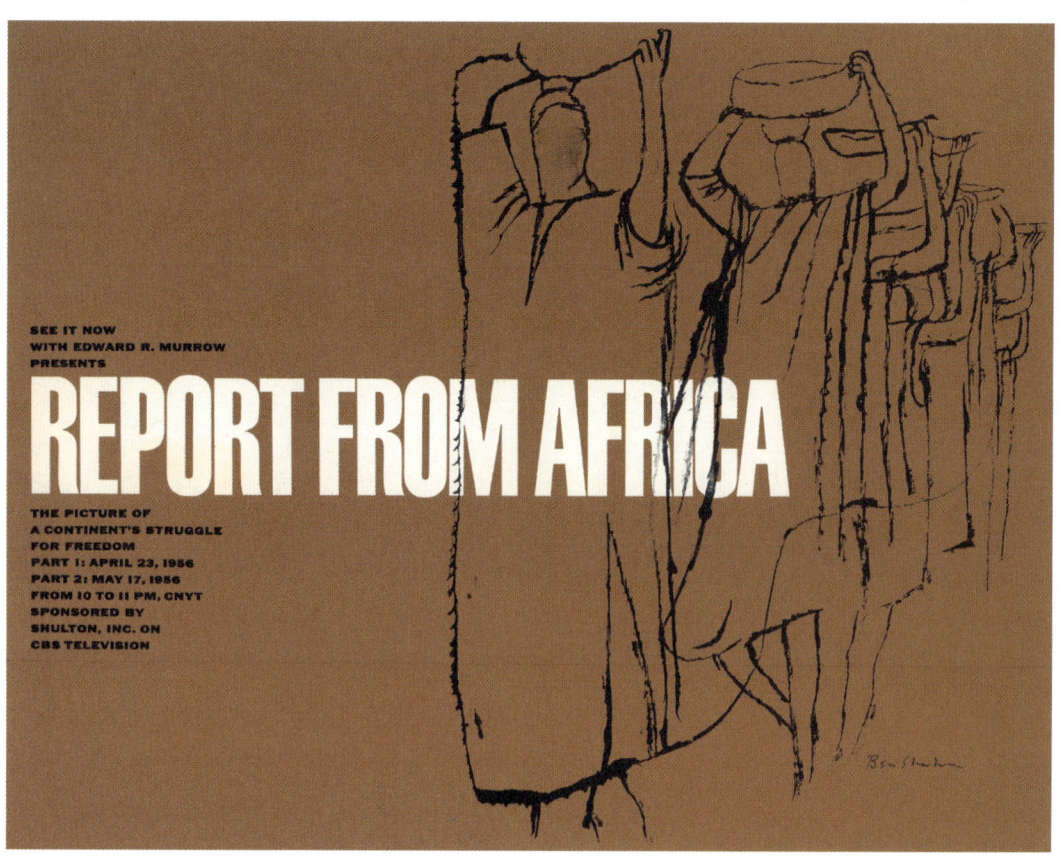

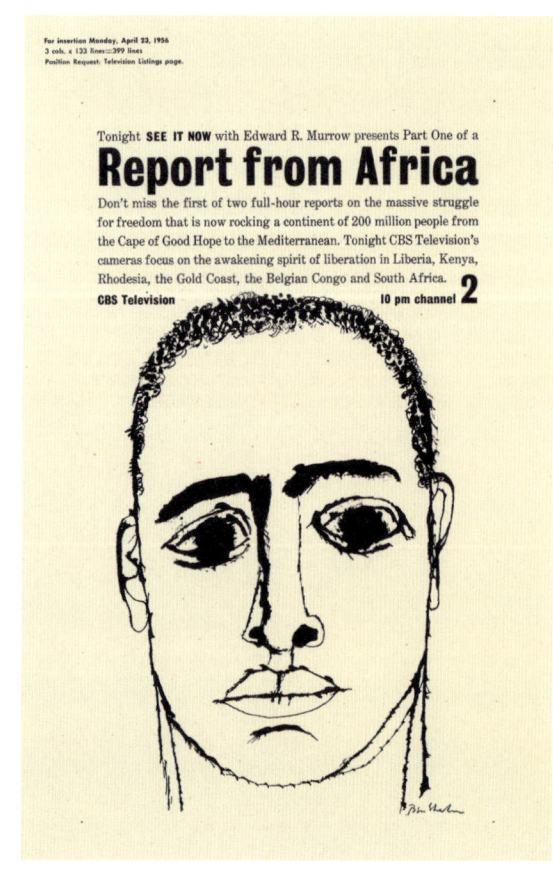

Report from Africa [advertisement for CBS]
April and May 1956

Report from Africa [advertisement for CBS]
April 1956

Report on South Africa [advertisement for CBS]
December 1954

Louis Armstrong
c. 1956

Ralph Ellison
Invisible Man. Harmondsworth, Middlesex:
Penguin Books Ltd., 1965

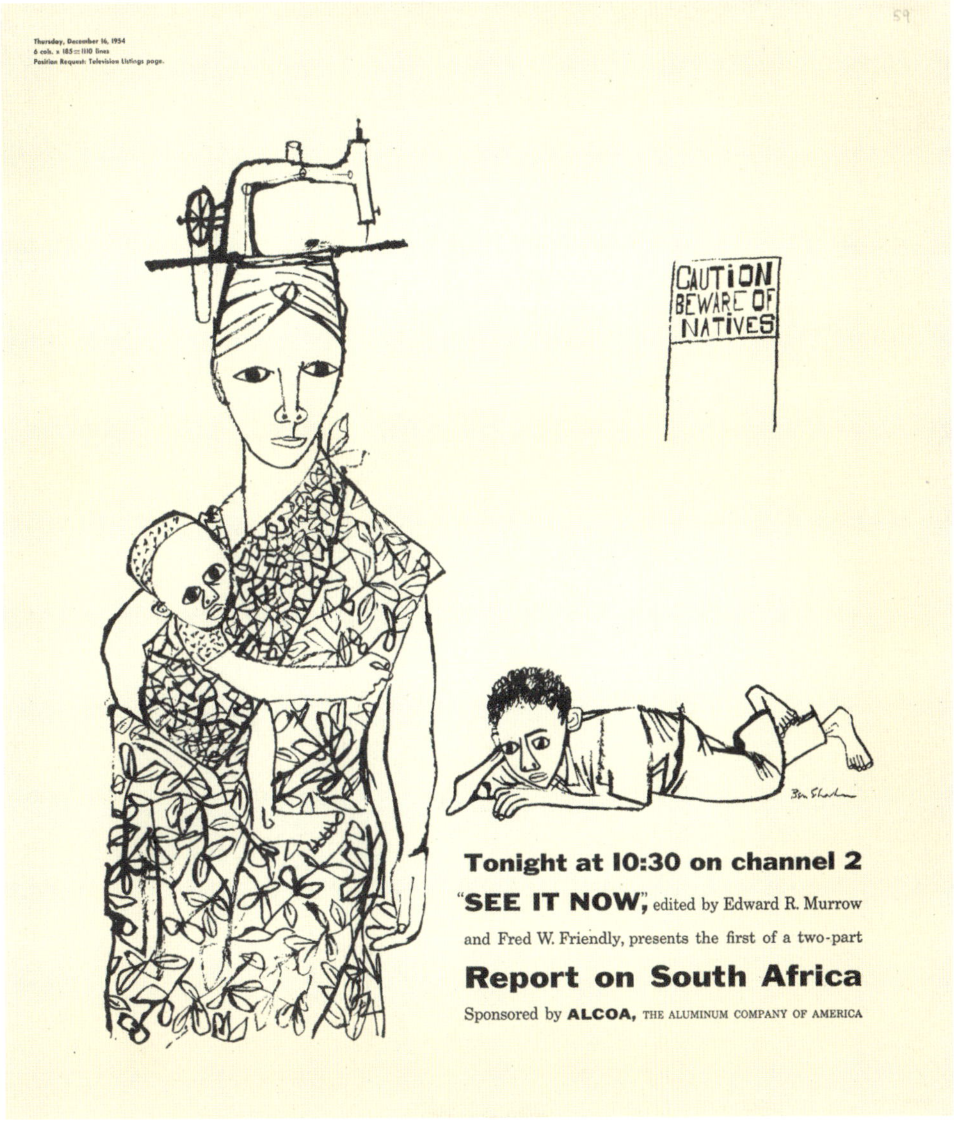

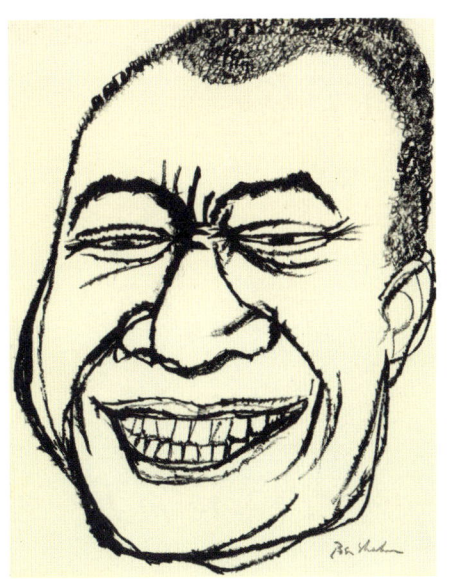

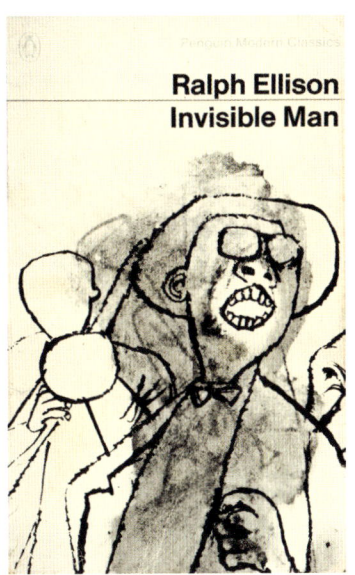

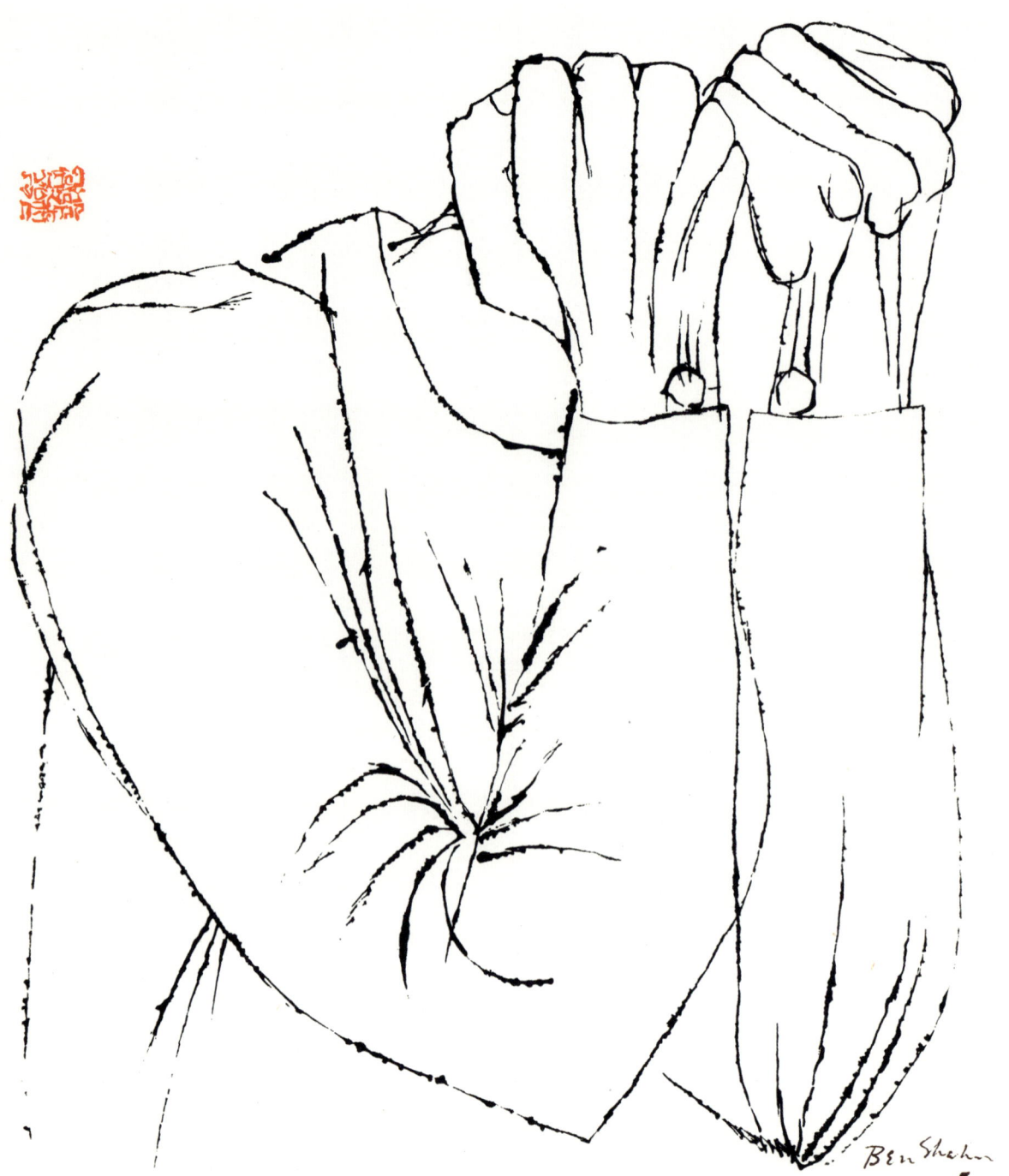

אלה אזכרה ונפשי עלי אשפכה
כי בלענו זרים כעוגה בלי
הפוכה כי בימי השר לא
עלתה ארוכה להרוגי מלוכה

Ben Shahn's early schooling in Russian-controlled Lithuania focused on Biblical and Talmudic studies, which immersed him in the prayers, psalms, and stories from the Hebrew Bible. He absorbed the *Yiddishkeit* (Jewishness) of the immigrant neighborhoods in Brooklyn where he grew up. These experiences sealed his enduring appreciation for the rituals, languages, and cultural traditions of Judaism, and were among the factors that inspired his lifelong commitment to social justice. Shahn rejected observant Judaism at a young age, as he precociously questioned the existence of an Almighty God. He loved speaking and joking in Yiddish with his neighbors in the New Deal town of Jersey Homesteads; its earliest residents shared his heritage and socialist ideals. For certain scholars Shahn "represent[ed] Jewishness as a body of [leftist] political convictions, group identification, lived experiences, and common history rather than religiosity."[1] But in later years, according to Bernarda Bryson Shahn, he was able to return "freely" to the "religious ties and traditions" of his youth "without the sense of moral burden and entrapment." She called his heretical conception of religion "pagan in spirit."[2]

In 1931 Shahn made expressive watercolors for a *Haggadah*—the prayer book for the Passover feast that narrates the ancient Israelites' Exodus from bondage in Egypt. He addressed modern antisemitism and European Jewish immigration to the U.S. in his 1936–38 Resettlement Administration (RA) mural for Jersey Homesteads. Shahn depicted a Nazi figure and alluded to antisemitic violence in this RA mural—references that are apparently not found in other official New Deal murals. He painted prisoners behind the barbed wire of forced labor camps in studies for his unrealized St. Louis mural (1939) and in several easel paintings from the early 1940s.[3] He condemned Nazi brutality in his wartime poster designs. Shahn was thus alert to the rising tide of fascism and persecution led by Germany in the 1930s, which ultimately claimed the lives of six million European Jews in the Holocaust as well as the lives of large numbers of Sinti and Roma, Jehovah's Witnesses, homosexuals, and disabled people, among others. In the postwar years, the artist turned to symbolic motifs to grapple with such incomprehensible acts of evil, using ancient and medieval Hebrew texts to respond to history or contemporary life. In *Warsaw, 1943* (1963), for example, he combined the thirteenth-century "Ten Martyrs' Prayer" said on the Day of Atonement with an anguished, head-in-clenched-hands figure to commemorate the twentieth anniversary of the uprising of the Warsaw Ghetto Jews against Nazi occupiers.

Shahn used passages from the Hebrew Bible and ancient mythology to express his fears about potential nuclear destruction and also to reflect

Warsaw, 1943, 1963
These I will remember and my soul overflows with sorrow. For evil people have swallowed us, like a cake, unturned, for during the days of Caesar there was no reprieve for the ten martyrs, put to death by the [Roman] government.

on the eternal problem of undeserved suffering. *Where Wast Thou?* (1964) features a radiant constellation (representing scientific theories of the universe) and a whirlwind emanating black linear flames (symbolizing divinity). The Hebrew text from Book of Job 38:4–7 is God's thundering response to the ever-struggling Job, who challenged God's fairness as the creator of all things. With rich blue-purple hues and gold leaf, Shahn used abstraction to give visual form to the unknowable mysteries of the universe and the enigmas of God's ways. The work exhibits the fluid yet controlled forms of Japanese calligraphy and the linear rhythms and movements of the paintings of Jackson Pollock, Georges Mathieu, and Franz Kline—whom he noted in his 1963 book *Love and Joy About Letters*. An homage to the expressive delights of, and deep mysteries in, the alphabets of various languages, the book opens with a quote from the medieval Spanish mystic, Rabbi Abraham Abulafia, and a brief discussion of Hebrew letters, with which Shahn took playful artistic liberties.[4]

Shahn's masterful combination of calligraphy and images as equal partners appears in his many illustrated and hand-scripted books. In 1954 he designed his version of the twenty-two-letter Hebrew alphabet for an interpretation of *The Alphabet of Creation*, a noble legend from the *Sefer ha-Zohar*, or *The Book of Splendor*, about how God created the world through the letters of the alphabet. Presumably written by Spanish scholar Moses de León in the thirteenth century, the *Zohar* is central to the literature of the *Kabbalah* or Jewish mysticism. In 1965 Shahn illustrated *Ecclesiastes, or, The Preacher*, a pictorial recreation of the Book of Ecclesiastes, whose author, conveying the futility or vanity of trying to understand life's meaning, imparted the practical wisdom of enjoying God's gifts on earth. In his majestic book about Psalm 150, *Hallelujah* (1970), Shahn paired pages of Hebrew calligraphy with lyrical lithographs of musicians praising the Lord through the triumphant sounds of ancient instruments.

While Shahn engaged in such joyous celebrations of higher spiritual forces, his Judaism, scholars have noted, is best expressed by the writings of Hillel the Elder, the influential first-century BCE rabbi, sage, and scholar. Shahn used Hillel's words from Ethics of the Fathers 1:14 in one of his last paintings, *Identity* (1968), which conveys the artist's ever-urgent concern for the world around him: "If I am not for myself, who is for me? If I care only for myself, what am I? If not now, when?" Scripted in Hebrew above five sets of individual arms with clasped hands raised in solidarity and protest, this credo gives *Identity* an antiwar tenor. Made in 1968, when public support for U.S. involvement in the Vietnam War significantly eroded after North Vietnam's Tet Offensive, the painting speaks to the coexistence of the political and spiritual in Shahn's later art. Indeed, Shahn's skeptical attitude toward organized religion matches his politics in his last years. In his final interview he described himself as "more of an anarchist, more of a perpetual radical than a visionary utopian."[5]

1. Diana L. Linden, *Ben Shahn's New Deal Murals: Jewish Identity in the American Scene* (Detroit: Wayne State University Press, 2015), 127, 132. On Shahn's Jewish identity, see also Sara Blair, *How the Other Half Looks: The Lower East Side and the Afterlives of Images* (Princeton: Princeton University Press, 2018), 119–51, and the work of Matthew Baigell and Ziva Amishai-Maisels.

2. Bernarda Bryson Shahn, "Introduction," in Ben Shahn, *Hallelujah* (New York: Kennedy Graphics, 1970), unpaginated. Shahn disliked being labeled a "Jewish artist," which he found limiting.

3. Linden, *Ben Shahn's New Deal Murals*, 54, 111.

4. Shahn consulted on the accuracy of his Hebrew with his dear friend and Roosevelt neighbor Morris (Moishe) Bressler, a Hebrew scholar and singer of Yiddish and Russian folksongs, and with renowned rabbi Louis Finkelstein. Thanks to Dalya Luttwak and Frances Flannery for sharing their expertise on the Hebrew texts that Shahn used.

5. Richard Kostelanetz, "Ben Shahn: Master 'Journalist' of American Art (1969)," in *On Innovative Art(ist)s: Recollections of an Expanding Field* (Jefferson, N.C.: McFarland & Company, 1992), 169. In his last presidential campaign poster, *McCarthy Peace* (1968), Shahn supported Democratic nominee Senator Eugene McCarthy and his anti-Vietnam War platform, which galvanized a generation of college students and young peace activists.

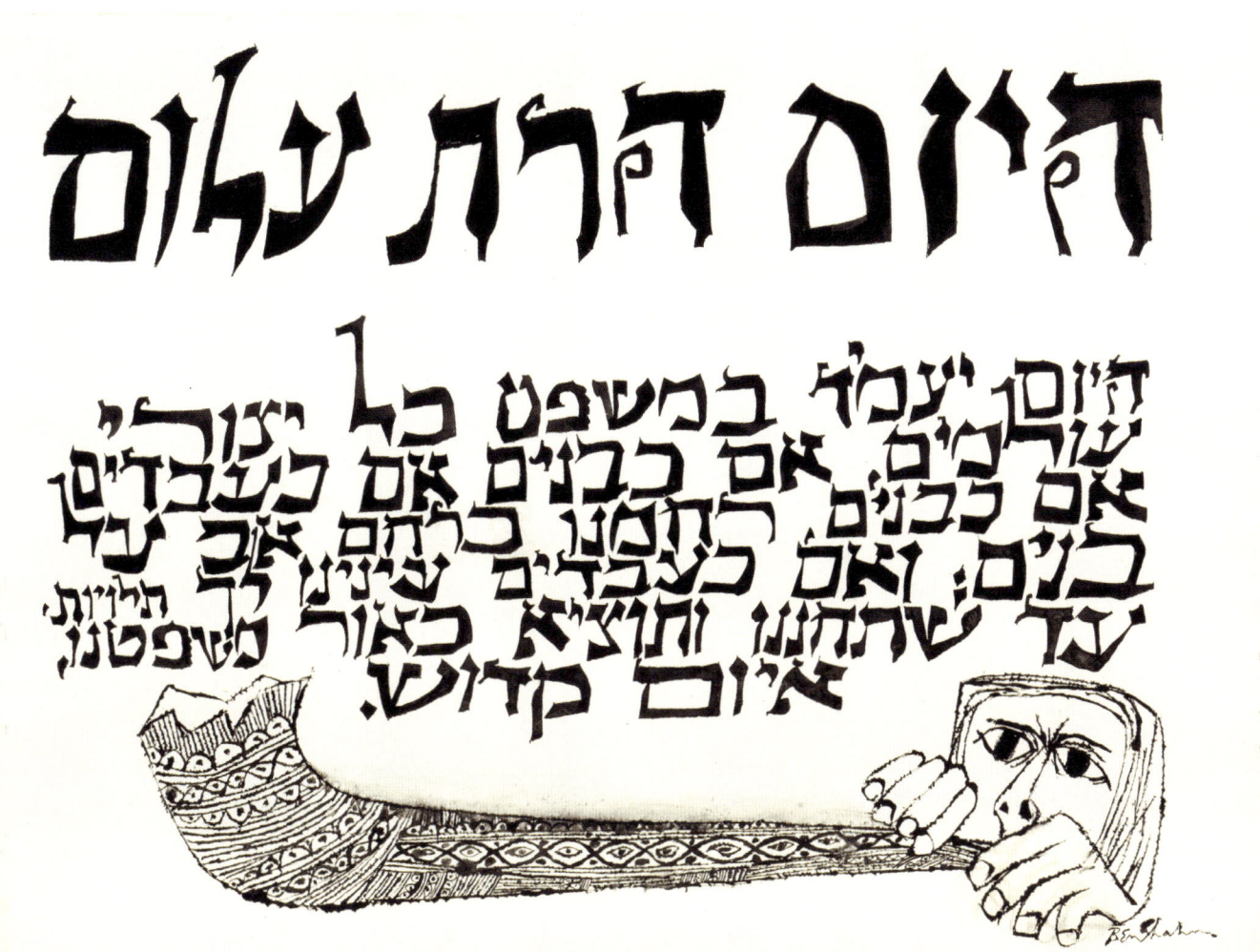

Today is the Birth[day] of the World, 1955

Today the world is born; today shall stand before You. All the beings of the cosmos, whether as Your children or as Your servants. If as Your children, show them mercy, like a mother toward her children. If as Your servants, then our eyes are turned toward You in great anticipation. That You may be gracious, rendering judgment for good, on our behalf, as clear as light of day.

Poem recited on Rosh Hashanah. Origin unknown

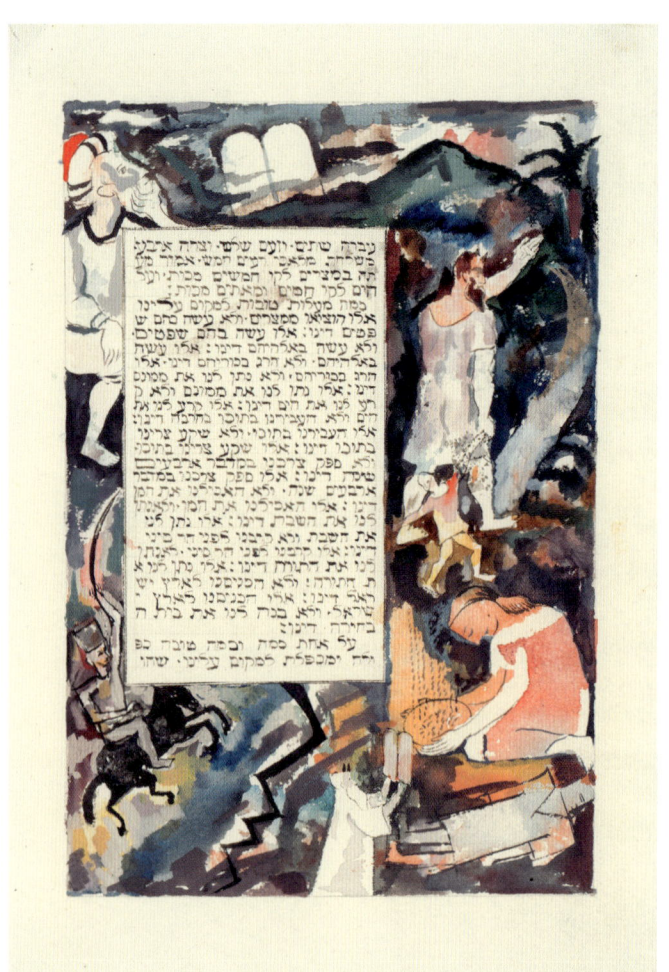

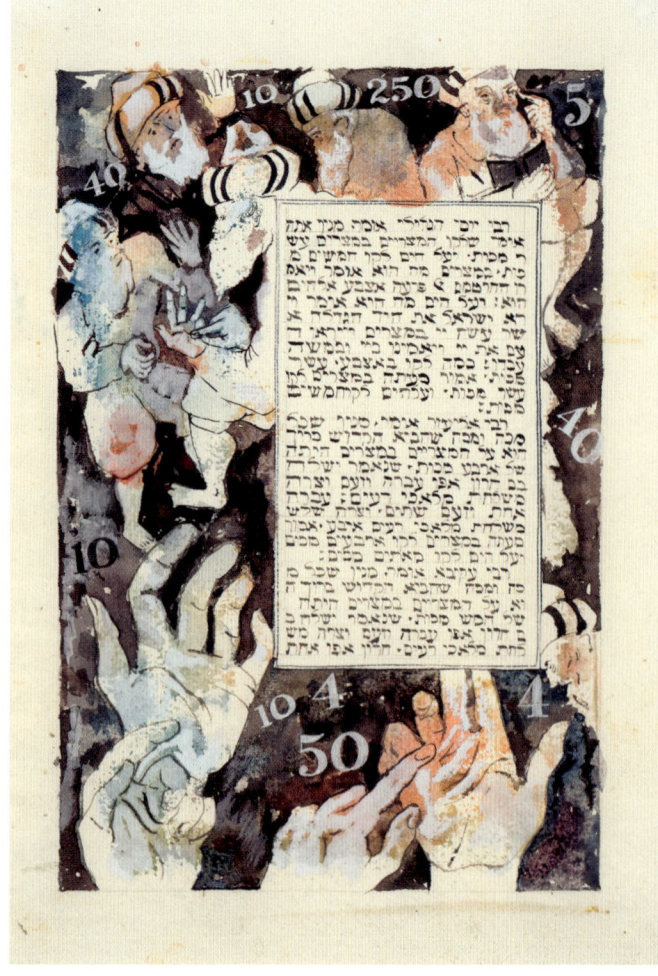

How Many Are God's Goodnesses to Us
[from the *Haggadah* series]
1931

The Reckoning of the Miracles
[from the *Haggadah* series]
1931

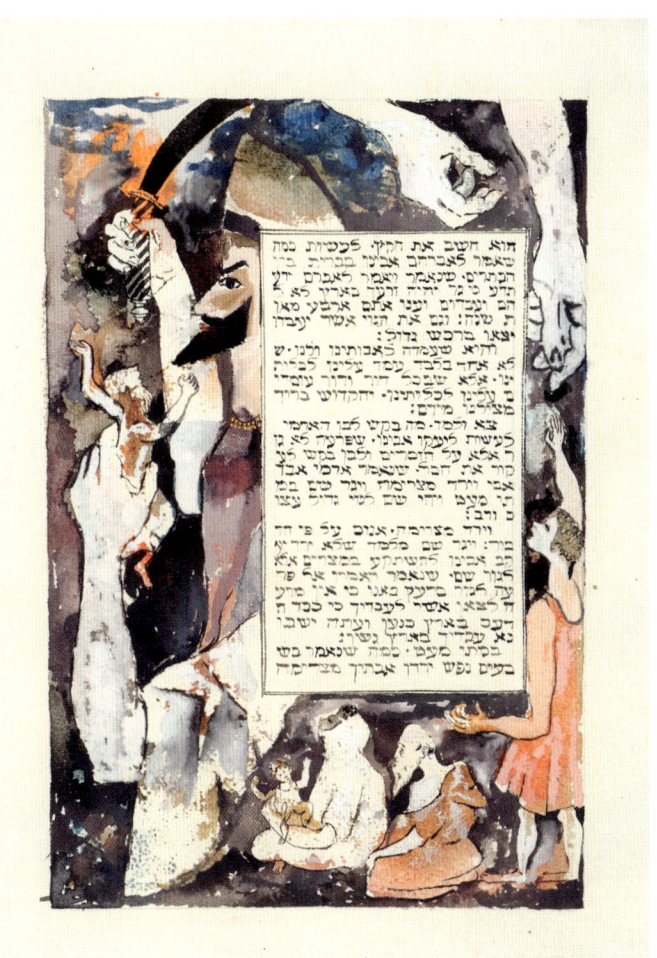

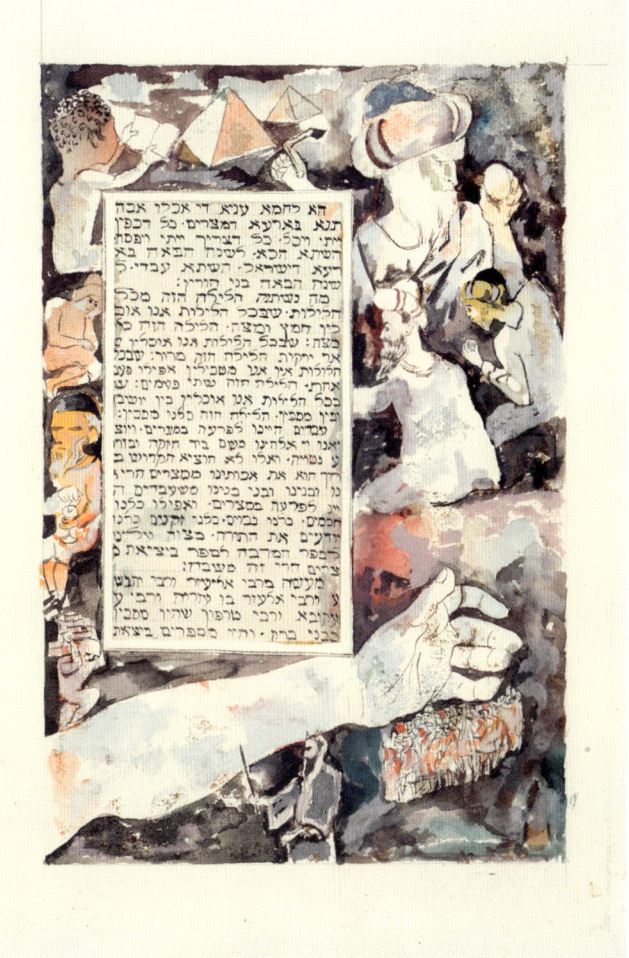

In Every Generation Men Rise Up Against Us
[from the *Haggadah* series]
1931

The Bread of Affliction
[from the *Haggadah* series]
1931

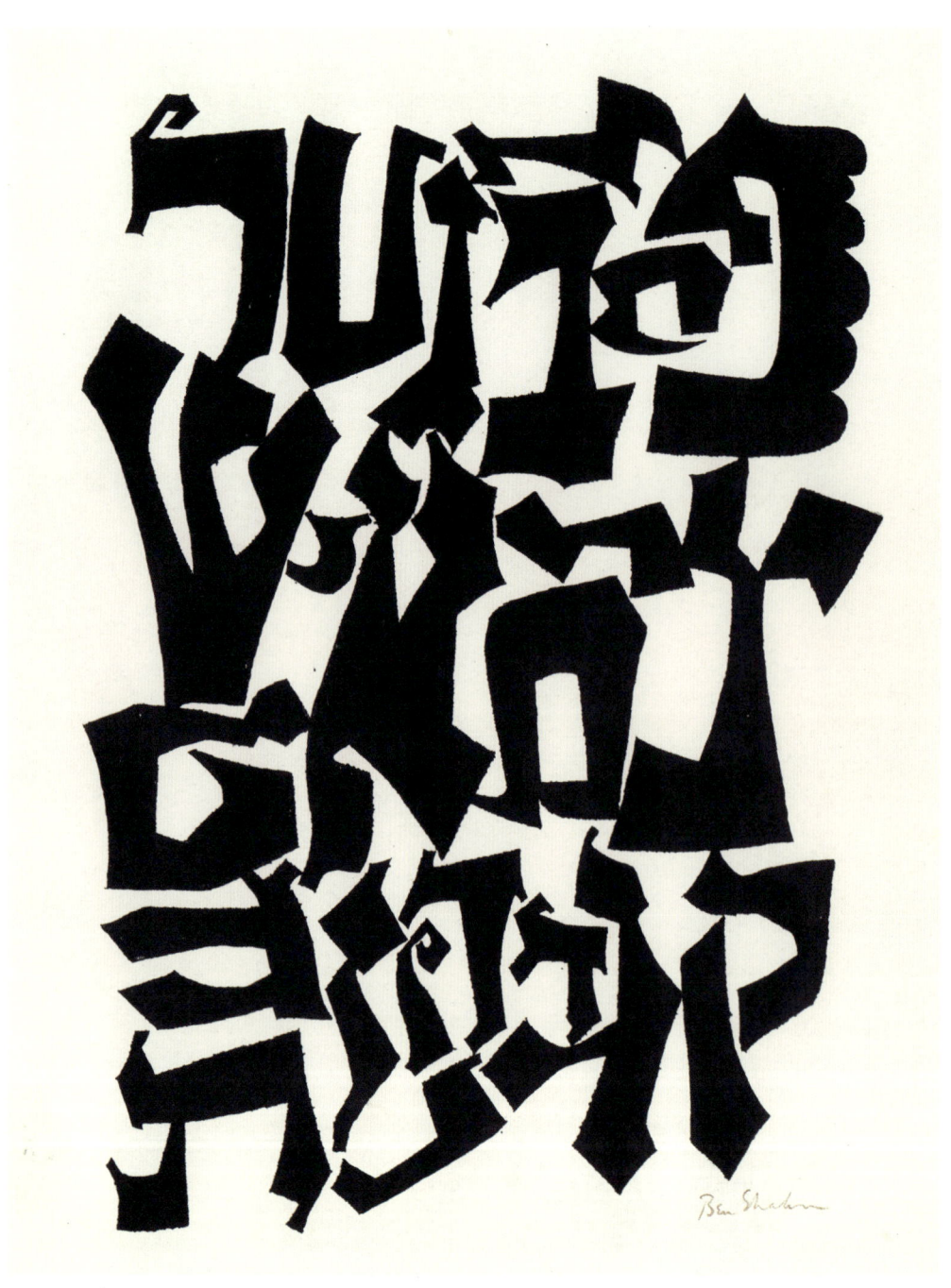

Alphabet of Creation
1957

Ben Shahn and Stefan Martin
Maimonides with Calligraphy [Ecclesiastes], 1965
The words of Kohelet, son of David, King of Jerusalem, futilities
of futilities—said Kohelet—futility of futility all is futile.
Ecclesiastes [The Book of Kohelet] 1:1

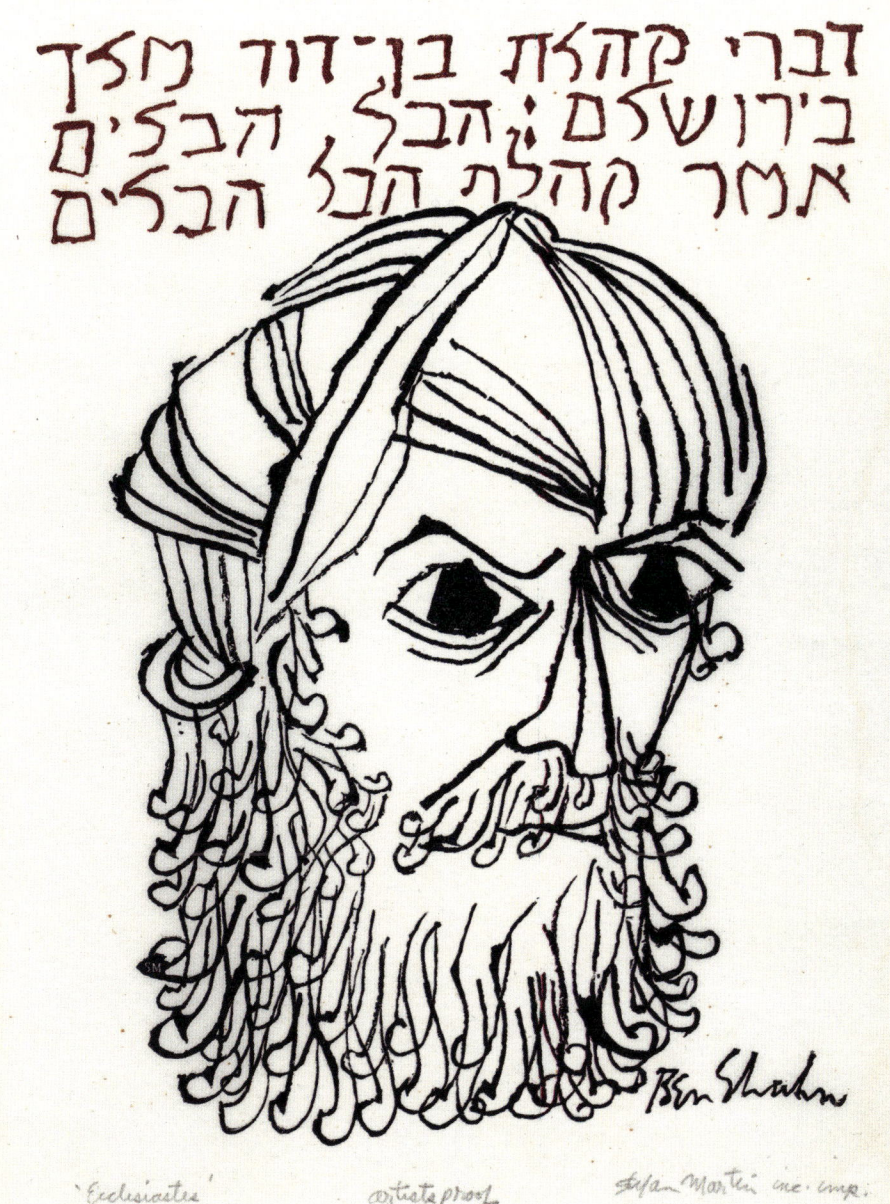

דִּבְרֵי קֹהֶלֶת בֶּן־דָּוִד מֶלֶךְ
בִּירוּשָׁלָ͏ִם: הֲבֵל הֲבָלִים
אָמַר קֹהֶלֶת הֲבֵל הֲבָלִים
הַכֹּל הָבֶל

Ben Shahn

'Ecclesiastes'   artist's proof   Stefan Martin inc. imp.

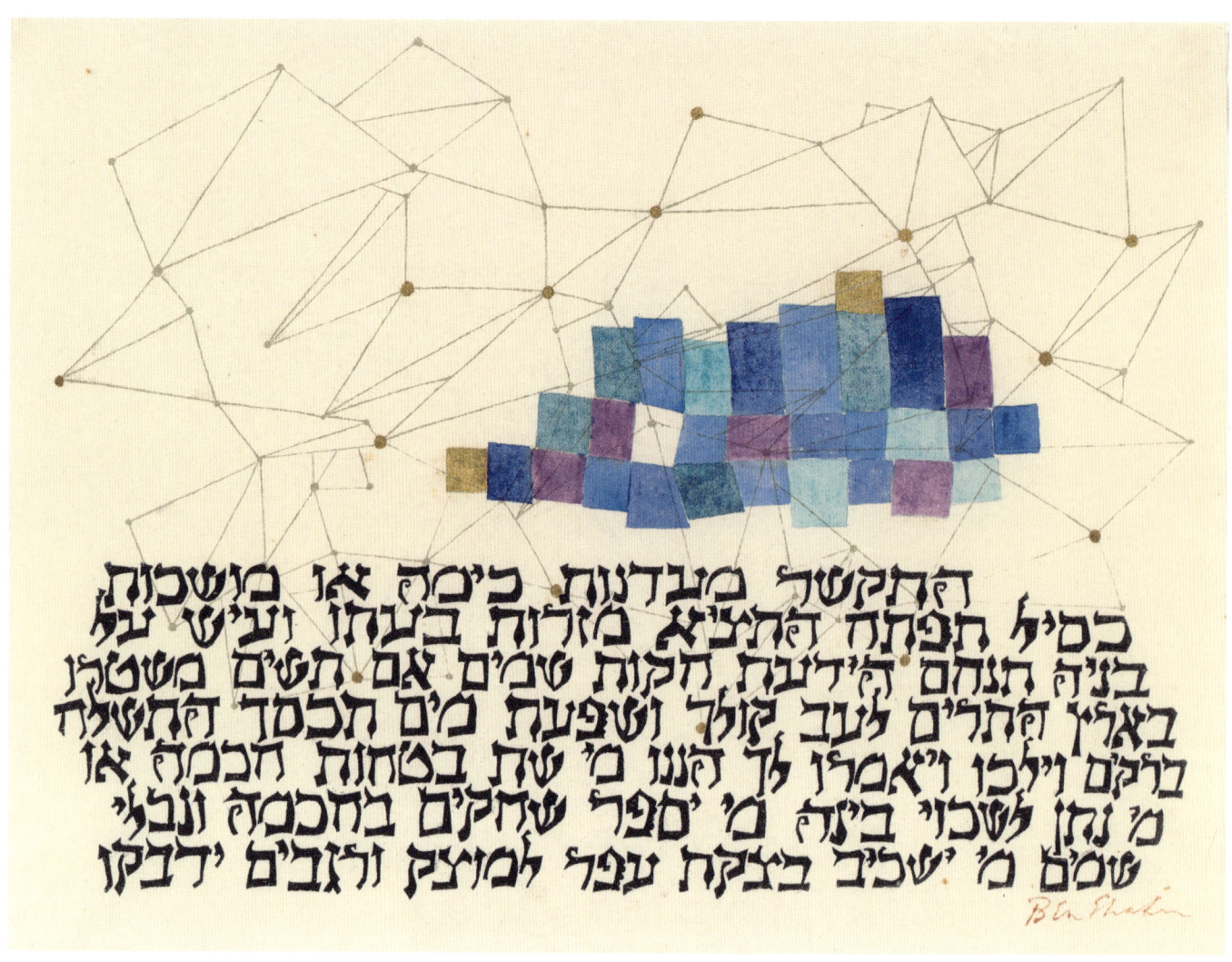

Pleiades, 1960

Can you bind the chains of the Pleiades? Can you loosen Orion's belt?

Can you bring forth the constellations in their seasons or lead out the Bear with its cubs?

Do you know the laws of the heavens? Can you set up God's dominion over the earth?

Can you raise your voice to the clouds and cover yourself with a flood of water?

Do you send the lightning bolts on their way? Do they report to you, "Here we are?"

Who gives the ibis wisdom or gives the rooster understanding?

Who has the wisdom to count the clouds? Who can tip over the water jars of the heavens

when the dust becomes hard and the clods of earth stick together?

Book of Job 38:31–38

Where Wast Thou?, 1964

Where were you when I laid the earth's foundations? Speak, if you have understanding.

Do you know who fixed its dimensions? Or who measured it with a line?

Onto what were its bases sunk? Or who set its cornerstone;

when the morning stars sang together, and all the sons of God shouted for joy?

Book of Job 38:4–7

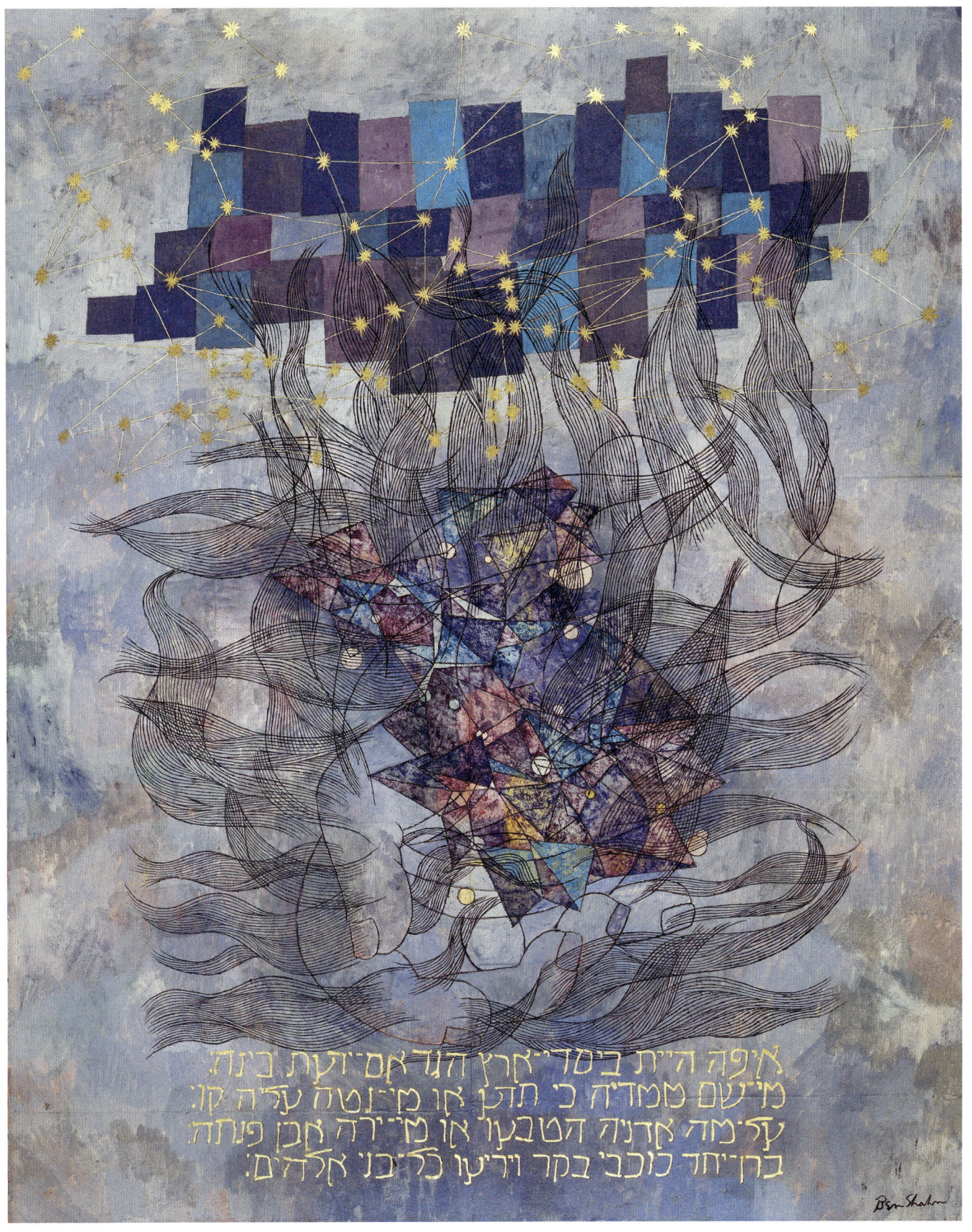

אֵיפֹה הָיִיתָ בְּיָסְדִי־אָרֶץ הַגֵּד אִם־יָדַעְתָּ בִינָה:
מִי־שָׂם מְמַדֶּיהָ כִּי תֵדָע אוֹ מִי־נָטָה עָלֶיהָ קָּו:
עַל־מָה אֲדָנֶיהָ הָטְבָּעוּ אוֹ מִי־יָרָה אֶבֶן פִּנָּתָהּ:
בְּרָן־יַחַד כּוֹכְבֵי בֹקֶר וַיָּרִיעוּ כָּל־בְּנֵי אֱלֹהִים:

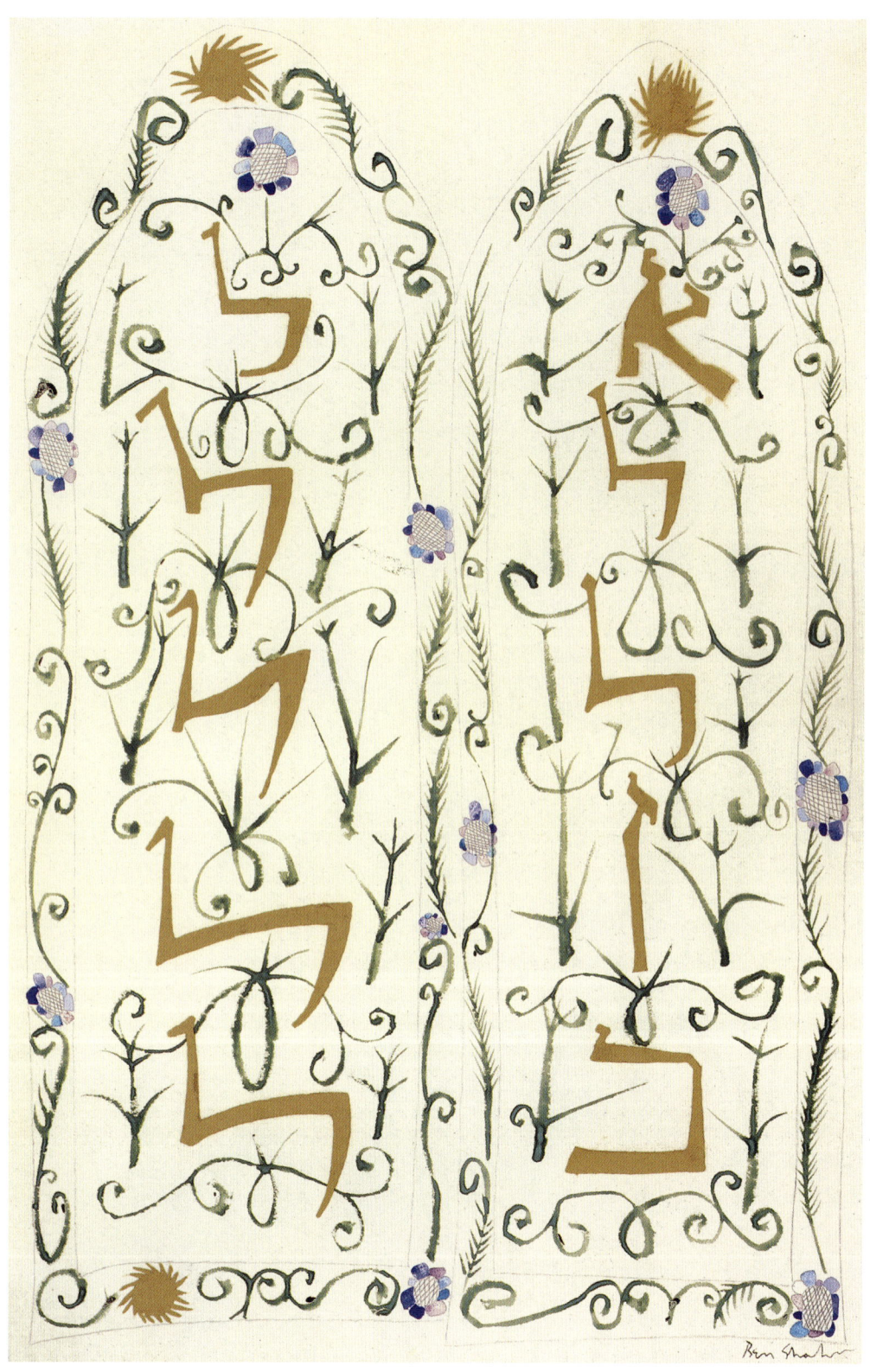

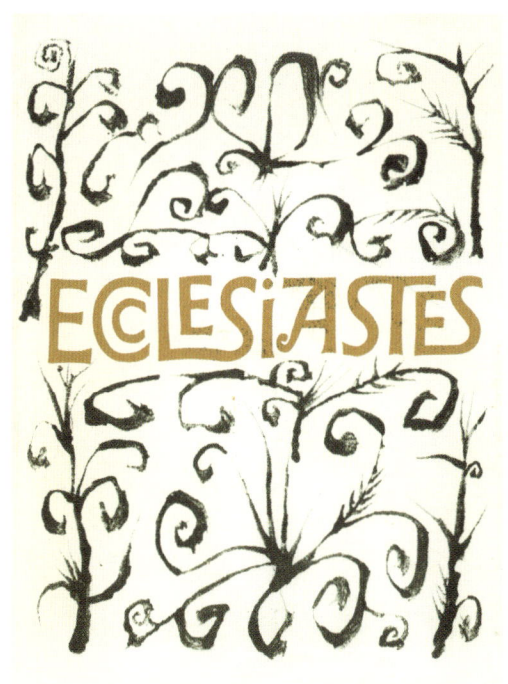

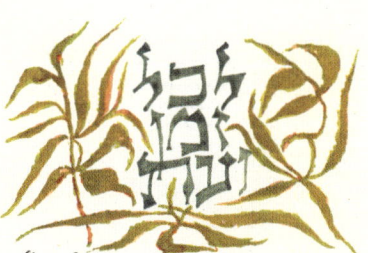

Chapter 3. To every thing there is a season, and a time to every purpose under the heaven: a time to be born, and a time to die; a time to plant, and a time to pluck up that which is planted; a time to kill, and a time to heal; a time to break down, and a time to build up; a time to weep, and a time to laugh; a time to mourn, and a time to dance; a time to cast away stones, and a time to gather stones together; a time to embrace, and a time to refrain from embracing; a time to get, and a time to lose; a time to keep and a time to cast away; a time to rend, and a time to sew; a time to keep silence, and a time to speak; a time to love, and a time to hate; a time of war and a time of peace. What profit hath he that worked in that wherein he laboureth? I have seen the travail, which God hath given to the sons of men to be exercised in it. He hath made every thing beautiful in his time: also he

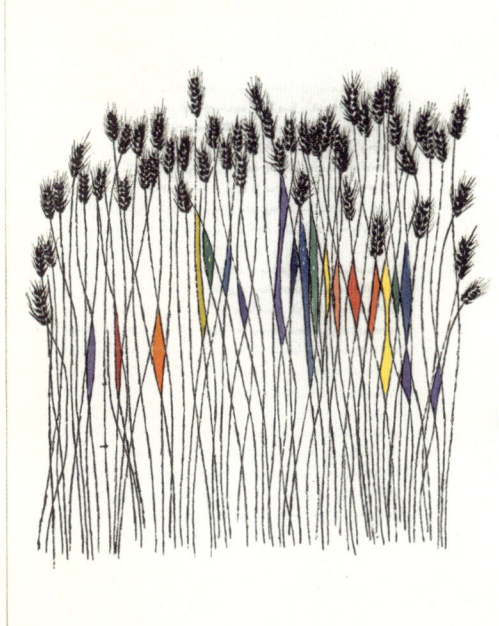

Decalogue
1961

Ecclesiastes, or, The Preacher. New York:
Grossman Publishers / The Trianon Press, 1971

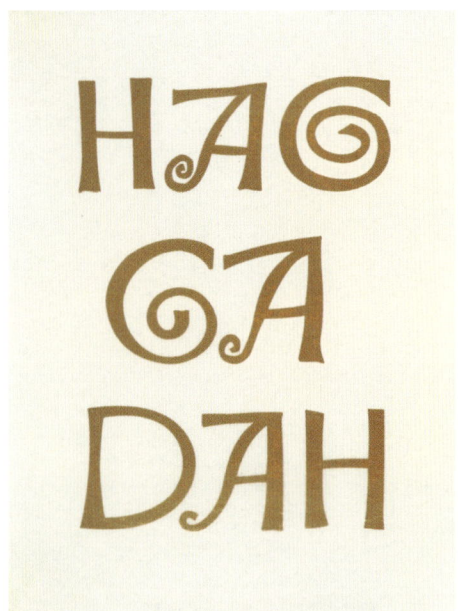

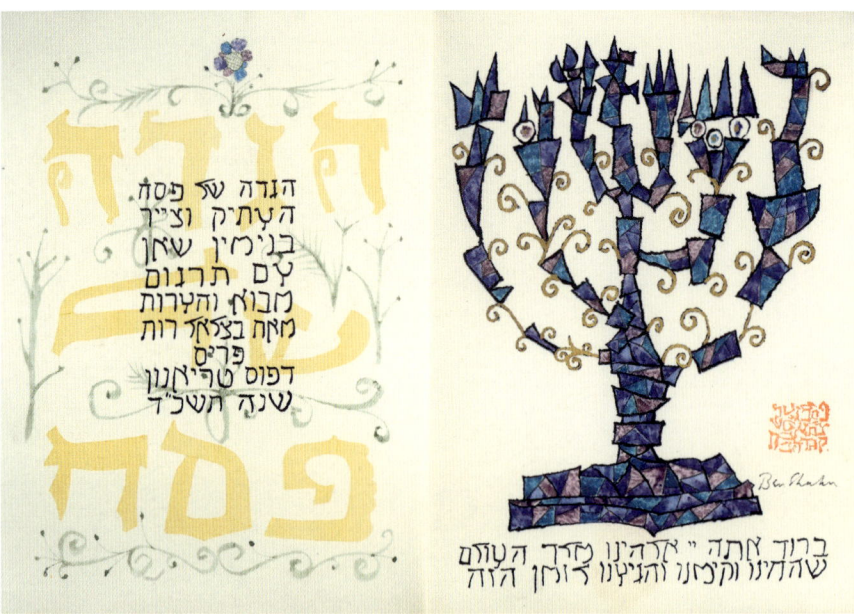

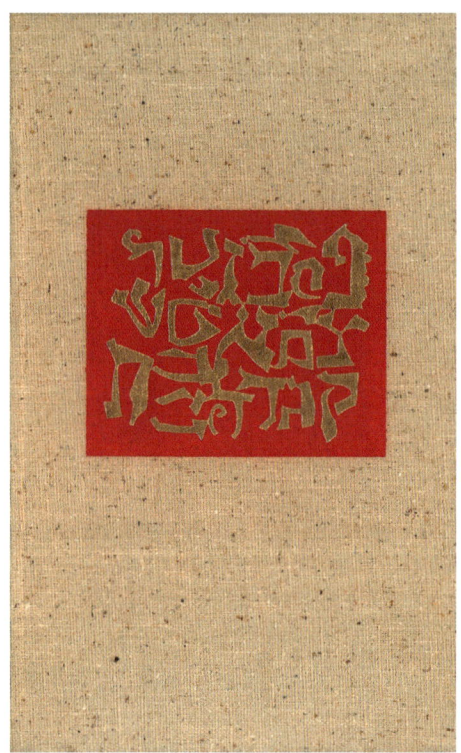

And when the Ayin had left, Samekh entered saying: "O Lord,

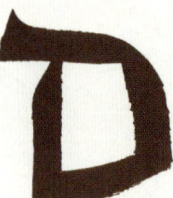

be it Thy divine will to create the world through me, seeing that Thou art called Samekh after me, the Upholder of all that fall!"

But God said, "Remain, Samekh, where you are. For you must continue to uphold all that fall."

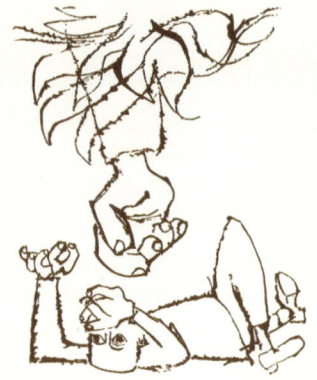

Haggadah. Paris and London: The Trianon Press, 1966

The Alphabet of Creation: An Ancient Legend from the Zohar.
New York: Pantheon, 1954

Hallelujah Suite [Psalm 150]
1970

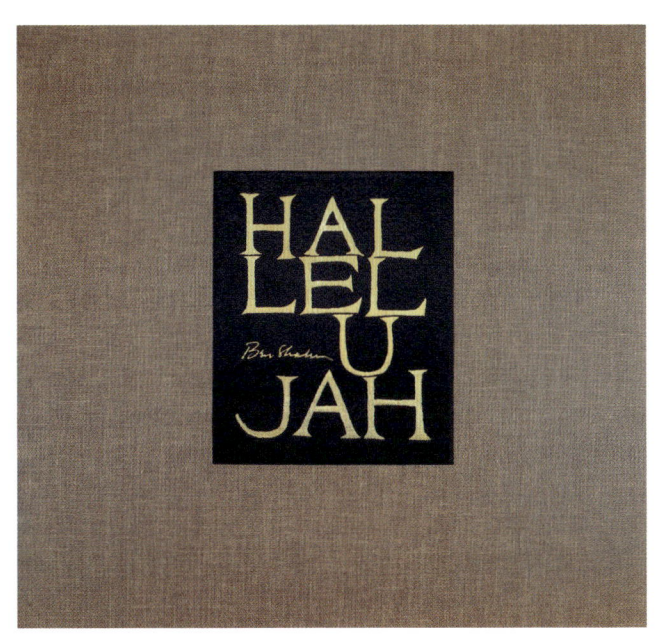

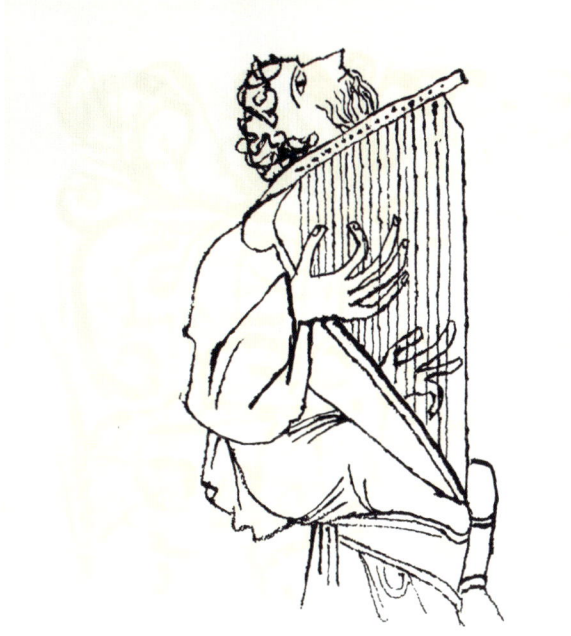

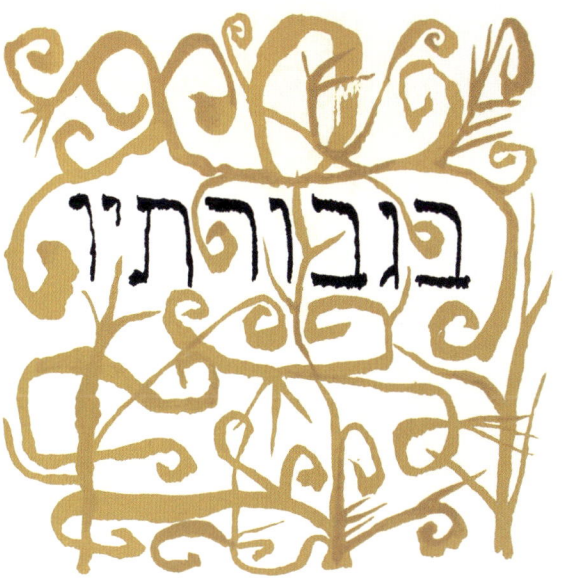

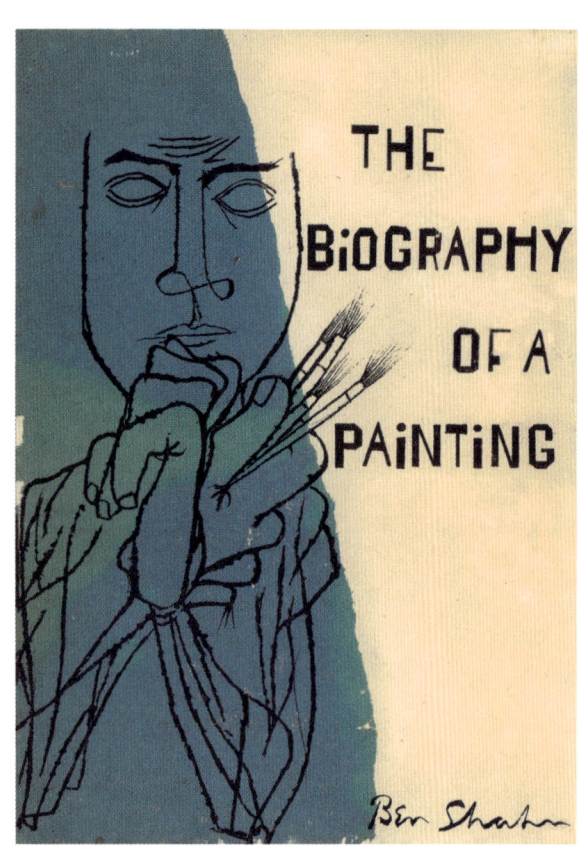

The Biography of a Painting.
New York: Paragraphic Books, 1966

Flowering Brushes, 1968
He [Rabbi Hillel] used to say: "If I am not for myself, who is
for me? If I care only for myself, what am I? If not now, when?"
Hillel the Elder, Ethics of the Fathers 1:14

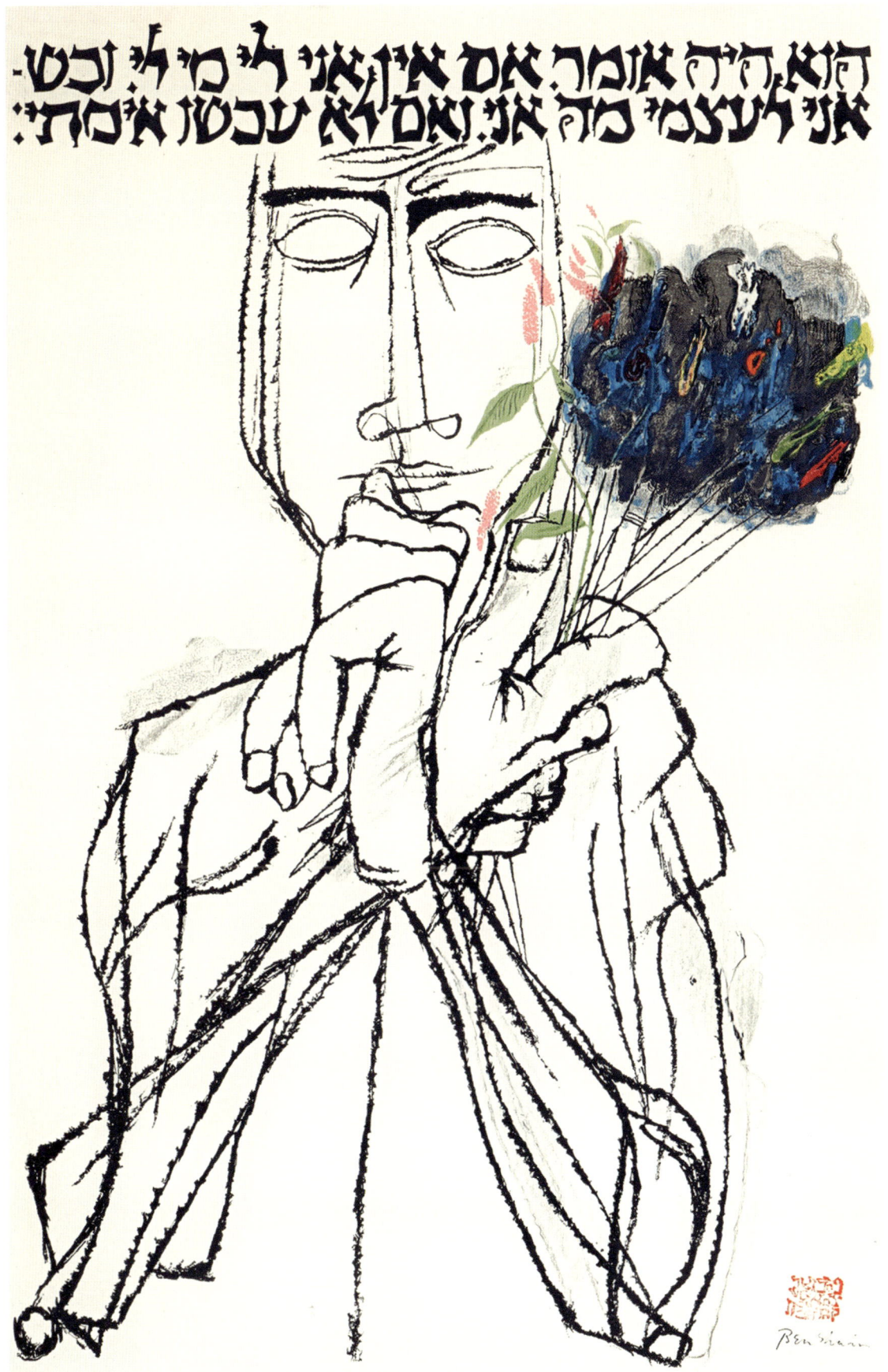

הוא היה אומר אם אין אני לי מי לי. וכש
אני לעצמי מה אני. ואם לא עכשו אימתי:

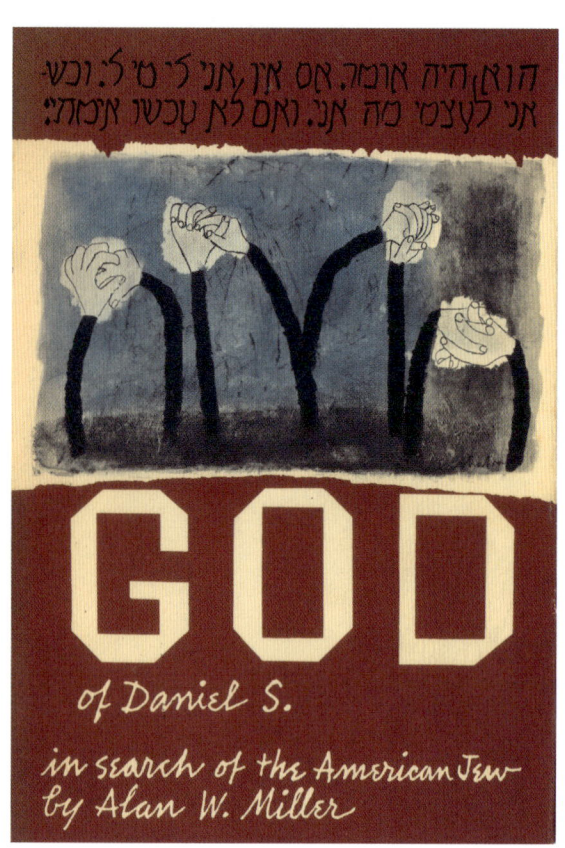

Alan W. Miller
God of Daniel S.: In Search of the American Jew. London:
Collier-Macmillan Ltd., 1969

Identity, 1968
He [Rabbi Hillel] used to say: "If I am not for myself, who is
for me? If I care only for myself, what am I? If not now, when?"
Hillel the Elder, Ethics of the Fathers 1:14

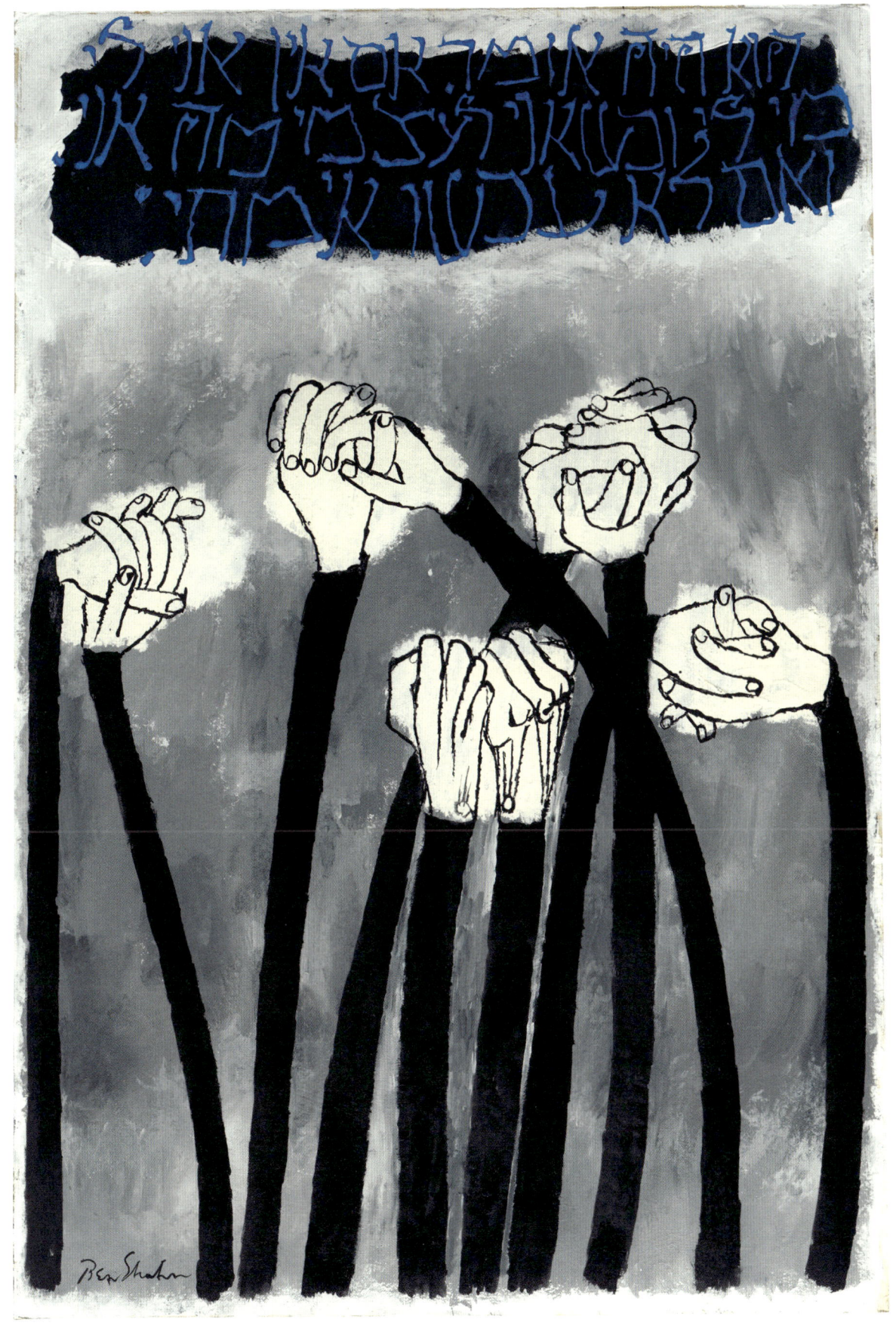

Except as noted, all works are
by Ben Shahn.

*Organize… Steel Workers Organizing
Committee*, 1930s
Gouache on board
39 ⅞ × 29 ⅞ in.
New Jersey State Museum.
Museum Purchase, FA1970.64.3
p. 176

How Many Are God's Goodnesses to Us
[from the *Haggadah* series], 1931
Watercolor and ink on paper
11 ⅞ × 8 ⅜ in.
Jewish Museum, New York. Gift of Mr.
Edward M. M. Warburg, JM 153-47.9
p. 254 left

*In Every Generation Men Rise Up
Against Us* [from the *Haggadah*
series], 1931
Watercolor and ink on paper
11 ¾ × 8 ½ in.
Jewish Museum, New York.
Gift of Edward M. M. Warburg,
JM 153-47.4
p. 255 left

The Bread of Affliction [from the
Haggadah series], 1931
Watercolor and ink on paper
11 ¾ × 8 ⅜ in.
Jewish Museum, New York. Gift
of Edward M. M. Warburg, JM 153-47.1
p. 255 right

The Reckoning of the Miracles
[from the *Haggadah* series], 1931
Watercolor and ink on paper
11 ¾ × 8 ½ in.
Jewish Museum, New York. Gift of
Edward M. M. Warburg, JM 153-47.8
p. 254 right

Three Witnesses, c. 1931–32
Watercolor on paper
10 ⅛ × 13 ½ in.
Montclair Art Museum, New Jersey.
Bequest of Moses and Ida Soyer
p. 71 bottom

*Untitled [Jewish Children, between
First and Second Avenues, Lower
East Side, New York City]*,
c. 1931–32
Gelatin silver print mounted
7 ⅜ × 9 ¾ in.

Ben Shahn papers, Archives
of American Art, Smithsonian
Institution

Bartolomeo Vanzetti and Nicola Sacco,
1931–32
Gouache on paper on board
10 ⅞ × 14 ⅝ in.
Museum of Modern Art, New York.
Gift of Abby Aldrich Rockefeller,
1935
p. 71 top

The Passion of Sacco and Vanzetti,
1931–32
Tempera on canvas mounted on
composition board
84 × 48 in.
Whitney Museum of American Art,
New York. Gift of Edith and Milton
Lowenthal in memory of Juliana
Force, 49.22
p. 70 left

Two Women, New York [possible study
for the *Sacco and Vanzetti* series],
c. 1932
Opaque and transparent watercolor
on masonite
10 ⅛ × 11 ½ in.
Museum of Fine Arts, Boston. Gift
of Mr. and Mrs. Stephen A. Stone

My Son is Innocent, 1932
Gouache on paper mounted on
masonite
16 ⅜ × 12 in.
Private collection, USA
p. 77

*Supreme Court of California:
Mooney Series*, 1932
Gouache on paper
16 × 24 in.
Hirshhorn Museum and Sculpture
Garden, Smithsonian Institution.
Gift of Joseph H. Hirshhorn, 1966
p. 72

*Two Witnesses, Mellie Edeau
and Sadie Edeau*, 1932
Tempera on paper on board
12 ⅛ × 16 ⅛ in.
Museum of Modern Art, New York.
Purchase, 1946
p. 75 top

Tom Mooney Handcuffed, 1932–33
Gouache on paper
16 ½ × 14 ¼ in.

New Jersey State Museum. The
Governor of New Jersey Purchase
Award. The Association for the Arts
of the New Jersey State Museum
Purchase Award, Art from New Jersey
Four, FA1969.124
p. 73

*Governor James Rolph, Jr.,
of California*, 1932–33
Gouache on board
16 ½ × 12 in.
Collection of Sally Kay and Scott
Hochhauser, New York
p. 74

14th St. [New York City], 1932–34
Gelatin silver print mounted
7 ¼ × 9 ¾ in.
Ben Shahn papers, Archives
of American Art, Smithsonian
Institution
p. 86 bottom

Greenwich Village [New York City],
1932–34
Gelatin silver print mounted
8 × 9 ⅞ in.
Ben Shahn papers, Archives
of American Art, Smithsonian
Institution
p. 87 bottom

*Untitled [Lower East Side, New York
City]*, c. 1932–35
Gelatin silver print
Exhibition copy
6 ¼ × 9 ⅜ in.
Image courtesy of Howard Greenberg
Gallery, New York
p. 172 bottom

6th Ave. [New York City], 1932–35
Gelatin silver print mounted
7 ⅞ × 10 in.
Ben Shahn papers, Archives
of American Art, Smithsonian
Institution

East Side Merchant [New York City],
1932–35
Gelatin silver print
7 ½ × 9 ½ in.
Harvard Art Museums/Fogg Museum.
Gift of Bernarda Bryson Shahn,
P1970.2854
p. 88 top

*Greenwich Village [Bethune Street,
New York City]*, 1932–35

Gelatin silver print
6 ¼ × 9 ½ in.
Harvard Art Museums/Fogg Museum.
Gift of Bernarda Bryson Shahn,
P1970.2476
p. 88 bottom

Greenwich Village [New York City],
1932–35
Gelatin silver print mounted
8 × 10 in.
Ben Shahn papers, Archives
of American Art, Smithsonian
Institution
p. 87 top

*Houston St. Playground [East Houston
Street, New York City]*, 1932–35
Gelatin silver print
Exhibition copy
6 ¼ × 9 ⅝ in.
Harvard Art Museums/Fogg Museum.
Gift of Bernarda Bryson Shahn,
P1970.2205
p. 126 bottom

*Untitled [Fourteenth Street, New York
City]*, 1932–35
Gelatin silver print
5 ⅞ × 9 in.
Harvard Art Museums/Fogg Museum.
Gift of Bernarda Bryson Shahn, by
exchange, P2000.14

*Untitled [Houston Street Playground,
East Houston Street, New York City]*,
1932–35
Gelatin silver print
Exhibition copy
6 × 9 in.
Harvard Art Museums/Fogg Museum.
Gift of Bernarda Bryson Shahn,
P1970.2478
p. 126 top

Untitled [New York City], 1932–35
Gelatin silver print
6 ½ × 8 ⅞ in.
Harvard Art Museums/Fogg Museum.
Gift of Bernarda Bryson Shahn,
P1970.2873
p. 122 bottom

Untitled [Seward Park, New York City],
1932–35
Gelatin silver print
5 ¼ × 8 in.
Harvard Art Museums/Fogg Museum.
Gift of Bernarda Bryson Shahn,
P1970.2958

Rena and Tom Mooney, 1933
Tempera on paper mounted
on masonite
20 ½ × 14 ½ in.
Private collection, USA
p. 76

Bootleggers [*Prohibition* mural study for
the Central Park Casino, unrealized],
c. 1934
Gouache and watercolor on masonite
16 ¼ × 15 ¾ in.
Museum of the City of New York.
Courtesy of the Fine Arts Program,
Public Building Services, U.S.
General Services Administration,
commissioned through the New Deal
Art Projects, 1934
p. 135

Delivering Barrels [*Prohibition* mural
study for the Central Park Casino,
unrealized], c. 1934
Gouache and watercolor on masonite
16 × 24 in.
Museum of the City of New York.
Courtesy of the Fine Arts Program,
Public Building Services, U.S.
General Services Administration,
commissioned through the New Deal
Art Projects, 1934
p. 134

*Federal Agents Pouring Wine Down
a Sewer* [*Prohibition* mural study for
the Central Park Casino, unrealized],
c. 1934
Gouache and watercolor on masonite
16 ¼ × 11 ¼ in.
Museum of the City of New York.
Courtesy of the Fine Arts Program,
Public Building Services, U.S.
General Services Administration,
commissioned through the New Deal
Art Projects, 1934
p. 80

Parade for Repeal [*Prohibition* mural
study for the Central Park Casino,
unrealized], c. 1934
Gouache and watercolor on masonite
16 ½ × 31 ¾ in.
Museum of the City of New York.
Courtesy of the Fine Arts Program,
Public Building Services, U.S.
General Services Administration,
commissioned through the New Deal
Art Projects, 1934
pp. 132–133

Village Speakeasy Closed for Violation
[*Prohibition* mural study for the
Central Park Casino, unrealized],
c. 1934
Gouache and watercolor on masonite
16 ¼ × 47 ¾ in.

Museum of the City of New York.
Courtesy of the Fine Arts Program,
Public Building Services, U.S.
General Services Administration,
commissioned through the New Deal
Art Projects, 1934
pp. 136–37

WCTU Parade [*Prohibition* mural study
for the Central Park Casino, unrealized],
c. 1934
Gouache and watercolor on masonite
16 ⅛ × 31 ¾ in.
Museum of the City of New York.
Courtesy of the Fine Arts Program,
Public Building Services, U.S. General
Services Administration, commissioned
through the New Deal Art Projects, 1934
pp. 130–31

*Untitled [New York City Reformatory,
New Hampton, New York]*, 1934
Gelatin silver print
6 ¼ × 9 ⅜ in.
Ben Shahn papers, Archives of
American Art, Smithsonian Institution
p. 89 top

*Untitled [New York City Reformatory,
New Hampton, New York]*, May–June
1934
Gelatin silver print
5 ⅞ × 9 in.
Harvard Art Museums/Fogg Museum.
Gift of Bernarda Bryson Shahn,
by exchange, P2000.18
p. 89 bottom

*Untitled [Artists' Union and Artists
Committee of Action Demonstrations,
NYC]*, 1934–35
Gelatin silver print
3 × 6 ¾ in.
Bernarda Bryson Shahn papers,
Archives of American Art, Smithsonian
Institution

*Untitled [Artists' Union and Artists
Committee of Action Demonstrations,
NYC]*, 1934–35
Gelatin silver print
4 ⅝ × 7 in.
Bernarda Bryson Shahn papers,
Archives of American Art, Smithsonian
Institution
p. 91 middle

*Untitled [Artists' Union and Artists
Committee of Action Demonstrations,
NYC]*, 1934–35
Gelatin silver print
6 ¼ × 4 ½ in.
Bernarda Bryson Shahn papers,
Archives of American Art, Smithsonian
Institution
p. 90

*Untitled [Artists' Union and Artists
Committee of Action Demonstrations,
NYC]*, 1934–35
Gelatin silver print
4 × 6 ¾ in.
Bernarda Bryson Shahn papers,
Archives of American Art,
Smithsonian Institution

*Untitled [Artists' Union and Artists
Committee of Action Demonstrations,
NYC]*, 1934–35
Gelatin silver print
4 ⅛ × 6 ¾ in.
Bernarda Bryson Shahn papers,
Archives of American Art,
Smithsonian Institution

*Untitled [Artists' Union and Artists
Committee of Action Demonstrations,
NYC]*, 1934–35
Gelatin silver print
4 ¾ × 7 in.
Bernarda Bryson Shahn papers,
Archives of American Art,
Smithsonian Institution
p. 91 top

*Untitled [Artists' Union and Artists
Committee of Action Demonstrations,
NYC]*, 1934–35
Gelatin silver print
4 ¼ × 6 ½ in.
Bernarda Bryson Shahn papers,
Archives of American Art,
Smithsonian Institution

*Untitled [Artists' Union and Artists
Committee of Action Demonstrations,
NYC]*, 1934–35
Gelatin silver print
4 ⅜ × 5 ⅝ in.
Bernarda Bryson Shahn papers,
Archives of American Art,
Smithsonian Institution
p. 91 bottom

*Untitled [Artists' Union and Artists
Committee of Action Demonstrations,
NYC]*, 1934–35
Gelatin silver print
6 × 8 ¾ in.
Bernarda Bryson Shahn papers,
Archives of American Art,
Smithsonian Institution

*Untitled [Welfare Hospital,
Welfare Island, New York City]*,
1934–35
Gelatin silver print
Exhibition copy
6 × 9 ⅝ in.
Harvard Art Museums/Fogg Museum.
Gift of Bernarda Bryson Shahn,
P1970.2810
p. 21 bottom

*Invest in Your Country's Future,
Pass the American Youth Act*,
c. 1935
Gouache, ink, and pencil on paper
11 × 17 ½ in.
Collection of Michael Berg, Fairfax
Station, Virginia
p. 118 bottom

Untitled [New York City], 1935
Gelatin silver print mounted
8 × 10 ⅛ in.
Ben Shahn papers, Archives of
American Art, Smithsonian Institution
p. 86 top

*Untitled [Artists' Union Demonstration,
Spanish Consulate, near Madison
Avenue and East Fifty-Third Street,
New York City]*, Spring 1935
Digitally inverted from 35 mm negative
Exhibition copy
1 × 1 ⅜ in.
Harvard Art Museums/Fogg Museum.
Gift of Bernarda Bryson Shahn,
P1970.3953
p. 94 top

*Untitled [Artists' Union Demonstration,
Spanish Consulate, near Madison
Avenue and East Fifty-Third Street,
New York City]*, Spring 1935
Digitally inverted from 35 mm negative
Exhibition copy
1 × 1 ⅜ in.
Harvard Art Museums/Fogg Museum.
Gift of Bernarda Bryson Shahn,
P1970.3955
p. 94 bottom

*Untitled [Artists' Union Demonstration,
Spanish Consulate, near Madison
Avenue and East Fifty-Third Street,
New York City]*, Spring 1935
Digitally inverted from 35 mm negative
Exhibition copy
1 ⅜ × 1 in.
Harvard Art Museums/Fogg Museum.
Gift of Bernarda Bryson Shahn,
P1970.3957
p. 95

*Bank in Smithland, Kentucky,
RA6080-M5*, October 1935
Gelatin silver print mounted
7 ⅞ × 9 ⅞ in.
Ben Shahn papers, Archives of
American Art, Smithsonian Institution
p. 109

*Boone County, Arkansas. The Family
of a Resettlement Administration
Client in the Doorway of Their Home*,
October 1935
Digital file from 35 mm negative
Exhibition copy

Library of Congress, Prints &
Photographs Division, FSA/OWI
Collection, LC-DIG-fsa-8a16229
p. 102 top

*Children of Destitute Ozark
Mountaineer, Arkansas*, October 1935
Digital file from 35 mm negative
Exhibition copy
Library of Congress, Prints &
Photographs Division, FSA/OWI
Collection, LC-DIG-fsa-8a16213
p. 101 top

*Child of Fortuna Family, Hammond,
Louisiana, RA6174-M3*, October 1935
Gelatin silver print
8 ⅛ × 10 in.
Elizabeth McCausland papers,
Archives of American Art,
Smithsonian Institution
p. 98 top

*Children of Rehabilitation Client,
Maria Plantation, Arkansas*,
October 1935
Digital file from 35 mm negative
Exhibition copy
Library of Congress, Prints &
Photographs Division, FSA/OWI
Collection, LC-DIG-fsa-8a16282
p. 101 bottom

*Children of Sharecropper,
Little Rock, Arkansas, RA6026-M3*,
October 1935
Gelatin silver print
8 × 9 ⅞ in.
Ben Shahn papers, Archives of
American Art, Smithsonian Institution

*Citizens of Camden, Tennessee,
RA6185-M2*, October 1935
Gelatin silver print
8 × 9 ⅞ in.
Ben Shahn papers, Archives of
American Art, Smithsonian Institution

*Cotton Pickers, 6:30 a.m., Alexander
Plantation, Pulaski County, Arkansas*,
October 1935
Digital file from 35 mm negative
Exhibition copy
Library of Congress, Prints &
Photographs Division, FSA/OWI
Collection, LC-DIG-fsa-8a16190
p. 104

*Cotton Pickers, Pulaski County,
Arkansas*, October 1935
Digital file from 35 mm negative
Exhibition copy
Library of Congress, Prints &
Photographs Division, FSA/OWI
Collection, LC-DIG-fsa-8a17074
p. 106 top

*Family of Rehabilitation Client,
Boone County, Arkansas, RA6034-M1*,
October 1935
Gelatin silver print
8 × 9 ¾ in.
Ben Shahn papers, Archives
of American Art, Smithsonian
Institution

Huntingdon, Tennessee, October 1935
Digital file from 35 mm negative
Exhibition copy
Library of Congress, Prints &
Photographs Division, FSA/OWI
Collection, LC-DIG-fsa-8a16812
p. 112 bottom

*Kentucky Coal Miner, Jenkins,
Kentucky*, October 1935
Digital file from 35 mm negative
Exhibition copy
Library of Congress, Prints &
Photographs Division, FSA/OWI
Collection, LC-DIG-fsa-8a16946
p. 180

*Kentucky Coal Miners, Jenkins,
Kentucky*, October 1935
Digital file from 35 mm negative
Exhibition copy
Library of Congress, Prints &
Photographs Division, FSA/OWI
Collection, LC-DIG-fsa-8a16947
p. 179

*Medicine Show, Huntingdon,
Tennessee*, October 1935
Digital file from 35 mm negative
Exhibition copy
Library of Congress, Prints &
Photographs Division, FSA/OWI
Collection, LC-DIG-fsa-8a16825
p. 112 top

*Medicine Show, Huntingdon,
Tennessee*, October 1935
Digital file from 35 mm negative
Exhibition copy
Library of Congress, Prints &
Photographs Division, FSA/OWI
Collection, LC-DIG-fsa-8a16807
p. 113 top

*Picking Cotton on Alexander
Plantation, Pulaski County, Arkansas*,
October 1935
Digital file from 35 mm negative
Exhibition copy
Library of Congress, Prints &
Photographs Division, FSA/OWI
Collection, LC-DIG-fsa-8a17057
p. 107

*Rehabilitation Clients, Boone County,
Arkansas*, October 1935
Digital file from 35 mm negative

Exhibition copy
Library of Congress, Prints &
Photographs Division, FSA/OWI
Collection, LC-DIG-fsa-8a16222
p. 99

*Sam Nichols, Tenant Farmer,
Boone County, Arkansas*,
October 1935
Digital file from 35 mm negative
Exhibition copy
Library of Congress, Prints &
Photographs Division, FSA/OWI
Collection, LC-DIG-fsa-8a16238
p. 150

Scene at Smithland, Kentucky,
October 1935
Digital file from 35 mm negative
Exhibition copy
Library of Congress, Prints &
Photographs Division, FSA/OWI
Collection, LC-DIG-fsa-8a16410
p. 108 top

*Sharecroppers' Children on
Sunday, near Little Rock, Arkansas*,
October 1935
Digital file from 35 mm negative
Exhibition copy
Library of Congress, Prints &
Photographs Division, FSA/OWI
Collection, LC-DIG-fsa-8a16174
p. 103

*Son of Destitute Ozark Family,
Arkansas, RA6070-M3*,
October 1935
Gelatin silver print
8 × 9 ¾ in.
Elizabeth McCausland papers,
Archives of American Art,
Smithsonian Institution

*Striking Miners, Scotts Run,
West Virginia*, October 1935
Digital file from 35 mm negative
Exhibition copy
Library of Congress, Prints &
Photographs Division, FSA/OWI
Collection, LC-DIG-fsa-8a16625
p. 122 top

Sunday in Scotts Run, West Virginia,
October 1935
Digital file from 35 mm negative
Exhibition copy
Library of Congress, Prints &
Photographs Division, FSA/OWI
Collection, LC-DIG-fsa-8a16580

*Untitled [Plaquemines Parish,
Louisiana]*, October 1935
Gelatin silver print
Exhibition copy
7 ½ × 9 ⅝ in.

Harvard Art Museums/Fogg Museum.
Gift of Bernarda Bryson Shahn,
P1970.1583
p. 114

Untitled [possibly related to: *Cotton
Pickers, Pulaski County, Arkansas*],
October 1935
Digital file from 35 mm negative
Exhibition copy
Library of Congress, Prints &
Photographs Division, FSA/OWI
Collection, LC-DIG-fsa-8a16160
p. 105

Untitled [possibly related to: *Doped
Singer, "Love oh, love, oh keerless
love," Scotts Run, West Virginia. Relief
Investigator Reported a Number of
Dope Cases at Scotts Run*], October 1935
Digital file from 35 mm negative
Exhibition copy
Library of Congress, Prints &
Photographs Division, FSA/OWI
Collection, LC-DIG-fsa-8a16602
p. 168

*Watching Medicine Show, Huntingdon,
Tennessee, RA6166-M4*, October 1935
Gelatin silver print
8 × 9 ⅞ in.
Ben Shahn papers, Archives of
American Art, Smithsonian Institution
p. 97

*Wife and Child of Sharecropper,
Arkansas*, October 1935
Digital file from 35 mm negative
Exhibition copy
Library of Congress, Prints &
Photographs Division, FSA/OWI
Collection, LC-DIG-fsa-8a16211
p. 100

*Miner / A Good House / Good
Gardening Land is Ready / for You
through Resettlement*, c. 1936
Gelatin silver print (poster)
34 ¼ × 21 in.
Harvard Art Museums/Fogg Museum.
Gift of Bernarda Bryson Shahn
p. 117 right

*The Sheriff's Sale / Faces over a Million
American Farmers / Resettlements
Farm Debt Adjustment / Will Help Save
Their Farms*, c. 1936
Gelatin silver print (poster)
34 ⅛ × 23 in.
Harvard Art Museums/Fogg Museum.
Gift of Bernarda Bryson Shahn
p. 117 left

Bernarda Bryson Shahn
A Mule and a Plow, 1936
Photo-offset lithograph on paper

37 ⅞ × 24 ⅝ in.
Maier Museum of Art at Randolph
College, founded as Randolph-Macon
Woman's College, Lynchburg,
Virginia
p. 115

East Side Soap Box, 1936
Gouache on paper
17 ½ × 11 ⅜ in.
Jewish Museum, New York. Purchase:
Deana Bezark Fund in memory of
Leslie Bezark; Mrs. Jack N. Berkman,
Susan and Arthur Fleischer, Dr. Jack
Allen and Shirley Kapland, Hanni and
Peter Kaufmann, Hyman L. and Joan
C. Sall Funds, and Margaret Goldstein
Bequest, 1995-61
p. 62

Seward Park, 1936
Lithograph on Rives paper
15 ¼ × 22 ¾ in.
New Jersey State Museum. Gift
of Dorothy and Sydney Spivack,
FA1969.288.10
p. 118 top

Street Corner Speaker, 1936
Watercolor on paper
15 ½ × 11 ½ in.
Colby College Museum of Art,
Waterville, Maine. Gift of Barbro
and Bernard Osher, 2011.053
p. 79 right

Years of Dust, 1936
Photo-offset lithograph on paper
38 × 24 ⅝ in.
Maier Museum of Art at Randolph
College, founded as Randolph-Macon
Woman's College, Lynchburg,
Virginia
p. 116

Bowery [New York City], April 1936
Gelatin silver print mounted
7 ⅞ × 10 ¼ in.
Ben Shahn papers, Archives
of American Art, Smithsonian
Institution
p. 84 bottom

*East Side Merchants [Lower East Side,
New York City]*, April 1936
Gelatin silver print
8 ¼ × 10 ⅛ in.
Ben Shahn papers, Archives
of American Art, Smithsonian
Institution
p. 84 top

*Untitled [Lower East Side, New York
City]*, April 1936
Gelatin silver print
8 × 10 ⅛ in.

Ben Shahn papers, Archives
of American Art, Smithsonian
Institution
p. 83

*Untitled [Lower East Side, New York
City]*, April 1936
Gelatin silver print
6 ⅞ × 9 ¾ in.
Ben Shahn papers, Archives of
American Art, Smithsonian Institution
p. 172 top

*Study for Great State of Wisconsin
mural*, c. 1937
Gouache, ink, and graphite
on illustration board
4 × 17 ½ in.
Collection of halley k harrisburg
and Michael Rosenfeld, New York.
Courtesy of Michael Rosenfeld Gallery,
LLC, New York
pp. 138–39

*Music for the Square Dance, Skyline
Farms, Alabama, RA6285-M2*, 1937
Gelatin silver print
8 ⅛ × 10 ¼ in.
Ben Shahn papers, Archives
of American Art, Smithsonian
Institution

*Practicing for the Westmoreland
Fair, Pennsylvania*, 1937
Digital file from 35 mm negative
Exhibition copy
Library of Congress, Prints &
Photographs Division, FSA/OWI
Collection, LC-DIG-fsa-8a17492
p. 166

Scotts Run, West Virginia, 1937
Tempera on paper mounted on wood
22 ⅝ × 28 ¼ in.
Whitney Museum of American Art,
New York. Purchase, 38.11
p. 123

Wear Goggles, 1937
Offset lithograph on paper
20 × 14 in.
New Jersey State Museum.
Museum Purchase,
FA1970.320.22

Untitled [Steel Strike, Warren, Ohio],
Summer 1937
Gelatin silver print
8 × 10 in.
Ben Shahn papers, Archives
of American Art, Smithsonian
Institution
p. 40 top left

Untitled [Steel Strike, Warren, Ohio],
Summer 1937

Gelatin silver print
7 ⅞ × 10 ⅛ in.
Ben Shahn papers, Archives of
American Art, Smithsonian Institution
p. 40 bottom left

Puddlers' Sunday, 1937 or 1938
Tempera on board
16 × 23 ¾ in.
Frances Lehman Loeb Art Center,
Vassar College. Gift of Mr. and Mrs.
Albert Hackett (Frances Goodrich,
class of 1912)
p. 40 top right

Unemployed, c. 1938
Tempera on board
13 ¾ × 16 ½ in.
Schoen Collection
p. 119

Sunday Painting, 1938
Egg tempera on rag paper mounted
on board
16 × 24 in.
Kennedy Museum of Art, Ohio
University. Bequest of Bernarda Bryson
Shahn Estate, 2006
p. 121

*At Ashville July 4th Celebration,
Ashville, Ohio*, July–August 1938
Digital file from 35 mm negative
Exhibition copy
Library of Congress, Prints &
Photographs Division, FSA/OWI
Collection, LC-DIG-fsa-8a17825
p. 163

Farmpeople at Fair in Central Ohio,
August 1938
Digital file from 35 mm negative
Exhibition copy
Library of Congress, Prints &
Photographs Division, FSA/OWI
Collection, LC-DIG-fsa-8a18994

*Itinerant Photographer in Columbus,
Ohio*, August 1938
Digital file from 35 mm negative
Exhibition copy
Library of Congress, Prints &
Photographs Division, FSA/OWI
Collection, LC-DIG-fsa-8a18478
p. 110 top

*"Business was Bad," World
War Veterans' Homecoming
and Carnival, London, Ohio*,
Summer 1938
Digital file from 35 mm negative
Exhibition copy
Library of Congress, Prints &
Photographs Division, FSA/OWI
Collection, LC-DIG-fsa-8a17949
p. 162 top

*"Roadside Inn," Central Ohio.
The Figure of the Body was Originally
Distributed to Advertise the Neward
Indian Mounds. Redecorated*,
Summer 1938
Digital file from 35 mm negative
Exhibition copy
Library of Congress, Prints &
Photographs Division, FSA/OWI
Collection, LC-DIG-fsa-8a18487
p. 111

*Scene at Buckeye Lake Amusement
Park, near Columbus, Ohio*, Summer
1938
Digital file from 35 mm negative
Exhibition copy
Library of Congress, Prints &
Photographs Division, FSA/OWI
Collection, LC-DIG-fsa-8a18579
p. 162 bottom

Street Scene, Circleville, Ohio,
Summer 1938
Digital file from 35 mm negative
Exhibition copy
Library of Congress, Prints &
Photographs Division, FSA/OWI
Collection, LC-DIG-fsa-8a17674
p. 110 bottom

Sunday Morning, c. 1938–43
Tempera on paper mounted
on masonite
15 ¾ × 23 ¾ in.
Georgia Museum of Art, University
of Georgia; Eva Underhill Holbrook
Memorial Collection of American Art.
Gift of Alfred H. Holbrook, GMOA
1947.154
p. 120

Seurat's Lunch, c. 1939
Tempera on masonite
19 ⅞ × 29 ⅞ in.
Museum of Contemporary Art
Chicago. Gift of Mary and Earle Ludgin
Collection, 1988.3
p. 128

Father Coughlin, 1939
Watercolor and ink
15 ½ × 12 in.
Columbus Museum of Art. Museum
Purchase, Derby Fund, from the Philip
J. and Suzanne Schiller Collection
of American Social Commentary Art,
1930–1970
p. 78 bottom

Handball, 1939
Gouache on paper on board
22 ¾ × 31 ¼ in.
Museum of Modern Art, New York.
Abby Aldrich Rockefeller Fund, 1940
p. 127

Untitled [Grinning Puddler], c. 1940
Gouache and ink on paper
16 ⅛ × 10 ⅜ in.
Collection of Michael Berg, Fairfax
Station, Virginia
p. 181 top left

*Democracies Fear New Peace Offensive
[Spring, 1940]*, 1940
Tempera on paper
14 ¼ × 21 ⅜ in.
Museum of Contemporary Art Chicago.
Gift of the Mary and Earle Ludgin
Collection, 2008.34
p. 124

Pretty Girl Milking the Cow, 1940
Tempera on paper mounted on
masonite
21 ⅝ × 29 ½ in.
Frances Lehman Loeb Art
Center, Vassar College.
Gift of Edgar Kaufmann, Jr.
p. 125

Willis Avenue Bridge, 1940
Gouache on paper on board
23 × 31 ¼ in.
Museum of Modern Art, New York.
Gift of Lincoln Kirstein, 1947
p. 21 top

Carpenter's Helper #2, c. 1940–42
Gouache on cardboard
10 ⅞ × 5 ½ in.
Columbus Museum of Art.
Museum Purchase, Howald Fund
p. 142 left

Steel Worker [study for *The Meaning
of Social Security* mural, Washington,
D.C.], 1940–42
Gouache on paper
11 × 8 in.
Collection of Adam and Erika Berg,
Washington, D.C.
p. 142 right

Housing [from *The Meaning
of Social Security* mural, West Wall],
1940–42
Fresco secco
Exhibition copy
105 × 184 in.
Wilbur J. Cohen Federal Building,
Washington, D.C.
p. 143

Public Works [from *The Meaning
of Social Security* mural, West Wall],
1940–42
Fresco secco
Exhibition copy
105 × 184 ½ in.
Wilbur J. Cohen Federal Building,
Washington, D.C.

Vandenberg, Dewey, and Taft, 1941
Screen print in colors
16 × 22 ½ in.
Collection of Michael Berg, Fairfax
Station, Virginia
p. 196

We Fight for a Free World!, c. 1942
Gouache and tempera on board
13 ½ × 29 ¾ in.
Collection of halley k harrisburg and
Michael Rosenfeld, New York. Courtesy
of Michael Rosenfeld Gallery, LLC,
New York
p. 152

French Workers, 1942
Gouache on board
14 ¾ × 20 ¾ in.
Colby College Museum of Art,
Waterville, Maine. Museum purchase
from the Jere Abbott Acquisitions
Fund, 2011.002
p. 147

French Workers, 1942
Tempera on masonite
40 × 57 in.
Museo Nacional Thyssen-Bornemisza,
Madrid
p. 148 top

This is Nazi Brutality, 1942
Offset photolithograph in colors
37 × 27 ¾ in.
Madison Art Collection, James Madison
University. Gift of Michael Berg, 2013
p. 144

*We French Workers Warn You…
Defeat Means Slavery, Starvation,
Death*, 1942
Offset lithograph on paper
26 ¾ × 41 in.
Museo Nacional Centro de Arte Reina
Sofía, Madrid
p. 148 bottom

1943 AD, c. 1943
Tempera on pressboard
30 ¾ × 27 ¾ in.
Syracuse University Art Museum.
Gift of Chancellor William Pearson
Tolley '22, 1960.034
p. 151

Ben Shahn and Muriel Rukeyser
Our Manpower, c. 1943
Poster
Exhibition copy
14 ⅝ × 20 ⅛ in.
Muriel Rukeyser papers, Henry
W. and Albert A. Berg Collection
of English and American Literature,
New York Public Library
p. 187 bottom

Girl Skipping Rope, 1943
Tempera on board
15 ⅞ × 23 ⅞ in.
Museum of Fine Arts, Boston.
Gift of the Stephen and Sybil Stone
Foundation
p. 158

India, 1943
Tempera on board
20 × 36 in.
Neuberger Museum of Art,
Purchase College, State University
of New York. Gift of Roy R. Neuberger,
1970.02.27
p. 29 top

Morning, 1943
Opaque watercolor on paper
mounted on hardboard
5 ¾ × 13 ¼ in.
Phillips Collection, Washington,
D.C.
p. 153

Italian Landscape, 1943–44
Tempera on paper
27 ½ × 36 in.
Walker Art Center, Minneapolis.
Gift of the T. B. Walker Foundation,
Gilbert M. Walker Fund,
1944
p. 156, cover

Bountiful Harvest, 1944
Tempera on board
38 × 28 in.
Bernard Goldberg Fine Arts, LLC,
New York
p. 189

Cherubs and Children, 1944
Tempera on paper mounted
on board
15 ½ × 23 ¼ in.
Whitney Museum of American Art,
New York. Purchase, 45.17
p. 159

*For Full Employment After the War,
Register, Vote [Welders]*, 1944
Offset photolithograph in colors
28 ¾ × 39 in.
Collection of Michael Berg, Fairfax
Station, Virginia
p. 187 top

Four Piece Orchestra, 1944
Tempera on masonite
18 × 23 ⅝ in.
Museo Nacional Thyssen-Bornemisza,
Madrid
p. 167

From Workers to Farmers… Thanks!,
1944

Offset photolithograph in colors
39 × 28 ⅞ in.
Collection of Adam and Erika Berg,
Washington, D.C.
p. 190 left

Italian Landscape II: Europa,
1944
Tempera on academy board
22 ½ × 30 ⅝ in.
Montgomery Museum of Fine Arts,
Alabama; The Blount Collection
p. 157

Our Friend, 1944
Offset photolithograph in colors
29 ⅞ × 39 ½ in.
Collection of Michael Berg, Fairfax
Station, Virginia
p. 188

*Register… The Ballot is a Power
in Your Hands*, 1944
Offset photolithograph in colors
39 × 29 in.
Collection of Michael Berg, Fairfax
Station, Virginia

The Clinic, 1944
Tempera on paper mounted
on masonite
15 ⅝ × 22 ¾ in.
Georgia Museum of Art, University
of Georgia; Eva Underhill Holbrook
Memorial Collection of American
Art. University Purchase, GMOA
1948.204
p. 183

Ronny Jaques
*Ben Shahn [CIO-PAC Office, New York
City]*, c. 1945
Gelatin silver print
13 ⅞ × 11 in.
National Portrait Gallery, Smithsonian
Institution
p. 185

Liberation, 1945
Gouache on board
29 ¾ × 39 ⅞ in.
Museum of Modern Art, New York.
James Thrall Soby Bequest, 1979
p. 161

Remember the Wrapper, 1945
Tempera on paperboard mounted
on wood
19 ¾ × 26 ¼ in.
Hirshhorn Museum and Sculpture
Garden, Smithsonian Institution.
Gift of Joseph H. Hirshhorn, 1966
p. 160

We Want Peace, Register, Vote, c. 1946
Offset lithograph laid on canvas

41 ½ × 27 in.
Jule Collins Smith Museum
of Fine Art, Auburn University,
Alabama
p. 190 right

Break Reaction's Grip, 1946
Photo-offset lithograph on paper
41 ½ × 29 ⅛ in.
Maier Museum of Art, Randolph
College, founded as Randolph-Macon
Woman's College, Lynchburg,
Virginia
p. 195

Carnival, 1946
Tempera on masonite
22 × 29 ¾ in.
Museo Nacional Thyssen-Bornemisza,
Madrid
p. 165

*For All These Rights We've Just Begun
to Fight*, 1946
Photo-offset lithograph on paper
29 × 38 ¾ in.
Maier Museum of Art, Randolph
College, founded as Randolph-Macon
Woman's College, Lynchburg,
Virginia
p. 194

Hunger, 1946
Gouache on composition board
39 × 25 in.
Jule Collins Smith Museum
of Fine Art, Auburn University,
Alabama
p. 191

Man, 1946
Tempera on board
22 ¾ × 16 ⅜ in.
Museum of Modern Art, New York. Gift
of Mr. and Mrs. E. Powis Jones, 1958
p. 192

Nearly Everyone Reads the Bulletin,
1946
Gouache and ink on masonite
22 × 30 in.
Philadelphia Museum of Art.
The Louis E. Stern Collection, 1963
p. 164

The Church is the Union Hall, 1946
Tempera on board
20 × 16 in.
High Museum of Art, Atlanta.
Purchase with funds from Sherri and
Jess Crawford, High Museum of Art
Enhancement Fund, the American
Art Collectors, Mr. and Mrs. Henry
Schwob, and Mr. and Mrs. John L.
Huber
p. 234

Warning! Inflation Means Depression,
1946
Photo-offset lithograph on paper
41 ¼ × 27 ⅞ in.
Maier Museum of Art, Randolph
College, founded as Randolph-Macon
Woman's College, Lynchburg,
Virginia
p. 193

World's Greatest Comics, 1946
Tempera on panel
35 × 48 in.
Amon Carter Museum of American
Art, Fort Worth, Texas
p. 175

Laissez-faire, c. 1947
Screen print on laid paper
14 ⅛ × 21 in.
New Jersey State Museum.
Gift of Mr. and Mrs. Michael Lewis,
FA1969.323
p. 197 top

New York, 1947
Tempera on paper mounted on canvas
and panel
36 × 48 in.
Jewish Museum, New York. Purchase:
Oscar and Regina Gruss Charitable
and Educational Foundation Fund,
1996-23
p. 173

Study for New York, 1947
Wash and graphite on paper
5 ¼ × 8 ⅛ in.
Jewish Museum, New York. Purchase:
Miriam and Milton Handler Fund,
2000-70

The Miner, c. 1948
Lithograph
7 ½ × 4 ⅞ in.
Herbert F. Johnson Museum
of Art, Cornell University, Ithaca,
New York
p. 181 top right

A Good Man is Hard to Find, 1948
Lithograph in colors
43 ⅝ × 29 ¾ in.
Collection of Michael Berg, Fairfax
Station, Virginia
p. 202

Allegory, 1948
Tempera on panel
36 ⅛ × 48 ⅛ in.
Modern Art Museum of Fort Worth.
Gift of William P. Bomar, Jr.
in memory of Mrs. Jewel Nail
Bomar and Mr. Andrew Chilton
Phillips
p. 171

Untitled [sixteen drawings from John
Bartlow Martin, "The Hickman Story,"
Harper's Magazine, August 1948,
vol. 197, no. 1179, pp. 39–52]
1948
Pen and ink on wove paper
Exhibition copies
Framed: 13 ¾ × 11 ¾ in.
David and Alfred Smart Museum
of Art, University of Chicago.
Gift of Leon and Marian Despres
pp. 238–39

Let Your Help Match His Courage, 1949
Tempera on composition board
46 × 30 in.
Museum of Modern Art, New York.
Gift of the National Foundation
for Infantile Paralysis, 1958

Nocturne, 1949
Tempera on lightweight canvas,
mounted to panel
26 ⅞ × 39 ⅞ in.
Courtesy of the Office of the Dean of
Students. Gift of an anonymous donor
to the Willard Straight Hall Collection,
Cornell University, Ithaca, New York
p. 169

Bricklayers, c. 1951
Tempera on paper
14 × 11 in.
Collection of Debra and Michael
Skolnick, Elkins Park, Pennsylvania
p. 2

A.B.C., 1953
Watercolor on paper on board
25 ½ × 38 ⅞ in.
Des Moines Art Center Permanent
Collections. Purchased with funds
from Rose F. Rosenfield, 1957.13

Artist and Politicians, 1953
Ink on paper
23 ½ × 18 ½ in.
New Jersey State Museum.
Gift of Dr. and Mrs. Sidney Merians,
FA1982.62.1
p. 208

Discord, 1953
Watercolor
38 × 25 in.
Columbus Museum of Art. Museum
Purchase, Derby Fund, from the Philip
J. and Suzanne Schiller Collection
of American Social Commentary Art,
1930–1970
p. 205

Second Allegory, 1953
Tempera on canvas mounted on
masonite
53 ⅜ × 31 ⅜ in.

Krannert Art Museum, University
of Illinois Urbana-Champaign.
Festival of Arts Purchase Fund,
1953-7-1
p. 209

*Untitled [Portrait of J. Robert
Oppenheimer]*, c. 1954
Pencil on paper
9 × 6 in.
Private collection, USA
p. 228 bottom

Untitled [Portrait of Roy M. Cohn],
c. 1954
Ink on paper
6 ¼ × 4 ¾ in.
Private collection, USA
p. 207 right

Blind Botanist #2, 1954
Tempera on canvas, mounted to board
21 ⅛ × 17 ¼ in.
Neuberger Museum of Art,
Purchase College, State University
of New York. Gift from the Dina
and Alexander E. Racolin Collection,
1995.12.52
p. 225

Everyman, 1954
Tempera and oil on canvas mounted
to composition board
72 ⅛ × 24 in.
Whitney Museum of American Art,
New York. Purchase, 56.5
p. 212

J. Robert Oppenheimer, 1954
Ink on paper
12 ⅛ × 9 ¾ in.
National Portrait Gallery, Smithsonian
Institution
p. 229

National Pastime, 1955
Ink on paper mounted on board
26 ½ × 40 ¼ in.
Des Moines Art Center Permanent
Collections. Purchased with funds
from Rose F. Rosenfield, 1958.23

Today is the Birth[day] of the World, 1955
Ink on paper
22 ½ × 31 in.
Jewish Museum, New York.
Gift of Mr. and Mrs. Albert A. List,
JM 88-72
p. 253

Louis Armstrong, c. 1956
Gouache on paper
12 ⅛ × 10 in.
National Portrait Gallery,
Smithsonian Institution
p. 249 bottom left

Goyescas, 1956
Watercolor
25 ½ × 30 in.
Columbus Museum of Art.
Museum Purchase, Derby Fund,
from the Philip J. and Suzanne
Schiller Collection of American
Social Commentary Art,
1930–1970
p. 210

Mine Building, 1956
Screen print and tempera on
unbleached fiber paper
22 ⅜ × 30 ⅝ in.
New Jersey State Museum.
Gift of the Frelinghuysen
Foundation and the Dorothy and
Sydney Spivack Acquisition Fund,
FA1969.294

Alphabet of Creation, 1957
Screen print in black
32 ⅛ × 24 ¼ in.
Collection of Michael Berg, Fairfax
Station, Virginia
p. 256

Existentialists, 1957
Watercolor on heavy paperboard
46 ¼ × 33 ¼ in.
Brooklyn Museum. Dick S. Ramsay
Fund, 59.27
p. 214 top

Scientist, 1957
Screen print and watercolor
on paper
11 ⅞ × 10 in.
New Jersey State Museum.
Museum Purchase, FA1970.216.3
p. 220

The News [from *The Saga of the Lucky
Dragon* series], 1957
Pen and ink on cream laid paper
6 ¾ × 5 ⅞ in.
Madison Art Collection, James
Madison University. Gift of Michael
Berg, 2019
p. 230 bottom

Korea, c. 1958
Tempera on canvas mounted
on board
13 × 23 in.
Collection of Mark L. Brock,
Concord, Massachusetts
p. 211

Conversations, 1958
Opaque watercolor and brush and ink
on paper mounted on board
38 ¾ × 25 ½ in.
Whitney Museum of American Art,
New York. Purchase, with funds from

the Friends of the Whitney Museum
of American Art, 58.21
p. 213

Lute and Molecule #2, 1958
Screen print in black with hand coloring
26 × 39 ⅝ in.
Collection of Michael Berg, Fairfax
Station, Virginia
p. 228 top

Cat's Cradle in Blue, c. 1959
Egg tempera on composition board
39 ¾ × 25 ¾ in.
Pennsylvania Academy of the Fine Arts,
Philadelphia. Joseph E. Temple Fund
p. 215

After Titian, 1959
Tempera on fiberboard
53 ½ × 30 ½ in.
Smithsonian American Art Museum.
Gift of the Sara Roby Foundation
p. 216

*We Did Not Know What Happened
to Us*, c. 1960
Tempera on wood
48 × 72 ⅛ in.
Smithsonian American Art Museum.
Gift of S.C. Johnson & Son, Inc.
p. 231

Pleiades, 1960
Screen print in black and gray with
hand coloring (watercolor) and gold leaf
19 ½ × 26 in.
Collection of Michael Berg, Fairfax
Station, Virginia
p. 258

Stop H Bomb Tests, 1960
Screen print in red, blue, and black
43 ⅜ × 34 in.
Madison Art Collection, James Madison
University. Gift of Michael Berg, 2020
p. 224 top

Blind Botanist, 1961
Screen print in black and green
39 ⅝ × 26 in.
Collection of Michael Berg, Fairfax
Station, Virginia
p. 226

Decalogue, 1961
Gouache and gold leaf on paper
38 ¾ × 25 ¼ in.
Jewish Museum, New York. Gift
of Mr. and Mrs. Albert A. List Family,
JM 136-72
p. 260

It's No Use to Do Any More, 1961–62
Tempera on board
25 ½ × 39 ¼ in.

Maier Museum of Art, Randolph
College, founded as Randolph-Macon
Woman's College, Lynchburg,
Virginia
p. 232

Blind Botanist, 1963
Color lithograph
26 ⅝ × 20 ⅜ in.
Columbus Museum of Art. Museum
Purchase, Derby Fund, from the Philip
J. and Suzanne Schiller Collection
of American Social Commentary Art,
1930–1970
p. 227

Integration, Supreme Court, 1963
Tempera on paper mounted on
masonite
35 ½ × 47 ½ in.
Des Moines Art Center Permanent
Collections. Purchased with funds
from the Edmundson Art Foundation,
Inc., 1964.6
p. 245

Warsaw, 1943, 1963
Screen print in black and brown on
Japon paper
36 ⅛ × 27 ⅜ in.
Madison Art Collection, James
Madison University. Gift of Michael
Berg, 2016
p. 250

Untitled [Study for Gandhi], c. 1964
Pencil on paper
8 ⅝ × 7 ½ in.
Madison Art Collection, James
Madison University. Gift of Ben Shahn
Estate, 2015
p. 246 bottom left

Untitled [Study for Gandhi's Hand],
c. 1964
Pencil on paper
7 ⅜ × 8 ¾ in.
Madison Art Collection, James
Madison University. Gift of Ben Shahn
Estate, 2015
p. 246 bottom right

Hans Namuth
Ben Shahn [Roosevelt, New Jersey],
1964
Gelatin silver print
11 × 14 in.
National Portrait Gallery, Smithsonian
Institution. Gift of the Estate of Hans
Namuth
p. 61

Where Wast Thou?, 1964
Opaque watercolor and gold leaf on
paper mounted on masonite
51 ¾ × 42 in.

Amon Carter Museum of American Art,
Fort Worth, Texas
p. 259

Andrew Goodman [from the *Human
Relations Portfolio*], 1965
Photoscreen print in black and umber
on Japon paper
15 ¼ × 11 ¼ in.
Madison Art Collection, James
Madison University. Gift of Michael
Berg, 2014
p. 242 left

James Chaney [from the *Human
Relations Portfolio*], 1965
Photoscreen print in black and umber
on Japon paper
15 ¼ × 11 ¼ in.
Madison Art Collection, James
Madison University. Gift of Michael
Berg, 2014
p. 243 left

Michael Schwerner [from the *Human
Relations Portfolio*], 1965
Photoscreen print in black and umber
on Japon paper
15 ¼ × 11 ¼ in.
Madison Art Collection, James
Madison University. Gift of Michael
Berg, 2014
p. 242 right

Gandhi, 1965
Screen print in black
40 ⅛ × 26 in.
Madison Art Collection, James
Madison University. Gift of Michael
Berg, 2017
p. 247

Ben Shahn and Stefan Martin
*Maimonides with Calligraphy
[Ecclesiastes]*, 1965
Wood engraving in black and sepia
14 ½ × 10 ¼ in.
Madison Art Collection, James
Madison University. Gift of Michael
Berg, 2014
p. 257

Martin Luther King, 1965
Ink and ink wash on paper
26 ¼ × 20 ⅜ in.
Amon Carter Museum of American
Art, Fort Worth, Texas
p. 240

Menorah, 1965
Screen print with watercolor
and gold leaf on paper
26 ⅜ × 20 ½ in.
New Jersey State Museum.
Museum Purchase,
FA1965.14.8

We Shall Overcome [from the *Nine Drawings Portfolio*], 1965
Offset photolithograph in black and brown
22 ¼ × 16 ⅛ in.
Madison Art Collection, James Madison University.
Gift of Michael Berg, 2018
p. 243 right

Credo [Martin Luther], 1966
Screen print in black and blue
25 ½ × 20 in.
Madison Art Collection, James Madison University. Gift of Michael Berg, 2012
p. 219

Flowering Brushes, 1968
Lithograph on paper
39 ½ × 26 ⅝ in.
New Jersey State Museum. Museum Purchase, FA1969,190.1
p. 265

Identity, 1968
Mixed media on paper
40 × 27 ½ in.
Museo Nacional Thyssen-Bornemisza, Madrid
p. 267

Ben Shahn and Stefan Martin
Martin Luther King, 1968
Offset photolithograph in black
27 ½ × 21 in.
Collection of Adam and Erika Berg, Washington, D.C.
p. 241

Du Paty de Clam [from *The Dreyfus Affair* portfolio], 1984, based on c. 1930–31 watercolor
Pochoir print on paper
15 ⅜ × 11 ⅞ in.
Collection of Jean Shahn, Roosevelt, New Jersey
p. 69 right

Esterhazy [from *The Dreyfus Affair* portfolio], 1984, based on c. 1930–31 watercolor
Pochoir print on paper
15 ½ × 11 ⅞ in.
Collection of Jean Shahn, Roosevelt, New Jersey
p. 69 left

Georges Picquart [from *The Dreyfus Affair* portfolio], 1984, based on c. 1930–31 watercolor
Pochoir print on paper
15 ⅜ × 11 ⅞ in.
Collection of Jean Shahn, Roosevelt, New Jersey
p. 66 left

Labori et Picquart [from *The Dreyfus Affair* portfolio], 1984, based on c. 1930–31 watercolor
Pochoir print on paper
15 ⅜ × 12 in.
Collection of Jean Shahn, Roosevelt, New Jersey
p. 66 right

Le Capitaine Dreyfus [from *The Dreyfus Affair* portfolio], 1984, based on c. 1930–31 watercolor
Pochoir print on paper
15 ⅜ × 11 ¾ in.
Collection of Jean Shahn, Roosevelt, New Jersey
p. 65

Les Experts: Couard, Varinard, Belhomme, Teyssonnières [from *The Dreyfus Affair* portfolio], 1984, based on c. 1930–31 watercolor
Pochoir print on paper
15 ½ × 12 in.
Collection of Jean Shahn, Roosevelt, New Jersey
p. 67 left

Me. Labori [from *The Dreyfus Affair* portfolio], 1984, based on c. 1930–31 watercolor
Pochoir print on paper
15 ⅜ × 12 in.
Collection of Jean Shahn, Roosevelt, New Jersey
p. 67 right

Paleologue et Demange [from *The Dreyfus Affair* portfolio], 1984, based on c. 1930–31 watercolor
Pochoir print on paper
15 ⅜ × 11 ¾ in.
Collection of Jean Shahn, Roosevelt, New Jersey
p. 68 right

Untitled [Bowery, New York City], 1995, from April 1936 negative
Gelatin silver print from original 35 mm negative; made with permission of Bernarda Bryson Shahn
6 ¼ × 9 ¼ in.
Private collection, USA
Variant of image courtesy of Harvard Art Museums, P1970.2809
p. 85

BOOKS

Eugene Lyons
The Life and Death of Sacco and Vanzetti, 1927
New York: International Publishers
7 ⅝ × 5 ¼ in.
Private collection, USA

Marion D. Frankfurter and Gardner Jackson, eds.
The Letters of Sacco and Vanzetti: Written during the Seven Years (1920–1927) of Their Imprisonment, 1929
London: Constable & Company LTD
7 ¼ × 4 ⅞ in.
Private collection, USA
p. 70 right

Georges Charensol
L'Affaire Dreyfus et la Troisième République, 1930
Paris: Éditions Kra, "Les Documentaires"
7 ⅜ × 4 ¾ in.
Private collection, USA
p. 68 left

E. E. Cummings, with frontispiece by Ben Shahn
Tom [from ballet scenario based on *Uncle's Tom Cabin*], 1935
New York: Arrow Editions
8 ¾ × 8 ¼ in.
Private collection, USA
p. 78 top

Archibald MacLeish
Land of the Free, 1938
New York: Harcourt, Brace and Company
9 ⅜ × 7 ¼ in.
Private collection, USA / Stephen Lee Taller Ben Shahn Archive, Fine Arts Library, Harvard University
p. 98 bottom

Sherwood Anderson
Hometown, 1940
New York: Alliance Book Corporation
10 ¼ × 7 ⅛ in.
Private collection, USA
p. 237

Richard Wright and Edwin Rosskam
Twelve Million Black Voices: A Folk History of the Negro in the United States, 1941
New York: Viking Press
10 ¼ × 7 ¼ in.
Private collection, USA / Stephen Lee Taller Ben Shahn Archive, Fine Arts Library, Harvard University
p. 106 bottom

Henry A. Wallace, with cover design by Ben Shahn

Después de la Guerra Debe Comenzar el Siglo del Hombre del Pueblo, 1942
Mexico City: Publicaciones de la Universidad Obrera
7 ⅜ × 5 in.
Private collection, Madrid
p. 22 left

Cecil Beaton
Portrait of New York, 1948
London: B.T. Batsford Ltd.
9 × 6 in.
Private collection, USA

Adapted and illustrated by Ben Shahn
The Alphabet of Creation: An Ancient Legend from the Zohar, 1954
New York: Pantheon
10 ⅞ × 6 ½ in.
Collection of Michael Berg, Fairfax Station, Virginia
p. 262 bottom

Edward Steichen
The Family of Man: The Greatest Photographic Exhibition of All Time— 503 Pictures from 68 Countries— Created by Edward Steichen for the Museum of Modern Art, 1955
Exhibition catalogue. New York: Maco Magazine Corporation
11 ⅛ × 8 ½ in.
Private collection, USA
p. 102 bottom

Ben Shahn
The Shape of Content, 1957
Cambridge, Massachusetts: Harvard University Press
9 ¼ × 6 ⅜ in.
Private collection, USA
p. 218 left

Ben Shahn
Love and Joy about Letters, 1963
New York: Grossman Publishers
10 ¼ × 13 ¾ in.
Collection of Michael Berg, Fairfax Station, Virginia

Mulford Q. Sibley, with cover illustration by Ben Shahn
The Quiet Battle: Writings on the Theory and Practice of Non-violent Resistance, 1963
New York: Anchor Books, Doubleday & Company, Inc.
7 × 4 ⅛ in.
Private collection, USA
p. 218 right

Wendell Berry, with cover design and illustrations by Ben Shahn
November Twenty Six Nineteen Hundred Sixty Three, 1964
New York: George Braziller

7 1⁄8 × 8 3⁄4 in.
Private collection, USA / Collection of
Michael Berg, Fairfax Station, Virginia

Ralph Ellison, with cover illustration
by Ben Shahn
Invisible Man, 1965
Harmondsworth, Middlesex:
Penguin Books Ltd.
7 1⁄8 × 4 1⁄4 in.
Private collection, USA
p. 249 bottom right

Richard Hudson, with cover design
and illustrations by Ben Shahn
*Kuboyama and the Saga of the Lucky
Dragon*, 1965
New York: Thomas Yoseloff
11 1⁄8 × 8 5⁄8 in.
Private collection, USA
p. 233

Copied and illustrated by Ben Shahn
Haggadah, 1966
Paris and London: Trianon Press
Clamshell box: 16 3⁄4 × 13 in.
Book: 15 3⁄4 × 12 in.
Collection of Michael Berg, Fairfax
Station, Virginia
p. 262 top

Ben Shahn
The Biography of a Painting, 1966
New York: Paragraphic Books
8 3⁄8 × 11 in.
Private collection, USA
p. 264

Alan W. Miller, with cover jacket
design by Ben Shahn
*God of Daniel S.: In Search of the
American Jew*, 1969
London: Collier-Macmillan Ltd.
8 5⁄8 × 5 3⁄4 in.
Private collection, USA
p. 266

Lithographs and illustrations
by Ben Shahn
Hallelujah Suite [Psalm 150], 1970
New York: Kennedy Graphics, Inc.
Clamshell box: 17 7⁄8 × 18 3⁄4 in.
Book: 16 1⁄2 × 17 7⁄8 in.
Madison Art Collection, James Madison
University. Gift of Michael Berg and Dr.
Laura Katzman, 2023
p. 263

Handwritten and illuminated
by Ben Shahn
Ecclesiastes, or, The Preacher, 1971
New York: Grossman Publishers /
Trianon Press
12 1⁄4 × 9 1⁄4 in.
Private collection, USA
p. 261

EPHEMERA

Paul Thompson
"The Soap-Box Orator and His
Auditors," *National Geographic
Magazine*, July 1918, vol. 34, no. 1,
pp. 8–9
Magazine
10 × 7 in.
Private collection, USA
p. 79 left

Photographer unknown
"Two Blood-Hunting Vultures,
Mellie Edeau and Sadie Edeau,
Self-Confessed Perjurers," *Justice
and Labor in the Mooney Case*,
San Francisco, International Workers'
Defense League, January 1, 1919, p. 9
Pamphlet
Exhibition copy
11 7⁄8 × 9 1⁄2 in.
Ben Shahn papers, Archives of
American Art, Smithsonian Institution
p. 75 bottom

George Maurer
"Amnesty! On Sacco-Vanzetti Day!,"
Labor Defender, August 1931, vol. 6,
no. 8, p. 149
Magazine
Exhibition copy
12 1⁄4 × 9 1⁄4 in.
Stephen Lee Taller Ben Shahn
Archive, Fine Arts Library, Harvard
University

Photographer unknown, International
News Photograph Service
"'Mother' Mooney, 84, as She Waited
with Miss Anna Mooney, Daughter, in
the Corridors of the California Capitol
at Sacramento for Governor James
Rolph, Jr.'s Decision in the Motion
Plea of Her Son, Thomas J. Mooney...,"
c. 1931–32
Newspaper clipping
Exhibition copy
5 1⁄2 × 6 1⁄8 in.
Ben Shahn papers, Archives of
American Art, Smithsonian Institution

*Ben Shahn: The Passion of Sacco-
Vanzetti*, 1932
Exhibition brochure. New York:
Downtown Gallery
8 1⁄2 × 5 1⁄2 in.
Ben Shahn papers, Archives of
American Art, Smithsonian Institution

Ben Shahn: The Mooney Case, 1933
Exhibition brochure. New York:
Downtown Gallery
8 5⁄8 × 5 3⁄8 in.
Ben Shahn papers, Archives of
American Art, Smithsonian Institution

Photographer unknown
"Untitled [Children Sleeping],"
c. 1934–44
Newspaper clipping
3 3⁄4 × 5 7⁄8 in.
Ben Shahn papers, Archives of
American Art, Smithsonian Institution
p. 155 middle right

Art Front, November 1934, vol. 1, no. 1
Artists' Union magazine
16 x 11 in.
Hugo Gellert papers, Archives of
American Art, Smithsonian Institution
p. 92 right

Photographs by Lou Block, Lucienne
Bloch, and Ben Shahn
Art Front, January 1935, vol. 1, no. 2,
pp. 6–7
Artists' Union magazine
16 1⁄4 × 11 in.
Art Front collection, Archives of
American Art, Smithsonian Institution

Illustration by Ben Shahn
"The Committee of 100, Count 'Em,'"
Art Front, February 1935, vol. 1, no. 3,
pp. 4–5
Artists' Union magazine
16 1⁄8 × 10 7⁄8 in.
Art Front collection, Archives of
American Art, Smithsonian Institution
p. 93 top

Illustration by Ben Shahn
"Jonas 'Patrick Henry' Lie," *Art Front*,
April 1935, vol. 1, no. 4, p. 2
Artists' Union magazine
16 1⁄8 × 10 7⁄8 in.
Art Front collection, Archives of
American Art, Smithsonian Institution
p. 92 left

Stuart Davis, with illustrations
by Ben Shahn
"'We Reject'—The Art Commission,"
Art Front, July 1935, vol. 1, no. 6, pp. 4–5
Artists' Union magazine
16 1⁄8 × 11 in.
Art Front collection, Archives of
American Art, Smithsonian Institution
p. 93 bottom

Photographer unknown
"Spanish Refugees on Their Way
to Madrid," *New York Times*,
November 3, 1936
Newspaper clipping
7 × 8 1⁄8 in.
Ben Shahn papers, Archives of
American Art, Smithsonian Institution
p. 154 top

*Documentary Photographs from
the Files of the Resettlement*

*Administration: A College Art
Association Exhibition*,
December 1936
Exhibition brochure. New York:
WPA Federal Art Project Gallery
8 3⁄4 × 5 3⁄4 in.
Ben Shahn papers, Archives of
American Art, Smithsonian Institution
p. 113 bottom

Photographer unknown
"His Victory, Her Loss,"
c. 1935–36
Newspaper clipping
11 3⁄4 × 6 3⁄4 in.
Ben Shahn papers, Archives of
American Art, Smithsonian Institution
p. 154 bottom right

Photographer unknown, Times Wide
World Photos, Paris Bureau
"Where the Horrors of War Go
On. Women and Children of Jaen,
near Granada ... Air Raids and
Bombardments Which Destroyed
Their Homes," c. 1936–37
Newspaper clipping
8 1⁄2 × 5 1⁄2 in.
Ben Shahn papers, Archives of
American Art, Smithsonian Institution
p. 154 bottom left

Photographer unknown
"Having Fun? This Active Little
Rope-Skipper is Joan Lyons ...,"
c. 1937
Newspaper clipping
5 5⁄8 × 4 in.
Ben Shahn papers, Archives of
American Art, Smithsonian Institution
p. 155 left

Photographer unknown,
Wired Photo—Times Wide World
"Ford Employees Attacking C.I.O.
Leader Yesterday," *New York Times*,
May 27, 1937
Newspaper clipping
5 7⁄8 × 6 in.
Ben Shahn papers, Archives of
American Art, Smithsonian Institution
p. 197 bottom

Alfred T. Palmer
*Their Helmets Hoisted Back on Their
Heads, These Two Welders Take Time
Out for a Smoke and Breath of Fresh
Air. Hundreds of Welders are Employed
in the Building of Uncle Sam's New
Navy Craft. Newport News, Va.*,
October 1941
Gelatin silver print
8 1⁄8 × 10 1⁄4 in.
Ben Shahn papers, Archives of
American Art, Smithsonian Institution
p. 186

Royal Hellenic Government, ed.
Conditions in Greece: Confidential Photographic Record, 1942, pp. 26–27
Pamphlet
4 ¾ × 6 ½ in.
Ben Shahn papers, Archives of American Art, Smithsonian Institution
p. 155 bottom right

Photographer unknown
"Victims of India's Worst Famine in Decades. In Calcutta, a Family, Ravaged by Starvation, Lies Helpless in the Streets," *New York Times*, October 20, 1943
Newspaper clipping
6 ¼ × 8 in.
Ben Shahn papers, Archives of American Art, Smithsonian Institution
p. 29 bottom

Photographer unknown
Untitled [Ben Shahn's CIO Poster in Pool Hall Window, East Harlem, New York City], c. 1944
Gelatin silver print
10 ¼ × 10 ⅞ in.
Ben Shahn papers, Archives of American Art, Smithsonian Institution
p. 184 bottom

Photographer unknown
Untitled [Ben Shahn's CIO Poster on Wall, East Harlem, New York City], c. 1944
Gelatin silver print
10 ¼ × 8 ¼ in.
Ben Shahn papers, Archives of American Art, Smithsonian Institution
p. 184 top

Photographer unknown
Untitled [Workers in CIO-PAC Office, New York City], c. 1944
Gelatin silver print
10 ¼ × 8 ¼ in.
Ben Shahn papers, Archives of American Art, Smithsonian Institution
p. 184 top

Illustration by Ben Shahn
"Gasoline Travels in Paper Packages (North Africa)," *Fortune*, April 1944, vol. 29, no. 4, pp. 218–19
Advertisement for the Container Corporation of America, *United Nations* series
13 × 10 ⅜ in.
Private collection, USA
p. 149

Photographer unknown, ACME
Parade of Jeeps through Cisterna Castle, Italy, June 9, 1944
Gelatin silver print with paper label
Print: 7 ⅛ × 9 in., with label: 10 × 9 in.

Ben Shahn papers, Archives of American Art, Smithsonian Institution
p. 155 top

Author unknown
"Aftermath of War: A Portfolio of Paintings by Ben Shahn," *Fortune*, December 1945, vol. 32, no. 6, pp. 170–71
Magazine
13 × 10 ½ in.
Private collection, USA

Author unknown
"Photos for Art," *U.S. Camera*, May 1946, vol. 9, pp. 30–31
Magazine
13 ½ × 10 ½ in.
Stephen Lee Taller Ben Shahn Archive, Fine Arts Library, Harvard University

Walter Abell, with cover image by Ben Shahn
"Art and Labor," *Magazine of Art*, October 1946, vol. 39, no. 6
Magazine
12 × 9 in.
Private collection, USA

Author unknown, with illustrations by Ben Shahn
"Labor Drives South," *Fortune*, November 1946, vol. 34, no. 5, pp. 134–35, 140–41
Magazine
13 × 10 ½ in.
Private collection, USA
pp. 198–99

Cover image by Ben Shahn
Fortune, August 1947, vol. 36, no. 2
Magazine
13 × 10 ½ in.
Private collection, USA
p. 200

John Bartlow Martin, with illustrations by Ben Shahn
"The Blast in Centralia No. 5: A Mine Disaster No One Stopped," *Harper's Magazine*, March 1948, vol. 196, no. 1174, pp. 194–95
Magazine
Exhibition copy
10 ¼ × 7 ¼ in.
Stephen Lee Taller Ben Shahn Archive, Fine Arts Library, Harvard University
p. 181 bottom

Cover image by Ben Shahn
Fortune, January 1951, vol. 43, no. 1
Magazine
13 × 10 ⅛ in.

Private collection, USA
p. 201

Illustration by Ben Shahn
Watch out for The Man on a White Horse!, 1952
Photo-offset lithograph on newsprint; newspaper proof
18 × 14 in.
Stephen Lee Taller Ben Shahn Archive, Fine Arts Library, Harvard University
p. 206 right

Cover illustration by Ben Shahn
The Nation, August 23, 1952, vol. 175, no. 8
Magazine
12 × 8 ¾ in.
Stephen Lee Taller Ben Shahn Archive, Fine Arts Library, Harvard University
p. 206 left

Illustration and article by Ben Shahn
"The Artist and the Politicians," *Art News*, September 1953, vol. 52, no. 5, pp. 34–35
Magazine
12 ¼ × 9 ¼ in.
Stephen Lee Taller Ben Shahn Archive, Fine Arts Library, Harvard University

Edgar Kemler, with illustrations by Ben Shahn
"Will Joe Bolt the G.O.P.? lke Would Be Delighted," *The Nation*, May 15, 1954, vol. 178, no. 20, pp. 420–21
Magazine
11 ½ × 8 ½ in.
Private collection, USA
p. 207 left

Author unknown
"Ben Shahn: Painter of Protest Turns to Reflection," *Life*, October 4, 1954, vol. 37, no. 14, pp. 98–99
Magazine
13 ⅞ × 10 ½ in.
Private collection, USA

Illustration by Ben Shahn
Report on South Africa, December 1954
Advertisement for CBS. Offset lithograph on newsprint; newspaper proof
15 ⅝ × 13 ¾ in.
Stephen Lee Taller Ben Shahn Archive, Fine Arts Library, Harvard University
p. 249 top

Illustration by Ben Shahn
Report from Africa, April 1956

Advertisement for CBS. Offset lithograph on newsprint, newspaper proof
12 ⅛ × 7 ¾ in.
Stephen Lee Taller Ben Shahn Archive, Fine Arts Library, Harvard University
p. 248 bottom

Illustration by Ben Shahn
Report from Africa, April and May 1956
Advertisement for CBS. Offset lithograph on paper, cover proof
9 × 11 ¾ in.
Stephen Lee Taller Ben Shahn Archive, Fine Arts Library, Harvard University
p. 248 top

Cover image and article by Ben Shahn
"Nonconformity," *The Atlantic Monthly*, September 1957, vol. 200, no. 3
Magazine
11 × 8 ⅛ in.
Private collection, USA
p. 214 bottom

Ralph E. Lapp, with cover design and illustrations by Ben Shahn
"The Voyage of the Lucky Dragon," *Harper's Magazine*, December 1957, vol. 215, no. 1291
Magazine
11 × 8 ¼ in.
Private collection, USA
p. 230 top

Illustration by Ben Shahn
Fallout, part 2 of the two-part series *Atomic Timetable*, 1958
Advertisement for CBS. Lithograph on paper
11 ¼ × 11 ⅜ in.
Jewish Museum, New York. Gift of Dolores S. Taller in memory of Stephen Lee Taller, 2001-1
p. 223

Illustration by Ben Shahn
"You Have Not Converted a Man Because You Have Silenced Him," *Time*, April 11, 1960, vol. 75, no. 15, pp. 16–17
Advertisement for the Container Corporation of America. *Great Ideas of Western Man* series
11 ⅛ × 8 ¼ in.
Private collection, USA
p. 217

Stewart Meacham, with illustration by Ben Shahn
The Social Aspects of Nuclear Anxiety, 1964
Pamphlet

9 × 5 ⅛ in.
Ben Shahn papers, Archives of
American Art, Smithsonian Institution
p. 224 bottom

Leo Rosten, with illustration
by Ben Shahn
"They Made Our World... Gandhi,"
Look, August 25, 1964, vol. 28, no. 17,
pp. 60–61
Magazine
13 ¼ × 10 ½ in.
Private collection, USA
p. 246 top

Cover illustration by Ben Shahn
Time, March 19, 1965, vol. 85, no. 12
Magazine
11 × 8 ¼ in.
Private collection, USA

OTHER WORKS REPRODUCED
IN THE CATALOGUE

John Heartfield
*Adolf, der Übermensch: Schluckt Gold
und redet Blech* (Adolf, the Superman:
He Swallows Gold and Spouts Junk),
Arbeiter-Illustrierte-Zeitung (AIZ),
July 17, 1932, vol. 11, no. 29, p. 675
Rotogravure
p. 45 left

Untitled [related to *Prohibition* mural,
Central Park Casino, unrealized],
c. 1934
Watercolor and ink on paper
7 ½ × 5 in.
Collection of Michael Berg, Fairfax,
Virginia
p. 129

*Untitled [Greenwich Village, New York
City]*, 1935
Gelatin silver print
Exhibition copy
6 × 9 ⅛ in.
Harvard Art Museums/Fogg Museum.
Gift of Bernarda Bryson Shahn,
P1970.2934
p. 174

Unemployment [from *The Meaning
of Social Security* mural, East Wall],
1940–42
Fresco secco
Exhibition copy
105 × 283 in.
Wilbur J. Cohen Federal Building,
Washington, D.C.
pp. 140–41

Henry Koerner
Someone Talked!, 1942
Lithograph
Grinnell Lithographic Co., New York
32 ¾ × 23 ½ in.
Museum of Modern Art, New York.
Given anonymously, 878.1979
p. 45 right

Charles Olson and Ben Shahn
*Spanish Speaking Americans in the
War: The Southwest*, 1943
Pamphlet
11 × 8 ⅜ in.
Washington, D.C.: Office of the
Coordinator of Inter-American Affairs
Morgan Library & Museum, New York
p. 22 right

Photographer unknown
*Ben Shahn, James Thrall Soby, and
Amédée Ozenfant [Opening of the
Exhibition "Ben Shahn," the Museum
of Modern Art, New York]*, 1947
Gelatin silver copy print

8 × 10 in.
Ben Shahn papers, Archives of
American Art, Smithsonian Institution
p. 54 bottom

Miners' Wives, c. 1948
Tempera on panel
48 × 36 in.
Philadelphia Museum of Art,
Pennsylvania. Gift of Wright S.
Ludington, 1951
p. 40 bottom right

Robert Motherwell
The Voyage, 1949
Oil, tempera, and charcoal on paper
on board
48 × 94 in.
Museum of Modern Art, New York.
Gift of Blanchette Hooker Rockefeller,
39.1955
p. 54 top

Photographer unknown
*Untitled [Ben Shahn in Roosevelt,
New Jersey]*, c. 1950s
Gelatin silver print
11 × 13 ⅞ in.
Private collection, USA
p. 13

Defaced Portrait, 1955
Tempera
40 × 27 in.
Private collection
p. 25 left

*Dag Hammarskjöld, Doctor of
Philosophy, Public Government Official,
United Nations Secretary-General*, 1962
Tempera on wood
59 ⅞ × 48 in.
Nationalmuseum, Stockholm, Sweden
p. 30

Casals with Cello, 1969
Ink on paper
7 ⅛ × 5 ½ in.
Location unknown
p. 25 right

Amishai-Maisels, Ziva. "The Jewish Reaction: Shahn's Substitutions." In *Depiction and Interpretation: The Influence of the Holocaust on the Visual Arts*, 76–80. Oxford: Pergamon Press, 1993.

Anreus, Alejandro, ed. *Ben Shahn and the Passion of Sacco and Vanzetti*. With essays by Alejandro Anreus, Laura Katzman, Diana L. Linden, Nunzio Pernicone, and Frances K. Pohl. Exh. cat. Jersey City, NJ: Jersey City Museum, 2001.

Anreus, Alejandro, and Diana L. Linden. *The World through My Eyes: Celebrating the Legacy of Ben Shahn*. Exh. cat. Wayne, NJ: University Galleries, William Paterson University, 2019.

Araki, Yasuko. "On Ben Shahn's *Lucky Dragon* Series." *Annual of the Kajima Foundation for the Arts* (2003): 194–205.

Baigell, Matthew. "Ben Shahn's Postwar Jewish Paintings." In *Artist and Identity in Twentieth-Century America*, 213–31. Contemporary Artists and Their Critics. New York: Cambridge University Press, 2001.

Bailey, Julia Tatiana. "'Realism Reconsidered': Ben Shahn in London, 1956." *Modern American Art at Tate, 1945–1980*, edited by Alex J. Taylor. Online publication. London: Tate, 2019. tate.org.uk/research/publications /modern-american-art-at-tate/essays /realism-reconsidered.

Barradas, Efraín. "Lorenzo Homar y Ben Shahn: Admiración, aprendizaje, asimilación." In "Plástica digital." Special issue, *Plástica: Revista de la Liga de Arte de San Juan*, no. 2 (2024). https://www.revistaplasticapr.org /post/lorenzo-homar-y-ben-shahn -admiraci%C3%B3n-aprendizaje -asimilaci%C3%B3n.

Blair, Sara. "Looking Back: Henry Roth, Ben Shahn, and the Interwar Ghetto." In *How the Other Half Looks: The Lower East Side and the Afterlives of Images*, 119–51. Princeton, NJ: Princeton University Press, 2018.

Chevlowe, Susan. *Common Man, Mythic Vision: The Paintings of Ben Shahn*. With essays by Howard Greenfeld, Diana L. Linden, Frances K. Pohl, and Stephen Polcari. Exh. cat. New York: Jewish Museum; Princeton, NJ: Princeton University Press, 1998.

Decker, Christof. "A Unique Universalism: Ben Shahn and the Rhetoric of Visual Anecdotes." In *Anecdotal Modernity: Making and Unmaking History*, edited by James Dorson, Florian Sedlmeier, MaryAnn Snyder-Körber, and Birte Wege, 263–78. Anglia Book Series / Buchreihe der Anglia 68. Berlin: De Gruyter, 2020.

Decker, Christof. "Fighting for a Free World: Ben Shahn and the Art of the Poster." *American Art* 33, no. 2 (2019): 84–105.

Decker, Christof. "In Search of a Common Vision: Ben Shahn, Photography, and *The Family of Man* Exhibition in 1955." In *Imaging the Scenes of War: Aesthetic Crossovers in American Visual Culture*, 61–89. American Studies 38. Bielefeld: Transcript, 2022.

Di Stefano, Chiara. "L'altro volto dell'arte di tipo americano: La partecipazione di Ben Shahn alla Biennale di Venezia del 1954." In *Crocevia biennale*, edited by Francesca Castellani and Eleonora Charans, 181–90. Collana Acta Studiorum. Milan: Scalpendi, 2017.

Edwards, Susan H. "Ben Shahn and the American Racial Divide." In *Intersections: Lithography, Photography, and the Traditions of Printmaking*, edited by Kathleen Stewart Howe, 77–85. Tamarind Papers 17. Albuquerque: University of New Mexico Press, 1998.

Edwards, Susan H. *Ben Shahn and the Task of Photography in Thirties America*. Exh. cat. New York: Hunter College of the City University of New York, 1995.

Edwards, Susan H. "Ben Shahn: The Road South." *History of Photography* 19 (Spring 1995): 13–19.

Ellis, James W. "Ben Shahn's Sunday Paintings: Transformation of a Social Realist." *European-American Journals* 7, no. 2 (May 2019). eajournals.org /ijhphr/vol-7-issue-2-may-2019 /ben-shahns-sunday-paintings -transformation-of-a-socia-realist/.

Fagg, John. "Ben Shahn and Jacob Lawrence: Beyond Genre Painting." In *Re-envisioning Everyday Life: American Genre Scenes, 1905–1945*, 159–77. University Park: Pennsylvania State University Press, 2023.

Fagg, John. "Sport and Spectatorship as Everyday Ritual in Ben Shahn's Painting and Photography." In "Sport and the Visual." Special issue, *International Journal of the History of Sport* 28, nos. 8–9 (May–June 2011): 1353–69.

Fernández-Barkan, Davida. "Of Murals and Men: Carceral Aesthetics and Ben Shahn's Rikers Island Project." *American Art* 37, no. 1 (Spring 2023): 32–57.

Greenfeld, Howard. *Ben Shahn: An Artist's Life*. New York: Random House, 1998.

Inokoshi, Yuka, Yuji Maeyama, and Tomoko Yoshioka. *Ben Shahn: The Magic of Lines*. Exh. cat. Asaka, Japan: Marunuma Art Park, 2012.

Kao, Deborah Martin, Laura Katzman, and Jenna Webster. *Ben Shahn's New York: The Photography of Modern Times*. Exh. cat. Cambridge, MA: Fogg Art Museum, Harvard University Art Museums; New Haven: Yale University Press, 2000.

Katzman. Laura. "Art in the Atomic Age: Ben Shahn's *Stop H-Bomb Tests*." *Yale Journal of Criticism* 11, no. 1 (Spring 1998): 139–58.

Katzman, Laura. "Ben Shahn." In *150 Stories: Lives of the Artists at the League*, edited by Stephanie Cassidy. New York: Arts Students League of New York, forthcoming.

Katzman, Laura. *Ben Shahn, On Nonconformity*. With essays by Beatriz Cordero Martín, Christof Decker, and John Fagg. Exh. cat. Madrid: Editorial Activities Department, Museo Nacional Centro de Arte Reina Sofía, 2023.

Katzman, Laura. "Deconstructing Documentary: Ben Shahn's Use of Photography." In *Transatlantic Modernism*, edited by Martin Klepper and Joseph Schöpp, 173–90. American Studies 89. Heidelberg: C. Winter, 2001.

Katzman, Laura. *Drawing on the Left: Ben Shahn and the Art of Human Rights*. Exh. cat. Harrisonburg, VA: Duke Hall Gallery of Fine Art, James Madison University, 2017.

Katzman, Laura. "'Mechanical Vision': Photography and Mass Media Appropriation in Ben Shahn's *Sacco and Vanzetti* Series." In *Ben Shahn and the Passion of Sacco and Vanzetti*, edited by Alejandro Anreus, 51–80. Exh. cat. Jersey City, NJ: Jersey City Museum, 2001.

Katzman, Laura. "Source Matters: Ben Shahn and the Archive." *Archives of American Art Journal* 54, no. 2 (Fall 2015): 4–33.

Levinson, Cynthia. *The People's Painter: How Ben Shahn Fought for Justice with Art*. New York: Abrams Books for Young Readers, 2021.

Linden, Diana L. *Ben Shahn's Contemporary American Sculpture, 1940*. With research by Elizabeth D. Hamilton and Valerie G. Stanos. Exh. brochure. New York: Jonathan Boos, 2016.

Linden, Diana L. *Ben Shahn's New Deal Murals: Jewish Identity in the American Scene*. Detroit: Wayne State University Press, 2015.

Linden, Diana L. "Modern? American? Jew?: Museums and Exhibitions of Ben Shahn's Late Paintings." In *The Art of Being Jewish in Modern Times*, edited by Barbara Kirshenblatt-Gimblett and Jonathan Karp, 197–207. Philadelphia: University of Pennsylvania Press, 2008.

Mintie, Katherine. "Art and Politics in the 1940s: Ben Shahn." *Index* (April 22, 2020). harvardartmuseums.org /article/art-and-politics-in-the-1940s -ben-shahn/.

Nagata, Kozo. *Ben Shahn*. Tokyo: Otsuki Shoten, 2014.

Natanson, Nicholas. "The Photo-Series: Ben Shahn's Southern Meditations." In *The Black Image in the New Deal: The Politics of FSA Photography*, 85–112. Knoxville: University of Tennessee Press, 1992.

Nodohara, Shoso, and Tsukasa Senni. *Ben Shahn: Process for Design*. Exh. cat. Tokyo: Tama Art University Museum, 1996.

Nomiyama, Gyoji, et al. *Ben Shahn*. Contemporary Art 1. Tokyo: Kodansha, 1992.

Palmer, Daniel S. "The Integration of Art, Architecture, and Identity: Alfred Kastner, Louis Kahn, and Ben Shahn at Jersey Homesteads." PhD diss., Graduate Center, City University of New York, 2021.

Pohl, Francis K. *Ben Shahn*. With writings by Ben Shahn. San Francisco: Pomegranate Artbooks, 1993.

Pohl, Frances K. "Ben Shahn and *Fortune* Magazine: Representations of Labor in 1946." *Labor's Heritage* 1, no. 1 (January 1989): 46–55.

Pohl, Francis K. *Ben Shahn: New Deal Artist in a Cold War Climate, 1947–1954*. American Studies. Austin: University of Texas Press, 1989.

Pohl, Frances K. *Love and Joy about Letters: The Work of Ben Shahn and Mirella Bentivoglio*. Exh. cat. Claremont, CA: Pomona College Museum of Art, 2003.

Prescott, Kenneth W. *Ben Shahn Retrospective Exhibition*. Exh. cat. Tokyo: Isetan Museum of Art, 1991.

Raeburn, John. *Ben Shahn's American Scene: Photographs, 1938*. Urbana: University of Illinois Press, 2010.

Sakai, Tetsuo, et al. *Ben Shahn: Cross Media Artist: Photographs, Paintings and Graphic Arts*. With essays by Yasuko Araki, Deborah Martin Kao, and Mina Lee. Exh. cat. Tokyo: Bijutsu Shuppan-Sha, 2012.

Stimson, Blake. "Ben Shahn." In *Citizen Warhol*, 124–45. London: Routledge, 2014.

The Photographs of Ben Shahn. With an introduction by Timothy Egan. Fields of Vision. Washington, D.C.: Library of Congress; London: Giles, 2008.

Thomas, Ben. "'The Muses' 'Sterner Laws'—W. H. Auden and Ben Shahn." In *Edgar Wind and Modern Art: In Defence of Marginal Anarchy*, 117–55. London: Bloomsbury Visual Arts, 2020.

Wallner, Susan, dir. *Ben Shahn: Passion for Justice*. With interviews by Alejandro Anreus, Howard Greenfeld, Laura Katzman, Frances K. Pohl, Bernarda Bryson Shahn, Judith Shahn, et al. Princeton, NJ: Films for the Humanities and Sciences, 2002. DVD, 57 min.

Whiting, Cécile. "Ben Shahn: Aggrieved Men and Nuclear Fallout during the Cold War." *American Art* 30, no. 3 (Fall 2016): 2–25.

The first edition of the catalogue was published by the Editorial Activities Department of the Museo Reina Sofía to coincide with the exhibition *Ben Shahn, On Nonconformity*, organized by the Museo Reina Sofía from October 4, 2023, to February 26, 2024.

EXHIBITION

Curator
Laura Katzman

Project Director
Teresa Velázquez

Coordination
Beatriz Velázquez
Ana Uruñuela

Coordination Support
Ana Lázaro

Management
Natalia Guaza

Administrative Support
Nieves Fernández

Exhibition Design
Ignacio de Antonio

Registration
Iliana Naranjo
Camino Prieto

Conservation
Conservator in charge:
Juan Antonio Sáez Dégano
Conservators: Paula Ercilla,
Alicia García, Eugenia Gimeno,
Rosa Rubio, Virginia Uriarte

Installation Coordination
Nieves Sánchez

Shipping
Técnica de Transportes
Internacionales TTI, s.a.u.

Installation
Rehabilitaciones Rees S.L.

Insurance
Liberty Specialty Markets

CATALOGUE

Catalogue published by
the Editorial Activities Department
of the Museo Reina Sofía

Editorial Director
Alicia Pinteño Granado

Editorial Coordination
Mercedes Pineda

Translations from Spanish to English
Jethro Soutar

From Hebrew and Yiddish to English
Dalya Luttwak and Frances Flannery

Copyediting
Nicholas Acker

Proofreading
Jonathan Fox

Graphic Design
gráfica futura

Production Management
Julio López

Administrative Support
Victoria Wizner

Plates
Museoteca

Printing and Binding
Impresos Izquierdo

The Museo Nacional Centro de Arte Reina Sofía wishes to express its deep gratitude to Laura Katzman, the curator of the exhibition, for her enthusiasm and involvement in the project, to the institutional lenders and their teams, and to all the collectors who have entrusted us with their works for the exhibition.

Amon Carter Museum of American Art, Fort Worth, Texas
Archives of American Art, Smithsonian Institution, Washington, D.C.
Adam and Erika Berg, Washington, D.C.
Michael Berg, Fairfax Station, Virginia
Bernard Goldberg Fine Arts, LLC, New York
Mark L. Brock, Concord, Massachusetts
Brooklyn Museum, Brooklyn, New York
Colby College Museum of Art, Waterville, Maine
Columbus Museum of Art, Columbus, Ohio
Des Moines Art Center, Des Moines, Iowa
Fine Arts Library, Harvard University, Cambridge, Massachusetts
The Frances Lehman Loeb Art Center, Vassar College, Poughkeepsie, New York
Georgia Museum of Art, University of Georgia, Athens, Georgia
Harvard Art Museums/Fogg Museum, Cambridge, Massachusetts
Herbert F. Johnson Museum of Art, Cornell University, Ithaca, New York
High Museum of Art, Atlanta, Georgia
Hirshhorn Museum and Sculpture Garden, Smithsonian Institution, Washington, D.C.
Jewish Museum, New York
Jule Collins Smith Museum of Fine Art, Auburn University, Auburn, Alabama
Sally Kay and Scott Hochhauser, New York
Kennedy Museum of Art, Ohio University, Athens, Ohio
Krannert Art Museum, University of Illinois Urbana-Champaign, Illinois
Madison Art Collection, James Madison University, Harrisonburg, Virginia
Maier Museum of Art, Randolph College, founded as Randolph-Macon Woman's College, Lynchburg, Virginia
Michael Rosenfeld Gallery, LLC, New York
Modern Art Museum of Fort Worth, Texas
Montclair Art Museum, Montclair, New Jersey
Montgomery Museum of Fine Arts, Montgomery, Alabama
Museo Nacional Thyssen-Bornemisza, Madrid
Museum of Contemporary Art Chicago, Illinois
Museum of Fine Arts, Boston, Massachusetts

The Museum of Modern Art, New York
Museum of the City of New York, New York
National Portrait Gallery, Smithsonian Institution, Washington, D.C.
Neuberger Museum of Art, Purchase College, State University of New York Purchase, New York
New Jersey State Museum, Trenton New Jersey
Pennsylvania Academy of the Fine Arts, Philadelphia, Pennsylvania
Philadelphia Museum of Art, Philadelphia, Pennsylvania
The Phillips Collection, Washington, D.C.
Private collection, USA
Private collection, USA
The Schoen Collection
Jean Shahn, Roosevelt, New Jersey
Debra and Michael Skolnick, Elkins Park, Pennsylvania
Smithsonian American Art Museum, Washington, D.C.
Syracuse University Art Museum, Syracuse, New York
Walker Art Center, Minneapolis, Minnesota
Whitney Museum of American Art, New York
Willard Straight Hall Collection, Cornell University, Ithaca, New York

We would also like to express our gratitude to those who in various ways have collaborated in the materialization of the project.

Nicholas Acker
Jonathan R. Alger
Mary Jane Appel
Robyn Asleson
Erin Beasley
Benton Museum of Art, Pomona College, Claremont, California
Makeda Best
Jenny Bird
Manuel Borja-Villel
Elizabeth Botten
Marisa Bourgoin
Sarah Brooks
Taína Caragol
Susan Cary
Heather Coltman
Steve Comba
Beatriz Cordero Martín
Emily Cushman
The David and Alfred Smart Museum of Art, The University of Chicago, Illinois
Lydia Davis
Christof Decker
Emily Dittman
Jessica Evans Brady
John Fagg
Kathleen Foster
Catherine Futter
Karen Gerard
Amelia Goerlitz

Rubén Graciani
Wendy Grossman
Evelyn Hankins
Lindsay R. Harris
Maria Harvey
Michelle Harvey
Barbara Haskell
Jodi Hauptman
James Heffernan
Anne L. Helmreich
Beth Hinderliter
Karen Hines
Jonathan Horowitz
Howard Greenberg Gallery, New York
Peter Huestis
Jesús Jiménez
Martha Johnson
Connie Kay and Jules Kay (1934–2023)
Liza Kirwin
Katie L. Kujala
Germán Labrador Méndez
Shelley Langdale
MiKyoung Lee
Cynthia Levinson
Dominique Lopes DelGiudice
Dalya Luttwak
Kate Markoski
Fabiola Martínez Rodríguez
Sheryl McMahan
Virginia Mecklenburg
Jordana Mendelson
Laura Neufeld
The New York Public Library, New York
Cindy Ott
Frances K. Pohl
Prints & Photographs Division, The Library of Congress, Washington, D.C.
Shirley Reece-Hughes
Tomás Regalado-Lopez
Kelly Reynolds
Edward Saywell
Kathy Schwartz
Abigail Shahn
Jasper Shahn
Jean Shahn
Zachary Shahn
Virginia Soenksen
Richard Sorensen
Deborah Spanich
Wren Stevens
Sarah Vogelman
Felix Wang
JY Zhou